The HUMAN RECORD

Volume II

The HUMAN RECORD

SOURCES OF GLOBAL HISTORY

SIXTH EDITION / Volume II: Since 1500

Alfred J. Andrea

Emeritus Professor of History, University of Vermont

James H. Overfield

Professor of History, University of Vermont

HOUGHTON MIFFLIN COMPANY BOSTON NEW YORK

As always, our love and thanks to
Juanita B. Andrea and Susan L. Overfield

Executive Publisher: Patricia A. Coryell
Publisher: Suzanne Jeans
Senior Sponsoring Editor: Nancy Blaine
Senior Marketing Manager: Katherine Bates
Discipline Product Manager: Lynn Baldridge
Senior Development Editor: Tonya Lobato
Senior Project Editor: Margaret Park Bridges
Senior Media Producer: Lisa Ciccolo
Senior Content Manager: Janet Edmonds
Art and Design Manager: Jill Haber
Cover Design Director: Tony Saizon
Senior Photo Editor: Jennifer Meyer Dare
Senior Composition Buyer: Chuck Dutton
New Title Project Manager: Susan Peltier
Associate Editor: Adrienne Zicht
Marketing Associate: Lauren Bussard

Cover image: Metropolitan Museum of Art, Photograph © The Metropolitan Museum of Art

Source credits appear on pages 489–493, which constitute an extension of the copyright page.

Printed in the U.S.A.

Library of Congress Control Number: 2006939646

Instructor's examination copy
ISBN-10: 0-618-83425-7
ISBN-13: 978-0-618-83425-9

For orders, use student text ISBNs
ISBN-10: 0-618-75111-4
ISBN-13: 978-0-618-75111-2

123456789-CRS-12 11 10 09 08

Contents

Geographic Contents

Western Hemisphere

Topical Contents

Resistance to Western Colonialism/ Imperialsim

Women

Migration

Preface

The sixth edition of *The Human Record: Sources of Global History* follows the principles that have guided the book since its inception in 1990. Foremost is our commitment to the proposition that all students of history must meet the challenge of analyzing primary sources, thereby becoming active inquirers into the past. Working with primary source evidence enables students to see that historical scholarship is an intellectual process of drawing inferences and discovering patterns from clues yielded by the past, not of memorizing someone else's judgments. Furthermore, such analysis motivates students to learn by stimulating their curiosity and imagination, and it helps them develop into critical thinkers who are equipped to deal with the complex intellectual challenges of life.

Themes and Structure

We have compiled a source collection that traces the course of human history from the rise of the earliest civilizations to the present. Volume I follows the evolution of cultures that most significantly influenced the history of the world from around 3500 B.C.E. to 1700 C.E., with emphasis on the development of the major social, religious, intellectual, and political traditions of the societies that flourished in Eurasia and Africa. Although our focus in Volume I is on the Eastern Hemisphere, we do not neglect the Americas. Volume I concurrently develops the theme of the growing links and increasingly important exchanges among the world's cultures down to the early modern era. Volume II, which begins just before 1500 C.E. and covers the two centuries of overlap in far greater detail than Volume I, picks up this theme of growing human interconnectedness by tracing the gradual establishment of Western global hegemony; the simultaneous historical developments in other civilizations and societies around the world; the anti-Western, anticolonial movements of the twentieth century; and the emergence of the twenty-first century's integrated but still often bitterly divided world.

To address these themes in the depth and breadth they deserve, we have chosen primary sources that present an overview of global history in mosaic form. Each source serves two functions: It presents an intimate glimpse into some meaningful aspect of the human past and simultaneously contributes to the creation of a single large picture — an integrated history of the world. With this dual purpose in mind, we have tried to avoid isolated sources that provide a taste of some culture or age but, by their dissociation, shed no light on patterns of cultural creation, continuity, change, and interchange — the essential components of world history.

In selecting and arranging the various pieces of our mosaic, we have sought to create a balanced picture of human history that reflects many different perspectives and experiences. Believing that the study of history properly concerns every aspect of past human activity and thought, we have chosen sources that mirror the practices and concerns of as wide a variety of representative persons and groups as availability and space allow.

Our pursuit of historical balance has also led us into the arena of artifactual evidence. Although most historians center their research on documents, the discipline of history requires us to consider all of the clues surrendered by the past, and these include its artifacts. Moreover, we have discovered that students enjoy analyzing artifacts and remember vividly the insights they draw from them. For these reasons, we have included works of art and other artifacts that users of this book can and should analyze as historical sources.

New to This Edition

We have been gratified with the positive response by colleagues and especially students to the first five editions of *The Human Record*. Many have taken the trouble to write or otherwise contact us to express their satisfaction. No textbook is perfect, however, and these correspondents have been equally generous in sharing their perceptions of how we might improve our book and meet more fully the needs of its readers. Such suggestions, when combined with continuing advances in historical scholarship and our own deeper reflections on a variety of issues, have mandated periodic revisions. In the current revision, as was true in the previous four, our intent has been to make the book as interesting and useful as possible to students and instructors alike.

In this continuing (and never-ending) pursuit of trying to find the best and most useful documents and artifacts, we have added eighty-three new sources to these volumes, thirty-one in Volume I and fifty-two in Volume II. Needless to say, in order to keep these volumes within manageable boundaries, we have had to excise almost a like number of sources, many of which undoubtedly have their advocates, who will be disappointed at their excision from the present edition. Persons who disagree with our judgments as to what to cut and what to add should feel free to contact us (see "Feedback" below) and to argue their case. There will be a seventh edition.

Instructors who have used earlier editions of *The Human Record* will recognize immediately that we have added a new feature that we call "Multiple Voices." Two of the most important skills that every student of history must acquire and sharpen are an ability to identify, evaluate, and use evidence that reflects different perspectives and an ability to trace historical development over time. Earlier editions of *The Human Record* have contained occasional clusters of sources that have challenged students to grapple with problems that require these skills, but now we have endeavored to increase substantially the number of such exercises, to give each a certain uniformity and coherence, and to highlight each as a distinctive entity. Together, the two volumes contain fifteen Multiple Voices units, with each containing three to five sources and clearly set apart from other elements in the chapter. We believe that this will enable instructors to use them easily as in-class lessons and as focal points for out-of-class essays. Beyond that, we believe that each Multiple Voices unit will help students acquire and deepen habits of the mind that are necessary for not only their successful mastery of history but also, more important, their functioning in the world as educated individuals and citizens. These include, but are not limited to, a high degree of comfort with nuance and ambiguity; a sensitivity to the ways in which personality, time, place, culture, and other circumstances influence perspectives; an understanding that change and continuity are equally important elements in the dynamics of human history; a willingness to offer provisional answers to complex phenomena in which some or much of the desired evidence is not available; and an intellectual humility that allows one to modify and even radically change previous judgments once new evidence or insights become available.

Beyond helping to stimulate these skills and habits of the mind, we also have an obligation to reflect in our work the most up-to-date scholarly discoveries and controversies. With that in mind, we have revised many of our introductions and commentaries. More than one-third of the pages dedicated to editorial commentary and notes have been rewritten.

Learning Aids

Source analysis can be a daunting challenge for any student. With this in mind, we have labored to make these sources as accessible as possible by providing the student-user with a variety of aids. First there is the *Prologue*, in which we explain, initially in a theoretical manner and then through concrete examples, how a historian interprets written and artifactual sources. Instructors who have used previous editions of our book will note that the new Prologue offers a sample Multiple Voices exercise as a means of introducing student-readers to the art of source analysis. Next we offer *part, chapter, sub-chapter*, and *individual source introductions* — all to help the reader place each selection into a meaningful context and understand each source's significance. Because we consider *The Human Record* to be an interpretive overview of global history and therefore a survey of the major patterns of global history that stands on its own as a text, our introductions are significantly fuller than what one normally encounters in a book of sources.

Suggested *Questions for Analysis* precede each source; their purpose is to help the student make sense of each piece of evidence and wrest from it as much insight as possible. The questions are presented in a three-tiered format designed to resemble the historian's approach to source analysis and to help students make historical comparisons on a global scale. The first several questions are usually quite specific and ask the reader to pick out important pieces of information. These initial questions require the student to address two issues: What does this document or artifact say, and what meaningful facts can I garner from it? Addressing concrete questions of this sort prepares the student researcher for the next, more significant, level of critical thinking and analysis: drawing inferences. Questions that demand inferential conclusions follow the fact-oriented questions. Finally, whenever possible, we offer a third tier of questions that challenge the student to compare the individual or society that produced a particular source with an individual, group, or culture encountered earlier in the volume. We believe such comparisons help students fix more firmly in their minds the distinguishing cultural characteristics of the various societies they encounter in their survey of world history. Beyond that, it underscores the fact that global history is, at least on one level, comparative history.

Another form of help we offer is to *gloss the sources*, explaining words and allusions that students cannot reasonably be expected to know. To facilitate reading and to encourage reference, the notes appear at the bottom of the page on which they are cited. A few documents also contain *interlinear notes* that serve as transitions or provide needed information.

Some instructors might use *The Human Record* as their sole textbook. Most, however, will use it as a supplement to a standard narrative textbook, and most of these will probably decide not to require their students to analyze every source. To assist instructors (and students) in selecting sources that best suit their interests and needs, we have prepared *two analytical tables of contents* for each volume. The first lists readings and artifacts by geographic and cultural area, the second by topic. The two tables suggest to professor and student alike the rich variety of material available within these pages, particularly for essays in comparative history.

In summary, our goal in crafting *The Human Record* has been to do our best to prepare the student-reader for success — *success* being defined as comfort with historical analysis, proficiency in critical thinking, learning to view history on a global scale, and a deepened awareness of the rich cultural varieties, as well as shared characteristics, of the human family.

Using The Human Record: *Suggestions from the Editors*

Specific suggestions for assignments and classroom activities appear in the online manual *Using* The Human Record: *Suggestions from the Editors*, which may be accessed through the textbook website at www.college.hmco.com/history/instructors. It is also available in print format. In it we explain why we have chosen the sources that appear in this book and what insights we believe students should be capable of drawing from them. We also describe classroom exercises for encouraging student thought and discussion on the various sources. The advice we present is the fruit of our own use of these sources in the classroom.

Feedback

As already suggested, we want to receive comments and suggestions from instructors and students who use this book. Comments on the Prologue and Volume I should be addressed to A. J. Andrea, whose e-mail address is <Alfred.Andrea@uvm.edu>; comments on Volume II should be addressed to J. H. Overfield at <James.Overfield@uvm.edu>.

Acknowledgments

We are in debt to the many professionals who offered their expert advice and assistance during the various incarnations of *The Human Record.* Scholars and friends at The University of Vermont who generously shared their expertise with us over the years as we crafted these six editions include Abbas Alnasrawi, Doris Bergen, Holly-Lynn Busier, Ernesto Capello, Robert V. Daniels, Carolyn Elliott, Bogac Ergene, Erik Esselstrom, Shirley Gedeon, Erik Gilbert, William Haviland, Walter Hawthorn, Richard Horowitz, William Mierse, George Moyser, Kristin M. Peterson-Ishaq, Abubaker Saad, Wolfe W. Schmokel, Peter Seybolt, John W. Seyller, Sean Stilwell, Mark Stoler, Marshall True, Diane Villemaire, Janet Whatley, and Denise Youngblood. Additionally, Ms. Tara Coram of the Arthur M. Sackler Gallery and Freer Gallery of Art of the Smithsonian Institution deserves special thanks for the assistance she rendered A. J. Andrea in his exploration of the Asian art holdings of the two museums.

We wish also to acknowledge the following instructors whose comments on the fifth edition helped guide our revision: Janet Bednarek, University of Dayton; Sharon Cohen, Springbrook High School; Michael Davidson, Southern Illinois University; Jay Harmon, Catholic High School; Brian Hodson, Fort Hays State University; Patrick Patterson, Honolulu Community College; Daniel Sarefield, The Ohio State University; and John Wilson, Rowen University.

Finally, our debt to our spouses is beyond payment, but the dedication to them of each edition of this book reflects in some small way how deeply we appreciate their constant support and good-humored tolerance.

A. J. A.
J. H. O.

The HUMAN RECORD

Volume II

Prologue

Primary Sources and How to Read Them

Imagine a course in chemistry in which you never set foot in a laboratory or a course on the history of jazz in which you never listen to a note of music. You would consider such courses deficient and would complain to your academic advisor or college dean about flawed teaching methods and wasted tuition. And you would be right. No one can understand chemistry without doing experiments; no one can understand music without listening to performances.

In much the same way, no one can understand history without reading and analyzing *primary sources*. Simply defined, *in most instances, primary sources are historical records produced at the same time the event or period that is being studied took place or soon thereafter*. They are distinct from *secondary sources* — books, articles, television documentaries, and even historical films — produced well after the events they describe and analyze. Secondary sources — *histories* in the conventional sense of the term — organize the jumble of past events into understandable narratives. They provide interpretations, sometimes make comparisons, and almost always discuss motive and causation. When done well, they provide pleasure and insight. But such works, no matter how well done, are still *secondary*, in that they are written well after the fact and derive their evidence and information from primary sources.

History is an ambitious discipline that deals with all aspects of past human activity and belief. This means that the primary sources historians use to recreate the past are equally wide-ranging and diverse. Most primary sources are written — government records, law codes, private correspondence, literary works, religious texts, merchants' account books, memoirs, and the list goes on almost endlessly. So important are written records to the study of history that many historians refer to societies and cultures with no system of writing as prehistoric. This does not mean they lack a history; it means there is no way to construct a detailed narrative of their histories due to the lack of written records. Of course, even so-called prehistoric societies leave behind evidence of their experiences, creativity, and belief systems in their *oral traditions* and their *artifacts*.

Let us look first at oral traditions, which can include legends, religious rituals, proverbs, genealogies, and a variety of other forms of wisdom and knowledge. Simply put, they constitute a society's remembered past as passed down by word of mouth. The difficulty of working with such evidence is significant. You are aware of how stories change as they are transmitted from person to person. Imagine how difficult it is to use such stories as historical evidence. Yet, despite the challenge they offer us, these sources cannot be overlooked.

Although the oral traditions of ancient societies were often written down long after they were first articulated, they are often the only recorded evidence that we have of a far-distant society or event. So, the farther back in history we go, the more we see the inadequacy of the definition of primary sources that we offered above ("historical records produced at the same time the event or period that is being studied took place or soon thereafter"). The early chapters of Volume I contain quite a few primary sources based on oral traditions; in some cases, they were recorded many centuries after the events and people they deal with. We will inform you when this is the case and offer you sufficient information and suggestions as to which questions you can validly ask of them to enable you to use them effectively.

Artifacts — essentially anything, other than a document, that was crafted by hand or machine — can help us place oral traditions into a clearer context by producing tangible evidence that supports or calls into question this form of testimony. Artifacts can also tell us something about prehistoric societies whose oral traditions are lost to us. They also serve as primary sources for historians who study literate cultures. Written records, no matter how extensive and diverse, never allow us to draw a complete picture of the past, and we can fill at least some of those gaps by studying what human hands have fashioned. Everyday objects — such as fabrics, tools, kitchen implements, weapons, farm equipment, jewelry, pieces of furniture, and family photographs — provide windows into the ways that people lived. Grander cultural products — paintings, sculpture, buildings, musical compositions, and, more recently, film — are equally important because they also reflect the values, attitudes, and styles of living of their creators and those for whom they were created.

To be a historian is to work with primary sources in all their diverse forms. But to do so effectively is not easy. Each source provides only one glimpse of reality, and no single source by itself gives us the whole picture of past events and developments. Many sources are difficult to understand and can be interpreted only after the precise meaning of their words has been deciphered and their backgrounds thoroughly investigated. Many sources contain distortions and errors that can be discovered only by rigorous internal analysis and comparison with evidence from other sources. Only after all these source-related difficulties have been overcome can a historian hope to achieve a coherent and reasonably accurate understanding of the past.

To illustrate some of the challenges of working with primary sources, let us imagine a time in the future when a historian decides to write a history of your college class in connection with its fiftieth reunion. Since no one has written a book or article about your class, our historian has no secondary sources to consult and must rely entirely on primary sources. What primary sources might he or she use? The list is a long one: the school catalogue, class lists, academic transcripts, yearbooks, college rules and regulations, and similar official documents; lecture notes, syllabi, examinations, term papers, and textbooks; diaries and private letters; articles from the campus newspaper and programs for sporting events, concerts, and plays; posters and handbills; recollections written down or otherwise recorded by some of your classmates long after they graduated. With a bit of thought you could add other items to the list, among them some artifacts, such as souvenirs sold in the campus store, and other unwritten sources, such as recordings of music popular at the time and photographs and videotapes of student life and activity.

Even with this imposing list of sources, our future historian will have only an incomplete record of the events that made up your class's experiences. Many of those moments — telephone conversations, meetings with professors, and gossip exchanged at the student union — never made it into any written record. Also consider the fact that all the sources available to our future historian will be fortunate survivors. They will represent only a small percentage of the material generated by you, your classmates, professors, and administrators over a two- or four-year period. Wastebaskets and recycling bins will have claimed much written material; the "delete" key, inevitable changes in computer technology, and old websites dumped as "obsolete" will make it impossible to retrieve some basic sources, such as your college's website, e-mail, and a vast amount of other online materials. It is also probable that it will be difficult to find information about certain groups within your class, such as part-time students, nontraditional students, and commuters. The past always has its so-called silent or near-silent groups of people. Of course, they were never truly silent, but often nobody was listening to them. It is the historian's task to find whatever evidence exists that gives them a voice, but often that evidence is tantalizingly slim.

For these reasons, the evidence available to our future historian will be fragmentary at best. This is always the case when doing historical research. The records of the past cannot be retained in their totality, not even records that pertain to the recent past.

How will our future historian use the many individual pieces of surviving documentary evidence about your class? As he or she reviews the list, it will quickly become apparent that no single primary source provides a complete or unbiased picture. Each source has its own perspective, value, and limitations. Imagine that the personal essays submitted by applicants for admission were a historian's only sources of information about the student body. On reading them, our researcher might draw the false conclusion that the school attracted only the most gifted, talented, interesting, and intellectually committed students imaginable.

Despite their flaws, however, essays composed by applicants for admission are still important pieces of historical evidence. They reflect the would-be students' perceptions of the school's cultural values and the types of people it hopes to attract, and usually the applicants are right on the mark because they have studied the college's or university's website and read the brochures prepared by its admissions office. Admissions materials and, to a degree, even the school's official catalogue (assuming it still has a printed catalogue and has not gone totally online) are forms of creative advertising, and both present an idealized picture of campus life. But such publications have value for the careful researcher because they reflect the values of the faculty and administrators who composed them. The catalogue also provides useful information regarding rules and regulations, courses, instructors, school organizations, and similar items. Such factual information, however, is the raw material of history, not history itself, and certainly it does not reflect anything close to the full historical reality of your class's collective experience.

What is true of the catalogue is equally true of the student newspaper and every other piece of evidence pertinent to your class. Each primary source is a part of a larger whole, but as we have already seen, we do not have all the pieces. Think of historical evidence in terms of a jigsaw puzzle. Many of the pieces are missing, but it is possible to put the remaining pieces together to form a fairly accurate and coherent picture. The picture that emerges will not be complete, but it is valid and useful, and from it one can often make educated guesses as to what the missing pieces look like. The keys to putting together this historical puzzle are hard work and imagination. Each is absolutely necessary.

Examining Primary Sources

Hard work speaks for itself, but students are often unaware that historians also need imagination to reconstruct the past. After all, many students ask, doesn't history consist of irrefutable dates, names, and facts? Where does imagination enter into the process of learning these facts? Again, let us consider your class's history and its documentary sources. Many of those documents provide factual data — dates, names, grades, statistics. While these data are important, individually and collectively they have no historical meaning until they have been *interpreted*. Your college class is more than a collection of statistics and facts. It is a group of individuals who, despite their differences, shared and molded a collective experience. It was and is a community evolving within a particular time and place. Any valid or useful history must reach beyond dates, names, and facts and interpret the historical characteristics and role of your class. What were its values? How did it change and why? What impact did it have? These are some of the important questions a historian asks of the evidence.

To arrive at answers, the historian must examine every piece of relevant evidence in its full context and wring from that evidence as many *inferences* as possible. *An inference is a logical conclusion drawn from evidence*, and it is the heart and soul of historical inquiry. Facts are the raw materials of history, but inferences are its finished products.

Every American schoolchild learns at an early age that "in fourteen hundred and ninety-two, Columbus sailed the ocean blue." In subsequent history classes, he or she might learn other facts about the famous explorer: that he was born in Genoa in 1451; that he made three other transatlantic voyages in 1493, 1497, and 1503; that he died in Spain in 1506. Knowing these facts is of little value, however, unless it contributes to our understanding of the motives, causes, and significance of Columbus's voyages. Why did Columbus sail west? Why did Spain support such enterprises? Why were Europeans willing and able to exploit, as they did, the so-called New World? What were the short- and long-term consequences of the European presence in the Americas? Finding answers to questions such as these are the historian's ultimate goal, and these answers can be reached only by studying primary sources.

One noted historian, Robin Winks, has written a book entitled *The Historian as Detective*, and the image is appropriate although inexact. Like a detective, the historian examines evidence to reconstruct events. Like a detective, the historian is interested in discovering "what happened, who did it, and why." Like a detective interrogating witnesses, *the historian also must carefully examine the testimony of sources.*

First and foremost, the historian must evaluate the *validity* of the source. Is it what it purports to be? Artful forgeries have misled many historians. Even authentic sources still can be misleading if the author lied or deliberately misrepresented reality. In addition, the historian can easily be led astray by not fully understanding the *perspective* reflected in the document. As is soon learned by any detective who has examined eyewitnesses to an event, even honest witnesses' accounts can differ widely. The detective has the opportunity to re-examine witnesses and offer them the opportunity to change their testimony in the light of new evidence and deeper reflection. The historian is not so fortunate. Even when the historian compares a piece of documentary evidence with other evidence in order to uncover its flaws, there is no way to cross-examine its author. Given this fact, it is absolutely necessary for the historian to understand as fully as possible the source's perspective. Thus, the historian must ask several key questions — all of which share the letter *W*.

- *What* kind of document is it?
- *Who* wrote it?
- For *whom* and *why*?
- *Where* was it composed and *when*?

What is important because understanding the nature of a source gives the historian an idea of what kind of information he or she can expect to find in it. Many sources simply do not address the questions a historian would like to ask of them, and knowing this can prevent a great deal of frustration. Your class's historian would be foolish to try to learn much about the academic quality of your school's courses from a study of the registrar's class lists and grade sheets. Student and faculty class notes, copies of syllabi, examinations, student papers, and textbooks would be far more useful.

Who, for whom, and *why* are equally important questions. The official catalogue (if, as noted above, the school still prints one) and publicity materials prepared by the admissions office undoubtedly address some issues pertaining to student social life. But should documents like these — designed to attract potential students and to place the school in the best possible light — be read and accepted uncritically? Obviously not. They must be tested against student testimony discovered in such sources as private letters, memoirs, posters, the student newspaper, and the yearbook.

Where and *when* are also important questions to ask of any primary source. As a rule, distance from an event in space and time colors perceptions and can diminish the reliability of a source. Recollections of a person celebrating a twenty-fifth class reunion could be an insightful and valuable source of information for your class's historian. Conceivably this graduate would have a perspective and information that he or she lacked a quarter of a century earlier. Just as conceivably, that person's memory of what college was like might have faded to the point where his recollections have little value.

You and the Sources

This book will actively involve you in the work of historical inquiry by asking you to draw inferences based on your analysis of primary source evidence. This might prove difficult at first, but it is well within your capability.

You will analyze two types of evidence: documents and artifacts. Each source will be authentic, so you do not have to worry about validating it. Editorial material in this book also supplies you with the information necessary to place each piece of evidence into its proper context and will suggest questions you legitimately can and should ask of each source.

It is important to keep in mind that historians approach each source with questions, even though they might be vaguely formulated. Like detectives, historians want to discover some particular truth or shed light on an issue. This requires asking specific questions of the witnesses or, in the historian's case, of the evidence. These questions should not be prejudgments. *One of the worst errors a historian can make is setting out to prove a point or to defend an ideological position.* Questions are essential, but they are starting points, nothing else. Therefore, as you approach a source, have your question or questions fixed in your mind, and constantly remind yourself as you work your way through a source what issue or issues you are investigating, but at the same time, keep an open mind. You are not an advocate or a debater. Your mission is to discover the truth, insofar as you can, by following the evidence and asking the right questions of it. Each source in this anthology is preceded by a number of suggested *Questions for Analysis*. You or your professor might want to ask other questions. Whatever the case, keep focused on your questions and issues, and take notes as you read a source. Never rely on unaided memory; it will almost inevitably lead you astray.

Above all else, you must be honest and thorough as you study a source. Read each explanatory footnote carefully to avoid misunderstanding a word or an allusion. Try to understand exactly what the source is saying and what its author's perspective is. Be careful not to wrench items, words, or ideas out of context, thereby distorting them. Be sure to read the entire source so that you understand as fully as possible what it says and does not say.

This is not as difficult as it sounds. But it does take concentration and work. And do not let the word "work" mislead you. True, primary source analysis demands attention to detail and some hard thought, but it is also rewarding. There is great satisfaction in developing a deeper and truer understanding of the past based on a careful exploration of the evidence. What is more, an ability to analyze and interpret evidence is a skill that will serve you well in whatever career you follow.

Analyzing Sample Sources

To illustrate how you should go about this task and what is expected of you, we will now take you through an exercise. One of the new features of the sixth edition of this source book is a feature we call "Multiple Voices." Each volume is divided into four Parts, and each Part contains one or more Multiple Voices sections. Each Multiple Voices feature is a set of short source excerpts that illustrates one of three phenomena: (1) multiple, more-or-less contemporary perspectives on a common event or phenomenon; (2) multiple sources that illustrate how something changes over time; (3) multiple perspectives from different cultures regarding a common concern or issue. The sample exercise we have constructed for this Prologue is a Multiple Voices feature. We have chosen three documents and an artifact that shed light on the importance and economic policies of the Indian port city of Calicut in the years preceding the entry on a large scale of Europeans into the Indian Ocean. We present this grouping of sources as it would appear in the book: first a bit of background; next a discussion of the individual sources; then suggested Questions for Analysis; and finally the sources themselves, with explanatory notes.

Everyone Meets in Calicut

BACKGROUND

On May 20, 1498, after almost eleven months of sailing, the Portuguese captain-major Vasco da Gama anchored his three ships a few miles from Calicut on India's Malabar, or southwestern, Coast, thereby inaugurating Europe's entry into the markets of the Indian Ocean. At the time of da Gama's arrival, Calicut (or Kozhikode), which had been established in the thirteenth century, was the capital of the most important state in a region dotted with small powers. Despite lacking a good natural harbor, Calicut prospered as a center of trade for reasons suggested in the following sources. However, with the establishment of competitive Portuguese trading stations along the Malabar Coast and elsewhere in the Indian Ocean following da Gama's initial contact with India, Calicut's fortunes rapidly declined, and its prominence ended.

THE SOURCES

We begin with an account of Calicut contained in the anonymous ***Logbook (Roteiro) of the First Voyage of Vasco da Gama***, often referred to simply as the ***Roteiro***. The journal, which is incomplete, was kept by one of da Gama's crew members aboard the ***San Rafael***. Several persons, namely the notary João de Sã and the soldier Álvaro Velho, have been offered as candidates, but neither has a definitive claim on its authorship. What is certain, however, is that the ***Roteiro*** is authentic.

The second source, Ibn Battuta's ***Rihla***, or ***A Gift to Those Who Contemplate the Wonders of Cities and the Marvels Encountered in Travel***, predates the ***Roteiro*** by a century and a half. Abu Abdallah Muhammad Ibn Battuta (1304–1368?) left his home in Tangier on the coast of Morocco in 1325 at the age of twenty-one to begin a twenty-six-year journey throughout the Islamic World and beyond. When he returned to Morocco in 1349, he had logged about 73,000 miles of travel, including more than seven years spent as a *qadi*, or religious judge, in the Islamic sultanate of Delhi in north India. In 1341 Sultan Muhammad Tughluq (r. 1325–1351) invited Ibn Battuta to travel to China as his ambassador. On his way to China, Ibn Battuta stopped at Calicut. In 1354 the traveler began to collaborate with a professional scribe, Ibn Juzayy, to fashion his many adventures into a *rihla*, or book of travels, one of the most popular forms of literature in the Islamic World. It took almost two years to complete his long and complex story. Some of that story was fabricated, as even contemporaries noticed, but most of the *rihla* has the ring of authenticity. The excerpt describes Calicut as seen in 1341 and remembered about fifteen years later, and there is no good reason to doubt that this is an eyewitness account.

The third source, ***The Overall Survey of the Ocean's Shores***, is Chinese. Its author, Ma Huan (ca. 1380–after 1451), accompanied the fourth (1413–1415), sixth (1421–1423), and seventh (1431–1433) expeditions of the great Ming fleets that the Yongle Emperor (r. 1402–1424) and his successor sent into the Indian Ocean under the command of Admiral Zheng He (1371–1433). The main purpose of the seven expeditions, which began in 1405 and ended in 1433, was to reassert Chinese hegemony in coastal lands touched by the Indian Ocean. Ma Huan, who was a Chinese Muslim, served as an Arabic translator on his first voyage and upon his return home transcribed his notes into book form. After sailing on two other expeditions, he amended his account accordingly and published a book in 1451 that encapsulated all three expeditions and described in detail the lands visited and actions taken by the fleets during those voyages. In this excerpt he describes Calicut, known to the Chinese as Guli.

The fourth source, an artifact, is a detail of the western portions of India and the adjoining Arabian Sea from the ***Catalan World Atlas***, which was drawn in 1375 on the island of Majorca, probably by Abraham Cresques (1325–1387), a Jewish "master of maps of the world" who served the king of Aragon in northeast Spain (Catalonia), which had seized Majorca from the Moors in 1229. Cresques's map, which wound up in the possession of the king of France in 1380 (and today is one of the treasures of Paris's Bibliothèque Nationale), was based on the best available literary and cartographic sources and reflected the facts and fictions regarding the Afro-Eurasian World that circulated in educated circles in late-fourteenth-century Western Europe. In the segment shown here, we see at the top the Three Magi on their way to visit the Christ Child. Below them is the sultan of Delhi, whose Muslim state dominated north India; below him is the raja of Vijayanagara, who presided over the most powerful Hindu state in south India. Between them are an elephant and its handler. In the Arabian Sea at the bottom of the map are pearl divers, as described by Marco Polo. Above the pearl divers is a vessel with two men in conical hats.

QUESTIONS FOR ANALYSIS

1. According to the *Roteiro*, why was Calicut so important, and, by implication, why was it necessary for Portugal to gain direct access to it?
2. What does Ibn Battuta tell us about the roles of foreigners in Calicut, and specifically which foreigners?
3. From what all three documentary sources tell us, what factors contributed to Calicut's prosperity?
4. What does the *Catalan World Atlas* tell us about Western Europe's knowledge of the Malabar Coast and India in general by the late fourteenth century?
5. Overall, what can we say with certainty about Calicut prior to its rapid decline in the sixteenth century?

I ▾ ROTEIRO

From this country of Calicut . . . come the spices that are consumed in the East and the West, in Portugal, as in all other countries of the world, as also [are] precious stones of every description. The following spices are to be found in this city of Calicut, being its own produce: much ginger and pepper and cinnamon, although the last is not of so fine a quality as that brought from an island called Çillon [Ceylon],[1] which is eight days journey from Calicut. Calicut is the staple for all this cinnamon. Cloves are brought to this city from an island called Melqua [Malacca].[2] The Mecca vessels carry these spices from there to a city in Mecca[3] called Judeâ [Jeddah],[4] and from the said island to Judeâ is a voyage of 50 days sailing before the wind. . . . At Judeâ they discharge their cargoes, paying customs duties to the Grand Sultan.[5] The merchandise is then transshipped to smaller vessels, which carry it through the Red Sea to a place close to Santa Catarina of Mount Sinai,[6] called Tuuz [El Tûr][7] where customs dues are paid once more. From

[1]The modern island nation of Sri Lanka. At this time, Ceylon alone produced true cinnamon. The other cinnamon-like spice is cassia, which is made from the bark of a related tree that originated in China.
[2]The straits and city of Malacca were not the source. Cloves came from the Southeast Asian islands known as the Moluccas (or Spice Islands), which today constitute the province of Maluku in the Republic of Indonesia.
[3]Actually Arabia, Mecca [or Makkah] being the inland holy city of Islam in the Arabian Peninsula. Today Mecca is located in Saudi Arabia.
[4]Jeddah (or Jidda) is the Arabian Peninsula's main port city on the Red Sea.
[5]The Mamluk dynasty of sultans that ruled Egypt from 1250 to 1517.
[6]Saint Catherine's Monastery — an ancient Christian monastery in Egypt that still exists.
[7]A port on Egypt's Sinai Peninsula.

that place the merchants carry the spices on the backs of camels . . . to Quayro [Cairo], a journey occupying ten days. At Quayro duties are paid again. On this road to Cairo they are frequently robbed by thieves. . . .

At Cairo the spices are embarked on the river Nile . . . and descending[8] that river for two days they reach a place called Roxette [Rosetta], where duties have to be paid once more. There they are placed on camels, and are conveyed in one day to a city called Alexandria, which is a sea-port.[9] This city is visited by the galleys of Venice and Genoa, in search of these spices, which yield the Grand Sultan [an annual] revenue of 600,000 cruzados.[10]

[8]Sailing north.
[9]On the Mediterranean.
[10]A Portuguese gold coin that received its name from the crusader's cross emblazoned on it.

2 ▾ *Ibn Battuta, A GIFT TO THOSE WHO CONTEMPLATE THE WONDERS OF CITIES AND THE MARVELS ENCOUNTERED IN TRAVEL*

The sultan of Calicut is an infidel,[1] known as "the Sámarí."[2] . . . In this town too lives the famous ship-owner Mithqál,[3] who possesses vast wealth and many ships for his trade with India, China, Yemen, and Fars.[4] When we reached the city, the principal inhabitants and merchants and the sultan's representative came out to welcome us, with drums, trumpets, bugles and standards on their ships. We entered the harbor in great pomp. . . . We stopped in the port of Calicut, in which there were at the time thirteen Chinese vessels, and disembarked. Every one of us was lodged in a house, and we stayed three months as the guests of the infidel, awaiting the season of the voyage to China.[5] On the Sea of China traveling is done in Chinese ships only. . . .

The Chinese vessels are of three kinds: large ships called *chunks* [junks], middle-sized ones called *zaws* [dhows], and small ones called *kakams*. The large ships have from twelve down to three sails, which are made of bamboo rods plaited like mats. They are never lowered, but turned according to the direction of the wind. . . . A ship carries a complement of a thousand men, six hundred of whom are sailors and four hundred men-at-arms, including archers . . . and arbalists, who throw naptha.[6] . . . The vessel has four decks and contains rooms, cabins, and salons for merchants; a cabin has chambers and a lavatory, and can be locked by its occupant, who takes along with him slave girls and wives. Often a man will live in his cabin unknown to

[1]A Hindu.
[2]In the local language, the title was *Samudri raja*, which means "Lord of the Sea." The Portuguese would corrupt this to "Zamorin."
[3]A strange name, very much like being called "Goldie" in English. A measure of weight throughout the Islamic world, a *mithqal* was 4.72 grams of gold. This might mean the man was a Muslim from across the Arabian Sea.
[4]Yemen is the southwestern tip of the Arabian Peninsula; Fars is the southern region of Iran along the Gulf of Oman.
[5]They awaited the lessening of the northeast monsoon winds, which blow from late November to April. The period around 11 April was considered the best time to begin a voyage from the Malabar Coast to the Bay of Bengal, which lay east of India.
[6]Crossbowmen who shoot missiles containing a mixture of fiery materials.

any of the others on board until they meet on reaching some town. The sailors have their children on board ship, and they cultivate green stuffs, vegetables, and ginger in wooden tanks. The owner's factor [agent-in-charge] on board ship is like a great amir.[7] When he goes on shore he is preceded by archers and Abyssinians[8] with javelins, swords, drums, trumpets, and bugles. On reaching the house where he stays, they stand their lances on both sides of the door, and continue thus during his stay. Some of the Chinese own large numbers of ships on which their factors are sent to foreign countries. There is no people in the world wealthier than the Chinese.

When the time came for the voyage to China, the sultan Sámarí made provision for us on one of the thirteen junks in the port of Calicut. The factor on the junk was called Sulayman of Safad,[9] in Syria. . . .

▹ Disaster strikes. Ibn Battuta's ship sinks in a storm in the harbor before he boards it, but it carries with it to the bottom all of his baggage, servants, and slaves.

Next morning we found the bodies of Sumbal and Zahir ad-Din,[10] and having prayed over them buried them. I saw the infidel, the sultan of Calicut . . . a fire lit before him on the beach; his police officers were beating the people to prevent them from plundering what the sea had cast up. In all the lands of Malabar, except in this one land alone, it is the custom that whenever a ship is wrecked all that is taken from it belongs to the treasury. At Calicut, however, it is retained by its owners, and for that reason Calicut has become a flourishing city and attracts large numbers of merchants.

[7]Lord or commander.

[8]Persons from the Horn of Africa — modern Ethiopia, Eritrea, and Somalia — and maybe even farther south along the Swahili Coast.

[9]Zefat in present-day Israel.

[10]Envoys whom the sultan of Delhi had dispatched to accompany him.

3 ▾ *Ma Huan, THE OVERALL SURVEY OF THE OCEAN'S SHORES*

THE COUNTRY OF GULI

The king of the country is a Nankun[1] man; he is a firm believer in the Buddhist religion[2] and he venerates the elephant and the ox. . . .

The king of the country and the people of the country all refrain from eating the flesh of the ox. The great chiefs are Muslim people; they all refrain from eating the flesh of the pig. Formerly there was a king who made a sworn compact with the Muslim people [who said to him], "You do not eat the ox; I do not eat the pig; we will reciprocally respect the taboo"; [and this compact] has been honored right down to the present day. . . .

The king has two great chiefs who administer the affairs of the country; both are Muslims.

The majority of the people in the country all profess the Muslim religion. There are twenty or thirty temples of worship,[3] and once in seven days they go to worship. . . .

[1]High caste — probably a member of the Kshatriya, or warrior-ruler, caste.

[2]Actually, he was a Hindu. His veneration of an ox (probably a bull) suggests he was a devotee of Shiva.

[3]The preceding sentence and the following reference to the weekly day of worship make it appear that these temples were mosques. It seems unlikely, however, that the majority of the population was Muslim and that Calicut had twenty or thirty mosques. More likely, it had several mosques and many Hindu temples. As a Muslim, Ma Huan might have thought, incorrectly, that Hindus, like Muslims, have a once-a-week day of communal prayer.

If a [Chinese] treasure-ship goes there,[4] it is left entirely to the two men to superintend the buying and selling; the king sends a chief and a Zhedi Weinoji[5] to examine the account books in the official bureau; a broker comes and joins them; [and] a high officer who commands the ships discusses the choice of a certain date for fixing prices. When the day arrives, they first of all take the silk embroideries . . . and other such goods that have been brought there [by the ship], and discuss the price of them one by one; when [the price] has been fixed, they write out an agreement stating the amount of the price, [which] is retained by these persons.

The chief and the Zhedi, with his excellency the eunuch,[6] all join hands together, and the broker then says, "In such and such a moon, on such and such a day, we have all joined hands and sealed our agreement with a hand-clasp; whether [the price] be dear or cheap, we will never repudiate or change it."

After that, the Zhedi and the men of wealth then come bringing precious stones, pearls, corals, and other such things, so that they may be examined and the price discussed; [this] cannot be settled in a day; [if done] quickly, [it takes] one moon; [if done] slowly, two or three moons.

Once the money-price has been fixed after examination and discussion, if a pearl or other such article is purchased, the price that must be paid for it is calculated by the chief and the Weinoji who carried out the original transaction. As to the quantity of the hemp-silk or other such article that must be given in exchange for it, goods are exchanged according to [the price fixed by] the original hand-clasp — there is not the slightest deviation. . . .

The king uses gold of 60 percent to cast a coin for current use. . . . He also makes a coin of silver . . . for petty transactions. . . .

The people of the country also take the silk of the silk-worm, soften it by boiling, dye it all colors, and weave it into kerchiefs with decorative stripes at intervals . . . ; each length is sold for 100 gold coins.

As to pepper; the inhabitants of the mountainous countryside have established gardens, and it is extensively cultivated. When the period of the tenth moon arrives, the pepper ripens. It is collected, dried in the sun, and sold. Of course, big pepper-collectors come and collect it, and take it to the official storehouse to be stored; if there is a buyer, an official gives permission for the sale. The duty is collected according to the amount [of the purchase price] and is paid to the authorities. . . .

Foreign ships from every place come there; and the king of the country also sends a chief and a writer and others to watch the sales; thereupon they collect the duty and pay it to the authorities.

---

[4]The fleets commanded by Zheng He contained a significant number of treasure ships — large ships along the lines described by Ibn Battuta that carried Chinese trade goods and gifts, but which also were meant to carry back tribute, foreign trade goods, exotic items, and persons of importance invited (or compelled) to visit the imperial court at Nanjing. By extension, Ma Huan means any Chinese trading vessel.

[5]Probably his attempt to transliterate *Waligi Chitty*, or accountant.

[6]The reference is to Zheng He, a eunuch, who commanded the treasure ships that visited Calicut during these voyages, but more broadly it probably also refers to the commander of any Chinese ship.

4 ▾ THE CATALAN WORLD ATLAS

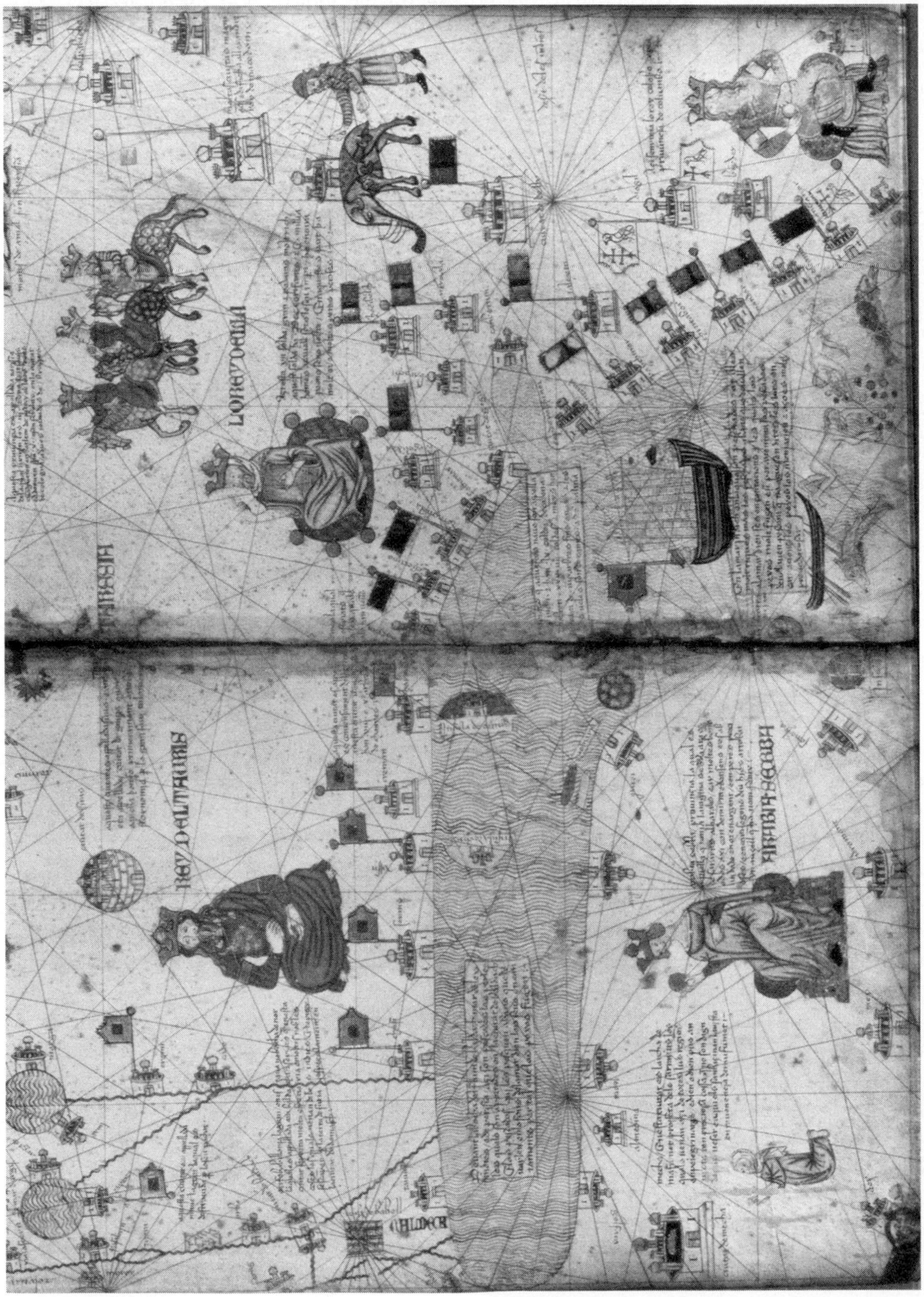

Interpreting the Sources

These four pieces of evidence allow us to say quite a bit about Calicut before Europeans established a strong presence in the Indian Ocean. Let us begin with the two Western sources.

The *Catalan World Atlas* depicts what is unmistakably a Chinese vessel off the west coast of India. The plaited bamboo sails, which Ibn Battuta described, as well as the distinctive hats worn by the two men, make that identification easy. Clearly, Westerners realized as early as the fourteenth century that the Chinese were major players in the commerce of the Indian subcontinent. The West's knowledge of the great wealth of India, as well as its high degree of urbanization and its political fragmentation, is obvious from the portraits of the sultan of Delhi and the raja of Vijayanagara, as well as the symbols for the many cities dotting the coastline and interior. The pearl divers, elephant, and Three Magi only add to the overall picture of India's riches and wonders. The fact is that between roughly 1250 and 1350 a significant number of Europeans, especially missionaries and merchants, had traveled, largely by land, to China and India, and some of them, such as Marco Polo, had written widely circulated accounts of their experiences. Even if you did not know that, you can infer from this map segment alone that the fourteenth-century West was not totally ignorant of India's geography and dynamics, including the importance of Chinese merchants in the commerce of the Malabar Coast.

The *Roteiro* illustrates why the Portuguese desired direct overseas access to the rich markets of India and beyond. Given the numerous duties and profit margins placed on spices that made their way to Egypt and from there to Europe, the Portuguese realized that access to the markets of the Malabar Coast and beyond would enable them cut out many of the middle agents who profited greatly from this lucrative trade. At this point there is no good reason for you to know that the overland trade routes between Europe and the "Indies" (India, China, and other distant lands in Asia and East Africa) had largely broken down after about 1350 (see Vol. I, Chapter 12) and that the closing down of those routes spurred Portugal and Spain to find alternate ways by sea. What you can easily infer from this source is that the Portuguese expected to make much more per year than the 600,000 *cruzados* that the sultan of Egypt enjoyed, once they had direct access to Calicut. As we learn from this anonymous author, not only was Calicut a major commercial emporium, it was also a center of spice and gemstone production.

The *Roteiro* makes clear how important Calicut was to the commerce of Arabia and Egypt, Venice, Genoa, and the Spice Islands; Ibn Battuta and Ma Huan show us how central Calicut was to the overseas trade of China and other segments of the Islamic world. Our Moroccan and Chinese eyewitnesses further depict Calicut as an international city, where Muslims served both Chinese shipowners and the Hindu ruler of Calicut as trusted, high-ranking officials in charge of commercial activities. Both authors also shed light on policies adopted by the rulers of Calicut to encourage commerce and friendly relations with neighboring and far-distant powers.

Ibn Battuta tells us how his diplomatic party was received with great ceremony and how the *Samudri raja* arranged for his transportation aboard a Chinese vessel. Even more revealing are his descriptions of the sizes and types of the Chinese ships that did business at Calicut; the high status and honor accorded the factors, or agents-in-charge, of these Chinese ships; and the manner in which the ruler of Calicut protected the goods of shipwrecked merchants. The size of their ships alone suggests that the Chinese invested heavily in their trade with Calicut, but they did so because they knew that they would be welcomed and treated fairly at the port city. And why not? The rulers of Calicut understood that the prosperity of their city depended on the satisfaction of visiting merchants.

Ma Huan provides additional detail in this regard. The rajas of Calicut maintained a policy of religious toleration, which, given how much they depended on Muslim officials and merchants, was the only logical policy to follow. And this was in an age when bitter wars were fought between the sultanate of Delhi and Vijayanagara. The rajas also provided for a well-run and honest marketplace by commissioning officials who were responsible for facilitating all commercial transactions and guaranteeing all contracts. Inasmuch as a tax on all sales was paid into the ruler's treasury, it was in his best interest to grease the wheels of trade and to guarantee that once a deal was struck, it was inviolate. The fact that the raja minted gold and silver coins suggests that these policies worked well.

Finally, Ma Huan supports and supplements evidence from the *Roteiro* regarding Calicut's industries. Pepper production, which was carefully regulated by the state in regard to collection, storage, and sale (although the trees were apparently cultivated in small family garden plots), was a major staple of Calicut's economy. Likewise, Calicut's silk industry produced expensive bolts of silk, and the region was also a major source for coral and gemstones, especially pearls. Despite its native silk production, however, Calicut was a center for trade in Chinese embroidered silk. Apparently the high quality of this product allowed it to compete favorably with Indian silk.

Well, as you can see, interpreting historical sources is not an arcane science or esoteric art. Yes, it is challenging, but it is a skill that you can master. Look at it this way: It is an exercise that mainly requires close attention and common sense. You must first read and study each source carefully and thoroughly. Then, using the evidence you have picked up from the documents and artifacts, answer the Questions for Analysis. It is that straightforward. If you work with us, trusting us to provide you with all of the necessary background information and clues that you need to make sense out of these sources, you will succeed.

One last word: Have fun doing it because you should find it enjoyable to meet the challenge of reconstructing the past through its human records.

Part One

A New Era of Interaction and Exchange: The Fifteenth Through Seventeenth Centuries

A NEW ERA IN WORLD HISTORY began in 1419 when two small Portuguese ships under the command of João Gonçalves Zarco and Tristão Vaz Teixeira left Lagos harbor, at the southwest corner of the Iberian Peninsula, and sailed into the ocean waters off Africa's northwest coast. Driven off course by a storm, the Portuguese reached a tiny uninhabited island some 440 miles west of Morocco that they named Porto Santo — Blessed Port. Leaving Teixeira and a small crew behind, Zarco sailed back to Portugal and returned a year later with a charter from Prince Henry the Navigator (1394–1460), the third son of King João and the driving force behind the 1419 expedition and many of those that followed. More important, some years later, probably around 1429, Zarco brought with him a small number of colonists, who settled on Porto Santo and a larger island to the south, Madeira. Within a decade, these settlers had introduced grapevines from Crete and sugar cane from Sicily and were reaping handsome profits from the export of wine, high-quality wood, dyestuffs, fish, timber, and sugar to Europe.

With these events began the era of European exploration, expansion, and colonization. Although mariners from France, Spain, Portugal, and Italy had reached the Canary Islands — an archipelago in the Atlantic even farther south than Madeira — as early as the thirteenth century, they went no farther, and for more than 200 years the Canaries remained the southernmost limit of Europeans' knowledge of the western Atlantic. But during the fifteenth century, the Portuguese pushed farther west and south, establishing fortified trading posts on Africa's coast and claiming and colonizing the Azores, Cape Verde, and the islands of São Tomé and Príncipe. In doing so, they learned more about wind patterns, ocean currents, commercial opportunities, and the peoples of Africa. In 1488 Bartolomeu Dias rounded the Cape of Good Hope, on Africa's southwestern tip, and in 1497–1498 four ships under the command of Vasco da Gama sailed around Africa and reached Calicut, on India's west coast. Lured by the prospect of trading directly with Asia, the Portuguese pushed on, reaching the Malay coast in 1511, China in 1513, and Japan in 1542. They soon established commercial routes to Africa and Asia and began to reap huge profits from the sale of African ivory, pepper, gold, slaves, and especially Asian spices.

Even before da Gama reached India, other Europeans were seeking new ocean routes to Asia. Columbus's voyage of 1492 was the first of dozens of expeditions that established a vast Spanish empire not in Asia but in the Americas. Northern Europeans also joined the competition. The French, Dutch, English, Danes, and Swedes claimed lands in the Americas and the Caribbean, and the French, Dutch, and English challenged the Portuguese in Asia. Thus, the modest Portuguese expedition of 1419 initiated two centuries of European exploration, conquest, and commercial expansion, the consequences of which were so momentous that no other development in the early modern era rivals its significance.

Early European expansion had its greatest impact on Mexico and Central and South America, where Spanish and Portuguese conquests, accompanied by economic exploitation and the introduction of Old World diseases, killed millions of Native Americans and destroyed much of their ancient cultures. The indigenous peoples of North America faced similar threats only after 1600, when European settlers arrived and began their slow but relentless expansion into the continent's interior. Here, the Native Americans' loss of territory and identity was not as sudden or dramatic, but the process was no less painful, and the results no less devastating.

Africa also was deeply affected by European expansion, even though Europeans remained largely on the coast and relied on Africans to bring them items for trade. In addition to gold, ivory, and pepper, these items included slaves, who in the 1400s and 1500s were shipped first to Europe, then to São Tomé, Madeira, and the Canaries, and finally in ever greater numbers to the New World.

Asia underwent important changes in the sixteenth and seventeenth centuries, but most of them had little to do with European expansion. In Southwest Asia, the Ottoman Empire extended and consolidated an empire that was centered in Anatolia but also included territory in Syria-Palestine, the Arabian Peninsula, northern Africa, and southeastern Europe. Farther east, two new states, the Safavid Empire in Persia and the Mughal Empire in India, took shape. In Southeast Asia, the continuing expansion of Islam was the most important development. In Japan, a century of civil war ended in 1603 when the Tokugawa clan established a new regime that unified and stabilized Japan. In China, Manchu invaders from the north displaced the Ming Dynasty in 1644 and established China's last imperial dynasty, the Qing. By 1650 only the Philippines, conquered by Spain; Siberia, conquered by Russia; and parts of Indonesia, controlled by the Dutch, were under direct European rule.

The Europeans, although successful in extending their worldwide influence, experienced wrenching changes and bitter conflicts at home. Overseas trade and the influx of gold and silver from the Americas fueled economic growth, but this growth had mixed results. Inflation caused difficulties for individuals and governments alike, and some regions, such as Italy, declined economically as commerce shifted from the Mediterranean to the Atlantic.

Knowledge of new lands and peoples added to the intellectual ferment and conflict fueled by Renaissance humanism, Protestantism, and scientific discoveries. Wars, religious conflict, and revolts were endemic, and some states, such as France, almost disintegrated. By 1650 Europe had resolved many of these conflicts. European society had not only survived a century and a half of rapid change but had also grown stronger from it. Europe's emergence as a world power had begun.

Chapter 1

Europe in an Age of Conflict and Expansion

FROM THE 1400S THROUGH THE MID 1600s, Europe changed in many ways. Religious uniformity under the Roman Catholic Church gave way to religious diversity as new Protestant churches rejected papal authority and Catholic doctrine. A political order characterized by local aristocratic power, decentralized authority, and weak monarchies was undermined by the emergence of increasingly centralized and fiercely competitive nation-states. Armies grew in size, and battles were fought by soldiers armed with artillery and firearms, not longbows, pikes, and lances. Intellectuals lost interest in the abstract theological and philosophical speculations that had preoccupied their thirteenth-century predecessors and, inspired by new interests in Greek and Roman antiquity, they broke new ground in science, moral philosophy, and political thought. Writers, artists, and architects developed new styles and themes, and explorers discovered new ocean routes that took them to Africa, Asia, and the Americas.

Taken together, these changes mark the end of the Middle Ages, that long, formative period of European civilization that began with the fall of the Western Roman Empire in the fifth century C.E. These changes are generally viewed as indicators of progress, growth, and advancement in an age of renaissance, or rebirth, after centuries of medieval stagnation. Such a view is problematic. Aside from belittling the impressive achievements of the Middle Ages, it ignores the many tensions, doubts, and conflicts that accompanied the political, economic, and cultural changes of the immediate postmedieval era.

In many ways these years are better characterized as an "era of contradiction" or an "era of conflict" than as an age of rebirth. The emergence of Protestantism, for example, ultimately led to an acceptance of religious diversity and religious toleration in most of Europe, but in the sixteenth and early seventeenth centuries it resulted in war, rebellion, and persecution. Tens of thousands of Europeans were exiled, imprisoned, or executed because of their religious convictions, and millions died as a result of the religious wars that stretched from the 1520s to the 1640s. The discoveries of Copernicus, Kepler, Galileo, and others in the long run provided the foundation for one of Europe's most enduring achievements — experimental, mathematics-based science. During their own lifetimes, however, their rejection of ancient authorities and their many disagreements led to the pessimistic view that humans could know little if anything with certainty. Nor did these scientists' discoveries dispel the irrational fears and superstitions of the age. Witch hunts and witch trials claimed the lives of thousands of individuals thought to have given themselves over to the Devil in return for supernatural powers.

The sixteenth century witnessed spectacular economic growth that generated new forms of business organization such as the joint stock company and created huge fortunes for many merchants and investors. But mounting inflation caused hardship for landlords and peasants, and around 1600 plague, famine, war, and depression caused a decline in Europe's overall standard of living. Political changes also caused tensions. Advocates of centralized monarchy contended with defenders of local autonomy, divine right absolutists faced believers in regicide, and kings battled parliaments. Wars were fought to gain or protect territory, to advance the cause of Catholicism or Protestantism, to settle dynastic claims, or to fulfill personal ambitions. The Thirty Years' War (1618–1648) involved every major European state and caused human suffering unmatched in Europe until the wars of the twentieth century.

Expansionist Europe was not, as one might have expected, a stable, cohesive, and self-confident society. By luck the Europeans, in their efforts to reach Asia by sailing west, discovered the Americas, whose peoples were easily subdued after millions of them died from imported Old World diseases. Elsewhere, the Europeans' success in developing the military potential of gunpowder, in particular the ability to mount artillery on oceangoing ships, enabled them to expand their economic activities and establish a measure of political power on the fringes of Africa and Asia. But these accomplishments, rightly deemed significant by historians, gave scant comfort to the majority of Europeans, who faced a troubled present and anticipated the future with more foreboding than hope.

Religious Controversy in the Reformation Era

During the High Middle Ages, "the age of faith," the devotion accorded the Catholic Church resulted in part from the clergy's moral example and leadership and in part from the Church's promise that its doctrines and practices, if followed, assured eternal salvation. During the fourteenth and fifteenth centuries, however, the Church was rocked by schism, scandal, deficits, political challenges, and uninspired and corrupt leadership. Anger over abuses intensified, and many Europeans began to question the Church's ability to deliver the salvation they fervently sought. These doubts go far in explaining the success of the Protestant revolt, sparked in 1517 when a German friar, Martin Luther, challenged Catholic teachings, especially the doctrine that people could atone for their sins by purchasing indulgences. By 1650 Protestants dominated northern Germany, Scandinavia, England, Scotland, the Netherlands, and major Swiss cities and were a significant minority in France and parts of central Europe.

No area of European life was unaffected by the Protestant Reformation. In the religious sphere, new Protestant churches proliferated, and Catholic reforms revitalized an institution that had lost its spiritual focus and vitality. Education expanded because of the Protestants' emphasis on Bible reading by the laity and the need of competing churches for educated leadership. Literacy among women increased as a result of Protestant educational efforts, and according to some historians, a more positive view of women resulted from the Protestant affirmation of clerical marriage. Conversely, Protestant women made no appreciable legal or economic gains and were just as likely as their Catholic sisters to be victimized by witch hunts and witch trials. The religious struggles of the Reformation era also affected politics. With religious passions exacerbating dynastic rivalries and internal conflicts, Europe endured a century of religious wars, including both civil wars and wars between states.

Most importantly, the Reformation era contributed to Europe's ongoing secularization. In the short run, the Protestant and Catholic reformations intensified religious feeling and thrust religion into the forefront of European life. In the long run, however, the proliferation of competing faiths divided and weakened Europe's churches, and the long years of religious intolerance and war discredited religion in the eyes of many. The gradual acceptance of religious diversity within individual states and Europe as a whole was a sign of growing secularism. Paradoxically, the very intensity of the era's religious passions helped undermine the role of religion in European life and thought.

A Protestant View of Christianity

▼▼▼

1 ▼ *Martin Luther, TABLE TALK*

The Protestant Reformation had many voices, but its first prophet was Martin Luther (1483–1546), whose Ninety-five Theses of 1517 sparked the momentous anti-Catholic rebellion. Born into the family of a German miner and educated at the University of Erfurt, Luther was preparing for a career as a lawyer when suddenly in 1505 he changed course and became an Augustinian friar. Luther's decision followed a terrifying experience in a thunderstorm but at a deeper level resulted from his dissatisfaction over his relationship with God and doubts about his salvation. He hoped that life as a friar would shield him from the world's temptations and allow him to win God's favor by devoting himself to prayer, study, and the sacraments. His spiritual doubts soon returned, however. Intensely conscious of his own inadequacies and failings, he became convinced that he could never earn his salvation or live up to the high standards of selflessness, charity, and purity prescribed by Jesus' teachings and the Catholic Church. He despaired of ever satisfying an angry, judging God and was terrorized by the prospect of eternal damnation.

During the 1510s, however, while teaching theology at the University of Wittenberg, Luther found spiritual peace through his reflections on the Scriptures. He concluded that human beings, burdened by weakness and sin, were incapable of earning their own salvation by leading a blameless life and performing the pious acts enjoined by the Catholic Church. Rather, he came to view salvation as an unmerited divine gift, resulting from God-implanted faith in Jesus, especially in the redemptive power of his death and resurrection. This doctrine of "justification by faith alone" inspired the Ninety-five Theses, in which Luther attacked contemporary Catholic teaching, especially the doctrine of indulgences, which taught that people could atone for their sins and ensure their own and loved ones' salvation by contributing money to the Church. Within five years Luther was the recognized leader of a religious movement — Protestantism — that broke with the Catholic Church not only over the theology of salvation but also over a host of other fundamental issues concerning Christianity and the Christian life.

As Protestantism spread from Germany to other parts of Europe, Luther remained in Wittenberg as a pastor and professor and wrote hundreds of sermons, books, and treatises in defense of his beliefs. He and his wife, Katharina, a former nun, made their home in the Augustinian convent where Luther had lived as a friar. Here they raised a family and entertained scores of religious leaders and students with whom Luther loved to discuss the issues of the day. From 1522 to 1546, some of these guests recorded Luther's most notable sayings as they remembered them, and from their journals we have what is known as Luther's *Tischreden*, or *Table Talk*.

QUESTIONS FOR ANALYSIS

1. **According to Luther, what role should the Bible play in a Christian's life? In his view how does the Roman Catholic Church obscure the Bible's meaning and message?**
2. **What does Luther mean by "good works"? Why does he believe that the Roman Catholic Church distorts the role of good works in a Christian's life?**
3. **What role does faith play in a Christian's life, according to Luther? Why is he convinced that faith is superior to external acts of devotion?**
4. **What are Luther's criticisms of the pope and other high officials of the Catholic Church?**
5. **Why does Luther single out monks and members of religious orders for special criticism? What are their shortcomings?**

SALVATION AND DAMNATION

Because as the everlasting, merciful God, through his Word[1] and Sacraments,[2] talks and deals with us, all other creatures excluded, not of temporal things which pertain to this vanishing life . . . but as to where we shall go when we depart from here, and gives unto us his Son for a Savior, delivering us from sin and death, and purchasing for us everlasting righteousness, life, and salvation, therefore it is most certain, that we do not die away like the beasts that have no understanding; but so many of us . . . shall through him be raised again to life everlasting at the last day, and the ungodly to everlasting destruction.

FAITH VERSUS GOOD WORKS

He that goes from the gospel to the law,[3] thinking to be saved by good works,[4] falls as uneasily as he who falls from the true service of God to idolatry; for, without Christ, all is idolatry and fictitious imaginings of God, whether of the Turkish Quran, of the pope's decrees, or Moses' laws; if a man think thereby to be justified and saved before God, he is undone.

▾ ▾ ▾

The gospel preaches nothing of the merit of works; he that says the gospel requires works for salvation, I say, flat and plain, is a liar.

Nothing that is properly good proceeds out of the works of the law, unless grace be present; for what we are forced to do, goes not from the heart, nor is acceptable.

---

[1]The *Word* is God's message, especially as revealed through Jesus' life.

[2]Sacraments are sacred rites that are outward visible signs of an inward spiritual grace to which the promise of Christ is attached. Of the seven Catholic sacraments, Luther retained two, baptism and the eucharist.

[3]By *law* Luther meant religious rules and regulations; he believed that futile human efforts to live strictly according to the dictates of the law undermined true faith.

[4]All the ceremonies and pious activities such as pilgrimages, relic veneration, and attendance at Mass that the Catholic Church promoted as vehicles of God's grace and eternal salvation.

▾ ▾ ▾

A Capuchin[5] says: wear a grey coat and a hood, a rope round thy body, and sandals on thy feet. A Cordelier says: put on a black hood; an ordinary papist says: do this or that work, hear mass, pray, fast, give alms, etc. But a true Christian says: I am justified and saved only by faith in Christ, without any works or merits of my own; compare these together, and judge which is the true righteousness.

▾ ▾ ▾

I have often been resolved to live uprightly, and to lead a true godly life, and to set everything aside that would hinder this, but it was far from being put in execution; even as it was with Peter,[6] when he swore he would lay down his life for Christ.

▾ ▾ ▾

I will not lie or dissemble before my God, but will freely confess, I am not able to effect that good which I intend, but await the happy hour when God shall be pleased to meet me with his grace.

▾ ▾ ▾

A Christian's worshiping is not the external, hypocritical mask that our friars wear, when they chastise their bodies, torment and make themselves faint, with ostentatious fasting, watching, singing, wearing hair shirts, scourging themselves, etc. Such worshiping God does not desire.

THE BIBLE

Great is the strength of the divine Word. In the epistle to the Hebrews,[7] it is called "a two-edged sword." But we have neglected and scorned the pure and clear Word, and have drunk not of the fresh and cool spring; we are gone from the clear fountain to the foul puddle, and drunk its filthy water; that is, we have diligently read old writers and teachers, who went about with speculative reasonings, like the monks and friars.

▾ ▾ ▾

The ungodly papists prefer the authority of the church far above God's Word; a blasphemy abominable and not to be endured; void of all shame and piety, they spit in God's face. Truly, God's patience is exceeding great, in that they are not destroyed; but so it always has been.

THE PAPACY AND THE MONASTIC ORDERS

How does it happen that the popes pretend that they form the Church, when, all the while, they are bitter enemies of the Church, and have no knowledge, certainly no comprehension, of the holy gospel? Pope, cardinals, bishops, not a soul of them has read the Bible; it is a book unknown to them. They are a pack of guzzling, gluttonous wretches, rich, wallowing in wealth and laziness, resting secure in their power, and never, for a moment, thinking of accomplishing God's will.

▾ ▾ ▾

Kings and princes coin money only out of metals, but the pope coins money out of everything — indulgences, ceremonies, dispensations, pardons; all fish come to his net. . . .

▾ ▾ ▾

A gentleman being at the point of death, a monk from the next convent came to see what he could pick up, and said to the gentleman: Sir, will you give so and so to our monastery? The dying man,

[5]The Capuchins and Cordeliers were both branches of the Franciscan order noted for their austerity and strict poverty. A distinctive feature of the Capuchins' dress was their peaked hood, or *capuche*.

[6]One of Jesus' twelve apostles; following Jesus' arrest before his crucifixion by Roman soldiers, Peter three times denied any relationship with Jesus, despite having vowed shortly before to lay down his life for his teacher. Eventually, Peter died a martyr in Rome.

[7]Paul's Letter to the Hebrews, a part of the Christian Bible, or New Testament.

unable to speak, replied by a nod of the head, whereupon the monk, turning to the gentleman's son, said: You see, your father makes us this bequest. The son said to the father: Sir, is it your pleasure that I kick this monk down the stairs? The dying man nodded as before, and the son immediately drove the monk out of doors.

▾ ▾ ▾

The papists took the invocation of saints from the pagans, who divided God into numberless images and idols, and ordained to each its particular office and work. . . .

The invocation of saints is a most abominable blindness and heresy; yet the papists will not give it up. The pope's greatest profit arises from the dead; for the calling on dead saints brings him infinite sums of money and riches, far more than he gets from the living. . . .

▾ ▾ ▾

In Italy, the monasteries are very wealthy. There are but three or four monks to each; the surplus of their revenues goes to the pope and his cardinals.

▾ ▾ ▾

The fasting of the friars is more easy to them than our eating to us. For one day of fasting there are three of feasting. Every friar for his supper has two quarts of beer, a quart of wine, and spice-cakes, or bread prepared with spice and salt, the better to relish their drink. Thus go on these poor fasting brethren; getting so pale and wan, they are like the fiery angels.

▾ ▾ ▾

In Popedom they make priests, not to preach and teach God's Word, but only to celebrate mass, and to roam about with the sacrament. For, when a bishop ordains a man, he says: Take the power to celebrate mass, and to offer it for the living and the dead. But we ordain priests according to the command of Christ and St. Paul, namely, to preach the pure gospel and God's Word. The papists in their ordinations make no mention of preaching and teaching God's Word, therefore their consecrating and ordaining is false and wrong, for all worshiping which is not ordained of God, or erected by God's Word and command, is worthless, yea, mere idolatry.

THE REFORM OF THE CHURCH

The pope and his crew can in no way endure the idea of reformation; the mere word creates more alarm at Rome than thunderbolts from heaven or the day of judgment. A cardinal said the other day: Let them eat, and drink, and do what they will; but as to reforming us, we think that is a vain idea; we will not endure it. Neither will we Protestants be satisfied, though they administer the sacrament in both kinds, and permit priests to marry;[8] we will also have the doctrine of the faith pure and unfalsified, and the righteousness that justifies and saves before God, and which expels and drives away all idolatry and false-worshiping; with these gone and banished, the foundation on which Popedom is built also falls.

▾ ▾ ▾

The chief cause that I fell out with the pope was this: the pope boasted that he was the head of the church, and condemned all that would not be under his power and authority; . . . Further, he took upon him power, rule, and authority over the Christian church, and over the Holy Scriptures, the Word of God; no man must presume to expound the Scriptures, but only he, and according to his ridiculous conceits; this was not to be endured. They who, against God's word, boast of the church's authority, are mere idiots.

[8]Two of the many changes that Protestants demanded were allowing all Christians to receive the sacrament of the eucharist in the forms of bread and wine (in medieval Roman Catholic practice, only the priest drank the eucharistic wine) and allowing priests to marry. The principle behind both changes was Luther's teaching that all Christians are in a sense priests — that is, responsible for their own religious faith.

Art as Protestant Propaganda

▼▼▼

2 ▾ *Lucas Cranach the Younger, TWO KINDS OF PREACHING: EVANGELICAL AND PAPAL*

Some seventy years before Luther posted his Ninety-five Theses, another German, Johannes Gutenberg (ca. 1395–1468), perfected a method of printing books through movable metal type. Printing shops soon were established in hundreds of European towns and cities, and by the mid sixteenth century hundreds of thousands of books and pamphlets had been published.

Many of these publications played key roles in the era's religious struggles. The Ninety-five Theses, intended by Luther to spark academic debate at the University of Wittenberg, brought him instant prominence when they were translated into German and made available in cheap printed editions. Subsequently, Protestants, much more than Catholics, used the printed page to promote their ideas in Latin treatises for learned audiences and, more tellingly, in German books and pamphlets for the general population. Illustrations in the form of woodcuts were included in many of these works to make Protestant teachings accessible even to the illiterate.

One of the most famous of these illustrations is ***Two Kinds of Preaching: Evangelical and Papal***, the work of a lifelong resident of Wittenberg and a close friend of Luther's, Lucas Cranach the Younger (1515–1586). Produced in 1547, it was distributed not as a book illustration but as a broadsheet — a single large printed sheet sold for a few small coins.

We have reproduced the woodcut on two pages, but in its original form it is undivided. The preacher facing left is Luther. Before him rests an open Bible, and on his side of the pulpit are words from the New Testament Book of Acts: "All prophets attest to this, that there is no other name in heaven than that of Christ." Above Luther is a dove, representing the Holy Spirit, the third person of the Holy Trinity, whose major functions are illumination, solace, and sanctification. Luther is pointing to three heavenly figures: the Paschal Lamb (a symbol of the risen Christ), the crucified Christ, and God the Father, who holds an orb symbolizing his dominion over creation. The crucified Christ directs the following words to God the Father: "Holy Father, save them. I have sacrificed myself for them with my wounds." Directly below is written, "If we sin, we have an advocate before God, so let us turn in consolation to this means of grace." In the center and lower left corner, the two Lutheran sacraments, baptism and the Eucharist, are depicted. It is noteworthy that in celebrating the Eucharist, the Lutheran pastor offers to the laypeople both the communion wafer, representing Christ's body, and wine, representing Christ's blood, as opposed to the Catholic practice of restricting the drinking of the wine to the priest. Above the communion table and to the left of the crucified Christ are the words uttered by Christ at the Last Supper according to Matthew 26: "Drink of it, all of you."

The right side of the woodcut is a Lutheran perspective on how Roman Catholicism has perverted Christianity. The preaching friar receives inspiration from an imp-like demon that pumps air into his ear with a bellows. The words above his head summarize his message that the practices going on about him are theologically sound and offer an easy path to salvation. His audience consists mainly of clergy, with only a handful of laypeople included. In the upper right corner, an angry God rains down thunderbolts while Francis of Assisi, the founder of the Franciscan order and a revered medieval saint, attempts in vain to intercede on behalf of wayward humanity. The rest of the scene ridicules various Catholic practices. They include, in the lower right corner, the sale of indulgences by the pope, who holds a sign reading: "Because the coin rings, the soul to heaven springs." The sign on the money bag reads: "This is shame and vice, squeezed from your donations." Directly behind the pope are a priest celebrating a private Mass and an altar being consecrated by a birdlike demon. Deeper in the background is a dying man having his hair clipped in the style of a monk and having a monk's cowl, or hood, placed on his head, steps that supposedly would ensure his salvation. The attending nun sprinkles the man with holy water and holds a banner reading: "The cowl, the tonsure, and the water aid you." To the right of this scene, a bishop consecrates a bell. In the far background, two pilgrims approach a small chapel, around which marches a procession honoring the saint depicted on the banner. To Lutherans, all these practices represent misguided rituals that replace faith with meaningless "works."

QUESTIONS FOR ANALYSIS

1. What differences do you see in the makeup of the crowds surrounding the pulpits on the two sides of the picture (see pages 14 and 15)? What point is Cranach trying to make?
2. What views of the Bible are presented in the woodcuts?
3. Examine the attire of the clergy crowded around the pulpit in the right half of the woodcut. What point is Cranach attempting to make?
4. The woodcuts depict the Catholic Church as full of abuses. What are these abuses, and how are they illustrated?
5. How many specific points made by Luther in his *Table Talk* can you find illustrated in the Cranach woodcut?

Lucas Cranach the Younger, Two Kinds of Preaching: Evangelical

Lucas Cranach the Younger, Two Kinds of Preaching: Papal

Emerging Capitalism and Its Critics

The oft-repeated formula that medieval society was divided into three orders — those who prayed (the clergy), those who fought (the nobility), and those who worked (the peasantry) — was first stated around 1000 C.E. by the churchman Adelbert of Laon in a poem dedicated to King Robert II of France. If the bishop had written his poem almost any time later in the Middle Ages, he would have had to modify his analysis to include another important group — those who traded (merchants). Around 1000 C.E. Europe was already in the early stages of a prolonged period of economic expansion fueled by increased agricultural production, the rise of towns and cities, improvements in roads and bridges, the achievement of relative political stability, and regional specialization.

Trade played a key role in this economic growth. Local trade was centered in town and city markets, usually held once a week in the shadow of the town hall or church, where carts were parked, stalls were erected, and villagers from the countryside sold grain, cattle, swine, chickens, fruits, vegetables, hides, wool, and flax in exchange for silver or copper coins or articles made in the towns or from more distant places. Long-distance trade was centered in fairs, markets where at predetermined times during the year merchants gathered to exchange goods, money, gossip, and news. Trade fairs existed in every part of Europe, but the most famous were those of the Champagne region of northern France. Situated on the major trade routes between northern and southern Europe — and with access to the markets of the Baltic region, the Low Countries, and Germany — the towns of Bar-sur-Seine, Troyes, Provins, and Lagny hosted fairs lasting up to six weeks that together stretched from January to October. Trade items were not limited to European goods. By far the most glamorous (and expensive) goods at the fairs were silks, spices, drugs, tapestries, jade, and ivory — goods that originated in regions as far away as China and the East Indies, had been purchased in eastern Mediterranean ports, and were sold by the merchants of Venice, Genoa, Florence, and other Italian cities.

Trade declined in the fourteenth and early fifteenth centuries in the face of crop failures, plague, war, and political instability. Even during this prolonged recession, however, demand for luxury goods remained strong, and by the mid fifteenth century commerce revived as part of the general economic expansion that lasted until the early 1600s. Trade was stimulated by population growth, the opening of direct commercial contacts with Asia by the Portuguese, the influx of gold and silver into Europe from the mines of the Americas, and new demand for tropical products such as coffee, tobacco, and cocoa.

As a result of the broad expansion of European trade, all but a few Europeans came to depend on merchants to provide them with the products they needed and wanted. This does not mean, however, that merchants were highly regarded. Theologians drew on Christ's many teachings about the nobility of poverty and the spiritual dangers of wealth to castigate merchants for their single-minded pursuit of profit. Church lawyers wrote laws against usury — the loaning of money at interest. Preachers denounced merchants for raising prices when goods were scarce or in high demand, thereby defying the doctrine of the *just price*, which taught that it was wrong to sell anything for more than its value as defined by the general community. Moralists criticized merchants for selling overpriced and unneeded luxury goods to consumers who might better use their money for charity. Many laypeople disdained merchants out of simple jealousy or because of their inability to comprehend the complex financial transactions that were part of a merchant's life. The Austrian theologian Henry of Langenstein (1325–1383) expressed the views of many when he wrote,

> He who has enough to satisfy his wants and nevertheless ceaselessly labors to acquire riches either to obtain a higher social position, or that subsequently he may live without labor, or that his sons may become men of wealth and importance — all such are incited by a damnable avarice, sensuality, or pride. . . .[1]

As the sources in this section show, such views still existed in the fifteenth and sixteenth centuries.

---

[1]Raymond De Roover, "The Concept of the Just Price: Theory and Economic Policy," *Journal of Economic History* 18, December 1958.

Two German Critics of Merchants and Their Ethos

3 ▾ *REFORMATION OF THE EMPEROR SIGISMUND; Martin Luther, ADDRESS TO THE CHRISTIAN NOBILITY OF THE GERMAN NATION*

The *Reformation of the Emperor Sigismund* is a blueprint for religious, political, and economic reform supposedly written by Sigismund of Luxemburg, the king of Hungary and Bohemia and Holy Roman Emperor between 1410 and 1437. Although the document may have reflected some of Sigismund's ideas, it is likely that the treatise was written by an anonymous south German clergyman. Filled with great passion, it calls for the purification of the Church and a return to an idealized past in which good government and justice prevailed. After it appeared in the 1430s, the treatise circulated as a manuscript and appeared in eight printed editions between 1476 and 1522.

The *Address to the Christian Nobility of the German Nation* was one of three major treatises written by Martin Luther in 1521, four years after his posting of the Ninety-five Theses. In *Bondage of the Will*, he spelled out his belief in justification by faith rather than works; in *The Babylonian Captivity of the Church*, he sought to undercut the papacy's claim to absolute religious authority; and in the *Address to the Christian Nobility of the German Nation*, he outlined a program for the reform of the Church and society to be implemented by Germany's rulers. Like the author of the *Reformation of the Emperor Sigismund*, Luther, whose father was a peasant and small mine owner, expressed dismay about the influences and practices of Germany's merchants, best exemplified by the Fugger family of Augsburg, whose economic interests included banking, mining, textile manufacturing, and international trade.

QUESTIONS FOR ANALYSIS

1. When the author of the *Reformation of the Emperor Sigismund* and Luther discuss the potential damaging effects of trade, what kinds of trade are they thinking of?
2. According to each author, what motivates merchants, and how do their motives affect their personal behavior?
3. What are the social and economic consequences of merchants' activities?
4. How would Luther and the author of the *Reformation of the Emperor Sigismund* characterize the ideal social and economic order? How do the values and activities of merchants run counter to their ideal order?
5. What concrete steps do they recommend to attain such an order?
6. What kinds of arguments might have been raised by merchants to counter the critique of their profession offered by these two authors?

REFORMATION OF THE EMPEROR SIGMUND

We all know that Christendom must be supplied with necessities such as wine, salt, grain, lard, meat, and so on. These activities are carried on by means of buying and selling. Now it may happen that the harvest in one country is better than the harvest in another; and a merchant will hear of this, go into the country of plenty to buy up the supply, and sell elsewhere at a higher price. . . . Merchants who engage in this kind of trade defraud the world and exploit the poor. This and other kinds of deception which men carry on against one another in our society bring disasters upon us all, tempests, floods, hailstorms, bad harvests. And we ourselves are to be blamed for these, for our sins have offended God. . . .

I say this emphatically: Whenever you take something from your fellow man by means of dishonest buying and selling, you will not be able to use or enjoy it. It will burn, or be destroyed, or you will consume it in sickness and agony. And this will happen because of the ill faith we show toward each other. . . .

To put an end to all this, let us banish those merchants who roam from country to country, buying up surplus grain and meat and other necessities. Let us force them to stay at home and not journey about to seek their profits. And let no one sell grain or wine in another country. Grain and wine may be brought to local markets, but no one ought to be allowed to buy more than he can use in his own home, save only landlords and tavern keepers. . . .

A uniform price should be set in all imperial cities on wine and grain, meat and salt, and on all of the necessities that come to market. Four honorable men should be chosen in each place to fix this price, which should be posted in public so that no one will pay more for what he needs than is right. . . .

One might object: What happens when there is a hailstorm or a bad harvest? Will products not be dearer in some years and in some places than in others? I answer: If you hold to the procedures I have suggested, peace and honesty will reign among citizens, no man will deprive another of anything, and all will lead a common, equal life. The air will become pure, the elements will be kind to us, and nature will be bountiful. . . .

Another evil prevalent in our cities — and in the country, too — is that everyone seems to want to carry on more trades than is fitting for him. One man is a wine merchant by trade but deals in salt as well. Another is a tailor but sells cloth on the side. A shoemaker does his own tanning. Look at any of our crafts and trades: you will see that not a man is content with his lot. He goes after whatever he thinks he can get. In many cities four or five individuals control so much trade that twenty men could easily make a living from it.

Do you want to know what the old imperial laws say on the subject? Our forefathers were not fools. Crafts and trades were instituted for one purpose only; to assure every man of the opportunity to earn his daily bread. No one was allowed to trespass on another man's trade. In this way society takes care of its needs, and every individual may earn his livelihood. Whatever trade a man has learned, that trade he should practice. There ought to be no exceptions to this rule. All the imperial cities should enforce it, on pain of forfeiting forty marks of gold to the imperial treasury if the city is shown to have overlooked an infraction. No person must deprive another of his daily bread.

ADDRESS TO THE CHRISTIAN NOBILITY OF THE GERMAN NATION

In the first place, there is urgent need of a general order and decree on behalf of the German people against the overflowing abundance and the great expensiveness of the clothing worn by so many nobles and rich folk. To us, as to other people, God has given enough wool, fur, flax, and everything that that would provide proper, suitable, and worthy garments for each class. We do not need to waste such huge sums for silk, and velvet, and articles of gold, and other imports from abroad. I believe that, even if the pope did not rob us Germans with his intolerable, fraudulent practices, we should still have had too many of these native robbers, the silk and velvet merchants. As things stand, we see that each wants to keep up with the others, to the awakening and increase of pride and envy among us, as we have deserved. . . .

In the same way, the spice traffic ought to be reduced, for it is another of the great channels by which money is conveyed out of Germany. By the grace of God, more things to eat and drink are indigenous to our own country than to any other, and are just as precious and wholesome. Perhaps I am now bringing forward foolish and impossible suggestions which would endanger the principal trade of the merchants. But I am expressing my own views. . . . I do not see many goodly habits which have been introduced into the country by commerce. In olden days, God caused the children of Israel to dwell far from the sea, and did not allow them to engage in much commerce. . . .

At this point, I would say that we must surely bridle the Fuggers and similar trading companies. How can it happen in a godly and righteous manner, and in a single lifetime, that great wealth, worthy of a king, should be accumulated into a single pile? I am no man for figures. But I do not understand how a hundred guilder's[1] can make twenty profit in a single year, or even one guilder make another. Nothing like this takes place by cultivating the soil, or by raising cattle, where the increase does not depend on human wits, but on God's blessing. I commend that observation to men of affairs. . . . I do know that it would be much more godly to increase farming and decrease commerce; and more of those are on the right side, who till the earth as the Bible says, and seek their livelihood in this way.

---

[1]Guilder is the English word for gulden, a coin in wide use in northern Europe. Originally gold coins, they also were minted in silver and other metals in Luther's day.

Antwerp and Its Merchants

▼▼▼

4 ▼ *Lodovico Guicciardini, DESCRIPTION OF ALL THE LOW COUNTRIES*

In the sixteenth century, Europe's economy boomed, and the Flemish city of Antwerp was its center. Until the fifteenth century, Bruges, another Flemish city some fifty miles to the east of Antwerp, had been northern Europe's most important center for international trade and finance. In the 1400s, however, Bruges entered into a period of rapid decline, in part because of Antwerp's aggressive moves to attract merchants and financiers and in part due to the gradual silting of the Zwyn River, Bruges' link to the sea. Beginning in the 1440s, a number of foreign firms, including the four great German banking houses — the Meutings, Welsers, Hochstetters, and Fuggers — all established operations in Antwerp, and by 1500 Antwerp's rise to economic prominence was well under way.

The city's real boom began in the early 1500s when the Portuguese, having established direct commercial contact with India and Southeast Asia by a direct sea route around Africa, broke the Venetian monopoly on the spice trade and began to ship pepper and other spices to Antwerp, where they were purchased for resale throughout northern Europe. Additionally, in the sixteenth century the city imported from England large quantities of unfinished cloth that was dyed and treated for resale; and after Antwerp came under the control of Spain in the early 1500s, large amounts of American products, including gold and silver, flooded into the city. By the 1500s the city's population had swelled to 110,000. Approximately 15,000 were foreign merchants, bankers, and speculators who did much of their business in two bourses, or exchanges: the English or Wool Street market, mainly for the sale and purchase of goods, and the New Bourse, established in 1531 for financial transactions. Here fortunes were won and lost as businessmen from all over Europe exchanged goods, made loans, and speculated in Europe's many currencies.

Antwerp's economic golden age was short-lived. With a substantial Protestant population, the city was a victim of the political and religious strife that plagued the Low Countries in the late sixteenth and early seventeenth centuries. Having joined the revolt of the eighteen Dutch provinces against Spain, Antwerp was sacked by Spanish troops in 1576 and by French troops in 1583. When the Spanish took the city in 1585, Dutch Protestants responded by placing Antwerp under a blockade, and Amsterdam gradually emerged as Europe's commercial and banking center.

The beginning of Antwerp's decline was just a few years away when the Italian merchant Lodovico Guicciardini published his book *Descrittione di tutti i Paesi Bassi (Description of All the Low Countries)* in 1567. Born in 1521 into a distinguished Florentine family with a tradition of business success and political eminence, Lodovico represented family business interests in Lyons and Antwerp until the firm went bankrupt in the 1540s. Until his death in 1589, he remained in Antwerp, where he pursued various business interests and wrote several books,

including *Description of All the Low Countries*. In the long chapter on Antwerp, Guicciardini praised the wealth and sophistication of the city, while criticizing some aspects of Europe's emerging capitalist economy.

QUESTIONS FOR ANALYSIS

1. **What factors, according to Guicciardini, contributed to Antwerp's rise to economic prominence?**
2. **What information does Guicciardini provide about the values and mores of Antwerp's merchants?**
3. **What most impresses Guicciardini about Antwerp's merchant community?**
4. **What criticisms does Guicciardini make of the values and mores of Antwerp's merchants?**
5. **According to Guicciardini, how do merchants manipulate currency values and commodity prices to maximize profits? What does he tell us about the results of such practices?**
6. **Even though Guicciardini is critical of some merchants' practices, overall he seems to think they serve a useful and necessary service. What are his reasons for this conclusion?**

Let us next briefly consider by what ways and means this city has risen to such high dignity and rank, Certainly, the first of her major advantages were the markets and market days granted to her by local princes and later expanded upon by the grace and authority of emperors and popes. . . . The second of the major advantages which have made the city of Antwerp so prominent and wealthy began around 1503 and 1504, at which time through remarkable and amazing navigation skills and weaponry, having already occupied Calicut, the Portuguese made a treaty with the kings of the region. They commenced to ship spices and medicinal drugs from India straight to Portugal twice a year over 16,000 miles and then to transport them directly to this city. Previously, these spices and drugs were brought by way of the Red Sea, as it's called, to Beirut and Alexandria, and from these places Venetians transported them to Venice to supply Italy, France, Germany, and other Christian provinces. . . . And thus around 1516, all the merchants who previously had been living in Bruges took up residence in Antwerp, much to the harm of Bruges and to the good of Antwerp. . . .

The citizens of Antwerp are highly involved in mercantile pursuits; among them are certainly great merchants and traders, of whom a few are very rich, with fortunes of close to 400,000 *écus*[1] per person and more. They are humane, civil, ingenious, and quick to imitate foreigners and intermarry with them. They are very comfortable living abroad, and most of them, even the women, no matter how much they have been outside the country, can speak two, three, or four languages, and some even five, six, or seven, This is both useful and admirable. . . . All of these people who earn money invest it not just in commerce, but also in construction, in buying lands and properties; in all these ways they improve their position, and thus on a daily basis the city keeps on growing, prospers, and flourishes remarkably.

---

[1]A gold coin first minted in France in the 1300s.

Furthermore, although some of the lesser folk and others given to frugality live according to the old custom of dining sparingly, it is nevertheless a fact that presently the people live lavishly, perhaps more than proper. Men and women of all ages dress very well, each one according to wealth and status, always following new and stylish fashions, but many of them much more richly and luxuriously than decorum and respectability can or should allow. Here one can see at all hours of the day weddings, feastings, and dancing. Everywhere one can hear the sound of musical instruments and singing, and the noise of merrymaking. In sum, the riches, power, splendor, and magnificence of the city appear in all possible ways. . . .

Now to discuss the handling and buying and selling of merchandise which routinely goes on every day in Antwerp. I may say that all these merchants, both foreign and native, carry on commerce and trade that is unbelievable and amazing. . . ; we shall describe briefly how it is done, which is as follows: Every morning and evening they go at a certain hour to the English Exchange, and there for more than an hour at a time, by means of brokers who speak every language, of whom there are great numbers, negotiate mainly the buying and selling of all sorts of types of merchandise. Then a little later, they go to the New Exchange, and similarly using brokers negotiate the buying and selling of currency, setting interest rates and especially making loans.

Now there is currency exchange[2] at Antwerp on several other exchanges in Italy—Rome, Venice, Milan, Florence, Genoa; in Germany—Augsburg, Nuremberg, Frankfurt; frequently on the four well-known fairs of Spain, two of them at Medina del Campo, the third at Villanon, and the fourth at Riosecco; in addition at Burgos, Cadiz, and Seville some business on money exchange takes place; money exchanges are also negotiated on various exchanges in France, such as the annual fairs in Lyons, Lutèce, and Rouen, and finally on London and Besançon. Now the reckoning in this money exchange consists principally in giving or receiving as many grossi[3] that clearly are enough to make up an écu, crown, ducat, as they say, or angelet, for which at locations in Italy and other areas you deliver goods, receive merchandise, or pay debts of the same or approximately the same value. So giving or taking here [in Antwerp] in order to receive or pay out somewhere else is properly called "exchange," a practice invented principally for the benefit of merchants. But as a result of the cunning of many merchants, especially the wealthiest, not content with this convenience but driven by an insatiable and extraordinary drive for profit, they have perverted and corrupted this laudable method of exchange. For by borrowing funds for which they have no need or by adding or removing large sums of money [from one location], they can through these means raise or lower the price of money artificially for their own private profit but to the loss of all others. In a way, nevertheless, this business of trading through money exchange is not only tolerable but also reasonable and very useful, nor can it (as the theologians might wish) be called unjust gain when used properly. Despite the risk,

---

[2]"Exchange" refers to the exchange of one currency for another, a common occurrence in a Europe in which cities, princes, and even private individuals issued coins of different values and quality. "Bills of exchange," to which Guicciardini is referring in this passage, are basically short-term loans that enabled a merchant to borrow money in one city, usually for the purchase of goods, with the promise to repay the loan within a certain period, usually no more than a few months, in some foreign city, in the currency of that city. By the sixteenth century, merchants and merchant houses had accounts with bankers in several cities where they did business, with their agents settling their accounts when bills of exchange came due. Since some risk was involved with the loans connected with bills of exchange, interest was charged. In addition, as Guicciardini describes, speculative gains or losses were possible if the value of currencies fluctuated from the time the loan was taken until the time the account was settled.

[3]Plural of *grosso*, a silver coin minted by a number of Italian cities. Ecus, crowns, and ducats were more valuable gold or silver coins.

rarely do you make much profit, and indeed sometimes one loses not insubstantial sums. But now let us say a few words about the practice of "deposit."[4]

"Deposit" today refers to those practices (to cover up with a fine word the baseness of the true facts), when one provides a certain sum of money for a fixed time at an agreed-upon cost or interest, for example, following the example of Emperor Charles V and confirmed by his son King Phillip,[5] at twelve percent per year. This rate of interest was permitted to merchants in difficult times to prevent more serious misfortunes, but time and experience, in addition to past examples, show clearly enough that such enormous interest rates, being corrupted and manipulated by the deviousness of men by many ways and means, is a grievous matter, and of great harm to men of limited means and to commerce. Certainly this way of doing business would benefit the public if men making the loans would agree to a reasonable rate such as six or six and a quarter percent . . . or even, a bit more up to eight and a third percent. But they are not satisfied with these interest rates, and frequency surpassing all limits of restraint, transform the business of loans into something disagreeable and even violent. In former times noblemen if they had any surplus funds would invest in farmlands and their estates, in agriculture and livestock, and things such as these, by which many found employment and the countryside was made bountiful. Merchants too, if they were well off, freely spent their money to ship out and bring in goods in abundance, and they supplied them here and there wherever need required it; and by this abundant two-way trade, many men were given employment, and since the countryside and cities were filled with plenty and well-supplied with merchandise, the wealth of the state and of the prince increased. Now however, a good part of the nobility, enticed and corrupted by great and certain profit that comes from these excessive and usurious loans, put their extra money out at interest secretly (for it is illegal for nobles to do so) or have someone loan the money for them. Similarly, many merchants, driven by the same prospects and hoping to avoid greater risks and inconveniences, lend their money at a fixed exorbitant rate of interest or exchange money at the highest price. Hence, as it pertains to the nobility, many fields lie uncultivated and pastures are lacking livestock, a condition that results in shortages of food and sometimes misery for the public. And as far as the merchants are concerned, the land is no longer supplied with goods and merchandise, a condition which, in addition to other harm, causes the goods that are available to be expensive and sometimes excessive in price; all of this causes great and severe harm to the public good, especially to the poor, who are in many ways ruined by the rich. One could cite many clear examples of this, but because we see it so often, with many bankruptcies and disorders, we shall speak no more about it.

Instead, returning to our main subject, commerce, since we have already related how some merchants profit unjustly and injure the public, we should also add that an infinite number of them earn their money justly, and are of use to the world, and this by means of the trade in merchandise which they buy in quantity and sell in good faith, and import from everywhere and export to all places and countries. . . .

---

[4]In this context "deposit" refers to the temporary charges for the use of money, in other words, "interest." Charging interest on loans was condemned in the Bible, and was illegal for Christians according to the teachings and laws of the medieval Roman Catholic Church. As trade expanded, however, such laws were infrequently enforced, and many theologians and lawyers adopted the position that charging a reasonable rate of interest was acceptable when risk was involved.

[5]Charles I, king of Spain from 1516 to 1556 and as Charles V, was Holy Roman Emperor from 1519 to 1556. His son, Philip II was king of Spain from 1556 to 1598.

Marriage and Families in Early Modern Europe

The popular assumption that general progress marked Europe's transition from the Middle Ages to the Renaissance and early modern era is contradicted by the experiences of most European women. Although medieval women were far from having equality with men, they enjoyed more freedom and higher status than in antiquity and the postmedieval period. Aristocratic women in the Middle Ages often managed their families' estates while their husbands were on military campaigns, and some owned land themselves. Urban women joined guilds, were apprenticed to learn craft skills, and in some cities monopolized whole professions, such as leatherworking, brewing, weaving, and cloth finishing. Religious women were admired for their charity and piety, and many achieved distinction as models of spirituality.

During the fourteenth and fifteenth centuries, however, in the era that saw the decline of medieval civilization and the flowering of the Renaissance in Italy, women's economic and social prospects declined, and continued to do so in the early modern period. In cities guilds excluded women from membership, and municipal councils barred women from work as physicians and apothecaries. For more and more urban women, work meant domestic service, spinning, shopkeeping, or prostitution, all poorly paid, low-status jobs. In the countryside women's work remained essential to the peasant household's economic survival. Women tended gardens, raised poultry, helped with planting and harvesting, cooked, preserved food, and cared for children and the elderly. Many rural women also worked for wages as servants or laborers.

Irrespective of a woman's social status, everyone agreed that her main purpose was to marry and have children. Large families, especially ones with more sons than daughters, were viewed as economic necessities by rich and poor alike. Peasants relied on children as workers, while wealthy aristocrats and businessmen considered children as guarantees of the continuation of the family line and of the preservation of its wealth and property. Moralists and religious leaders agreed that matrimony offered men and women the best opportunity for fulfillment and happiness and provided the foundation for a sound, God-fearing society.

Many writers praised the institution of marriage so fervently because they were convinced that it was weakening. In Renaissance Italy upper-class parents deplored the reluctance of their sons to marry. In northern Europe the age of first marriage steadily rose, and the proportion of unmarried individuals grew. Estimates of the number of single European women during the 1500s and early 1600s range from 20 to 40 percent, equally divided between widows and spinsters. For those who did marry, contemporary writers and preachers give the impression that more and more husbands and wives were unhappy. Although moralists affirmed that a strong marriage depended on mutual affection and clearly defined spousal responsibilities and rights, custom deprived young women of a meaningful say in the choice of a spouse, and laws clearly made wives subservient to husbands. The endless stream of commentaries on unhappy marriages, abusive husbands, and disobedient wives suggests that harmonious marriages were far from universal.

The sources in this section, one representing Renaissance Italy and the other sixteenth-century Germany, provide insight into the institution of marriage and in more general terms women's place in society.

Upper-Class Marriage in Renaissance Florence

5 ▾ *Leon Battista Alberti, BOOK OF THE FAMILY*

More so than any other city, Florence was the heart and soul of the Italian Renaissance. Its painters, sculptors, and architects produced works of great beauty, and its humanist scholars inspired a new appreciation and understanding of Greek and Roman antiquity. None of this would have been possible without a relatively small number of elite Florentine families who made fortunes in business and, under the guidance and control of the Medici family, made up the city's political oligarchy. These families, along with the Catholic Church, provided the money to support the scholarship of humanists, the work of painters and sculptors, and the construction and remodeling of countless buildings.

Some members of the Florentine elite were more than patrons; they were artists and scholars in their own right. Such was the case with Leon Battista Alberti (1404–1472), viewed by many as a personification of the ideal "Renaissance man." The illegitimate son of one of Florence's wealthiest merchants, Alberti studied at the universities of Padua and Bologna before becoming a papal official in Rome. He wrote books on mathematics, ancient literature, painting, and architecture and designed churches and private residences in Florence and other Italian cities. He also wrote the *Book of the Family* (1443), a dialogue among Alberti men that supposedly took place in 1421 at the funeral of Alberti's father. Written in Italian rather than Latin and translated into the major European languages, Alberti's work expresses views of marriage and children common among wealthy and privileged Europeans of his era, especially those who had made their fortunes in business.

In the first section of the following excerpt from *Book of the Family*, Lionardo, a man in his late twenties or thirties, discusses marriage and the choice of wives; in the second section, an older gentleman, Gionnozzo, recalls the steps he took as a new husband to train his wife.

QUESTIONS FOR ANALYSIS

1. According to the speaker Lionardo, what discourages young men from marrying?
2. What is the main purpose of marriage, according to the characters in the dialogue?

3. **In arranging marriages, how much input did the future wife and husband have? Who else influenced the final choice of a mate?**
4. **According to Lionardo, what considerations should affect the choice of a future wife? What qualities of a future wife are most important?**
5. **What did Gionnozzo hope to accomplish when he showed his new bride around the house, especially his private apartment?**
6. **What views of women underlie Alberti's description of marriage?**

ARRANGING A MARRIAGE

LIONARDO: Most times, the young do not appreciate the welfare of the family. Perhaps it seems to them that by bowing to matrimony they will lose much of their freedom in life. Perhaps they are overcome at times and caught in the clutches of a woman they love, as the comic poets are pleased to portray them. Perhaps the young find it most annoying having to maintain themselves, and therefore think that providing for a wife and children in addition to themselves is an overwhelming and hateful burden and are afraid they cannot properly take care of the needs which keep pace with the family's growth. Because of this, they consider the marriage bed too bothersome and avoid their duty honestly to enlarge the family. For these reasons, we must convince the young to marry by using reason, persuasion, rewards, and all other arguments so that the family may not be reduced to few members, which, as we said, is a most unfortunate condition, but grow in glory and the number of its young. . . .

▾ ▾ ▾

Once the young men have been persuaded through the efforts and advice of all the elders of the family, the mothers and other old relatives and friends, who know the customs and behavior of almost all the girls of the city from the time they were born, must select all the well-born and properly-raised girls and propose their names to the youth who is to be married. The latter will choose the one he prefers, and the elders must not reject her as a daughter-in-law, unless she brings with her the breath of scandal or blame. . . . He should, however, follow the example of a good family-head who, when buying something, insists on examining the property many times before signing any contract. . . . One who wishes to marry must be even more diligent. My advice to him is to show forethought and, over a period of time and in various ways, learn what kind of woman his intended bride is, for he will be her husband and companion for the rest of his life. In his mind he must have two reasons for marrying: the first is to beget children, the other, to have a faithful and steadfast companion throughout his life. We must, therefore, seek a woman suited to childbearing and pleasant enough to be our constant companion.

For this reason, then, they say that in a wife we must seek beauty, family, and wealth. . . . The first prerequisite of beauty in a woman is good habits. It is possible for a foolish, ignorant, slovenly, and drunken woman to have a beautiful body, but no one will deem her to be a beautiful wife. . . . As for physical beauty, we should not only take pleasure in comeliness, charm, and elegance, but should try to have in our house a wife well built for bearing children and strong of body to insure that they will be born strong and robust. An ancient proverb states: "As you want your children, so choose their mother." . . . Physicians say that a wife should not be thin, but neither should she be burdened with fat, for the fat are very weak, have many obstructions, and are slow in conceiving. . . . They believe that a woman who is tall but full in all her limbs is very useful for begetting many children. They always prefer one of girlish age for many reasons, such as ease in conforming with her husband's wishes and others which we do not have to discuss here. Girls are pure because of their age, simple through inexperience, modest by nature and without malice. They are eager to learn their husbands' habits and desires and acquiesce without any reluctance. Thus we must follow all the precepts mentioned, for they are most useful for recognizing and choosing a prolific wife. To this we may add that it is a good sign for the girl to have many brothers, for you may then hope that she will be like her mother.

Thus we have finished speaking of beauty. Next comes the bride's family. . . . I believe first of all we must examine with care the life and ways of all those who will become our relatives. Many marriages have been the cause of great misfortunes to families because they became related with quarrelsome, contentious, proud, and hateful men, as we hear and read every day. . . .

Therefore, to conclude this part of my argument in a few words, for I want to be very brief, let one try to find new relatives who are not of vulgar blood, little wealth, or humble profession. In other things let them be modest and not too far above you so that their greatness will not cast a shadow on your honor and dignity and will not disturb your family's peace and tranquility. . . . Nor do I want these relatives to be inferior to you, for if it is an expense to aid the fallen relatives I mentioned above, these others will keep you in slavery. Let them, therefore, be your equals, modest, noble, and of honorable profession, as we have said.

Next comes the dowry,[1] which I believe should be modest, sure, and given at once rather than large, doubtful, and to be given in the future. . . . Let them not be too large, for the larger they are, the greater is the delay in receiving payment, the chance of litigation, and the reluctance to pay. In addition, in the case of a large dowry you will be much more inclined to undergo great expense in order to collect it. . . . Having discussed how a wife is to be chosen and how she is to be received, we must now learn how she is to be treated at home.

INSTRUCTIONS FOR A NEW WIFE

. . .

LIONARDO [Addressing Giannozzo]: You can be glad you had a most virtuous wife, perhaps more virtuous than others. I do not know where you could find another woman as industrious and prudent in managing the family as your wife was.

GIANNOZZO: She certainly was an excellent mother by nature and upbringing, but even more through my instruction. . . .

LIONARDO: How did you go about it?

GIANNOZZO: I shall tell you. When after a few days my wife began to feel at ease in my house and did not miss her mother and family so much, I took her by the hand and showed her the whole house. I showed her that upstairs was the place for storing grain and down in the cellar that for wine and firewood. I showed her where the tableware was and everything else in the house, so that she saw where everything was kept and knew its use. Then we returned to my room, and there, after closing the door, I showed her our valuables, silver, tapestries, clothes, and jewels, and pointed out their proper storage places.

I kept only the ledgers and business papers, my ancestors' as well as mine, locked so that my wife could not read them or even see them then or at any time since. . . . I never allowed my wife to enter my study either alone or in my company, and I ordered her to turn over to me at once any papers of mine she should ever find. . . .

No matter how trifling a secret I had, I never shared it with my wife or with any other woman. I

[1]The dowry is the payment in money, goods, or land made by the bride's family to the groom. During the marriage the dowry was controlled by the husband, but if the husband predeceased the wife, it returned to the wife under most circumstances. The amount of the dowry depended on the wealth of the families involved. The increasing size of dowry payments in Italy during the fifteenth century became a hardship for families with several daughters. Daughters whose families could not raise a suitable dowry typically joined a religious order and entered a convent.

disapprove of those husbands who consult their wives and do not know how to keep any secret to themselves. They are mad to seek good advice and wisdom in women, and even more so if they think a wife can guard a secret with greater jealousy and silence than her husband. O foolish husbands, is there ever a time when you chat with a woman without being reminded that women can do anything but keep silent? For this reason, then, I always took care that none of my secrets should ever become known to women. . . .

LIONARDO: What an excellent warning! And you are no less prudent than fortunate if your wife was never able to draw out any of your secrets.

GIANNOZZO: She never did, my dear Lionardo, and I shall tell you why. First of all, she was very modest, and so never cared to know more than she should. Then, I never spoke to her about anything but household matters, habits, and our children. Of these subjects I spoke to her often and at length so that she might learn what to do. . . . As for the household goods, I deemed it proper, then and later, to entrust them to my wife's care, but not entirely, for I often wanted to know and see where the least thing was kept and how safe it was. After my wife had seen and understood where everything was to be kept, I said to her: "My dear wife, you must take no less care than myself of those things which will be useful and convenient to you and to me both while we preserve them in good condition and whose neglect would bring harm and inconvenience. You have seen our possessions, which, thank God, are such that we can well be satisfied. If we know how to take care of them, they will be useful to you, to me, and to our children. Therefore, my dear wife, it is your duty as well as mine to be diligent and take care of them."

LIONARDO: What did your wife answer?

GIANNOZZO: She answered that she had learned to obey her father and mother, and that they had instructed her to obey me always. She was ready, therefore, to do whatever I commanded. And I said to her: "Well then, my dear wife, one who knows how to obey her father and mother will soon learn to satisfy her husband." . . .

A Sixteenth-Century Commentary on Marriage

▼▼▼

6 ▼ *Erhard Schön,*
NO MORE PRECIOUS TREASURE IS ON THE EARTH THAN A GENTLE WIFE WHO LONGS FOR HONOR

Many Europeans were introduced to the new technology of printing not through books but through broadsheets. Printed on a single sheet and usually consisting of a woodcut illustration and a brief text, these inexpensive publications were meant for a mass audience. As seen earlier in this chapter, such broadsheets served as instruments of propaganda during the Reformation Era. They also offered up satire, social commentary, moral instruction, and news about murders, witchcraft trials, astronomical portents, monsters, strange births, and countless other matters.

The following broadsheet is the work of Erhard Schön (ca. 1491–1550), a Protestant from Nuremberg who produced hundreds of woodcuts for books and broadsheets, including the following commentary on marriage, *No More Precious Treasure Is on the Earth Than a Gentle Wife Who Longs for Honor*, which appeared in 1531. It shows, from left to right, a husband (pulling a cart that carries a diaper-filled laundry tub), the wife, a young man, his sweetheart, an old woman wearing a fool's cap, and finally an old man. In a text from an unknown author, these six characters state their opinions about marriage.

QUESTIONS FOR ANALYSIS

1. What qualities of his wife does the husband in Schön's woodcut most bitterly complain about?
2. What is the significance of the britches, purse, and sword that the wife holds in Schön's print?
3. According to Schön, how does the wife justify her actions and behavior? How do her justifications compare to the expectations about marriage set forth by the young girl?
4. Compare and contrast the arguments for and against marriage presented by the old man and the female fool in Schön's print. To what extent do the comments of the old man confirm the fears about marriage expressed by the young man?

Erhard Schön, No More Precious Treasure Is on the Earth Than a Gentle Wife Who Longs for Honor

NO MORE PRECIOUS TREASURE

The Wretched Idol {the Husband}
Oh woe, oh woe to me, wretched fool,
With what difficulty I pull this cart
To which point marriage has brought me.
I wish I had never thought of it!
A shrewish scold has come into my house
and has taken my sword, pants and purse.
Night and day I have no peace
And no good word from her.
My fidelity does not please her;
My words provoke hostility from her.
Thus is the fate of many a man
Who has, knows and can do nothing,
And yet in time must have a wife.

The Wife Speaks
Hey, beloved mate, but is this really true?
Be quiet! Or I will pull you by the hair.
If you want a nice and gentle wife
Who will always be subservient to you
Then stay at home in your own house
And stop your carousing.
Naked I go running around to peddle things,
Suffering from hunger and quaffing water.
It's difficult for a nice young wife
To maintain her wifely honor.
If you won't work to support me,
Then you have to wash, spin and pull the cart
And must let your back be bared.

The Journeyman
What do you say about this, young lady?
Would you like to be like her
And yourself hold sword, pants, purse and authority?
With words that bite, rasp and cut?
That I should and would never suffer.
Should I fight and brawl with you,
Then perhaps I would end up
Pulling a cart like this poor man,
Who has lost all joy and pleasure.
Should I waste my life of freedom
With spinning, washing, cooking and carting?
I would rather swear off from taking up marriage.

The Girl
Boy, believe me on my honor.
I don't wish for such power.
If you want to fight over rank,
Then you will be the man in all things.
What a wife deserves,
To love, to experience hardship together and honor,
I will demand nothing besides this.
You should have no doubt about it.
I will devote my life to serving you
And love you in constant friendship.
And you won't be scolded by a single word.

The Woman Fool
Watch yourself, young man.
I, a poor fool speak the truth.
Much good is said about marriage
But it means more correctly "Woe."
You must suffer 'til you die
Much anxiety, uncertainty, worry and want.
From this no married person is spared.
Now when you see a pretty girl,
She will gladly do what you want
For a bottle of wine.
Afterwards you can let her go
And take on another.
A wife you have forever.

The Wise Man
Young man I will teach you better.
Do not listen to this woman fool.
Beware of the tricks of whores,
Who are always there to deceive you.
Take a young lady into marriage.
God will guide your lives.
Stay with her in love and pain
And always be patient.
If you experience aggravation,
Consider it to be God's will.
Provide for your wife by the sweat of your brow,
As God commands in the Book of Genesis.
Patience and suffering make a door
Through which we arrive at that place
Where the angels have their home.

The Beginnings of the Scientific Revolution

Although intellectuals in the Middle Ages and Renaissance had many disagreements and controversies, all but a few shared a number of common beliefs and assumptions. They believed that Roman Catholic Christianity provided a complete revelation of God's purposes and true and perfect guidelines for human conduct. All of them revered antiquity. They looked to the Greeks for guidance in logic, philosophy, and science and to the Romans for inspiration in literature, government, and law. All believed that the Earth was the center of the universe and that on Earth Catholic Christians came closest to realizing God's design for humanity.

In the sixteenth and seventeenth centuries, intellectuals were forced to reevaluate all of these perspectives. The secularism of the Renaissance, the religious divisions growing out of the Reformation, and surprising encounters with Africans, Native Americans, and Asians all challenged Europe's intellectual assumptions. As important as these developments were, however, none approached the significance of the remarkable scientific discoveries that collectively have come to be known as the Scientific Revolution.

Science, or natural philosophy as it was known at the time, was nothing new for Europeans in the 1500s and 1600s. Many medieval and Renaissance scholars had sought to understand the natural world, but their need to make science conform to Catholic doctrine discouraged speculation, and their conviction that everything worth knowing in science had already been revealed by the ancients hampered new discoveries.

The first major break from ancient Greek science was made by the Polish astronomer Nicolaus Copernicus, who, in his *On the Revolutions of the Heavenly Spheres*, theorized that the sun, not the Earth, was the center of the universe. By the time of Galileo Galilei (1564–1642), most scientists accepted Copernican heliocentrism, even though it raised perplexing theoretical questions. Most of these questions were answered by Isaac Newton (1642–1727), whose *Mathematical Principles of Natural Philosophy* (1687) explained planetary and earthly motion through the law of universal gravitation. Newton's work was the crowning achievement of a 150-year period in which European thinkers transformed their understanding of astronomy and mechanics; made spectacular advances in mathematics; invented the telescope, microscope, and many other scientific instruments; and achieved new insights in anatomy and chemistry.

As the two documents in this section show, the Scientific Revolution, like all revolutions, had wide-ranging effects. Galileo's letter to the Grand Duchess Christina of Tuscany shows how the new theories clashed with orthodox Christian beliefs and, according to some critics, challenged the literal truth of the Bible. The excerpts from Francis Bacon's *New Organon* reveal how the scientific inquiries of the age inspired new standards and methods for gaining knowledge and promoted a belief that progress was possible if nature could be understood and manipulated for the benefit of humanity.

Science and the Claims of Religion

7 ▾ *Galileo Galilei,* *LETTER TO THE GRAND DUCHESS CHRISTINA*

The greatest European scientist in the early 1600s was the Italian physicist and astronomer Galileo Galilei (1564–1642). Mechanics was the subject of his most important work, in which he developed the theory of inertia and described the laws that dictate the movement of falling bodies. In astronomy he pioneered the use of the telescope and defended the theory of a sun-centered universe advanced by Copernicus in 1543. His public support of Copernicus disturbed Catholic theologians, who were convinced it undermined correct belief and the authority of the Church. The Church officially condemned Copernican theory in 1616 and forced Galileo to renounce many of his ideas in 1632. Galileo's works continued to be read, however, and despite his condemnation, his writings contributed to the acceptance of Copernican theory and the new methodology of science.

In the following selection, Galileo, a devout Catholic, defends his approach to science in a published letter addressed to Christina, the grand duchess of Tuscany, in 1615.

QUESTIONS FOR ANALYSIS

1. According to Galileo, what are his enemies' motives? Why in his view do they use religious arguments against him?
2. According to Galileo, why is it dangerous to apply passages of Scripture to science?
3. To Galileo, how does nature differ from the Bible as a source of truth?
4. In Galileo's view, what is the proper relationship between science and religion?

Some years ago, as Your Serene Highness well knows, I discovered in the heavens many things that had not been seen before our own age. The novelty of these things, as well as some consequences which followed from them in contradiction to the physical notions commonly held among academic philosophers, stirred up against me no small number of professors — as if I had placed these things in the sky with my own hands in order to upset nature and overturn the sciences. They seemed to forget that the increase of known truths stimulates the investigation, establishment, and growth of the arts; not their diminution or destruction.

Showing a greater fondness for their own opinions than for truth, they sought to deny and disprove the new things which, if they had cared to look for themselves, their own senses would have demonstrated to them. To this end they hurled various charges and published numerous writings filled with vain arguments, and they made the grave mistake of sprinkling these with passages taken from places in the Bible which they had failed to understand properly, and which were ill suited to their purposes.

Persisting in their original resolve to destroy me and everything mine by any means they can think of, these men are aware of my views in astronomy and philosophy. They know that as to the arrangement of the parts of the universe, I hold the sun to be situated motionless in the center of the revolution of the celestial orbs while the Earth rotates on its axis and revolves about the sun. They know also that I support this position not only by refuting the arguments of Ptolemy[1] and Aristotle, but by producing many counter-arguments; in particular, some which relate to physical effects whose causes can perhaps be assigned in no other way. In addition there are astronomical arguments derived from many things in my new celestial discoveries that plainly confute the Ptolemaic system while admirably agreeing with and confirming the contrary hypothesis. Possibly because they are disturbed by the known truth of other propositions of mine which differ from those commonly held, and therefore mistrusting their defense so long as they confine themselves to the field of philosophy, these men have resolved to fabricate a shield for their fallacies out of the mantle of pretended religion and the authority of the Bible. These they apply, with little judgment, to the refutation of arguments that they do not understand and have not even listened to.

First they have endeavored to spread the opinion that such propositions in general are contrary to the Bible and are consequently damnable and heretical. . . . Next, becoming bolder, . . . they began scattering rumors among the people that before long this doctrine would be condemned by the supreme authority.[2] They know, too, that official condemnation would not only suppress the two propositions which I have mentioned, but would render damnable all other astronomical and physical statements and observations that have any necessary relation or connection with these. . . .

To this end they make a shield of their hypocritical zeal for religion. They go about invoking the Bible, which they would have minister to their deceitful purposes. Contrary to the sense of the Bible and the intention of the holy Fathers, if I am not mistaken, they would extend such authorities until even in purely physical matters — where faith is not involved — they would have us altogether abandon reason and the evidence of our senses in favor of some biblical passage, though under the surface meaning of its words this passage may contain a different sense. . . .

The reason produced for condemning the opinion that the Earth moves and the sun stands still is that in many places in the Bible one may read that the sun moves and the earth stands still. Since the Bible cannot err, it follows as a necessary consequence that anyone takes an erroneous and heretical position who maintains that the sun is inherently motionless and the earth movable.

With regard to this argument, I think in the first place that it is very pious to say and prudent to affirm that the holy Bible can never speak untruth — whenever its true meaning is understood. But I believe nobody will deny that it is often very abstruse, and may say things which are quite different from what its bare words signify. Hence in expounding the Bible if one were always to confine oneself to the unadorned grammatical meaning, one might fall into error. Not only contradictions and propositions far from true might thus be made to appear in the Bible, but even grave heresies and follies. Thus it would be necessary to assign to God feet,

[1]Ptolemy (ca. 100 to 170 C.E.), who spent most of his life in Alexandria, Egypt, was the Greek astronomer who propounded key aspects of the geocentric planetary system that prevailed in Europe until the time of Copernicus.

[2]The pope.

hands, and eyes, as well as corporeal and human affections, such as anger, repentance, hatred, and sometimes even the forgetting of things past and ignorance of those to come. . . .

This being granted, I think that in discussions of physical problems we ought to begin not from the authority of scriptural passages but from sense-experiences and necessary demonstrations; for the holy Bible and the phenomena of nature proceed alike from the divine Word, the former as the dictate of the Holy Ghost[3] and the latter as the observant executrix of God's commands. It is necessary for the Bible, in order to be accommodated to the understanding of every man, to speak many things which appear to differ from the absolute truth so far as the bare meaning of the words is concerned. But Nature, on the other hand, is inexorable and immutable; she never transgresses the laws imposed upon her, or cares a whit whether her abstruse reasons and methods of operation are understandable to men. For that reason it appears that nothing physical which sense-experience sets before our eyes, or which necessary demonstrations prove to us, ought to be called in question (much less condemned) upon the testimony of biblical passages which may have some different meaning beneath their words. For the Bible is not chained in every expression to conditions as strict as those which govern all physical effects; nor is God any less excellently revealed in Nature's actions than in the sacred statements of the Bible.

[3]The Holy Ghost (or Holy Spirit) is the third divine person of the Trinity (God the Father, God the Son, God the Holy Ghost), who sanctifies and inspires humankind. Christians believe the authors of the Bible wrote under the sacred and infallible inspiration of the Holy Ghost.

The Promise of Science

8 ▾ *Francis Bacon, NEW ORGANON*

Along with the Frenchman René Descartes (1596–1650), the English thinker Francis Bacon (1561–1626) was instrumental in formulating the strategies and methods of the new science. Both rejected the medieval and Renaissance doctrine that scientific truth was attainable from the study and analysis of authoritative ancient texts. Descartes, a superb mathematician and an advocate of the deductive method, stated in his *Discourse on Method* (1637) that humans could find scientific truth by carefully drawing conclusions from a few general, self-evident propositions. Bacon, a proponent of the inductive method, believed that experiment, observation, and the collection of data would reveal nature's laws. In his view, only after studying many individual phenomena could students of nature generalize about underlying principles. He also believed that understanding principles would enable humans to use and control nature to better their condition.

Bacon's *New Organon* (1620), or "New Method of Inquiry," was meant to replace the "old organon," which refers to the "old method of inquiry" based on the logical system devised by Aristotle. Written in Latin and hence directed to a learned audience, the *New Organon* consists of 130 aphorisms — concise statements of principles — that summarize Bacon's views on scientific knowledge and its potential.

QUESTIONS FOR ANALYSIS

1. What does Bacon see as the major impediments to scientific progress?
2. According to Bacon, what are the roles of experiment, mathematics, and technology in scientific generalization?
3. What does Bacon mean when he says that a scientist must be like a bee rather than an ant or a spider?
4. What role in humanity's future does Bacon see for science?
5. According to Bacon, what are the roadblocks to scientific progress? How do his views on this matter differ from those of Galileo?

---

1. Man, being the servant and interpreter of Nature, can do and understand so much and so much only as he has observed in fact or in thought of the course of nature: beyond this he neither knows anything nor can do anything. . . .

3. Human knowledge and human power meet in one; for where the cause is not known the effect cannot be produced. . . .

9. The cause and root of nearly all evils in the sciences is this — that while we falsely admire and extol the powers of the human mind we neglect to seek for its true helps. . . .

19. There are and can be only two ways of searching into and discovering truth. The one flies from the senses and particulars to the most general axioms, and from these principles, the truth of which it takes for settled and immovable, proceeds to judgment and to the discovery of middle axioms. And this way is now in fashion. The other derives axioms from the senses and particulars, rising by a gradual and unbroken ascent, so that it arrives at the most general axioms last of all. This is the true way, but as yet untried. . . .

22. Both ways set out from the senses and particulars, and rest in the highest generalities; but the difference between them is infinite. For the one just glances at experiment and particulars in passing, the other dwells duly and orderly among them. The one, again, begins at once by establishing certain abstract and useless generalities, the other rises by gradual steps to that which is prior and better known in the order of nature. . . .

31. It is idle to expect any great advancement in science from the superinducing[1] and engrafting of new things upon old. We must begin anew from the very foundations, unless we would revolve for ever in a circle with mean and contemptible progress. . . .

36. One method of delivery alone remains to us; which is simply this: we must lead men to the particulars themselves, and their series and order; while men on their side must force themselves for a while to lay their notions by and begin to familiarize themselves with facts. . . .

95. Those who have handled sciences have been either men of experiment or men of dogmas. The men of experiment are like the ant; they only collect and use: the reasoners resemble spiders, who make cobwebs out of their own substance. But the bee takes a middle course; it gathers its material from the flowers of the garden and of the field, but transforms and digests it by a power of its own. Not unlike this is the true business of philosophy; for it neither relies solely or chiefly on the powers of the mind, nor does it take the matter which it gathers from natural history and mechanical experiments and lay it up in the memory whole, as it finds it; but lays it up in the understanding altered and digested. Therefore from a closer and purer league

---

[1]To introduce a concept over and above some already existing concept.

between these two faculties, the experimental and the rational, (such as has never yet been made) much may be hoped. . . .

108. So much then for the removing of despair and the raising of hope through the dismissal or rectification of the errors of past time. We must now see what else there is to ground hope upon. And this consideration occurs at once — that if many useful discoveries have been made by accident or upon occasion when men were not seeking for them but were busy about other things; no one can doubt but that when they apply themselves to seek and make this their business, and that too by method and in order and not by desultory impulses, they will discover far more.

109. Another argument of hope may be drawn from this, — that some of the inventions already known are such as before they were discovered it could hardly have entered any man's head to think of; they would have been simply set aside as impossible. . . .

If, for instance, before the invention of ordnance,[2] a man had described the thing by its effects, and said that there was a new invention, by means of which the strongest towers and walls could be shaken and thrown down at a great distance; men would doubtless have begun to think over all the ways of multiplying the force of catapults and mechanical engines by weights and wheels and such machinery for ramming and projecting; but the notion of a fiery blast suddenly and violently expanding and exploding would hardly have entered into any man's imagination or fancy. . . .

In the same way, if before the discovery of silk, any one had said that there was a kind of thread discovered for the purposes of dress and furniture, which far surpassed the thread of linen or of wool in fineness and at the same time in strength, and also in beauty and softness; men would have begun immediately to think of some silky kind of vegetable, or of the finer hair of some animal, or of the feathers and down of birds; but of a web woven by a tiny worm, and that in such abundance, and renewing itself yearly, they would assuredly never have thought. Nay, if any one had said anything about a worm, he would no doubt have been laughed at as dreaming of a new kind of cobwebs.

So again, if before the discovery of the magnet, any one had said that a certain instrument had been invented by means of which the quarters and points of the heavens could be taken and distinguished with exactness; men would have been carried by their imagination to a variety of conjectures concerning the more exquisite construction of astronomical instruments; but that anything could be discovered agreeing so well in its movements with the heavenly bodies, and yet not a heavenly body itself, but simply a substance of metal or stone, would have been judged altogether incredible. . . .

There is therefore much ground for hoping that there are still laid up in the womb of nature many secrets of excellent use, having no affinity or parallelism with any thing that is now known, but lying entirely out of the common track of our imagination, which have not yet been found out. They too no doubt will some time or other, in the course and revolution of many ages, come to light of themselves, just as the others did; only by the method of which we are now treating they can be speedily and suddenly and simultaneously presented and anticipated.

---

[2]Cannon and artillery.

Multiple Voices I ▾▾▾ European Views of Native Americans

BACKGROUND

Europeans during the era of exploration and expansion were surprised and intrigued by what their mariners, merchants, and missionaries encountered in Asia and Africa, but nothing prepared them for their explorers' discoveries across the Atlantic. No one knew what to make of two vast continents filled with strange plants and animals and, even more intriguingly, peoples whose values, beliefs, customs, crops, clothes, weapons, and appearances differed from anything they had experienced or even imagined. The result was an outpouring of published books, treatises, and commentaries that catered to Europeans' interest in the Americas. Some read these books out of simple curiosity or because they were titillated by tales of nudity and cannibalism. Others, however, sought answers to weightier questions. Were the Indians, as Columbus called them, fully human? Did they have souls and the gift of reason? Or were they essentially savages, who by their very nature were inferior to Europeans and other inhabitants of the Old World? Finding answers to these questions was important because such perceptions greatly influenced how the Native Americans were treated once they came under the political control of Spain and Portugal and later France, England, and the Netherlands.

Finding answers was difficult, however, for there was little consensus among European writers about the Native Americans' essential characteristics. This is hardly surprising, given the many differences among the Native Americans themselves. What one writer said about the Aztecs — whose agrarian-based economy supported a capital city, Tenochtitlán, with a population between 200,000 and 250,000 — would be far different from another writer's commentary on Native Americans who lived in small bands of hunters, fishermen, and foragers. Views of the Native Americans also depended on an author's individual experiences and perspective. Many writers made pronouncements about Native Americans and many artists depicted them in paintings, woodcuts, and engravings without having stepped foot in the Americas. They relied on others' firsthand accounts and interpreted those accounts in ways that reflected what they knew of "different" peoples of Africa or Asia or what they had read in medieval travel literature or ancient geographies. Even those who encountered Native Americans in person drew conclusions about their characteristics that were affected by the observers' backgrounds, expectations, and self-interest.

THE SOURCES

Fittingly, the first excerpt comes from a letter written by Christopher Columbus. It was written to Luis de Santangel, a counselor to King Ferdinand of Aragon, who, along with Queen Isabella of Castile, had sponsored Columbus's first transatlantic voyage in 1492. Columbus, who composed this letter during his return trip to Europe in January 1493, was eager to convince his readers that his discoveries would pay rich dividends in gold, spices, and converts to Christianity. As a result, his letter exaggerates the wealth of the newly discovered islands, and it ignores the fact that he had lost his flagship, the *Santa Maria*, when it was wrecked on a reef off present-day Haiti. You can judge if he also describes the native peoples he encountered in such a way that his royal patrons would hear what they wanted to hear.

The next source is a woodcut, believed to have been printed by the Froschauer publishing firm of Augsburg, Germany, in 1505. The first printed illustration of Native Americans, it was published not as part of a book, but as a broadsheet — a single page that was sold for a few pennies. No one knows who carved the woodcut, but it probably was based on two recently published letters ascribed to the Florentine merchant, explorer, and cartographer Amerigo Vespucci, after whom the Americas are named. Vespucci made two documented trips to the east coast of South America between 1499 and 1502 and claims to have made two more. If Vespucci's writings did indeed inspire the woodcut, then the people depicted are probably the Tupinamba of Brazil.

The next two excerpts were written by participants in a famous debate before King Charles I of Spain in 1550 over the true nature of Native Americans and whether the Spaniards were justified in enslaving them. The Spanish scholar and philosopher Juan Ginés de Sepúlveda argued in the affirmative. Born in 1490 into an aristocratic family, Sepúlveda studied at the University of Alcalá and then pursued an academic career in Italy. He spent his last years in Spain, where he was court historian for King Charles I and his son Philip II. He was famous for his studies of the ancient Greek philosopher Aristotle, who had written in the *Politics*, "Where then there is such a difference as that between soul and body, or between men and animals . . . the lower sort are by nature slaves, and it is better for them as for all inferiors that they should be under the rule of a master." Sepúlveda first stated his position on the treatment of Native Americans in 1547 in *Democrates Secundus, or The Just Causes of War Against the Indians.*

Arguing against Sepúlveda was Bartolomé de Las Casas (1474–1566), a Spanish Dominican friar famous for defending Native Americans' rights. Las Casas had been a soldier before sailing to Hispaniola in 1502 in the entourage of Nicholas de Ovando, the new Spanish governor of the island. He received grants of land from the governor and fought in the Spanish conquest of Cuba between 1511 and 1515, but in 1515 he returned to Spain, where he lobbied for more humane treatment of the Indians. In 1519, with royal approval, he established a cooperative Spanish-Indian farming community in Venezuela, which he hoped would be a model for similar collaborative experiments. After his farm failed, he became a Dominican and dedicated himself to writing and working on behalf of the Indians. His many books revealed (and probably exaggerated) the Spaniards' cruelties in the New World. His views so struck the conscience of Charles I that the king arranged the

Las Casas–Sepúlveda debate in 1550. The following excerpt is drawn from Las Casas's response to Sepúlveda in the debate. Entitled *In Defense of the Indians*, it was circulated as a manuscript in the 1500s but was not published until the twentieth century.

The final source is an engraving by Theodore de Bry (1528–1598), who produced many hundreds of illustrations of New World scenes in dozens of books, all of which were published by him or his descendants. Born into a Protestant family in Liège, a city in present-day Belgium, he fled to Germany in 1567 to escape religious persecution. In the late 1580s, he began a project of publishing illustrated editions of explorers' narratives. Only six volumes of *The Grand Voyages* had been completed at the time of de Bry's death, but the project was continued by his descendants, who published the fourteenth and final volume in 1634. Never having visited the Americas, de Bry based his illustrations strictly on the words of the explorers whose memoirs he was publishing. Several of the works he published contributed to the so-called Black Legend — the idea especially popular among Protestant writers and some Catholic missionaries that Spanish interaction with Native Americans was characterized by cruelty, intolerance, greed, and fanaticism. The engraving shown here, which illustrates Columbus's first interaction with Native Americans, appeared in the first volume of *The Grand Voyages*.

QUESTIONS FOR ANALYSIS

1. For each of the written sources and woodcuts, what point or points was the author or artist trying to make about Native Americans?
2. How many different "interpretations" of Native Americans' essential characteristics can you discover?
3. In each case, how might the author's or illustrator's views have been affected by his background, prejudices, or ambitions?
4. How might each of the opinions represented in these sources have been used to justify the way Native Americans were treated by Spanish authorities?

I ▾ Christopher Columbus, A LETTER CONCERNING RECENTLY DISCOVERED ISLANDS

The people of this island, and of all the other islands which I have found and of which I have information, all go naked, men and women, as their mothers bore them, although some women cover a single place with the leaf of a plant or with a net of cotton which they make for the purpose. They have no iron or steel or weapons, nor are they fitted to use them, not because they are not well built men and of handsome stature, but because they are very marvelously timorous. They have no other arms than weapons made of canes, cut in seeding time, to the ends of which they fix a small sharpened stick. . . .

It is true that, after they have been reassured and have lost their fear, they are so guileless and so generous with all they possess, that no one would believe it who has not seen it. They never refuse anything which they possess, if it be asked of them; on the contrary, they invite anyone to share it, and display as much love as if they would give their hearts, and whether the thing be of value or whether it be of small price, at once with whatever trifle of whatever kind it may be that is given to them, with that they are content. . . .

And they do not know any creed and are not idolaters; only they all believe that power and good are in the heavens, and they are very firmly convinced that I, with these ships and men, came from the heavens, and in this belief they everywhere received me, after they had overcome their fear. And this does not come because they are ignorant; on the contrary, they are of a very acute intelligence and are men who navigate all those seas, so that it is amazing how good an account they give of everything, but it is because they have never seen people clothed or ships of such a kind. . . .

In all these islands, I saw no great diversity in the appearance of the people or in their manners and language. On the contrary, they all understand one another, which is very curious thing, on account of which I hope that their highnesses will determine upon their conversion to our holy faith, towards which they are very inclined. . . .

In these islands I have so far found no human monstrosities, as many expected, but on the contrary the whole population is very well-formed, nor are they negroes as in Guinea. . . .

As I have found no monsters, so I have had no report of any, except in an island "Quaris," the second at the coming into the Indies, which is inhabited by a people who are regarded in all the islands as very fierce and who eat human flesh. They have many canoes with which they range through all the islands of India and pillage and take as much as they can. They are no more malformed than the others, except that they have the custom of wearing their hair long like women, and they use bows and arrows of the same cane stems, with a small piece of wood at the end, owing to lack of iron which they do not possess. . . .

In conclusion, to speak only of that which has been accomplished on this voyage, which was so hasty, their highnesses can see that I will give them as much gold as they may need, if their highnesses will render me very slight assistance; moreover, spice and cotton, as much as their highnesses shall command; and mastic, as much as they shall order to be shipped . . . ; and aloe wood,[1] as much as they shall order to be shipped, and slaves, as many as they shall order to be shipped and who will be from the idolaters. . . .

[1]Mastic and aloe wood are aromatics (fragrant materials used for making scents) that were prized in Europe.

2 ▾ *Anonymous, WOODCUT OF SOUTH AMERICAN INDIANS*

3 ▾ *Juan Ginés de Sepúlveda, DEMOCRATES SECUNDUS, OR THE JUST CAUSES OF WAR AGAINST THE INDIANS*

. . . Now compare these qualities of prudence, skill, magnanimity, moderation, humanity, and religion with those of those little men of America in whom one can scarcely find any remnants of humanity. They not only lack culture but do not even use or know about writing or preserve records of their history — save for some obscure memory of certain deeds contained in painting. They lack written laws and their institutions and customs are barbaric. And as for their virtues . . . what can be expected of men committed to all kinds of passion and nefarious lewdness and of whom not a few are given to the eating of human flesh. Do not believe that their life before the coming of the Spaniards was one of . . . peace, of the kind that poets sang about. On the contrary, they made war with each other almost continuously, and with such fury that they considered a victory to be empty if they could not satisfy their prodigious hunger with the flesh of their enemies. . . . But in other respects they are so cowardly and timid that they can scarcely offer any resistance to the hostile presence of our side, and many times thousands and thousands of them have been dispersed and have fled like women on being defeated by a small Spanish force scarcely amounting to one hundred.

So as not to detain you longer in this matter, consider the nature of those people in one single instance and example, that of the Mexicans, who are regarded as the most prudent and courageous. . . . Cortés for his part, after taking possession of the city [Tenochtitlan], held the people's cowardliness, ineptitude, and rudeness in such contempt that he not only compelled the king and his principal subjects, through terror, to receive the yoke and rule of the king of Spain, but also imprisoned King Moctezuma himself. . . . This he could do because of the stupor and inertia of the people, who were indifferent to the situation and preoccupied with other things than the taking up of arms to liberate their king. . . . Could there be a better or clearer testimony of the superiority that some men have over others in talent, skill, strength of spirit, and virtue? Is it not proof that they are slaves by nature? For the fact that some of them appear to have a talent for certain manual tasks is no argument for their greater human prudence. We see that certain insects, such as the bees and the spiders, produce works that no human skill can imitate. . . .

How can we doubt that these people — so uncivilized, so barbaric, contaminated with so many impieties and obscenities — have been justly conquered by a nation excellent in every kind of virtue, with the best law and best benefit for the barbarians? Prior to the arrival of the Christians they had the nature, customs, religion, and practice of evil sacrifice as we have explained. Now, on receiving with our rule our writing, laws, and morality, imbued with the Christian religion, having shown themselves to be docile to the missionaries that we have sent them, as many have done, they are as different from their primitive condition as civilized people are from barbarians, or as those with sight from the blind, as the inhuman from the meek, as the pious from the impious, or to put it in a single phrase, in effect, as men from beasts.

4 ▾ *Bartolomé de las Casas, IN DEFENSE OF THE INDIANS*

From the fact that the Indians are barbarians it does not necessarily follow that they are incapable of government and have to be ruled by others, except to be taught about the Catholic faith and to be admitted to the holy sacraments. They are not ignorant, inhuman, or bestial. Rather, long before they had heard the word Spaniard they had properly organized states, wisely ordered by excellent laws, religion, and custom. They cultivated friendship and, bound together in common fellowship, lived in populous cities in which they wisely administered the affairs of both peace and war justly and equitably, truly governed by laws that at very many points surpass ours, and could have won the admiration of the sages of Athens. . . .

The Indian race is not that barbaric, nor are they dull witted or stupid, but they are easy to teach and very talented in learning all the liberal arts, and very ready to accept, honor, and observe the Christian religion and correct their sins . . . once priests have introduced them to the sacred mysteries and taught them the word of God. They have been endowed with excellent conduct, and before the coming of the Spaniards, as we have said, they had political states that were well founded on beneficial laws.

Furthermore, they are so skilled in every mechanical art that with every right they should be set ahead of all the nations of the known world on this score, so very beautiful in their skill and artistry are the things this people produces in the grace of its architecture, its painting, and its needlework. . . .

In the liberal arts that they have been taught up to now, such as grammar and logic, they are remarkably adept. With every kind of music they charm the ears of their audience with wonderful sweetness. They write skillfully and quite elegantly, so that most often we are at a loss to know whether the characters are handwritten or printed. . . .

Again, if we want to be sons of Christ and followers of the truth of the gospel, we should consider that, even though these peoples may be completely barbaric, they are nevertheless created in God's image. They are not so forsaken by divine providence that they are incapable of attaining Christ's kingdom, They are our brothers, redeemed by Christ's most precious blood, no less than the wisest and most learned men in the whole world. . . .

5 ▾ *Theodore de Bry, COLUMBUS GREETED BY NATIVES*

▲▲▲

Chapter 2

The Islamic Heartland and India

FOLLOWING YEARS OF CONQUEST and upheaval, three dominant empires emerged in South and Southwest Asia between the mid fifteenth and early sixteenth centuries. The first empire to take shape was that of the Ottoman Turks, a seminomadic people who after migrating to Anatolia from Persia and central Asia in the 1100s quickly embarked on successful conquests in Anatolia and surrounding regions. In 1453 they conquered the last remnant of the Byzantine Empire when they captured the imperial city, Constantinople, and, as Istanbul, made it the seat of government. After further conquests, by the mid 1500s the Ottomans ruled an empire that included Egypt, Anatolia, Syria, and lands in North Africa, the western coast of the Arabian Peninsula, and southeastern Europe. Meanwhile, on the Ottoman Empire's eastern flank in the early sixteenth century, Ismail I created the Safavid Empire in Persia, which was distinguished by its rulers' fervent devotion to Shia Islam. Finally, during the 1500s, the Mughal Empire emerged in India as a result of the exploits of Babur (1483–1530), a military adventurer from central Asia who conquered northwest India, and those of his grandson, Akbar (1542–1605), who extended Mughal authority to the east and south.

In addition to their leaders' allegiance to Islam, these empires were similar in several respects. Each was established through military conquest, each was governed by an all-powerful ruler, and each was a formidable military power. In each, the arts and literature flourished. Each at first rested on a strong economic foundation, and each experienced an erosion of that foundation by inflation, high taxation, bureaucratic corruption, and changes in the world economy.

Differences among the empires also existed. In the sphere of religion, the Safavid Empire was a bastion of Shiism, in contrast to the Ottomans' devotion to Sunni Islam. Safavid

Persia also was unique in that its population had relatively few non-Muslims. In contrast, the Ottomans' subjects in southeastern Europe were mostly Christian, and smaller numbers of Christians and Jews were scattered throughout the rest of their empire. Most of the Mughals' subjects were Hindus.

The three empires also had different experiences with Europeans. The Ottomans and Europeans were archrivals, each representing to the other a despised religion and, moreover, a threat to their territory and commerce. European and Ottoman fleets clashed in the Mediterranean, and their armies fought for control of southeastern Europe. Nonetheless, European merchants continued to trade and even reside in Ottoman cities, and European powers such as France forged military alliances with the Ottoman sultan when it suited their purposes.

Relations between Europeans and Safavid Persia, on the other hand, were generally more cordial, mainly because they shared a common enemy in the Ottomans. Although Shah Abbas I (r. 1587–1629) resented Portuguese incursions in the Persian Gulf, he drew on the expertise of European military advisors and sent missions to Europe in 1599 and 1608 to discuss joint military action against the Ottomans.

In India the Portuguese quickly capitalized on the success of Vasco da Gama's voyage around Africa to Calicut in 1498. They undercut the monopoly of Arab merchants in the spice trade on the west Indian coast and established a base of operations in the city of Goa, which they forcibly annexed from the local Muslim ruler. The Dutch, English, and French became seriously involved in India only after 1600. They, too, established commercial operations on the coast, but only with the permission of a local ruler or a Mughal official. Akbar was intrigued by Christianity, and the Mughal emperor Jahangir was impressed by European art, but overall, emperors and local rulers were indifferent to the small number of Europeans who came to their shores.

By the mid seventeenth century, all three Islamic empires were deteriorating. By the mid eighteenth century, the Safavids had been overthrown, and the Mughals ruled an "empire" that consisted of little more than the imperial capital and its vicinity. The Ottoman Empire survived until after World War I, but its days of military prowess and economic vitality had ended long before its final demise.

Rulers and Their Challenges in the Ottoman, Safavid, and Mughal Empires

Many factors — resources, wealth, technological development, social coherence, cultural unity, and military strength — contribute to the rise and fall of states. But as the histories of the Ottoman, Safavid, and Mughal empires all confirm, quality of rule is also significant, especially when authority is exercised by a single all-powerful ruler.

The early history of all three empires confirms the importance of leadership, especially on the battlefield. The expansion of the Ottoman Empire around 1500 resulted from the conquests of three men — Mehmet II (r. 1451–1481), who directed the successful siege of Constantinople in 1453; Selim I (r. 1512–1520), who conquered Egypt, Syria, Palestine, and parts of southern and western Arabia; and Suleiman I (r. 1520–1566), who added Hungary, the Mediterranean island of Rhodes, and some Persian territory to Ottoman domains. The Safavid Empire was forged by Shah Ismail (r. 1501–1524), a charismatic leader whose original power base was Azerbaijan in northern Persia. Believed by his followers to be a descendant of the Prophet Muhammad's son-in-law, Ali, he defeated his rivals and in 1501 assumed the title *shah*, or emperor. Babur (1483–1530), the founder of the Mughal Empire in India, was a military adventurer of Mongol-Turkish ancestry who invaded India after having lost his original kingdom in Afghanistan. In 1526 he led an army of 12,000 troops into northern India and, with superior tactics and firepower, defeated the army of the Lodis, the Delhi sultanate's last dynasty.

Individual rulers also contributed to the cultural achievements of all three empires. Akbar, a brilliant military commander, patronized painters, poets, historians, and religious thinkers. Under his free-spending successors, Jahangir (r. 1605–1627) and Shah Jahan (r. 1627–1658), Mughal culture reached new heights. Under Shah Abbas I (r. 1587–1629), the Safavid capital, Isfahan, was transformed through the construction of mosques, formal gardens, palaces, royal tombs, and public squares. Similarly, the early Ottoman sultans, following the precedent of Mehmet II, who had the magnificent Greek Orthodox church of Hagia Sophia in Constantinople converted into a mosque, all sought to leave their mark on Islamic culture by sponsoring ambitious building programs and the work of scholars, poets, and artists.

The sources in this section provide insights into the personalities and policies of three of the most renowned Islamic rulers of the sixteenth and seventeenth centuries — Suleiman I, Abbas I, and Jahangir. They provide an opportunity to analyze their styles of leadership and the strengths and weaknesses of their regimes.

A European Diplomat's Impressions of Suleiman I

▼▼▼

9 ▾ *Ogier Ghiselin de Busbecq, TURKISH LETTERS*

Suleiman I, known to Europeans as Suleiman the Magnificent, is remembered mainly for his military exploits, but his accomplishments go beyond the battlefield. He was a patron of history and literature, oversaw the codification of Ottoman law, and contributed to the architectural grandeur of Istanbul, the seat of Ottoman government. He was one of the outstanding rulers of the age.

The following observations of Suleiman and Ottoman society were recorded by Ogier Ghiselin de Busbecq (1522–1590), a Flemish nobleman who spent most of his life in the service of the Hapsburg dynasty, in particular Ferdinand I, who was the archduke of Austria, king of Hungary and Bohemia, and, from 1558 to 1564, Holy Roman Emperor. In 1555 Ferdinand sent Busbecq to Istanbul to represent his interests in an ongoing dispute with Suleiman over the division of the Kingdom of Hungary, which had broken apart after the Ottoman victory at the Battle of Mohács in 1526. After six years of discussions, the two sides agreed on a compromise in which Austria dominated the western third of Hungary and portions of today's Croatia, while the Ottomans held central Hungary and were allowed to collect tribute from semi-independent Transylvania.

During his six years in Ottoman lands, Busbecq recorded his observations and impressions, which he sent in the form of four long letters to his friend Nicholas Michault, a Hapsburg official in a position to communicate Busbecq's views to Ferdinand and his advisors. All four letters were later published in Paris in 1589. Subsequently appearing in numerous Latin versions and translated into the major European languages, Busbecq's letters provide a wealth of information about Ottoman society.

The following excerpt begins with a description of Busbecq's first meeting with Suleiman I in 1555 and then goes on to comment on Ottoman military power. It concludes with a summary of the events surrounding the assassination in 1553 of Suleiman's oldest son and most likely successor, Mustafa. It is an example of the conflict and intrigue surrounding issues of succession in the Ottoman state, in which one of the sons of the sultan would succeed his father, but not necessarily the eldest. As Busbecq explains, Mustafa's interests clashed with the ambitions of Roxelana, Suleiman's Russian-Ukrainian concubine and later wife, who bore him two sons and a daughter. To ensure that her son Selim would become sultan after Suleiman's death, she convinced her aging husband that Mustafa was plotting against him and had to be killed.

QUESTIONS FOR ANALYSIS

1. What does Busbecq's first meeting with Suleiman reveal about the sultan's attitudes toward Europeans? What further insights into his attitudes are provided later in the excerpt?
2. What does Busbecq see as the main difference between Ottoman and European attitudes toward social privilege and inherited status? How, in his view, do these attitudes affect Ottoman government?
3. What insights does Busbecq provide about the Ottoman military?
4. In Busbecq's view, what should be the European military response to the Ottoman threat? What can one infer from his recommendations?
5. What does the episode of Mustafa's assassination reveal about the power and influence of Roxelana? About Ottoman attitudes toward the imperial succession? About Suleiman's character?
6. What advantages and disadvantages were there in the Ottoman practice of not making the eldest son the automatic heir of the reigning sultan?
7. Shortly after Suleiman's reign, the Ottoman Empire began to decline. What in Busbecq's account points to future problems?

FIRST IMPRESSIONS

On our arrival . . . we were taken to call on Achmet Pasha (the chief Vizier) and the other pashas[1] — for the Sultan himself was not then in the town — and commenced our negotiations with them touching the business entrusted to us by King Ferdinand. The pashas . . . told us that the whole matter depended on the Sultan's pleasure. On his arrival we were admitted to an audience; but the manner and spirit in which he . . . listened to our address, our arguments, and our message was by no means favorable. . . .

On entering we were separately conducted into the royal presence by the chamberlains, who grasped our arms. . . . After having gone through a pretense of kissing his [Suleiman's] hand, we were conducted backwards to the wall opposite his seat, care being taken that we should never turn our backs on him. The Sultan then listened to what I had to say; but the language I used was not at all to his taste, for the demands of his Majesty[2] breathed a spirit of independence and dignity, which was by no means acceptable to one who deemed that his wish was law; and so he made no answer beyond saying in an impatient way, "Giusel, giusel," i.e., well, well. After this we were dismissed to our quarters.

The Sultan's hall was crowded with people, among whom were several officers of high rank. Besides these there were all the troopers of the Imperial guard, and a large force of Janissaries, but there was not in all that great assembly a single man who owed his position to anything save his valor and his merit. No distinction is attached to birth among the Turks; the respect to be paid to a man is measured by the position he holds in the public service. There is no fighting for precedence; a man's place is marked out by the duties he discharges. . . . It is by merit that men rise in the service, a system which ensures that posts should only be assigned to the competent. . . . Those who receive the highest offices from the Sultan are for the most part the sons of shepherds or herdsmen, and so far from being ashamed of their parentage, they actually glory

[1]*Pasha* was an honorary title for a high-ranking military or government official; the *grand vizier* was the sultan's chief advisor and head of the Ottoman administration.

[2]Archduke Ferdinand, Busbecq's employer.

in it, and consider it a matter of boasting that they owe nothing to the accident of birth; for they do not believe that high qualities are either natural or hereditary, nor do they think that they can be handed down from father to son, but that they are partly the gift of God, and partly the result of good training, great industry, and unwearied zeal. . . . Among the Turks, therefore, honors, high posts, and judgeships are the rewards of great ability and good service.[3]

OTTOMAN MILITARY STRENGTH

Against us stands Suleiman, that foe whom his own and his ancestors' exploits have made so terrible; he tramples the soil of Hungary with 200,000 horses, he is at the very gates of Austria, threatens the rest of Germany, and brings in his train all the nations that extend from our borders to those of Persia. The army he leads is equipped with the wealth of many kingdoms. Of the three regions, into which the world is divided,[4] there is not one that does not contribute its share towards our destruction. . . .

▾ ▾ ▾

The Turkish monarch going to war takes with him over 40,000 camels and nearly as many baggage mules, of which a great part, when he is invading Persia, are loaded with rice and other kinds of grain. These mules and camels also serve to carry tents and armor, and likewise tools and munitions for the campaign. The territories, which bear the name of Persia, . . . are less fertile than our country, and even such crops as they bear are laid waste by the inhabitants in time of invasion in hopes of starving out the enemy, so that it is very dangerous for an army to invade Persia if it is not furnished with abundant supplies. . . .

▾ ▾ ▾

After dinner I practice the Turkish bow, in the use of which weapon people here are marvelously expert. From the eighth, or even the seventh, year of their age they begin to shoot at a mark, and practice archery ten or twelve years. This constant exercise strengthens the muscles of their arms, and gives them such skill that they can hit the smallest marks with their arrows. . . . So sure is their aim that in battle they can hit a man in the eye or in any other exposed part they choose.

▾ ▾ ▾

No nation in the world has shown greater readiness than the Turks to avail themselves of the useful inventions of foreigners, as is proved by their employment of cannons and mortars, and many other things invented by Christians. . . . The Turks are much afraid of carbines and pistols, such as are used on horseback. The same, I hear, is the case with the Persians, on which account someone advised Rustem,[5] when he was setting out with the Sultan on a campaign against them, to raise from his household servants a troop of 200 horsemen and arm them with firearms, as they would cause much alarm . . . in the ranks of the enemy. Rustem, in accordance with this advice, raised a troop of dragoons,[6] furnished them with firearms, and had them drilled. But they had not completed half the journey when their guns began to get out of order. Every day some essential part of their weapons was lost or broken, and it was not often that armorers could be found capable of repairing them. So, a large part of the firearms having been rendered unserviceable, the men took a dislike to the weapon; and this prejudice was increased by the dirt which its use entailed, the Turks being a very cleanly people; for the dragoons had their hands and clothes begrimed

[3]What Busbecq fails to mention is that all the officials he observed were the sultan's slaves, taken from non-Muslim families as young boys and converted to Islam according to the *devshirme,* or "child contribution" system. The brightest were educated in foreign languages, the law, and administrative skills, after which they took jobs in the sultan's "Inner Service" and could rise to the level of pasha. The less gifted were given jobs in the military and made up the core of the famous Ottoman janissary corps.

[4]Asia, Europe, and Africa.

[5]Rustem, the grand vizier, was also Suleiman's son-in-law. He married the daughter of Suleiman and Roxelana, originally a Russian slave girl in the sultan's harem.

[6]Heavily armed mounted troops.

with gunpowder, and moreover presented such a sorry appearance, with their ugly boxes and pouches hanging about them, that their comrades laughed at them and called them apothecaries. So, . . . they gathered around Rustem and showing him their broken and useless firearms, asked what advantage he hoped to gain from them when they met the enemy, and demanded that he should relieve them of them, and give them their old arms again. Rustem, after considering their request carefully, thought there was no reason for refusing to comply with it, and so they got permission to resume their bows and arrows.

PROBLEMS OF THE SUCCESSION

Suleiman had a son by a concubine who came from the Crimea. . . . His name was Mustafa, and at the time of which I am speaking he was young, vigorous, and of high repute as a soldier. But Suleiman had also several other children, by a Russian woman.[7] . . . To the latter he was so much attached that he placed her in the position of wife. . . .

Mustafa's high qualities and matured years marked him out to the soldiers who loved him, and the people who supported him, as the successor of his father, who was now in the decline of life. On the other hand, his step-mother [Roxelana], by throwing the claim of a lawful wife onto the balance, was doing her utmost to counterbalance his personal merits and his rights as eldest son, with a view to obtaining the throne for her own children. In this intrigue, she received the advice and assistance of Rustem, whose fortunes were inseparably linked with hers by his marriage with a daughter she had had by Suleiman. . . .

Inasmuch as Rustem was chief Vizier, . . . he had no difficulty . . . in influencing his master's mind. The Turks, accordingly, are convinced that it was by the calumnies of Rustem and the spells of Roxelana, who was in ill repute as a practitioner of sorcery, that the Sultan was so estranged from his son as to entertain the design of getting rid of him. A few believe that Mustafa, being aware of the plans, . . . decided to anticipate them, and thus engaged in designs against his father's throne and person. The sons of Turkish Sultans are in the most wretched position in the world, for, as soon as one of them succeeds his father, the rest are doomed to certain death. The Turk can endure no rival to the throne, and, indeed, the conduct of the Janissaries renders it impossible for the new Sultan to spare his brothers; for if one of them survives, the Janissaries are forever asking generous favors. If these are refused, the cry is heard, "Long live the brother!" "God preserve the brother!" — a tolerably broad hint that they intend to place him on the throne. So that the Turkish Sultans are compelled to celebrate their succession by staining their hands with the blood of their nearest relatives. . . .

Being at war with Shah Tahmasp, Shah of the Persians, he [Suleiman] had sent Rustem against him as a commander-in-chief of his armies. Just as he was about to enter Persian territory, Rustem suddenly halted, and hurried off dispatches to Suleiman, informing him that affairs were in a very critical state; that treason was rife; . . . that the soldiers had been tampered with, and cared for no one but Mustafa; . . . and he must come at once if he wished to preserve his throne. Suleiman was seriously alarmed by these dispatches. He immediately hurried to the army, sent a letter to summon Mustafa to his presence, inviting him to clear himself of those crimes of which he was suspected. . . .

There was great uneasiness among the soldiers, when Mustafa arrived. . . . He was brought to his father's tent, and there everything betokened peace. . . . But there were in the tent certain mutes — . . . strong and sturdy fellows, who had been appointed as his executioners. As soon as he entered the inner tent, they threw

[7]A reference to Roxelana.

themselves upon him, and endeavored to put the fatal noose around his neck. Mustafa, being a man of considerable strength, made a stout defense and fought — there being no doubt that if he escaped . . . and threw himself among the Janissaries, the news of this outrage on their beloved prince would cause such pity and indignation, that they would not only protect him, but also proclaim him Sultan. Suleiman felt how critical the matter was, being only separated by the linen hangings of his tent from the stage on which this tragedy was being enacted. When he found that there was an unexpected delay in the execution of his scheme, he thrust out his head from the chamber of his tent, and glared on the mutes with fierce and threatening eyes; at the same time, with signs full of hideous meaning, he sternly rebuked their slackness. Hereon the mutes, gaining fresh strength from the terror he inspired, threw Mustafa down, got the bowstring round his neck, and strangled him. Shortly afterwards they laid his body on a rug in front of the tent, that the Janissaries might see the man they had desired as their Sultan. . . .

Meanwhile, Roxelana, not content with removing Mustafa from her path, . . . did not consider that she and her children were free from danger, so long as his offspring survived. Some pretext, however, she thought necessary, in order to furnish a reason for the murder, but this was not hard to find. Information was brought to Suleiman that, whenever his grandson appeared in public, the boys of Ghemlik[8] — where he was being educated — shouted out, "God save the Prince, and may he long survive his father;" and that the meaning of these cries was to point him out as his grandsire's future successor, and his father's avenger. Moreover, he was bidden to remember that the Janissaries would be sure to support the son of Mustafa, so that the father's death had in no way secured the peace of the throne and realm. . . .

Suleiman was easily convinced by these arguments to sign the death warrant of his grandson. He commissioned Ibrahim Pasha to go to the Ghemlik with all speed, and put the innocent child to death.[9]

[8]A town in northwest Turkey.

[9]The assassination was carried out by a eunuch hired by Ibrahim Pasha, who had succeeded Rustem as grand vizier.

Shah Abbas I: Policies and Personality

▼▼▼

10 ▾ *Eskandar Beg Monshi, HISTORY OF SHAH ABBAS THE GREAT*

When Shah Abbas I ascended the Safavid throne in 1587 after the forced abdication of his father, he inherited a disintegrating empire. He faced rebellion from Turkoman tribal leaders and invasions by the Ottomans from the west and the Uzbeks from the east. Within fifteen years, however, he crushed the rebels and routed the Uzbeks and Ottomans. Subsequently, Abbas defeated the Mughals in 1621, seized the Persian Gulf island of Bahrain in 1622, and with English help expelled the Portuguese from their trading post at Ormuz in the same year. In addition to his military exploits, Abbas encouraged foreign and domestic trade, cultivated useful contacts with foreigners, supported industry, and presided over a glorious era in Persian culture.

The author of the following excerpt, Eskandar Beg, known as Monshi (secretary) because of his service as an advisor to Shah Abbas, was born in 1560 and

died around 1632. Few details are known about his life. He tells us in the introduction to his *History* that as a young man he abandoned his studies of history and literature in favor of bookkeeping after having been "led astray by some shortsighted, materialistic persons." After entering government service, he gained the attention of a number of the shah's advisors, who found him employment as a secretary to the shah. As secretary, he traveled with the shah, drew up documents, handled correspondence, and provided counsel. Sometime around 1600, with the approval of Abbas, he began to research and write a history of the shah's reign, a project he completed in 1629, the year of Abbas's death. Beg was an eyewitness to many of the events he describes, and for others he drew on interviews with officials, soldiers, merchants, and travelers. Not surprisingly, his portrayal of Abbas is highly laudatory. As shown in the following excerpt, however, he does not hesitate to criticize some of his patron's decisions and point out some of his flaws.

QUESTIONS FOR ANALYSIS

1. According to Eskandar Beg, what were the major challenges that Abbas faced when he assumed the throne?
2. What specific policies did Abbas institute to meet these challenges?
3. In all that he did, what were Abbas's ultimate purposes?
4. What were the salient characteristics of Abbas's personality? How, according to Eskandar Beg, did his personality serve him well in his rule?

When Shah Abbas undertook the personal direction of affairs of state . . . he succeeded in restoring such order to the state that men stood in amazement at it. It should not be forgotten that Iran [Persia] had been without a strong king for more than ten years. As a result, the ignorant military, the army officers and the leading men of the tribes, had formed two factions and blotted their scutcheon[1] by treachery and mad ambition. Their actions rent the fabric of the state and gave their enemies the opportunity to attack Iran on two fronts; every year, some new province was lost.

Shah Abbas took steps to remedy the situation: first, he judged it better to deal with his domestic foes. One by one, he got into his power and destroyed those seditious emirs and army officers who had risen to the rank of emir, sultan, or khan, whether by virtue of seniority or corrupt practices, and had then proceeded to stir up trouble between the *kizilbash*[2] tribes. In their place, he appointed to the highest offices, and to the emirate, promising officers who owed their rise to himself alone. Gradually, as the former class of officer faded into oblivion, he managed

[1]A scutcheon, or escutcheon, is a shield or shield-shaped emblem bearing a coat of arms. To "blot one's scutcheon" means to tarnish one's reputation.

[2]The term *kizilbash* refers to the Turkish-speaking Turkoman tribes from western Iran and eastern Asia Minor who in the thirteenth century converted to Shiism and subsequently became strong supporters of the Safavids in their struggle to gain control of Iran. *Kizilbash* means "red heads," referring to the red turbans they wore. With the triumph of the Safavids, each *kizilbash* leader was awarded a province or fief with extensive powers. Efforts of Ismail's son, Shah Tahmasp (r. 1524–1576), to curb the independence of the *kizilbash* and replace them with Persians led to civil strife, assassinations, and the breakdown of central government. Abbas's predecessor, Muhammad, ruled as a Turkoman puppet until he was poisoned by a Turkoman faction in 1587.

to reduce the dissension among the kizilbash, and the king's commands were once more obeyed by the army. . . .

▾ ▾ ▾

The greater part of governing is the preservation of stability within the kingdom and security on the roads. Prior to the accession of Shah Abbas, this peace and security had disappeared in Iran, and it had become extremely difficult for people to travel about the country. As soon as he came to the throne, Shah Abbas turned his attention to this problem. He called for the principal highway robbers in each province to be identified, and he then set about eliminating this class of people. Within a short space of time, most of their leaders had been arrested. Some of them, who had been driven by misfortune to adopt this way of life, were pardoned by Shah Abbas and their troubles solved by various forms of royal favor. . . . Others, however, were handed over to the *šaḥna* [a police official] for punishment, and society was rid of this scourge. With security restored to the roads, merchants and tradesmen traveled to and from the Safavid empire.

▾ ▾ ▾

The welfare of his people was always a prime concern of the Shah, and he was at pains to see that the people enjoyed peace and security, and that oppression by officialdom, the major cause of anxiety on the part of the common man, was totally stamped out in his kingdom. Substantial reductions were made in the taxes due . . . first, the tax on flocks in Iraq, amounting to nearly fifteen thousand Iraqi *tomān*,[3] was remitted to the people of that province, and the population of Iraq, which is the flourishing heart of Iran and the seat of government, by this gift was preferred above the other provinces. Second, all *dīvān*[4] levies were waived for all Shi'ites throughout the empire during the month of Ramadan.[5] The total revenues for one month, which according to the computation of the *dīvān* officials amounted to some twenty thousand *tomān,* were given to the people as alms. The object was that they should be free from demands for taxes during this blessed month, which is a time to be devoted to the service and worship of God.

Shah Abbas was constantly trying to alleviate the hardships of the poor and to ensure that none of his subjects should live in want. . . . On many occasions, he allocated substantial sums as subsistence allowances to the poor and to true believers. He also gave alms to these persons, and obtained the reward of these two good works. These are the charitable works the Shah has performed up to the time of writing; may he be spared to perform many others!

▾ ▾ ▾

From birth, the Shah has been inclined toward despotic behavior and has had a quick temper; he has never been slow to punish wrongdoers. The punishment of wrongdoers constitutes a major part of the command of armies, the government of empire, and ministry to one's people, and Shah Abbas has never been diverted, by worldly motives or by respect for rank, from inflicting punishment. The knowledge that this was the case has had a salutary effect from the early days of his reign. Reports of his sternness and severity have had a restraining influence on those who oppressed their subordinates, and have meant that his orders were carried out without delay. For example, if a father were commanded to slay his son, the order would be obeyed instantly; if the father procrastinated out of compassion, the order would be reversed; and if the son hesitated in his turn, another would be sent to put them both to death. His writ therefore became law, and no one dared to oppose his orders for an instant.

[3]A gold coin; the basic unit of the Persian currency.

[4]A government council; in this context, one dealing with finance.

[5]Ramadan is the month in which Muslims fast from sunrise to sundown to commemorate the flight of Muhammad and his followers from Mecca to Medina in 622 C.E. Fasting is a means of expiating one's sins for the year.

Before Abbas came to the throne, the *kizilbash* tribes were frequently slow in answering a mobilization call, and many men drew their pay but stayed at home. . . . Shah Abbas therefore conducted an inquiry into the state of the army and issued orders that, whenever there was a call to arms, all men, whether regulars or irregulars, should report without delay out of zeal for their faith, and to save their honor and that of their tribe. If anyone failed to answer a mobilization call, he would be put to death forthwith if he could not show cause for his absence, and his property would be made over to the person who reported him to the authorities. If his tribe took his side and concealed his offense, the whole tribe would be punished. After a few men had been executed and their property handed over to informers, mobilization orders were obeyed with alacrity.

▾ ▾ ▾

One of his principal pieces of legislation has been his reform of the army. Because the rivalries of the *kizilbash* tribes had led them to commit all sorts of enormities, and because their devotion to the Safavid royal house had been weakened by dissension, Shah Abbas decided (as the result of divine inspiration, which is vouchsafed to kings but not to ordinary mortals); to admit into the armed forces groups other than the *kizilbash*. He enrolled in the armed forces large numbers of Georgian, Circassian, and other *ḡolāms,*[6] and created the office of . . . commander-in-chief of *ḡolām* regiments, which had not previously existed under the Safavid regime. Several thousand men were drafted into regiments of musketeers from the *Caḡatāy*[7] tribe, and from various Arab and Persian tribes. . . . Into the regiments of musketeers, too, were drafted all the riff-raff from every province — sturdy, serviceable men who were unemployed and preyed on the lower classes of society. By this means the lower classes were given relief from their lawless activities, and the recruits made amends for their past sins by performing useful service in the army. . . .

Shah Abbas tightened up provincial administration. Any emir or noble who was awarded a provincial governorship, or who was charged with the security of the highways, received his office on the understanding that he discharge his duties in a proper manner. If any merchant or traveler or resident were robbed, it was the duty of the governor to recover his money for him or replace it out of his own funds. This rule was enforced throughout the Safavid empire. As a result, property was secure, and people could travel without hindrance to and from Iran. . . .

▾ ▾ ▾

The character of the Shah contains some contradictions; for instance, his fiery temper, his imperiousness, his majesty and regal splendor are matched by his mildness, leniency, his ascetic way of life, and his informality. . . . When he is in a good temper, he mixes with the greatest informality with the members of his household, his close friends and retainers and others, and treats them like brothers. In contrast, when he is in a towering rage, his aspect is so terrifying that the same man who, shortly before, was his boon companion and was treated with all the informality of a close friend, dares not speak a word out of turn for fear of being accused of insolence or discourtesy. At such times, the emirs, sultans, and even the court wits and his boon companion keep silent, for fear of the consequences. . . .

▾ ▾ ▾

As regards his knowledge of the outside world, he possesses information about the rulers (both Muslim and non-Muslim) of other countries, about the size and composition of their armies, about their religious faith and the organization of their kingdoms, about their highway systems, and about the prosperity or otherwise of their realms. He has cultivated diplomatic relations with most of the princes of the world, and the

[6]Persian for slaves, that is, slaves of the shah. The Georgians and Circassians, both largely Christian peoples, were also slaves.

[7]A Turkic group living in Afghanistan and northwest India.

rulers of the most distant parts of Europe, Russia, and India are on friendly terms with him. . . .

Shah Abbas mixes freely with all classes of society, and in most cases is able to converse with people in their own particular idiom. He is well versed in Persian poetry; he understands it well, indulges in poetic license, and sometimes utters verses himself. He is a skilled musician, an outstanding composer of rounds, rhapsodies, and part-songs; some of his compositions are famous. As a conversationalist, he is capable of elegant and witty speech.

A Self-Portrait of Jahangir

11 ▾ *Jahangir, MEMOIRS*

Jahangir, Mughal emperor from 1605 to 1627, modestly increased the size of the empire through conquest, snuffed out half a dozen rebellions, and on the whole continued the policies of his illustrious father, Akbar (r. 1556–1605). His lands provided him the wealth to indulge his tastes for formal gardens, entertaining, ceremony, sports, literature, and finely crafted books. In addition to subsidizing the work of hundreds of painters and writers, Jahangir himself contributed to the literature of his age by writing a memoir. Intended to glorify himself and instruct his heirs, it covered the first thirteen years of his reign, before his addiction to alcohol and opium sapped his energy and effectiveness.

QUESTIONS FOR ANALYSIS

1. Other than to glorify the person of the emperor, what political purposes might have been served by Jahangir's elaborate coronation ceremony?
2. What do the "twelve special regulations" issued at the beginning of Jahangir's reign reveal about his priorities as emperor?
3. How does Jahangir view his Hindu subjects? What are his reasons for allowing them to practice their religion?
4. What does the episode of the Afghan bandits reveal about Jahangir's view of the emperor's responsibilities?
5. What similarities and differences do you see in the authority and leadership style of Suleiman I (source 9), Abbas I (source 10), and Jahangir?

JAHANGIR'S CORONATION

On the eighth of the latter month of Jammaudy, of the year of the Hegira one thousand and fourteen,[1] in the metropolis of Agra, and in the forenoon of the day, being then at the age of thirty-eight, I became Emperor, and under the most felicitous auspices, took my seat on the throne of my wishes. . . . Hence I assumed the titles of Jahangir Padshah, and Jahangir Shah: the world-subduing emperor; the world-subduing king. I ordained that the following legend

[1]October 10, 1605. Jahangir uses the Muslim calendar, dated from the Hegira, Muhammad's flight from Mecca to Medina in 1622.

should be stamped on the coinage of the empire: "Stricken at Agra by that . . . safeguard of the world; the sovereign splendor of the faith, Jahangir, son of the imperial Akbar."

On this occasion I made use of the throne prepared by my father, and enriched at an expense without parallel, for the celebration of the festival of the new year. . . . In the fabrication of the throne a sum not far short of ten krours of ashrefies[2] was expended in jewels alone. . . .

Having thus seated myself on the throne of my expectation and wishes, I caused also the imperial crown, which my father had caused to be made after the manner of that which was worn by the great kings of Persia, to be brought before me, and then, in the presence of the whole assembled Emirs,[3] having placed it on my brows, as an omen auspicious to the stability and happiness of my reign, kept it there for the space of a full . . . hour. On each of the twelve points of this crown was a single diamond . . . the whole purchased by my father with the resources of his own government, not from anything accruing to him by inheritance from his predecessors. At the point in the center of the top part of the crown was a single pearl . . . and on different parts of the same were set altogether two hundred rubies. . . .

For forty days and forty nights I caused the . . . great imperial state drum to strike up, without ceasing, the strains of joy and triumph; and . . . around my throne, the ground was spread by my directions with the most costly brocades and gold embroidered carpets. Censers[4] of gold and silver were disposed in different directions for the purpose of burning fragrant drugs, and nearly three thousand camphorated wax lights, . . . in branches of gold and silver perfumed with ambergris, illuminated the scene from night till morning. Numbers of blooming youth, . . . clad in dresses of the most costly materials, woven in silk and gold, with . . . amulets sparkling with the lustre of the diamond, the emerald, the sapphire, and the ruby, awaited my commands, rank after rank, and in attitude most respectful. And finally, the Emirs of the empire . . . stood round in brilliant array, also waiting for the commands of their sovereign. . . .

THE EMPEROR'S DECREES

The very first ordinance that issued from me . . . related to the chain of justice, one end of which I caused to be fastened to the battlements of the royal tower of the castle of Agra, and the other to a stone post near the bed of the river Jumnah; to the end that whenever those charged with administering the courts were slack in dispensing justice to the downtrodden, he who had suffered injustice by applying his hand to the chain would find himself in the way of obtaining speedy redress.[5] . . .

I issued twelve special regulations to be implemented and observed in all the realm.

1. I canceled the tamgha, the mirabari,[6] and all other imposts the jagirdars[7] of every province and district had imposed for their own profit.
2. I ordered that when a district lay wasted by thieves and highway bandits or was destitute of inhabitants, that towns should be built, . . . and every effort made to protect the subjects from injury. I directed the jagirdars in such deserted places to erect mosques and caravansaries, or places for the accommodation of travelers, in order to render the district once more an inhabited country, and that men might again be able to travel back and forth safely. . . .

[2]A *krour* is a measurement of weight, and an *ashrefy* is a unit of money. Although it is impossible to determine the exact value of ten "krours of ashrefies," it is an enormous sum.

[3]High government officials.

[4]A container for burning incense.

[5]Presumably pulling the chain would be the first step in bringing the perceived injustice to the emperor's attention.

[6]The *tamgha* and *mirabari* were both customs duties.

[7]A *jagir* was a grant of land by the emperor that entitled the holder to the income from the land. The income was to be used mainly to maintain troops. A *jagirdar* was the holder of a jagir.

3. Merchants travelling through the country were not to have their bales or packs opened without their consent.
4. When a person shall die and leave children, whether he is an infidel[8] or Muslim, no man was to interfere a pin's point in his property; but when he has no children or direct and unquestionable heirs his inheritance is to be spent on approved expenditures such as construction of mosques and caravansaries, repair of bridges, and the creation of watertanks and wells.
5. No person was permitted either to make or to sell wine or any other intoxicating liquor. I undertook to institute this regulation, although it is sufficiently well known that I myself have the strongest inclination for wine, in which from the age of sixteen I have liberally indulged. . . .
6. No official was permitted to take up his abode in the house of any subject of my realm. On the contrary, when individuals serving in the state armies come to any town, and can rent a place to live, it would be commendable; otherwise they were to pitch their tents outside the town. . . .
7. No person was to suffer, for any offence, the cutting off of a nose or ear. For theft, the offender was to be scourged with thorns, or deterred from further transgressions by an oath on the Quran.[9]
8. I decreed that superintendents of royal lands and jagirdars were prohibited from seizing the lands of their subjects or cultivating the lands themselves for their own benefit. . . . On the contrary, his attention was to be wholly and exclusively devoted to the cultivation and improvement of the district allotted to him.
9. The tax collectors of royal lands and jagirdars may not intermarry with the people of the districts in which they reside without my permission.[10]
10. Governors in all the large cities were directed to establish infirmaries and hospitals with physicians appointed to treat the sick. Expenses are to be covered by income from royal lands.
11. During the month of my birth there could be no slaughter of animals in my realm. . . . In every week also, on Thursday, that being the day of my accession, and Sunday, my father's birthday, . . . and also because it is the day attributed to the sun and the day on which the creation of the world was begun. . . .
12. I issued a decree confirming the dignitaries and jagirs of my father's government in all that they had enjoyed while he was living; and where I found sufficient merit, I conferred an advance of rank. . . .

POLICY TOWARD THE HINDUS

I am here led to relate that at the city of Banaras[11] a temple had been erected [in which] . . . the principal idol . . . had on its head a tiara or cap, enriched with jewels. . . . [Also] placed in this temple, moreover, as the associates and ministering servants of the principal idol, [were] four other images of solid gold, each crowned with a tiara, in like manner enriched with precious stones. It was the belief of these non-believers that a dead Hindu, provided when alive he had been a worshiper, when laid before this idol would be restored to life. As I could not possibly give credit to such a pretense, I employed a confidential person to ascertain the truth; and, as I justly supposed, the whole was detected to be an impudent fraud. . . .

On this subject I must however acknowledge, that having on one occasion asked my father the reason why he had forbidden anyone to prevent or interfere with the building of these haunts of idolatry, his reply was in the following terms: "My dear child," said he, "I find myself a powerful monarch, the shadow of God upon earth. I

[8]A Hindu.
[9]Islam's sacred book.
[10]This was to prevent any tax collector or jagirdar from gaining a vested interest in the fortunes of a particular region or family.
[11]A city on the Ganges River.

have seen that he bestows the blessing of his gracious providence upon all his creatures without distinction. . . . With all of the human race, with all of God's creatures, I am at peace: why then should I permit myself, under any consideration, to be the cause of molestation or aggression to any one? Besides, are not five parts in six . . . either Hindus or aliens to the faith; and were I to be governed by motives of the kind suggested in your inquiry, what alternative can I have but to put them all to death! I have thought it therefore my wisest plan to let these men alone. Neither is it to be forgotten, that the class of whom we are speaking . . . are usefully engaged, either in the pursuits of science or the arts, or of improvements for the benefit of mankind, and have in numerous instances arrived at the highest distinctions in the state, there being, indeed, to be found in this city men of every description, and of every religion on the face of the earth." . . .

▾ ▾ ▾

In the practice of being burnt on the funeral pyre of their husbands[12] as sometimes exhibited among the widows of the Hindus, I had previously directed that no woman who was the mother of children should be thus made a sacrifice, however willing to die; and I now further ordained, that in no case was the practice to be permitted, when compulsion was in the slightest degree employed, whatever might be the opinions of the people. In other respects they were in no way to be molested in the duties of their religion, nor exposed to oppression or violence in any manner whatever. . . .

THE DUTIES OF THE EMPEROR

. . . It had been made known to me that the roads about Kandahar[13] were grievously infested by the Afghans, who by their vexatious exactions rendered the communications in that quarter extremely unsafe for travelers of every description. . . .

Lushker Khan . . . was despatched by my orders toward Kabul for the purpose of clearing the roads in that direction, which had been rendered unsafe by the outrages of licentious bandits. It so happened that when this commander had nearly reached the point for which he was destined he found opposed to him a body of mountaineers . . . , who had assembled to the number of forty thousand, horse and foot and musketeers, had shut up the approaches against him, and prevented his further advance. . . . A conflict began, which continued . . . from dawn of day until nearly sunset. The enemy were however finally defeated, with the loss of seventeen thousand killed, a number taken prisoners, and a still greater proportion escaping to their hiding-places among the mountains. The prisoners were conducted to my presence yoked together, with the heads of the seventeen thousand slain in the battle suspended from their necks. After some deliberation as to the destiny of these captives, I resolved that their lives should be spared, and that they should be employed in bringing forage for my elephants.

. . . The shedding of so much human blood must ever be extremely painful; but until some other resource is discovered, it is unavoidable. Unhappily the functions of government cannot be carried on without severity, and occasional extinction of human life: for without something of the kind, some species of coercion and chastisement, the world would soon exhibit the horrible spectacle of mankind, like wild beasts, worrying each other to death with no other motive than rapacity and revenge. God is witness that there is no repose for crowned heads. There is no pain or anxiety equal to that which attends the possession of sovereign power, for to the possessor there is not in this world a moment's rest. . . .

---

[12]A woman who burned herself in this way was known as *sati* (Sanskrit for "virtuous woman"). The word *sati* also is used to describe the burning itself.

[13]A city in Afghanistan.

Religion and Society in South and Southwest Asia

Although many religions — Hinduism, Buddhism, Zoroastrianism, Judaism, Islam, and Christianity — originated in South and Southwest Asia, by the sixteenth century two faiths dominated the region. They were Islam, ascendant everywhere except India, and Hinduism, India's ancient religion that endured despite centuries of competition from Buddhism, Jainism, and Islam.

At first glance one is struck by the differences between Islam and Hinduism. Islam is distinguished by uncompromising monotheism; the centrality of a single holy book, the Quran; and its origin in the prophecies of a single human being, Muhammad. In contrast, Hinduism is characterized by its embrace of thousands of gods, its slow and continuous evolution, and its lack of a single creed or holy book. Yet on a deeper level, the two religions are similar. Both reject any separation between the religious and secular spheres. Islam and Hinduism not only guide each believer's spiritual development but also define that believer's role as a parent, spouse, subject, and man or woman. Secularism as such does not exist in either religious tradition.

Islam is based on the prophecies and doctrines revealed by Allah (Arabic for God) to Muhammad (ca. 570–632 C.E.) and later recorded in Islam's most holy book, the Quran. *Islam* in Arabic means "submission," and a Muslim is one who submits to God's will. Islam's basic creed is the statement that every follower must utter daily: "There is no God but God, and Muhammad is the Prophet of God." All Muslims are expected to accept the Quran as the word of God, perform works of charity, fast during the holy month of Ramadan, say daily prayers, and, if possible, make a pilgrimage to Mecca, the city on the Arabian Peninsula where Muhammad received Allah's revelation. Islam teaches that at death each person will be judged by Allah, with the faithful rewarded by Heaven and the unbelievers damned to Hell.

Hinduism, which evolved over many centuries, has no single creed, set of rituals, holy book, or organized church. Unlike Judaism, Christianity, and Islam, which affirm the existence of only one God, Hinduism includes thousands of deities in its pantheon, although all are believed to be manifestations of the Divine Essence or Absolute Reality, called Brahman. Hindus believe many paths can lead to enlightenment, and Hinduism thus encompasses a wide range of beliefs and rituals.

All Hindus are part of the caste system, a religiously sanctioned order of social relationships that goes back to the beginnings of Indian civilization between 1500 and 1000 B.C.E. A person's caste, into which he or she is born, determines the individual's social and legal status, restricts marriage partners to other caste members, limits the individual to certain professions, and, in effect, minimizes contacts with members of other castes. Hindus use two different words for caste: *varna* (color) and *jati* (birth). *Varna* refers only to the four most ancient and fundamental social-religious divisions: ***Brahmins*** (priests and teachers), ***Kshatriyas*** (warriors, nobles, and rulers), ***Vaisyas*** (landowners, merchants, and artisans), and ***Sudras*** (peasants and laborers). Outside the caste system and at the bottom of the Hindu hierarchy are the untouchables, who are relegated to despised tasks such as gathering manure, sweeping streets, and butchering animals. ***Jati*** refers to many subdivisions of the four major varna groups; by the 1500s and 1600s, these local hereditary occupational groups numbered around 3,000.

The caste system is related to the doctrine of the transmigration of souls, or reincarnation. This is the belief that each individual soul, or ***atman***, a fragment of the Universal Soul, or Brahman, strives through successive births to reunite with Brahman and win release from the chains of material existence and the cycle of death and rebirth. Reincarnation is based on one's ***karma***, the fruit of one's actions, or the soul's destiny, which is decided by how well or poorly a person has conformed to ***dharma***, the duty to be performed by members of each jati and varna. If a person fulfills his or her dharma, in the next incarnation he or she will move up the cosmic ladder, closer to ultimate reunion with the One.

Sunni-Shia Conflict in the Early Sixteenth Century

▼▼▼

12 ▾ *Sultan Selim I,* *LETTER TO SHAH ISMAIL OF PERSIA*

The following letter, written by the Ottoman sultan Selim I (r. 1512–1520) to the founder of the Persian Safavid Empire, Ismail I (r. 1501–1524), exemplifies the ongoing bitterness between Shia and Sunni Muslims. Selim, who in the Ottoman tradition was a Sunni, was deeply disturbed by the emergence of a Shia state in Persia under Ismail. Ismail, believed by his followers to have descended from Ali, Muhammad's son-in-law, had many supporters among the Turks of eastern Anatolia and had aided Selim's brother and rival, Ahmed, in the succession conflict following Sultan Bayezid's death in 1512. When Ismail invaded eastern Ottoman territory in 1513, war seemed inevitable. Nonetheless, Selim wrote the following letter to Ismail in early 1514 threatening to destroy him militarily unless he embraced Sunni Islam and abandoned his conquests. Ismail did neither, and later in 1514 Selim's armies defeated Ismail's forces at the Battle of Chaldiran. Despite this loss, Ismail remained in power and affirmed his commitment to Shiism. Chaldiran was only the first act in a long and bitter struggle between the two empires.

QUESTIONS FOR ANALYSIS

1. Even though Selim's letter is designed to malign Shiism, not define Islam, it contains many references to essential Muslim beliefs. Which ones can you find?

2. **What does Selim's letter reveal about the differences between Sunnis and Shias?**
3. **How does Selim perceive himself within the Islamic world?**
4. **Selim must have realized that the deeply religious Ismail was unlikely to abandon Shiism. Why might he have written the letter, despite the likelihood that its appeal would fall on deaf ears?**

The Supreme Being who is at once the sovereign arbiter of the destinies of men and the source of all light and knowledge, declares in the holy book[1] that the true faith is that of the Muslims, and that whoever professes another religion, far from being hearkened to and saved, will on the contrary be cast out among the rejected on the great day of the Last Judgment; He says further . . . that he who abandons the good way will be condemned to hell-fire and eternal torments. Place yourself, O Prince, among the true believers, those who walk in the path of salvation, and who turn aside with care from vice and infidelity. . . .

I, sovereign chief of the Ottomans, master of the heroes of the age; . . . I, the exterminator of idolators, destroyer of the enemies of the true faith, the terror of the tyrants and pharaohs of the age; I, before whom proud and unjust kings have humbled themselves, and whose hand breaks the strongest sceptres. . . . I address myself graciously to you, Emir Ismail, chief of the troops of Persia . . . and predestined to perish . . . in order to make known to you that the works emanating from the Almighty are not the fragile products of caprice or folly, but make up an infinity of mysteries impenetrable to the human mind. The Lord Himself says in his holy book: "We have not created the heavens and the earth in order to play a game" [Quran, 21:16]. Man . . . is the only being who can comprehend the attributes of the divinity and adore its sublime beauties; but he possesses this rare intelligence, he attains this divine knowledge only in our religion and by observing the precepts of the prince of prophets . . . the right arm of the God of Mercy [Muhammad]; it is then only by practicing the true religion that man will prosper in this world and merit eternal life in the other. As to you, Emir Ismail, such a recompense will not be your lot; because you have denied the sanctity of the divine laws; . . . have deserted the path of salvation and the sacred commandments; . . . have impaired the purity of the dogmas of Islam; . . . have dishonored, soiled, and destroyed the altars of the Lord, usurped the sceptre of the East by unlawful and tyrannical means; . . . have raised yourself by odious devices to a place shining with splendor and magnificence; . . . have opened to Muslims the gates of tyranny and oppression; . . . have joined iniquity, perjury, and blasphemy to your sectarian impiety; . . . have raised the standard of irreligion and heresy; . . . have dared to throw off the control of Muslim laws and to permit lust and rape, the massacre of the most virtuous and respectable men, the destruction of pulpits and temples, the profanation of tombs, the ill-treatment of the *ulama,* the doctors and emirs[2] descended from the Prophet, the repudiation of the Quran, the cursing of the legitimate Caliphs.[3] Now as the first duty of a Muslim and above all of a pious prince is to obey the commandment, "O, you faithful who believe, be the executors of the decrees of God!" the *ulama* and

---

[1]The Quran.

[2]Shias originally broke away from mainstream Islam over disagreements concerning the early caliphate. They believe that Ali, Muhammad's cousin and son-in-law (the fourth caliph), should have been the first. As a result, the Shias believe that the first three caliphs (all legitimate according to the Sunnis) are illegitimate.

[3]*Ulama* were bodies of religious teachers and interpreters of Muslim law; *doctors* here means teachers; *emirs* were military commanders and princes.

our doctors have pronounced sentence of death against you, . . . and have imposed on every Muslim the sacred obligation to arm in defense of religion and destroy heresy and impiety in your person and that of all your partisans.

Animated by the spirit of this *fatwa,*[4] conforming to the Quran, the code of divine laws, and wishing on one side to strengthen Islam, on the other to liberate the lands and peoples who writhe under your yoke, we have resolved to lay aside our imperial robes in order to put on the shield and coat of mail [armor], to raise our ever victorious banner, to assemble our invincible armies, to take up the gauntlet of the avenger, to march with our soldiers, whose sword strikes mortal blows, and whose point will pierce the enemy. . . . In pursuit of this noble resolution, we have entered upon the campaign, and guided by the hand of the Almighty, we hope soon to strike down your tyrannous arm, blow away the clouds of glory and grandeur which trouble your head and cause your fatal blindness, release from your despotism your trembling subjects, smother you in the end in the very mass of flames which your infernal *jinn*[5] raises everywhere along your passage. . . . However, anxious to conform to the spirit of the law of the Prophet, we come, before commencing war, to set out before you the words of the Quran, in place of the sword, and to exhort you to embrace the true faith; this is why we address this letter to you. . . .

We urge you to look into yourself, to renounce your errors, and to march towards the good with a firm and courageous step; we ask further that you give up possession of the territory violently seized from our state and to which you have only illegitimate pretensions, that you deliver it back into the hands of our lieutenants and officers; and if you value your safety and repose, this should be done without delay.

But if, to your misfortune, you persist in your past conduct, puffed up with the idea of your power and your foolish bravado, you wish to pursue the course of your iniquities, you will see in a few days your plains covered with our tents and inundated with our battalions. Then prodigies of valor will be done, and we shall see the decrees of the Almighty, Who is the God of Armies, and sovereign judge of the actions of men, accomplished. For the rest, victory to him who follows the path of salvation!

[4]Religious decree.

[5]Supernatural spirit.

A Muslim's Description of Hindu Beliefs and Practices

13 ▾ *Abul Fazl, AKBARNAMA*

As Akbar, Mughal ruler from 1556 to 1605, expanded and strengthened his empire, at his side was Abul Fazl, his close friend and advisor from 1579 until his assassination in 1602. Abul Fazl is best known as the author of the *Akbarnama*, a laudatory history of Akbar's reign full of information about the emperor's personality and exploits. At the time of Abul Fazl's assassination, instigated by Akbar's son and future emperor Jahangir, his history had covered only the first forty-six years of Akbar's life, but that was enough to ensure his work's standing as one of the masterpieces of Mughal literature.

The *Akbarnama* is more than a chronicle of Akbar's life; it also contains numerous descriptions of Indian society such as the following passage on Hinduism.

Abul Fazl, who shared Akbar's tolerant religious views, was interested in presenting Hinduism favorably to his Islamic readers, many of whom were uncomfortable with Akbar's toleration of his Hindu subjects. Even more disturbing to many Muslims was his genuine interest not just in Hinduism but also in Christianity, Jainism, and Zoroastrianism, all of which he drew upon to found a new religious cult, *Din Illahi*, or Divine Faith. In the *Akbarnama*, Abul Fazl sought to lessen the concerns of orthodox Muslims that Hindus were guilty of the two greatest sins against the majesty and oneness of God — idolatry (the worship of idols) and polytheism (a belief in many gods). He also explained the religious basis of the Hindu caste system, whose rigid hierarchies were far removed from the Muslim belief in the equality of all believers before Allah.

QUESTIONS FOR ANALYSIS

1. How does Abul Fazl counter the charge that Hindus are polytheists? Do you find his arguments convincing? Why or why not?
2. How does Abul Fazl address the charge that Hindus are idol worshipers?
3. In what ways do caste and karma provide Hindus a moral understanding of the universe?
4. What do the dharmas of the castes reveal about Hindu social values?
5. Where do women fit into the structure of the ladder of reincarnation? What does this suggest about their status in Hindu society?
6. On the basis of Abul Fazl's account, what conclusions can you reach about the ways Hindus perceive and relate to Divine Reality?

They [Hindus] one and all believe in the unity of God, and as to the reverence they pay to images of stone and wood and the like, which simpletons regard as idolatry, it is not so. The writer of these has exhaustively discussed the subject with many enlightened and upright men, and it became evident that these images . . . are fashioned as aids to fix the mind and keep the thoughts from wandering, while the worship of God alone is required as indispensable. In all their ceremonial observances and usage they ever implore the favor of the world-illumining sun and regard the pure essence of the Supreme Being as transcending the idea of power in operation.

Brahma . . . they hold to be the Creator; Vishnu, the Nourisher and Preserver; and Rudra,[1] called also Mahadeva, the Destroyer. Some maintain that God who is without equal, manifested himself under these three divine forms, without thereby sullying the garment of His inviolate sanctity, as the Nazarenes [Christians] hold of the Messiah.[2] Others assert that these were human creatures exalted to these dignities through perfectness of worship, probity of thought and righteousness of deed. The godliness and self-discipline of this people is such as is rarely to be found in other lands.

---

[1]Also known as Shiva.

[2]Abul Fazl makes two comparisons here. First he compares this Hindu trinity with the Christian Trinity (three divine and full separate persons in one God); then he points out the similarities in Christian and Hindu beliefs in incarnation, whereby God or a god becomes embodied in an earthly form. His Muslim readers would have known basic Christian beliefs.

They hold that the world had a beginning, and some are of opinion that it will have an end. . . . They allow of no existence external to God. The world is a delusive appearance, and as a man in sleep sees fanciful shapes, and is affected by a thousand joys and sorrows, so are its seeming realities. . . .

Brahman is the Supreme Being; and is essential existence and wisdom and also bliss. . . .

Since according to their belief, the Supreme Deity can assume an elemental form . . . they first make various idols of gold and other substances to represent this ideal and gradually withdrawing the mind from this material worship, they become meditatively absorbed in the ocean of His mysterious Being. . . .

They believe that the Supreme Being in the wisdom of His counsel, assumes an elementary form of a special character[3] for the good of the creation, and many of the wisest of the Hindus accept this doctrine. . . .

CASTE

The Hindu philosophers reckon four states of auspiciousness which they term *varna.* 1. *Brahmin.* 2. *Kshatriya.* 3. *Vaisya.* 4. *Sudra.* Other than these are termed *Mlechchha.*[4] At the creation of the world the first of these classes was produced from the mouth of Brahma . . . ; the second, from his arms; the third, from his thigh and the fourth from his feet; the fifth from the cow *Kamadhenu,* the name of Mlechchha being employed to designate them.

The *Brahmins* have six recognized duties. 1. The study of the Vedas[5] and other sciences. 2. The instruction of others (in the sacred texts). 3. The performance of the *Jag,* that is oblation [a religious offering] of money and kind to the Devatas.[6] 4. Inciting others to the same. 5. Giving presents. 6. Receiving presents.

Of these six the *Kshatriya* must perform three. 1. Perusing the holy texts. 2. The performance of the Jag. 3. Giving presents. Further they must, 1. Minister to Brahmins. 2. Control the administration of worldly government and receive the reward thereof. 3. Protect religion. 4. Exact fines for delinquency and observe adequate measure therein. 5. Punish in proportion to the offense. 6. Amass wealth and duly expend it. 7. Supervise the management of elephants, horses, and cattle and the functions of ministerial subordinates. 8. Levy war on due occasion. 9. Never ask for alms. 10. Favor the meritorious and the like.

The *Vaisya* also must perform the same three duties of the Brahmin, and in addition must occupy himself in: 1. Service. 2. Agriculture. 3. Trade. 4. The care of cattle. 5. The carrying of loads. . . .

The Sudra is incapable of any other privilege than to serve these three castes, wear their cast-off garments and eat their leavings. He may be a painter, goldsmith, blacksmith, carpenter, and trade in salt, honey, milk, butter-milk, clarified butter and grain.

Those of the fifth class, are reckoned as beyond the pale of religion, like infidels, Jews, and the like.[7] By the inter-marriages of these, sixteen other classes are formed. The son of Brahmin parents is acknowledged as a Brahmin. If the mother be a Kshatriya (the father being a Brahmin), the progeny is called *Murdhavasikta.* If the mother be a Vaisya, the son is named *Ambastha,* and if a Sudra girl, *Nishada.* If the father and mother are both Kshatriya, the progeny is Kshatriya. If the mother be a Brahmin (and the father a Kshatriya), the son is called *Suta.* If the mother be a Vaisya, the son is *Mahisya.* If the mother be a Sudra, the progeny is *Ugra.* If both parents be Vaisya, the progeny is *Vaisya.* If the mother be a Brahmin (which is illicit), the progeny is *Vaideha* but if she be a Kshatriya, which also is regarded

[3]That is, the Hindu Supreme Being assumes various bodies known as *avataras.*

[4]The "untouchables" or outcasts of Hindu society.

[5]The four collections of ancient poetry that are sacred texts among Hindus.

[6]Hindu deities.

[7]Abul Fazl is drawing an analogy for his Muslim readers. Just as Muslims consider all nonbelievers as outside the community of God, so Hindus regard the Mlechchha as outside their community.

as improper, he is *Magadha.* From the Vaisya by a Sudra mother is produced a *Karana.* When both parents are Sudra, the progeny is *Sudra.* If the mother be a Brahmin, the progeny is *Chandala.* If she be a Kshatriya, it is called *Chatta.* From a Sudra by a Vaisya girl is produced the *Ayogava.*

In the same way still further ramifications are formed, each with different customs and modes of worship and each with infinite distinctions of habitation, profession, and rank of ancestry that defy computation. . . .

KARMA

. . . This is a system of knowledge of an amazing and extraordinary character, in which the learned of Hindustan concur without dissenting opinion. It reveals the particular class of actions performed in a former birth which have occasioned the events that befall men in this present life, and prescribes the special expiation of each sin, one by one. It is of four kinds.

The first kind discloses the particular action which has brought a man into existence in one of the five classes into which mankind is divided, and the action which occasions the assumption of a male or female form. A *Kshatriya* who lives continently, will, in his next birth, be born a *Brahmin.* A *Vaisya* who hazards his transient life to protect a Brahmin, will become a *Kshatriya.* A *Sudra* who lends money without interest and does not defile his tongue by demanding repayment, will be born a *Vaisya.* A *Mlechchha* who serves a *Brahmin* and eats food from his house till his death, will become a *Sudra.* A *Brahmin* who undertakes the profession of a *Kshatriya* will become a *Kshatriya,* and thus a *Kshatriya* will become a *Vaisya,* and a *Vaisya* a *Sudra,* and a *Sudra* a *Mlechchha.* Whosoever accepts in alms . . . the bed on which a man has died[8] . . . will, in the next birth, from a man become a woman. Any woman or *Mlechchha,* who in the temple . . . sees the form of *Narayana,*[9] and worships him with certain incantations, will in the next birth, if a woman, become a man, and if a *Mlechchha,* a *Brahmin.* . . .

The second kind shows the strange effects of actions on health of body and in the production of manifold diseases.

Madness is the punishment of disobedience to father and mother. . . .

Pain in the eyes arises from having looked upon another's wife. . . .

Dumbness is the consequence of killing a sister. . . .

Colic results from having eaten with an impious person or a liar. . . .

Consumption is the punishment of killing a *Brahmin.* . . .

The third kind indicates the class for actions which have caused sterility and names suitable remedies. . . .

A woman who does not menstruate, in a former existence . . . roughly drove away the children of her neighbors who had come as usual to play at her house. . . .

A woman who gives birth to only daughters is thus punished for having contemptuously regarded her husband from pride. . . .

A woman who has given birth to a son that dies and to a daughter that lives, has, in her former existence, taken animal life. Some say that she had killed goats. . . .

The fourth kind treats of riches and poverty, and the like. Whoever distributes alms at auspicious times, as during eclipses of the moon and sun, will become rich and bountiful (in his next existence). Whoso at these times, visits any place of pilgrimage . . . and there dies, will possess great wealth, but will be avaricious and of a surly disposition. Whosoever when hungry and with food before him, hears the supplication of a poor man and bestows it all upon him, will be rich and [generous].

---

[8]An "unclean" object.

[9]The personification of solar and cosmic energy underlying creation.

Women and Islamic Law in the Ottoman Empire

▼▼▼

14 ▼ *Khayr al-Din Ramli, LEGAL OPINIONS*

Many of Muhammad's teachings were favorable to women. He taught the spiritual equality between men and women, and in his treatment of his own wives and daughters he exemplified his teachings about the moral and ethical dimensions of marriage. Women were among his earliest and most important followers. As Islam expanded and evolved, however, women's status declined. Women, especially from the upper classes, were secluded in their homes and expected to wear veils in public. Their role in religious affairs virtually disappeared, and vocational and educational opportunities declined. Some Islamic scholars came to believe that Heaven itself was closed to females.

As the following legal opinions show, however, women in the Ottoman Empire were not without legal rights during the seventeenth century. The empire had a complex and sophisticated court system staffed by *qadi* (judges), whose job was to interpret Islamic law, or Sharia, and apply it to specific cases. In making their decisions, they drew on their knowledge of the Quran and Hadith (traditions connected with Muhammad's life and teachings), legal precedent, and textbooks and commentaries on Islamic law. They also took into account *fatwas*, legal opinions provided by learned men known as *muftis*. Such legal opinions could be solicited by the judges themselves or by an individual involved in a court case. A fatwa was not a binding legal judgment but rather one scholar's opinion that would be included in the record of the trial and might affect the judge's decision. In some provincial courts, however, the standing of a mufti might be so high that his fatwa would actually override a decision of the court.

The following fatwas were written by Khayr al-Din Ramli (1585–1671), who, after advanced studies in Cairo, returned to his native city of Ramla in Palestine, where he supported himself through farming, income from property, and teaching Islamic law. His fame, however, was based on his work as a jurisconsult, or mufti. By the 1650s his reputation had spread throughout Syria and Palestine and was so great that no judge would go against one of his opinions. The following are examples of the many opinions he offered on questions having to do with women's position in society. They reveal judgments that took male dominance in society for granted but also accorded legal rights and protections to women.

Many of the decisions involve marriage, a state into which every adult Muslim was expected to enter. Most marriages were arranged by legal guardians (usually fathers or grandfathers), often when the future wife and husband were still children. On reaching a marriagable age, the young girl or boy had no choice but to acquiesce to his or her guardian's wishes and accept the planned marriage. For marriages arranged for adults, however, individuals had the right to reject the proposed match. Similarly, if a marriage was arranged by someone other than a father or grandfather for a minor, then on reaching adulthood the person could refuse.

Islamic law affirmed that no social good was served by continuing defective or unhappy marriages. Hence divorce was permissible and fairly common. A husband could divorce his wife by saying before her and a witness "I divorce you, I divorce you, I divorce you." This meant that the woman was irrevocably and finally divorced ("thrice-divorced") and could remarry if she wished. For a specified time or until the divorced wife remarried, the former husband was obligated to support her. A woman could also demand a divorce by demonstrating in court that her husband had failed to fulfill his financial or sexual obligations. Or alternatively, she could convince her husband to annul the marriage by offering him financial concessions. For example, she might return some or all of the dowry payment she had received or release the husband from support obligations after the annulment.

Many of the cases on which Khayr al-Din Ramli commented centered on relations between unmarried men and women, child custody, crimes against women, and sexuality. Together they provide many insights into male-female relations in seventeenth-century Syria-Palestine.

QUESTIONS FOR ANALYSIS

1. In making arrangements for marriage, how much legal authority is exercised by the following: the future husband and wife; fathers and grandfathers; male relatives of the future husband and wife?
2. What do the divorce cases reveal about the obligations of husbands to their wives?
3. What rights does a married woman have against an abusive husband?
4. How did Khayr al-Din Ramli view rapists and abductors of women? What penalties are prescribed for perpetrators of such crimes?
5. In one case a widow is appointed by her dying husband to be guardian of their children. What does this reveal about inheritance practices?
6. Taking all the cases together, what do they tell about women's legal standing in seventeenth-century Syria-Palestine? What situations and legal opinions underscore women's legal inferiority to men? What situations and decisions accord women legal rights in their dealings with men?

ARRANGING MARRIAGES

QUESTION: There is a minor girl whose brother married her off, and she came of age and chose annulment in her "coming-of-age" choice. Her husband claimed that her brother had acted as the agent of her father and she does not have a choice. She then claimed that [her brother] married her off during [her father's] brief absence on a journey. If the husband provides evidence for his claim, is her choice canceled or not? If he does not have evidence, and wants her oath on that, must she swear an oath?

ANSWER: Yes, if the husband proves his claim, then her choice is canceled. . . . Only the father's and grandfather's marriage arrangements cannot be canceled . . . [and] if the marriage was arranged by way of a proxy for her father, then she has no choice. If the marriage was arranged as a result of [the brother's] guardianship, then she has a choice.

▾▾▾

Question: A virgin in her legal majority and of sound mind was abducted by her brother and married off to an unsuitable man. Does her father have the right to annul the marriage contract on the basis of the [husband's] unsuitability?

Answer: Yes, if the father asks for that, then the judge should separate the spouses whether or not the marriage was consummated, so long as she has not borne children, and is not pregnant, and did not receive the dower[1] before the marriage. . . . This is the case if her brother has married her off with her consent. But if she was given in marriage without her consent, she can reject [the marriage], and there is no need for the father [to ask for] separation [and raise] opposition, for he is not [in this case] a commissioned agent. [But] if she authorizes him to represent her, then he has the right to request from the judge an annulment of the marriage and a separation, and the judge should separate them. . . .

DIVORCE AND ANNULMENT

Question: There is a poor woman whose husband is absent in a remote region and he left her without support or a legal provider, and she has suffered proven harm from that. She has made a claim against him for that [support], but the absent one is very poor. The resources [intended] for her support were left in his house and in his shop, but they are not sufficient for her to withstand her poverty. She therefore asked the Shafi[2] judge to annul the marriage, and he ordered her to bring proof. Two just men testified in conformity with what she had claimed, and so the judge annulled the marriage. . . . Then, following her waiting period, she married another man. Then the first husband returned and wanted to nullify the judgment. Can that be done for him, when it was all necessary and had ample justification?

Answer: When the harm is demonstrated and the evidence for that is witnessed, the annulment of the absent [one's marriage] is sound. . . . It is not for the Hanafi[3] or others to nullify this. . . .

▾▾▾

Question: There is a poor man who married a virgin in her legal majority, but he did not pay her stipulated dower expeditiously, nor did he provide support, nor did he clothe her. This caused her great harm. Must he follow one of God's two commands: "Either you maintain her well or you release her with kindness?" And if the judge annuls the marriage, is it on account of the severe harm being done to her?

Answer: Yes, the husband should do one of the two things, according to God's command: "maintain her well or release her with kindness." . . . You cannot sustain [indefinitely] such needs through borrowing, and it appears that she does not have anyone to lend her money, and the husband has no actual wealth. . . .

▾▾▾

Question: A man consummated his marriage with his virgin legally major wife, and then claimed that he found her deflowered. He was asked, "How was that?" And he said, "I had intercourse with her several times and I found her deflowered." What is the legal judgment on that?

Answer: The judgment is that all of the dower is required, and it is fully and entirely incumbent on him. Her testimony on her own virginity [is sufficient] to remove the shame. And if he accuses her without [evidence], he is punished and his testimony is not accepted, as is her right.

---

[1]In contrast to practice in Europe, according to Islamic law, dowry payments were paid by the husband to the wife.

[2]One of the four schools of Sunni Muslim jurisprudence; it tended to be more favorable to women seeking divorce.

[3]Another school of Sunni Muslim jurisprudence, less favorable to women seeking divorce.

If he defamed her with a charge of adultery, he must now make a sworn allegation of adultery if she so requests, [and take the consequences].[4] Such is the case, and God knows best.

VIOLENCE AGAINST WOMEN

QUESTION: A man approached a woman, a virgin in her legal majority who was married to someone else,[5] abducted her in the month of Ramadan, and took her to a village near her own village. He brought her to the shaykh[6] of the village, who welcomed him and gave him hospitality and protection. There the man consummated the "marriage," saying "between us there are relations." Such is the way of the peasants. . . . What is the punishment for him and the man who helped him? . . . Should Muslim rulers halt these practices of the peasants . . . even by combat and killing?[7]

ANSWER: The punishment of the abductor and his accomplice for this grave crime is severe beating and long imprisonment, and even worse punishment until they show remorse. It is conceivable that the punishment could be execution because of the severity of this act of disobedience to God. This practice — and one fears for the people of the region if it spreads and they do not halt it — will be punished by God. The one who commits this act, and those who remain silent about it, are like one who punches a hole in a ship, [an act] that will drown all the passengers. . . .

▾ ▾ ▾

QUESTION: There is a *muhsan*[8] criminal who kidnapped a virgin and took her virginity. She fled from him to her family and now her seducer wants to take her away by force. Should he be prevented, and what is required of him?

ANSWER: Yes, he should be prevented [from taking] her. If he claimed *shubha*[9] [judicial doubt], there is no *hadd* punishment but he must [pay] a fair dower. If he did not claim *shubha,* and admission and testimony prove [his actions], the specified *hadd* punishment[10] is required: if he is *muhsan,* then he is stoned; if not, he is flogged. In the event the *hadd* penalty is canceled, a dower is required.

▾ ▾ ▾

QUESTION: There is an evil man who harms his wife, hits her without right and rebukes her without cause. He swore many times to divorce her until she proved that a thrice divorce [a final and irrevocable divorce] had taken effect.

ANSWER: He is forbidden to do that, and he is rebuked and enjoined from her. If she has proved that a thrice divorce has taken place, it is permissible for her to kill him, according to many of the *'ulama'* [jurists] if he is not prevented [from approaching her] except by killing.

---

[4]In order to prove adultery, an accuser had to present four witnesses to testify that it occurred. A failure to prove such an accusation carried severe legal penalties.

[5]The marriage had been legally contracted but not consummated.

[6]In this context, the village leader, often a man with some religious training and standing.

[7]In other words, by sending in troops to enforce the law.

[8]A legally married person.

[9]An issue about which legal authorities disagree.

[10]A *hadd* punishment is one prescribed by Islamic law.

Chapter 3

Continuity and Change in East and Southeast Asia

IMPORTANT CHANGES TOOK PLACE in East and Southeast Asia in the early modern era: Islam continued to make converts in Southeast Asia and western China; a new dynasty, the Tokugawa, brought stability to Japan after decades of civil war; the Chinese Ming Dynasty declined precipitously in the late 1500s and was overthrown in 1644; and most important, European merchants and missionaries, taking advantage of the ocean route around the tip of Africa and across the Indian Ocean, appeared in ever greater numbers. All these changes, however, took place in a region that largely remained what it had been for more than a millennium. For most of East and Southeast Asia, continuity rather than change was the hallmark of the early modern era.

One constant was the primacy of China. In terms of size, wealth, population, technology, trade, military might, and cultural influence, China, as it had for centuries, overshadowed the smaller states and nomadic societies that surrounded it. With some justification the Chinese considered China the "central kingdom" and viewed all other peoples as their inferiors. On China's periphery were three neighboring states — Japan, Korea, and Vietnam — that were politically independent but whose religious practices, formal thought, writing systems, and political institutions all reflected long centuries of Chinese influence. In Southeast Asia, an area of small kingdoms, chiefdoms, and independent cities rather than large territorial states, Chinese influence was less apparent. The strength of Hinduism, Buddhism, and Islam in the region was the result of centuries of contact with India. Nonetheless, China remained the most important market for Southeast Asian merchants, and Southeast Asian rulers paid tribute to the Chinese emperor as a token of their loyalty and subservience. The sparsely populated arid regions to the west and north of China lacked large cities and centralized states. It was populated by Uighurs, Turks, Khitans, Jurchens, and Mongols who supported themselves through pastoralism and, where feasible, agriculture. Their raids on agricultural lands were a constant threat to China and sometimes developed into full-blown invasions. No less than four Chinese dynasties — the Liao, Jin, Yuan, and Qing — originated among these so-called barbarian peoples of the steppe.

Another constant was East and Southeast Asia's important role in the world economy. Southeast Asia was a commercial crossroads linking Chinese and Japanese markets to the north with those of India, Southwest Asia, Europe, and Africa to the west. It was a source of cotton, rice, fish, forest products, copper, and lead, and other items that were exchanged for Indian textiles and Chinese silks, ceramics, medicines, paper, and tea. More important, Southeast Asia grew spices — pepper, nutmeg, cloves, and mace — that were coveted throughout the Afro-Eurasian world. When Europeans sought ocean routes to Asia, their primary goal was to gain direct access to the spice markets of Southeast Asia.

China, however, was the region's economic powerhouse. Its population in 1500 was between 100 and 125 million, well above Europe's estimated 80 million. Its two largest cities, Beijing and Nanjing, with populations around 700,000 each, were slightly smaller than Istanbul, the world's most populous city, but were six times larger than Paris, which in 1500 had approximately 125,000 residents and was Europe's largest city. Much Chinese economic activity was devoted to supplying this vast domestic market, but China also played a major role in international trade. China's main exports were silks, satins, and brocades, whose lustrous textures and colorful designs were unmatched, and ceramics, whose quality was recognized throughout Eurasia and Africa. Although the Chinese imported spices from Southeast Asia and cotton textiles from India, they were interested in few other foreign products. Thus, foreign merchants paid for their goods with gold and silver, meaning that year after year China had a favorable balance of trade.

Until the sixteenth century, contact between these Asian societies and Europe had been rare. Although trade between the two regions had existed for centuries, the goods exchanged had always been carried by Arab, Indian, or central Asian intermediaries. The number of European travelers to China increased in the thirteenth century, when the Mongol

Empire made travel across Eurasia less dangerous and arduous. But with the breakup of the Mongol Empire in the middle of the fourteenth century, the onslaught of the Eurasian pandemic of the bubonic plague, and the antipathy toward foreigners shown by China's new Ming Dynasty (1368–1644), European contact with China was reduced to a trickle.

Then in the early 1500s, the Portuguese arrived in the region's coastal cities seeking trade and converts to Christianity. The Spanish, Dutch, and English soon followed, and in time these and other Westerners would have immense impact on the region. In the sixteenth and seventeenth centuries, however, the Europeans' arrival had little immediate significance. The exception was Southeast Asia, where the Portuguese captured the port city of Melaka in 1511, and the Spaniards gradually subjugated the Philippines beginning in the 1560s. Even in Southeast Asia, however, the Portuguese failed in their attempt to dominate the region's spice trade, and European Catholic missionaries made few converts except in the Philippines. Greater changes came only in the early 1600s when the Dutch took over the island of Java, expelled the Portuguese from Melaka, and took control of key ports and regions in Sumatra, the Moluccas, and the Malay Peninsula.

Elsewhere, the Europeans' arrival was a relatively minor event. In Japan the most significant development was its political recovery after decades of civil war. In 1603 the Tokugawa clan and its followers seized power and installed Tokugawa Ieyasu as shogun, or military ruler. Tokugawa rulers expelled the European missionaries and limited trade with Europe to one Dutch ship a year. Ming emperors permitted the Portuguese to carry on limited trade at a single port, Macao, and allowed a small number of Jesuit missionaries to reside at the imperial court in Beijing. Here they impressed the Chinese elite with their mechanical clocks and astronomical knowledge but had little effect on Chinese politics or culture.

Confucianism in China and Japan

No philosopher has influenced the values and behavior of more human beings than the Chinese thinker Kong Fuzi (ca. 551–479 B.C.E.), known in the West by his Latinized name Confucius. Like many other thinkers of his day, Confucius, a scholar intent on a career in public service, was distressed by the political fragmentation and turbulence that plagued China during the Eastern Zhou Era

(771–256 B.C.E.). Only after his efforts to achieve a position as a ruler's trusted advisor had failed did he turn to teaching. He proved to be a gifted teacher, one who is reputed to have had more than 3,000 students, some of whom collected his sayings in a book entitled *Lun-yu*, or *Analects*.

Confucius taught that China's troubles were rooted in the failure of its people and leaders to understand and act according to the rules of proper conduct. Proper conduct meant actions conforming to the standards of an idealized past, when China was structured along lines of behavior and authority paralleling those of a harmonious family. He taught that just as fathers, wives, sons, and daughters have specific roles and obligations within families, individuals have roles and obligations in society that depend on age, gender, marital status, ancestry, and social standing. Subjects owed rulers obedience, and rulers were expected to be models of virtue and benevolence. Children owed parents love and reverence, and parents, especially fathers, were expected to be kind and just. Children learned from parents, and subjects from rulers. Confucius also taught that whatever one's status, one must live according to the principles of *jen*, which means humaneness, benevolence, and love, and *li*, a term that encompasses the concepts of ceremony, propriety, and good manners. Because the wisdom and practices of ancient sages were central to his teaching, Confucius taught that one could achieve virtue by studying the literature, history, and rituals of the past. Education in traditional values and behavior was the path to sagehood, the quality of knowing what is proper and good and acting accordingly.

Although Confucius's philosophy competed with many other schools of thought in his own time, during the Han Dynasty (206 B.C.E.–220 C.E.) it became the official program of studies for anyone seeking an office in the imperial administration. Mastery of the Confucian Classics was the path to success on the civil service examinations by which China chose its officials. Although the examination system was abolished by China's Mongol rulers during the Yuan Era (1264–1368), it was revived under the Ming (1368–1644) and continued in use until 1905. For almost 2,000 years, China was administered by a literary elite devoted to Confucianism.

Confucianism's influence was not limited to China. Although it had to compete with Buddhism and other indigenous religions, Confucianism deeply affected the thought, politics, and everyday life of Korea, Vietnam, and Japan.

"Doing Good" in Seventeenth-Century China

▾▾▾

15 ▾ *MERITORIOUS DEEDS AT NO COST*

During the sixteenth and seventeenth centuries, interpreters of Confucianism drew mainly on the work of scholars from the Song Era (960–1279 C.E.). Known as Neo-Confucianists, these scholars had brought new energy and rigor to Confucianism after several centuries of stagnation and declining influence. The greatest Neo-Confucianist was Zhu Xi (1130–1200), who presided over a huge project of historical research and wrote detailed commentaries on most of the Confucian Classics. His commentaries came to be viewed as the orthodox version of Confucianism and the official interpretation for evaluating performance on the civil service examinations during the Ming and Qing eras.

Confucian scholarship in the 1500s and 1600s, however, was more than rehashing and refining Neo-Confucian formulas. With generous support from the emperor and high officials, Ming scholars completed vast research projects on history, medicine, ethics, and literature. In reinterpreting Confucianism, they sought to apply the Sage's wisdom to a society experiencing population growth, commercialization, urbanization, and ultimately dynastic decline and foreign conquest. Many endeavored to make Confucianism less elitist and more "popular."

Traditional Confucianism had taught that the erudition and virtue necessary for sagehood were theoretically attainable by anyone, but that in reality they could be achieved only by a small number of privileged males who had the wealth and leisure for years of study and self-cultivation. Women, artisans, peasants, and even merchants were capable of understanding and internalizing some Confucian principles by observing the behavior of their superiors, but serious scholarship, true morality, and sagehood were beyond them. In the early 1500s, such ideas were challenged by Wang Yangming (1472–1529), who taught that everyone, regardless of his station, was capable of practicing exemplary morality and achieving sagehood. An official as well as a scholar, Wang also was convinced that a healthy Chinese polity depended on teaching sound moral principles to all classes of people.

Wang's ideas were well received in a China where urbanization, increased literacy, and growing wealth were creating a burgeoning demand for books, many of which brought Confucian ideas to the broad reading public. These included summaries of the Confucian Classics, editions of the Classics themselves, manuals to prepare candidates for the civil service examinations, and "morality books." Morality books, which first appeared in the Song and Yuan eras, discussed proper behavior not only for the learned elite but also for all people. With titles such as *A Record of the Practice of Good Deeds* and *Establishing One's Own Destiny*, morality books taught their many readers that good deeds would be rewarded by worldly success, robust health, many sons, and a long life.

Among the most popular morality books was the anonymous *Meritorious Deeds at No Cost*, which appeared in the mid seventeenth century. Unlike other such books, which recommended costly good deeds such as paying for proper family rituals in connection with marriage, coming of age, funerals, and ancestral rites, it discussed laudable acts that required little or no money. It lists actions considered good for "people in general" but mainly concentrates on good deeds appropriate to specific groups, ranging from local gentry and scholars to soldiers and household servants. Its prescriptions provide insights into both Confucian values and also contemporary Chinese views of class, family, and gender.

Meritorious Deeds at No Cost begins with the "local gentry," individuals who have the rank and status of government officials but who reside at home and may not have any specific political responsibilities. The next group is "scholars," which refers to individuals at various stages of preparing for the civil service examinations. As educated individuals and potential officials, their status placed them below the gentry but above the common people. The recommended meritorious deeds for this group reveal that many "scholars" were also teachers.

QUESTIONS FOR ANALYSIS

1. **In what ways do the responsibilities of the various groups differ from one another? In what ways do they reflect certain underlying assumptions about what makes a good society?**
2. **According to this document, what should be the attitude of the upper classes (gentry and scholars) to those below them? Conversely, how should peasants, merchants, and artisans view their social superiors?**
3. **What views of women and sexuality are stated or implied in this treatise?**
4. **What views of money and moneymaking are stated or implied in this treatise?**
5. **According to this treatise, what specific kinds of behaviors and attitudes are components of filial piety?**
6. **Taking the document as a whole, what conclusions can be drawn about the ultimate purpose or highest good the author hopes to achieve through the various kinds of behaviors he describes?**

LOCAL GENTRY

Rectify your own conduct and transform the common people. . . .

If people have suffered a grave injustice, expose and correct it.

Settle disputes among your neighbors fairly.

When villagers commit misdeeds, admonish them boldly and persuade them to desist. . . .

Be tolerant of the mistakes of others.

Be willing to listen to that which is displeasing to your ears.

Do not make remarks about women's sexiness.

Do not harbor resentment when you are censured. . . .

Hold up for public admiration women who are faithful to their husbands and children who are obedient to their parents. . . .

Prevent plotting and intrigue. . . .

Prevent the younger members of your family from oppressing others by taking advantage of your position. . . .

Do not be arrogant, because of your own power and wealth, toward relatives who are poor or of low status. . . .

Do not ignore your own relatives and treat others as if they were your kin.

Influence other families to cherish good deeds. . . .

Do not disport yourself with lewd friends. . . .

Instruct your children, grandchildren, and nephews to be humane and compassionate toward all and to avoid anger and self-indulgence.

Do not deceive or oppress younger brothers or cousins.

Encourage others to read and study without minding the difficulties.

Urge others to esteem charity and disdain personal gain. . . .

Persuade others to settle lawsuits through conciliation.

Try to settle complaints and grievances among others. . . .

Curb the strong and protect the weak.

Show respect to the aged and compassion for the poor.

Do not keep too many concubines.

SCHOLARS

Be loyal to the emperor and filial to your parents.

Honor your elder brothers and be faithful to your friends. . . .

Instruct the common people in the virtues of loyalty and filial piety. . . .

Be wholehearted in inspiring your students to study. . . .

Try to improve your speech and behavior.
Teach your students also to be mindful of their speech and behavior. . . .
Be patient in educating the younger members of poor families. . . .
Do not write or post notices which defame other people. . . .
Do not encourage the spread of immoral and lewd novels [by writing, reprinting, expanding, etc.]. . . .
Do not attack or vilify commoners; do not oppress ignorant villagers. . . .
Do not ridicule other people's handwriting. . . .
Make others desist from unfiliality toward their parents or unkindness toward relatives and friends.
Educate the ignorant to show respect to their ancestors and live in harmony with their families. . . .

PEASANTS

Do not miss the proper time for farm work. . . .
Do not obstruct or cut off paths. Fill up holes that might give trouble to passersby. . . .
Do not damage crops in your neighbors' fields by leaving animals to roam at large, relying on your landlord's power and influence to protect you.
Do not encroach [on others' property] beyond the boundaries of your own fields and watercourses, thinking to ingratiate yourself with your landlord. . . .
In plowing, do not infringe on graves or make them hard to find. . . .
Do not damage the crops in neighboring fields out of envy because they are so flourishing. . . .
Do not become lazy and cease being conscientious because you think your landlord does not provide enough food and wine or fails to pay you enough.
Fill up holes in graves.
Take good care of others' carts and tools. . . .
Keep carts and cattle from trampling down others' crops.

CRAFTSMEN

. . . Whenever you make something, try to make it strong and durable.
Do not be resentful toward your master if he fails to provide enough food and drink. . . .
Do not reveal and spread abroad the secrets of your master's house.
Do not make crude imitations.
Finish your work without delay.
In your trade with others, do not practice deceit through forgery.
Do not mix damaged articles with good.
Do not break or damage finished goods.
Do not recklessly indulge in licentiousness. . . .
Do not steal the materials of others.
Do not use the materials of others carelessly. . . .

MERCHANTS

Do not deceive ignorant villagers when fixing the price of goods.
Do not raise the price of fuel and rice too high.
When the poor buy rice, do not give them short measure. . . .
When sick people have urgent need of something, do not raise the price unreasonably.
Do not deceitfully serve unclean dishes or leftover food to customers who are unaware of the fact.
Do not dispossess or deprive others of their business by devious means.
Do not envy the prosperity of others' business and speak ill of them wherever you go. . . .
Treat the young and the aged on the same terms as the able-bodied.
When people come in the middle of the night with an urgent need to buy something, do not refuse them on the ground that it is too cold. . . .
Give fair value when you exchange silver for copper coins. Especially when changing money for the poor, be generous to them.
When a debtor owes you a small sum but is short of money, have mercy and forget about the difference. Do not bring him to

bankruptcy and hatred by refusing to come to terms.

When the poor want to buy such things as mosquito nets, clothing, and quilts, have pity on them and reduce the price. Do not refuse to come to terms.

PEOPLE IN GENERAL

Do not show anger or worry in your parents' sight.

Accept meekly the reproaches and anger of your parents.

Persuade your parents to correct their mistakes and return to the right path.

Do not divulge your parents' faults to others.

Do not let your parents do heavy work.

Do not be disgusted with your parents' behavior when they are old and sick.

Do not yell at your parents or give them angry looks.

Love your brothers. . . .

If you are poor, do not entertain thoughts of harming the rich.

If you are rich, do not deceive and cheat the poor. . . .

Do not speak of others' humble ancestry.

Do not talk about the private [women's] quarters of others. [Commentary: When others bring up such things, if they are of the younger generation, reprimand them with straight talk, and if they are older or of the same generation as you, change the subject.] . . .

Respect women's chastity. . . .

Do not stir up your mind with lewd and wanton thoughts.

Do not besmirch others' honor or chastity.

Do not intimidate others to satisfy your own ambition.

Do not assert your own superiority by bringing humiliation upon others. . . .

Do not dwell on others' faults while dilating [expounding at length] on your own virtues.

Try to promote friendly relations among neighbors and relatives. . . .

When you hear someone speaking about the failings of others, make him stop.

When you hear a man praising the goodness of others, help him to do so. . . .

When you see a man about to go whoring or gambling, try to dissuade him. . . .

Do not deceive cripples, fools, old men, the young, or the sick. . . .

Make peace between husbands and wives who are about to separate. . . .

Help the blind and disabled to pass over dangerous bridges and roads. . . .

Cut down thorns by the roadside to keep them from tearing people's clothes. . . .

Put stones in muddy places [to make them passable].

Lay wooden boards where the road is broken off.

At night, light a lamp for others. . . .

Do not listen to your wife or concubines if they should encourage you to neglect or abandon your parents. . . .

Do not humiliate or ridicule the aged, the young, or the crippled. . . .

Do not be impudent toward your superiors. . . .

Do not sell faithful dogs to dog butchers. . . .

Even if you see that the good sometimes suffer bad fortune and you yourself experience poverty, do not let it discourage you from doing good.

Even if you see bad men prosper, do not lose faith in ultimate recompense.[1] . . .

In all undertakings, think of others.

[1]Reward for one's good deeds.

Teaching the Young in Tokugawa Japan

16 ▾ *Kaibara and Token Ekiken, COMMON SENSE TEACHINGS FOR JAPANESE CHILDREN and GREATER LEARNING FOR WOMEN*

Although Chinese Neo-Confucianism had been brought to Japan by Zen Buddhist monks in the fourteenth and fifteenth centuries, it had little influence on Japan's aristocratic ruling class until the Tokugawa Era, when the new regime actively supported it. Tokugawa rulers were attracted to Confucianism because it emphasized the need for social hierarchy and obedience to the ruler of a centralized state. Hayashi Razan (1583–1657), a leading Confucian scholar, was an advisor to Tokugawa Ieyasu, and the school founded by the Hayashi family at Edo in 1630 with shogunal support became the nation's center of Confucian scholarship and teaching. Many provincial lords founded similar academies in their domains, and the education that samurai received in these schools and from private tutors helped transform Japan's warrior aristocracy into a literate bureaucratic ruling class committed to Confucian values.

Among the Confucian scholars of the early Tokugawa Era, few matched the literary output and popularity of Kaibara Ekiken (1630–1714). After studying in Kyoto and Edo, he served the Kuroda lords of the Fukuoka domain in southwestern Japan as physician, tutor, and scholar-in-residence. He wrote more than 100 works on medicine, botany, philosophy, and education.

This selection draws on material from two of Ekiken's works. The first part is excerpted from his *Common Sense Teachings for Japanese Children*, a manual for tutors of children in aristocratic households. The second part is taken from *Greater Learning for Women*, a discussion of moral precepts for girls. It is thought that this treatise was written in collaboration with Token, Ekiken's wife.

QUESTIONS FOR ANALYSIS

1. According to *Common Sense Teachings for Japanese Children*, what moral qualities should be inculcated in students?
2. What attitudes toward the lower classes are expressed in these two treatises?
3. How do the goals and purposes of education differ for Japanese boys and girls? How are they similar?
4. What do these treatises say about Japanese marriage customs and family life?
5. What is there in Ekiken's educational treatises that would have furthered the Tokugawa shoguns' ambition to provide Japan with stable and peaceful government (see source 19)?

COMMON SENSE TEACHINGS FOR JAPANESE CHILDREN

In January when children reach the age of six, teach them numbers one through ten, and the names given to designate 100, 1,000, 10,000 and 100,000,000. Let them know the four directions, East, West, North and South. Assess their native intelligence and differentiate between quick and slow learners. Teach them Japanese pronunciation from the age of six or seven, and let them learn how to write. . . . From this time on, teach them to respect their elders, and let them know the distinctions between the upper and lower classes and between the young and old. Let them learn to use the correct expressions.

When the children reach the age of seven, do not let the boys and girls sit together, nor must you allow them to dine together. . . .

For the eighth year. This is the age when the ancients began studying the book *Little Learning.*[1] Beginning at this time, teach the youngsters etiquette befitting their age, and caution them not to commit an act of impoliteness. Among those which must be taught are: daily deportment, the manners set for appearing before one's senior and withdrawing from his presence, how to speak or respond to one's senior or guest, how to place a serving tray or replace it for one's senior, how to present a wine cup and pour rice wine and to serve side dishes to accompany it, and how to serve tea. Children must also learn how to behave while taking their meals.

Children must be taught by those who are close to them the virtues of filial piety and obedience. To serve the parents well is called filial piety, and to serve one's seniors well is called obedience. The one who lives close to the children and who is able to teach must instruct the children in the early years of their life that the first obligation of a human being is to revere the parents and serve them well. Then comes the next lesson which includes respect for one's seniors, listening to their commands and not holding them in contempt. One's seniors include elder brothers, elder sisters, uncles, aunts, and cousins who are older and worthy of respect. . . . As the children grow older, teach them to love their younger brothers and to be compassionate to the employees and servants. Teach them also the respect due the teachers and the behavior codes governing friends. The etiquette governing each movement toward important guests — such as standing, sitting, advancing forward, and retiring from their presence — and the language to be employed must be taught. Teach them how to pay respect to others according to the social positions held by them. Gradually the ways of filial piety and obedience, loyalty and trustworthiness, right deportment and decorum, and sense of shame must be inculcated in the children's minds and they must know how to implement them. Caution them not to desire the possessions of others, or to stoop below one's dignity in consuming excessive amounts of food and drink. . . .

Once reaching the age of eight, children must follow and never lead their elders when entering a gate, sitting, or eating and drinking. From this time on they must be taught how to become humble and yield to others. Do not permit the children to behave as they please. It is important to caution them against "doing their own things."

At the age of ten, let the children be placed under the guidance of a teacher, and tell them about the general meaning of the five constant virtues and let them understand the way of the five human relationships.[2] Let them read books by the Sage [Confucius] and the wise men of old and cultivate the desire for learning. . . . When not engaged in reading, teach them the literary and military arts. . . .

[1]The *Little Learning* was written in 1187 by the Song scholar Liu Zucheng. A book for children, it contains rules of behavior and excerpts from the Classics and other works.

[2]The *five virtues* are human heartedness, righteousness, propriety, wisdom, and good faith. The *five relationships* are ruler–subject, father–son, husband–wife, older brother–younger brother, and friend–friend.

Fifteen is the age when the ancients began the study of the *Great Learning.*[3] From this time on, concentrate on the learning of a sense of justice and duty. The students must also learn to cultivate their personalities and investigate the way of governing people. . . .

Those who are born in the high-ranking families have the heavy obligations of becoming leaders of the people, of having people entrusted to their care, and of governing them. Therefore, without fail, a teacher must be selected for them when they are still young. They must be taught how to read and be informed of the ways of old, of cultivating their personalities, and of the way of governing people. If they do not learn the way of governing people, they may injure the many people who are entrusted to their care by the Way of Heaven. That will be a serious disaster. . . .

GREATER LEARNING FOR WOMEN

Seeing that it is a girl's destiny, on reaching womanhood, to go to a new home, and live in submission to her father-in-law, it is even more incumbent upon her than it is on a boy to receive with all reverence her parents' instructions. Should her parents, through their tenderness, allow her to grow up self-willed, she will infallibly show herself capricious in her husband's house, and thus alienate his affection; while, if her father-in-law be a man of correct principles, the girl will find the yoke of these principles intolerable. She will hate and decry her father-in-law, and the end of those domestic dissensions will be her dismissal from her husband's house and the covering of herself with ignominy. Her parents, forgetting the faulty education they gave her, may indeed lay all the blame on the father-in-law. But they will be in error; for the whole disaster should rightly be attributed to the faulty education the girl received from her parents.

▾ ▾ ▾

More precious in a woman is a virtuous heart than a face of beauty. . . . The only qualities that befit a woman are gentle obedience, chastity, mercy, and quietness.

▾ ▾ ▾

From her earliest youth a girl should observe the line of demarcation separating women from men. The customs of antiquity did not allow men and women to sit in the same apartment, to keep their wearing apparel in the same place, to bathe in the same place, or to transmit to each other anything directly from hand to hand. A woman . . . must observe a certain distance in her relations even with her husband and with her brothers. In our days the women of lower classes, ignoring all rules of this nature, behave disorderly; they contaminate their reputations, bring down reproach upon the head of their parents and brothers, and spend their whole lives in an unprofitable manner. Is not this truly lamentable?

▾ ▾ ▾

It is the chief duty of a girl living in the parental house to practice filial piety towards her father and mother. But after marriage her duty is to honor her father-in-law and mother-in-law, to honor them beyond her father and mother, to love and reverence them with all ardor, and to tend them with practice of every filial piety. . . . Even if your father-in-law and mother-in-law are inclined to hate and vilify you, do not be angry with them, and murmur not. If you carry piety towards them to its utmost limits, and minister to them in all sincerity, it cannot be but that they will end by becoming friendly to you.

▾ ▾ ▾

[3]The *Great Learning* consists of a short main text thought to have been written by Confucius and nine chapters of commentary written by Confucius's disciple, Zeng Zi.

The great lifelong duty of a woman is obedience. . . . When the husband issues his instructions, the wife must never disobey them. In a doubtful case, she should inquire of her husband and obediently follow his commands. . . .

Should her husband be roused at any time to anger, she must obey him with fear and trembling, and not set herself up against him in anger and forwardness. A woman should look upon her husband as if he were Heaven itself, and never weary of thinking how she may yield to her husband and thus escape celestial castigation.

Her treatment of her servant girls will require circumspection. Those low-born girls have had no proper education; they are stupid, obstinate, and vulgar in their speech. . . . Again, in her dealings with those lowly people, a woman will find many things to disapprove of. But if she be always reproving and scolding, and spend her time in hustle and anger, her household will be in a continual state of disturbance. When there is real wrongdoing, she should occasionally notice it, and point out the path of amendment, while lesser faults should be quietly endured without anger. . . .

▼▼▼

Merchants in a Confucian World

▼▼▼

17 ▼ *Wang Daokun, BIOGRAPHIES OF ZHU JIEFU AND GENTLEMAN WANG*

The Confucian tradition considered merchants as necessary evils at best. Farmers were the backbone of a healthy society, but merchants, according to many Confucians, were unproductive, uncultured, and preoccupied with profit rather than the good of society. Their travels kept them away from the ancestral heart and prevented them from performing their duties to parents and ancestral spirits. Until 775 C.E., merchants were not permitted to take the civil service examinations and both their consumption habits and business activities were closely regulated by generally unsympathetic government officials. Despite merchants' low status, commerce flourished in most periods of Chinese history, and during the Ming Era, in which population grew and trade expanded, the merchant's calling came to be viewed more favorably. Sons and daughters of merchants married more frequently into the families of officials and great landowners, and more sons of merchants became government officials after passing the civil service examinations. Some Confucian thinkers praised commerce as necessary for the well-being of society, and others even proposed that successful merchants were equal to or just slightly below officials and gentry in terms of status. Such positive views remained in the minority, however, and throughout the Ming Era, suspicion of merchants and doubts about their calling remained strong among intellectuals and commoners alike.

Wang Daokun (1525–1593) exemplifies this ambivalence about merchants in both his life and writings. He combined a merchant's background with a Confucian education and a career in the imperial bureaucracy. His father and grandfather had been salt merchants, but the gifted Wang passed the civil service examinations while in his twenties and entered government service. Having served as governor of several provinces and as a army official, in 1575 he resigned to care for his aged parents and to write books on a wide variety of topics, including card playing, drinking games, and ancestral rites. He also wrote a series of biographies of Ming Era merchants, many of whom combined business success with Confucian morality. Wang's sketches provide many insights into Confucian ethics and the business climate of late Ming China.

QUESTIONS FOR ANALYSIS

1. According to Wang, what are the virtues of Zhu Jiefu and Gentleman Wang? To what extent do the two merchants represent different virtues?
2. What is the point about the incident involving Gentleman Wang and Magistrate Xu?
3. What do these biographies reveal about Chinese attitudes toward the elderly? Toward political authority? Toward wealth? Toward women?
4. What do these biographies reveal about the government's attitudes and policies in regard to merchants? What episodes illustrate these attitudes?
5. Do the author's sympathies lie with the merchants or the government officials in their dealings with one another?

THE BIOGRAPHY OF ZHU JIEFU

Zhu Jiefu . . . started as a Confucian scholar. He was from Tunxi . . . and his father Hsing . . . was a salt merchant who lived away from home at Wulin. Hsing had taken Shaoji of Wulin as his concubine[1] but she was barren. Later, when he returned home for his father-in-law's birthday, his primary wife became pregnant and gave birth to Zhu Jiefu. In his early childhood, Zhu Jiefu lived in Wulin with his father and went to school there. Shaoji . . . did not treat him as her son. Jiefu, however, served her respectfully and worked diligently in school. At the age of fourteen, he officially registered Wulin as his native place and was designated an official student of that place.[2] Shortly thereafter, his father died at Wulin. His concubine took the money and hid it with some of her mother's relatives and would not return to her husband's hometown. Jiefu wept day and night, saying, "However unworthy I may be, my late father was blameless." Finally the concubine arranged for the funeral and burial. . . . Thus, everything was done properly.

After the funeral, Jiefu was short of funds. Since for generations his family had been in commerce, he decided not to suffer just to preserve his scholar's cap. Therefore he handed in his resignation to the academic officials and devoted himself to the salt business. He thoroughly studied the laws on salt merchandising and was always able to talk about the strengths and weaknesses of the law. . . . Therefore, all the other salt merchants respected him as their leader.

---

[1]It was common for men to have concubines, in some cases several of them, in addition to their wives. Laws did not prohibit children of concubines from inheriting their father's property.

[2]This meant that Zhu Jiefu was being groomed to take the civil service examinations.

During the Jiaqing period [1522–1567], salt affairs were handled by the Central Law Officer,[3] who increased the taxes suddenly, causing great inconvenience for the merchants. They gathered in Jiefu's house and asked him to serve as their negotiator. Jiefu entered the office and stated the advantages and disadvantages of the new law eloquently in thousands of words. Leaning against his couch, the Central Law Officer listened to Jiefu's argument and finally adopted his suggestion.

At that time, the merchants suffered greatly from two scoundrels who often took them to court in the hopes of getting bribes from them. During tense moments at trials, the merchants usually turned to Jiefu as their spokesman. Being lofty and righteous, he always disclosed the scoundrels' crimes and condemned them. The merchants thus esteemed Jiefu for his virtue and wanted to give him a hundred taels[4] of gold as a birthday present. But he protested: "Even if my acts have not been at the lofty level of a knight-errant, I did not do them for the sake of money." Thus, the merchants respected him even more and no longer talked about giving him money.

When there was a dispute among the merchants which the officials could not resolve, Jiefu could always mediate it immediately. Even when one group would go to his house and demand his compliance with their views, he would still be able to settle the dispute by indirect and gentle persuasion. Hence, people both far and near followed each other, coming to ask him to be their arbitrator. Yet, after settling a dispute, Jiefu would always step aside and never take credit himself.

The populace in Tunxi city where Jiefu lived was militant and litigious. When he returned home for his father's funeral, slanderous rumors were spread about him, but Jiefu humbled himself and never tried to get back at the instigators. Later, when he grew rich rapidly, people became even more critical. Jiefu merely behaved with even greater deference. When the ancestral shrine fell into disrepair, Jiefu on his own sent workmen to repair it. When members of his lineage started talking about it, he had the workmen work during the day and consulted with his relatives in the evening. Finally the whole lineage got together and shared the task with him.

Once Jiefu bought a concubine in Wulin who bore a child after only a few months. His family was about to discard the child but Jiefu upbraided them, saying, "I love my children dearly. How could I cause someone else's child to die in the gutter?" He brought the child up and educated him until he was able to support himself. . . .

Jiefu finally discontinued his salt business and ordered his son to pursue a different career. By that time he was already planning to retire to his hometown. Then in 1568 a Central Law Officer who was appointed to inspect the salt business started to encourage secret informants. Soon Jiefu was arrested, an enemy having laid a trap for him. However, the official could not find any evidence against him. But then Ho, whose son Jiefu had once scolded, came forward to testify. Consequently, Jiefu was found guilty. When the litigation against him was completed, he was sentenced to be a frontier guard at Dinghai. . . .

When Jiefu received his sentence to enter the army, he controlled his feelings and immediately complied. His son, fearing his father would acquire a bad name, suggested that he send a petition to the Emperor. Jiefu merely sighed and said, "Your father must have offended Heaven. The truth is that the Central Law Officer is a representative of his Heavenly Majesty, not that your father is falsely charged."

---

[3]An imperial official.

[4]A tael was a coin weighing approximately one and a half ounces.

. . . [Before he died] he advised his son, Zhengmin: "Your father's name has been recorded in the official labor records. Now he is about to die as a prisoner. Never let your father's example stop you from behaving righteously. Remember this." Then, at the age of sixty-five, he died.

THE BIOGRAPHY OF GENTLEMAN WANG

. . . At first, Mr. Wang's capital was no greater than the average person's. Later, as he grew more prosperous every day, the number of his associates also steadily increased. To accommodate his apprentices, Mr. Wang built buildings with doors on four sides. Whenever customers came, they could be taken care of from all four directions; thus, no one ever had to wait very long.

Mr. Wang set up the following guidelines for his associates: do not let anyone who lives in another county control the banking; when lending money, never harass law-abiding people unnecessarily or give them less than they need; charge low interest on loans; do not aim at high profit and do not ask for daily interest. These principles led customers to throng to him, even ones from neighboring towns and provinces. Within a short time, Mr. Wang accumulated great wealth; in fact, of all the rich people in that area he became the richest.

Mr. Wang liked to help people and to give assistance to the poor. If anyone among his kinsmen could not afford a funeral for his parents, Mr. Wang would always buy some land and build a tomb for him. As soon as he heard someone could not make ends meet, he would buy land to rent to him. . . .

During the Jiaqing period there was a serious drought, and the Prefect[5] proposed opening the granary. Considering the hardship this would cause the people, Mr. Wang sent a written report to the Prefect, as follows:

> This proposal will cause starving people to travel here from hundreds of li[6] away to wait for the distribution. Even if there are no delays on route, they may die before they get here. Yet if we make them stay home and wait for a pint of food, it will be like abandoning them to die in the gutters. I suggest that we exchange the grain for money and distribute it around the area. All the wealthy people ought to donate some money to help the poor. I myself will start with a donation of a hundred taels of gold.

The Prefect accepted his suggestion and everyone said that this was much more convenient. Then Mr. Wang also prepared some food to feed people in his own county and caused similar actions to be taken throughout the whole of Shanghai. Thus most people in this area survived. . . .

Whenever there was a dispute, Mr. Wang could always resolve it immediately, even if it was quite serious. When Magistrate Xu was in charge of Shanghai, he imprisoned someone named Zhu, who died in jail. The victim's, father then presented a petition to the Emperor which worried the Magistrate. The officials, elders, and local leaders were willing to offer the father a thousand taels of gold on the Magistrate's behalf, but on discussing it, they decided only Mr. Wang could settle the matter, and indeed he persuaded the father to accept the terms. Then the Magistrate was transferred to another position. Upon learning this fact, the officials, elders, and local leaders all quickly dispersed. Mr. Wang sighed and said, "It isn't easy to collect a thousand taels of gold but I will not break the promise made to the Magistrate in trouble." He then paid the thousand taels of gold and the Magistrate was out of his difficulties. Even when Magistrate Xu was dismissed soon thereafter, Mr. Wang did not voice any concern, and after two years Xu returned the thousand taels of gold to him. . . .

[5]An imperial official.

[6]A measure of distance, approximately one third of a mile.

When Mr. Wang is at home he is always in high spirits. . . . In his later years he has become particularly fond of chess, often staying up all night until he either wins or loses a game. The youths say that Mr. Wang is no ordinary person, that he must have received instruction from Heaven.

Now Mr. Wang is almost one hundred years old. He has at least thirty sons and grandsons living at home with him. It is said, "One who seeks perfection will attain it." This describes Mr. Wang perfectly.

Political Decline and Recovery in China and Japan

Eighteenth-century China and Japan were models of well-governed, prosperous states with enlightened rulers and obedient subjects. This had seemed highly unlikely a century and a half earlier, when severe political problems plagued both societies: Japan, plagued by civil war, seemed on the brink of disintegrating; China, meanwhile, was suffering from the incompetent rule of a declining Ming Dynasty.

The incessant civil strife of sixteenth-century Japan was rooted in long-standing tensions inherent in Japan's feudal society. In the 1300s power began to shift away from the shogun, a military commander who ruled in the name of the emperor, to local military families who controlled districts and provinces. With a weakened central government, local wars and feuds became endemic among the *daimyo*, the emerging provincial lords, who enlisted both commoners and *samurai*, lesser members of the nobility, to fight in their armies. The warfare intensified between 1467 and 1568, a period sometimes called the Warring States Era.

This ruinous feudal anarchy ended as a result of the efforts of three strong military leaders bent on unifying Japan. Oda Nobunaga (1534–1582) brought approximately half of Japan under his rule before a traitorous vassal assassinated him. His successor, Toyotomi Hideyoshi (1536–1598), a commoner who had risen through the ranks to become Nobunaga's ablest general, continued the work of consolidation. It was completed by Tokugawa Ieyasu (1542–1616), who conquered his rivals after Hideyoshi's death and declared himself shogun in 1603. Ieyasu and his successors stabilized Japan by imposing a sociopolitical order that lasted until 1867.

China's political problems had multiple causes, ranging from foreign military threats and fluctuations in the value of silver to a series of poor harvests after the weather turned cold and wet in the early 1600s. Just as these problems were mounting, the quality and effectiveness of Ming rulers plummeted, especially during the interminable reign of Emperor Wanli (1573–1620). Disgusted with his bickering and quarrelsome advisors, Wanli withdrew from politics, ceased meeting with high officials, and failed to fill vacancies in the administration. Paralyzed by feuding between court eunuchs and Confucian officials, the central government drifted as China's problems worsened. Factional strife, oppressive taxation, corruption, unchecked banditry, famine, and bankruptcy led to rebellion, the dynasty's collapse, and foreign conquest. In 1644 a rebel leader, Li Zicheng (1605–1645) captured Beijing, and in despair the last Ming emperor hanged himself. Within months, however, Li was driven from the city by the Manchus, northern invaders from the Amur River region. In the following decades, the Manchus extended their authority over all of China; established China's last dynasty, the Qing; and breathed new life into the imperial system.

Symptoms of Ming Decline

18 ▾ *Yang Lien,* *MEMORIAL TO EMPEROR MING XIZONG CONCERNING EUNUCH WEI ZHONGXIAN*

Governing China had always been a formidable task. Expenditures had to be kept in line with revenues; borders needed to be defended; bridges, roads, and dams had to be maintained; countless daily decisions were required of the emperor and his top officials. In the late sixteenth century, governing China became even harder. Mongol military pressure grew in the north, pirates increased their raids on coastal cities, and in the 1590s the Japanese invaded China's client state, Korea. Peasant discontent boiled over into peasant rebellion as rural misery deepened in the face of poor harvests, worsening banditry, rising taxes, and currency fluctuations. From the 1580s onward, however, emperors ignored or were distracted from dealing with these extraordinary new challenges. They paid a price for their indifference. Rebellion overwhelmed the government and brought about the fall of the Ming in 1644.

The following selection, a memorial (memorandum) directed to the Xizong emperor by a high official, Yang Lien, highlights another problem of late Ming government, the rising power of court eunuchs. Eunuchs, castrated males who had traditionally been given the job of managing the day-to-day business of the palace, assumed a greater importance in government when Emperor Wanli secluded himself and refused to communicate with his officials except through eunuch intermediaries. Eunuch influence was opposed by Confucian officials, especially elite members of the Donglin Society, a group of scholar-officials and former officeholders connected with the Donglin Academy at Wusih on the lower Yangzi River.

The conflict between court eunuchs and the scholar-officials came to a head in the 1620s when the eunuch Wei Zhongxian rose to power during the reign of Emperor Xizong (1568–1627). With the backing of spies and a small eunuch army in the palace, Wei, a former butler for the emperor's mother and a close friend of the emperor's former wet nurse, purged his enemies, levied new taxes, and flouted rules and procedures.

In 1624 Yang Lien, a member of the Donglin Society, took the bold step of denouncing Wei in a memorandum to the emperor. He was fulfilling his duties as a member of the Board of Censors, a branch of the administration that served as the "eyes and ears" of the emperor by investigating officials' conduct and hearing subjects' complaints. The emperor ignored the memorandum, however, and in 1625, on Wei's orders, Yang was accused of treason, tortured, and executed. Wei fell from power in 1627 when the new emperor Chongzhen (r. 1627–1644) exiled him to Anhui province; there Wei hanged himself rather than face an official inquiry. But the Ming government had suffered another wound.

QUESTIONS FOR ANALYSIS

1. According to Yang, what motivated him to write this memorandum to the emperor?
2. This excerpt specifically lists only a few of Wei's twenty-four alleged "crimes." Based on your reading of the entire excerpt, what other "crimes" were on the list?
3. What is it about Wei's actions that violated Yang's Confucian sensibilities?
4. What does the memorandum reveal about the basis of Wei's authority and political strength?
5. What does the memorandum tell us about the qualities of Emperor Ming Xizong?

A treacherous eunuch has taken advantage of his position to act as emperor. He has seized control and disrupted the government, deceived the ruler, and flouted the law. He recognizes no higher authority, turns his back on the favors the emperor has conferred on him, and interferes with the inherited institutions. I beg Your Majesty to order an investigation so that the dynasty can be saved.

When Emperor Hongwu[1] first established the laws and institutions, eunuchs were not allowed to interfere in any affairs outside the palace; even within it they did nothing more than clean up. Anyone who violated these rules was punished without chance of amnesty, so the eunuchs prudently were cautious and obedient. The succeeding emperors never changed these laws. . . .

How would anyone have expected that, with a wise ruler like Your Majesty on the throne, there would be a chief eunuch like Wei Zhongxian, a man totally uninhibited, who destroys court precedents, ignores the ruler to pursue his selfish ends, corrupts good people, ruins the emperor's reputation . . . and brews unimaginable disasters? The entire court has been intimidated. No one dares denounce him by name. My responsibility really is painful. . . . If today out of fear I also do not speak out, I will be abandoning my determination to be loyal and my responsibility to serve the state. I would also be turning my back on your kindness in bringing me back to office after retirement. . . .

I shall list for Your Majesty Zhongxian's twenty-four most heinous crimes. Zhongxian

---

[1]The first Ming emperor, who ruled from 1368 to 1398.

was originally an ordinary, unreliable sort. He had himself castrated in middle age in order to enter the palace. He is illiterate. . . . Your Majesty was impressed by his minor acts of service and plucked him out of obscurity to confer honors on him. . . .

Our dynastic institutions require that rescripts[2] be delegated to the grand secretaries. This not only allows for calm deliberation and protects from interference, but it assures that someone takes the responsibility seriously. Since Zhongxian usurped power, he issues the imperial edicts. If he accurately conveys your orders, it is bad enough. If he falsifies them, who can argue with him?. . . It is possible for a scrap of paper in the middle of the night to kill a person without Your Majesty or the grand secretaries knowing anything of it. The harm this causes is huge. The grand secretaries are so depressed that they ask to quit. Thus Wei Zhongxian destroys the political institutions that had lasted over two hundred years. . . .

One of your concubines, of virtuous and pure character, had gained your favor. Zhongxian was afraid she would expose his illegal behavior, so conspired with his cronies. They said she had a sudden illness to cover up his murdering her. Thus Your Majesty is not able to protect the concubines you favor. . . .

During the forty years that your father the former emperor was heir apparent, Wang An[3] was unique in worrying about all the dangers he faced, protecting him from harm, never giving in to intimidation or temptation. Didn't he deserve some of the credit for your father's getting to the throne? When he died and Your Majesty succeeded, Wang An protected you, so he cannot be called disloyal. Even if he had committed some offense, Your Majesty should have explained what he had done wrong publicly for all to see. Instead Zhongxian, because of his personal hatreds, forged an imperial order and had him killed in Nanhai park. His head and body were separated, his flesh given to the dogs and pigs. This not only revealed his enmity toward Wang An, but his enmity toward all the former emperor's old servants, even his old dogs and horses. It showed him to be without the slightest fear. From that time on, which of the eunuchs was willing to be loyal or principled? I do not know how many thousands or hundreds of the rest of the eunuchs, important and unimportant alike, were slaughtered or driven away for no crime. . . .

Doesn't Your Majesty remember the time when Zhongxian, against all rules, rode his horse in the palace grounds? Those who are favored too much become arrogant; those who receive too many favors grow resentful. I heard that this spring when he rode a horse in front of Your Majesty, you shot and killed the horse, but forgave Zhongxian. Despite your generosity, Zhongxian did not beg to die for his offense, but rather acted more arrogantly in Your Majesty's presence and spoke resentfully of Your Majesty when away. . . . In the past traitors and bandits have struggled to wreak havoc and take over. This is in fact what Your Majesty now faces. . . . Even if Zhongxian were cut into mincemeat, it would not atone for his sins. . . .

. . . Zhongxian . . . kills or replaces any eunuch he fears will expose his treachery. Thus those close at hand are terrified and keep silent. He expels or imprisons any of the officials he fears will expose his villainy, so the officials also all look the other way and keep silent. There are even ignorant spineless fellows eager to get rich and powerful who attach themselves to him or hang around his gate. They praise whatever he likes and criticize whatever he hates, doing whatever is needed. Thus whatever he inside wants they do outside, whatever they outside say he responds to inside. Disaster or good luck can depend on

[2]Official decrees and edicts.

[3]The eunuch Wang An was a supporter of the Donglin party and a bitter opponent of Wei Zhongxian. He was killed on Wei's orders in 1621.

slight movements. And if per chance the evil deeds of the inner court are revealed, there is still Lady Ke[4] to make excuses or cover up.

As a consequence, everyone in the palace recognizes the existence of Zhongxian but not of Your Majesty; everyone in the capital recognizes the existence of Zhongxian but not of Your Majesty. Even the major and minor officials and workers, by turning toward the sources of power, unconsciously show that they do not recognize the existence of Your Majesty, only of Zhongxian. Whenever they see that some matter needs urgent attention or an appointment needs to be made, they always say, "It must be discussed with the eunuch." . . . All matters, large and small, in both the palace and the government offices, are decided by Zhongxian alone. . . .

In the tenth year of the first emperor of the dynasty [1377], there was a eunuch who had been in service a long time but carelessly mentioned a governmental matter. The emperor dismissed him that very day. . . . How brilliant! A eunuch who mentioned a governmental matter became a warning for the future. What about Zhongxian who deceives his ruler, recognizes no one above him, and piles up crimes? How can he be left unpunished?

I beg Your Majesty to take courage and thunder forth. Take Zhongxian to the ancestral temple in fetters. Assemble the military and civil officials of all ranks and have the judicial officials interrogate him. Check all the precedents from previous reigns on eunuchs having contacts with the outside, usurping imperial authority, breaking dynastic laws, disrupting court business, alienating the people, and violating the trust of the ruler. Sentence him in a way that will please the gods and satisfy public indignation. . . .

If all this is done and yet Heaven does not show its pleasure, the people do not rejoice, and there is not a new era of peace within the country and at its borders, then I ask that you behead me as an offering to Zhongxian. I am well aware that once my words become known, Zhongxian's clique will detest me, but I am not afraid. . . . My lifetime goal has been to serve loyally. I would not regret having to die as a way of paying back the extraordinary favors I have received during two reigns. I hope Your Majesty recognizes my passion and takes prompt action.

[4]Lady Ke, who had been the emperor's wet nurse, was instrumental in Wei's rise to power and reputedly his lover.

The Reunification of Japan Under Hideyoshi and the Tokugawa Clan

▼▼▼

19 ▾ EDICT ON THE COLLECTION OF SWORDS; LAWS GOVERNING MILITARY HOUSEHOLDS; CLOSED COUNTRY EDICT

The reunification of Japan under Oda Nobunaga, Toyotomi Hideyoshi, and Tokugawa Ieyasu involved more than battlefield victories over rival aristocrats and rebellious Buddhist sects. It also required the reordering of Japanese society, politics, foreign relations, and religious life through the enforcement of dozens of edicts that stabilized Japan and solidified the rulers' own authority. Excerpts from

three of the most significant edicts follow. The first, issued by Hideyoshi in 1588, required all farmers to relinquish their military weapons and devote themselves to agriculture exclusively. The second edict, Laws Governing Military Households, proclaimed by Tokugawa Ieyasu (who continued to rule Japan until his death in 1616 despite having named his son Hidetada shogun in 1605 to avoid a succession dispute), spelled out rules for members of Japan's aristocratic (daimyo) families. The third edict, known as the Closed Country Edict, was issued by Tokugawa Iemitsu in 1635 and addressed issues relating to trade, foreign relations, and the status of Christianity, which had been introduced by the Portuguese in the 1500s and claimed approximately 500,000 converts by the early 1600s.

QUESTIONS FOR ANALYSIS

1. What is the stated purpose of the edict on the collection of swords?
2. What are the potential effects of the edict on the collection of swords for class relationships within Japanese society?
3. In what ways does the edict on military households ensure the shogun's control of the daimyo?
4. Even though Tokugawa policies limited the independence of the daimyo, the daimyo still retained certain political powers. How many such powers can be identified in the Laws Governing Military Households?
5. According to the Closed Country Edict, what is the greater threat to Japan: Christianity or trade with foreigners?
6. Did the Closed Country Edict really close Japan?
7. What overriding purpose do all three edicts serve?
8. What sort of social order for Japan is envisioned in the three edicts?

EDICT ON THE COLLECTION OF SWORDS (1588)

1. The farmers of all provinces are strictly forbidden to have in their possession any swords, bows, spears, firearms or other types of weapons. If unnecessary implements of war are kept, the collection of annual rent may become more difficult, and without provocation uprisings can be fomented. Therefore those who perpetrate improper acts against samurai who receive a grant of land must be brought to trial and punished. . . .

2. The swords and short swords collected in the above manner will not be wasted. They will be used as nails and bolts in the construction of the Great Image of Buddha. In this way, the farmers will benefit not only in this life but also in the lives to come.

3. If farmers possess only agricultural implements and devote themselves exclusively to cultivating the fields, they and their descendants will prosper. This compassionate concern for the well-being of the farmers is the reason for issuance of this edict, and such a concern is the foundation for the peace and security of the country and the joy and happiness of all the people. . . .

LAWS GOVERNING MILITARY HOUSEHOLDS (1615)

1. The study of literature and the practice of the military arts, archery and horsemanship, must be cultivated diligently. . . .

From of old the rule has been to practice "the arts of peace on the left hand, and the arts of war on the right"; both must be mastered. . . .

2. Drinking parties and wanton revelry should be avoided.

In the codes that have come down to us this kind of dissipation has been severely proscribed. Sexual indulgence and habitual gambling lead to the downfall of a state.

3. Offenders against the law should not be harbored or hidden in any domain.

Law is the basis of social order. . . . Those who break the law deserve heavy punishment.

4. Great lords [daimyo], the lesser lords, and officials should immediately expel from their domains any among their retainers or henchmen who have been charged with treason or murder.

Wild and wicked men may become weapons for overturning the state and destroying the people. How can they be allowed to go free?

5. Henceforth no outsider, none but the inhabitants of a particular domain, shall be permitted to reside in that domain. . . .

6. Whenever it is intended to make repairs on a castle of one of the feudal domains, the [shogunate] should be notified. The construction of any new castles is to be halted and stringently prohibited. . . .

7. Immediate report should be made of innovations which are being planned or of factional conspiracies being formed in neighboring domains. . . .

8. Do not enter into marriage privately [i.e., without notifying the shogunate] author. . . . To form an alliance by marriage is the root of treason.

9. Visits of the daimyo to the capital are to be in accordance with regulations.[1]

. . . Daimyo should not be accompanied by a large number of soldiers. Twenty horsemen shall be the maximum escort for daimyo with an income of from one million to two hundred thousand *koku* of rice.[2] For those with an income of one hundred thousand koku or less, the escort should be proportionate to their income. On official missions, however, they may be accompanied by an escort proportionate to their rank.

10. Restrictions on the type and quality of dress to be worn should not be transgressed.

Lord and vassal, superior and inferior, should observe what is proper to their station in life. [There follows an injunction against the wearing of fine white damask or purple silk by retainers without authorization.]

11. Persons without rank shall not ride in palanquins.[3]

From of old there have been certain families entitled to ride in palanquins without special permission, and others who have received such permission. Recently, however, even the ordinary retainers and henchmen of some families have taken to riding about in palanquins, which is truly the worst sort of presumption. Henceforth permission shall be granted only to the lords of the various domains, their close relatives and ranking officials, medical men and astrologers, those over sixty years of age, and those ill or infirm. In the cases of ordinary household retainers or henchmen who willfully ride in palanquins, their masters shall be held accountable. . . .

12. The samurai of the various domains shall lead a frugal and simple life.

When the rich make a display of their wealth, the poor are humiliated and envious. Nothing engenders corruption so much as this, and therefore it must be strictly curbed.

13. The lords of the domains should select officials with a capacity for public administration.

Good government depends on getting the right men. Due attention should be given to their merits and faults; rewards and punishments must be properly meted out. If a domain has able men, it flourishes; if it lacks able men it

---

[1]This refers to the policy that required daimyo to reside every other year in Edo, the seat of shogunal government.

[2]One *koku* equals five bushels.

[3]Enclosed carriages, usually for one person, borne on the shoulders of carriers by means of poles.

is doomed to perish. This is the clear admonition of the wise men of old.

CLOSED COUNTRY EDICT (1635)

1. Japanese ships are strictly forbidden to leave for foreign countries.

2. No Japanese is permitted to go abroad. If there is anyone who attempts to do so secretly, he must be executed. The ship so involved must be impounded and its owner arrested, and the matter must be reported to the higher authority.

3. If any Japanese returns from overseas after residing there, he must be put to death.

4. If there is any place where the teachings of the [Catholic] priests is practiced, the two of you[4] must order a thorough investigation.

5. Any informer revealing the whereabouts of the followers of the priests must be rewarded accordingly. If anyone reveals the whereabouts of a high ranking priest, he must be given one hundred pieces of silver. For those of lower ranks, depending on the deed, the reward must be set accordingly. . . .

7. If there are any Southern Barbarians [Europeans] who propagate the teachings of the priests, or otherwise commit crimes, they may be incarcerated in the prison. . . .

8. All incoming ships must be carefully searched for the followers of the priests.

9. No single trading city shall be permitted to purchase all the merchandise brought by foreign ships.

10. Samurai[5] are not permitted to purchase any goods originating from foreign ships directly from Chinese merchants in Nagasaki. . . .

12. After settling the price, all white yarns [raw silk] brought by foreign ships shall be allocated to the five trading cities[6] and other quarters as stipulated.

13. After settling the price of white yarns, other merchandise [brought by foreign ships] may be traded freely between the [licensed] dealers. . . .

14. The date of departure homeward of foreign ships shall not be later than the twentieth day of the ninth month. Any ships arriving in Japan later than usual shall depart within fifty days of their arrival. . . .

[4]Refers to the two commissioners of Nagasaki, to whom the edict is addressed.

[5]Aristocratic warriors.

[6]The cities of Kyoto, Edo, Osaka, Sakai, and Nagasaki.

Multiple Voices II ▾▾▾ Asian Views of Christianity

BACKGROUND

For many Europeans, the Portuguese discovery of an all-sea route to Asia excited dreams of unlimited profit through trade. Others, however, were more excited about spiritual, not material, gains. Members of Catholic religious orders, popes, Catholic princes, and devout laypeople all saw the Portuguese and Spanish presence in Asia as an opportunity to bring the Gospel of Christ to Asia's millions. Such an ambition was centuries old. According to tradition, as early as 52 C.E. St. Thomas, one of Jesus' twelve disciples, established a church on India's west coast. In the fifth and sixth centuries, Nestorian Christian merchants and missionaries, who were deemed heretical by the Roman Catholic and Orthodox churches, introduced their faith to Persia and central Asia and later to China. Between 1000 and 1350, the impetus for missionary activity in Asia came mainly from the Roman Catholic Church, which sent missionaries to India, Persia, Ethiopia, and China. Beginning in the 1240s, Catholic missions to Asia became part of a broader strategy to convert the Mongols and persuade them to join an anti-Muslim alliance against the Turks. Although these diplomatic initiatives failed, Catholic missionaries continued to seek converts in Mongolia and China until the mid 1300s, when the collapse of the Mongol Empire made travel across Eurasia too difficult for merchants and missionaries alike.

Despite the meager results of these initiatives, efforts to Christianize Asia were renewed in the sixteenth century. In these efforts, a key role was played by a newly established religious order, the Society of Jesus, whose founder, Ignatius of Loyola, saw missionary work as one of the order's main purposes. The missionaries of the sixteenth and seventeenth centuries had a number of advantages over their medieval predecessors. Not only did they have greater accessibility to Asia by an all-sea route, but they also were more numerous. Furthermore, their efforts were better coordinated because of the leadership of the well-trained and dedicated Jesuits. The obstacles they faced were still daunting, however. Preaching was difficult because of language barriers, and even in the best of circumstances it was challenging to overcome the skepticism and indifference of Buddhists, Hindus, Muslims, and Confucians. Furthermore, except in Goa, the Indian coastal city taken by the Portuguese in 1510, and the Philippines, which came under Spanish rule in the late 1580s, missionaries could carry on their activities only so long as they enjoyed the good graces of local rulers. Thus, the Jesuits and others adopted a "top-down" strategy, seeking to gain converts among Japanese aristocrats, Chinese scholar-officials, and Mughal and Safavid courtiers before taking their message to the broader population.

Like earlier efforts, the Catholic drive to Christianize Asia after 1500 failed except in the Philippines and Goa. A few major rulers evinced an interest in Christian doctrine, and several more weighed the economic and political advantages that conversion might bring, but none converted. The following excerpts all shed light on some of the reasons that this was the case.

THE SOURCES

The first reading is taken from two edicts issued by Toyotomi Hideyoshi, who ruled Japan between 1582 and 1598. A larger-than-life figure, Hideyoshi played a key role in unifying Japan after decades of civil war, launched two invasions of Korea as the first steps toward conquering China, and took measures to solidify the Japanese social order. In 1587 he also made the first moves against Japanese Christianity by issuing the two edicts excerpted here.

By 1587 Christianity in Japan had made impressive progress. In less than four decades after the Jesuits arrived, they had converted a number of daimyo from Kyushu, the southernmost and westernmost of Japan's four major islands. These daimyo, at least some of whom converted to attract Portuguese trade to their ports, in turn forced their subjects to become Christians. The Jesuit fathers also won the support from Oda Nobunaga, the daimyo who had unified much of Japan before his death in 1582; for a time they also had the support of his successor, Hideyoshi. Both rulers were interested in things European and, more important, viewed Christians as a counterweight to the Buddhist sectarians who were their political rivals. By the 1580s Japanese Christians numbered around 300,000.

Progress abruptly stopped in July 1587, when Hideyoshi issued two edicts that attacked Christianity and sought to limit further conversions to Christianity. His motives were primarily political. His edicts were one part of a broader strategy to establish his authority over all segments of Japan's population. An important part of this strategy was to crush certain Buddhist sects that had established independent political bases or were connected with popular rebellion. These included the True Sect Buddhists, who gained military control of Kaga province in 1488, and one of its offshoots, the Ikko ("Single-Minded") Sect, which gained control of smaller areas and was connected with popular insurrection and antitax movements. By 1587 Hideyoshi had come to see the growing body of Christians as a similar threat.

The second excerpt is from the journal of Matteo Ricci (1552–1610), an Italian Jesuit who took control of the Jesuits' missionary efforts in China soon after his arrival in 1582. Under his leadership the Jesuits targeted intellectuals, officials, and, ultimately, members of the imperial court, whom the Jesuits sought to impress by learning Chinese, adopting Chinese dress, giving gifts of clocks and other mechanical devices, and displaying their scientific and mathematical knowledge. By the early 1600s, approximately two dozen Jesuit priests were in China, with residences in several cities, including Beijing. In 1601, on the strength of Ricci's knowledge of astronomy and mathematics, the emperor invited him to establish a residence in the capital city. Ricci remained there until his death in 1610, by which time several thousand Chinese, including some members of the imperial family, had become Christians.

The Jesuits also made enemies. An example is an episode that took place in Nanchang, a major city in Jiangxi province, in 1607, when local magistrates sought to close the Jesuit residence that had been founded in 1595. In Ricci's account of the Nanchang incident, we can see some of the cultural barriers and attitudes that made the Jesuits' efforts to accommodate Christianity to Chinese civilization so difficult. The excerpt begins with a summary of the anti-Christian allegations made at a monthly meeting of the Nanchang magistrates.

The last excerpt comes from a report written by a Carmelite friar, Paul Simon, to Pope Paul V shortly after Simon's return from a visit to the court of Shah Abbas I of Persia in 1605. Simon's visit was one of several missions sent to the Safavid court in Isfahan to gauge the possibility of converting Shah Abbas I, who shared a common enemy with European Christian rulers in the Ottoman Turks and had given tantalizing hints of an interest in Christianity. Abbas, for his part, encouraged hopes by sending two embassies to Europe to explore military cooperation, welcoming missionaries from several Catholic religious orders, and permitting the construction of monasteries and churches in Isfahan, Shiraz, and Ormuz. Simon, however, found Abbas a religious enigma, and the shah never converted to Christianity.

QUESTIONS FOR ANALYSIS

1. What, if any, value did Asians see in Christian teaching and doctrine?
2. To what extent did Asian rulers and aristocrats support Christian missionary endeavors for nonreligious gain?
3. What did Asian rulers and aristocrats see as the major weaknesses of Christian teaching?
4. To what extent did Asian rulers and aristocrats see Christianity as a threat to their power or goals?
5. On the basis of what you have read, what conclusions can you draw about the reasons why missionary efforts in Asia had such limited results?

I ▾ Hideyoshi, 1587 EDICTS ON CHRISTIANITY

NOTICE

1. The matter of [becoming] a sectarian of the Bateren[1] shall be the free choice of the individual concerned.

2. That enfeoffed recipients[2] of provinces, districts, and estates should force peasants registered in [Buddhist] temples, and others of their tenantry, against their will into the ranks of the Bateren sectarians is unreasonable beyond words and is outrageous. . . .

4. Persons holding above 200 *cho* of land or can expect 2 or 3 thousand *kan* of rice harvest each year,[3] may become [sectarians of the] Bateren

---

[1]Japanese approximation of the word "padre"; used to designate Christian priests, especially Jesuits.

[2]Those invested by a higher authority with territory and, with it, various rights and duties connected with that territory; sometimes translated as "vassals."

[3]One *cho* equals approximately 2.9 acres; one *kan* equals approximately 8.25 pounds. Clearly, this provision refers to individuals with substantial wealth from landholding—members of the aristocracy.

upon obtaining official permission, acceding to the pleasure of the lord of the *Tenka*.[4] . . .

6. The Bateren sectarians, it has come to the attention [of the lord of the *Tenka*], are even more given to conjurations [deceits] . . . than the Ikkō Sect. The Ikkō Sect established temple precincts[5] in the provinces and districts and did not pay the yearly dues to their enfeoffed recipients. Moreover, they made the entire Province of Kaga into [Ikkō] sectarians, chased out . . . the lord of the province, delivered the stipends over to bonzes [monks] of the Ikkō Sect, and, beyond that, even took over Echizen.[6] That this was harmful to the *Tenka* is the undisguisable truth.

7. The bonzes of the Ikkō sectarians had temples built in every cove and inlet. Though they have been pardoned, they no longer regulate matters in their temple precincts in the same manner as before.

8. That daimyo in possession of provinces and districts or of estates should force their retainers into the ranks of the Bateren sectarians is even more undesirable by far than the Honganji[7] sectarians' establishment of temple precincts, and is bound to be of great harm to the *Tenka*. These individuals . . . shall be subject to punishment.

9. Bateren sectarians by their free choice, [insofar as they] are of the lower classes, shall be unmolested. . . .

10. The sale of Japanese to China, South Barbary,[8] and Korea is outrageous[9]. . . .

11. Trade and slaughter of cattle and horses for use as food shall also be considered criminal.[10]

The above items shall rest under strict prohibition. Any transgressor shall immediately be put to severe punishment.

ORDAINED

1. Japan is the Land of the Gods. Diffusion here from the Kirishitan [Christian] Country of a pernicious doctrine is most undesirable.

2. To approach the people of our provinces and districts and, making them into [Kirishitan] sectarians, cause them to destroy the shrines of the gods and the temples of the Buddhas is a thing unheard of in previous ages. . . . But to corrupt and stir up the lower classes is outrageous.

3. It is the judgement [of the lord of the *Tenka*] that since the Bateren by means of their clever doctrine amass parishioners as they please, the aforementioned violation of the Buddhist Law in these Precincts . . . has resulted. That being outrageous, the Bateren can hardly be allowed to remain on Japanese soil. Within twenty days they must make their preparations and return to their country. . . .

4. The purpose of the Black Ships[11] is trade, and that is a different matter. As years and months pass, trade may be carried on in all sort of articles.

5. From now on all those who do not disturb Buddhism (merchants as a matter of course, and all others as well) may freely travel from the Kirishitan Country and return. Act accordingly.

[4]A reference to Hideyoshi; *tenka* means the "whole realm."

[5]Refers to villages or larger regions that were under the political control of Buddhist clergy connected with a temple or monastery.

[6]A small western province on the Sea of Japan.

[7]Honganji, literally "temple of the original vow," was the main temple of the Jodo Shinshu (True Pure Land Sect) in Kyoto. Nobunaga considered the temple a threat, and after a ten-year siege, he ordered it burned to the ground and all its inhabitants killed.

[8]Europeans were called "Southern Barbarians," so South Barbary may refer to Europe itself, but it more likely refers to the Southern parts of Asia where the Portuguese had established a presence.

[9]There is evidence that European merchants for a time did purchase small numbers of Japanese and sell them into slavery to some of their Asian trading partners. When confronted by Hideyoshi on this matter, the Jesuits denied any involvement in the trade in slaves and claimed they had no direct influence on the practices of European merchants.

[10]The Japanese, who considered the slaughter of animals as work suitable for the lowest groups in their social hierarchy, viewed the eating of useful animals such as horses and cattle as a sign of barbarism. The Japanese diet consisted almost exclusively of rice, vegetables, and seafood.

[11]The term used by the Japanese for the ships of the Europeans.

2 ▾ *Matteo Ricci, JOURNAL*

▹ Ricci's account begins with a lengthy quotation in which he summarizes the criticisms of Christianity presented by his detractors at a monthly meeting of the Nanchang magistrates in 1607.

"Matthew Ricci, Giovanni Soerio, Emanuele Dias, and certain other foreigners from western kingdoms, men who are guilty of high treason against the throne, are scattered amongst us, in five different provinces. They are continually communicating with each other and are here and there practicing brigandage on the rivers, collecting money, and then distributing it to the people, in order to curry favor with the multitudes. They are frequently visited by the Magistrates, by the high nobility and by the Military Prefects, with whom they have entered into a secret pact, binding unto death.

These men teach that we should pay no respect to the images of our ancestors, a doctrine which is destined to extinguish the love of future generations for their forebears. Some of them break up the idols, leaving the temples empty and the gods to be pitied, without any patronage. In the beginning they lived in small houses, but by this time they have bought up large and magnificent residences. The doctrine they teach is something infernal. It attracts the ignorant into its fraudulent meshes, and great crowds of this class are continually assembled at their houses. Their doctrine gets beyond the city walls and spreads itself through the neighboring towns and villages and into the open country, and the people become so wrapt up in its falsity, that students are not following their course, laborers are neglecting their work, farmers are not cultivating their acres, and even the women have no interest in their housework. The whole city has become disturbed, and, whereas in the beginning there were only a hundred or so professing their faith, now there are more than twenty thousand. These priests distribute pictures of some Tartar or Saracen, [a reference to Jesus], who they say is God, who came down from heaven to redeem and to instruct all of humanity, and who alone, according to their doctrine, can give wealth and happiness; a doctrine by which the simple people are very easily deceived. These men are an abomination on the face of the earth, and there is just ground for fear that once they have erected their own temples, they will start a rebellion. . . . Wherefore, moved by their interest in the maintenance of the public good, in the conservation of the realm, and in the preservation, whole and entire, of their ancient laws, the petitioners are presenting this complaint and demanding, in the name of the entire province, that a rescript of it be forwarded to the emperor, asking that these foreigners be sentenced to death, or banished from the realm, to some deserted island in the sea." . . .

▹ The allegations were considered by the mayor of Nanchang, who referred the case to a local court. The justices heard testimony from the mayor; Father Emanuele Dias, the head of the Jesuit mission in Nanchang; several of the magistrates who had submitted the original complaint; and several who opposed punishing the Jesuits. The latter argued that since the emperor had welcomed Ricci to the imperial court in Beijing, it made little sense to expel the Jesuits from Nanchang. Ricci summarizes the court's decision in the following excerpt.

A few days later, the court decision was pronounced and written out. . . . The following is a summary of their declaration. Having examined the cause of Father Emanuele and his companions, it was found that these men had come here from the West because they had heard so much about the fame of the great Chinese Empire, and that they had already been living in the realm for some years, without any display of ill-will. Father Emanuele should be permitted to practice his own religion, but it was not considered to be the right thing for the common people, who are attracted by novelties, to adore the God of Heaven. For them to go over to the religion of foreigners would indeed be most unbecoming. . . . It would therefore seem to be . . . [in] . . . the best interests of the Kingdom, to . . . [warn] . . . everyone in a public edict not to abandon the sacrifices of their ancient religion by accepting the cult of foreigners. Such a movement might, indeed, result in calling together certain gatherings, detrimental to the public welfare, and harmful also to the foreigner, himself. Wherefore, the Governor of this district, by order of the high Magistrates, admonishes the said Father Emanuele to refrain from perverting the people, by inducing them to accept a foreign religion. . . . It is not permitted for any of the native people to go over to the religion of the foreigners, nor is it permitted to gather together for prayer meetings. Whoever does contrary to these prescriptions will be severely punished. . . . To his part of the edict, the Director of the Schools added, that . . . a sign should be posted above the door of the Father's residence, notifying the public that these men were forbidden to have frequent contact with the people.

The Fathers were not too disturbed by this pronouncement, because they were afraid that it was going to be much worse. In fact, everyone thought it was rather favorable . . . since the Fathers were not banished from the city, as the literati had demanded. . . .

3 ▾ Paul Simon, REPORT TO POPE PAUL V

Regarding the religion of the king [Shah Abbas I] I think that no one knows what he believes: he does not observe the Muslim law in many things, nor is he a Christian. Six or seven years ago he displayed many signs of not being averse to our Faith. . . .

It is true that when the Augustinian Fathers[12] went to Persia the king showed himself extraordinarily affectionate with them, and gave many signs of being well disposed toward the Christian Faith and of wanting to embrace it. . . . He gave them 2,000 scudi[13] yearly for their subsistence, and entertained them several times at banquets, always making them sit near him. . . . When the Fathers proposed to him [that he should adopt] our Faith, he made show to agree to everything. He gave them . . . a writing in which he promised to construct a church with bells in every town he should capture from the Turks, to allow the Gospel to be preached, if the King of Spain kept to that which he had promised him by the same Fathers, i.e., to take up arms against the Turks, and to send him artillery and engineers, which up till now has not been fulfilled. As evidence that he still had the mind to fulfil what he was promising, he said that on the following day he would go to their church — as in fact he did. . . .

▷ By the time Father Simon arrived in Isfahan in 1605, Abba's views of Christianity had changed.

In Tabriz it was told the king that the Augustinian Fathers had put up a bell in their church in Isfahan and that for this reason there were many people sick in that town. The Shah bit his finger, muttering two or three times: "Church with a bell! church with a bell!"; and gave orders that they should immediately take it down, as they did. In many other actions he demonstrated

[12]These Augustinian friars were from Portugal, which had established itself in the Persian port of Hormuz in 1507. Between 1580 and 1640, the thrones of Portugal and Spain were combined.

[13]A *scudo* was a silver coin minted in Italy.

the small goodwill he had for Christians; and this increased to such an extent that, when we arrived in the city of Isfahan, he had given instructions for publication of an edict to the effect that all 'Frankish' [European] Christians and the Augustinian Fathers should quit his realm. . . .

. . . The cause of so great a change . . . God alone knows; the Augustinian Fathers say that in the beginning the king was merely pretending and that those demonstrations of affection and goodwill did not come from his heart. Other people attribute it to the many causes for annoyance the officials of his Catholic Majesty in Ormuz have given him; to the Christian princes, His Holiness [the pope], the Emperor, the king of Spain not having kept the word they had given to various ambassadors that they would make war on the Turks, when they exhorted him himself to do the same, as he in fact has done; to many of the Franks, who had gone to his country, having committed a great many follies; and, more recently still, to the Emperor having agreed to a treaty[14] of peace between himself and the Turks, without giving him notice. . . . Certain it is that the mullahs — this the name they give in their tongue to the learned men of their belief — went to the Shah, and told him to reflect on what he was doing — that he knew very well that the [Ottoman] Sultan was the head of the Muslim belief; if he should bring about the destruction of the latter in this warfare, the Christians would do the same to him, and to all of their belief. For they observed what poor sort of friends they were. . . . It would be better to make peace with the Turkish Sultan, and then both of them together to attack the Christians. . . .

With all that he does not detest them [the Christians], for he converses and eats with them, he suffers us to say frankly what we believe about our Faith and his own: sometimes he asks us about this. To us he has given a house: he knows that we say Mass publicly, he allows whoever may wish among the Persians to come to it, and we can teach them freely regarding our holy Faith, whenever they make inquiries about it. . . . Till now none of them has been converted: I think they are waiting for one of the nobles or of their mullahs to break the ice. . . .

[14]Treaty of Zsitvatorok, signed in November 1606, ended fifteen years of warfare between the Ottomans and the Hapsburg prince Rudolph II, who was Holy Roman Emperor and king of Hungary and Bohemia.

▲▲▲

Chapter 4

Africa and the Americas

BETWEEN THE FIFTEENTH AND SEVENTEENTH CENTURIES, Africa and the Americas were the two areas of the world to experience the most profound effects of European expansion. On both sides of the Atlantic, the arrival of Europeans resulted in demographic changes, the introduction of new species of plants and animals, political disruption, efforts to spread Christianity, new weaponry, and changing patterns of trade. But the magnitude of Europe's impact on the two regions varied greatly. The arrival of the Europeans affected Africa significantly but utterly transformed the Americas.

The European presence in Africa primarily meant trade — trade in which Europeans exchanged iron, hardware, textiles, and other goods for pepper, gold, ivory, and, above all, human beings. European involvement in the slave trade began in 1441, when a Portuguese raiding party captured twelve Africans on a small coastal island and sold them into slavery in Portugal. After the plantation system of agriculture was established on São Tomé, Cape Verde, and other South Atlantic islands and later spread to the West Indies and the Americas, the demand for slaves grew from fewer than 1,000 a year in the fifteenth century, to 7,500 a year in the mid seventeenth century, to more than 50,000 a year in the eighteenth and early nineteenth centuries. The slave trade, however, did not translate into European political dominance or permanent European settlements in Africa. Except for small numbers of Dutch farmers who began to migrate to South Africa in 1652, Europeans in Africa stayed on the coast, completed their business, and then departed. Missionary efforts were meager, and Portuguese dominance in Angola, in southwest Africa, is the only example of anything that approximated a European colony. As a result, despite the slave trade, Africans kept control of their political lives and experienced few changes in their distinctive cultures and religions until the late nineteenth century, when a new wave of European expansion occurred.

In the Americas, however, the Europeans' arrival had immediate and catastrophic consequences for the indigenous peoples. By 1650 Spaniards and Portuguese directly ruled Mexico and Central and South America, and the English, French, Dutch, and other northern Europeans had begun to settle North America's Atlantic coast and the St. Lawrence River basin. In the 200 years following Columbus's discoveries, throughout the Western Hemisphere wealth was plundered, political structures were destroyed, millions of Native Americans were killed by Old World diseases, and traditional patterns of life and belief disappeared or managed only a tenuous survival.

Of the many factors that explain the differences in the African and the American experiences in the age of European expansion, two stand out. First, unlike the Americas, where more than half a dozen European states from Portugal to Sweden competed for trade and territory, in Africa only one European state, Portugal, was involved. Portugal led the way in African exploration and trade and by the end of the fifteenth century had established commercial contacts and trading posts that discouraged European competitors. Only in the seventeenth century did other states, notably the Netherlands, France, and England, show an interest in African trade. Second, Europeans, including the Portuguese, were convinced that in comparison to other parts of the world Africa offered few economic rewards other than gold and the slave trade. Furthermore, Portugal's merchants and politicians concluded in the sixteenth century that their money and energy would be better spent on Asian trade and Brazilian development than on Africa. Neither they nor any other Europeans were willing to make the economic and military commitments necessary to support European settlement and establish European political authority. Europeans faced a far different situation in the Americas. They soon discovered that the region contained easily exploitable sources of wealth such as gold, silver, and furs and was capable of growing profitable crops such as tobacco and sugar. All these things were more or less theirs for the taking, not only in the thinly populated regions of North America and eastern and southern South America but also in the more populous regions of Mexico, Peru, and the Caribbean.

The Europeans' guns, steel swords, and horses certainly gave them an initial advantage over the American Indians. The relative ease of the European conquest, however, resulted only in part from the European superior technology. In Mexico, under normal circumstances several hundred Spaniards, even with their firearms and Native American allies, would have been no match for thousands of Aztec warriors with arrows, clubs, lances, and spears. Disease, not firearms, was the deciding factor. In the midst of fighting, the Aztecs were struck by a debilitating smallpox epidemic, a disease introduced by the Spaniards. It was a sorely weakened and demoralized Aztec Empire that succumbed to the Spaniards and their allies in 1521.

All American Indians, not just the Aztecs, had to contend with the bacteria, viruses, and parasites the Europeans carried in their bodies from across the Atlantic. Because of their long isolation, they lacked immunity to Old World diseases such as diphtheria, measles, chickenpox, whooping cough, yellow fever, influenza, dysentery, and smallpox. Thus, the arrival of a few Europeans and Africans had devastating consequences for the indigenous peoples of the Americas. On the island of Hispaniola, where Columbus established the first Spanish settlement in the New World, the Arawak Indians had a population of between 300,000 and 400,000 in 1492 but had virtually disappeared fifty years later. In Mexico, within fifty years after the arrival of the Spaniards, the region's population fell by 90 percent, and in this case millions, not tens of thousands, were victimized. No part of the Americas was untouched.

Such human devastation not only made it relatively easy for the Europeans to conquer or displace the Native Americans but also led to the enslavement of Africans in the New World. The epidemics created labor shortages that Europeans sought to overcome by importing enslaved Africans. Before the transatlantic slave trade ended, as many as 11 million Africans had been sold into slavery in the Americas, and millions more died in slave raids and the holds of slave ships crossing the Atlantic. These Africans, too, were indirect victims of the bacteria, viruses, and parasites brought to the New World in the early years of European expansion.

Africans and the Portuguese

When the Portuguese began sending ships into the Atlantic to explore Africa's offshore islands and west coast in the early fifteenth century, their goals were shaped by their limited and often inaccurate perceptions of Africa. They knew about Madeira and the Canary Islands, which French, Spanish, and Genoese mariners had visited in the late 1300s and perhaps even earlier. They knew that the North African coast was a Muslim stronghold, that beyond the coast lay a vast desert, and that south of the desert was a region rich in gold and pepper. Many also were convinced that somewhere in eastern Africa there existed a potential ally in the struggle against Islam — a Christian kingdom ruled by Prester John, whose existence had intrigued Europeans ever since the twelfth century. Based on this meager information and legend, the Portuguese gambled that their voyages down the African coast would enable them to bypass Muslim traders in North Africa and give them direct access to African gold and pepper. They also dreamed of making contact with the mighty kingdom of Prester John and joining him in a new crusade against their common Muslim enemy. Thus, the Portuguese became explorers to make money and serve God.

In time the Portuguese expanded their knowledge of Africa, and as they did, some of their original goals were abandoned and new ones emerged. They did find a Christian kingdom in eastern Africa, but it was not the realm of Prester John, but the kingdom of Ethiopia, a weak state vulnerable to attack by its Muslim neighbors. No Portuguese-Ethiopian alliance would tip the military balance in favor of Christians. On Africa's west coast, the Portuguese discovered economic opportunities beyond trading for gold, pepper, and ivory. The ample rainfall and rich volcanic soil of the islands of Cape Verde, Madeira, and São Tomé made them ideal for growing and processing sugar, a commodity with a ready and expanding market in Europe. The sugar plantations of these South Atlantic islands created a demand for African slaves, and beginning in the 1400s purchasing or capturing slaves in Africa and transporting and reselling them throughout the Atlantic world became a major Portuguese enterprise.

In 1498 the Portuguese made an even more important discovery — namely, that by sailing around the Cape of Good Hope they could reach the rich markets of India, Southeast Asia, China, and Japan by an all-ocean route. This transformed Portuguese thinking about Africa. Having direct access to the luxury goods and spices of Asia generated opportunities for profits that trade in African goods could never match. As a result, from the sixteenth century onward, the Portuguese came to view Africa mainly as a source of slaves for the New World and a place to sail around in order to reach Asia.

Africa in the age of European discovery assumed a more prominent role in the world economy, but at great cost — the enslavement of millions of Africans. The growth of slavery in the New World, and the slave trade that made it possible, gave birth to the myth of the Africans' moral and intellectual inferiority, used by defenders of slavery to justify a cruel and vicious institution. Thus, the Europeans' involvement in Africa resulted in no massive epidemics, no toppling of empires, and no wholesale religious changes as it did in the Americas. It was, however, no less traumatic and tragic.

Political Breakdown in the Kingdom of Kongo

▼▼▼

20 ▼ *Nzinga Mbemba (Afonso I), LETTERS TO THE KING OF PORTUGAL*

The largest state in central West Africa around 1500 was the Kingdom of Kongo, stretching along the estuary of the Congo River in territory that lies within present-day Angola and the Democratic Republic of Congo. In 1483 the Portuguese navigator Diogo Cão made contact with Kongo and several years later visited its inland capital. When he sailed home, he was accompanied by Kongo emissaries whom King Nzinga a Kuwu dispatched to Lisbon to learn European ways. They returned in 1491, along with Portuguese priests, artisans, and soldiers, who brought with them numerous European goods, including a printing press. In the same year, the king and his son, Nzinga Mbemba, were baptized as Catholics.

Around 1506 Nzinga Mbemba, who took the name Afonso after his baptism, succeeded his father and ruled until about 1543. Afonso promoted European culture in his kingdom by proclaiming Christianity the state religion (a step that affected few of his subjects), imitating the etiquette of Portuguese royalty, and using the Portuguese language in state business. His son Henrique was educated in Portugal and returned to serve as sub-Saharan Africa's first black Roman Catholic bishop. European firearms, horses, and cattle were introduced, and Afonso dreamed of achieving a powerful and prosperous state with European help. By the time of his death, however, his kingdom verged on disintegration, in no small measure because of the Portuguese. As many later African rulers were to discover, the introduction of European products and customs caused dissension and social instability. Worse, Portuguese involvement in the slave trade undermined Afonso's authority and made his subjects restive. In 1526 Afonso wrote the following letters to King João III (r. 1521–1528), urging him to control his subjects. They are two of twenty-four letters Afonso and his Portuguese-educated, native secretaries dispatched to the kings of Portugal on a variety of issues.

QUESTIONS FOR ANALYSIS

1. According to Afonso, what have been the detrimental effects of the Portuguese presence in his kingdom?
2. What do the letters reveal about the workings of the slave trade in the kingdom? Who participated in it?
3. What do the letters reveal about Afonso's attitude toward slavery? Does he oppose the practice as such or only certain aspects of it?
4. What steps had Afonso taken to deal with the problems caused by the Portuguese? What do the letters suggest about the effectiveness of these steps?

5. **How would you characterize Afonso's attitude toward the power and authority of the king of Portugal? Does he consider himself inferior to the Portuguese king or his equal?**
6. **How would you characterize King Afonso's conception of the ideal relationship between the Portuguese and his kingdom?**

Sir, Your Highness should know how our Kingdom is being lost in so many ways that it is convenient to provide for the necessary remedy, since this is caused by the excessive freedom given by your agents and officials to the men and merchants who are allowed to come to this Kingdom to set up shops with goods and many things which have been prohibited by us, and which they spread throughout our Kingdoms and Domains in such an abundance that many of our vassals, whom we had in obedience, do not comply because they have the things in greater abundance than we ourselves; and it was with these things that we had them content and subjected under our vassalage and jurisdiction, so it is doing a great harm not only to the service of God, but the security and peace of our Kingdoms and State as well.

And we cannot reckon how great the damage is, since the mentioned merchants are taking every day our natives, sons of the land and the sons of our noblemen and vassals and our relatives, because the thieves and men of bad conscience grab them wishing to have the things and wares of this Kingdom which they are ambitious of; they grab them and get them to be sold; and so great, Sir, is the corruption and licentiousness that our country is being completely depopulated, and Your Highness should not agree with this nor accept it as in your service. And to avoid it we need from those [your] Kingdoms no more than some priests and a few people to teach in schools, and no other goods except wine and flour for the holy sacrament. That is why we beg of Your Highness to help and assist us in this matter, commanding your factors that they should not send here either merchants or wares, because it is *our will that in these Kingdoms there should not be any trade of slaves nor outlet for them.* Concerning what is referred [to] above, again we beg of Your Highness to agree with it, since otherwise we cannot remedy such an obvious damage. Pray Our Lord in His mercy to have Your Highness under His guard and let you do forever the things of His service. I kiss your hands many times.

At our town of Kongo, written on the sixth day of July, João Teixeira did it in 1526.
The King. Dom Afonso.

▾▾▾

Moreover, Sir, in our Kingdoms there is another great inconvenience which is of little service to God, and this is that many of our people, keenly desirous as they are of the wares and things of your Kingdoms, which are brought here by your people, and in order to satisfy their voracious appetite, seize many of our people, freed and exempt men, and very often it happens that they kidnap even noblemen and the sons of noblemen, and our relatives, and take them to be sold to the white men who are in our Kingdoms; and for this purpose they have concealed them; and others are brought during the night so that they might not be recognized.

And as soon as they are taken by the white men they are immediately ironed and branded with fire, and when they are carried to be embarked [on ships], if they are caught by our guards' men the whites allege that they have bought them but they cannot say from whom, so that it is our duty to do justice and to restore to the freemen their freedom, but it cannot be done if your subjects feel offended, as they claim to be.

And to avoid such a great evil we passed a law so that any white man living in our Kingdoms and wanting to purchase goods in any way should first inform three of our noblemen and officials of our court whom we rely upon in this matter, . . . who should investigate if the mentioned goods are captives or free men, and if cleared by them there will be no further doubt nor embargo [an act prohibiting the departure of a trading vessel] for them to be taken and embarked. But if the white men do not comply with it they will lose the aforementioned goods. And if we do them this favor and concession it is for the part Your Highness has in it, since we know that it is in your service too that these goods are taken from our Kingdom, otherwise we should not consent to this. . . .

▾▾▾

Sir, Your Highness has been kind enough to write to us saying that we should ask in our letters for anything we need, and that we shall be provided with everything, and as the peace and the health of our Kingdom depend on us, and as there are among us old folks and people who have lived for many days, it happens that we have continuously many and different diseases which put us very often in such a weakness that we reach almost the last extreme; and the same happens to our children, relatives and natives owing to the lack in this country of physicians and surgeons who might know how to cure properly such diseases. And as we have got neither dispensaries nor drugs which might help us in this forlornness, many of those who had been already confirmed and instructed in the holy faith of Our Lord Jesus Christ perish and die; and the rest of the people in their majority cure themselves with herbs and . . . and other ancient methods, so that they put all their faith in the mentioned herbs and ceremonies if they live, and believe that they are saved if they die; and this is not much in the service of God.

And to avoid such a great error and inconvenience, since it is from God in the first place and then from your Kingdoms and from Your Highness that all the good and drugs and medicines have come to save us, we beg of you to be agreeable and kind enough to send us two physicians and two apothecaries and one surgeon, so that they may come with their drugstores and all the necessary things to stay in our kingdoms, because we are in extreme need of them all and each of them. We shall do them all good and shall benefit them by all means, since they are sent by Your Highness, whom we thank for your work in their coming. We beg of Your Highness as a great favor to do this for us, because besides being good in itself it is in the service of God as we have said above.

{Extracts from letter of King Afonso to the King of Portugal dated Oct. 18, 1526. By hand of Dom João Teixeira.}

Military Conflict in Southeast Africa

▾▾▾

21 ▾ *João dos Santos, EASTERN ETHIOPIA*

An example of African response to the Portuguese presence is provided by the military campaigns in southeast Africa launched in the late sixteenth century by the people known as the Zimba. The Portuguese used the term *Zimba* to describe any and all marauders from north of the Zambezi River, but the Zimba were in fact warriors of the Mang'aja tribe, whose attacks on the Portuguese and other African peoples to their east were ordered by their lundu, or chief, in the late 1580s in response to disruption of their traditional trade. During the sixteenth century, the market for Mang'aja ivory was ruined when the gold-obsessed Portuguese took over the coastal cities with which the Mang'aja had traded. The Zimba's military campaigns were intended to force the reopening of these mar-

kets. The Portuguese efforts to suppress the Zimba's attacks failed spectacularly. The Mang'aja continued their attacks until the early 1600s, but they never succeeded in re-establishing the traditional market for their ivory.

The following excerpt is from *Eastern Ethiopia* by João dos Santos, about whom little is known except that he was a Catholic clergyman who traveled along the east African coast and resided for a time in Sofala during the late sixteenth century. He uses the term *eastern Ethiopia* to include all of Africa's east coast from the Cape of Good Hope to the Red Sea.

QUESTIONS FOR ANALYSIS

1. According to dos Santos's account, why do the Portuguese decide to resist the Zimba?
2. What seems to have been the Zimba's attitude toward the Portuguese?
3. How would you characterize the attitude of the African allies of the Portuguese toward the Zimba? How dedicated were the allies to the Portuguese themselves?
4. How great an advantage did Portuguese firearms give them over their enemy?
5. What tactics of the Zimba were most effective in the conflict with the Portuguese and their allies? What purposes did cannibalism play in the Zimba's overall strategy?
6. What hints does dos Santos's account provide about the motives of the Zimba's military campaign?

Opposite the fort of Sena, on the other side of the river, live some Kaffirs,[1] lords of those lands, good neighbors and friends of the Portuguese, and always most loyal to them. It so happened at the time I was there that the Zimba Kaffirs, . . . who eat human flesh, invaded this territory and made war upon one of these friendly Kaffirs, and by force of arms took from him the kraal[2] in which he resided and a great part of his land, besides which they killed and ate a number of his people. The Kaffir, seeing himself thus routed and his power destroyed, proceeded to Sena[3] to lay his trouble before the captain, who was then André de Santiago, and to beg for assistance in driving out of his house the enemy who had taken possession of it. The captain, upon hearing his pitiful request, determined to assist him, both because he was very friendly to us and because he did not wish to have so near to Sena a neighbor as wicked as the Zimba.

Therefore, having made all necessary preparations for this war, he set out, taking with him a great number of the Portuguese of Sena with their guns and two pieces of heavy cannon from the fort. On arriving at the place where the Zimba were, they found them within a strong double palisade of wood, with its ramparts and loopholes for arrows, surrounded by a very deep and wide trench, within which the enemy were most defiant. André de Santiago, seeing that the

[1]Based on the Arab word *kafir*, meaning "black," Kaffir was used to refer to the Bantu-speaking peoples of southeastern Africa and more generally to non-Muslim black Africans. Today in South Africa it is a derogatory term used by some whites for all blacks.

[2]Based on the Portuguese word *curral,* an enclosed pen for cattle, kraal refers to the enclosed area surrounding a royal residence.

[3]Sena and Tete were towns on the Zambezi River where the Portuguese had established trading posts.

enterprise was much more formidable than he had anticipated and that he had brought with him but few men to attack so strong an enemy and his fortress, fixed his camp on the bank of a rivulet which ran by the place, and sent a message to the captain of Tete, Pedro Fernandes de Chaves, to come to his assistance with the Portuguese of Tete and as many Kaffir vassals of his fort as he could bring.

Pedro Fernandes de Chaves immediately prepared to go . . . and assembled more than a hundred men with their guns, Portuguese and half-castes,[4] and the eleven vassal chiefs. They all crossed to the other side of the river and proceeded by land until they were near the place where the Zimba had fortified themselves. These had information of their approach, and greatly feared their arrival. For this reason they sent out spies secretly upon the road, that when they approached they might see them, and report concerning the men who were coming. And learning from these spies that the Portuguese were in front of the Kaffirs in palanquins[5] and hammocks and not disposed in order of battle, they sallied out of their fortress by night secretly, without being heard by André de Santiago, and proceeded to conceal themselves in a dense thicket at about half a league's[6] distance, through which the men of Tete would have to pass. When they were thus stationed the Portuguese came up nearly half a league in advance of the Kaffirs of their company, quite unsuspicious of what might befall them in the thicket. Just as they were entering it the Zimba fell upon them suddenly with such violence that in a short time they were all killed, not one surviving, and when they were dead the Zimba cut off their legs and arms, which they carried away on their backs with all the baggage and arms they had brought with them, after which they returned secretly to their fortress. When the chiefs reached the thicket and found all the Portuguese and their captain dead, they immediately turned back from the place and retreated to Tete, where they related the lamentable event that had occurred.

At the time that preparations for this war were being made there was a friar of St. Dominic preaching at Tete, named Nicolau do Rosario, . . . In the ambush he was severely wounded, and seizing him yet alive the Zimba carried him away with them to put him to death more cruelly afterwards, which they did upon arriving at their fortress, where they bound him hand and foot to a tree and killed him with their arrows in the most cruel manner. This they did to him rather than to others because he was a priest and head of the Christians, as they called him, laying all the blame for the war upon him and saying that Christians did nothing without the leave and counsel of their [priests]. . . .

After the Zimba had put Father Nicolau to death they rested during the remainder of that sad day, and on the night that followed they celebrated their victory and success, playing upon many cornets and drums, and the next day at dawn they all sallied out of their fortress, the chief clothed in the chasuble[7] that the father had brought with him to say mass, carrying the golden chalice in his left hand and an assagai[8] in his right, all the other Zimba carrying on their backs the limbs of the Portuguese, with the head of the captain of Tete on the point of a long lance, and beating a drum they had taken from him. In this manner, with loud shouts and cries they came within sight of André de Santiago and all the Portuguese who were with him, and showed them all these things. After this they retired within their fortress, saying that what they had done to the men of Tete who had come to help their enemies, they would do to them, and

[4] People of mixed Portuguese/African ancestry.

[5] Covered litters or couches that were mounted on long horizontal poles so they could be carried about.

[6] A measure of the distance a man or horse could walk in an hour. In Spain and Portugal, a league was approximately three miles.

[7] One of the vestments worn by a Catholic priest while celebrating Mass.

[8] A spear.

that it was the flesh of those men that they were about to eat.

André de Santiago . . . was greatly shocked, as also were all the other Portuguese, at this most horrible and pitiful spectacle, for which reason they decided to retreat as soon as night came on. In carrying this decision into execution they were in so great a hurry to reach the other side of the river that they were heard by the Zimba, who sallied out of their fortress and falling upon them with great violence killed many of them on the bank of the river. Among the slain was André de Santiago, who died as the valiant man he was. . . .

Great sorrow was felt at the death of Father Nicolau, whom all looked upon as a saint, and for all the Portuguese who lost their lives in this most disastrous war, both because some of them were married and left wives and children at these rivers, and because the Zimba were victorious, more insolent than before, and were within fortifications close to Sena, where with greater audacity they might in the future do much damage to the Portuguese who passed up and down these rivers with their merchandise. For these reasons Dom Pedro de Sousa, captain of Mozambique, determined to chastise these Zimba, conquer them, and drive them from the vicinity of Sena. . . .

After obtaining information of the condition of the Zimba, he commanded all the necessary preparations to be made for this war, and assembled nearly two hundred Portuguese and fifteen hundred Kaffirs, with whom he crossed to the other side of the Zambesi and proceeded by land to the fortress of the Zimba, where he formed a camp at the same place that André de Santiago had formed his. Then he commanded that the various pieces of artillery which he had taken with him for the purpose should be fired against the wall of the fortress, but this had no effect upon it, as it was made of large wood, strengthened within by a strong and wide rampart which the Zimba had constructed with the earth from the trench.

Dom Pedro, seeing that his artillery had no effect upon the enemy's wall, determined to enter the fortress and take it by assault, and for this purpose he commanded part of the trench to be filled up, which was done with great difficulty and danger to our men, as the Zimba from the top of the wall wounded and killed some of them with arrows. When this part of the trench was filled up, a number of men crossed over with axes in their hands to the foot of the palisade, which they began to cut down, but the Zimba from the top of the wall poured so great a quantity of boiling fat and water upon them that nearly all were scalded and badly wounded, especially the naked Kaffirs, so that no one dared go near the palisade, because they were afraid of the boiling fat and through fear of certain iron hooks similar to long harpoons, which the Zimba thrust through the loopholes in the wall and with which they wounded and caught hold of all who came near and pulled from within with such force that they drew them to the apertures, where they wounded them mortally. For this reason the captain commanded all the men to be recalled to the camp to rest, and the remainder of that day was spent in tending the wounded and the scalded.

The following day the captain commanded a quantity of wood and branches of trees to be collected, with which huge wicker-work frames were made, as high as and higher than the enemy's palisade, and he commanded them to be placed in front of the wall and filled with earth that the soldiers might fight on them with their guns, and the Zimba would not dare to appear on the wall or be able to pour boiling fat upon the men cutting down the palisade. When this stratagem of war was almost in readiness, another peaceful or cowardly device was planned in the following manner. The war had lasted two months, for which reason the residents of these rivers, who were there rather by force than of their own free will, being away from their homes and trade, which is their profession, and not war, pretended to have received letters from their wives in Sena relating the danger they were in from a rebel Kaffir who they said was coming with a number of men to rob Sena, knowing that the Portuguese were absent, for which reason they ought immediately to return home. This false information was spread through the camp, and the residents of Sena went to the captain and begged him to abandon the siege of the Zimba and attend to what was of greater importance, as otherwise they would be compelled to return to their homes and leave him.

Dom Pedro, seeing their determination and believing the information said to be given in the letters to be true, abandoned the siege and commanded the men to pass by night to the other side of the river and return to Sena, but this retreat could not be effected with such secrecy as to be unknown to the Zimba, who sallied out of their fortress with great cries, fell upon the camp, killed some men who were still there, and seized the greater part of the baggage and artillery, that had not been taken away.

With this defeat and disappointment the captain returned to Sena, and thence to Mozambique, without accomplishing what he desired; and the Zimba's position was improved and he became more insolent than before. . . .

Encounters in the Americas

For many millennia, perhaps beginning as early as 40,000 B.C.E., peoples from Asia crossed the land bridge between northeast Siberia and present-day Alaska. Then after 10,000 B.C.E., as the Ice Age ended and the oceans rose, this link between Eurasia and the Americas was submerged under the Bering Sea, and the peoples of the Americas were cut off from the rest of the world. This isolation ended after 1492, when Europeans and Africans, along with their animals, plants, and pathogens, arrived in the wake of Columbus's first voyage to the New World.

First on Caribbean islands, then in Mexico and Peru, and ultimately throughout the Americas, American Indians after 1492 faced the decision to resist or cooperate with the Europeans. Cooperation usually meant trade, in which Native Americans exchanged dyes, foodstuffs, and furs for hardware, firearms, trinkets, and alcoholic beverages. Cooperation also took the form of military alliances. In Mexico, for example, thousands of warriors fought on Cortés's side against their hated enemy, the Aztecs, while in North America the Hurons allied with the French and the Iroquois allied with the Dutch and later the English in a long series of wars.

Many Native Americans also chose to resist, however, and did so until well into the nineteenth century. In Mexico and Peru, such resistance meant military defeat with Cortés's conquest of the Aztec Empire between 1519 and 1521 and Pizarro's overthrow of the Inca Empire between 1531 and 1533. In North America, Indian raids inflicted considerable casualties and damage on the early European settlements in New England, the middle colonies, and the Chesapeake region. But the colonists' reprisals were equally bloody and destructive, and in conflicts such as the Pequot War (1637) in Connecticut and the Algonquin-Dutch wars (1643–1645) in present-day New York and New Jersey, the Indians were routed and massacred. The long-term outcome of their resistance was never in doubt. The Europeans' single-mindedness and weaponry, when combined with the toll of epidemics from Old World diseases, made their victory inevitable.

The Battle for Tenochtitlán

22 ▾ Bernardino de Sahagún, GENERAL HISTORY OF THE THINGS OF NEW SPAIN

Bernardino de Sahagún (ca. 1499–1590), a member of the Franciscan religious order, was one of the earliest Spanish missionaries in Mexico, arriving in 1529. He soon developed a keen interest in the culture of the peoples of Mexico, for whom he had deep affection and respect. Having mastered the Nahuatl language, spoken by the Aztecs and other central Mexican peoples, he began around 1545 to collect oral and pictorial information about Mexican culture. The result was his *General History of the Things of New Spain*, a major source of information about Mexican culture at the time of the Spanish conquest. Many Spaniards considered Sahagún's work dangerous because they feared that his efforts to preserve the memory of native culture threatened their plans to exploit and Christianize the Indians. As a result, in 1578 his writings and notes were confiscated by royal decree and sent back to Spain, where they gathered dust in an archive until they were rediscovered and published in the nineteenth century.

The following selection comes from the twelfth and last book of the *General History*. Based on interviews with Aztecs who had lived through the conquest some twenty-five years earlier, Book Twelve recounts the conquest of Mexico from the time Cortés arrived on the Mexican coast in April 1519 until the days following the Aztecs' capitulation in August 1521. Although the exact role of Sahagún and his Indian assistants in composing and organizing Book Twelve has been hotly debated by scholars, most agree that it accurately portrays Aztec views and perceptions of the events that unfolded between 1519 and 1521.

The following excerpt picks up the story in November 1519. By then the Spaniards had allied with the Tlaxcalans, the Aztecs' bitter enemies, and were leaving Cholula, a city that the Spaniards and their allies had sacked and looted because of its leaders' lack of cooperation. They were on their way to Tenochtitlán, the splendid Aztec capital on Lake Texcoco, for an anticipated meeting with Emperor Moctezuma.

QUESTIONS FOR ANALYSIS

1. What does the source reveal about the motives of the Spaniards and their Indian allies for their attack on the Aztecs?
2. What was Moctezuma's strategy for dealing with the Spaniards? Why did it fail?
3. Aside from their firearms, what other military advantages did the Spaniards have over their opponents?
4. On several occasions the Aztecs routed the Spaniards. What explains these Aztec victories?
5. How did the Aztec view of war differ from that of the Spaniards?

6. **What does the source reveal about Aztec religious beliefs and values?**
7. **What similarities and differences do you see between the Aztec-Spanish conflict and the armed clashes between the Zimba and the Portuguese (see source 20)?**

And after the dying in Cholula, the Spaniards set off on their way to Mexico,[1] coming gathered and bunched, raising dust. . . .

Thereupon Moteucçoma[2] named and sent noblemen and a great many other agents of his . . . to go meet [Cortés] . . . at Quauhtechcac. They gave [the Spaniards] golden banners of precious feathers, and golden necklaces.

And when they had given the things to them, they seemed to smile, to rejoice and to be very happy. Like monkeys they grabbed the gold. It was as though their hearts were put to rest, brightened, freshened. For gold was what they greatly thirsted for; they were gluttonous for it, starved for it, piggishly wanting it. They came lifting up the golden banners, waving them from side to side, showing them to each other. They seemed to babble; what they said to each other was in a babbling tongue. . . .

Another group of messengers — rainmakers, witches, and priests — had also gone out for an encounter, but nowhere were they able to do anything or to get sight of [the Spaniards]; they did not hit their target, they did not find the people they were looking for, they were not sufficient. . . .

▷ Cortés and his entourage continue their march.

Then they set out in this direction, about to enter Mexico here. Then they all dressed and equipped themselves for war. They girded themselves, tying their battle gear tightly on themselves and then on their horses. Then they arranged themselves in rows, files, ranks.

Four horsemen came ahead going first, staying ahead, leading. . . .

Also the dogs, their dogs, came ahead, sniffing at things and constantly panting.

By himself came marching ahead, all alone, the one who bore the standard on his shoulder. He came waving it about, making it spin, tossing it here and there. . . .

Following him came those with iron swords. Their iron swords came bare and gleaming. On their shoulders they bore their shields, of wood or leather.

The second contingent and file were horses carrying people, each with his cotton cuirass,[3] his leather shield, his iron lance, and his iron sword hanging down from the horse's neck. They came with bells on, jingling or rattling. The horses, the deer,[4] neighed, there was much neighing, and they would sweat a great deal; water seemed to fall from them. And their flecks of foam splatted on the ground, like soapsuds splatting. . . .

The third file were those with iron crossbows, the crossbowmen. Their quivers went hanging at their sides, passed under their armpits, well filled, packed with arrows, with iron bolts. . . .

The fourth file were likewise horsemen; their outfits were the same as has been said.

The fifth group were those with harquebuses,[5] the harquebusiers, shouldering their harquebuses; some held them [level]. And when they went into the great palace, the residence of the ruler, they repeatedly shot off their harquebuses. They exploded, sputtered, discharged, thundered, disgorged. Smoke spread, it grew dark

[1] *Mexico* refers to Tenochtitlán, the capital of the Aztec empire. *Mexica* (pronounced Mezh ee´ ka) refers to the people of Tenochtitlán and Tlatelolco, a suburb of Tenochtitlán.

[2] One of several spellings of the Aztec emperor's name, including Montezuma and Moctezuma.

[3] A piece of armor covering the body from neck to waist.

[4] Having never seen horses, some Aztecs considered them to be large deer.

[5] A heavy matchlock gun that was portable but capable of being fired only with a support.

with smoke, everyplace filled with smoke. The fetid smell made people dizzy and faint.

Then all those from the various altepetl[6] on the other side of the mountains, the Tlaxcalans, the people of Tliliuhquitepec, of Huexotzinco, came following behind. They came outfitted for war with their cotton upper armor, shields, and bows, their quivers full and packed with feathered arrows, some barbed, some blunted, some with obsidian[7] points. They went crouching, hitting their mouths with their hands yelling, singing, . . . whistling, shaking their heads.

Some bore burdens and provisions on their backs; some used tump[8] lines for their forehead, some bands around their chests, some carrying frames, some board cages, some deep baskets. Some made bundles, perhaps putting the bundles on their backs. Some dragged the large cannons, which went resting on wooden wheels, making a clamor as they came.

▷ Cortés and his army entered Tenochtitlán in November 1519 and were amicably received by Moctezuma, who was nonetheless taken captive by the Spaniards. Cortés's army was allowed to remain in a palace compound, but tensions grew the following spring. Pedro de Alvarado, in command while Cortés left to deal with a threat to his authority from the governor of Cuba, became concerned for the Spaniards' safety as the Aztecs prepared to celebrate the annual festival in honor of the god Huitzilopochtli.

And when it had dawned and was already the day of his[9] festivity, very early in the morning those who had made vows to him unveiled his face. Forming a single row before him they offered him incense; each in his place laid down before him offerings of food for fasting and rolled amaranth dough. And it was as though all the youthful warriors had gathered together and had hit on the idea of holding and observing the festivity in order to show the Spaniards something, to make them marvel and instruct them. . . .

When things were already going on, when the festivity was being observed and there was dancing and singing, with voices raised in song, the singing was like the noise of waves breaking against the rocks.

When it was time, when the moment had come for the Spaniards to do the killing, they came out equipped for battle. They came and closed off each of the places where people went in and out. . . . Then they surrounded those who were dancing, going among the cylindrical drums. They struck a drummer's arms; both of his hands were severed. Then they struck his neck; his head landed far away. Then they stabbed everyone with iron lances and struck them with iron swords. They struck some in the belly, and then their entrails came spilling out. They split open the heads of some, they really cut their skulls to pieces, their skulls were cut up into little bits. And if someone still tried to run it was useless; he just dragged his intestines along. There was a stench as if of sulfur. Those who tried to escape could go nowhere. When anyone tried to go out, at the entryways they struck and stabbed him.

And when it became known what was happening, everyone cried out, "Mexica warriors, come running, get outfitted with devices, shields, and arrows, hurry, come running, the warriors are dying; they have died, perished, been annihilated, O Mexica warriors!" Thereupon there were war cries, shouting, and beating of hands against lips. The warriors quickly came outfitted, bunched together, carrying arrows and shields. Then the fighting began; they shot at them with barbed darts, spears, and tridents, and they hurled darts with broad obsidian points at them.

[6]The Nahuatl term for any sovereign state, especially for the local ethnic states of central Mexico.

[7]A volcanic glass, generally black.

[8]A strap or sling passed around the chest or forehead to help support a pack being carried on a person's back.

[9]A reference to the god Huitzilopochtli. An image of the god, made from amaranth seed flour and the blood of recently sacrificed victims, played a central role in the festival.

▷ The fighting drove the Spaniards and their allies back to the palace enclave. Without a reliable supply of food and water, in July 1520 Cortés, who had returned with his power intact, led his followers on a desperate nocturnal escape from the city, but they were discovered and suffered heavy losses. They retreated to the other side of the lake, and the Aztecs believed the Spanish threat had passed.

Before the Spanish appeared to us, first an epidemic broke out, a sickness of pustules.[10] . . . Large bumps spread on people; some were entirely covered. They spread everywhere, on the face, the head, the chest, etc. The disease brought great desolation; a great many died of it. They could no longer walk about, but lay in their dwellings and sleeping places, no longer able to move or stir. They were unable to change position, to stretch out on their sides or face down, or raise their heads. And when they made a motion, they called out loudly. The pustules that covered people caused great desolation; very many people died of them, and many just starved to death; starvation reigned, and no one took care of others any longer.

On some people, the pustules appeared only far apart, and they did not suffer greatly, nor did many of them die of it. But many people's faces were spoiled by it, their faces and noses were made rough. Some lost an eye or were blinded.

This disease of pustules lasted a full sixty days; after sixty days it abated and ended. When people were convalescing and reviving, the pustules disease began to move in the direction of the Chalco.[11] And many were disabled or paralyzed by it, but they were not disabled forever. . . . The Mexica warriors were greatly weakened by it.

And when things were in this state, the Spaniards came, moving toward us from Tetzcoco. . . .

▷ Having resupplied his Spanish/Tlaxcalan army and having constructed a dozen cannon-carrying brigantines for use on the lake, Cortés resumed his offensive late in 1520. In April 1521 he reached Tenochtitlán and placed the city under a blockade.

The Tlatelolca fought in Çoquipan, in war boats. And in Xoloco the Spaniards came to a place where there was a wall in the middle of the road, blocking it. They fired the big guns at it. At the first shot it did not give way, but the second time it began to crumble. The third time, at last parts of it fell to the ground, and the fourth time finally the wall went to the ground once and for all. . . .

Once they got two of their boats into the canal at Xocotitlan. When they had beached them, then they went looking into the house sites of the people of Xocotitlan. But Tzilacatzin and some other warriors who saw the Spaniards immediately came out to face them; they came running after them, throwing stones at them, and they scattered the Spaniards into the water. . . .

When they got to Tlilhuacan, the warriors crouched far down and hid themselves, hugging the ground, waiting for the war cry, when there would be shouting and cries of encouragement. When the cry went up, "O Mexica, up and at them!" the Tlappanecatl Ecatzin, a warrior of Otomi[12] rank, faced the Spaniards and threw himself at them, saying, "O Tlatelolca warriors, up and at them, who are these barbarians? Come running!" Then he went and threw a Spaniard down, knocking him to the ground; the one he threw down was the one who came first, who came leading them. And when he had thrown him down, he dragged the Spaniard off.

And at this point they let loose with all the warriors who had been crouching there; they

[10]The disease was smallpox.
[11]A city on the southeast corner of Lake Texcoco.
[12]Elite warriors bound by oath never to retreat.

came out and chased the Spaniards in the passageways, and when the Spaniards saw it the Mexica seemed to be intoxicated. The captives were taken. Many Tlaxcalans, and people of Acolhuacan, Chalco, Xochimilco, etc., were captured. A great abundance were captured and killed. . . .

Then they took the captives to Yacacolco, hurrying them along, going along herding their captives together. Some went weeping, some singing, some went shouting while hitting their hands against their mouths. When they got them to Yacacolco, they lined them all up. Each one went to the altar platform where the sacrifice was performed. The Spaniards went first, going in the lead; the people of the different altepetl just followed, coming last. And when the sacrifice was over, they strung the Spaniards' heads on poles on skull racks; they also strung up the horses' heads. They placed them below, and the Spaniards' heads were above them, strung up facing east. . . .

▷ Despite this victory, the Aztecs could not overcome the problems of shortages of food, water, and warriors. In mid July 1521 the Spaniards and their allies resumed their assault, and in early August the Aztecs decided to send into battle a quetzal-owl warrior, whose success or failure, it was believed, would reveal if the gods wished the Aztecs to continue fighting.

And all the common people suffered greatly. There was famine; many died of hunger. They no longer drank good, pure water, but the water they drank was salty. Many people died of it, and because of it many got dysentery and died. Everything was eaten: lizards, swallows, maize, straw, grass that grows on salt flats. And they chewed at wood, glue flowers, plaster, leather, and deerskin, which they roasted, baked, and toasted so that they could eat them, and they ground up medicinal herbs and adobe bricks. There had never been the like of such suffering. The siege was frightening, and great numbers died of hunger. . . .

And . . . the ruler Quauhtemoctzin[13] and the warriors Coyohuehuetzin, Temilotzin, Topantemoctzin, the Mixcoatlailotlac Ahuelitoctzin, Tlacotzin, and Petlauhtzin took a great warrior named Tlapaltecatl Opochtzin . . . and outfitted him, dressing him in a quetzal-owl costume. . . . When they put it on him he looked very frightening and splendid. . . . They gave him the darts of the devil,[14] darts of wooden rods with flint tips. And the reason they did this was that it was as though the fate of the rulers of the Mexica were being determined.

When our enemies saw him, it was as though a mountain had fallen. Every one of the Spaniards was frightened; he intimidated them, they seemed to respect him a great deal. Then the quetzal-owl climbed up on the roof. But when some of our enemies had taken a good look at him they rose and turned him back, pursuing him. Then the quetzal-owl turned them again and pursued them. Then he snatched up the precious feathers and gold and dropped down off the roof. He did not die, and our enemies did not carry him off. Also three of our enemies were captured. At that the war stopped for good. There was silence, nothing more happened. Then our enemies went away. It was silent and nothing more happened until it got dark.

And the next day nothing more happened at all, no one made a sound. The common people just lay collapsed. The Spaniards did nothing more either, but lay still, looking at the people. Nothing was going on, they just lay still. . . .

▷ Two weeks passed before the Aztecs capitulated on August 13, 1521.

[13]Quauhtemoctzin was now the Aztec emperor.

[14]Darts sacred to Huitzilopochtli.

Conflict in New Netherland

23 ▾ David Pieterzen DeVries, VOYAGES FROM HOLLAND TO AMERICA

As a result of the efforts of Henry Hudson, who in 1609 explored what is now New York Harbor and the Hudson River, the Dutch claimed New Netherland, an area that included Long Island, eastern New York, and parts of New Jersey and Connecticut. To encourage colonization, the Dutch government granted wealthy colonists huge tracts of land, known as patroonships, with the understanding that each patroon would settle at least fifty tenants on the land within four years. At first, relations with the Algonquins and Raritans in the area around New Amsterdam (present-day New York City) were generally cordial, but they deteriorated after the arrival of Willem Kieft as governor in 1642. He sought to tax the Algonquins to pay for the construction of a fort and attempted to force them off their land to create new patroonships, even though few of them had attracted the minimum number of tenants. When the Algonquins resisted, Kieft ordered the massacre described by David DeVries in the following excerpt from his *Voyages from Holland to America*. Born in Rochelle, France, in 1592 or 1593, DeVries spent most of his life as a merchant in the Netherlands before becoming a patroon in the Dutch colony in the early 1640s.

QUESTIONS FOR ANALYSIS

1. Why does DeVries oppose the governor's plan to attack the Algonquins?
2. What does this suggest about DeVries's attitude toward the Native Americans?
3. How did the Algonquins react immediately after the massacre?
4. What does the Algonquins' behavior suggest about their early relations with the Dutch?
5. What were the long-term results of the massacre?

The 24th of February, sitting at a table with the Governor, he [Governor Kieft] began to state his intentions, that he had a mind to *wipe the mouths* of the savages; that he had been dining at the house of Jan Claesen Damen, where Maryn Adriaensen and Jan Claesen Damen, together with Jacob Planck, had presented a petition to him to begin this work. I answered him that they were not wise to request this; that such work could not be done without the approbation of the Twelve Men;[1] that it could not take place without my assent, who was one of the Twelve Men; that moreover I was the first patroon, and no one else hitherto had risked there so many thousands, and also his person, as I was the first to come from Holland or Zeeland to plant a colony; and that he should consider what profit he could derive from this business, as he well

[1]The board of directors responsible for governing New Netherland.

knew that on account of trifling with the Indians we had lost our colony in the South River at Swanendael, in the Hoere-kil, with thirty-two men, who were murdered in the year 1630; and that in the year 1640, the cause of my people being murdered on Staten Island was a difficulty which he had brought on with the Raritan Indians, where his soldiers had for some trifling thing killed some savages. . . . But it appeared that my speaking was of no avail. He had, with his co-murderers, determined to commit the murder, deeming it a Roman deed,[2] and to do it without warning the inhabitants in the open lands [so] that each one might take care of himself against the retaliation of the savages, for he could not kill all the Indians. When I had expressed all these things in full, sitting at the table, and the meal was over, he told me he wished me to go to the large hall, which he had been lately adding to his house. Coming to it, there stood all his soldiers ready to cross the river to Pavonia to commit the murder. Then spoke I again to Governor Willem Kieft: "Let this work alone; you wish to break the mouths of the Indians, but you will also murder our own nation, for there are none of the settlers in the open country who are aware of it. My own dwelling, my people, cattle, corn, and tobacco will be lost." He answered me, assuring me that there would be no danger; that some soldiers should go to my house to protect it. But that was not done. So was this business begun between the 25th and 26th of February in the year 1643. I remained that night at the Governor's, sitting up. I went and sat by the kitchen fire, when about midnight I heard a great shrieking, and I ran to the ramparts of the fort, and looked over to Pavonia. Saw nothing but firing, and heard the shrieks of the savages murdered in their sleep. I returned again to the house by the fire. Having sat there awhile, there came an Indian with his squaw, whom I knew well, and who lived about an hour's walk from my house, and told me that they had fled in a small skiff, which they had taken from the shore at Pavonia; that the Indians from Fort Orange had surprised them; and that they had come to conceal themselves in the fort. I told them that they must go away immediately; that this was no time for them to come to the fort to conceal themselves; that they who had killed their people at Pavonia were not Indians, but the Swannekens, as they call the Dutch, had done it. They then asked me how they should get out of the fort. I took them to the door, and there was no sentry there, and so they betook themselves to the woods. When it was day the soldiers returned to the fort, having massacred or murdered eighty Indians, and considering they had done a deed of Roman valor, in murdering so many in their sleep; where infants were torn from their mothers' breasts, and hacked to pieces in the presence of the parents, and the pieces thrown into the fire and in the water, and other sucklings, being bound to small boards, were cut, stuck, and pierced, and miserably massacred in a manner to move a heart of stone. Some were thrown into the river, and when the fathers and mothers endeavored to save them, the soldiers would not let them come on land but made both parents and children drown — children from five to six years of age, and also some old and decrepit persons. Those who fled from this onslaught, and concealed themselves in the neighboring sedge [marsh grass], and when it was morning, came out to beg a piece of bread, and to be permitted to warm themselves, were murdered in cold blood and tossed into the fire or the water. Some came to our people in the country with their hands, some with their legs cut off, and some holding their entrails in their arms, and others had such horrible cuts and gashes, that worse than they were could never happen. And these poor simple creatures, as also many of our own people, did not know any better than that they had been attacked by a party of other Indians — the Maquas. After this exploit, the soldiers were rewarded for their services, and Director Kieft thanked them by taking them by the hand and congratulating them. At another

[2]A glorious deed in the manner of the ancient Romans.

place, on the same night, on Corler's Hook near Corler's plantation, forty Indians were in the same manner attacked in their sleep, and massacred there in the same manner. Did the Duke of Alva[3] in the Netherlands ever do anything more cruel? This is indeed a disgrace to our nation, who have so generous a governor in our Fatherland as the Prince of Orange,[4] who has always endeavored in his wars to spill as little blood as possible. As soon as the savages understood that the Swannekens had so treated them, all the men whom they could surprise on the farmlands, they killed; but we have never heard that they have ever permitted women or children to be killed. They burned all the houses, farms, barns, grain, haystacks, and destroyed everything they could get hold of. So there was an open destructive war begun. They also burnt my farm, cattle, corn, barn, tobacco-house, and all the tobacco. My people saved themselves in the house where I alone lived, which was made with embrasures, through which they defended themselves. Whilst my people were in alarm the savage whom I had aided to escape from the fort in the night came there, and told the other Indians that I was a good chief, that I had helped him out of the fort, and that the killing of the Indians took place contrary to my wish. Then they all cried out together to my people that they would not shoot them; that if they had not destroyed my cattle they would not do it, nor burn my house; that they would let my little brewery stand, though they wished to get the copper kettle, in order to make darts for their arrows; but hearing now that it had been done contrary to my wish, they all went away, and left my house unbesieged. When now the Indians had destroyed so many farms and men in revenge for their people, I went to Governor Willem Kieft, and asked him if it was not as I had said it would be, that he would only effect the spilling of Christian blood. Who would now compensate us for our losses? But he gave me no answer. He said he wondered that no Indians came to the fort. I told him that I did not wonder at it; "why should the Indians come here where you have so treated them?"

[3]Spanish general in the service of Philip II of Spain responsible for carrying out harsh anti-Protestant measures in the Netherlands in the 1560s.

[4]Frederick Henry, *stadholder,* or elected executive and military commander of the Netherlands.

Land and Labor in Spanish America

Throughout its more than 300 years of existence, Spain's empire in the Americas was based on the exploitation of Native Americans. Such exploitation began in the 1490s when Columbus sought to establish a settlement on Hispaniola, an island he discovered in 1492. The first Spanish settlers were determined to enrich themselves, and this spelled disaster for the island's Arawaks, who were robbed of their food, forced to work as slaves in the Spaniards' homes, fields, and mines as slaves, and, in the case of women, sexually abused. In 1497 Columbus attempted to curb the rapaciousness of his countrymen by allocating groups of Arawaks to individual Spaniards, who could demand tribute and labor from these Indians and these Indians alone. Abuses continued, however, and in 1512 the Crown issued the Laws of Burgos, which sought to regulate the treatment of Indians. Rea-

sonable labor expectations, adequate food and housing, and restrictions on punishments were among the set of laws' many provisions. The laws were impossible to enforce, and by the mid 1500s were irrelevant. By then slaves from Africa were doing the Spaniards' work on Hispaniola. The Arawaks, who numbered between 300,000 and 400,000 in 1492, had virtually disappeared as a result of agricultural disruption, excessive labor, and epidemics.

Elsewhere in Spanish America the effects of forced labor were less catastrophic, but economic realities were no different. Without cheap labor and tribute from the Indians, none of the Spaniards' objectives — income for the Crown, profit for individual Spanish landowners and merchants, and winning souls to Christ — could be attained. Although this rarely meant enslavement, Indians could be assigned to an individual Spaniard, or *encomendero*, who in the *encomienda* system could demand tribute and labor from the Indians assigned to him in return for protection and religious instruction. Indians also could be required to pay tribute to the state or be subjected to state-controlled labor drafts (*repartimiento*). Some Indians were forced to accept pittance wages for their work in the open market.

Reliance on native labor was a perplexing and hotly debated topic among Spanish settlers, clergy, and royal officials. Through what mechanisms should the Indians be compelled to work for the Spaniards? What kind of work could they reasonably be asked to do? What responsibilities did Spaniards have to protect Indians from mistreatment and abuse? Most fundamentally, how was it possible to reconcile the need to compel Indians to work with the Spaniards' responsibility to convert them to Christianity, civilize them, and treat them as human beings? The Spaniards never found satisfactory answers to these questions, even after 300 years of colonial rule.

Indian Labor and Tribute in Mexico

24 ▾ *Alonso de Zorita, THE BRIEF AND SUMMARY RELATION OF THE LORDS OF NEW SPAIN*

As the Spanish Empire expanded from the Caribbean islands to Mexico and Central and South America, the debate over Spain's Indian policy continued unabated. Despite the reservations of royal officials and the failure of the system on Hispaniola, Cortés, the conqueror of the Aztecs, established a version of the *encomienda* system in Mexico when he assigned the rights to Indian tribute and labor to his soldiers. With little legislative guidance or judicial oversight, abuses were inevitable. In response, pro-Indian reformers, many drawn from the Catholic religious orders, sought the suppression of the encomiendas and the end of all forms of Indian servitude. These reformers were opposed by the encomenderos, some Spanish officials, and a number of churchmen who staunchly defended their rights to Indian labor and tribute.

In the 1520s and 1530s, the royal government pursued a middle course in this debate, allowing the encomienda system to continue but trying to regulate it to protect the Indians. Then in 1542 the Crown issued the New Laws, a comprehensive legal code for Spanish America that addressed Indian issues in twenty-three of its fifty-four articles. It prohibited the future enslavement of Indians, ordered the release of slaves if owners could not provide documentary proof of ownership, established further regulations for tribute, and ordered that all encomienda agreements were to lapse after the deaths of current holders. The New Laws set off a storm of protest from encomenderos, and the Crown had no choice but to back down from some of its provisions, including the abolition of the encomiendas themselves. Thus, the *encomienda* system survived until the eighteenth century, but legislation continued to whittle away at the encomenderos' privileges, gradually transferring the assessment and collection of Indian tribute to royal officials.

To enforce these and other laws pertaining to life in the Americas, the Crown established a system of courts that ranged from small regional courts to *audiencias*, which served as supreme courts in their administrative districts. Staffed by royal appointees who served both as judges and as advisors to regional administrators, audiencias were probably the most important single civil institution in the Spanish American colonies.

In the midst of the debate over the New Laws, a young Spanish lawyer, Alonso de Zorita, arrived in the New World to serve as *odior*, or judge, in the Audiencia of Santo Domingo on the island of Hispaniola. This graduate of the University of Salamanca spent the next twenty years as judge in Spanish America, with postings in Guatemala, the region of present-day Colombia, and Mexico City. Although he handed down stiff penalties to Indians in several cases, he was known as a defender of Indian rights and an adversary of the encomenderos, whose campaign against him probably caused his reassignment from Guatemala to Mexico City in 1556. With his hearing failing, he returned to Spain in 1566 and died there sometime in the 1580s. In his retirement he maintained an interest in American affairs and also wrote several lengthy works, including *The Brief and Summary Relation of the Lords of New Spain*. Begun during his tenure in Mexico as a report requested by the Crown on Indian conditions, the manuscript probably was completed around 1570 and sent to members of the Council of the Indies, the supreme governing council of Spain's empire. Although several laws issued in the late 1500s resemble suggestions made by Zorita in his book, a direct influence cannot be proved. Several manuscript versions of the work existed in various European libraries, but the work did not appear in print until the 1800s.

Because Zorita was an advocate of Indian rights, it is legitimate to raise the question of the book's objectivity and accuracy. The scholarly consensus is that he presented an overly idyllic picture of preconquest Mexico but that his portrayal of the Indians' plight under the Spaniards, although written with intense feeling, is not distorted. Certainly evidence of the practices he describes can be found in court records and the works of many contemporaries.

QUESTIONS FOR ANALYSIS

1. Based on Zorita's account, enumerate the ways in which Spaniards depended on the Indians to generate wealth for private individuals and colonial administrators.
2. What evidence does Zorita provide of the royal government's efforts to protect the Indians from abuse and excessive exploitation?
3. According to Zorita, why did such efforts fail?
4. According to Zorita, why did Indian efforts to redress grievances also fail?
5. According to Zorita, what was the effect of Spanish policies on Indian family life and, more generally, on Indian society?
6. How does Zorita characterize the encomenderos?
7. How did the requirement that Indians pay their tribute in silver money cause hardship for the Indians?

INDIAN LABOR

It is said that the Indians are being worked to death cultivating fields for their caciques and principales,[1] and enriching these lords, but those who say this are very mistaken. . . .

Others say that drunkenness is the cause of their dying out, because many do die of it, and they kill one another when they are drunk. But this conclusion too is erroneous, for the same condition exists in other places where the people are not dying out. . . .

Neither drunkenness nor their well-organized communal labor is killing them off. The cause is their labor on Spanish public works and their personal service to the Spaniards, which they fulfill in a manner contrary to their own ways and tempo of work. . . .

Their numbers have . . . been diminished by their enslavement for work in the mines and in the personal service of the Spaniards. In the first years there was such haste to make slaves that they poured into Mexico City from all directions, and throughout the Indies they were taken in flocks like sheep to be branded. The Spaniards pressed the Indian lords to bring in all the slaves, and such was the Indians' fear that to satisfy the Spaniards they brought their own vassals and even their own children when they had no others to offer. Much the same thing happens today in the provision of Indians for the Spaniards' service, and in the enslavement of Indians on the pretext that they had risen in rebellion, contrary to Your Majesty's orders.

They have been reduced by the thousands by their toil in the gold and silver mines; and on the journey to the mines 80 or 100 leagues[2] away they were loaded with heavy burdens to which they were not accustomed. They died in the mines or along the road, of hunger and cold or extreme heat, and from carrying enormous loads of implements for the mines or other extremely heavy things; for the Spaniards, not satisfied with taking them so far away to work, must load them down on the way. . . .

The Spaniards still compel the Indians to go to the mines on the pretext that they are being sent to construct buildings there and are going

---

[1]*Caciques* (pronounced kah´ si kays) was originally an Arawakian word borrowed by the Spaniards to designate Native American chiefs; *principales* (pronounced prin si pah´ lays) refers to descendants of the Aztec warrior aristocracy and certain community officials. Neither term does justice to the complexities of pre- and postconquest Mesoamerican society.

[2]A measure of distance used in Spain and Spanish America. It was approximately the distance a man or horse could walk in an hour, approximately three miles.

voluntarily; these Spaniards claim that Your Majesty does not prohibit such labor, but only forbids work in the mines. In actual fact the Indians never go voluntarily, for they are forced to go under the repartimiento system by order of the Audiencia, contrary to Your Majesty's orders.

They have also been exhausted by the long journeys they have had to make, a thousand carriers at a time, sometimes more, sometimes less, carrying backbreaking loads of merchandise for days on end. . . .

The Spaniards also loaded them down with their household furnishings, beds, chairs, tables, and all the other appointments for their household and kitchen service. Thus weighted down, women and boys as well as children, they trudged over field and mountain, and returned to their homes half dead, or died on the way. . . .

The Indians have also been laid low by the labor of making sheep, cattle, and pig farms, of fencing these farms, of putting up farm buildings, and by their labor on roads, bridges, watercourses, stone walls, and sugar mills. For this labor, in which they were occupied for many days and weeks, they were taken away from their homes, their accustomed tempo of work and mode of life were disrupted. . . .

Now they are paid, but so little that they cannot buy enough to eat, for they are still used for such labor with permission from the Audiencias. . . .

Yet another multitude has been killed off and continues to be killed off by being taken as carriers on conquests and expeditions, and still others to serve the soldiers. They were taken from their homes by force and separated from their women and children and kin, and few if any returned, for they perished in the conquests or along the roads, or died on their return home. . . .

I could mention other things that are causing the extinction of these wretched people, but the great increase in the number of farms owned by Spaniards is in itself a sufficient cause. Ten, fifteen, and twenty years ago there were fewer farms, and there were many more Indians. The Indians were forced to work on them and suffered hardships therefrom, but since they were many and the farms few, it was not so noticeable. Now the Spanish farms are many and large and the Indians very few, and they must clear, cultivate, and weed as well as harvest and store the crops, so that all this labor now falls on the few that remain. . . .

Since the Spanish construction projects, farms, ranches, and herds are so numerous and large, the Audiencias outdo themselves dispatching orders to the corregidores and alcaldes mayores[3] to provide Indian laborers for the Spaniards. These officials fully understand the injury this is causing and know that the Indians are dying out, but their only concern is to aid the Spaniards. . . .

. . . The wishes of Your Majesty and his Royal Council are well known and are made very plain in the laws that are issued every day in favor of the poor Indians and for their increase and preservation. But these laws are obeyed and not enforced,[4] wherefore there is no end to the destruction of the Indians, nor does anyone care what Your Majesty decrees. . . .

Indeed, the more laws and decrees are sent, the worse is the condition of the Indians by reason of the false and sophistical interpretation that the Spanish officials give these laws, twisting their meaning to suit their own purposes. It seems to me that the saying of a certain philosopher well applies to this case: Where there is a plenty of doctors and medicines, there is a plenty of ill health. Just so, where there are many laws and judges, there is much injustice.

INDIAN TRIBUTE

The first assessment was made by the Bishop of Mexico, who came with the title of Protector of the

[3]*Corregidores* were Spanish magistrates; *alcades mayores* were Indian village leaders.

[4]A reference to the Spanish phrase *Obedezco pero no cumplo*, a formula employed by Spanish officials when a royal order was inconvenient or unenforceable.

Indians.[5] . . . There were great frauds connected with this assessment, because many caciques and principales, fearing their encomenderos or wishing to please them, declared that the Indians could pay the amounts they were paying. Under pressure from their encomenderos, these caciques even overstated the amounts the Indians were paying, so that if some reduction were made, the assessment would remain what it had been.

Since that time the Audiencia and some visitadores[6] have made other assessments. Because the first ones were so high, these officials thought they were doing the Indians a great favor by reducing the amounts slightly. As a result of failure to solve the problem once and for all, the Indians constantly clamor for relief from their heavy burdens. The Audiencia has sometimes lowered the assessments, sometimes raised them. In recent years the frauds and tricks practiced by the Spaniards have led to the increase or even doubling of the assessments, thus returning them to their former level or slightly below. This is the cause of the constant comings and goings of the Indians to and from the Audiencia, in which they waste their money and even lose their lives, but never obtain justice. . . .

The system . . . has another defect, which is that the tribute is per capita. The number of Indians daily grows less, but the tribute remains the same. To be sure, the law makes provision for a reduction of tribute in such cases, but the law is not complied with. The Indians, being generally a people of great simplicity, do not know how to demand their rights and so bear their woes in silence. If some of them . . . do complain in the name of all, this leads to another evil, namely, that the Indians squander their lives and money in suits, and all the while continue to pay tribute according to the first count. In the end they never obtain justice, for they drop the suit because they have run out of money or the encomenderos have bribed their leaders; or their leaders may have died; or they may be unable to prove that some of their people have fled or died, or that there was an error in the count. . . .

Your Majesty has also ordered that assessments should be made, not on the basis of reports concerning the capacity to pay of the towns, but on the basis of personal observation and study of the character and capacities of each town, the fertility of its soil, and the like, in order that a just assessment may be made and each Indian may be made to understand precisely what he owes and is obliged to give, so much and no more. Your Majesty has also decreed that the Indians . . . should give only those things that are found in their native lands and regions and that they can easily obtain, namely, the produce of their fields or the products of their crafts. . . . Your Majesty has also ordered that the Indians must not be made to pay up to the limits of their capacity, that they should be allowed to get richer and not poorer, that they should be left with enough to take care of their needs, cure their ills, and marry off their children, and that they should enjoy rest and repose, with due regard for their preservation, increase, and religious instruction. . . .

. . . Many penalties, including loss of encomiendas, are prescribed for violation of these orders, but all of them together have not secured compliance. . . .

Throughout the Indies the natives are dying out and declining in number, though some assert that this is not so. Since the Indians are so heavily burdened with tribute payments that they cannot support themselves and their wives and children, they often leave them (although they loved them dearly), and abandon their wretched little homes and their fields. They depart for some other region and wander about from place to place or flee to the woods, where jaguars or other beasts eat them. Some Indians have hanged themselves in desperation because

[5]Juan de Zumárrago (1468–1548), a Spanish Franciscan.

[6]Spanish administrators who "visited" Indian villages to collect data on population and other matters.

of the great hardships they suffer on account of the tribute. . . .

As I said before, the Indians have little stamina. As a result, an Indian's planting is so small that his harvest will barely cover his needs for the year, for he cannot cultivate an area larger than the little plot that he and his wife and children (if he has them) can work. From this harvest half a fanega[7] of maize is taken for tribute. This amount is taken in good and bad years alike . . . . One might think they would not miss half a fanega, but it is a great deal to them because of their small harvest. Maize is their staff of life, the source of their food and clothing, and if they do not grow it themselves, they have no means of obtaining it. Consequently, if the crop fails, they suffer from famine and eat herbs, roots, and fruit that rot their guts. . . . They have very little food other than maize, for in general they are all very poor. . . . though some have a piece of farm land around their houses. For the rest, an Indian has a very sorry mantle [cloak] with which he covers himself, a sleeping mat, a stone to grind maize . . . and a few chickens. . . . The value of the whole may come to 10 pesos,[8] and not all possess even this much. Consequently, the tribute they pay and the means to support themselves and their families come from their labor alone.

To ask the Indians for tribute in reales is also a great injury to them. Unless an Indian lives in a town not far from a Spanish town, or on a main traveled road, or raises cacao[9] or cotton, or makes cotton cloth, or raises fruit, he does not receive money. There are regions where the Indians have never seen a real in all their lives, and do not even know what a real is. In order to earn money, therefore, they must quit their towns and homes, leaving their wives and children without means of support, and go 30, 40, and even more leagues to climates different from their own, where they sometimes lose their lives. Sometimes in their despair they prefer not to return home, or perhaps one will take to living with another woman and lead a depraved life, leaving all the burdens of supporting his family to his poor wife.

If an Indian cannot pay the money tribute because he lacks the means, or does not know where to go to earn reales, goes to jail and his time at forced labor is sold to some Spaniard to cover the tribute and jailer's costs. He must toil for two, three, or four months or even longer, according to what he owes and what he is paid for his work, because he has no property that can be seized and sold by the authorities. . . .

[7]A dry measure of approximately 1.5 bushels.

[8]*Peso* was a name of a coin equal to eight *reales*. In 1537 King Charles I set the weight of a peso at just under 27.47 grams, slightly less than an ounce. In comparison, an American penny weighs 2.5 grams.

[9]The bean from the cacao plant is used to make cocoa and chocolate. The cacao bean was a form of currency before the conquest.

The "Mountain of Silver" and the Mita System

25 ▾ *Antonio Vazquez de Espinosa, COMPENDIUM AND DESCRIPTION OF THE WEST INDIES*

In 1545 an Indian herder lost his footing on a mountain in the eastern range of the Andes while chasing a llama. To keep from falling, he grabbed a bush, which he uprooted to reveal a rich vein of silver. This is one story of how the world learned of the world's richest silver mine, at Potosí, in present-day Bolivia. Located two

miles above sea level in a cold, desolate region, Potosí became the site of the Western Hemisphere's first mining boomtown. By 1600 Potosí had a population of 150,000 (more than half of whom were Indians), making it the largest, wildest, gaudiest city in the New World. With one-fifth of its silver going to the Spanish crown, Potosí had a major impact on the European Wars of Religion, in that it bankrolled the Spanish military campaigns against the Protestants, and on world trade, since its silver was used by Europeans to purchase goods in India, Southeast Asia, and China.

The backbone of the Potosí operation was a system of government-controlled draft labor known as the *repartimiento*, which was practiced in Mexico and other parts of Spanish America. In Peru it was referred to as the *mita* (Quechua for "time" or "distribution"), a term used by the Incas for their preconquest system of required state labor. In the repartimiento and mita systems, native communities were required to supply a portion of their population at fixed intervals for assignment to particular tasks. In theory, required work was distributed evenly throughout each community, and an individual might go months or even years without being called for labor service.

The following description of the mita system is provided by Antonio Vazquez de Espinosa (d. 1630), a Spanish Carmelite friar who abandoned an academic career to perform priestly work in the Americas. During his retirement in the 1620s, he wrote several books on Spanish America and his experiences as a priest. His best-known work is *Compendium and Description of the West Indies*, which recorded his observations of conditions in Mexico and Spanish South America. In this excerpt he describes mercury mining at Huancavelica and the "mountain of silver" at Potosí.

QUESTIONS FOR ANALYSIS

1. What was the range of annual wages for each laborer at Huancavelica? How do their wages compare with the annual salary of the royal hospital chaplain? How does the sum of the workers' annual wages compare with the cost of tallow candles at Potosí? Compare the wages of the mita workers at Potosí with the wages paid those Native Americans who freely hired themselves out. What do you conclude from all these figures?
2. What were the major hazards connected with the extraction and production of mercury and silver?
3. What evidence does this source provide of Spanish concern for the welfare of the Indian workers? What evidence of indifference does it provide? Where does the weight of the evidence seem to lie?
4. What does the document tell us about the impact of the mita system on native society?
5. What similarities and differences do you see between the Mexican repartimiento described by Zorita (source 24) and the mita described by Vazquez?

HUANCAVELICA

. . . It contains 400 Spanish residents, as well as many temporary shops of dealers in merchandise and groceries, heads of trading houses, and transients, for the town has a lively commerce. It has a parish church . . . a Dominican convent, and a Royal Hospital under the Brethren of San Juan de Diós for the care of the sick, especially Indians on the range; it has a chaplain with a salary of 800 pesos[1] contributed by His Majesty; he is curate of the parish of San Sebastian de Indios, for the Indians who have come to work in the mines and who have settled down there. . . .

Every two months His Majesty sends by the regular courier from Lima[2] 60,000 pesos to pay for the mita of the Indians, for the crews are changed every two months, so that merely for the Indian mita payment . . . 360,000 pesos are sent from Lima every year, not to speak of much besides, which all crosses . . . that cold and desolate mountain country which . . . has nothing on it but llama ranches.

Up on the range there are 3,000 or 4,000 Indians working in the mine; it is colder up there than in the town, since it is higher. The mine where the mercury is located is a large layer which they keep following downward. When I was in that town [in 1616] I went up on the range and down into the mine, which at that time was considerably more than 130 stades[3] deep. The ore was very rich black flint, and the excavation so extensive that it held more than 3,000 Indians working away hard with picks and hammers, breaking up that flint ore; and when they have filled their little sacks, the poor fellows, loaded down with ore, climb up those ladders or rigging, some like masts and others like cables, and so trying and distressing that a man empty-handed can hardly get up them. . . . Nor is that the greatest evil and difficulty; that is due to thievish and undisciplined superintendents. As that great vein of ore keeps going down deeper and they follow its rich trail, in order to make sure that no section of that ore shall drop on top of them, they keep leaving supports or pillars of the ore itself, even if of the richest quality, and they necessarily help to sustain and insure each section with less risk. This being so, there are men so heartless that for the sake of stealing a little rich ore, they go down out of hours and deprive the innocent Indians of this protection by hollowing into these pillars to steal the rich ore in them, and then a great section is apt to fall in and kill all the Indians, and sometimes the unscrupulous and grasping superintendents themselves . . . and much of this is kept quiet so that it shall not come to the notice of the manager and cause the punishment of the accomplices. . . .

. . . On the other side of the town there are structures where they grind up the mercury ore and then put it in jars with . . . many little holes . . . and a channel for it to drip into and pass into the jar or place where it is to fall. Then they roast the ore with a straw fire. . . . Under the onset of this fire it melts and the mercury goes up in vapor or exhalation until, passing through the holes in the first mold, it hits the body of the second, and there it coagulates, rests, and comes to stop where they have provided lodging for it; but if it does not strike any solid body while it is hot, it rises as vapor until it cools and coagulates and starts falling downward again. Those who carry out the reduction of this ore have to be very careful and test cautiously; they must wait till the jars are cold before uncovering them for otherwise they may easily get mercury poisoning and if they do, they are of no further use; their teeth fall out, and some die.

---

[1]See source 24, note 8.

[2]The capital city of the Viceroyalty of Peru, one of the two major administrative units of Spanish America covering all of South America except part of the Caribbean coast.

[3]A measure of length, approximately 200 feet.

POTOSÍ

According to His Majesty's warrant, the mine owners on this massive range have a right to the mita of 13,300 Indians in the working and exploitation of the mines. . . . It is the duty of the Corregidor[4] of Potosí to have them rounded up and to see that they come in from all the provinces between Cuzco over the whole of El Collao and as far as the frontiers of Tarija and Tomina;[5] this Potosí Corregidor has power and authority over all the Corregidors in those provinces mentioned; for if they do not fill the Indian mita allotment assigned each of them in accordance with the capacity of their provinces as indicated to them, he can send them, and does, salaried inspectors to report upon it, and when the remissness is great or remarkable, he can suspend them, notifying the Viceroy[6] of the fact.

These Indians are sent out every year under a captain whom they choose in each village or tribe, for him to take them and oversee them for the year each has to serve; every year they have a new election, for as some go out, others come in. This works out very badly, with great losses and gaps in the quotas of Indians, the villages being depopulated; and this gives rise to great extortions and abuses on the part of the inspectors toward the poor Indians, ruining them and thus depriving the . . . chief Indians of their property and carrying them off in chains because they do not fill out the mita assignment, which they cannot do, for the reason given and for others which I do not bring forward.

These 13,300 are divided up every 4 months into 3 mitas, each consisting of 4,433 Indians, to work in the mines on the range and in the 120 smelters in the Potosí and Tarapaya areas; it is a good league [about three miles] between the two. These mita Indians earn each day, or there is paid each one for his labor, 4 reals.[7] Besides these there are others not under obligation, who . . . hire themselves out voluntarily: these each get from 12 to 16 reals, and some up to 24, according to their reputation of wielding the pick and knowing how to get the ore out. These . . . will be over 4,000 in number. They and the mita Indians go up every Monday morning to the locality of Guayna Potosí which is at the foot of the range; the Corregidor arrives with all the provincial captains or chiefs who have charge of the Indians assigned them, and he there checks off and reports to each mine and smelter owner the number of Indians assigned him for his mine or smelter; that keeps him busy till 1 p.m., by which time the Indians are already turned over to these mine and smelter owners.

After each has eaten his ration, they climb up the hill, each to his mine, and go in, staying there from that hour until Saturday evening without coming out of the mine; their wives bring them food, but they stay constantly underground, excavating and carrying out the ore from which they get the silver. They all have tallow candles, lighted day and night; that is the light they work with, for as they are underground, they have need of it all the time. The mere cost of these candles used in the mines on this range will amount every year to more than 300,000 pesos, even though tallow is cheap in that country, being abundant; but this is a very great expense, and it is almost incredible, how much is spent for candles in the operation of breaking down and getting out the ore.

These Indians have different functions in the handling of the silver ore; some break it up with bar or pick, and dig down in, following the vein in the mine; others bring it up; others up above keep separating the good and the poor in piles; others are occupied in taking it down from the range to the mills on herds of llamas; every day

[4] A Spanish official with military and executive functions.
[5] The region consisted of approximately 139 villages.
[6] The official who governs a province in the name of the king.
[7] A real is one-eighth of a peso.

they bring up more than 8,000 of these native beasts of burden for this task. These teamsters who carry the metal do not belong to the mita, but are mingados — hired.

So huge is the wealth which has been taken out of this range since the year 1545, when it was discovered, up to the present year of 1628, which makes 83 years that they have been working and reducing its ores, that merely from the registered mines, as appears from an examination of most of the accounts in the royal records, 326,000,000 assay[8] pesos have been taken out. At the beginning when the ore was richer and easier to get out, for then there were no mita Indians and no mercury process, in the 40 years between 1545 and 1585, they took out 111,000,000 of assay silver. From the year 1585 up to 1628, 43 years, although the mines are harder to work, for they are deeper down, with the assistance of 13,300 Indians whom His Majesty has granted to the mine owners on that range, and of other hired Indians, who come there freely and voluntarily to work at day's wages, and with the great advantage of the mercury process, in which none of the ore or the silver is wasted, and with the better knowledge of the technique which the miners now have, they have taken out 215,000,000 assay pesos. That, plus the 111 extracted in the 40 years previous to 1585, makes 326,000,000 assay pesos, not counting the great amount of silver secretly taken from these mines . . . and to other countries outside Spain; and to the Philippines and China, which is beyond all reckoning. . . .

Over and above that, such great treasure and riches have come from the Indies in gold and silver from all the other mines in New Spain and Peru, Honduras, the New Kingdom of Granada, Chile, New Galicia, New Vizcaya,[9] and other quarters since the discovery of the Indies, that they exceed 1,800 millions.

[8]Measured so the silver content met official standards.
[9]New Galicia and New Vizcaya were regions and administrative jurisdictions located in north-central and northwestern Mexico.

Part Two

A World of Transformation and Tradition: Mid Seventeenth to Early Nineteenth Century

TWO THEMES — TENSION BETWEEN tradition and innovation and the acceleration of interaction among human societies — stand out in world history from the mid seventeenth to the early nineteenth century. Such tensions and such interaction were nothing new, of course. Human societies had always interacted with one another, and most at some point had faced the challenge of resolving conflicts between tradition and innovation. But from the mid 1600s to the early 1800s, interaction was increasingly global rather than local or regional, and the forces of innovation were more powerful and pervasive, more threatening to old ways, and less avoidable than at any time in the past.

Tradition was most threatened in Europe and its offshoots in the Americas. On both sides of the Atlantic, intellectuals abandoned medieval and Renaissance assumptions about philosophy and religion for a world view that was increasingly secular and scientific. In politics, revolutions resulted in the rejection of divine right monarchy and legally sanctioned privilege in favor of popular sovereignty, constitutionalism, and legal equality. In the area of economics, commerce expanded, agricultural productivity increased, and populations grew. At the end of the eighteenth century, the appearance of steam-driven machinery in English textile mills marked the beginning of a major transformation in human affairs — the most profound since the invention of agriculture millennia earlier — the Industrial Revolution.

Innovation and tradition also clashed in other parts of the world. In Russia Tsar Peter the Great's drive to transform Russia by government-mandated Europeanization set off a bitter debate over Russia's past and future that lasted well beyond his death in 1725. In the Ottoman Empire, reformers pushed for military and administrative changes to breathe new life into the sultan's government but faced strong opposition from those who valued or benefited from the status quo. In India the swift decline of the Mughal Empire and the gradual expansion of British authority introduced a new political dimension to the politics of the subcontinent, while in China the establishment of the Qing

Dynasty in the seventeenth century as well as the growing problems faced by the dynasty from the late 1700s onward created tensions and conflict.

The Manchu conquest of China and the continuing expansion of Russia into Siberia are two examples of the growing interaction among the world's peoples from the mid seventeenth to the early nineteenth century. But the major force behind globalization was the ongoing commercial, demographic, and political expansion of Europe. Europeans continued to migrate to the New World, and as they and their descendants added to the population of the Americas, they created an expanding market for Europe's manufactured goods and served as a source of agricultural products and raw materials. This in turn caused a dramatic increase in transatlantic trade, which in the eighteenth century included more than 6 million Africans who were sold into slavery in the Americas.

European expansion also occurred in other parts of the world. During the 1600s the Dutch drove the Portuguese from much of Southeast Asia and established political control over Java in the East Indies. By the late eighteenth century, the British ruled Bengal, Hyderabad, Myore, and several smaller Indian states; were flooding the Chinese market with opium; and were pressuring the Chinese government to open its ports to foreign trade. Europeans in the late 1700s and early 1800s also were exploring, exploiting, and settling in New Zealand, Australia, and Oceania, bringing the world's last isolated region into global networks of political influence, cultural interchange, and commerce. More so than at any time in world history, isolation among the world's peoples was melting away.

Chapter 5

Europe and the Americas in an Age of Science, Economic Growth, and Revolution

On October 24, 1648, the work of hundreds of diplomats and dozens of heads of state ended when signatures were affixed to the last agreements that collectively make up the Treaty of Westphalia, named after the northwest German territory where negotiations had taken place for the previous six years. With this treaty, one of Europe's most devastating and demoralizing wars, the Thirty Years' War, came to an end. In no small measure because of this war's horrors and destructiveness, it was the last of the religious wars that had plagued Europe after the Protestants' break from the Roman Catholic Church in the sixteenth century. After more than a century of attempting to exterminate each other with armies, the executioner's axe, and instruments of the torture chamber, Protestants and Catholics accepted the permanence of Europe's religious divisions.

Religion was not the only area in which tensions eased in the second half of the seventeenth century. Conflicts between centralizing monarchs and independent-minded nobles and provinces ended in most European states with the triumph of absolutism — a form of government in which monarchs claimed the exclusive right to make and enforce laws. In only a handful of states, notably the Netherlands and England, were wealthy landowners and merchants able to strengthen representative assemblies and limit royal authority. In these states too, however, many conflicts over fundamental constitutional issues were resolved in the late 1600s.

A resolution of uncertainties also took place in the realm of ideas. The work of Isaac Newton (1642–1727) settled perplexing scientific issues that had emerged in the sixteenth century when Nicolaus Copernicus and others revealed the flaws of ancient Greek science but sought in vain for a coherent, all-encompassing model to replace it. Newton's theory of universal gravitation provided such a model. It enabled scientists to understand a host of natural phenomena, including the Earth's tides, the acceleration of falling bodies, and lunar and planetary movement. In the 1700s the broad acceptance of Newton's theories along with advances in mathematics and other branches of science inspired confidence in human reason and the secularism of Europe's Age of Enlightenment.

Building on late-seventeenth-century foundations, Europe in the eighteenth century was more civil, orderly, and tranquil than it had been in hundreds of years. Wars were fought, but with military discipline tightened, religious tensions eased, and pitched battles rare, none matched the devastation of the Reformation era's religious wars. Steady economic growth — much of it fueled by trade with the Americas, modest inflation, and greater agricultural productivity — increased per capita wealth within Europe's expanding population. Peasant revolts and urban violence declined, and old class antagonisms seemed to have abated.

The Atlantic community's outward tranquillity, however, was deceptive. A host of issues — commercial, political, and ideological — increasingly divided the governments of Spain, Brazil, and Great Britain from colonists across the Atlantic, many of whom now considered themselves more American than European. The result was a series of anticolonial revolts between the 1770s and 1810s that led to the establishment of more than a dozen new independent states in the Americas.

Discontent was also growing in Europe. Peasants, who as always were taxed to their limit and beyond, faced land shortages and higher rents as a result of rural population growth. Artisans felt pinched by decades of gradual inflation. Many merchants, manufacturers, lawyers, and other members of the middle class prospered, but they resented the nobles' privileges and their rulers' ineffectiveness. Their resentment, especially in France, was justified. While promoting themselves as defenders of liberty against royal tyranny, French nobles selfishly guarded their privileges and tax exemptions, even at the cost of bankrupting the state. Faced with spiraling deficits, Louis XV (r. 1715–1774) pursued his pleasures, and Louis XVI (r. 1774–1792) embraced and then abandoned one solution after another. The intellectual atmosphere of the Age of Enlightenment, with its belief in reason and progress, heightened political expectations, as did events in North

America, where between 1776 and 1783 the thirteen colonies threw off British rule and established the United States of America, a new type of state based on constitutionalism and popular sovereignty. The meeting of France's representative assembly, the Estates General, in May 1789 was the first step toward a revolution that reverberated throughout the world.

In England another revolution, an economic revolution, was also under way by century's end. The adoption of new spinning and weaving devices driven by water power and steam was transforming the textile industry, while new methods of smelting and casting brought fundamental changes to the production of iron. By the early nineteenth century, as guilds and domestic industry gave way to factory production, output soared, urban populations swelled, and work was redefined. Collectively known as the Industrial Revolution, these economic changes reshaped the human condition even more than had the political revolution in France.

An Age of Monarchy — Absolute and Limited

In many history books, the era of European history from the mid 1600s to the end of the eighteenth century is known as the Age of Absolutism, a term that accurately describes the political systems of France, Spain, Sweden, Denmark, Austria, Hungary, Prussia, Russia, and many small principalities in Germany and Italy. In these states monarchs were absolute in the dictionary sense of "having no restriction, exception, or qualification." Representative assemblies such as the French Estates General and the Spanish *cortes* no longer met to offer advice or approve new taxes; great nobles no longer maintained private armies; church leaders became royal appointees; and monarchs were free to use their subjects' money to build lavish palaces and fight wars to advance their families' interests. These monarchs ruled by divine right, meaning that God had chosen them for their role and, as a corollary, that opposition to such rulers was an affront to the Divinity. Louis XIV, who built Europe's most extravagant royal palace at Versailles and plunged France into years of warfare to increase his territory and glory, captured the spirit of absolutism when he told his minister of finance Colbert, "After I have heard your arguments and those of your colleagues, and having given my opinion on all your claims, I do not wish to hear further talk about it. . . . [A]fter a decision I give you I wish no word of reply."[1] More famously and simply, he is said to have proclaimed, "*L'état, c'est moi*" ("I am the state").

[1]C. B. Cole, *Colbert and a Century of French Mercantilism* (1939), vol. 1, 290.

Like every other historical label, however, the term "age of absolutism" is deficient in some respects. Not all European governments were absolutist monarchies. Among the more than 300 large and small sovereign states in Europe, a few were republics, in which at least part of the population exercised political authority without benefit of a prince or king. They included the Italian mercantile states of Venice and Genoa, a number of small German city-states, and one major economic and political power, the United Provinces, or the Netherlands. In other states monarchs reigned, but with limited authority. They included Europe's largest state, Poland, whose king was elected by the nobility and lacked the authority to raise a standing army, name ministers, or impose new taxes. They also included England, which after a century of political turmoil forged a government in which royal power was limited by law and the authority of an elected assembly, the Parliament. As had been true for hundreds of years, European politics in the early modern era was marked by pluralism and diversity.

A Classic Statement of Absolutist Principles

26 ▾ *Jacques-Bénigne Bossuet, POLITICS DERIVED FROM THE WORDS OF HOLY SCRIPTURE*

Living through decades of civil war, regicide, religious conflict, and rebellion, European intellectuals in the sixteenth and seventeenth centuries sought to understand the underlying causes of Europe's political turmoil and theorized about what form of government was best able to bring this turmoil to an end. Many saw Europe's political salvation in strong, centralized monarchies, a type of government they defended from a number of theoretical perspectives. Some drew an analogy between the state and well-run families: Just as a father exercised unquestioned authority over his spouse, children, and servants, so a king should have similar authority over his subjects. Others, most notably the Englishman Thomas Hobbes in *Leviathan* (1660), developed pro-absolutist arguments based on purely rational principles. Most, however, defended absolutism with religious arguments based on Scripture or analogies between royal and divine power.

Among the dozens of writers who defended absolutism on religious grounds, none was so widely cited as Jacques-Bénigne Bossuet, a French churchman. Born into a family of successful lawyers in Dijon in 1627, Bossuet entered the priesthood and soon gained a reputation as one of the great orators and preachers of his day. After moving to Paris in 1659, he frequently was asked to preach before the royal family, and in 1670 Louis XIV chose him to tutor his son and heir to the throne. As part of his duties, Bossuet in 1678 composed a treatise on the authority and duties of kings, which later was published under the title *Politics Derived from the Words of Holy Scripture*. After his duties as royal tutor ended in 1681, he was appointed bishop of Meaux and became emboiled in a number of theological controversies with Protestants, Jesuits, and Catholic freethinkers who questioned the reality of miracles and the literal truth of the Bible. He died in 1704.

QUESTIONS FOR ANALYSIS

1. According to Bossuet, in what ways are kings "divine"?
2. How does he prove his assertion concerning the divinity of kings?
3. In terms of monarchs' relationship with their subjects, what are the implications of kings' divine nature?
4. According to Bossuet, what are the main purposes of government?
5. Bossuet asserts that royal authority is "absolute," but not "arbitrary." What does he mean by this distinction?
6. According to Bossuet, what is the appropriate response on the part of royal subjects when their king would seem to act against justice and the true faith?

ON THE NATURE AND THE PROPERTIES OF ROYAL AUTHORITY

God establishes kings as his ministers, and reigns through them over the peoples. We have already seen that all power comes from God. The Prince, adds Saint Paul,[1] "is a minister of God to you for good. But if you do that which is evil, be afraid; for he bears not the sword in vain: for he is a minister of God, an avenger for wrath to him that does evil" [Romans 13:4]. So princes act as ministers of God and his lieutenants on earth. It is through them that He rules His empire. This is why we have seen that the royal throne is not the throne of a man, but the throne of God Himself. . . . He governs all peoples, and gives kings to all. . . .

It appears from all this that the person of the king is sacred, and that it is a sacrilege to attack him. God has His prophets anoint them with a sacred unction,[2] as He has His pontiffs and His altars anointed. But, even without the external application of this unction, their charge renders them sacred, as being the representatives of the divine majesty, delegated by His providence to the execution of His designs. . . .

Kings must be guarded as being sacred; and he who neglects to guard them deserves to die. He who guards the life of the prince, places his own in the safe-keeping of God. . . .

Saint Paul, after having said that the prince is the minister of God, concludes thus: "Wherefore you need to be in subjection, not only because of the wrath, but also for conscience's sake" [Romans 13:5]. . . . And again, "servants, obey in all things your temporal masters and whatever you do, do it heartily as to the Lord, and not as unto men." If the apostle speaks thus of servitude, which is an unnatural condition; what should we think of legitimate subjection to princes and to the magistrates who are the protectors of public liberty? This is why Saint Peter[3] says, "submit yourselves to every ordinance of man for the Lord's sake: whether it be to the king as supreme, or unto governors, as unto them that are sent by him for the punishment of evildoers and for the praise of them that do well" [1 Peter 2:13]. And, even if they did not carry out their duty, we must respect in them their charge and their ministry. . . . There is thus a religious character about the respect we show to the prince. The service of God and the respect for kings are

---

[1]Paul (ca. 10–67 C.E.) was, along with Peter (see footnote 3), the most famous early Christian missionary. Fourteen letters attributed to him are included in the Christian New Testament.

[2]Ointment used in a consecration ceremony.

[3]Peter was one of Jesus' twelve apostles and one of the Church's most important early missionaries. Two letters attributed to him, thought to have been written while he served as the first bishop of Rome, are included in the Christian New Testament.

one; and Saint Peter puts these two duties together: "Fear God; honor the king" [1 Peter 2:17]. . . . Indeed, God has infused something of divinity into princes. . . .

The kings must respect their own power and use it only to the public good. Their power coming from above, as we have said, they must not believe that it belongs to them to be used as they please; but they must use it with fear and restraint, as a thing which comes from God and for which God will call them to account. Kings should therefore tremble when using the power that God has given them, and think how horrible is the sacrilege of misusing a power which comes from God.

The Royal Authority Is Paternal, and Its Inherent Character Is Goodness

We have seen that kings take the place of God, who is the true father of all mankind. We have also seen that the first idea of power arrived at by men is that of paternal power; and that kings have been made on the model of fathers. Also, everybody agrees that the obedience which is due to the public power is to be found, in the Ten Commandments, in the commandment which obliges men to honor their parents. From all this, it follows that the title of king is the title of a father, and that goodness is the most natural characteristic of kings. . . .

Because God is great and sufficient unto Himself, He turns, so to speak, entirely towards doing good to men, according to the word. . . . He places an image of His greatness in kings in order to force them to imitate His goodness. He raises them to a level where they have nothing more to desire for themselves. . . .

The Royal Authority Is Absolute

In order to render this idea odious and unbearable, many pretend to confuse absolute government with arbitrary government. But there are no two more dissimilar things. . . . The prince need render no account to anyone for the orders he gives. "I counsel you to keep the king's commandment and that in regard to the oath of God. Be not hasty to go out of his sight: . . . for he does whatsoever pleases him. Where the word of a king is, there is power; and who may say unto him, What are you doing?" [Ecclesiastes 8:2] Without this absolute authority the king can do no good, nor punish evil; his power must be such that no one can hope to escape it. . . .

Men must therefore obey princes as they obey justice itself, without which there can be no order or purpose in things. They are Gods, and share in a fashion the divine independence. . . .

The Royal Authority Must Be Invincible

If there is in a State any authority which can stand in the path of public power and hinder it in its exercise, no one is safe. . . .

If the prince himself, who is the judge of judges, fears powerful men, what stability could there be in the State? It is therefore necessary that authority should be invincible, and that nothing should be able to breach the rampart behind which the public peace and private weal are safe.

Of Majesty

Majesty is the reflection of the greatness of God in the prince. God is infinite, God is all. The prince, as a prince, is not regarded as a private individual: he is a public figure, the whole State rests in him; the will of the whole people is comprehended in his. Just as all perfection and all virtue are concentrated in God, so all the power of private individuals is concentrated in the person of the prince. What greatness, that one man should carry so much! The power of God makes itself felt in an instant from one end of the world to the other: the royal power acts in the same way throughout the whole kingdom. It keeps the whole kingdom in being, as God keeps the whole world. If God were to withdraw His hand, the world would fall back into nothingness: if authority ceased in the kingdom, everything would be confusion. . . .

Now, put together all the great and august things that we have said on the subject of royal authority. See a great people united in one person: see this sacred, paternal, and absolute power: see the secret purpose which governs the whole body of the State comprehended in one head: you see the image of God in the kings; and you get an idea of royal majesty. . . . God is holiness itself, goodness itself, power itself, reason itself. The majesty of God is in these things. The majesty of the prince is in the image of these things. This majesty is so great that its source cannot be in the prince; it is borrowed from God who gives it to him for the good of the peoples, for whom it is salutary that they should be held in by a superior power. . . .

Therefore, use your power boldly, oh, kings! For it is divine and salutary to mankind; but use it with humility. You are endowed with it from outside. Fundamentally, it leaves you weak; it leaves you mortal; it leaves you sinners; and burdens you with greater responsibility towards God.

On the Obedience Due to the Prince

The subjects owe unlimited obedience to the prince. If the prince is not punctually obeyed, the public order is overthrown and there is no more unity, and consequently no more cooperation or peace in a State. . . .

Open godlessness, and even persecution, do not absolve the subjects from the obedience they owe to princes. The character of royalty is holy and sacred, even in infidel princes; and we have seen that Isaiah[4] calls Cyrus "the anointed of the Lord." Nebuchadnezzar[5] was godless, and proud to the point of wanting to equal God and put to death those who refused him a sacrilegious worship; and nevertheless Daniel addresses him thus: "You are the king of kings: and the God of Heavens has given you the kingdom and the power and the empire and the glory" [Daniel 2:37]. . . .

The subjects may oppose to the violence of princes only respectful remonstrances, without murmurs or rebellion, and prayers for their conversion.

If God does not hearken to the prayers of His faithful; if in order to try and chasten His children He permits their persecution to grow worse, they must then remember that Jesus Christ has "sent them as lambs in the midst of wolves." [Luke 10:3] Here is a truly holy doctrine, truly worthy of Jesus Christ and of His disciples.

On the Duties of the Prince

The purpose of government is the welfare and conservation of the State. . . .

The good constitution of the body of the State consists in two things: religion and justice. These are the internal and constitutive principles of States. By the one we render to God what is owed to Him, and by the other we render to men that which they deserve. . . . The prince must employ his authority to destroy false religion in his State. . . .

The prince is the minister of God: "He bears not the sword in vain: for he is a revenger to execute wrath upon him that doeth evil" [Romans 13:4]. He is the protector of the public peace which is based upon religion; and he must maintain his throne, of which, as we have seen, religion is the foundation. Those who will not allow the prince to act strictly in religious matters, because religion should be free, make an impious error. Otherwise, one would have to tolerate in all the subjects and in all the country idolatry, Mohammedanism, Judaism, any false religions; blasphemy, even atheism, and the greatest crimes would be the least punished.

---

[4]A Hebrew prophet to whom is attributed the Book of Isaiah, part of the Hebrew Scriptures and the Christian Old Testament. In it he discusses Cyrus the Great (r. 550–529 B.C.E.), founder of the first Persian Empire. After conquering Babylon, Cyrus freed the Jews from captivity and allowed them to return to Palestine.

[5]Ruler of Babylon from 605 to 562 B.C.E. One of his advisors, Daniel, is the main character in the Book of Daniel, part of the Hebrew Scriptures and the Christian Old Testament, written in the Maccabean period (167–63 B.C.E.).

The Foundations of Parliamentary Supremacy in England

▼▼▼

27 ▾ ENGLISH BILL OF RIGHTS

The acceptance of the English Bill of Rights in 1689 kept England on a political path that set it apart from the absolutist governments then taking hold in France and elsewhere on the European continent. It also ended a clash between the Crown and Parliament that had convulsed English politics for almost a century. Ever since the reigns of James I (r. 1603–1625) and his son Charles I (r. 1625–1649), the landowners, merchants, and lawyers who dominated the House of Commons had fought the monarchy over religious, economic, diplomatic, and political issues that all centered on the fundamental question of Parliament's place in England's government. A political impasse over new taxes led to civil war between parliamentarians and royalists in 1642. After a triumphant Parliament ordered the execution of Charles I in 1649, a faction of Puritans led by Oliver Cromwell seized power and imposed its strict Protestant beliefs on the English people for the next eleven years. The Puritans' grip on England loosened after the death of Cromwell in 1658 and was lost altogether when a newly elected Parliament restored the Stuarts in 1660.

Charles II (r. 1660–1685) and his brother James II (r. 1685–1688), however, alienated their subjects through pro-French and pro-Catholic policies and a disregard for Parliament. James II was a professed Catholic, and when a male heir was born in 1688, this raised the possibility of a long line of English Catholic kings. Many of his predominantly Protestant subjects found this unacceptable, and the result was the Glorious Revolution of 1688–1689. In a change that resembled a coup d'état more than a revolution, Parliament offered the crown to James's Protestant daughter Mary and her husband, William of Orange of Holland. After James mounted only token resistance and then fled the country, his son-in-law and daughter became King William III and Queen Mary II after signing the Bill of Rights, presented to them by Parliament in 1689. By doing so, they accepted parliamentary limitations on royal authority that became a permanent part of England's constitution.

QUESTIONS FOR ANALYSIS

1. What abuses of royal power seem to have most disturbed the authors of the English Bill of Rights?
2. Were the authors most concerned with political, economic, or religious issues?
3. What role does the Bill of Rights envision for the English Crown?
4. When the Bill of Rights speaks of "rights," to whose rights does it refer?
5. In what ways might the common people of England benefit from the Bill of Rights?
6. If given the opportunity, how might Bossuet (source 26) have criticized the premises of the English Bill of Rights?

Whereas the late King James the Second, by the assistance of diverse evil counselors, judges and ministers employed by him, did endeavor to subvert and extirpate the Protestant religion and the laws and liberties of this kingdom;

By assuming and exercising a power of dispensing with and suspending of laws and the execution of laws without consent of Parliament;

By committing and prosecuting diverse worthy prelates for humbly petitioning to be excused from concurring to the said assumed power;

By issuing and causing to be executed a commission under the great seal for erecting a court called the Court of Commissioners for Ecclesiastical Causes;[1]

By levying money for and to the use of the Crown by pretense of prerogative for other time and in other manner than the same was granted by Parliament;

By raising and keeping a standing army within this kingdom in time of peace without consent of Parliament, and quartering soldiers contrary to law;

By causing several good subjects being Protestants to be disarmed at the same time when papists were both armed and employed contrary to law;

By violating the freedom of election of members to serve in Parliament; . . .

And whereas of late years partial corrupt and unqualified persons have been returned and served on juries in trials, and particularly diverse jurors in trials for high treason which were not freeholders;

And excessive bail hath been required of persons committed in criminal cases to elude the benefit of the laws made for the liberty of the subjects;

And excessive fines have been imposed;

And illegal and cruel punishments inflicted;

And several grants and promises made of fines and forfeitures before any conviction or judgment against the persons upon whom the same were to be levied;

All which are utterly and directly contrary to the known laws and statutes and freedom of this realm;

And whereas the said late King James the Second having abdicated the government and the throne being thereby vacant, his Highness the prince of Orange (whom it hath pleased Almighty God to make the glorious instrument of delivering this kingdom from popery and arbitrary power) did . . . cause letters to be written to the Lords Spiritual and Temporal being Protestants, and other letters to the several counties, cities, universities, boroughs and cinque ports,[2] for the choosing of such persons to represent them as were of right to be sent to Parliament, to meet and sit at Westminster upon the two and twentieth day of January in this year one thousand six hundred eighty and eight,[3] in order to make such an establishment as that their religion, laws and liberties might not again be in danger of being subverted, upon which letters elections having been accordingly made;

And thereupon the said Lords Spiritual and Temporal and Commons,[4] pursuant to their respective letters and elections, being now assembled . . . , taking into their most serious consideration the best means for attaining the ends aforesaid, do in the first place (as their ancestors in like case have usually done) for the vindicating and asserting their ancient rights and liberties declare;

That the pretended power of suspending of laws or the execution of laws by regal authority without consent of Parliament is illegal;

[1]A special royal court established to try religious cases.

[2]Five maritime towns in southeast England that during the Middle Ages gained the right to send representatives to Parliament in return for aiding the naval defense of the realm.

[3]Until the eighteenth century the English new year began on March 25, not January 1; by modern reckoning the year should be 1689.

[4]The Lords Spiritual were the prelates of the Anglican Church who sat in the House of Lords; the Lords Temporal were titled peers who sat in the House of Lords; Commons refers to the House of Commons, to which nontitled Englishmen were elected.

That the pretended power of dispensing with laws or the execution of laws by regal authority, as it hath been assumed and exercised of late, is illegal;

That the commission for erecting the late Court of Commissioners for Ecclesiastical Causes, and all other commissions and courts of like nature, are illegal and pernicious;

That levying money for or to the use of the Crown by pretense of prerogative, without grant of Parliament, for longer time, or in other manner than the same is or shall be granted, is illegal;

That it is the right of the Subjects to petition the king, and all commitments and prosecutions for such petitioning are illegal;

That the raising or keeping a standing army within the kingdom in time of peace, unless it be with consent of Parliament, is against law;

That the subjects which are Protestants may have arms for their defense suitable to their conditions and as allowed by law;

That election of members of Parliament ought to be free;

That the freedom of speech and debates or proceedings in Parliament ought not to be impeached or questioned in any court or place out of Parliament;

That excessive bail ought not to be required, nor excessive fines imposed nor cruel and unusual punishments inflicted;

That jurors ought to be duly impaneled and returned, and jurors which pass upon men in trials for high treason ought to be freeholders;[5]

That all grants and promises of fines and forfeitures of particular persons before conviction are illegal and void;

And that for redress of all grievances, and for the amending, strengthening and preserving of the laws, Parliaments ought to be held frequently. . . .

[5]Property holders.

Peter the Great's Blueprint for Russia

28 ▾ *Peter the Great, EDICTS AND DECREES*

Brought to a near halt during two centuries of Mongol domination and impeded by decades of turmoil and foreign invasion following the death of Ivan IV in 1584, the growth of strong central government in Russia under the tsar resumed during the reigns of Alexis (r. 1645–1676) and his son Peter the Great (r. 1682–1725). Alexis streamlined the central bureaucracy, extended control over church affairs, issued a new law code (which imposed serfdom on all Russian peasants), and increasingly bypassed advisory bodies such as the Council of State and Assembly of the Land. Alexis also made efforts to reconstruct the Russian military and founded a number of state-sponsored factories for the manufacture of weapons, glass, brick, textiles, and agricultural tools.

Despite Alexis's accomplishments, when his son Peter the Great became tsar, Russia still lagged behind the nations of western Europe. Manufacturing was negligible; commerce was limited to small amounts of trade in amber, furs, and timber; and agricultural productivity was limited by long winters and the inefficiencies of a rural order based on serf labor. Russia still lacked the economic base and government institutions to match the size, weaponry, and training of its ri-

vals' armies. Peter the Great learned this bitter truth in November 1700 at the Battle of Narva, the first major battle in the Great Northern War, when a Swedish army of just over 8,000 routed a poorly trained and equipped Russian army four times its size. Peter responded with characteristic energy. Already enamored of Western technology, military drill, shipbuilding, fashion, and government as a result of boyhood contacts with European visitors to Moscow and his travels through Europe in 1697 and 1698, Peter threw himself into a campaign to transform Russia along European lines. Issuing no fewer than 3,000 decrees in the next twenty-five years on everything from the structure of government to male shaving habits, Peter stands out as the first ruler in history who sought to transform his state and subjects through a process that came to be known as Westernization.

QUESTIONS FOR ANALYSIS

1. What do these decrees reveal about Peter the Great's motives for his reforms?
2. What can be learned from these decrees about Russian social relationships and the state of the Russian economy?
3. Why do you think Peter believed it was necessary for Russians to change their dress, shaving habits, and calendar?
4. What evidence do these edicts provide about opposition or indifference to Peter's reforms on the part of his subjects?
5. What do these edicts reveal about Peter's views of the state and its relationship to his subjects?
6. What groups within Russia might have been most likely to oppose Peter's reforms? Why?

LEARNING FROM EUROPE

(Decree on the New Calendar {1699})

It is known to His Majesty that not only many European Christian lands, but also Slavic nations which are in total accord with our Eastern Orthodox Church . . . agree to count their years from the eighth day after the birth of Christ, that is from the first day of January, and not from the creation of the world,[1] because of the many difficulties and discrepancies of this reckoning. It is now the year 1699 from the birth of Christ, and from the first of January will begin both the new year 1700 and a new century; and so His Majesty has ordered, as a good and useful measure, that from now on time will be reckoned in government offices and dates be noted on documents and property deeds, starting from the first of January 1700. And to celebrate this good undertaking and the new century . . . in the sovereign city of Moscow . . . let the reputable citizens arrange decorations of pine, fir, and juniper trees and boughs along the busiest main streets and by the houses of eminent church and lay persons of rank. . . . Poorer persons should place at least one shrub or bough on their gates or on their house. . . . Also, . . . as a sign of rejoicing, wishes for the new year and

---

[1]Before January 1, 1700, the Russian calendar started from the date of the creation of the world, which was reckoned at 5508 B.C.E. The year began on September 1.

century will be exchanged, and the following will be organized: when fireworks are lit and guns fired on the great Red Square, let the boyars,[2] the Lords of the Palace, of the Chamber, and the Council, and the eminent personages of Court, Army, and Merchant ranks, each in his own grounds, fire three times from small guns, if they have any, or from muskets and other small arms, and shoot some rockets into the air.

(Decree on the Invitation of Foreigners {1702})

Since our accession to the throne all our efforts and intentions have tended to govern this realm in such a way that all of our subjects should, through our care for the general good, become more and more prosperous. For this end we have always tried to maintain internal order, to defend the state against invasion, and in every possible way to improve and to extend trade. With this purpose we have been compelled to make some necessary and salutary changes in the administration, in order that our subjects might more easily gain a knowledge of matters of which they were before ignorant, and become more skillful in their commercial relations. We have therefore given orders, made dispositions, and founded institutions indispensable for increasing our trade with foreigners, and shall do the same in the future. Nevertheless we fear that matters are not in such a good condition as we desire, and that our subjects cannot in perfect quietness enjoy the fruits of our labors, and we have therefore considered still other means to protect our frontier from the invasion of the enemy, and to preserve the rights and privileges of our State, and the general peace of all Christians. . . .

To attain these worthy aims, we have endeavored to improve our military forces, which are the protection of our State, so that our troops may consist of well-drilled men, maintained in perfect order and discipline. In order to obtain greater improvement in this respect, and to encourage foreigners, who are able to assist us in this way, as well as artisans profitable to the State, to come in numbers to our country, we have issued this manifesto, and have ordered printed copies of it to be sent throughout Europe. . . . And as in our residence of Moscow, the free exercise of religion of all other sects, although not agreeing with our church, is already allowed, so shall this be hereby confirmed anew in such manner that we, by the power granted to us by the Almighty, shall exercise no compulsion over the consciences of men, and shall gladly allow every Christian to care for his own salvation at his own risk.

(An Instruction to Russian Students Abroad Studying Navigation {1714})

1. Learn how to draw plans and charts and how to use the compass and other naval indicators.

2. Learn how to navigate a vessel in battle as well as in a simple maneuver, and learn how to use all appropriate tools and instruments; namely, sails, ropes, and oars, and the like matters, on row boats and other vessels.

3. Discover . . . how to put ships to sea during a naval battle. . . . Obtain from foreign naval officers written statements, bearing their signatures and seals, of how adequately you are prepared for naval duties.

4. If, upon his return, anyone wishes to receive from the Tsar greater favors, he should learn, in addition to the above enumerated instructions, how to construct those vessels [aboard] which he would like to demonstrate his skills.

5. Upon his return to Moscow, every foreign-trained Russian should bring with him at his own expense, for which he will later be reimbursed, at least two experienced masters of naval science. They the returnees will be assigned soldiers, one soldier per returnee, to teach them what they have learned abroad. . . .

---

[2]Members of the hereditary nobility.

CREATING A NEW RUSSIAN

(Decree on Western Dress {1701})

Western dress shall be worn by all the boyars, members of our councils and of our court . . . gentry of Moscow, secretaries . . . provincial gentry, gosti,[3] government officials, streltsy,[4] members of the guilds purveying for our household, citizens of Moscow of all ranks, and residents of provincial cities . . . excepting the clergy and peasant tillers of the soil. The upper dress shall be of French or Saxon cut, and the lower dress . . . — waistcoat, trousers, boots, shoes, and hats — shall be of the German type. They shall also ride German saddles. Likewise the womenfolk of all ranks, including the priests', deacons', and church attendants' wives, the wives of the dragoons, the soldiers, and the streltsy, and their children, shall wear Western dresses, hats, jackets, and underwear — undervests and petticoats — and shoes. From now on no one of the above-mentioned is to wear Russian dress or Circassian[5] coats, sheepskin coats, or Russian peasant coats, trousers, boots, and shoes. It is also forbidden to ride Russian saddles, and the craftsmen shall not manufacture them or sell them at the marketplaces.

(Decree on Shaving {1705})

Henceforth, in accordance with this, His Majesty's decree, all court attendants . . . provincial service men, government officials of all ranks, military men, all the gosti, members of the wholesale merchants' guild, and members of the guilds purveying for our household must shave their beards and moustaches. But, if it happens that some of them do not wish to shave their beards and moustaches, let a yearly tax be collected from such persons; from court attendants. . . . Special badges shall be issued to them from the Administrator of Land Affairs of Public Order . . . which they must wear. . . . As for the peasants, let a toll of two half-copecks[6] per beard be collected at the town gates each time they enter or leave a town; and do not let the peasants pass the town gates, into or out of town, without paying this toll.

MILITARY AND ECONOMIC REFORMS

(Decree on Promotion to Officer's Rank {1714})

Since there are many who promote to officer rank their relatives and friends — young men who do not know the fundamentals of soldiering, not having served in the lower ranks — and since even those who serve [in the ranks] do so for a few weeks or months only, as a formality; therefore . . . let a decree be promulgated that henceforth there shall be no promotion [to officer rank] of men of noble extraction or of any others who have not first served as privates in the Guards. This decree does not apply to soldiers of lowly origin who, after long service in the ranks, have received their commissions through honest service or to those who are promoted on the basis of merit, now or in the future. . . .

(Statute for the College of Manufactures[7] {1723})

His Imperial Majesty is diligently striving to establish and develop in the Russian Empire such manufacturing plants and factories as are found in other states, for the general welfare and prosperity of his subjects. He [therefore] most graciously charges the College of Manufactures to exert itself in devising the means to introduce, with the least expense, and to spread in the Russian Empire these and other ingenious arts, and especially those for which materials can be found within the empire. . . .

---

[3]Merchants who often served the tsar in some capacity.
[4]Members of the imperial guard stationed in Moscow.
[5]Circassia was a Russian territory between the Caspian and Black seas.
[6]One-twentieth of a ruble, the basic unit of Russian money.
[7]One of several administrative boards created by Peter in 1717. Modeled on Swedish practice.

His Imperial Majesty gives permission to everyone, without distinction of rank or condition, to open factories wherever he may find suitable. . . .

Factory owners must be closely supervised, in order that they have at their plants good and experienced [foreign] master craftsmen, who are able to train Russians in such a way that these, in turn, may themselves become masters, so that their produce may bring glory to the Russian manufactures. . . .

By the former decrees of His Majesty commercial people were forbidden to buy villages [i.e. to own serfs], the reason being that they were not engaged in any other activity beneficial for the state save commerce; but since it is now clear to all that many of them have started to found manufacturing establishments and build plants, . . . which tend to increase the welfare of the state . . . therefore permission is granted both to the gentry and to men of commerce to acquire villages for these factories without hindrance. . . .

In order to stimulate voluntary immigration of various craftsmen from other countries into the Russian Empire, and to encourage them to establish factories and manufacturing plants freely and at their own expense, the College of Manufactures must send appropriate announcements to the Russian envoys accredited at foreign courts. The envoys should then, in an appropriate way, bring these announcements to the attention of men of various professions, urge them to come to settle in Russia, and help them to move.

An Age of Science and Enlightenment

Although secularism had been a growing force in European intellectual life since the Italian Renaissance of the fourteenth and fifteenth centuries, only in the eighteenth century — the Age of Enlightenment — did it eclipse religion as the dominant influence on thought and culture. Organized churches, both Catholic and Protestant, still had millions of followers, and new religious movements such as English Methodism were signs of continuing religious vitality. Nonetheless, the leading intellectuals of the eighteenth century were indifferent or openly hostile to religion, artists painted few religious scenes, and rulers gave little thought to religion in making political and diplomatic decisions.

The main inspiration for the secularism of the eighteenth century was the Scientific Revolution, especially the work of Isaac Newton (1642–1727). When Newton revealed the underlying laws that determined the movement of bodies throughout the universe, and did so without relying on religious authority or ancient texts, he demonstrated to eighteenth-century intellectuals the full power of human reason. These intellectuals, known as *philosophes* (French for philosophers), came from every corner of Europe and disagreed on many issues, but all were convinced that reason could be applied to social, political, and economic problems with results as spectacular as those achieved by Newton and other seventeenth-century scientists. Specifically, reason could expose the weaknesses, flaws, and injustices carried over from Europe's "unenlightened" past. The philosophes, therefore, were social and political critics who scrutinized and frequently condemned their era's legal codes, schools, churches, government policies, wars, sexual mores, class privileges, and much else.

The Enlightenment was not, however, purely negative. The philosophes rejected passive acceptance of the status quo and proclaimed that human beings through reason could plan and achieve a better future. They disagreed about what that future would be like, but none doubted that improvement of the human condition was not just possible, but inevitable, if only reason were given freedom to inquire, question, plan, and inspire.

Two Images of Seventeenth-Century Science

29 ▾ *Sébastien Le Clerc, THE ROYAL ACADEMY AND ITS PROTECTORS and A DISSECTION AT THE JARDIN DES PLANTES*

Many early participants in Europe's scientific revolution were solitary scholars who had few contacts with others who shared their interests. By the late 1600s, however, leading scientists were all members of one of several scientific societies that supported and publicized their work and provided opportunities for exchanging ideas. The four most prestigious academies were the Academy of Experiment, founded in 1657 in Florence by Prince Leopold de Medici; the Royal Society of London, licensed but not financially supported by Charles II in 1660; the French Royal Academy of Sciences, founded in 1661 and supported by Louis XIV; and the Berlin Academy of Sciences, created in 1700 under the auspices of Elector Frederick III of Brandenburg-Prussia. Although these academies varied in size, organization, and activities, they all encouraged scientific investigation and contributed significantly to Europe's ongoing scientific development.

Many Europeans were introduced to the ideals and goals of the French Royal Academy of Sciences through the engravings of Sébastien Le Clerc (1637–1714), a gifted artist with a lifelong interest in science. He made the engravings for many of the Academy's books and set a new standard for accurate scientific illustration. Among his works was a series of engravings depicting the activities of the academicians themselves. These engravings appeared in several of the Academy's publications, with individual copies made for the king, interested courtiers, and collectors. Two of them are reproduced here.

The first, ***The Royal Academy and Its Protectors*** (1671), centers on Louis XIV, with two aristocrats, the Prince of Condé and the Duke of Orléans, to his right and Colbert, the French controller general of finance, to his left. They are surrounded by members of the Academy and their scientific instruments. Seen through the window are a formal garden and the Royal Observatory, which is under construction. At the center of the second engraving, entitled ***A Dissection at the Jardin des Plantes*** (1671), two academicians are dissecting a fox, with their observations being recorded by the individual seated at their right. In the foreground a member of the Academy points to a printed book, in which the observations made during the dissection will be published, and behind the table stands

Le Clerc himself, pointing to a page of his scientific engravings. On the far left two figures are making observations with a magnifying glass and a microscope, and on the right stand Colbert and another courtier.

Neither engraving is realistic. Louis XIV made his first visit to the Academy in 1681, ten years after *The Royal Academy and Its Protectors* was engraved. And none of the Academy's rooms would have afforded a window view of the Royal Observatory. Furthermore, the room where dissections were carried out was notoriously rank, probably closer in appearance and smell to a butcher shop than the genteel scene portrayed by Le Clerc. The artist's goal, however, was not to depict the day-to-day reality of the Academy's activities but to communicate an idealized vision of the methods and purposes of contemporary science.

QUESTIONS FOR ANALYSIS

1. How many different pieces of scientific equipment can you identify in the engravings? What do the equipment and other paraphernalia reveal about the scientific interests and methodology of the academicians?
2. What is the significance of the picture toward which Colbert is pointing? What might be the significance of the map on the floor?
3. What point is Le Clerc trying to make about the Academy in the following details from the engraving of the dissection room: the two figures at the window, the figure pointing to the book, and the artist pointing to the page of engravings?
4. Note the formal gardens that can be seen through the windows in both engravings. What attitude toward nature is expressed in gardens such as these?

Sébastien Le Clerc, The Royal Academy and Its Protectors

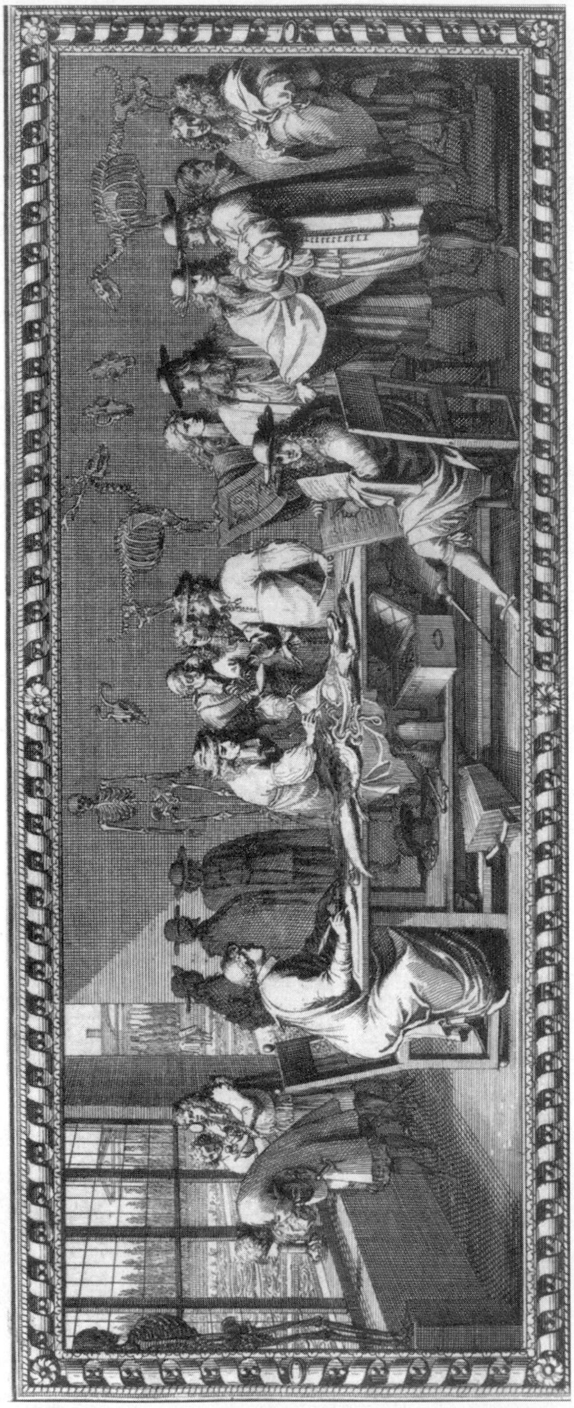

Sébastien Le Clerc, A Dissection at the Jardin des Plantes

A Plea for Religious Understanding and Tolerance

30 ▾ *Voltaire, TREATISE ON TOLERATION*

François-Marie Arouet (1694–1778), better known by his pen name, Voltaire, combined wit, literary elegance, and a passionate social conscience in a long literary career that best represents the values and spirit of the Age of Enlightenment. Born into a well-to-do Parisian bourgeois family, Voltaire published his first work, the tragic drama *Oedipus*, in 1717. In the next sixty-one years, he wrote thousands of poems, histories, satires, novels, short stories, essays, and reviews. The European reading public avidly bought his works, making him one of the first authors to make a large fortune through the sale of his writings.

Although Voltaire's enormous output and popularity ensured his influence on the Enlightenment at many different levels, one particular contribution stands out: his devotion to the principles of religious toleration and freedom of thought. Voltaire was convinced that throughout history the intolerance of organized religions, not just Christianity, had caused much of the world's suffering. He was angered that even in the "enlightened" eighteenth century, Protestant-Catholic enmity still resulted in episodes such as the torture and execution of Jean Calas, a French Protestant convicted unjustly of murdering his son, supposedly after learning of the son's intent to become a Catholic. Voltaire's devotion to religious toleration is revealed in the following selection, taken from his *Treatise on Toleration*, written in 1763 in response to the execution of Calas.

QUESTIONS FOR ANALYSIS

1. Does Voltaire believe that intolerance is a special trait of Christianity, or does he think that it characterizes other organized religions as well?
2. What point is Voltaire trying to make in his reference to the various dialects of the Italian language?
3. What does Voltaire suggest as the essence of a truly religious person?
4. What attitude toward humankind does Voltaire express in the "Prayer to God"?
5. What does the excerpt tell us about Voltaire's views of the nature of God?

OF UNIVERSAL TOLERANCE

No great art or studied eloquence is needed to prove that Christians should tolerate one another. I go even further and declare that we must look upon all men as our brothers. But the Turk, my brother? the Chinese, the Jew, the Siamese? Yes, of course; are we not all the children of one father and creatures of the same God?

But these people despise us; they call us idolators! Then I'll tell them they are quite wrong. I think I could at least shock the proud obstinacy of an imam[1] if I said to them something like this:

This little globe, nothing more than a point, rolls in space like so many other globes; we are lost in this immensity. Man, some five feet tall, is surely a very small part of the universe. One of these imperceptible beings says to some of his neighbors in Arabia or Africa: "Listen to me, for the God of all these worlds has enlightened me: there are nine hundred million little ants like us on the earth, but only my anthill is beloved of God; He will hold all others in horror through all eternity; only mine will be blessed, the others will be eternally wretched."

At that, they would cut me short and ask what fool made that stupid remark. I would be obliged to reply, "You yourselves." Then I would try to mollify them; but that would not be easy.

I would speak now to the Christians and dare say, for example, to a Dominican Inquisitor,[2] "My brother, you know that every province in Italy has its dialect, and people in Venice and Bergamo speak differently from those in Florence. The Academy della Crusca[3] has standardized the language; its dictionary is an inescapable authority, and Buonmattei's[4] grammar is an absolute and infallible guide; but do you believe that the head of the Academy and in his absence, Buonmattei, would have been able in all good conscience to cut out the tongues of all those from Venice and Bergamo who persisted in using their own dialect?"

The Inquisitor replies: "There is a great difference; here it's a question of your salvation. It's for your own good the Director of the Inquisition orders that you be seized on the testimony of a single person, no matter how infamous or criminal he may be; that you have no lawyer to defend you; that the very name of your accuser be unknown to you; that the Inquisitor promise you grace and then condemn you; that you undergo five different degrees of torture and then be whipped or sent to the galleys, or ceremoniously burned at the stake. . . .

I would take the liberty of replying: "My brother, perhaps you are right: I am convinced that you wish me well, but couldn't I be saved without all that?"

To be sure, these horrible absurdities do not soil the face of the earth everyday, but they are frequent enough, and a whole volume could easily be written about them much longer than the Gospels which condemn them. Not only is it very cruel to persecute in this brief existence of ours those who differ from us in opinion, but I am afraid it is being bold indeed to pronounce their eternal damnation. It hardly seems fitting for us atoms of the moment, for that is all we are, to presume to know in advance the decrees of our own Creator. . . .

Oh, sectarians of a merciful God, if you had a cruel heart, if, while adoring Him whose only law consists in the words: "Love God and thy neighbor as thyself (Luke X, 27)," you had overloaded this pure and holy law with sophisms and incomprehensible disputations; if you had lighted the torch of discord either over a new word or a single letter of the alphabet; if you had made eternal punishment the penalty for the omission of a few words or ceremonies which other nations could not know about, I would say to you, as I wept in compassion for mankind: "Transport yourselves with me to the day when all men will be judged and when God will do unto each man according to his works."

"I see all the dead of all centuries, past and present, appear before His presence. Are you quite sure that our Creator and Father will say to the wise and virtuous Confucius, to Solon the law-giver, to Pythagoras, Zaleucus, Socrates, and Plato, to the divine Antoninus, good Trajan, and Titus, the flowering of mankind, to Epictetus and so many other model men:[5] "Go, you monsters; go and suffer punishment, limitless in

[1] In this context, a Muslim prayer leader at a mosque.

[2] A Catholic official responsible for uncovering and punishing erroneous belief, or heresy.

[3] The Florentine Academy of Letters, founded in 1582.

[4] A seventeenth-century Italian grammarian.

[5] These were moralists, enlightened political leaders, and philosophers who had lived before the coming of Christianity.

time and intensity, eternal as I am eternal. And you, my beloved, Jean Chatel, Ravaillac, Damiens, Cartouche, etc.,[6] who died according to the prescribed formulas, share forever at my right hand my empire and my felicity."

You draw back in horror from these words, and since they escaped me, I have no more to say.

PRAYER TO GOD

I no longer address myself to men, but to thee, God of all beings, all worlds, and all ages. If indeed it is allowable for feeble creatures, lost in immensity and imperceptible to the rest of the universe, to dare ask anything of Thee who hast given all things, whose decrees are as immutable as they are eternal, deign to look with compassion upon the failings inherent in our nature, and grant that these failings lead us not into calamity.

Thou didst not give us hearts that we should hate each other or hands that we should cut each other's throats. Grant that we may help each other bear the burden of our painful and brief lives; that the slight difference in the clothing with which we cover our puny bodies, in our inadequate tongues, in all our ridiculous customs, in all our imperfect laws, in all our insensate opinions, in all our stations in life so disproportionate in our eyes but so equal in Thy sight, that all these little variations that differentiate the atoms called *man*, may not be the signals for hatred and persecution. . . .

May all men remember that they are brothers; may they hold in horror tyranny that is exercised over souls, just as they hold in execration the brigandage that snatches away by force the fruits of labor and peaceful industry. If the scourge of war is inevitable, let us not hate each other, let us not tear each other apart in the lap of peace; but let us use the brief moment of our existence in blessing in a thousand different tongues, from Siam to California, Thy goodness which has bestowed this moment upon us.

[6]Five notorious criminals from Voltaire's day.

Capitalism's Prophet

▼▼▼

31 ▼ *Adam Smith, THE WEALTH OF NATIONS*

A major figure in the Scottish Enlightenment, Adam Smith is regarded as the founder of the academic study of economics. Previous writers on economics had speculated about specific issues such as the causes of inflation and had discussed at length the ethical implications of the profit motive, the accumulation of wealth, and the lending of money for interest. In contrast, in his major work, *An Inquiry into the Nature and Causes of the Wealth of Nations*, Smith introduced an approach to the study of economics in which he systematically analyzed wages, labor, trade, population, rents, and money supply. The work's importance also lies in its indictment of mercantilism, a system of economic regulation implemented by many European governments in the seventeenth century to strengthen the state by encouraging industry, commerce, and agriculture. A main goal of the mercantilists was to increase the nation's gold and silver supply by exporting more than it imported. To achieve this favorable balance of trade, governments subsidized industries that produced exportable goods, protected native industries from foreign competition through tariffs, and instituted policies that favored their own countries' merchants over foreign competitors. Governments viewed colonies as

sources of raw materials and markets for their nation's own manufactures. Smith, in contrast, favored free trade among nations and economic freedom for individuals, making the paradoxical argument that by encouraging individuals to pursue their own self-interest, society as a whole benefited through economic growth. Thus, he is viewed not only as the founder of modern economic thought but also as one of the first proponents of capitalism.

Despite his prominence, few biographical details are known about Smith. Born in 1723 in a Scottish fishing village and educated at the universities of Glasgow and Oxford, he taught logic and moral philosophy at the University of Glasgow between 1751 and 1763. The publication of his *Theory of Moral Sentiments* in 1759 ensured his literary and philosophical reputation. In 1763 he became the tutor of an English aristocrat's son and lived for three years in France, where he met many prominent French intellectuals. From 1767 to 1776, he lived in semiretirement in Scotland and completed *The Wealth of Nations*, published in 1776. In 1778 he became commissioner of customs in Scotland and died in Edinburgh in 1790.

In the following excerpt, he describes the value of the division of labor and makes his case for free trade among nations.

QUESTIONS FOR ANALYSIS

1. Smith denies that a nation's wealth consists of the amount of gold and silver it controls. What arguments does he present to defend his position, and what are their implications for trade policy?
2. Smith proposes that each individual, by pursuing his or her own self-interest, promotes the general welfare of society. What examples of this paradox does he provide?
3. What implications does this paradox have for government policy?
4. What groups in society would you expect to be most enthusiastic about Smith's ideas? Why? What groups might be expected to oppose them?

SELF-INTEREST AND THE FREE MARKET

This division of labor,[1] from which so many advantages are derived, is not originally the effect of any human wisdom, which foresees and intends that general opulence to which it gives occasion. It is the necessary, though very slow and gradual consequence of a certain propensity in human nature which has in view no such extensive utility; the propensity to truck,[2] barter, and exchange one thing for another.

. . . It is common to all men, and to be found in no other race of animals, which seem to know neither this nor any other species of contracts. . . . Nobody ever saw a dog make a fair and deliberate exchange of one bone for another with another dog. Nobody ever saw one animal by its gestures and natural cries signify to another, this is mine, that yours; I am willing to give this for

---

[1]This section follows Smith's discussion of the *division of labor*. He uses this term in reference to economic specialization, both in terms of different professions and in terms of the separate tasks carried out by different individuals in the process of manufacturing or preparing commodities for the market.

[2]A synonym for barter.

that. . . . In almost every other race of animals each individual, which it is grown up to maturity, is entirely independent, and in its natural state has occasion for the assistance of no other living creature. But man has almost constant occasion for the help of his brethren, and it is in vain for him to expect it from their benevolence only. He will be more likely to prevail if he can interest their self-love in his favor, and show them that it is for their own advantage to do for him what he requires of them. Whoever offers to another a bargain of any kind, proposes to do this. Give me that which I want, and you shall have this which you want, is the meaning of every such offer; and it is in this manner that we obtain from one another the far greater part of those good offices which we stand in need of. It is not from the benevolence of the butcher, the brewer, or the baker, that we expect our dinner, but from their regard to their own interest. We address ourselves, not to their humanity but to their self-love, and never talk to them of our own necessities but of their advantages. . . .

PRICES AND THE FREE MARKET

. . . It is the interest of all those who employ their land, labor, or stock,[3] in bringing any commodity to market, that the quantity never should exceed the effectual demand; and it is the interest of all other people that it never should fall short of that demand.

If at any time it exceeds the effectual demand, some of the component parts of its price must be paid below their natural rate. If it is rent,[4] the interest of the landlords will immediately prompt them to withdraw a part of their land; and if it is wages or profit, the interest of the laborers in the one case, and of their employers in the other, will prompt them to withdraw a part of their labor or stock from this employment. The quantity brought to market will soon be no more than sufficient to supply the effectual demand. All the different parts of its price will rise to their natural rate, and the whole price to its natural price.

If, on the contrary, the quantity brought to market should at any time fall short of the effectual demand, some of the component parts of its price must rise above their natural rate. If it is rent, the interest of all other landlords will naturally prompt them to prepare more land for the raising of this commodity; if it is wages or profit, the interest of all other laborers and dealers will soon prompt them to employ more labor and stock in preparing and bringing it to market. The quantity brought thither will soon be sufficient to supply the effectual demand. All the different parts of its price will soon sink to their natural rate, and the whole price to its natural price. . . .

The monopolists, by keeping the market constantly under-stocked, by never fully supplying the effectual demand, sell their commodities much above the natural price, and raise their emoluments,[5] whether they consist in wages or profit, greatly above their natural rate.

The price of monopoly is upon every occasion the highest which can be got. The natural price, or the price of free competition, on the contrary, is the lowest which can be taken, not upon every occasion, indeed, but for any considerable time together. The one is upon every occasion the highest which can be squeezed out of the buyers, or which, it is supposed, they will consent to give: The other is the lowest which the sellers can commonly afford to take, and at the same time continue their business.

The exclusive privileges of corporations, statutes of apprenticeship,[6] and all those laws which restrain . . . the competition to a smaller number than might otherwise go into them, have the same tendency, though in a less degree. They are a sort of enlarged monopolies, and may frequently, for ages together and in whole classes

[3]Money or capital invested or available for investment or trading.

[4]In this sense, the cost of land; payments made by tenants to their landlord.

[5]The returns from employment, usually in the form of compensation.

[6]Laws that restricted the number of individuals who could receive training in trades through apprenticeship.

of employments, keep up the market price of particular commodities above the natural price, and maintain both the wages of the labor and the profits of the stock employed about them somewhat above their natural rate.

MERCANTALIST FALLACIES

. . . A rich country, in the same manner as a rich man, is supposed to be a country abounding in money; and to heap up gold and silver in any country is supposed to be the readiest way to enrich it. . . .

In consequence of these popular notions, all the different nations of Europe have studied, though to little purpose, every possible means of accumulating gold and silver in their respective countries. Spain and Portugal, the proprietors of the principal mines which supply Europe with those metals, have either prohibited their exportation under the severest penalties, or subjected it to a considerable duty. The like prohibition seems anciently to have {been} made a part of the policy of most other European nations. When those countries became commercial, the merchants found this prohibition, upon many occasions, extremely inconvenient. . . .

They represented {stated forcefully}, first, that the exportation of gold and silver in order to purchase foreign goods, did not always diminish the quantity of those metals in the kingdom. . . .

They represented, secondly, that this prohibition could not hinder the exportation of gold and silver, which, on account of the smallness of their bulk in proportion to their value, could easily be smuggled abroad. . . .

Those arguments . . . were solid. . . . But they were sophistical in supposing, that either to preserve or to augment the quantity of those metals required more the attention of government, than to preserve or to augment the quantity of any other useful commodities, which the freedom of trade, without any such attention, never fails to supply in the proper quantity. . . .

A country that has no mines of its own must undoubtedly draw its gold and silver from foreign countries, in the same manner as one that has no vineyards of its own must draw its wines. It does not seem necessary, however, that the attention of government should be more turned towards the one than towards the other object. A country that has wherewithal to buy wine, will always get the wine which it has occasion for; and a country that has wherewithal to buy gold and silver, will never be in want of those metals. They are to be bought for a certain price like all other commodities, and as they are the price of all other commodities, so all other commodities are the price of those metals. We trust with perfect security that the freedom of trade, without any attention of government, will always supply us with the wine which we have occasion for: and we may trust with equal security that it will always supply us with all the gold and silver which we can afford to purchase or to employ, either in circulating our commodities, or in other uses.

▾▾▾

By restraining, either by high duties, or by absolute prohibitions, the importation of such goods from foreign countries as can be produced at home, the monopoly of the home market is more or less secured to the domestic industry employed in producing them. . . . But whether it tends either to increase the general industry of the society, or to give it the most advantageous direction, is not, perhaps, altogether so evident. . . .

Every individual is continually exerting himself to find out the most advantageous employment for whatever capital he can command. It is his own advantage, indeed, and not that of the society, which he has in view. But the study of his own advantage, naturally, or rather necessarily, leads him to prefer that employment which is most advantageous to the society.

First, every individual endeavors to employ his capital as near home as he can, and consequently as much as he can in the support of domestic industry, provided always that he can thereby obtain the ordinary, or not a great deal less than the ordinary, profits of stock.

Secondly, every individual who employs his capital in the support of domestic industry, necessarily endeavors so to direct that industry, that its produce may be of the greatest possible value. . . .

As every individual, therefore, endeavors as much as he can both to employ his capital in the support of domestic industry, and so to direct that industry that its produce may be of the greatest value, every individual necessarily labors to render the annual revenue of the society as great as he can. He generally, indeed, neither intends to promote the public interest, nor knows how much he is promoting it. By preferring the support of domestic to that of foreign industry, he intends only his own security; and by directing that industry in such a manner as its produce may be of the greatest value, he intends only his own gain, and he is in this, as in many other cases, led by an invisible hand to promote an end which was no part of his intention. . . . By pursuing his own interest he frequently promotes that of the society more effectually than when he really intends to promote it. . . .

To give the monopoly of the home market to the produce of domestic industry, in any particular art or manufacture, is in some measure to direct private people in what manner they ought to employ their capital, and must, in almost all cases, be either a useless or a hurtful regulation. If the produce of domestic [industry] can be brought there as cheap as that of foreign industry, the regulation is evidently useless. If it cannot, it must generally be hurtful. It is the maxim of every prudent master of a family, never to attempt to make at home what it will cost him more to make than to buy. . . .

What is prudence in the conduct of every private family, can scarce be folly in that of a great kingdom. If a foreign country can supply us with a commodity cheaper than we ourselves can make it, better buy it of them with some part of the produce of our own industry, employed in a way in which we have some advantage. . . .

To expect, indeed, that the freedom of trade should ever be entirely restored in Great Britain, is as absurd as to expect that an Oceania or Utopia should ever be established in it. Not only the prejudices of the public, but what is much more unconquerable, the private interests of many individuals, irresistibly oppose it. . . .

The undertaker of a great manufacture, who, by the home markets being suddenly laid open to the competition of foreigners, should be obliged to abandon his trade, would no doubt suffer very considerably. That part of his capital which had usually been employed in purchasing materials and in paying his workmen might, without much difficulty perhaps, find another employment. But that part of it which was fixed in workhouses, and in the instruments of trade, could scarce be disposed of without considerable loss. The equitable regard, therefore, to his interest requires that changes of this kind should never be introduced suddenly, but slowly, gradually, and after a very long warning.

Revolution in France

Political revolutions involve more than changing leaders or replacing one ruling faction with another. Revolutions, usually through violence, bring about fundamental changes in the political order itself, often resulting in the transfer of power from one social group to another. Moreover, they affect more than just politics. Revolutions reshape legal systems, education, religious life, and economic practices and redefine relationships between rich and poor, males and females, old

and young. Because revolutions occur in societies already undergoing intellectual, economic, and social transformations, it is not surprising that history's first revolutions took place in western Europe and the Americas in the seventeenth through nineteenth centuries, when economic change undermined old social hierarchies and the emergence of new secular values weakened the foundations of divine right monarchies and privileged churches. Nor is it surprising that in recent history revolutions have spread to other parts of the world, as new ideologies and economic and social changes have affected one society after another.

The events that unfolded in France between 1789 and 1799 were not the Western world's first political revolutions. The clash in England between royalists and parliamentarians in the 1640s and 1650s, the overthrow of James II in 1688–1689, and the successful rebellion of the thirteen American colonies against British rule — respectively the Puritan Revolution, the Glorious Revolution, and the American Revolution — all occurred earlier. No previous revolution, however, came close to matching the impact and importance of the revolution in France. More social groups — peasants, urban workers, and women — participated, and it inspired more people around the globe. More important, the French Revolution went beyond the principles of constitutionalism and representative government. It championed the democratic idea that every person, irrespective of social standing, should have a voice in government and that all people should be treated equally before the law. It also aroused the first nationalist movements in Europe and inspired disaffected groups throughout the world to seek political and social change through revolution.

The French Revolution began because of a problem that has plagued rulers since the beginning of organized government — King Louis XVI (r. 1774–1792) and his ministers could not balance their budget. Having exhausted every other solution, the king in 1788 agreed to convene a meeting of the Estates General, France's representative assembly, which had last met in 1614. He hoped it would solve the government's fiscal plight by approving new taxes. The nobility, having fended off efforts to curtail its tax exemptions and privileges, saw the convening of the Estates General as an opportunity to increase its power at the expense of the monarchy. For both king and nobility, the calling of the Estates General had unexpected results: The nobility lost its privileges, and the king lost power and, ultimately, his life, when in 1793 a revolutionary assembly judged him a traitor to the revolution and ordered his execution.

Neither Louis nor the nobles had comprehended the depth of the French people's disgust with royal absolutism and aristocratic privilege. Nor had they sensed the degree to which the Enlightenment and the English and American revolutions had committed the people to fundamental change. Having convened in May 1789, the Estates General transformed itself into a National Assembly, and within months it replaced the laws and institutions of the Old Regime with a new political order based on constitutionalism, equality, and natural rights.

The Principles of the French Revolution

▾▾▾

32 ▾ *DECLARATION OF THE RIGHTS OF MAN AND OF THE CITIZEN*

The Estates General convened at Versailles on May 5, 1789. After six weeks of wrangling over voting procedures, in mid June representatives of the Third Estate (commoners), along with a handful of clergy and nobles, broke away to form a National Assembly and pledged to continue meeting until they wrote a constitution for France. On June 27 the king gave his grudging approval to the new assembly and ordered all representatives of the clergy and nobility to join its deliberations. The revolution was under way.

Among the National Assembly's most notable achievements was the approval of the Declaration of the Rights of Man and of the Citizen on August 26, 1789. Drawing on the principles of English constitutionalism, the American Revolution, and the Enlightenment, this document (which served as preamble to the Constitution of 1791) summarizes the original political and social goals of the French Revolution and countless others in the decades to follow.

QUESTIONS FOR ANALYSIS

1. **In what ways does the Declaration limit the power of the Crown and the authority of government?**
2. **According to the Declaration, what rights and responsibilities does citizenship entail?**
3. **What does the Declaration state about the origin and purpose of law?**
4. **How does the concept of rights in the Declaration differ from the concept of rights in the English Bill of Rights (source 27)?**

The representatives of the people of France, empowered to act as a national assembly, taking into consideration that ignorance, oblivion, or scorn of the rights of man are the only cause of public misery and the corruption of government, have resolved to state in a solemn declaration the natural, inalienable, and sacred rights of man, so that this declaration, continually offered to all the members of society, may forever recall them to their rights and duties; so that the actions of the legislative and executive power, able to be compared at every instant to the goal of any political institution, may be more respected; so that the demands of the citizens, from now on based on straightforward and incontestable principles, will revolve around the maintenance of the constitution and the happiness of everyone.

Consequently, the National Assembly recognizes and declares, in the presence and under the auspices of the Supreme Being, the following rights of man and citizen:

Article 1. Men are born and remain free and equal in rights; social distinctions can be established only for the common benefit.

2. The goal of every political association is the conservation of the natural and indefeasible rights of man; these rights are liberty, property, security, and resistance to oppression.

3. The source of all sovereignty is located essentially in the nation; no body, no individual can exercise authority which does not emanate from it expressly.

4. Liberty consists in being able to do anything that does not harm another. Thus the exercise of the natural rights of each man has no limits except those which assure to other members of society the enjoyment of these same rights; these limits can be determined only by law.

5. The law has the right to prohibit only those actions harmful to society. All that is not prohibited by the law cannot be hindered, and no one can be forced to do what it does not order.

6. The law is the expression of the general will; all citizens have the right to concur personally or through their representatives in its formation; it must be the same for everyone, whether it protects or punishes. All citizens, being equal in its eyes, are equally admissible to all honors, offices, and public employments, according to their abilities and without any distinction other than those of their virtues and talents.

7. No man can be accused, arrested, or detained except in instances determined by the law, and according to the practices which it has prescribed. Those who solicit, draw up, carry out, or have carried out arbitrary orders must be punished; but any citizen summoned or seized by virtue of the law must obey instantly; he renders himself guilty by resisting.

8. The law must establish only penalties that are strictly and plainly necessary, and no one can be punished except in virtue of a law established and published prior to the offense and legally applied.

9. Every man being presumed innocent until he has been declared guilty, if it is judged indispensable to arrest him, all harshness that is not necessary for making secure his person must be severely limited by the law.

10. No one may be disturbed because of his opinions, even religious, provided that their public manifestation does not disturb the public order established by law.

11. The free communication of thoughts and opinions is one of the most precious rights of man: every citizen can therefore freely speak, write, and print, except he is answerable for abuses of this liberty in instances determined by the law.

12. The guaranteeing of the rights of man and citizen requires a public force; this force is therefore instituted for the advantage of everyone, and not for the private use of those to whom it is entrusted.

13. For the maintenance of the public force, and for the expenses of administration, a tax supported in common is indispensable; it must be apportioned among all citizens on grounds of their capacities to pay.

14. All citizens have the right to determine for themselves or through their representatives the need for taxation of the public, to consent to it freely, to investigate its use, and to determine its rate, basis, collection, and duration.

15. Society has the right to demand an accountability from every public agent of his management.

16. Any society in which guarantees of rights are not assured nor the separation of powers determined has no constitution.

17. Property being an inviolable and sacred right, no one may be deprived of it except when public necessity, legally determined, requires it, and on condition of a just and predetermined compensation.

Nationalism and Revolution in France

33 ▾ *DECREE FOR PROCLAIMING THE LIBERTY AND SOVEREIGNTY OF ALL PEOPLES; PROPOSAL FOR THE LEVÉE EN MASSE; REPORT OF THE COMMITTEE OF PUBLIC SAFETY ON DRAFTING POETS AND CITIZENS FOR THE CAUSE OF REVOLUTION; REPORT OF THE COMMITTEE OF PUBLIC SAFETY ON REVOLUTIONARY EDUCATION*

Nationalism combines dedication to the interests, purposes, and well-being of one's nation-state and a sense of belonging to a larger national community that shares common values, traditions, and purposes. Such sentiments are deeply emotional and often take precedence over competing loyalties of family, church, locality, and class. This powerful ideology emerged only in the 1790s during the first years of the French Revolution, when the French people transformed themselves from subjects to citizens by abolishing monarchy and establishing a regime based on equality and popular sovereignty. For millions of French, the *patrie*, or fatherland, became more than their ancestral territory. It was their spiritual homeland and a beacon of liberty and equality for which citizens were willing to sacrifice and soldiers were prepared to die.

When war broke out in April 1792 between France and avowedly antirevolutionary Austria and Prussia, previously apathetic Frenchmen eagerly volunteered to serve in the army, especially after the Austrians and Prussians pushed across the French frontier and threatened Paris. Under General Dumouriez, the French repulsed the Austro-Prussian threat and in the fall of 1792 pushed into German territory to the east and the Austrian Netherlands to the north. It was then that the newly elected National Convention, having voted the execution of Louis XVI in September, turned the war into an ideological crusade by pledging aid to all peoples "who wish to recover their liberty." In its Decree for Proclaiming the Liberty and Sovereignty of All Peoples of December 15, 1792 (first excerpt), the National Convention ordered its generals to implement the full program of the revolution in conquered territories.

In 1793, however, disaster again threatened. With new enemies, including Britain, Holland, and Spain, and reversals on every front, the Committee of Public Safety, the twelve-man committee that had taken over the executive functions of government, took dramatic action. In August it proposed a decree (second excerpt) that ordered a program of unprecedented national mobilization. Approved by the Convention on August 23, the *levée en masse*, as it came to be known, permanently requisitioned all French to aid the military effort to protect the *patrie* and its revolution. Despite some resistance, the *levée* resulted in an army of 1,169,000 within a year; although only about 800,000 troops were trained and equipped for battle, this still was the largest army Europe had ever seen. The army was unique in other ways. The fighting men were largely citizen-soldiers committed to their cause and country, not indifferent mercenaries or unwilling recruits; officers won their commissions on merit, not through purchase or aristocratic privilege. By 1797, when the War of the First Coalition ended, Prussia had been forced to withdraw; Spain, Holland, and many German states were French satellites or allies; Austria had ceded to France the Austrian Netherlands and a good part of Italy; and Great Britain, although still at war with France, was isolated.

Throughout the fighting the Committee of Public Safety made ongoing efforts to maintain the nation's fervor by ordering schools to instill patriotism in their students and by sponsoring patriotic clubs, festivals, ceremonies, music, theatrical productions, and monuments. The third excerpt describes a plan to enlist France's poets on behalf of the revolution. The fourth and last excerpt describes a plan to found a School of Mars, a special school to train elite sixteen- and seventeen-year-old boys for service to the revolution.

QUESTIONS FOR ANALYSIS

1. How do these various decrees and proposals characterize France and its mission?
2. According to these documents, what principles does the French Revolution represent?
3. How do these documents represent France's prerevolutionary government and France's foreign enemies?
4. What does the French fatherland (*patrie*) provide for its citizens? What does it expect in return?
5. Do these edicts and proposals represent what you understand to be "propaganda"? Why or why not?

DECREE FOR PROCLAIMING THE LIBERTY AND SOVEREIGNTY OF ALL PEOPLES (December 15, 1792)

The National Convention, . . . faithful to the principles of the sovereignty of the people . . . and wishing to determine the rules to be followed by generals of the armies of the Republic in the countries where they shall carry its arms, decrees:

In the countries which are or shall be occupied by the armies of the Republic, the generals shall proclaim at once, in the name of the French nation, the sovereignty of the people, the suppression of all the established authorities and of the existing imposts and taxes, the abolition of the tithe, of feudalism, of seignioral rights, . . . of real and personal servitude, of the privileges of hunting and fishing, of *corvées*, of the nobility, and generally of all privileges.[1] . . .

---

[1]In other words, generals were charged with imposing on conquered territories what already had been accomplished by the National Assembly in 1789 — the abolition of "feudalism." This meant the end of the privileges enjoyed by noble and ecclesiastical landowners. These included a variety of payments and unpaid labor (*corvées*) owed by peasants to their lords and certain other privileges, such as exclusive hunting and fishing rights on the estate.

The French nation declares that it will treat as enemies the people who, refusing liberty and equality, or renouncing them, may wish to preserve, recall, or deal with the prince and the privileged estates;[2] it promises . . . not to subscribe to any treaty, and not to lay down its arms until after the establishment of the sovereignty and independence of the people whose territory the troops of the Republic have entered upon and who shall have adopted the principles of equality, and established a free and popular government.

PROPOSAL FOR THE LEVÉE EN MASSE (August 23, 1793)

Let us state a great truth: liberty has become the creditor of all citizens. Some owe it their labor, others their wealth, some their counsel, others the strength of their arms; all owe it the blood which flows in their veins. Thus all the French, men and women alike, people of all ages, are summoned by the *Patrie* to defend liberty. All physical and moral faculties, all political and economic means, belong to it by right; . . . Let everyone take up his post; let everyone behave as he should in this national and military outpouring that the ending of the campaign demands of us, and all will soon be proud that they had worked together to save the *Patrie*. . . .

Thus all are requisitioned, but all will not march off to war. . . .

Young men will fight, young men are called to conquer. Married men will forge arms, transport military baggage and guns and will prepare food supplies. Women, who finally are to take their rightful place in the revolution and follow their true destiny, will forget their everyday tasks: their delicate hands will work at making clothes for soldiers; they will make tents and they will extend their tender care to shelters where the defenders of the *Patrie* will receive the help that their wounds require. Children will make lint of old cloth. It is for them that we fight: children, . . . destined to gather all the fruits of the revolution, will raise their pure hands toward the skies. And old men, performing their missions again, as in the past, will be guided to the public squares of cities where they will inspire the courage of young warriors and preach the doctrines of hate for kings and the unity of the Republic.

REPORT OF THE COMMITTEE OF PUBLIC SAFETY ON DRAFTING POETS AND CITIZENS FOR THE CAUSE OF REVOLUTION (May 16, 1794)

The Committee of Public Safety summons poets to celebrate the principal events of the French Revolution, to compose hymns and poems and republican dramas, to make known the heroic deeds of the soldiers of liberty, the courage and loyalty of republicans, and the victories gained by French arms. It also summons citizens who cultivate literature to preserve for posterity the most noteworthy facts and great epochs in the rebirth of the French people, to give to history that firm and stern character which befits the annals of a great people engaged in winning the liberty which all the tyrants of Europe are attacking. It bids them to . . . inject republican morality into works intended for public instruction, while the Committee will be preparing for the Convention a type of national award to be decreed for their labors, and the date and form of the competition.

---

[2]The privileged estates are the clergy and the nobility.

REPORT OF THE COMMITTEE OF PUBLIC SAFETY ON REVOLUTIONARY EDUCATION (June 1, 1794)

What is involved here is the procedure that must be followed quickly to rear truly republican defenders of the *Patrie* and to revolutionize the youth as we have revolutionized the armies. . . .

. . . The young man of sixteen, seventeen, or seventeen and a half, is best prepared to receive a republican education. Nature's work is accomplished. At that moment the *Patrie* asks each citizen: What will you do for me? What means will you employ to defend my unity and my laws, my territory and my independence?

The Convention gives its reply to the *Patrie* today, a School of Mars is going to open its doors. Three thousand young citizens, the strongest, the most intelligent and the most commendable in conduct, are going to attend this new establishment. Three thousand children of honorable parents are going to devote themselves to shared tasks, to fashion themselves for military service. They will come from the heart of the new generation . . . to dedicate their nightly toil and their blood to their country. . . .

Love for the *Patrie*, this pure and generous sentiment which knows no sacrifice that it cannot make . . . ; love for the *Patrie* which was only a myth in the monarchies and which has filled the annals of the Republic with heroism and virtue, will become the ruling passion of the pupils of the School of Mars. . . .

In founding this outstanding revolutionary establishment, the National Convention ought thus to address the families of . . . the young citizens whom it calls to the School of Mars: "Citizens, for too long has ignorance dwelt in the countryside and the workshops; for too long fanaticism and tyranny have prevailed over the convictions of young citizens to enslave them or arrest their development. It is not for slaves or mercenaries to nurture free men; the *Patrie* itself today assumes this important function, which it will never relinquish to prejudice, deviousness, and aristocracy. Loyalty to your own families must end when the great family calls you. The Republic leaves to parents the guidance of your first years, but as soon as your intelligence develops, it loudly proclaims the right it has over you. You are born for the Republic and not to be the pride of family despotism or its victims. It takes you at that happy age when your ardent feelings are directed to virtue and respond naturally to enthusiasm for the good of and love of the *Patrie*."

Anticolonialism and Revolution in the Americas

Despite the many contrasts between the British colonies of North America and the Portuguese/Spanish colonies of Mexico and Central and South America, all of them won their independence between the 1770s and the 1830s. Although the independence movements in North and Latin America unfolded differently, throughout the Americas the rebels had similar grievances and ideals. Grievances included mercantilist restrictions on trade, high taxes, and a lack of self-government; the ideals were inspired by English constitutionalism, the Enlightenment, and, in the case of Latin America, the revolutions in North America and France.

Although rooted in similar causes, the revolutions resulted in governments that differed markedly. In the northern thirteen colonies, opponents of British rule co-

alesced in a unified movement under the Continental Congress and George Washington, and after independence this unity was preserved in the U.S. Constitution. In South America, where struggles for independence were waged on a regional basis under generals such as Simón Bolívar, Bernardo O'Higgins, and José de San Martín, the end of Spanish and Portuguese authority resulted in more than a dozen independent states. In North America, federal and state governments drew on the principles of English constitutionalism to guarantee basic freedoms and extend political rights to a majority of adult white males. In Latin America, with its traditions of Spanish/Portuguese absolutism and aristocracy, wealthy landowners controlled the new states and excluded the peasant masses from politics.

Social and economic relationships also differed markedly in the postcolonial era. Although the new U.S. government preserved slavery and continued to restrict women's legal and political rights, property holding was widespread. A fluid class structure and economic expansion ensured that not only the political elite but also the common people would benefit from independence. In Latin America, however, continuation of the colonial class structure meant that the economic and social chasm between the mass of propertyless Indian peasants and the tiny elite of white property owners remained intact. In this respect, the independence movement in Latin America ended colonialism but lacked important features of a true revolution.

"Simple Facts, Plain Arguments, and Common Sense"

▼▼▼

34 ▾ *Thomas Paine, COMMON SENSE*

After years of growing tensions over taxes, British imperial policy, the power of colonial legislatures, and a host of other issues, in April 1775 the American Revolution began with the clash between British regulars and American militiamen at the Battle of Lexington and Concord. In May the Green Mountain Boys under Ethan Allen took Fort Ticonderoga on Lake Champlain, and in June the British defeated colonial troops in the Battle of Bunker Hill outside of Boston at the cost of more than a thousand casualties.

Despite these events, in the summer and fall of 1775 most Americans still supported compromise and reconciliation with Great Britain. They were convinced that evil ministers, not the king, were responsible for British policy and hoped that views of conciliatory British politicians such as Edmund Burke would prevail. Then in January 1776 there appeared in Philadelphia a thirty-five-page pamphlet titled *Common Sense*, written by Thomas Paine (1737–1809), a bankrupt onetime corset-maker, sailor, tobacconist, and minor customs official who had migrated to Pennsylvania from England only fourteen months earlier to escape debtor's prison. It was the most brilliant political pamphlet written during the American Revolution, and perhaps ever in the English language.

In three months *Common Sense* sold more than 100,000 copies, one for every eight or ten adults in the colonies. It "burst from the press," wrote Benjamin

Rush, a Pennsylvania physician and signer of the Declaration of Independence, "with an effect which has rarely been produced in any age or country." Written with passion and vivid imagery, Paine's pamphlet brought into focus American reservations about England and expressed American aspirations to create a newer, freer, more open society as an independent nation. It accelerated the move toward the events of July 2, 1776, when the delegates to the Second Continental Congress created the United States of America, and of July 4, when they signed the Declaration of Independence.

During the Revolutionary War, Paine fought in Washington's army and composed pamphlets to bolster American spirits. In the late 1780s, he returned to England but in 1792 fled to France after his public support of the French Revolution led to his indictment for sedition. Chosen as a delegate to the French National Convention (although he knew no French), Paine was later imprisoned for ten months during the Reign of Terror, and on his release he resided with James Monroe, the American ambassador to France. While in France he attacked Christianity in his pamphlet *The Age of Reason*, whose notoriety was such that on his return to the United States in 1802 he was vilified as an atheist. Impoverished and disgraced, he died unheralded in New York City in 1809.

QUESTIONS FOR ANALYSIS

1. What are Paine's views of the origins and defects of monarchy as a form of government and hereditary succession as a principle of government?
2. What are his views of King George III?
3. What characteristics does Paine ascribe to Great Britain in general and the British government in particular? How might his background explain his negative views?
4. How does Paine counter the arguments of Americans who still sought reconciliation with Great Britain?
5. Despite Paine's rejection of the British government, do his ideas in *Common Sense* owe a debt to the principles of the English Bill of Rights (source 27)?
6. What is there about the pamphlet's language, tone, and arguments that might explain its enormous popularity?

OF MONARCHY AND HEREDITARY SUCCESSION

Government by kings was first introduced into the world by the heathens, from whom the children of Israel copied the custom. It was the most prosperous invention the Devil ever set on foot for the promotion of idolatry. The heathens paid divine honors to their deceased kings, and the Christian world has improved on the plan by doing the same to their living ones.[1] How impious is the title of sacred Majesty applied to a

[1]The reference is to the theory of divine right monarchy, which asserted that kings were God's specially chosen lieutenants to rule his subjects and were even in some limited sense divine figures themselves.

worm, who in the midst of his splendor is crumbling into dust! . . .

To the evil of monarchy we have added that of hereditary succession; and as the first is a degradation and lessening of ourselves, so the second, claimed as a matter of rights, is an insult and imposition on posterity. For all men being originally equals, no *one* by *birth* could have a right to set up his own family in perpetual preference to all others forever, and though himself might deserve *some* decent degree of honors of his contemporaries, yet his descendants might be far too unworthy to inherit them. . . .

Secondly, as no man at first could possess any other public honors than were bestowed upon him, so the givers of those honors could have no power to give away the right of posterity, and though they might say "we choose you for our head," they could not without manifest injustice to their children say "that your children and your children's children shall reign over our's forever." Because such an unwise, unjust, unnatural compact might perhaps, in the next succession put them under the government of a rogue or a fool. . . .

The most plausible plea which hath ever been offered in favor of hereditary succession is that it preserves a nation from civil wars; and were this true, it would be weighty; whereas, it is the most barefaced falsity ever imposed upon mankind. The whole history of England disowns the fact. Thirty kings and two minors have reigned in that distracted kingdom since the conquest,[2] in which time there have been (including the Revolution) no less than eight civil wars and nineteen rebellions. Wherefore instead of making for peace, it makes against it, and destroys the very foundation it seems to stand upon. . . .

In short, monarchy and succession have laid (not this or that kingdom only) but the world in blood and ashes. 'Tis a form of government which the word of god bears testimony against, and blood will attend it.

[2]A reference to the conquest of England in 1066 by the Duke of Normandy, who reigned as King William I until his death in 1087.

THOUGHTS ON THE PRESENT STATE OF AMERICAN AFFAIRS

In the following pages I offer nothing more than simple facts, plain arguments, and common sense; and have no other preliminaries to settle with the reader, than that he will divest himself of prejudice and prepossession, and suffer his reason and his feelings to determine for themselves; that he will put on, or rather that he will not put off, the true character of a man, and generously enlarge his views beyond the present day.

Volumes have been written on the subject of the struggle between England and America. Men of all ranks have embarked in the controversy, from different motives, and with various designs; but all have been ineffectual, and the period of debate is closed. Arms as the last resource decide the contest; the appeal was the choice of the king, and the continent has accepted the challenge. . . .

The sun never shined on a cause of greater worth. 'Tis not the affair of a city, a county, a province, or a kingdom; but of a continent — of at least one-eighth part of the habitable globe. 'Tis not the concern of a day, a year, or an age; posterity are virtually involved in the contest, and will be more or less affected even to the end of time by the proceedings now. Now is the seedtime of continental union, faith, and honor. The least fracture now will be like a name engraved with the point of a pin on the tender rind of a young oak; the wound would enlarge with the tree, and posterity read it in full grown characters. . . .

I have heard it asserted by some, that as America has flourished under her former connection with Great Britain, the same connection is necessary towards her future happiness. . . . Nothing can be more fallacious than this kind of argument. We may as well assert that because a child has thrived upon milk, that it is never to have meat, or that the first twenty years of our lives is to become a precedent for the next twenty. But even this is admitting more than is true; for I answer roundly that America would have flourished as much, and probably much more, had no European power taken any notice of her. The commerce by which she hath enriched herself are the necessaries of life, and will always have a market while eating is the custom of Europe.

But she has protected us, say some. That she hath engrossed[3] us is true, and defended the continent at our expense as well as her own is admitted; and she would have defended Turkey from the same motive, viz., for the sake of trade and dominion. . . .

We have boasted the protection of Great Britain without considering that her motive was *interest,* not *attachment;* and that she did not protect us from *our enemies* on *our account,* but from her enemies on her own account, from those who had no quarrel with us on any *other account,* and who will always be our enemies on the *same account.* . . .

As I have always considered the independency of this continent an event which sooner or later must arrive, so from the late rapid progress of the continent to maturity, the event cannot be far off. Wherefore, on the breaking out of hostilities, it was not worth the while to have disputed a matter which time would have finally redressed, unless we meant to be in earnest; otherwise it is like wasting an estate on a suit at law, to regulate the trespasses of a tenant whose lease is just expiring. No man was a warmer wisher for a reconciliation than myself, before the fatal nineteenth of April, 1775, but the moment the event of that day was made known, I rejected the hardened, sullen-tempered Pharaoh of England[4] forever; and disdain the wretch, that with the pretended title of FATHER OF HIS PEOPLE can unfeelingly hear of their slaughter, and composedly sleep with their blood upon his soul.

But admitting that matters were now made up, what would be the event? I answer, the ruin of the continent. And that for several reasons.

First. The powers of governing still remaining in the hands of the king, he will have a negative [veto] over the whole legislation of this continent. And as he hath shown himself such an inveterate enemy to liberty, and discovered such a thirst for arbitrary power, is he, or is he not, a proper person to say to these colonies, *You shall make no laws but what I please!* . . .

Secondly. That as even the best terms which we can expect to obtain can amount to no more than a temporary expedient, or a kind of government by guardianship, which can last no longer than till the colonies come of age, so the general face and state of things in the interim will be unsettled and unpromising. Emigrants of property will not choose to come to a country whose form of government hangs but by a thread, and who is every day tottering on the brink of commotion and disturbance; and numbers of the present inhabitants would lay hold of the interval to dispose of their effects, and quit the continent. . . .

If there is any true cause of fear respecting independence, it is because no plan is yet laid down. Men do not see their way out. Wherefore, as an opening into that business I offer the following hints; at the same time modestly affirming that I have no other opinion of them myself than that they may be the means of giving rise to something better. . . .

Let the assemblies be annual, with a president only. The representation more equal, their business wholly domestic, and subject to the authority of a continental congress.

Let each colony be divided into six, eight, or ten, convenient districts, each district to send a proper number of delegates to congress, so that each colony send at least thirty. The whole number in congress will be at least 390. Each congress to sit and to choose a president by the following method. When the delegates are met, let a colony be taken from the whole thirteen colonies by lot, after which let the congress choose (by ballot) a president from out of the delegates of that province. In the next congress,

[3]To occupy with troops.

[4]A reference to King George III of England.

let a colony be taken by lot from twelve only, omitting that colony from which the president was taken in the former congress, and so proceeding on till the whole thirteen shall have had their proper rotation. And in order that nothing may pass into a law but what is satisfactorily just, not less than three fifths of the congress to be called a majority. He that will promote discord, under a government so equally formed as this, would have joined Lucifer in his revolt. . . .

But where, say some, is the king of America? I'll tell you, friend, he reigns above, and doth not make havoc of mankind like the Royal Brute of Great Britain. Yet that we may not appear to be defective even in earthly honors, let a day be solemnly set apart for proclaiming the charter; let it be brought forth placed on the divine law, the Word of God; let a crown be placed thereon, by which the world may know, that so far as we approve of monarchy, that in America THE LAW IS KING. For as in absolute governments the king is law, so in free countries the law *ought* to BE king, and there ought to be no other. But lest any ill use should afterwards arise, let the crown at the conclusion of the ceremony be demolished, and scattered among the people whose right it is. . . .

Bolívar's Dreams for Latin America

▼▼▼

35 ▾ *Simón Bolívar, THE JAMAICA LETTER*

Simón Bolívar, the most renowned leader of the Latin American independence movement, was born to a wealthy Venezuelan landowning family in 1783. Orphaned at an early age, he was educated by a private tutor who inspired in his pupil an enthusiasm for the principles of the Enlightenment and republicanism. After spending three years in Europe, Bolívar returned in 1803 to New Spain, where the death of his new bride plunged him into grief and caused his return to France and Italy. In 1805 in Rome he took a vow to dedicate his life to the liberation of his native land from Spain. On his return he became a leading member of the republican-minded group in Caracas that in 1808 began to agitate for independence and in 1810 deposed the colonial governor. Until his death in 1830, Bolívar dedicated himself to the independence movement as a publicist, diplomat, theoretician, and statesman. His greatest contribution was as the general who led the armies that defeated the Spaniards and liberated the northern regions of South America.

The so-called Jamaica Letter was written in 1815 during a self-imposed exile in Jamaica. It was addressed to "an English gentleman," probably the island's governor, the Duke of Manchester. The Venezuelan Republic had collapsed in May as a result of a viciously fought Spanish counteroffensive, divisions among the revolutionaries, and opposition from many Indians, blacks, and mulattos, who viewed the Creole landowners, not the Spaniards, as their oppressors. The letter was written in response to a request from the Englishman for Bolívar's thoughts about the background and prospects of the liberation movement.

QUESTIONS FOR ANALYSIS

1. **Why does Bolívar believe that Spain's efforts to hold on to its American territories are doomed?**
2. **According to Bolívar, what Spanish policies made Spanish rule odious to him and other revolutionaries?**
3. **In Bolívar's view, what complicates the task of predicting Spanish America's political future?**
4. **Does Bolívar's letter reveal concern for the economic and social condition of South America's nonwhite population? What are some of the implications of Bolívar's attitudes?**
5. **Based on your reading of Bolívar, what guesses can you make about the reasons that the new nations of South America found it difficult to achieve stable republican governments?**

. . . Success will crown our efforts, because the destiny of America has been irrevocably decided; the tie that bound her to Spain has been severed. . . . That which formerly bound them now divides them. The hatred that the Peninsula[1] inspired in us is greater than the ocean between us. It would be easier to have the two continents meet than to reconcile the spirits of the two countries. The habit of obedience; a community of interest, of understanding, of religion; mutual goodwill; a tender regard for the birthplace and good name of our forefathers; in short, all that gave rise to our hopes, came to us from Spain. As a result there was born a principle of affinity that seemed eternal. . . . At present the contrary attitude persists: we are threatened with the fear of death, dishonor, and every harm; there is nothing we have not suffered at the hands of that unnatural stepmother — Spain. The veil has been torn asunder. We have already seen the light, and it is not our desire to be thrust back into darkness. . . .

The role of the inhabitants of the American hemisphere has for centuries been purely passive. Politically they were non-existent. We are still in a position lower than slavery, and therefore it is more difficult for us to rise to the enjoyment of freedom. . . . States are slaves because of either the nature or the misuse of their constitutions; a people is therefore enslaved when the government, by its nature or its vices, infringes on and usurps the rights of the citizen or subject. Applying these principles, we find that America was denied not only its freedom but even an active and effective tyranny. Under absolutism there are no recognized limits to the exercise of governmental powers. The will of the great sultan, khan, bey, and other despotic rulers is the supreme law, carried out more or less arbitrarily by the lesser pashas, khans, and satraps of Turkey and Persia, who have an organized system of oppression in which inferiors participate according to the authority vested in them. To them is entrusted the administration of civil, military, political, religious, and tax matters. But, after all is said and done, the rulers of Isfahan are Persians; the viziers of the Grand Turk are Turks; and the sultans of Tartary are Tartars. . . .

How different is our situation! We have been harassed by a conduct which has not only deprived us of our rights but has kept us in a sort of permanent infancy with regard to public affairs. If we could at least have managed our domestic affairs and our internal administration,

---

[1]Refers to the Iberian Peninsula, consisting of Spain and Portugal.

we could have acquainted ourselves with the processes and mechanics of public affairs. . . .

Americans today, and perhaps to a greater extent than ever before, who live within the Spanish system occupy a position in society no better than that of serfs destined for labor. . . . Yet even this status is surrounded with galling restrictions, such as being forbidden to grow European crops, or to store products which are royal monopolies, or to establish factories of a type the Peninsula itself does not possess. To this add the exclusive trading privileges, even in articles of prime necessity, and the barriers between American provinces, designed to prevent all exchange of trade, traffic, and understanding. In short, do you wish to know what our future held? — simply the cultivation of the fields of indigo, grain, coffee, sugar cane, cacao, and cotton; cattle raising on the broad plains; hunting wild game in the jungles; digging in the earth to mine its gold — but even these limitations could never satisfy the greed of Spain.

So negative was our existence that I can find nothing comparable in any other civilized society. . . . Is it not an outrage and a violation of human rights to expect a land so splendidly endowed, so vast, rich, and populous, to remain merely passive?

As I have just explained, we were cut off and, as it were, removed from the world in relation to the science of government and administration of the state. We were never viceroys or governors, save in the rarest of instances; seldom archbishops and bishops; diplomats never; as military men, only subordinates; as nobles, without royal privileges. In brief, we were neither magistrates nor financiers and seldom merchants — all in flagrant contradiction to our institutions. . . .

It is harder, Montesquieu[2] has written, to release a nation from servitude than to enslave a free nation. This truth is proven by the annals of all times, which reveal that most free nations have been put under the yoke, but very few enslaved nations have recovered their liberty. Despite the convictions of history, South Americans have made efforts to obtain liberal, even perfect, institutions, doubtless out of that instinct to aspire to the greatest possible happiness, which, common to all men, is bound to follow in civil societies founded on the principles of justice, liberty, and equality. But are we capable of maintaining in proper balance the difficult charge of a republic? Is it conceivable that a newly emancipated people can soar to the heights of liberty, and, unlike Icarus, neither have its wings melt nor fall into an abyss? Such a marvel is inconceivable and without precedent. There is no reasonable probability to bolster our hopes.

More than anyone, I desire to see America fashioned into the greatest nation in the world, greatest not so much by virtue of her area and wealth as by her freedom and glory. Although I seek perfection for the government of my country, I cannot persuade myself that the New World can, at the moment, be organized as a great republic. Since it is impossible, I dare not desire it; yet much less do I desire to have all America a monarchy because this plan is not only impracticable but also impossible. Wrongs now existing could not be righted, and our emancipation would be fruitless. The American states need the care of paternal governments to heal the sores and wounds of despotism and war. . . .

From the foregoing, we can draw these conclusions: The American provinces are fighting for their freedom, and they will ultimately succeed. Some provinces as a matter of course will form federal and some central republics; the larger areas will inevitably establish monarchies, some of which will fare so badly that they will disintegrate in either present or future revolutions. To

---

[2]Montesquieu (1689–1755) was a French philosopher, historian, and jurist best known for his *Spirit of the Laws* (1755) and his theory that the powers of government — executive, legislative, and judicial — must be separated to ensure individual freedom.

consolidate a great monarchy will be no easy task, but it will be utterly impossible to consolidate a great republic. . . .

When success is not assured, when the state is weak, and when results are distantly seen, all men hesitate; opinion is divided, passions rage, and the enemy fans these passions in order to win an easy victory because of them. As soon as we are strong and under the guidance of a liberal nation which will lend us her protection, we will achieve accord in cultivating the virtues and talents that lead to glory. Then will we march majestically toward that great prosperity for which South America is destined. . . .

Multiple Voices III

The Slave Trade Debate: European, African, and American Perspectives

BACKGROUND

In 1453, in his *Chronicle of the Discovery and Conquest of Guinea*, the Portuguese author Gomes Eannes de Azurara became one of the first Europeans to record his thoughts and feelings about the deportation and sale of African slaves by Europeans. Although his book was meant to glorify early Portuguese explorations and their sponsor, Prince Henry the Navigator, Eannes acknowledged that he was deeply saddened by the sight of African slaves disembarking from a Portuguese ship in the port city of Lagos. He deplored their "wretched state" and was reduced to tears by the sobs of families that soon would be broken apart and sold to different owners. His remorse was fleeting, however. He took comfort in the fact that in Portugal these slaves would be converted to Christianity, treated well ("not one of them was put in irons"), and given an opportunity to overcome their "bestial sloth."

For the next three centuries many Europeans depended on such rationalizations to dull their unease about their involvement in the slave trade. Others defended it as an economic necessity. Most ignored it. As a result, the slave trade steadily grew, until in the eighteenth century approximately 6 million Africans were transported across the Atlantic as slaves. As the slave trade peaked, however, abolitionist movements emerged in England, the United States, and France, and soon the institution of slavery was on the defensive. In the 1790s, French revolutionaries outlawed slavery throughout France's empire, and slaves and former slaves in the French colony of Saint Domingue rose up in rebellion, initiating a slave revolt that led to the formation of an independent Haiti in 1804. More significant was the decision of the British Parliament in 1807 to outlaw the slave trade throughout the British Empire. What had been the world's leading slave-trading nation now became its leading opponent, one that used its navy to block illegal slaving off Africa's coast, pressured other states to enact antislaving legislation, and encouraged "legitimate" trade between Africa and Europe.

What explains the sudden rise in abolitionist sentiment? Some Europeans turned against slavery out of religious conviction. Many early abolitionists were Quakers, members of a small English religious sect with a tradition of egalitarianism and pacifism. They wrote many of the first antislavery treatises and were prime movers in the founding of the first abolitionist societies, including the Pennsylvania Society for Promoting the Abolition of Slavery in 1784 and, in England, the Society for the Abolition of the Slave Trade in 1787. Methodism, an eighteenth-century offshoot of the Church of England with a broad popular following and a commitment to personal rebirth and social reform, also took a strong stance against slavery. Methodism's founder, John Wesley, denounced slavery both for brutalizing the slave and for threatening the salvation of slave owners and traders. Abolitionist sentiment also was encouraged by the intellectual atmosphere fostered by the Enlightenment, with its emphasis on freedom, natural rights, and progress. Finally, the campaign against the slave trade and slavery was strengthened by the American and French revolutions, movements dedicated to furthering the rights of man even though many of their leaders were slaveholders.

Inevitably, the abolitionists' goals were opposed by slave traders, planters, and some politicians, who marshaled a variety of religious, economic, and political arguments to support their cause. Ending the slave trade also was opposed by many Africans who had come to depend on the sale of slaves to Europeans as a source of wealth and power. The efforts of slavery's defenders were futile, however. When Brazil outlawed slavery in 1888, slavery and the slave trade in the Atlantic world had come to an end. By then, however, untold damage had been done, and slavery's racist legacy remained.

THE SOURCES

The excerpts that follow represent arguments both for and against the slave trade made between 1774 and 1820. The first excerpt is from the pamphlet "Thoughts Upon Slavery," written by the charismatic Methodist leader John Wesley in 1774. With much material borrowed from *Some Historical Accounts of Guinea*, published in 1771 by the American Quaker Anthony Benezet, Wesley's widely read treatise reveals the moral earnestness and emotional commitment of evangelical Protestant abolitionists. The second excerpt is from the *Address to the National Assembly in Favor of the Abolition of the Slave Trade*, a pamphlet published in 1790 by the Society of the Friends of Blacks, a French antislavery organization founded in 1788. Its anonymous author draws on moral principles derived from the Enlightenment and the early stages of the French Revolution.

The views of those who favored the continuation of the slave trade are represented by two sources. The first is taken from a memorandum prepared in 1797 by W. S. van Ryneveld, a director of the Dutch East India Company, at the request of the British government. The British had conquered the Dutch East India Company's settlement at the Cape of Good Hope in southern Africa in 1795 after their enemy the French had reduced the Netherlands to a puppet state in the wars of the French Revolution. The British sought van Ryneveld's views on a variety of issues, including the feasibility of eliminating slavery from the Cape colony, whose farmers had depended on slave labor imported from East Africa and Madagascar since the 1600s. Van Ryneveld, a South African slave owner himself, strongly opposed ending slavery for practical reasons. Following his advice, the British imported another 3,500 slaves to the Cape before 1807 and brought in another 2,100 Africans "rescued" by the British navy from outlawed slave ships but then forced to enter into fourteen-year apprenticeships with South African employers.

The final source contains the words of Osei Bonsu, the king of Asante, as recorded by Joseph Dupuis, a British envoy sent to the Asante capital city of Kumasi in 1820 to discuss Asante-British commerce. Beginning in the 1680s, Asante became the dominant state on the Guinea Coast, with approximately 100,000 square miles of territory and much of its income derived from the sale of prisoners of war, criminals, and other social outcasts to European slavers. Clearly Osei Bonsu was unhappy when he learned that in 1807 the British had suddenly decided that the slave trade must end.

QUESTIONS FOR ANALYSIS

1. Consider the arguments of slavery's detractors, Wesley and the author representing the Society of the Friends of Blacks. On what do they agree and disagree? What are their reasons for opposing the slave trade and slavery? What can be inferred about the intended audience for their writings? How do they try to appeal to that audience?
2. Obviously van Ryneveld and Osei Bonsu oppose the arguments of Wesley and the French abolitionists, but on what other matters do they agree and disagree?
3. On the basis of these four excerpts, what conclusions can you draw about the reasons that the abolitionists, not the defenders of slavery, were successful in attaining their goals?

1 ▾ John Wesley, THOUGHTS UPON SLAVERY

[After describing the cruelties of slavery, Wesley makes an appeal directly to the sea captains, merchants, and planters who profit from slavery.]

And, first, to the captains. . . . Most of *you* know, the country of *Guinea* . . . how populous, how fruitful, how pleasant it was a few years ago. You know the people were not stupid, not wanting in sense, considering the few means of improvement they enjoyed. Neither did you find them savage, fierce, cruel, treacherous, or unkind to strangers. On the contrary, they were in most parts a sensible and ingenious people. They were kind and friendly, courteous and obliging, and remarkably fair and just in their dealings. Such are the men whom you . . . tear away from this lovely country; part by stealth, part by force, part made captives in those wars, which you raise or foment on purpose. You have seen them torn away, children from their parents, parents from their children: Husbands from their wives,

wives from their beloved husbands, brethren and sisters from each other. You have dragged them who had never done you any wrong, perhaps in chains, from their native shore. You have forced them into your ships like a herd of swine, them who had souls immortal as your own. . . . You have carried the survivors into the vilest slavery, never to end but with life. . . .

May I speak plainly to you? I must. Love constrains me: Love to *you*, as well as to those you are concerned with. Is there a GOD? You know there is. Is He a just GOD? Then there must be a state of retribution: A state wherein the just GOD will reward every man according to his works. Then what reward will he render to you? O think betimes! Before you drop into eternity! Think now, *He shall have judgment without mercy, that showed no mercy.*

Are you a man? Then you should have a *human* heart. But have you indeed? What is your heart made of? Is there no such principle as compassion there? Do you never *feel* another's pain? . . . When you saw the flowing eyes, the heaving breasts, the bleeding sides and tortured limbs of your fellow-creatures, [were] you a stone, or a brute? Did you look upon them with the eyes of a tiger? When you squeezed the agonizing creatures down in the ship, or when you threw their poor mangled remains into the sea, had you no relenting? Did not one tear drop from your eye, one sigh escape from your breast? Do you feel no relenting now? If you do not, you must go on, till the measure of your iniquities is full. Then will the great GOD deal with *you*, as you have dealt with *them*, and require all their blood at your hands. And at that day it shall be more tolerable for *Sodom* and *Gomorrah*[1] than for you! But if your heart does relent, though in a small degree, know it is a call from the GOD of love. . . . Today resolve, GOD being your helper, to escape for your life. — Regard not money! All that a man hath will he give for his life? Whatever you lose, lose not your soul: nothing can countervail that loss. Immediately quit the horrid trade: At all events, be an honest man.

This equally concerns every merchant, who is engaged in the slave-trade. . . . O let his resolution be yours! Have no more any part in this detestable business. Instantly leave it to those unfeeling wretches, "Who laugh at human nature and compassion!" Be *you* a man! Not a wolf, a devourer of the human species! Be merciful, that you may obtain mercy!

And this equally concerns every gentleman that has an estate in our *American* plantations. . . . Instantly, at any price, were it the half of your goods, deliver thyself from blood-guiltiness! Thy hands, thy bed, thy furniture, thy house, thy lands are at present stained with blood. Surely it is enough; accumulate no more guilt; spill no more blood of the innocent! Do not hire another to shed blood: Do not pay him for doing it! Whether you are a Christian or no, show yourself a man; be not more savage than a lion or a bear!

O thou GOD of love, thou who art loving to every man . . . have compassion upon these outcasts of men, who are trodden down as dung upon the earth! Arise and help these that have no helper, whose blood is spilt upon the ground like water! . . . O burst thou all their chains in sunder; more especially the chains of their sins: Thou, Saviour of all, make them free, that they may be free indeed!

---

[1]According to the Book of Genesis, Sodom and Gomorrah were two cities destroyed by God for their sins.

2 ▾ Society of the Friends of Blacks, ADDRESS TO THE NATIONAL ASSEMBLY IN FAVOR OF THE ABOLITION OF THE SLAVE TRADE

The immediate emancipation of the blacks would not only be a fatal operation for the colonies; it would even be a deadly gift for the blacks, in the state of abjection and incompetence to which cupidity has reduced them. It would be to abandon to themselves and without assistance children in the cradle or mutilated and impotent beings.

It is therefore not yet time to demand that liberty; we ask only that one cease butchering thousands of blacks regularly every year in order to take hundreds of captives; we ask that one henceforth cease the prostitution, the profaning of the French name, used to authorize these thefts, these atrocious murders; we demand in a word the abolition of the slave trade. . . .

In regard to the colonists, we will demonstrate to you that if they need to recruit blacks in Africa to sustain the population of the colonies at the same level, it is because they wear out the blacks with work, whippings, and starvation; that, if they treated them with kindness and as good fathers of families, these blacks would multiply and that this population, always growing, would increase cultivation and prosperity. . . .

If some motive might on the contrary push them [the blacks] to insurrection, might it not be the indifference of the National Assembly about their lot? Might it not be the insistence on weighing them down with chains, when one consecrates everywhere this eternal axiom: *that all men are born free and equal in rights*. . . .

It is worthy of the first free Assembly of France to consecrate the principle of philanthropy which makes of humankind only one single family, to declare that it is horrified by this annual carnage which takes place on the coasts of Africa, that it has the intention of abolishing it one day, of mitigating the slavery that is the result, of looking for and preparing, from this moment, the means.

The humanity, justice, and magnanimity that have guided you [members of the National Assembly] in the reform of the most profoundly rooted abuses gives hope to the Society of the Friends of Blacks that you will receive with benevolence its demand in favor of that numerous portion of humankind, so cruelly oppressed for centuries. . . .

. . . You have engraved on an immortal monument[2] that all men are born and remain free and equal in rights; you have restored to the French people these rights that despotism had for so long despoiled; . . . you have broken the chains of feudalism that still degraded a good number of our fellow citizens; you have announced the destruction of all the stigmatizing distinctions that religious or political prejudices introduced into the great family of humankind. . . .

We are not asking you to restore to French blacks those political rights which alone, nevertheless, attest to and maintain the dignity of man; we are not even asking for their liberty. No; slander, bought no doubt with the greed of the shipowners, ascribes that scheme to us and spreads it everywhere; they want to stir up everyone against us, provoke the planters and their numerous creditors, who take alarm even at gradual emancipation. They want to alarm all the French, to whom they depict the prosperity of the colonies as inseparable from the slave trade and the perpetuity of slavery.

No, never has such an idea entered into our minds. . . .

[2]Declaration of the Rights of Man and of the Citizen (see source 32).

3 ▾ W. S. van Ryneveld, RESPONSE TO GOVERNOR MACARTNEY'S QUESTIONNAIRE

We know very well, that here, both within and without the Colony, no sufficient number of white people can be obtained to perform in culture [cultivation] the labour of the slaves; and, on the other hand, experience shows us every day that the procreation of slaves, in proportion to number, is very trifling, and even not worth mentioning; and that, moreover, a very considerable number of slaves is lost by continual disorders, especially by bile and putrid fevers, to which they are very subject.

The political state of this Colony, I think, is actually of that nature that, however injurious slavery of itself may be to the morals and industry of the inhabitants, still the keeping of slaves has now become, as it is styled, a necessary evil; and, at least, a sudden interdiction to the importation of slaves would occasion a general injury, as long as such a number of hands as is requisite for the culture cannot be obtained from another part, at a rate that may be thought proportionate to the produce arising from the lands. . . .

I perfectly acknowledge . . . that if there were no slaves at the Cape the peasants would then be more industrious and useful to the State, and that the facility of procuring slaves renders the inhabitants of this country lazy, haughty and brutal.

Every kind of vice and a perfect corruption of morals is owing to that. But how to help it? If slavery had been interdicted at the first settling of this Colony, then the inhabitants would doubtless have become more industrious and useful to each other. . . .

Yet, the business is done. Slavery exists and is now even indispensable. It is absolutely necessary because there are no other hands to till this extensive country, and therefore it will be the work, not of years, but as it were of centuries to remove by attentive and proper regulation this evil established with the first settling of the Colony. Should the slaves be now declared free, that would immediately render both the country and these poor creatures themselves miserable; not only all tillage would then be at an end, but also the number of freemen, instead of their being (as now) useful members of, would then really become a charge to, society. And should the importation of slaves be interdicted, on a sudden [at once], without any means being provided towards supplying other hands for the tillage, then the Colony would thereby be caused to languish . . . and especially the culture of grain would thereby be reduced to decay.

4 ▾ Joseph Dupuis, SUMMARY OF A CONVERSATION WITH OSEI BONSU, KING OF ASANTE

"Now," said the king, after a pause, "I have another palaver [long discussion], and you must help me to talk it. A long time ago the great king [of England] liked plenty of trade, more than now; then many ships came, and they bought ivory, gold, and slaves; but now he will not let the ships come as before, and the people buy gold and ivory only. This is what I have in my head, so now tell me truly, like a friend, why does the king, do so? . . . I only want to hear what you think as a friend: this is not like the other palavers." I [Dupuis] was confessedly at a loss for an argument that might pass as a satisfactory reason. . . . The king did not deem it plausible, that this obnoxious traffic should have been abolished from motives of humanity alone; neither would he admit that it lessened the number either of domestic or foreign wars.

Taking up one of my observations, he remarked, "the white men who go to council with your master, and pray to the great God for him, do not understand my country, or they would not say the slave trade was bad. But if they think it bad now, why did they think it good before. . . . If the great king would like to restore this trade, it would be good for the white men and for me too, because Ashanti is a country for war, and the people are strong; so if you talk that palaver for me properly, in the white country, if you go there, I will give you plenty of gold, and I will make you richer than all the white men.

. . . "And when he [the king of England] sees what is true, he will surely restore that trade. I cannot make war to catch slaves in the bush, like a thief. My ancestors never did so. But if I fight a king, and kill him when he is insolent, then certainly I must have his gold, and his slaves, and the people are mine too. Do not the white kings act like this? Because I hear the old men say, that before I conquered Fante[3] . . . white men came in great ships, and fought and killed many people; and then they took the gold and slaves to the white country: and sometimes they fought together. That is all the same as these black countries. . . . When I fought Gyaman,[4] I did not make war for slaves, but because Dinkera [the king] sent me an arrogant message and killed my people, and refused to pay me gold as his father did. Then . . . like my ancestors, and I killed Dinkera, and took his gold, and brought more than 20,000 slaves to Kumasi. Some of these people being bad men, I washed my stool[5] in their blood. . . . But then some were good people, and these I sold or gave to my captains: many, moreover, died, because this country does not grow too much corn . . . and what can I do? Unless I kill or sell them, they will grow strong and kill my people. Now you must tell my master [the king of England] that these slaves can work for him, and if he wants 10,000 he can have them. And if he wants fine handsome girls and women to give his captains, I can send him great numbers."

---

[3]The Fante arrived on the Guinea Coast sometime after 1600 and established a number of very small states before being conquered by Asante in the 1760s.

[4]A state to the northwest of Asante, and a rival to Asante power in this region.

[5]A reference to the Asante "Golden Stool," a symbol of Asante royal power.

Chapter 6

Africa, Southwest Asia, and India in the Seventeenth and Eighteenth Centuries

AROUND 1600, SOUTHWEST ASIA and India, regions dominated by the large and powerful Ottoman, Safavid, and Mughal empires, would seem to have had little in common with Africa, a continent divided into hundreds of kingdoms, confederations, chiefdoms, independent cities, and regions with no formal states. Southwest Asia and India, moreover, had but two major religions, Islam and Hinduism. Africa, on the other hand, had many religions: Islam in the Mediterranean north, in the Sudan, and on the east coast; Christianity in Ethiopia; and numerous varieties of animism throughout the continent. In comparison to Africa, India and Southwest Asia had more people, more cities, and more commercial and cultural contacts with Europe and East Asia.

Despite these differences, Africa, Southwest Asia, and India shared a number of common historical experiences in the seventeenth and eighteenth centuries. All three areas, for example, experienced political instability, which in some cases led to the collapse of once formidable states. The Safavid Empire was overrun and disappeared in the 1730s, and the Mughal Empire was reduced to impotence and irrelevance by the mid 1700s. The Ottoman Empire survived, but with shrunken borders, a demoralized populace, and an army that was a shadow of the force that had marched from victory to victory in the fifteenth and sixteenth centuries. In West Africa the Songhai Empire fell apart after a defeat by invading Moroccans in 1591, and in the southeast the Kingdom of Monomotapa, following years of Portuguese penetration, was overrun by a former client state, the Changamire Kingdom, in the 1680s. Other African states experienced civil war, invasion, or the erosion of central authority. These included Ethiopia, the Christian state in east Africa; Benin, a kingdom on the Gulf of Guinea; and Kanem-Bornu, in the central Sudan. Political decline in Africa was not universal. Dahomey, the Asante Confederation, and Oyo all emerged as formidable powers, and hundreds of chieftainships maintained their traditional lines of authority. Overall, however, African political life became less stable and more subject to conflict in the 1600s and 1700s.

Increased European involvement is another common thread in the histories of the three regions. This involvement was not necessarily harmful. With their purchasing power enhanced by the availability of American silver, European merchants increased their demand for the agricultural products, manufactured products, textiles, and a host of other products from Ottoman lands, Persia, and India. In other cases, however, European involvement meant actual political control. In India in the eighteenth century, officials of the British East India Company took advantage of the Mughal Empire's disintegration by establishing their authority over Bengal in the northeast and other regions on the subcontinent's east coast. In Africa the 1600s and 1700s saw the first permanent white settlements on the continent and a dramatic expansion of the slave trade. European settlement began in 1652 when Dutch farmers arrived at the southern tip of Africa and soon began to push into the interior in search of land and slaves. Meanwhile, on Africa's west coast Europeans presided over a substantial increase in the transatlantic slave trade in response to demands for slaves from sugar producers in Brazil and the West Indies. As many as 6 million Africans were transported to the Americas as slaves in the 1700s. Slave exports also increased on Africa's east coast. By the end of the eighteenth century, Dutch, Portuguese, Arab, and French merchants were selling thousands of African slaves every year to buyers in the Middle East, India, and French-controlled islands in the Indian Ocean. This spectacular growth in the slave trade underlined Africa's vulnerability in an age of growing global interaction.

Africa's Curse: The Slave Trade

Slavery has been practiced throughout history, in every corner of the globe. Slavery has existed in small farming villages in China and great imperial cities such as ancient Rome; it has been practiced by pastoral nomads, plantation owners, small farmers, emperors, and modern totalitarian dictators. Slavery is mentioned in ancient Sumerian law codes from the fourth millennium B.C.E. and is still the lot of millions of human beings today despite its official condemnation by the world's governments.

In recent history slavery has uniquely affected the people of Africa, who became a source of unpaid labor in many parts of the world, especially the Americas. The transatlantic slave trade began in the fifteenth century under the Portuguese, who at first made small shipments of Africans to Portugal to serve as domestics and then larger shipments to the Canary Islands, the Madeiras, and São Tomé to work on sugar plantations. By 1500, Portuguese merchants were exporting approximately 500 slaves each year. That number grew appreciably in the mid 1500s, when the plantation system was established in Brazil and subsequently spread to Spanish America, the West Indies, and British North America. In the 1700s, when Great Britain became the leading purveyor of slaves, the transatlantic slave trade peaked, with more than 6 million slaves transported to the Americas.

Almost every aspect of African slavery is the subject of debate among historians. Did the enslavement of Africans result from racism, or were Africans enslaved because they were available and convenient to the market across the Atlantic? Did the loss of millions of individuals to slavery over 500 years have serious or minimal demographic consequences for Africa? Was the political instability of African states linked to the slave trade or to other factors? Did reliance on selling slaves to Europeans impede Africa's economic development? Did European governments abolish the slave trade because of humanitarianism or hardheaded economic calculation?

One thing is certain. For the millions of Africans who were captured, shackled, wrenched from their families, branded, sold, packed into the holds of ships, sold once more, and put to work in American mines and fields, enslavement meant pain, debasement, and fear. For them, slavery was an unmitigated disaster.

The Path to Enslavement in America

▼▼▼

36 ▾ *Olaudah Equiano,* *THE INTERESTING NARRATIVE OF OLAUDAH EQUIANO WRITTEN BY HIMSELF*

In 1789 no fewer than 100 abolitionist books and pamphlets were published in England, but none was more widely read than the autobiography of the former slave Olaudah Equiano. In his memoir Equiano relates that he was born in 1745 in Iboland, an area east of the Niger River delta that today is part of Nigeria. He also describes how he was captured and sold into slavery when he was about eleven years old and, having survived the harrowing Atlantic crossing, served three masters, including an officer in the British navy; an English sea captain who took him to the West Indian island of Montserrat; and finally Robert King, a Quaker merchant from Philadelphia.

In many ways Equiano's experiences as a slave were exceptional. He never served as a plantation slave, and while owned by the naval officer, he learned to read and write. Under his three masters, he made numerous trips back and forth across the Atlantic and in the process learned skills relating to navigation, bookkeeping, and commerce. Having purchased his freedom from his last owner in 1766, he took up residence in England, where he supported himself as a barber, servant, and crew member on voyages to the Mediterranean and around the Atlantic. In the 1770s he joined the English abolitionist movement. As a result of the contacts he made with the movement's leaders, in the late 1780s he was given a government post with the responsibility of arranging the transfer of food and other provisions to Sierra Leone, a newly founded colony that abolitionists hoped would serve as an African homeland for freed slaves. Dismissed after a year, Equiano turned to writing his autobiography, which was published in 1789 with the financial support of leading abolitionists. Heavily promoted by Equiano on a lecture tour that took him to dozens of British towns and cities, his book went through eight editions in the 1790s. It is generally acknowledged that Equiano's autobiography strengthened the abolitionist cause and helped bring about the act of Parliament in 1807 that abolished the British slave trade.

How factual is Equiano's narrative? Historians must raise such a question about any historical source, especially autobiographies, whose authors cannot be expected to be totally objective when writing about themselves or to be totally accurate in recalling childhood events. Equiano's memoirs, furthermore, were written with a specific purpose, namely to discredit slavery and garner support for the abolitionist cause. One scholar, Vincent Carretta from the University of Maryland, has suggested that Equiano fabricated the account of his kidnapping in Africa and his voyage across the Atlantic on a slave ship. A baptismal certificate and a Royal Navy document, he argues, show that Equiano was actually born in South Carolina, not Africa.

Other scholars consider Carretta's evidence inconclusive and continue to believe that the memoir is generally accurate. Certainly comparing Equiano's description

of his slave experience with what we know from other sources suggests that his work is free of exaggeration and distortion. This includes the following excerpt, in which he describes his harsh introduction to slavery.

QUESTIONS FOR ANALYSIS

1. **On the basis of Equiano's account, what is the role of Africans in the slave trade?**
2. **What does Equiano's account reveal about the effect of slavery and the slave trade on African society?**
3. **What were the characteristics of slavery that Equiano encountered?**
4. **Once the slaves were on board the slave ship, what experiences contributed to their despair and demoralization, according to Equiano?**
5. **What factors might have contributed to the brutal treatment of the slaves by the ship's crew?**

TAKEN CAPTIVE

Generally when the grown people in the neighborhood were gone far in the fields to labor, the children assembled together in some of the neighbors' premises to play, and commonly some of us used to get up a tree to look out for any assailant or kidnapper that might come upon us, for they sometimes took those opportunities of our parents' absence to attack and carry off as many as they could seize. . . . One day, when all our people were gone out to their work as usual and only I and my dear sister were left to mind the house, two men and a woman got over our walls, and in a moment seized us both, and without giving us time to cry out or make resistance they stopped our mouths and ran off with us into the nearest wood. . . .

For a long time we had kept to the woods, but at last we came into a road which I believed I knew. I had now some hopes of being delivered, for we had advanced but a little way before I discovered some people at a distance, on which I began to cry out for their assistance: but my cries had no other effect than to make them tie me faster and stop my mouth, and then they put me into a large sack. They also stopped my sister's mouth and tied her hands, and in this manner we proceeded till we were out of the sight of these people. When we went to rest the following night they offered us some victuals, but we refused it, and the only comfort we had was in being in one another's arms all that night and bathing each other with our tears. But alas! we were soon deprived of even the small comfort of weeping together. The next day proved a day of greater sorrow than I had yet experienced, for my sister and I were then separated while we lay clasped in each other's arms. It was in vain that we besought them not to part us; she was torn from me and immediately carried away, while I was left in a state of distraction not to be described. I cried and grieved continually, and for several days I did not eat anything but what they forced into my mouth. At length, after many days' traveling, during which I had often changed masters, I got into the hands of a chieftain in a very pleasant country. This man had two wives and some children, and they all used me extremely well and did all they could to comfort me, particularly the first wife, who was something like my mother. . . . This first master of mine, as I may call him, was a smith, and my principal employment was working his bellows, which were the same kind as I had seen in my vicinity. . . . I believe it was gold he worked, for it was of a lovely bright yellow color and was worn by the women on their wrists and ankles. I was there I suppose about a month, and they at last used to trust me some little distance from the house. This liberty I used in embracing every opportunity to inquire the way to my own home: and I also sometimes, for the same purpose, went with the maidens in the cool of the evenings to bring pitchers of water from the springs for the use of the house.

▷ Equiano escapes but terrified of being alone in the forest at night returns to his household.

Soon after this my master's only daughter and child by his first wife sickened and died, which affected him so much that for some time he was almost frantic, and really would have killed himself had he not been watched and prevented. However, in a small time afterwards he recovered and I was again sold. I was now carried to the left of the sun's rising, through many different countries and a number of large woods. The people I was sold to used to carry me very often when I was tired either on their shoulders or on their backs. I saw many convenient well-built sheds along the roads at proper distances, to accommodate the merchants and travelers who lay in those buildings along with their wives, who often accompany them; and they always go well armed.

▷ Equiano encounters his sister, but again they are quickly separated.

I was now more miserable, if possible, than before. The small relief which her presence gave me from pain was gone, and the wretchedness of my situation was redoubled by my anxiety after her fate and my apprehensions lest her sufferings should be greater than mine, when I could not be with her to alleviate them. Yes, thou dear partner of all my childish sports! thou sharer of my joys and sorrow! happy should I have ever esteemed myself to encounter every misery for you, and to procure your freedom by the sacrifice of my own. . . .

I did not long remain after my sister [departed]. I was again sold and carried through a number of places till, after traveling a considerable time, I came to a town called Tinmah in the most beautiful country I had yet seen in Africa. . . . I was sold here . . . by a merchant who lived and brought me there. I had been about two or three days at his house when a wealthy widow, a neighbor of his, came there one evening, and brought with her an only son, a young gentleman about my own age and size. Here they saw me; and, having taken a fancy to me, I was bought of the merchant, and went home with them. . . . The next day I was washed and perfumed, and when meal-time came I was led into the presence of my mistress, and ate and drank before her with her son. This filled me with astonishment; and I could scarce help expressing my surprise that the young gentleman should suffer me, who was bound, to eat with him who was free; and not only so, but that he would not at any time either eat or drink till I had taken first, because I was the eldest, which was agreeable to our custom. Indeed everything here, and all their treatment of me, made me forget that I was a slave. . . . There were likewise slaves daily to attend us, while my young master and I with other boys sported with our darts and bows and arrows, as I had been used to do at home. In this resemblance to my former happy state I passed about two months; and I now began to think I was to be adopted into the family, and was beginning to be reconciled to my situation, and to forget by degrees my misfortunes, when all at once the delusion vanished; for without the least previous knowledge, one morning early, while my dear master and companion was still asleep, I was wakened out of my reverie to fresh sorrow, and hurried away. . . .

At last I came to the banks of a large river, which was covered with canoes in which the people appeared to live with their household utensils and provisions of all kinds. I was beyond measure astonished at this, as I had never before seen any water larger than a pond or a rivulet: and my surprise was mingled with no small fear when I was put into one of these canoes and we began to paddle and move along the river. We continued going on thus till night, and when we came to land and made fires on the banks, each family by themselves, some dragged their canoes on shore, others stayed and cooked in theirs and laid in them all night. . . . Thus I continued to travel, sometimes by land, sometimes by water, through different countries and various nations, till at the end of six or seven months after I had been kidnapped I arrived at the sea coast.

THE SLAVE SHIP

The first object which saluted my eyes when I arrived on the coast was the sea, and a slave ship which was then riding at anchor and waiting for its cargo. These filled me with astonishment, which was soon converted into terror when I was carried on board. I was immediately handled and tossed up to see if I were sound by some of the crew, and I was now persuaded that I had gotten into a world of bad spirits and that they were going to kill me. Their complexions too differing so much from ours, their long hair and the language they spoke (which was very different from any I had ever heard) united to confirm me in this belief. Indeed such were the horrors of my views and fears at the moment that, if ten thousand worlds had been my own, I would have freely parted with them all to have exchanged my condition with that of the meanest slave in my own country. When I looked round the ship too and saw a large furnace or copper boiling and a multitude of black people of every description chained together, every one of their countenances expressing dejection and sorrow, I no longer doubted of my fate; and quite overpowered with horror and anguish, I fell motionless on the deck and fainted. When I recovered a little I found some black people about me, who I believed were some of those who had brought me on board and had been receiving their pay; they talked to me in order to cheer me, but all in vain. . . .

I was soon put down under the decks, and there I received such a salutation in my nostrils as I had never experienced in my life: so that with the loathsomeness of the stench and crying together, I became so sick and low that I was not able to eat, nor had I the least desire to taste anything. I now wished for the last friend, death, to relieve me; but soon, to my grief, two of the white men offered me eatables, and on my refusing to eat, one of them held me fast by the hands and laid me across I think the windlass, and tied my feet while the other flogged me severely. I had never experienced anything of this kind before, and although, not being used to the water, I naturally feared that element the first time I saw it, yet nevertheless could I have got over the nettings I would have jumped over the side, but I could not; and besides, the crew used to watch us very closely who were not chained down to the decks, lest we should leap into the water: and I have seen some of these poor African prisoners most severely cut for attempting to do so, and hourly whipped for not eating. This indeed was often the case with myself. In a little time after, amongst the poor chained men I found some of my own nation, which in a small degree gave ease to my mind. I inquired of these what was to be done with us; they gave me to understand we were to be carried to these white people's country to work for them. I then was a little revived, and thought if it were no worse than working, my situation was not so desperate: but still I feared I should be put to death, the white people looked and acted, as I thought, in so savage a manner; for I had never seen among my people such instances of brutal cruelty, and this not only shown towards us blacks but also to some of the whites themselves. One white man in particular I saw, when we were permitted to be on deck, flogged so unmercifully with a large rope near the foremast that he died in consequence of it; and they tossed him over the side as they would have done a brute. This made me fear these people the more, and I expected nothing less than to be treated in the same manner. . . .

At last, when the ship we were in had got in all her cargo, they made ready with many fearful noises, and we were all put under deck so that we could not see how they managed the vessel. But this disappointment was the last of my sorrow. The stench of the hold while we were on the coast was so intolerably loathsome that it was dangerous to remain there for any time, and some of us had been permitted to stay on the deck for the fresh air; but now that the whole ship's cargo were confined together it became absolutely pestilential. The closeness of the place and the heat of the climate, added to the number in the ship, which was so crowded that each had scarcely room to turn himself, almost suffocated us. This produced copious perspirations, so that the air soon became unfit for respiration from a variety of loathsome smells, and brought on a sickness among the slaves, of which many died, thus falling victims to the improvident avarice, as I may call it, of their purchasers. This wretched situation was again aggravated by the galling of the chains, now become insupportable, and the filth of the necessary tubs, into which the children often fell and were almost suffocated. The shrieks of the women and the groans of the dying rendered the whole a scene of horror almost inconceivable. Happily perhaps for myself I was soon reduced so low here that it was thought necessary to keep me almost always on deck, and from my extreme youth I was not put in fetters. . . .

One day, when we had a smooth sea and moderate wind, two of my wearied countrymen who were chained together (I was near them at the time), preferring death to such a life of misery, somehow made through the nettings and jumped into the sea: immediately another quite dejected fellow, who on account of his illness was suffered to be out of irons, also followed their example; and I believe many more would very soon have done the same if they had not been prevented by the ship's crew, who were instantly alarmed. Those of us that were the most active were in a moment put down under the deck, and there was such a noise and confusion amongst the people of the ship as I never heard before, to stop her and get the boat out to go after the slaves. However two of the wretches were drowned, but they got the other and afterwards flogged him unmercifully for thus attempting to prefer death to slavery. In this manner we continued to undergo more hardships than I can now relate, hardships which are inseparable from this accursed trade. Many a time we were near suffocation from the want of fresh air, which we were often without for whole days together. This and the stench of the necessary tubs carried off many. . . .

At last we came in sight of the island of Barbados, at which the whites on board gave a great shout and made many signs of joy to us. We did not know what to think of this, but as the vessel drew nearer we plainly saw the harbor and other ships of different kinds and sizes, and we soon anchored amongst them off Bridgetown. Many merchants and planters now came on board, though it was in the evening. They put us in separate parcels and examined us attentively. They also made us jump, and pointed to the land, signifying we were to go there. . . .

We were not many days in the merchant's custody before we were sold after their usual manner, which is this: On a signal given, (as the beat of a drum) the buyers rush at once into the yard where the slaves are confined, and make choice of that parcel they like best. The noise and clamor with which this is attended and the eagerness visible in the countenances of the buyers serve not a little to increase the apprehensions of the terrified Africans, who may well be supposed to consider them as the ministers of that destruction to which they think themselves devoted. In this manner, without scruple, are relations and friends separated, most of them never to see each other again. I remember in the vessel in which I was brought over, in the men's apartment there were several brothers who, in the sale, were sold in different lots; and it was very moving on this occasion to see and hear their cries at parting. O, ye nominal Christians! might not an African ask you, learned you this from your God who says unto you, Do unto all men as you would men should do unto you?

The Economics of the Slave Trade on Africa's Coast

37 ▾ *Thomas Phillips,* *A JOURNAL OF A VOYAGE MADE IN THE* HANNIBAL *OF LONDON IN 1694*

As Olaudah Equiano's memoir reveals, the road to slavery in the Americas often began in inland villages where, as a result of military defeat, slave raids, or the decision of a chieftain or king, Africans were wrenched from their homes and marched to a slave market on the coast. There, while they were herded together in closely guarded holding pens or prisonlike structures, complex and sometimes lengthy business negotiations took place between European merchants whose ships lay anchored offshore and African slave merchants, many of whom were kings or major chieftains. Many European merchants recorded their experiences in such negotiations in memoirs or journals, and their recollections provide a wealth of information about the economics of the slave trade. These accounts also offer many insights into how African and European slave traders viewed each other and their profession. They reveal that for millions of human beings the transatlantic slave trade was a nightmare, but for many others it was one more way to make a profit in an increasingly commercialized world.

The following account of a slave voyage from England to Africa to the Caribbean island of Barbados in 1693 and 1694 is by Thomas Phillips, an English merchant. In 1693 he purchased the slave ship *Hannibal* in partnership with other London merchants who were members of the Royal African Company, a trading company chartered by King Charles II in 1672. The *Hannibal*, along with five other ships, departed England late in 1693 for Whydah, a kingdom on the Guinea coast that is located in present-day Benin some 200 miles east of Lagos, Nigeria. Whydah, the coastal village where the king resided, was rapidly developing into a major slave market and had been the site of an English trading station, or "factory," since 1682. The events Phillips describes took place in May 1694.

QUESTIONS FOR ANALYSIS

1. What evidence does the source provide about the attitudes of the Whydah king and nobility toward Europeans? Did they consider themselves equal, inferior, or superior to Europeans?
2. What do Phillips's words and actions reveal about his views of Africans?
3. What does the source reveal about Africans as businessmen? What did they hope to gain from trading with Europeans? How would you describe their business methods?
4. What can you infer from Phillips's account about the impact of the Whydah slave trade on Africa's interior?

5. **Compile a list of individuals or groups of individuals who benefited economically from the slave trade. Do not limit yourself to Europeans or simply to merchants and investors. You should end up with at least some Asians on your list.**
6. **Compare the attitudes toward slavery of the king of Whydah and his nobility with those of King Afonso of Kongo (source 20) some 200 years earlier. How might one account for these differences?**

Our factory [at Whydah] lies about three miles from the sea-side, where we were carry'd in hammocks, which the factor [agent] . . . sent to attend our landing, with several arm'd blacks that belong'd to him for our guard; . . .

Our factory . . . stands low near the marshes, which renders it a very unhealthy place to live in; the white men the African company send there, seldom returning to tell their tale: 'tis compass'd round with a mudwall, about six foot high, and on the southside is the gate; within is a large yard, a mud thatch'd house, where the factor lives, with the white men; also a storehouse, a trunk [a prison-like holding area] for slaves, and a place where they bury their dead white men, call'd, very improperly, the hog-yard; there is also a good forge, and some other small houses. . . .

As soon as the king understood of our landing, he sent two of his cappasheirs, or noblemen, to compliment us at our factory, where we design'd to continue [planned to stay], that night, and pay our devoirs [respects] to his majesty next day . . . ; whereupon he sent two more of his grandees to invite us there that night, saying he waited for us, and that all former captains used to attend him the first night: whereupon being unwilling to infringe the custom, or give his majesty any offence, we took our hammocks, and Mr. Peirson, myself, Capt. Clay, our surgeons, pursers,[1] and about 12 men, arm'd for our guard, were carry'd to the king's town, which contains about 50 houses. . . .

We returned him thanks by his interpreter, and assur'd him how great affection our masters, the royal African company of England, bore to him, for his civility and fair and just dealings with their captains; and that notwithstanding there were many other Places, more plenty of negro slaves that begg'd their custom [business patronage], yet they had rejected all the advantageous offers made them out of their good will to him, and therefore had sent us to trade with him, to supply his country with necessaries, and that we hop'd he would endeavour to continue their favour by his kind usage and fair dealing with us in our trade, that we may have our slaves with all expedition. . . . He answer'd that . . . we should be fairly dealt with, and not impos'd upon; But he did not prove as good as his word; . . . so after having examin'd us about our cargoe, what sort of goods we had, and what quantity of slaves we wanted, etc., we took our leaves and return'd to the factory. . . .

According to [our] promise we attended his majesty [the next morning] with samples of our goods, and made our agreement about the prices, tho' not without much difficulty . . . ; next day we paid our customs to the king and cappasheirs . . . then the bell [ringer] was order'd to go about to give notice to all people to bring their slaves to the trunk to sell us. . . .

Capt. Clay [the captain of another English ship] and I had agreed to go to the trunk to buy the slaves by turns, each his day, that we might have no distraction or disagreement in our trade,

---

[1]A ship's officer who kept accounts and business papers.

as often happens when there are here more ships than one, and their disagreements create animosities, underminings, and out-bidding each other, whereby they enhance the prices to their general loss and detriment, the blacks well knowing how to make the best use of such opportunities, and as we found make it their business, and endeavour to create and foment misunderstandings and jealousies between commanders, it turning to their great account in the disposal of their slaves.

When we were at the trunk, the king's slaves, if he had any, were the first offer'd to sale, . . . and we must not refuse them, tho' as I observ'd they were generally the worst slaves in the trunk, and we paid more for them than any others, which we could not remedy, it being one of his majesty's prerogatives: then the cappasheirs each brought out his slaves according to his degree and quality, the greatest first, etc. and our surgeon examin'd them well in all kinds, to see that they were sound [in] wind and limb, making them jump, stretch out their arms swiftly, looking in their mouths to judge of their age; for the cappasheirs are so cunning, that they shave them all close before we see them, so that let them be never so old we can see no grey hairs in their heads or beards; and then having liquor'd[2] them well and sleek with palm oil, 'tis no easy matter to know an old one from a middle-age one. . . .

When we had selected from the rest such as we liked, we agreed in what goods to pay for them, the prices being already stated before the king, how much of each sort of merchandize we were to give for a man, woman, and child, which gave us much ease, and saved abundance of disputes and wranglings . . . ; then we mark'd the slaves we had bought in the breast, or shoulder, with a hot iron, having, the letter of the ship's name on it, the place being before anointed with a little palm oil, which caus'd but little pain, the mark being usually well in four or five days, appearing very plain and white after. . . .

When our slaves were come to the sea-side, our canoes were ready to carry them off to the longboat, if the sea permitted, and she convey'd them aboard ship, where the men were all put in irons, two and two shackled together, to prevent their mutiny, or swimming ashore.

The negroes are so wilful and loath to leave their own country, that they have often leap'd out of the canoes, boat and ship, into the sea, and kept under water till they were drowned, to avoid being taken up and saved by our boats, which pursued them; they having a more dreadful apprehension of Barbadoes than we can have of hell, tho' in reality they live much better there than in their own country; but home is home, etc. . . .

I have been inform'd that some commanders have cut off the legs and arms of the most wilful, to terrify the rest, for they believe if they lose a member, they cannot return home again: I was advis'd by some of my officers to do the same, but I could not be persuaded to entertain the least thought of it, much less put in practice such barbarity and cruelty to poor creatures, who, excepting their want of Christianity and true religion (their misfortune more than fault) are as much the works of God's hands, and no doubt as dear to him as ourselves; nor can I imagine why they should be despis'd for their colour, being what they cannot help, and the effect of the climate it has pleas'd God to appoint them. I can't think there is any intrinsick value in one colour more than another, nor that white is better than black, only we think so because we are so, and are prone to judge favourably in our own case, as well as the blacks, who in odium [hatred and loathing] of the colour, say, the devil is white, and so paint him. . . .

After we are come to an agreement for the prices of our slaves, . . . we are oblig'd to pay our customs to the king and cappasheirs for leave to trade, protection and justice; which for every ship are as follow, *viz.*

[2]To dress (as leather) with oil or grease.

To the king six slaves value in cowries,[3] or what other goods we can persuade him to take, but cowries are most esteem'd and desir'd; all which are measur'd in his presence, and he would wrangle with us stoutly about heaping up the measure.

To the cappasheirs in all two slaves value, as above. . . .

The best goods to purchase slaves here are cowries, the smaller the more esteem'd; . . .

The next in demand are brass neptunes [large pans for obtaining salt] or basons [plates], very large, thin, and flat; for after they have bought them they cut them in pieces to make . . . bracelets, and collars for their arms legs and necks.

The other preferable goods are blue paper sletias, cambricks or lawns, caddy chints, broad ditto [all types of cloth], coral, large, smooth, and of a deep red, rangoes [beads] large and red, iron bars, powder [gunpowder], and brandy . . . but without the cowries and brass they will take none of the last goods, and but small quantities at best, especially if they can discover that you have a good store of cowries and brass aboard, then no other goods will serve their turn, till they have got as much as you have; and after, for the rest of the goods they will be indifferent, and make you come to their own terms, or else lie [offshore] a long time for your slaves, so that those you have on board are dying while you are buying others ashore; therefore every man that comes here, ought to be very cautious in making his report to the king at first, of what sorts and quantities of goods he has, and be sure to say his cargo consists mostly in iron, coral, rangoes, chints, etc. so that he may dispose of those goods as soon as he can, and at last his cowries and brass will bring him slaves as fast as he can buy them; but this is to be understood of a single ship: or more, if the captains agree, which seldom happens; for where there are divers [various] ships, and of separate interests, about buying the same commodity they commonly undermine, betray, and out-bid one the other; and the Guiney [Guinea] commanders words and promises are the least to be depended upon of any I know [who] use the sea; for they would deceive their fathers in their trade if they could. . . .

When our slaves are aboard we shackle the men two and two, while we lie in port, and in sight of their own country, for 'tis then they attempt to make their escape, and mutiny; to prevent which we always keep sentinels upon the hatchways, and have a chest full of small arms, ready loaden [loaded] and prim'd, constantly lying at hand upon the quarterdeck. . . . Their chief diet is call'd dabbadabb, being Indian corn ground as small as oatmeal, in iron mills, which we carry for that purpose; and after mix'd with water, and boil'd well in a large copper furnace, till 'tis as thick as a pudding, about a peckful of which in vessels, call'd crews, is allow'd to 10 men, with a little salt, malagetta [pepper], and palm oil, to relish; they are divided into messes of ten each, for the easier and better order in serving them: Three days a week they have horse-beans boil'd for their dinner and supper, great quantities of which the African company do send aboard us for that purpose; these beans the negroes extremely love and desire, beating their breast, eating them, and crying Pram! Pram! which is Very good! they are indeed the best diet for them, having a binding quality, and consequently good to prevent the flux [diarrhea], which is the inveterate distemper that most affects them, and ruins our voyages by their mortality. . . . We often at sea in the evenings would let the slaves come up into the sun to air themselves, and make them jump and dance for an hour or two to our bagpipes, harp, and fiddle, by which exercise to preserve them in health; but notwithstanding all our endeavour,

[3]*Cowrie* is a term for any number of marine snails that live in the coastal waters of the Indian and Pacific oceans. The snails produce thick polished shells, many of which are brightly colored and speckled. Particularly prized in Africa was a one-inch-long yellow shell produced off the Maldive Islands in the Indian Ocean. Many tons of these shells were harvested and processed for sale to Europeans, who transported them to Europe as ballast in the holds of their ships. There they were repurchased by slave traders before leaving for Africa.

'twas my hard fortune to have great sickness and mortality among them.

Having bought my compliment of 700 slaves, *viz.* 480 men and 220 women, and finish'd all my business at Whidaw, I took my leave of the old king, and his cappasheirs, and parted, with many affectionate expressions on both sides, being forced to promise him that I would return again the next year, with several things he desired me to bring him from England; and having sign'd bills of lading [loading] . . . for the negroes aboard, I set sail the 27th of July in the morning. . . .

I deliver'd alive at Barbadoes to the company's factors 372, which being sold, came out at about nineteen pounds per head. . . .

Political Change in the Ottoman and Mughal Empires

Empires are forged through military conquest, and most disintegrate and disappear as a result of military defeat. So it was for Muslim empires in Southwest Asia, Africa, and India from the late sixteenth century onward. The Songhai Empire of Africa, which had dominated the western Sudan since the late fifteenth century, fell apart and was replaced by a number of small regional states after a musket-bearing Moroccan army defeated its forces at the Battle of Tondibi in 1591. The Safavid Empire of Persia came to an abrupt end in 1722 when Afghan warriors took the capital city of Isfahan and the Safavids fled to the hills, leaving the region open to Ottoman invasion, decades of anarchy, and the establishment of the weak Qajar Dynasty in the 1790s. In India the Mughal Empire for all intents and purposes ceased to exist after the warlord Nadir Shah — who had seized power in Persia — invaded India in 1739 and sacked Delhi, the Mughal capital. The Ottoman Empire outlasted the other Islamic empires, but in the end it too disappeared in the wake of military defeat, in this case in World War I.

In each of these empires, decay had set in long before military defeat led to their demise. Like countless previous empires, all of them faced deteriorating financial situations once their expansion ended. Large armies were still needed to defend borders and maintain authority over newly conquered peoples, many of whom resented their new rulers and resisted integration into a new state. Rulers themselves added to the financial strain by spending large sums on court life, the arts, and ambitious building projects. When these empires were expanding, such costs could be met by confiscating the wealth of newly conquered peoples and adding these new subjects to the tax rolls. After expansion ended, however, expenses could be met only by raising taxes, running deficits, and selling offices and titles. Such expedients impeded economic growth, encouraged government corruption and inefficiency, and simply put off the day of fiscal reckoning.

The Songhai, Ottoman, Safavid, and Mughal empires all were plagued by succession struggles and deteriorating leadership. The Ottoman and Safavid practice of raising the rulers' sons as indulged prisoners in the palace to prevent rebellions contributed to a long series of uninformed, inexperienced, and often debauched sultans and shahs. In Songhai, of the eight sixteenth-century rulers who followed the empire's founders, Sunni Ali (r. 1469–1492) and Askia Muhammad (r. 1493–1528), all but three were murdered in office or deposed. Leadership also was a problem in Mughal India. Aurangzeb's (r. 1658–1707) persecution of his Hindu subjects and his costly military campaigns in the south set the stage for the mutinies and rebellions that undermined Mughal authority.

Although the causes of political decline in these empires were broadly similar, the consequences differed. After the breakup of the Songhai Empire, the western Sudan was ruled by a number of small regional states, some of which were conquered and merged around 1800 into a larger state, the Sokoto Caliphate. Persia survived the civil wars of the immediate post-Safavid Era but then languished for a century and a half under the Zand and Qajar dynasties. The Ottoman Empire continued, but efforts of reforming sultans and ministers failed to halt territorial losses or prevent growing Western interference. The fall of the Mughal Empire had especially significant consequences. It paved the way for the gradual British takeover of the Indian subcontinent — the first time a European state was able to extend its authority over an ancient center of civilization in Asia. It also marked the beginning of a new wave of European imperialism that by the late nineteenth century would bring Africa and much of Asia under Western control.

An Insider's View of Ottoman Decline

38 ▾ *Mehmed Pasha, THE BOOK OF COUNSEL FOR VIZIERS AND GOVERNORS*

Along with battlefield defeats, fiscal crises, internal turmoil, and palace intrigues, another sign of Ottoman decline in the seventeenth and eighteenth centuries was the appearance of numerous plans for reviving the empire's fortunes. Among the most candid and insightful works of this type was *The Book of Counsel for Viziers and Governors*, written in the early eighteenth century by an Ottoman treasury official, Mehmed Pasha. Although little is known about Mehmed Pasha's early life, it is likely that he was born into the family of a petty merchant in Istanbul in the 1650s. While in his teens, he was apprenticed to an official in the Ottoman treasury department, in which he worked for the rest of his career. His service was rewarded in 1702, when he was named chief *defterdar*, or treasurer of the empire. Over the next fifteen years, Mehmed Pasha lost and regained this office no fewer than seven times as different factions became ascendant in the sultan's administration. In 1717, however, he was executed on order of the sultan after he was blamed for the loss of a fortress in the Balkans.

It is unknown when exactly Mehmed Pasha wrote *The Book of Counsel for Viziers and Governors*, but internal evidence suggests it was around 1703 or 1704. It is a book written by a man who had firsthand knowledge of the failings of the Ottoman state and was deeply disturbed by what he knew.

QUESTIONS FOR ANALYSIS

1. Mehmed Pasha cites several examples of how the sultan's subjects suffer as a result of government policies and practices. What examples does he cite, and what are their causes?
2. What, according to the author, are the reasons for the government's financial problems? What solutions does he propose?
3. How does Mehmed Pasha's description of the Ottoman military and government differ from the observations made by Ogier Ghiselin de Busbecq in the sixteenth century (source 9)?
4. What do Mehmed Pasha's comments reveal about the economic situation in the Ottoman Empire around 1700?
5. Little was done to implement the changes suggested by Mehmed Pasha and other Ottoman reformers. What do you think made it so difficult to achieve meaningful reforms?

THE RESULTS OF BRIBERY

It is essential to guard against giving an office through bribery to the unfit and to tyrannical oppressors. For giving office to such as these because of bribes means giving permission to plunder the property of the subjects. . . . In addition to what is given as a bribe, he must make a profit for himself and his followers. . . . There is no more powerful engine of injustice and cruelty, for bribery destroys both faith and state. . . .

If it becomes necessary to give a position because of bribes, in this way its holder has permission from the government for every sort of oppression. Stretching out the hand of violence and tyranny against the poor subjects along his route of travel[1] and spreading fear among the poor, he destroys the wretched peasants and ruins the cultivated lands. As the fields and villages become empty of husbandmen, day by day weakness comes to land and property, which remain destitute of profits, revenues, harvest, and benefit. In addition to the fact that it causes a decline in the productivity of the subjects and in the revenues of the Treasury, through neglect of the employment of tilling and lack of the work of agriculture, there is the greatest probability . . . that it will cause scarcity, dearth, mishaps and calamities.

FINANCIAL ISSUES

The business of the Treasury is among the most important and essential affairs of the Exalted Government. The man who is chief treasurer needs to know and understand . . . the Treasury employees who for their own advantage are the cause of ruin and destruction to the government service in obtaining tax farms.[2] He must know how they behave in getting money from the Treasury through "invalid receipts"[3] and in other cases, and he must understand what are their tricks and wiles. . . . Every one of them is waiting and watching in the corner of opportunity, taking care to cause certain matters outside the regular procedure to appear correct. . . . In case the chief treasurer is not informed about such persons, they cause the wasting of the public wealth through various frauds, and of disordering affairs. . . .

[1]Officials traveling on government business were entitled to horses, food, and lodging from the people of the districts they visited.

[2]Tax farms were purchased by private individuals who in return for paying the government a lump sum received the right to collect taxes owed the government.

[3]Forged documents showing that a person had paid his taxes.

Those who are chief treasurers should be extremely circumspect in behavior, upright and devout, devoid of avarice and spite. . . . They . . . should strive to increase the income of the Treasury and to diminish expenditures.

But the reduction of expenditures cannot come about through the care and industry of the chief treasurer alone. These must be supplemented by the Sovereign and personal help of his imperial majesty the sultan, who is the refuge of the universe, and by the good management of his excellency the grand vizier.[4] . . .

Certain tax concessions, instead of being farmed out, should be committed to the charge of trustworthy and upright persons on government account.[5]

Let the janissary corps[6] not be increased. Let them be well disciplined, few but elite, and all present in time of need. In this connection also it is fitting to be extremely careful and to be attentive in keeping their rolls in proper order and in having the soldiers actually present. The late Lutfi Pasha, who was formerly grand vizier, has written: "Fifteen thousand soldiers are a great many soldiers. It is a heroic deed to pay the wages year by year of fifteen thousand men with no decrease." But under the present conditions the soldiers and pensioned veterans . . . who get pay and rations have exceeded all limits.

In order that the income and expenditure of the Treasury may be known and the totals inspected, the rolls of the bureaus must be investigated and the numbers known. There are on a war footing 53,200 janissary infantry, consisting of janissaries of the imperial court and pensioned veterans, including those who are in the fortresses protecting the ever-victorious frontier. There are 17,133 cavalrymen of the sipahis, silihdars,[7] and four other regiments of cavalry. The armorers of the imperial court and artillerymen and artillery drivers and bostanjis[8] of the bodyguard . . . and the aghas[9] of the imperial stirrup and müteferriqas[10] and sergeants and gatemen and those who belong to the imperial stables and the flourishing kitchens and to the dockyard and to the *peikan*[11] and to other units, making up 17,716 persons, the total of all these amounts to 96,727 persons.

The expense for meat and value of the winter allowance[12] together with the yearly pay of the janissaries of the lofty court and armorers and artillerymen and artillery drivers in the fortresses on the ever-victorious frontier exceeds a total of ten thousand purses of aspers.[13] And in addition to these, the local troops in the fortresses on the ever-victorious frontier number seventy thousand persons and certain veterans pensioned from the income of the custom house and tax farms, together with those who have the duty of saying prayers amount to twenty-three thousand five hundred. Their yearly pay amounts to five thousand nine hundred and ten purses. Those who are on the government galleys total six thousand persons and their yearly pay eight hundred purses. Accordingly, the total of those who receive pay and have duties is 196,227 and their yearly pay amounts to 16,710 purses.[14]

In addition to these salaries there are incomes of the illustrious princes and princesses and the grand vizier and the yearly allowance of the

[4]A *vizier* was a government minister. The *grand vizier* was chief minister.

[5]In other words, tax farming should be abandoned and taxes collected directly by the government. The author does not develop this point further.

[6]Infantry fighters in the Ottoman army, originally recruited from the sultan's Christian subjects, who were converted to Islam and given over to military training. Their effectiveness had severely declined by the eighteenth century.

[7]*Sipahis* and *silihdars* were cavalry troops supported by land grants from the sultan.

[8]Infantry troops who maintained the palace grounds in Istanbul.

[9]Generals.

[10]Mounted bodyguards who accompanied diplomats on missions.

[11]An elite bodyguard numbering thirty to forty men who wore distinctive gilded helmets.

[12]Payments over and above the troops' regular salaries.

[13]A *purse* was a unit of money made up of approximately 420 *piasters;* one piaster equaled 120 *aspers*.

[14]A sum that exceeded the estimated annual income of the government.

Tatar princes[15] and of the commanders of the sea and the expenditures of the imperial kitchens and stables, of the flourishing dockyards, of the prefect of the capital, of the chief butcher, of the agha of Istanbul, of the chief biscuit maker, of the cannon factory, some expenditures of müteferriqas, and in addition to these, chance expenditures which do not come to mind. . . . For this reason the income does not cover the expenditure, and of necessity the farmed taxes, and other taxes such as the capitation tax,[16] have each fallen a year or two in arrears.

THE STATE OF THE MILITARY

The troops on the frontiers are actually too numerous on their rolls and in the summaries given, although it is certain that in their appointed places each battalion is deficient, some being perhaps half lacking and others even more, nevertheless they let the salaries be sent from here for all. As for the extra money which they get, they have agreed to divide it among themselves. Care and thought and trustworthiness and uprightness in the officers is needed for the separation and distinguishing of those who are present and those who are absent. . . .

Everyone knows that there are very many people outside the corps who pretend they are janissaries. Especially in recent times, because of the long continuance of campaigns which have taken place against the Magyars[17] and in various other regions according to the necessity of the moment, outsiders have joined and mixed themselves among this janissary corps more than among all the others. Becoming mingled with all sorts of people, the janissaries have broken down their fixed regulations. In the towns and villages situated on the coasts of Anatolia and in many regions of Rumelia[18] likewise, many of the subject population, in order to free their necks from the obligations which are incumbent upon them, have changed their dress.[19] Because of their pretensions of being janissaries and because of aid from the commanders of the latter,[20] the civilians cannot be separated from the janissaries. There is no distinction between this sort of men and the faithful guardians of the frontier, veterans who have undergone fatigue and hard usage on campaigns, who have perhaps been several times wounded and injured, who have suffered cuts and bruises for the welfare of faith and state, who have pillowed their heads on stones and lain down to sleep upon the ground. . . .

At the present time special care is necessary in the repairing of castles. If they be built solidly they will not become dilapidated, and frequent repairs will not be needed. But the execution of repairs must not be committed to any chance person, for the appropriation from the Treasury may be embezzled and wasted. It must be committed to a man who abstains from profiteering and avarice.

When either the glorious commander-in-chief or the generals go on campaign, their true purpose should be the animating of religion and the execution of the words of the Prophet. . . . Let them not be unjust or oppressive to any one, but just and equitable, and let them seek to win affection and praises. . . .

For when soldiers are charged with a campaign, they join in bands and agree together to consider one of themselves as chief. Practicing brigandage, they are not satisfied with free fodder for their horses and food for their own bellies from the villages they meet. They covet the horse-cloth and rags of the peasants, and if they can get their hands on the granaries they become

[15]Chieftains on the borders of the empire who were allies of the Ottomans.

[16]A tax on individuals; a head tax.

[17]The term *Magyar,* meaning Hungarian, was used to refer to any of the Ottomans' Christian enemies in southeastern Europe.

[18]An area north of Greece, including the regions of Albania, Macedonia, and Thrace.

[19]The people have purchased and wear the uniforms of the janissaries and claim to be members of the corps to avoid paying taxes.

[20]The commanders have accepted bribes to enter their names on the corps' roles.

joyful, filling their sacks with barley and oats for provisions and fodder. While they behave in this way, . . . the sighs and groans of mankind attain the heavens and it is certain that they will be accursed. . . .

ECONOMIC REGULATIONS

It is essential at all times for every ruler to keep track of the small things relating to the general condition of the people. He must set the proper market prices. Everything must be sold at the price it is worth. For in case the sultan and the viziers say: "The fixing of market prices, though part of the public business, is insignificant," and are not diligent about it, the city judge alone cannot carry it out. . . . Under such circumstances everyone buys and sells as he pleases. Through senseless avarice the venom of vipers is added to lawful goods. The most contemptible of the people, useless both for the services of the sultan and for warfare, become possessors of all the wealth . . . while the great men of the people who deserve respect, becoming poor and powerless, pursue the road of bankruptcy. Then, when it comes about that both horsemen and footmen who go on campaign must sell all their property,[21] it is troublesome and difficult to determine all at once how to restrain those men who have them by the throat and how to change their demeanor and diminish their arrogance (may God forbid it!). . . . The fruiterers and merchants put a double price on provisions and supplies and reap a harvest of profits. They rob the people. . . .

[21]Many soldiers paid for their own military equipment and provisions before a campaign. They hoped to recoup their expenses through plunder.

European Designs on India

39 ▾ *Joseph François Dupleix, MEMORANDUM TO THE DIRECTORS OF THE FRENCH EAST INDIA COMPANY; Robert Clive, LETTER TO WILLIAM PITT THE ELDER*

As the Mughal Empire disintegrated in the eighteenth century, the relationship between India and Europe underwent a dramatic change. Until then Portuguese, Dutch, French, and English merchants had stayed out of Indian politics and were content to trade from coastal cities, where with the approval of the emperor and local rulers they built wharves, warehouses, and offices. As Mughal authority deteriorated, however, agents of the British East India Company, founded in 1600, and the French East India Company, founded in 1664, sought to expand their commercial activities by entering into agreements with local princes. By midcentury they were laying plans for actual territorial conquest.

A Frenchman, Joseph François Dupleix (1697–1763), and an Englishman, Robert Clive (1725–1774), were the two principal advocates of greater European involvement in Indian political affairs. Dupleix, the son of a merchant, was sent by his father on a voyage to India in 1715 to divert him from his interest in science to a career in commerce. The elder Dupleix's strategy proved successful. After amassing a huge fortune in Indian trade, Joseph François moved through the

ranks of the French East India Company and in 1742 was appointed governor-general of all the company's interests in India. He was convinced that the French could gain a decisive advantage over their British rivals if they could establish political control over Indian territories and use local tax revenues to pay the costs of fighting the British. He pursued this policy beginning in 1749, when in return for intervening in a local struggle France gained control of territories in and around the southeast coastal city of Pondicherry. In the next four years, under his direction the French extended their influence through south India through diplomacy and conquest. Worried about expenses and ongoing conflict with the British, the cautious directors of the French East India Company opposed such adventures, and to overcome their doubts Dupleix sent them the following memorandum in 1753. His efforts proved futile, however, and in 1754 Dupleix was recalled in disgrace when he defied the directors' orders to end his meddling in politics.

The dismissal of Dupleix, who died in obscurity and poverty in 1763, provided an opening for his rival, Robert Clive. The son of an English landowner and politician, Clive entered the service of the East India Company at age eighteen and sailed to India after an unspectacular career as a student. Commissioned in the company army four years later, he distinguished himself in the defeat of the French and their Indian allies at the Battle of Arcot in 1751. Six years later he led British forces to an even more decisive victory at the Battle of Plassey. They defeated the French and their ally, Siraj-ud-Daula, the *nawab*, or governor, of the large northeastern state of Bengal. After placing Mir Ja'far, their own puppet nawab, in power in Bengal, the British East India Company became the de facto ruler of Bengal, and its agents immediately set about plundering this new dependency for company and private profit. The British Empire in India had begun.

Clive's thoughts on empire are revealed in the following excerpts from a letter he wrote on January 7, 1759, to William Pitt the Elder (1708–1778), later Earl of Chatham, who since 1757 had been the government minister responsible for directing the fight against France in the Seven Years' War (1756–1763).

QUESTIONS FOR ANALYSIS

1. According to Dupleix, what are the anticipated benefits from the extension of French political authority in India?
2. According to Clive, what benefits will accrue to Great Britain once it establishes its authority in India? How do his views resemble and differ from those of Dupleix?
3. Why are Dupleix and Clive convinced that the Europeans will encounter little difficulty in establishing their political authority in India?
4. What does Clive's letter reveal about the state of the Mughal Empire in the mid 1700s?
5. What does Clive's letter reveal about his attitudes toward the Indians and their rulers?

MEMORANDUM TO THE DIRECTORS OF THE FRENCH EAST INDIA COMPANY (1753)

All the Company's commerce in India is shared with the English, the Dutch, the Portuguese and the Danes. . . . This division of trade, or rather this rivalry, has served to raise considerably the price of merchandise here and has contributed quite a little toward cheapening the quality — two unfortunate circumstances which, of course, further reduce the price and profits in Europe. . . . Our Company can hope for no monopoly in the Indian trade. We shall always share whatever we deal in with other countries. We can, therefore, hope for no other profits than those being made at present. We should even anticipate that instead of increasing, they are likely to decline and that very soon. . . . The only possible way of making profits on inferior merchandise would be to have a large and regular revenue; then the losses could be offset by our income. Those of our rivals who did not have such a resource would be obliged to give up this branch of commerce, or else restrict themselves to their national market. . . .

I think that I have shown the truth of the first point of this memorandum, and the complete proof can be found in the Company's books. I pass now to the second truth, which is that every commercial company should avoid the exportation of bullion [gold and silver] from the kingdom. It is a maxim long established that the more the specie [coined money] circulates in a state, the more flourishing is the state's condition, and the more the state can be helped and sustained by it. It is, then, good policy to seek every means of preventing its exportation. But it is very hard, not to say impossible, to trade in China and India without exporting a specie. . . . Since it is obviously impossible to keep all our specie in France, we should neglect nothing to reduce to a minimum its exportation to India, whence it will never flow back to Europe. Our manufactures in wool, gilt, etc., can diminish such exportation, but not to the extent we desire; we need something else, and this can only be found in a fixed, constant, and abundant local revenue. . . .

Let us suppose that the Company is obliged yearly to send twelve millions to India. Wool, cloth, and other exported manufactures amount to two millions, so there remains ten millions to be sent in specie, a large sum and one exported only too frequently. It could be reduced by at least half, and might even entirely cease, if the local revenue amounted to ten millions. . . .

. . . This work would have been already accomplished, if I had been better supported, not only here but in my native land, which has looked upon the benefits I have acquired for it with too great indifference. . . . I shall content myself by saying that, in spite of all the obstacles, I have succeeded in procuring for my nation a revenue of at least five millions. My intention was to raise it to ten millions, and I would have succeeded. . . . Yes, I can truly say that if what [military support] has arrived this year had been drawn from France's regular troops, all the fighting would now be over and the Company would be enjoying more than ten millions in revenue.

LETTER TO WILLIAM PITT THE ELDER (1759)

The great revolution that has been effected here by the success of the English arms, and the vast advantages gained to the Company by a treaty concluded in consequence thereof, have, I observe, in some measure, engaged the public attention; but much more may yet in time be done, if the Company will exert themselves in the manner the importance of their present possessions and future prospects deserves. I have represented to them in the strongest terms the expediency of sending out and keeping up constantly such a force as will enable them to embrace the first opportunity of further aggrandizing themselves; and I dare pronounce, from a thorough knowledge of this country's government, and of the genius of the people, acquired by two years' application and experience, that such an opportunity will soon offer. The reigning Subah,[1] whom the victory at Plassey invested with the sovereignty of these provinces, still, it is true, retains his attachment to us, and probably, while he has no other support, will continue to do so; but Muslims are so little influenced by gratitude, that should he ever think it his interest to break with us, the obligations he owes us would prove no restraint. . . . Moreover, he is advanced in years; and his son is so cruel, worthless a young fellow, and so apparently an enemy to the English, that it will be almost unsafe trusting him with the succession. So small a body as two thousand Europeans will secure us against any apprehensions from either the one or the other; and, in case of their daring to be troublesome, enable the Company to take the sovereignty upon themselves.

There will be the less difficulty in bringing about such an event, as the natives themselves have no attachment whatever to particular princes; and as, under the present Government, they have no security for their lives or properties, they would rejoice in so happy an exchange as that of a mild for a despotic Government: and there is little room to doubt our easily obtaining the Mughal's [Mughal emperor's] grant in confirmation thereof, provided we agreed to pay him the stipulated allotment out of the revenues, viz. fifty lacs[2] annually. . . .

But so large a sovereignty may possibly be an object too extensive for a mercantile Company; and it is to be feared they are not of themselves able, without the nation's assistance, to maintain so wide a dominion. I have therefore presumed, Sir, to represent this matter to you, and submit it to your consideration, whether the execution of a design, that may hereafter be still carried to greater lengths, be worthy of the Government's taking it into hand. . . . Now I leave you to judge, whether an income yearly of upwards of two millions sterling, with the possession of three provinces abounding in the most valuable productions of nature and of art, be an object deserving the public attention; and whether it be worth the nation's while to take the proper measures to secure such an acquisition — an acquisition which, under the management of so able and disinterested a minister, would prove a source of immense wealth to the kingdom, and might in time be appropriated in part as a fund towards diminishing the heavy load of debt under which we at present labor. Add to these advantages the influence we shall thereby acquire over the several European nations engaged in the commerce here, which these could no longer carry on but through our indulgence, and under such limitations as we should think fit to prescribe. It is well worthy of consideration, that this project may be brought about without draining the mother country, as has been too much the case with our possessions in America. A small force from home will be sufficient, as we always make sure of any number we please of black [Indian] troops, who, being both much better paid and treated by us than by the country powers, will very readily enter into our service. . . .

[1]A synonym for nawab, governor of an Indian province. The specific reference is to Mir Ja'far, the British puppet installed in power after the Battle of Plassey.

[2]Synonymous with *lakh*, meaning 100,000. Clive states that the British will pay 5 million rupees (in British currency approximately 260,000 pounds) per year to the emperor.

The Continuing Vitality of Islam

The resurgence of Islam in the late twentieth century, characterized by political militancy, intensification of personal devotion, and a drive to create societies based on Islamic law and teaching, has precedents that go far back in Islamic history. Time and again the religion has been revitalized and renewed by movements inspired by visionaries and reformers who have exhorted believers to purify doctrine and ritual and to rededicate their lives to God. The eighteenth century was such a period of Islamic revitalization, despite the demoralizing political and military failures of the major Muslim empires. Even though the Ottoman armies were falling behind those of Europe and the Safavid and Mughal empires collapsed, Islam continued to make converts in Southeast Asia and Africa and spread into areas such as eastern Bengal through migration. In addition, movements of reform and renewal took root in many parts of the Islamic world, including the religion's historic center in Arabia and its outermost fringes in Southeast Asia and West Africa.

Although eighteenth-century Muslim reform movements showed a great deal of variation, most were led by legal or Quranic scholars or devotees of Sufism, the mystical movement within Islam that emphasizes personal experience and closeness to God through devotion. Many reformers traveled widely and drew inspiration from experiences in religious centers such as Baghdad, Cairo, Mecca, and Medina. Some called for a purification of Muslim practices and a return to Islam's fundamentals as revealed in the Quran and the teachings and deeds of Muhammad. Many were convinced that Islam had been tainted by accommodating itself to local religious customs and beliefs. Some urged Muslims to seek social justice, while others preached a message of puritanical rigor and personal regeneration. A few called on their followers to take up the sword against unbelievers and heretics.

Eighteenth-century Islamic reform movements were not anti-Western in any meaningful sense. They did, however, affect interactions between the West and the Islamic world in later centuries. In the early history of Islam, many Muslim intellectuals and religious leaders considered certain Western and Islamic views compatible, and they had integrated aspects of Western thought, especially ancient Greek science, into Islamic learning. The message of many eighteenth-century reformers, however, was that Islam was sufficient unto itself. Islam should be more exclusivist, more centered on its own writings and traditions, and more suspicious of outside ideas and practices. Such views were one of many factors that shaped relations between the Muslim and Western worlds in the modern era.

A Call to Recapture Islam's Purity

▼▼▼

40 ▼ *Abdullah Wahhab, THE HISTORY AND DOCTRINES OF THE WAHHABIS*

Wahhabism, the dominant form of Islam in Saudi Arabia and Qatar and a growing influence on Islam as a result of Saudi funding of schools in Pakistan and Afghanistan, traces its origins to Muhammad Ibn Abd al-Wahhab (1703–1792), who with the aid of a tribal chief, Muhammad Ibn Saud, led a militant reform movement in Arabia in the eighteenth century. Wahhab's early followers called themselves *Muwahhidun*, or "those who advocate oneness," because they rejected any belief or practice that even slightly detracted from the exclusive worship of God. Adherents of the movement today generally refer to themselves as *Salafi*, or "followers of the predecessors," a reference to the early companions of the Prophet Muhammad.

Muhammad Ibn Abd al-Wahhab was a native of Nejd, a region in the east-central part of the Arabian Peninsula. As a student and teacher, he visited Mecca, Medina, Basra, Damascus, and Baghdad. After he returned to Arabia, Wahhab, influenced by the thought of the medieval theologian Ibn Tamiyya and the teachings of the Hanbali School of jurisprudence, began to denounce the Arabs' religious failings. These included magical rituals, faith in holy men, worship of saints and their tombs, and veneration of supposedly sacred wells and trees. Rejecting Sufi mysticism, Shiism, and rationalist attempts to understand God's nature and purposes, he urged his followers to declare *jihad* (holy war) on Arab tribes that refused to abandon such practices.

In 1802, ten years after Abd al-Wahhab's death, his followers captured Karbala in present-day Iraq and destroyed the tomb of the revered Shia Imam Husayn. One year later, they captured the holy city of Mecca, the immediate aftermath of which is described in the following selection. It is the work of the founder's grandson, Abdullah Wahhab, who participated in the conquest of Mecca and was executed when an army sent by the Ottoman sultan took the city in 1813. Abdullah Wahhab wrote this piece to answer critics and to clarify the beliefs of the Muwahhidun.

QUESTIONS FOR ANALYSIS

1. In the Wahhabi view, what are the most serious threats to the purity of Islam?
2. How did the Wahhabis attempt to change Mecca after they captured it? What do their acts reveal about their beliefs and purposes?
3. The Wahhabis have been characterized as puritanical and intolerant. Is such a view justified on the basis of this document?

4. **The Wahhabis strongly opposed Shiism and the use of logic as a means of discovering religious truth. Why? (See the introduction to source 12 for a discussion of Shiism.)**
5. **How do the Wahhabis perceive their role in the history of Islam?**

. . . Now I was engaged in the holy war, carried on by those who truly believe in the Unity of God, when God, praised be He, graciously permitted us to enter Mecca, the holy, the exalted, at midday, on the 6th day of the week on the 8th of the month Muharram, 1218, Hijrí [April 1803]. Before this, Saud,[1] our leader in the holy war, whom the Lord protect, had summoned the nobles, the divines, and the common people of Mecca; for indeed the leaders of the pilgrims and the rulers of Mecca had resolved on battle, and had risen up against us in the holy place, to exclude us from the house of God. But when the army of the true believers advanced, the Lord filled their hearts with terror, and they fled hither and thither. Then our commander gave protection to everyone within the holy place, while we, with shaven heads and hair cut short,[2] entered with safety, crying "Labbayka,"[3] without fear of any created being, and only of the Lord God. Now, though we were more numerous, better armed and disciplined than the people of Mecca, yet we did not cut down their trees, neither did we hunt,[4] nor shed any blood except the blood of victims, and of those four-footed beasts which the Lord has made lawful by his commands.

When our pilgrimage was over, we gathered the people together . . . , and our leader, whom the Lord saves, explained to the divines what we required of the people, . . . namely, a pure belief in the Unity of God Almighty. He pointed out to them that there was no dispute between us and them except on two points, and that one of these was a sincere belief in the unity of God, and a knowledge of the different kinds of prayer of which *dua*[5] was one. He added that to show the significance of *shirk*,[6] the prophet (may he be blessed!) had put people to death on account of it; that he had continued to call upon them to believe in the Unity of God for some time after he became inspired, and that he had abandoned shirk before the Lord had declared to him the remaining four pillars[7] of Islam. . . .

. . . They then acknowledged our belief, and there was not one among them who doubted or hesitated to believe that that for which we condemned men to death, was the truth pure and unsullied. And they swore a binding oath, although we had not asked them, that their hearts had been opened and their doubts removed, and that they were convinced whoever said, "Oh prophet of God!" or "Oh Ibn 'Abbes!" or "Oh 'Abdul Qadir!"[8] or called on any other created being, thus entreating him to turn away evil or grant what is good (where the power belongs to God alone), such as recovery from sickness, or victory over enemies, or protection from temptation, etc.; he is a *Mushrik*,[9] guilty of the most

---

[1]Saud bin Abdul Aziz bin Muhammad al Saud, head of the house of Saud from 1803 to 1814.

[2]A custom during the pilgrimage to Mecca.

[3]The loud cry uttered as Muslims begin their pilgrimage activities in Mecca.

[4]Not cutting down a defeated enemy's trees or hunting the enemy's animals was considered an act of mercy.

[5]A personal prayer uttered by a Muslim.

[6]*Shirk* is the opposite of surrender to God and the acceptance and recognition of His reality. It may mean atheism, paganism, or polytheism. It is the root of all sin and transgression.

[7]The first pillar of Islam is the creed, which affirms "There is no god but God, and Muhammad is the messenger of God." The other four pillars are daily prayer; almsgiving; fasting during the month of Ramadan; and pilgrimage, at least once in every Muslim's life if possible, to Mecca, the city of Muhammad's birth and revelation.

[8]Calling out in prayer the name of Muhammad or these early caliphs in the Abbasid line detracted from the majesty of God.

[9]A person guilty of shirk.

heinous form of shirk, his blood shall be shed and property confiscated. Nor is it any excuse that he believes the effective first cause in the movements of the universe is God, and only supplicates those mortals . . . to intercede for him or bring him nearer the presence of God, so that he may obtain what he requires from Him through them or through their intercession. Again, the tombs which had been erected over the remains of the pious, had become in these times as it were idols where the people went to pray for what they required; they humbled themselves before them, and called upon those lying in them, in their distress, just as did those who were in darkness before the coming of Muhammad.

When this was over, we razed all the large tombs in the city which the people generally worshipped and believed in, and by which they hoped to obtain benefits or ward off evil, so that there did not remain an idol to be adored in that pure city, for which God be praised. Then the taxes and customs we abolished, all the different kinds of instruments for using tobacco we destroyed, and tobacco itself we proclaimed forbidden.[10] Next we burned the dwellings of those selling *hashish*, and living in open wickedness, and issued a proclamation, directing the people to constantly exercise themselves in prayer. They were not to pray in separate groups according to the different Imams;[11] but all were directed to arrange themselves at each time of prayer behind any Imam who is a follower of any of the four Imams (may the Lord be pleased with them!). For in this way the Lord would be worshiped by as it were one voice, the faithful of all sects would become friendly disposed towards each other, and all dissensions would cease. . . .

We believe that good and evil proceed from God, the exalted; that nothing happens in His kingdom, but what He commands; . . . We believe that the faithful will see Him in the end, but we do not know under what form, as it was beyond our comprehension. And in the same way we follow Imam Ahmad Ibn Hanbal in matters of detail; but we do not reject anyone who follows any of the four Imams, as do the Shias, the Zaidiyyahs, and the Imamiyyahs,[12] &c. Nor do we admit them in any way to act openly according to their vicious creeds; on the contrary, we compelled them to follow one of the four Imams. We do not claim to exercise our reason in all matters of religion, and of our faith, save that we follow our judgment where a point is clearly demonstrated to us in either the Quran or the Sunnah.[13] . . . We do not command the destruction of any writings except such as tend to cast people into infidelity to injure their faith, such as those on Logic, which have been prohibited by all Divines. But we are not very exacting with regard to books or documents of this nature, if they appear to assist our opponents, we destroy them. . . . We do not consider it proper to make Arabs prisoners of war, nor have we done so, neither do we fight with other nations. Finally, we do not consider it lawful to kill women or children. . . .

We consider pilgrimage is supported by legal custom, but it should not be undertaken except to a mosque, and for the purpose of praying in it. Therefore, whoever performs pilgrimage for this purpose, is not wrong, and doubtless those who spend the precious moments of their existence in invoking the Prophet, shall, according to Hadith,[14] obtain happiness in this world and the

[10]The Wahhabis saw no Quranic basis for the use of tobacco; its use is still rare in present-day Saudi Arabia.

[11]The author uses the term *imam* to refer to the founders of the four major schools of Sunni Muslim jurisprudence: Abu Hanifah (d. 767), founder of the Hanafite school; Malik ibn Anas (d. 795), founder of the Malikite school; al-Shafi (d. 820), founder of the Shafiite school; and Ahmad ibn Hanbal (d. 855), founder of the Hanbali school. The Wahhabis were Hanbalis, but did not reject the authority of the other schools.

[12]Zaidiyyahs and Imamiyyahs were Shia sects.

[13]The body of traditional social and legal thought and practice that represent the proper observance of Islam.

[14]The tradition, or written record, of the thought and deeds of Muhammad as recorded by his companions.

next, and he will dispel their sorrows. We do not deny miraculous powers to the saints, but on the contrary allow them. They are under the guidance of the Lord, so long as they continue to follow the way pointed out in the laws and obey the prescribed rules. But whether alive or dead, they must not be made the object of any form of worship. . . .

We prohibit those forms of Bidah[15] that affect religion or pious works. Thus drinking coffee, reciting poetry, praising kings, do not affect religion or pious works and are not prohibited. . . .

All games are lawful. Our prophet allowed play in his mosque. So it is lawful to chide and punish persons in various ways; to train them in the use of different weapons; or to use anything which tends to encourage warriors in battle, such as a war-drum. But it must not be accompanied with musical instruments. These are forbidden, and indeed the difference between them and a war drum is clear. . . .

Whoever is desirous of knowing our belief, let him come to us at al Diriyya,[16] and he will see what will gladden his heart, and his eyes will be pleased in reading the compilations on the different kinds of knowledge. . . . He will see God praised in a pleasing manner; the assistance He gives in establishing the true faith; the kindness, which He exerts among the weak and feeble, between inhabitants and travelers. . . . He is our Agent, our Master, our Deliverer. May peace and the blessing of God be upon our prince Muhammad and on his family and his companions!

[15]Erroneous or improper customs that grew after the third generation of Muslims died out.

[16]The Wahhabi capital, some fifteen miles northeast of Riyadh.

Jihad in the Western Sudan

▼▼▼

41 ▾ *Usman dan Fodio, SELECTIONS FROM HIS WRITINGS*

Although merchants and teachers from North Africa and Arabia had introduced Islam to Africa's western and central Sudan (the region south of the Saharan and Libyan deserts) as early as the tenth century, by 1800 Islam was not truly dominant in these regions. It was still a religion of the cities, where Muslim merchants had established Islamic communities, built mosques, introduced Arabic, and made converts. Many converts, however, continued non-Muslim religious rites and festivals, and outside the cities peasants and herders remained animists. Rulers became Muslims in name, but often less for religious reasons than to ingratiate themselves with the merchant community and to attract Islamic scholars to their service as advisors, interpreters, and scribes. Most rulers tolerated their subjects' pagan practices, and many participated in such practices themselves.

This all changed as a result of a series of jihads, or holy wars, that swept across the Sudan in the eighteenth and especially the nineteenth centuries. Dedicated Muslims took up arms against nonbelievers and, after seizing power, imposed a strict form of Islam on their new subjects. In a matter of decades, these movements redrew the political and religious map of the Sudan.

The first major jihad of the era, known as the Sokoto Jihad, took place in Hausaland in the early nineteenth century under the leadership of Usman dan Fodio (1754–1817). Hausaland, an area that straddles the Niger River and today

makes up the northern part of Nigeria, had been settled by Hausa speakers in the tenth century but also had substantial numbers of Fulani, pastoralists who had begun to migrate into the area in the 1500s. It was divided into approximately a dozen principalities that had emerged after the Songhai Empire's collapse around 1600.

Usman dan Fodio, a member of a Fulani clan with a tradition of Islamic scholarship and teaching, was a member of the *Qadiriyya*, a Sufi brotherhood dating from the twelfth century. Beginning in the 1770s, he began to travel and preach in Hausaland, denouncing corrupt Islamic practices and the tyrannical and venal rulers who tolerated them. His calls for religious and political renewal won him followers among the Fulani, who considered themselves oppressed by their rulers, and some Hausa farmers, who were feeling the effects of drought and land shortages. In 1804, when the Sultan of Gobir denounced Usman and prepared to attack his followers, Usman called on his supporters to take up arms and begin a jihad against Hausaland's rulers. By the late 1810s, Usman controlled Hausaland and established the Kingdom of Sokoto. After his retirement from public life, Usman's son and brother extended the campaign to the south and east of the kingdom. The era of Sudanese jihads had begun in earnest.

Usman wrote nearly 100 treatises on politics, religion, marriage customs, and education. Brief excerpts from four of them are included here. Together they provide a sampling of his thoughts on religion, government, and society.

QUESTIONS FOR ANALYSIS

1. What policies and values of the Hausa sultans does Usman criticize? Why?
2. How do the religious failings of the Hausa princes prevent them from being just and equitable rulers?
3. What groups in Hausa society would have been most likely to respond positively to Usman's criticisms of the sultans?
4. What is Usman's message concerning the treatment of Muslim women? Is it a message of equality with men?

THE FAULTS OF THE HAUSA RULERS[1]

And one of the ways of their government is the building of their sovereignty upon three things: the people's persons, their honor, and their possessions; and whomsoever they wish to kill or exile or violate his honor or devour his wealth they do so in pursuit of their lusts, without any right in the *Sharia*.[2] . . . One of the ways of their government is their intentionally eating whatever food they wish, whether it is religiously permitted or forbidden, and wearing whatever clothes they wish, whether religiously permitted or forbidden, and drinking what beverages they wish, whether religiously permitted or forbidden, and riding whatever riding beasts they wish, whether religiously permitted or forbidden, and

[1]An excerpt from *Kitab al-farq*, "The Book of Difference between the Government of Muslims and Unbelievers," probably written around 1806.

[2]*Sharia*, literally "path" in Arabic, is the word for Islamic law.

taking what women they wish without marriage contract, and living in decorated palaces, whether religiously permitted or forbidden, and spreading soft carpets as they wish, whether religiously permitted or forbidden.

. . . One of the ways of their government is to place many women in their houses, until the number of women of some of them amounts to one thousand or more. . . . One of the ways of their government is to delay in the paying of a debt, and this is injustice. One of the ways of their government is what the superintendent of the market takes from all the parties to a sale, and the meat which he takes on each market day from the butchers, . . . and one of the ways of their government is the cotton and other things which they take in the course of the markets. . . . One of the ways of their government is the taking of people's beasts of burden without their permission to carry the sultan's food to him.

. . . One of the ways of their government which is also well known is that whoever dies in their country, they take his property, and they call it "inheritance," and they know that it is without doubt injustice.[3] One of the ways of their government is to impose tax on merchants, and other travellers. One of the ways of their government, which is also well known, is that one may not pass by their farms, nor cross them without suffering bad treatment from their slaves. One of the ways of their government, which is also well known, is that if the people's animals go among their animals, they do not come out again unless they give a proportion of them, and if the sultan's animals stray, and are found spoiling the cultivated land and other things, they are not driven off. . . .

One of the ways of their government, which is also well known, is that if you have an adversary in law and he precedes you to them, and gives them some money, then your word will not be accepted by them, even though they know for a certainty of your truthfulness, unless you give them more than your adversary gave. One of the ways of their government is to shut the door in the face of the needy. . . . Therefore do not follow their way in their government, and do not imitate them. . . .

ROYAL RELIGION[4]

It is well known that in our time Islam in these countries mentioned above is widespread among people other than the sultans. As for the sultans, they are undoubtedly unbelievers, even though they may profess the religion of Islam, because they practice polytheistic rituals and turn people away from the path of God and raise the flag of worldly kingdom above the banner of Islam. . . .

The government of a country is the government of its king without question. If the king is a Muslim, his land is Muslim; if he is an Unbeliever, his land is a land of Unbelievers. . . . There is no dispute that the sultans of these countries venerate certain places, certain trees, and certain rocks and offer sacrifice to them. This constitutes unbelief according to the consensus of opinion.

I say this on the basis of the common practice known about them, but I do not deny the existence of some Muslims here and there among them. Those however are rare and there is no place for what is rare in legal decisions.

THE TREATMENT OF WOMEN AND SLAVES[5]

Most of our educated men leave their wives, their daughters, and the slaves morally abandoned, like beasts, without teaching them what God prescribes should be taught them, and without instructing them in the articles of the

[3]A grievance of foreign Muslim merchants who might die while residing in a Hausa city.

[4]From *Tanbih al-ikhwan 'ala ahwal ard al-Sudan*, "Concerning the Government of Our Country and Neighboring Countries in the Sudan," written around 1811.

[5]From *Nur al-albab*, "Light of the Intellects."

Law which concern them. Thus, they leave them ignorant of the rules regarding ablutions,[6] prayer, fasting, business dealings, and other duties which they have to fulfil, and which God commands that they should be taught.

Men treat these beings like household implements which become broken after long use and which are then thrown out on the dung-heap. This is an abominable crime! Alas! How can they thus shut up their wives, their daughters, and their slaves in the darkness of ignorance? . . .

Muslim women — Do not listen to the speech of those who are misguided and who sow the seed of error in the heart of another; they deceive you when they stress obedience to your husbands without telling you of obedience to God and to his Messenger [Muhammad] (May God show him bounty and grant him salvation), and when they say that the woman finds her happiness in obedience to her husband.

They seek only their own satisfaction, and that is why they impose upon you tasks which the Law of God and that of his Prophet have never especially assigned to you. Such are — the preparation of food-stuffs, the washing of clothes, and other duties which they like to impose upon you, while they neglect to teach you what God and the Prophet have prescribed for you.

Yes, the woman owes submission to her husband, publicly as well as in intimacy, even if he is one of the humble people of the world, and to disobey him is a crime, at least so long as he does not command what God condemns; in that case she must refuse, since it is wrong of a human creature to disobey the Creator.

THE CALL TO HOLY WAR[7]

That to make war upon the heathen king who does not say "There is no God but Allah" on account of the custom of his town, and who makes no profession of Islam, is obligatory by assent,[8] and that to take the government from him is obligatory by assent.

And that to make war upon the king who is an apostate, and who has abandoned the religion of Islam for the religion of heathendom is obligatory by assent, and that to take the government from him is obligatory by assent; And that to make war against the king who is an apostate — who has not abandoned the religion of Islam as far as the profession of it is concerned, but who mingles the observances of Islam with the observances of heathendom, like the kings of Hausaland for the most part — is also obligatory by assent, and that to take the government from him is obligatory by assent. . . .

And to enslave the freeborn among the Muslims is unlawful by assent, whether they reside in the territory of Islam, or in enemy territory. . . .

---

[6]Washing one's body as part of a religious rite.

[7]From *Wathiqat ahl al-Sudan wa man sha' Allah min al-ikhwan*, "Dispatch to the Folk of the Sudan and to Whom so Allah Wills Among the Brethren," probably written in 1804 or 1805.

[8]"By assent" refers to the consensus of the Muslim community.

Chapter 7

Change and Continuity in East Asia

For the Ottoman, Safavid, and Mughal empires, the seventeenth and eighteenth centuries were times of decline and defeat after an era of strength and expansion. In East Asia this pattern was reversed. For Japan the sixteenth century was an era of civil war and social discord, made worse by the arrival of Europeans, who introduced firearms and converted tens of thousands of Japanese to Christianity. China entered a period of dynastic decline at the end of the sixteenth century when the quality and effectiveness of Ming emperors declined just when the empire was faced with pressing new financial and diplomatic problems. Factionalism paralyzed the central administration, and peasant violence escalated in the face of rising taxes, higher rents, natural catastrophes, and government corruption. The collapse of central authority and the suicide of the last emperor paved the way for the invasion of China by the Manchus, a seminomadic people who poured into China from their homeland to the northeast and established a new dynasty, the Qing, in 1644.

During the seventeenth century, however, conflicts and tensions abated in both China and Japan. In Japan recovery began in 1603, when the Tokugawa clan took power and ended the decades-long civil war, while in China it began soon after the Manchus established their authority. Although China and Japan did not lack problems in the seventeenth and eighteenth centuries, in comparison to what had occurred earlier and what would follow, these were years of orderly government and social harmony.

These were also years in which European pressures on the region eased. The Qing continued to limit European merchants' activities to Macao and Guangzhou, and beginning in the early 1700s they curtailed European missionary activity. They also checked Russian expansion in the Amur Valley. In 1689 they negotiated the Treaty of Nerchinsk, by which the

Russians agreed to abandon their trading posts in Manchuria in return for modest commercial privileges in Beijing. In Japan the Tokugawa shoguns in the first half of the seventeenth century expelled all foreigners, outlawed Christianity, and limited trade with Europeans to one Dutch ship a year. In the East Indies the Dutch, after forcing out the Portuguese and establishing a political base in Java, were content after the mid 1600s to protect rather than expand their gains. Spain's involvement in the region never extended beyond the Philippines.

By the end of the 1700s, however, signs of change were evident. In Japan economic expansion, urbanization, and political tranquillity created new tensions by enriching merchants and undermining the function and financial base of the military aristocracy. In China continuing population growth caused hardship among the peasants by driving up the cost of land; moreover, around 1800 budgetary shortfalls, higher taxes, abuses of the civil service examination system, and neglect of roads, bridges, and dikes were signs of impending dynastic decline.

In addition, European pressures in the region were building. In the 1780s the English began to settle Australia and New Zealand. French missionaries increased their activities in Vietnam. In 1800 the Dutch government stripped the Dutch East India Company of its administrative responsibilities in the East Indies and tightened its grip on the region's agriculture and trade. From their base in India, British merchants opened a new chapter in the history of trade with China after finding a product that millions of Chinese deeply craved. The product — grown and processed in India, packed into 133-pound chests, shipped to Guangzhou, and purchased for silver by Chinese traders who sold it to millions of addicts — was opium. For East and Southeast Asians and the peoples of the South Pacific islands, a new era of upheaval was about to begin.

China's Revival Under the Qing

After the last Ming emperor hanged himself in April 1644 and the bandit-emperor Li Zicheng fled Beijing in June, Manchu invaders placed the child emperor Shunzhi on the throne, and China's last dynasty, the Qing, began its rule. During the next thirty-five years, Manchu armies fought from Burma to Taiwan, hunting down and executing Ming supporters, crushing their armies, and suppressing rebellion. By 1680 Manchu authority over China had been secured.

The Manchus made it clear from the start that they were the rulers and the Chinese their subjects. They ordered courtiers and officials to abandon the loose-fitting robes of the Ming for the high-collared tight jackets favored by the Manchus. They also required all males to shave their foreheads and braid their hair in back in a style despised by the Chinese. In other ways, however, the Manchus themselves adapted to Chinese culture. They embraced the Chinese principle of centralized monarchy, learned Chinese, and supported Confucian scholarship. They reinstated the civil service examinations, which had been neglected during the last decades of Ming rule. Although Manchus were disproportionately represented in the bureaucracy, Chinese were allocated half of all important offices, and gradually Chinese scholar-officials began to support and serve the new dynasty.

From 1661 through 1799, China had but three emperors: Kangxi (r. 1661–1722), Yongzhen (r. 1722–1736), and Qianlong (r. 1736–1796), who resigned as emperor in 1796 to avoid exceeding the long reign of his grandfather Kangxi but who actually ruled until 1799. By any standard their reigns were among the most impressive in all of Chinese history. China reached its greatest size as a result of military campaigns in central Asia. Agriculture flourished, trade expanded, and China's population grew (how much and how fast it grew is a matter of ongoing scholarly debate). China's cultural vitality was no less remarkable. Painting and scholarship flourished, and the era's literary output included what many considered China's greatest novel, *The Dream of the Red Chamber* by Cao Xueqin.

Toward the end of Qianlong's reign, however, problems emerged. Rural poverty worsened, military effectiveness declined, and factionalism and favoritism at the imperial court resurfaced. Nonetheless, it was neither far-fetched nor fanciful when France's leading eighteenth-century writer, Voltaire, described Qing China as a model of moral and ethical government and praised Qianlong as the ideal philosopher-king.

Emperor Kangxi Views His World

42 ▾ *Kangxi, SELF-PORTRAIT*

In 1661 a seven-year-old boy became the second Qing emperor after the unexpected death of his father, Shunzhi. He took as his reign name Kangxi, and during his long reign, which lasted until 1722, he crushed the last vestiges of Ming resistance, fortified China's borders, revitalized the civil service examination system, won the support of China's scholar-officials, eased tensions between ethnic Chinese and their Manchu conquerors, and brought new vigor and direction to the government. A generous supporter of writers, artists, poets, scholars, and craftsmen, Kangxi himself was a scholar and writer of distinction. He studied Confucianism, Latin, music, mathematics, and science and left behind a rich store of writings, including poems, essays, aphorisms, and letters.

In 1974 the historian Jonathan Spence drew on these writings and statements to compile a self-portrait of the emperor. In the following excerpts, the emperor expresses his views on justice, government administration, and Europeans, with whom China's relations worsened during his reign.

As noted in "Multiple Voices II: Asian Views of Christianity" (page 93), the most prominent European visitors to China were members of the Society of Jesus, a Catholic religious order, who sought to make converts to Christianity by impressing the Chinese elite with their knowledge of astronomy and mathematics and their skills as cartographers, artists, and architects. They had been welcomed at the imperial court in Beijing, where they wore Chinese garb, learned Chinese, and paid homage to the emperor. They also managed to convert some 200 court officials, who in keeping with a policy initiated by the founder of the Jesuit mission in China, Matteo Ricci, were permitted to continue traditional ceremonies in honor of deceased ancestors and offer public homage to Confucius. Kangxi had an avid interest in Western learning, and in 1692 he granted the Jesuits permission to preach outside Beijing. By the early eighteenth century, as many as 300,000 Chinese may have been Roman Catholics.

In the early 1700s, however, the Catholic missionary effort experienced a fatal schism. Members of the Franciscan and Dominican religious orders, fresh from their successful missionary efforts in the Philippines, attacked the Jesuit position on Confucian rites and won over Pope Clement XI to their point of view. In 1706 the pope decreed that Confucian ceremonies were religious, not civil, rites and henceforth would be prohibited for Chinese Catholics. An angry Kangxi responded with a ban on Christian preaching, and the Qing assault on Christianity was under way. Under Kangxi's successor the Jesuits lost their position at Beijing, and the main source of contact between the imperial court and the intellectual world of the West disappeared.

QUESTIONS FOR ANALYSIS

1. What does Kangxi's treatment of delinquent and dishonest government officials reveal about his philosophy of government?
2. How do Confucian values affect Kangxi's decisions about whether to be lenient to men accused of killing their wives?
3. What are Kangxi's views of the civil service examination system? What ideas does he have about improving the system?
4. What role do eunuchs play in Kangxi's administration? How does this compare with the situation during the late Ming Era (source 18)?
5. According to Kangxi, what are the strengths and limitations of Western science and mathematics?
6. According to Kangxi, what specific issues were involved in the dispute over Chinese rites?
7. What other characteristics and actions of the missionaries led to Kangxi's decision to ban further Christian preaching?

AN EMPEROR'S RESPONSIBILITIES

Giving life to people and killing people — those are the powers that the emperor has. He knows that administrative errors in government bureaus can be rectified, but that a criminal who has been executed cannot be brought back to life any more than a chopped string can be joined together again. He knows, too, that sometimes people have to be persuaded into morality by the example of an execution. . . .

Hu Jianzheng was a subdirector of the Court of Sacrificial Worship whose family terrorized their native area in Jiangsu, seizing people's lands and wives and daughters, and murdering people after falsely accusing them of being thieves. . . . I ordered . . . that he be executed with his family and in his native place, so that all the local gentry might learn how I regarded such behavior. Corporal Yambu was sentenced to death for gross corruption in the shipyards. I not only agreed to the penalty but sent guards officer Uge to supervise the beheading, and ordered that all shipyard personnel from generals down to private soldiers kneel down in full armor and listen to my warning that execution would be their fate as well unless they ended their evil ways. . . .

Of all the things that I find distasteful, none is more so than giving a final verdict on the death sentences that are sent to me for ratification. . . .

Each year we went through the lists, sparing sixteen out of sixty-three at one session, eighteen out of fifty-seven at another, thirty-three out of eighty-three at another. For example, it was clear to me that the three cases of husbands killing wives that came up . . . were all quite different. The husband who hit his wife with an ax because she nagged at him for drinking, and then murdered her after another domestic quarrel . . . how could any extenuating circumstances be found? But Baoer, who killed his wife for swearing at his parents; and Meng, whose wife failed to serve him properly and used foul language so that he killed her — they could have their sentences reduced. . . .

EUNUCHS AND BUREAUCRATS

You have to define and reward people in accordance with their status in life. If too much grace is shown to inferiors they become lazy and uppity and will be sure to stir up trouble — and if you neglect them they will abuse you behind your back. That was why I insisted on such strictness when the eunuch Jian Wenzai beat a commoner to death, saying strangulation was not enough. For eunuchs are basically Yin[1] in nature. They are quite different from ordinary people; when weak with age they babble like babies. In my court I never let them get involved with government — even the few . . . with whom I might chatter or exchange family jokes were never allowed to discuss politics. I only have about four hundred, as opposed to the immense numbers there were in the Ming, and I keep them working at menial jobs; I ignore their frowns and smiles and make sure that they stay poor. Whereas in the later Ming Dynasty, besides being so extravagant and reckless, they obtained the power to write endorsements on the emperors' memorials, for the emperors were unable to read the one- or two-thousand-character memorials that flowed in; and the eunuchs in turn passed the memorials on to *their* subordinates to handle.

▾▾▾

There are too many men who claim to be pure scholars and yet are stupid and arrogant; we'd be better off with less talk of moral principle and more practice of it. . . .

This is one of the worst habits of the great officials, that if they are not recommending their teachers or their friends for high office then they recommend their relations. This evil practice used to be restricted to the Chinese: they've always formed cliques and then used their recommendations to advance the other members of the clique. Now the practice has spread to the Chinese Bannermen[2] . . . and even the Manchus, who used to be so loyal, recommend men from their own Banners, knowing them to have a foul reputation, and will refuse to help the Chinese. . . .

In 1694 I noted that we were losing talent because of the ways the exams were being conducted: even in the military exams most of the successful candidates were from Zhejiang and Jiangnan, while there was only one from Henan and one from Shanxi.[3] The successful ones had often done no more than memorize old examination answer books, whereas the best *should* be selected on the basis of riding and archery. Yet it is always the strong men from the western provinces who are eager to serve in the army, while not only are troops from Zhejiang and Jiangnan among the weakest, they also pass on their posts to their relatives who are also weak.

Even among the examiners there are those who are corrupt, those who do not understand basic works, those who ask detailed questions about practical matters of which they know nothing, those who insist entirely on memorization of the [Confucian] *Classics* and refuse to prescribe essays, those who put candidates from their own geographical area at the top of the list, or those who make false claims about their abilities to select the impoverished and deserving. . . . Other candidates hire people to sit [take] the exams for them, or else pretend to be from a province that has a more liberal quota than their own. It's usually easy enough to check the latter, since I've learnt to recognize the accents from thirteen provinces, and if you watch the person and study his voice you can tell where he is really from. As to the other problems, one can overcome some of them by holding the exams under rigorous armed supervision and then reading the exam papers oneself.

[1]In East Asian thought, Yin and Yang were the two complementary principles or forces that make up all aspects and phenomena of life. Yin is conceived of as Earth, female, dark, passive, and absorbing.

[2]The banner system was a method of military organization under the Qing in which fighting men were grouped in divisions identified by different colored banners. Bannermen were given grants of land and small stipends for their service. Chinese (as opposed to Manchu) bannermen were originally drawn from the ranks of Chinese soldiers and officers who had surrendered to the Manchus and joined their cause early in their struggle against Ming supporters.

[3]Zhejiang and Jiangnan were southeast coastal regions of China; Henan and Shanxi were north-central provinces.

DEALING WITH EUROPEANS

The rare can become common, as with the lions and other animals that foreign ambassadors like to give us and my children are now accustomed to; . . .

Western skills are a case in point: in the late Ming Dynasty, when the Westerners first brought the gnomon [sundial], the Chinese thought it a rare treasure until they understood its use. And when the Emperor Shunzhi got a small chiming clock in 1653, he kept it always near him; but now we have learned to balance the springs and to adjust the chimes and finally to make the whole clock, so that my children can have ten chiming clocks each to play with, if they want them. Similarly, we learned in a short time to make glassware that is superior to that made in the West, and our lacquer would be better than theirs, too, were it not that their wet sea climate gives a better sheen than the dry and dusty Chinese climate ever could. . . .

I realized, too, that Western mathematics has its uses. . . . I ordered the Jesuits Thomas, Gerbillon, and Bouvet to study Manchu also, and to compose treatises in that language on Western arithmetic and the geometry of Euclid.[4] In the early 1690's I often worked several hours a day with them. With Verbiest I had examined each stage of the forging of cannons, and made him build a water fountain that operated in conjunction with an organ, and erect a windmill in the court; with the new group . . . I worked on clocks and mechanics. Pereira taught me to play the tune, *"P'u-yen-chou"* on the harpsichord and the structure of the eight-note scale, Pedrini taught my sons musical theory, and Gherardini painted portraits at the Court. I also learned to calculate the weight and volume of spheres, cubes, and cones, and to measure distances and the angle of river banks. On inspection tours later I used these Western methods to show my officials how to make more accurate calculations when planning their river works. . . . I showed them how to calculate circumferences and assess the area of a plot of land, even if its borders were as jagged as dogs' teeth, drawing diagrams for them on the ground with an arrow; and calculated the flow of river water through a lock gate by multiplying the volume that flowed in a few seconds to get a figure for the whole day. . . .

But I was careful not to refer to these Westerners as "Great Officials." . . . For even though some of the Western methods are different from our own, and may even be an improvement, there is little about them that is new. The principles of mathematics all derive from the *Book of Changes,*[5] and the Western methods are Chinese in origin: this algebra — "A-erh-chu-pa-erh" — springs from an Eastern word.[6] And though it was indeed the Westerners who showed us something our ancient calendar experts did not know — namely how to calculate the angle of the northern pole — this but shows the truth what Zhu Xi[7] arrived at through his investigation of things: the earth is like the yolk within an egg.

▾▾▾

On the question of the Chinese Rites that might be practiced by the Western missionaries, de Tournon[8] would not speak, though I sent messages to him repeatedly. I had agreed with the

[4]The ancient Greek mathematician who lived around 300 B.C.E. and laid the foundation for the study of geometry.

[5]One of the Classics, the *Book of Changes* was a work of divination that relied on the analysis of trigrams and hexagrams.

[6]*Algebra* is derived from the Arabic word *Al-jabr.* Kangxi is correct when he asserts that China had a long tradition of achievement in algebra, geometry, and trigonometry dating back at least as far as the Han Dynasty (206 B.C.E.–220 C.E.).

[7]Zhu Xi (1130–1200 C.E.), a famous commentator on Confucius, was China's leading philosopher after the classical age.

[8]Charles de Tournon (1668–1710) was a papal envoy sent to India and China to oversee Catholic missions. His demand that Chinese Christians abandon traditional rites was deeply offensive to Kangxi. The emperor ordered him to prison, where he died in 1710.

formulation the Beijing fathers had drawn up in 1700: that Confucius was honored by the Chinese as a master, but his name was not invoked in prayer for the purpose of gaining happiness, rank, or wealth; that worship of ancestors was an expression of love and filial remembrance, not intended to bring protection to the worshiper; and that there was no idea when an ancestral tablet was erected, that the soul of the ancestor dwelt in that tablet. . . .

If de Tournon didn't reply, the Catholic Bishop Maigrot[9] did, . . . telling me that Heaven is a material thing and should not be worshiped, and that one should invoke only the name "Lord of Heaven" to show the proper reverence. Maigrot wasn't merely ignorant of Chinese literature, he couldn't even recognize the simplest Chinese characters; yet he chose to discuss the falsity of the Chinese moral system. . . .

Even little animals mourn their dead mothers for many days; these Westerners who want to treat their dead with indifference are not even equal to animals. How could they be compared with Chinese? We venerate Confucius because of his doctrines of respect for virtue, his system of education, his inculcation of love for superiors and ancestors. Westerners venerate their own saints because of their actions. They paint pictures of men with wings and say, "These represent heavenly spirits, swift as if they had wings, though in reality there are no men with wings." I do not find it appropriate to dispute this doctrine, yet with superficial knowledge Maigrot discussed Chinese sanctity. . . .

▾▾▾

Since I discovered on the Southern Tour of 1703 that there were missionaries wandering at will over China, I had grown cautious and determined to control them more tightly: to bunch them in the larger cities and in groups that included men from several different countries, to catalogue their names and residences, and to permit no new establishments without my express permission. . . . I made all missionaries who wanted to stay on in China sign a certificate, stating that they would remain here for life and follow Ricci on the Rites. Forty or fifty who refused were exiled to Guangzhou; de Tournon was sent to Macao,[10] his secretary, Appiani, we kept in prison in Beijing.

Despite these sterner restrictions, the Westerners continued to cause me anxiety. Our ships were being sold overseas; reports came of ironwood for keel blocks being shipped out of Guangdong; Luzon and Batavia[11] became havens for Chinese outlaws; and the Dutch were strong in the Southern Seas. I ordered a general inquiry among residents of Beijing who had once lived on the coast, and called a conference of the coastal governors-general. "I fear that some time in the future China is going to get into difficulties with these various Western countries," I said. "That is my prediction."

---

[9]Charles Maigrot (1652–1730) was the apostolic vicar to China.

[10]Macao was the trading settlement near Guangzhou where by imperial order Western merchants were permitted to do business.

[11]Luzon was the major island of the Spanish-ruled Philippines; Batavia was the Dutch name for the island of Java in the East Indies.

Negotiating with the Qianlong Emperor

43 ▾ *Sir Henry Dundas,* *LETTER TO LORD GEORGE MACARTNEY*

Chinese restrictions on Western commerce in the eighteenth century increasingly frustrated the British, who were strenuously seeking to expand their trade in East Asia. According to the Chinese government's Guangzhou System, agents of the British East India Company and other European merchants could do business in the environs of only one city, Guangzhou, and only during the trading season, which ran from October to March. Subject to Chinese laws, they were barred from entering Guangzhou, learning Chinese, being accompanied by their wives, and much else. Furthermore, they were required to deal only with a small number of merchant companies that formed a merchants' guild, the Cohong, which had a government monopoly on trading with Westerners. Any grievance or dispute had to be referred to these merchants, who would pass it on to the hoppo, a government-appointed official who oversaw Guangzhou trade. The hoppo might make a decision himself, forward the grievance to Beijing, or simply ignore it.

Efforts by the East India Company to have the system modified got nowhere. When the company sent James Flint to China in 1759 to negotiate trade issues with the emperor, the unfortunate envoy was imprisoned for three years on charges of learning Chinese, sailing to unapproved ports, and improperly addressing the emperor.

By the end of the century, the demand for Chinese tea was soaring, so at the urging of Sir Henry Dundas, president of the board of the East India Company and home minister in the government of William Pitt the Younger, the company and the government decided to dispatch another embassy to Beijing in 1792. Chosen to head the mission was Lord George Macartney, a friend of Dundas's and an experienced diplomat. Unlike previous emissaries to Beijing, Macartney would be the official representative of the king, not the East India Company. The government's planning for the trip included the following set of instructions prepared for Macartney by Dundas. Written as a letter, it describes British goals and provides insights into British thinking on how Macartney should approach the emperor and his officials.

QUESTIONS FOR ANALYSIS

1. What specific complaints about China's trade policies are expressed in the letter of instruction?
2. What are the specific goals of Macartney's mission?
3. If these goals had been attained, how would they have improved the situation of the English merchants trading with China?
4. According to the letter, what must Macartney do to have the best chance of having successful negotiations with the Chinese government? What should he avoid?

5. What British views of the Chinese underlie the instructions given to Macartney?
6. Which British proposals do you think the Chinese found most objectionable? Why?

My Lord.

The measures lately taken by Government [of Great Britain] respecting the Tea trade, having more than trebled the former legal importation of this article into Great Britain, it [has] become particularly desirable to cultivate a friendship, and increase the communication with China, which may lead to such a vent [market] throughout that extensive Empire, of the manufactures of the mother Country, and of our Indian Territories, as beside contributing to their prosperity will out of the sales of such produce, furnish resources for the investment to Europe, now requiring no less an annual sum than one million, four hundred thousand pounds.

Hitherto, however, Great Britain has been obliged to pursue the Trade with that Country under circumstances the most discouraging, hazardous to its agents employed in conducting it, and precarious to the various interests involved in it. The only place where His Majesty's subjects have the privilege of a factory [trading station] is Canton [Guangzhou]. The fair competition of the Market is there destroyed by associations of the Chinese; our Supercargoes[1] are denied open access to the tribunals of the Country, and to the equal execution of its laws, and are kept altogether in a most arbitrary state of depression, ill suited to the importance of the concerns which are entrusted to their care, and scarcely compatible with the regulations of civilized society. . . .

His Majesty from his earnest desire to promote the present undertaking and in order to give the greater dignity to the Embassy, has been graciously pleased to order one of His Ships of War to convey you and your Suite [entourage] to the Coast of China. With the same view he has ordered a Military Guard to attend your Person, to be composed of chosen Men from the light Dragoons, Infantry and Artillery, with proper Officers. . . . This guard will add splendour and procure respect to the Embassy; the order, appearance and evolutions of the Men may convey no useless idea of our military Character and discipline, and if it should excite in the Emperor a desire of adopting any of the exercise or maneuvers, among the Troops, an opportunity thus offers to him, for which a return of good offices on his part is natural to be expected. . . .

Should your answer be satisfactory, and I will not suppose the contrary, you will then assume the Character and public appearance of His Majesty's Ambassador Extraordinary, and proceed with as much ceremony as can be admitted without causing a material delay, or incurring an unreasonable expense. . . .

. . . You will take the earliest opportunity of representing to His Imperial Majesty, that your Royal Master, already so justly celebrated in Foreign Countries on account of the voyages projected under his immediate auspices, for the acquisition and diffusion of knowledge, was from the same disposition desirous of sending an embassy to the most civilized as well as most ancient and populous Nation in the World in order to observe its celebrated institutions, and to communicate and receive the benefits which must result from an unreserved and friendly intercourse between that Country and his own. You will take

---

[1]An officer on a merchant ship in charge of the commercial concerns of the voyage.

care to express the high esteem which His Majesty has conceived for the Emperor, from the wisdom and virtue with which his character has been distinguished. . . .

I do not mean to prescribe to you the particular mode of your negotiation; much must be left to your circumspection, and the judgement to be formed upon occurrences as they arise; but upon the present view of the matter, I am inclined to believe that instead of attempting to gain upon the Chinese Administration by representations founded upon the intricacies of either European or Indian Politicks, you should fairly state, after repeating the general assurances of His Majesty's friendly and pacific inclinations towards the Emperor, and his respect for the reputed mildness of his Administration, first the mutual benefit to be derived from a trade between the two Nations, in the course of which we receive beside other articles to the amount of twenty millions of Pounds weight of a Chinese herb [tea], which would find very little vent, as not being in general use in other Countries, European or Asiatic, and for which we return woolens, cottons, and other articles useful to the Chinese, but a considerable part is actually paid to China in bullion.

Secondly, that the great extent of our commercial concerns in China, requires a place of security as a depot for such of our Goods as cannot be sold off or shipped during the short season that is allowed for our shipping to arrive and depart, and that for this purpose we wish to obtain a grant of a small tract of ground or detached Island, but in a more convenient situation than Canton, where our present warehouses are at a great distance from our Ships, and where we are not able to restrain the irregularities which are occasionally committed by the seamen of the Company's Ships, and those of private traders.

Thirdly, that our views are purely commercial, having not even a wish for territory; that we desire neither fortification nor defense but only the protection of the Chinese Government for our Merchants or their agents in trading or travelling through the Country and a security to us against the encroachments of other powers, who might ever aim to disturb our trade; and you must here be prepared to obviate any prejudice which may arise from the argument of our present dominions in India by stating our situation in this respect to have arisen without our intending it, from the necessity of our defending ourselves against the oppressions of the revolted Nabobs,[2] who entered into Cabals [small, secret conspiratorial groups] to our prejudice with other Nations of Europe, and disregarded the privileges granted to us by different Emperors, or by such other arguments as your own reflections upon the subject will suggest. . . .

If any favorable opportunity should be afforded to your Excellency it will be advisable that the difficulties with which our trade has long laboured at Canton should be represented. . . .

Should a new establishment be conceded you will take it in the name of the King of Great Britain. You will endeavour to obtain it on the most beneficial terms, with a power of regulating the police, and exercising jurisdiction over our own dependents. . . .

It is necessary you should be on your Guard against one stipulation which, perhaps, will be demanded from you: which is that of the exclusion of the trade of opium from the Chinese dominions as being prohibited by the Laws of the Empire; if this subject should come into discussion, it must be handled with the greatest circumspection. It is beyond a doubt that no inconsiderable portion of the opium raised within our Indian territories actually finds its way to China: but if it should be made . . . any article of any proposed commercial treaty, that none of that drug should be sent by us to China, you must accede to it, rather than risk any essential benefit by contending for a liberty in this respect in which case the sale of our opium in Bengal must be left to take its chance in an open market,

[2]Another spelling of *nawab*, a term for an Indian provincial prince.

or to find a consumption in the dispersed and circuitous traffic of the eastern Seas. . . .

In case the embassy should have an amicable and prosperous termination, it may be proposed to his Imperial Majesty to receive an occasional or perpetual Minister from the King of Great Britain, and to send one on his own part to the Court of London, in the assurance that all proper honours will be paid to any person who may be deputed in that sacred character. . . .

Your Excellency's most obedient
and most humble Servant
Henry Dundas.

Qianlong's Rejection of British Demands

44 ▾ *Emperor Qianlong, EDICT ON TRADE WITH GREAT BRITAIN*

Lord Macartney sailed for China in September 1792 with an entourage of scientists, servants, artists, guards, and translators on a heavily armed man-of-war accompanied by two support ships. The support ships were loaded with 600 boxes of gifts for the eighty-two-year-old emperor and his officials designed to show the sophistication and quality of British manufacturing and instrument making. The British reached Beijing in June 1793. After reaching a compromise on the issue of whether Macartney could kneel and bow before the emperor rather than prostrate himself in the ritual known as the kowtow, Macartney made his requests to the emperor and his high officials. Shortly thereafter, Qianlong rejected each and every British proposal in an edict to King George III. Macartney's mission had failed, and Sino-British relations continued to deteriorate until the Opium War (1839–1842) settled the two nations' many disputes through force rather than diplomacy.

QUESTIONS FOR ANALYSIS

1. **What views of China's place in the world are revealed in Qianlong's letter?**
2. **What does the letter reveal about Qianlong's views of foreigners in general and the British in particular?**
3. **What are the emperor's stated reasons for rejecting any expansion of trade with Great Britain?**
4. **What unstated reasons might also have influenced his decision?**

You, O King, from afar have yearned after the blessings of our civilization, and in your eagerness to come into touch with our converting influence have sent an Embassy across the sea bearing a memorial.[1] I have already taken note of your respectful spirit of submission, have treated your mission with extreme favor and loaded it with gifts, besides issuing a mandate to you, O

[1]Memorandum.

King, and honoring you with the bestowal of valuable presents. Thus has my indulgence been manifested.

Yesterday your Ambassador petitioned my Ministers to memorialize me regarding your trade with China, but his proposal is not consistent with our dynastic usage and cannot be entertained. Hitherto, all European nations, including your own country's barbarian merchants, have carried on their trade with our Celestial Empire at Guangzhou. Such has been the procedure for many years, although our Celestial Empire possesses all things in prolific abundance and lacks no product within its own borders. There was therefore no need to import the manufactures of outside barbarians in exchange for our own produce. But as the tea, silk, and porcelain which the Celestial Empire produces are absolute necessities to European nations and to yourselves, we have permitted, as a signal mark of favor, that *hongs*[2] should be established at Guangzhou, so that your wants might be supplied and your country thus participate in our beneficence. But your Ambassador has now put forward new requests which completely fail to recognize the Throne's principle to "treat strangers from afar with indulgence," and to exercise a pacifying control over barbarian tribes the world over. Moreover, our dynasty, ruling over the myriad races of the globe, extends the same benevolence towards all. Your England is not the only nation trading at Guangzhou. If other nations, following your bad example, wrongfully importune my ear with further impossible requests, how will it be possible for me to treat them with easy indulgence? Nevertheless, I do not forget the lonely remoteness of your island, cut off from the world by intervening wastes of sea, nor do I overlook your excusable ignorance of the usages of our Celestial Empire. I have consequently commanded my Ministers to enlighten your Ambassador on the subject, and have ordered the departure of the mission. But I have doubts that after your Envoy's return he may fail to acquaint you with my view in detail or that he may be lacking in lucidity, so that I shall now proceed . . . to issue my mandate on each question separately. In this way you will, I trust, comprehend my meaning. . . .

Your request for a small island near Zhoushan,[3] where your merchants may reside and goods be warehoused, arises from your desire to develop trade. As there are neither *hongs* nor interpreters in or near Zhoushan, where none of your ships has ever called, such an island would be utterly useless for your purposes. Every inch of the territory of our Empire is marked on the map and the strictest vigilance is exercised over it all: even tiny islets and far-lying sand-banks are clearly defined as part of the provinces to which they belong. Consider, moreover, that England is not the only barbarian land which wishes to establish . . . trade with our Empire: supposing that other nations were all to imitate your evil example and beseech me to present them each and all with a site for trading purposes, how could I possibly comply? This also is a flagrant infringement of the usage of my Empire and cannot possibly be entertained.

The next request, for a small site in the vicinity of Guangzhou city, where your barbarian merchants may lodge or, alternatively, that there be no longer any restrictions over their movements at Macao,[4] has arisen from the following causes. Hitherto, the barbarian merchants of Europe have had a definite locality assigned to them at Macao for residence and trade, and have been forbidden to encroach an inch beyond the limits assigned to that locality. . . . If these restrictions were withdrawn, friction would inevitably occur between the Chinese and your barbarian subjects, and the results would militate against the benevolent regard that I feel towards you. From every point of view, therefore, it

[2]Approximately ten Chinese merchant guilds that alone were licensed to trade with Westerners.

[3]A group of islands in the East China Sea at the entrance to Hangzhou Bay.

[4]Island colony west of present-day Hong Kong where Europeans were allowed to carry on their trade.

is best that the regulations now in force should continue unchanged. . . .

Regarding your nation's worship of the Lord of Heaven, it is the same religion as that of other European nations. Ever since the beginning of history, sage Emperors and wise rulers have bestowed on China a moral system and inculcated a code, which from time immemorial has been religiously observed by the myriads of my subjects [Confucianism]. There has been no hankering after heterodox doctrines. Even the European officials [missionaries] in my capital are forbidden to hold intercourse with Chinese subjects; they are restricted within the limits of their appointed residences, and may not go about propagating their religion. The distinction between Chinese and barbarian is most strict, and your Ambassador's request that barbarians shall be given full liberty to disseminate their religion is utterly unreasonable.

It may be, O King, that the above proposals have been wantonly made by your Ambassador on his own responsibility, or peradventure [perhaps] you yourself are ignorant of our dynastic regulations and had no intention of transgressing them when you expressed these wild ideas and hopes. . . . If, after the receipt of this explicit decree, you lightly give ear to the representations of your subordinates and allow your barbarian merchants to proceed to Zhejiang and Tianjin,[5] with the object of landing and trading there, the ordinances of my Celestial Empire are strict in the extreme, and the local officials, both civil and military, are bound reverently to obey the law of the land. Should your vessels touch the shore, your merchants will assuredly never be permitted to land or to reside there, but will be subject to instant expulsion. In that event your barbarian merchants will have had a long journey for nothing. Do not say that you were not warned in due time! Tremblingly obey and show no negligence! A special mandate!

[5]Two Chinese port cities.

Social and Economic Change in Tokugawa Japan

Tokugawa Ieyasu and his immediate successors implemented a four-part plan to strengthen their authority and stabilize Japan. They tightened control of powerful daimyo families; severed almost all contacts between Japan and the outside world; officially sanctioned and supported Confucianism; and sought to freeze class divisions with military aristocrats at the top and farmers, artisans, and merchants below them. These policies were remarkably successful. Their subjects, who yearned for order as much as their rulers, experienced internal peace and stable government under the Tokugawa until 1867, when the regime was overthrown.

Paradoxically, the demise of the Tokugawa regime resulted in part from its success. Decades of peace fostered economic expansion accompanied by population growth, urbanization, and social mobility. Japan's population grew from approximately 18 million in 1600 to 30 million by the 1750s, and Edo (present-day Tokyo) grew from a small village into a city of over a million. These changes increased

demand for all types of goods, especially rice, and as a result, richer peasants and merchants prospered. Most peasants, however, could not take advantage of the commercialization of agriculture, and in the eighteenth century many experienced hardship from land shortages and rising rents. In addition, Japan's military aristocrats, the daimyo and samurai, failed to benefit from the economic boom. Lavish spending and the daimyo's need to maintain residences in both Edo and their own domain led to massive indebtedness.

While economic change was undermining the social basis of the Tokugawa regime, intellectual ferment was eroding its ideological underpinnings. As the memory of earlier civil wars faded, the conservativism of Confucianism lost some of its appeal, and foreign ideas seemed less dangerous. In the eighteenth century, two intellectual developments challenged state-sponsored Confucianism. Proponents of National Learning, or *Kokugaku*, rejected Chinese influence, especially Confucianism, and dedicated themselves to the study and glorification of Japan's ancient literature and religion. Other Japanese developed an interest in European ideas, especially in medicine but also in botany, cartography, and gunnery. These endeavors were known as Dutch Studies because the main source of information about Europe were the Dutch, who continued to trade on a limited basis with Japan even after the seclusion policy was adopted. By the late eighteenth century, those who were dissatisfied with the Tokugawa regime had models for a different future, something that solidly Confucian China lacked.

The National Learning Movement

45 ▾ *Kamo Mabuchi,* *A STUDY OF THE IDEA OF THE NATION*

The son of a Shinto priest, Kamo Mabuchi (1697–1769) received training in both ancient Japanese literature and Confucianism. He contributed to the National Learning Movement in two important ways. As a poet he sought to imitate the style of ancient Japanese poetry, and as a scholar he inspired a new interest in the systematic study of ancient Japanese verse. Kamo's greatest work is his commentary on the *Collection of Ten Thousand Leaves*, an anthology of Japanese poetry dating from the eighth century. As the following selection illustrates, his overriding purpose was to reveal the original simplicity and spontaneity of the Japanese people before their corruption by Chinese influence.

QUESTIONS FOR ANALYSIS

1. How does Kamo seek to "prove" the worthlessness of Confucianism?
2. According to Kamo, how was the very nature of the Japanese people affected when Confucianism was introduced?
3. What is Kamo's vision for Japan's future?
4. According to Kamo, what are the drawbacks of Chinese as a written language? What language reforms does he propose for the Japanese?

5. On the basis of your knowledge of Confucianism and Chinese history, in your view how valid are his criticisms of Chinese thought and the Chinese in general?

Someone remarked to me, "I pay no heed to such petty trifles as Japanese poetry; what interests me is the Chinese Way of governing a nation."

I smiled at this and did not answer. Later, when I met the same man he asked, "You seem to have an opinion on every subject — why did you merely keep smiling when I spoke to you?"

I answered, "You mean when you were talking about the Chinese Confucian teachings or whatever you call them? They are no more than a human invention which reduces the heart of Heaven and Earth to something trivial."

At these words he became enraged, "How dare you call our Great Way trivial?"

I answered, "I would be interested in hearing whether or not the Chinese Confucian learning has actually helped to govern a country successfully." He immediately cited the instances of Yao, Shun, Hsia, Yin, Chou, and so on.[1] I asked if there were no later examples, but he informed me that there were not.

I pursued the matter, asking this time about how far back Chinese traditions went. He answered that thousands of years had passed from Yao's day to the present. I then asked, "Why then did the Way of Yao continue only until the Chou and afterwards cease? I am sure that it is because you restrict yourself to citing events which took place thousands of years ago that the Way seems so good. But those are merely ancient legends. It takes more than such specious ideas to run a country!"

When I said this he grew all the more furious, and ranted on about ancient matters. I said, "You are utterly prejudiced." . . .

Despite the fact that their country has been torn for centuries by disturbances and has never really been well administered, they think that they can explain with their Way of Confucius the principles governing the whole world. Indeed, when one has heard them through, there is nothing to be said: anyone can quickly grasp their doctrines because they consist of mere quibbling. What they value the most and insist on is the establishment and maintenance of good government. Everybody in China would seem to have been in agreement on this point, but belief in it did not in fact lie very deep. It is obvious that many gave superficial assent who did not assent in their hearts. Yet when these principles were introduced to this country it was stated that China had obtained good government through the adoption of them. This was a complete fabrication. I wish it were possible to send to China anyone who clung to such a belief! . . .

Japan in ancient days was governed in accordance with the natural laws of Heaven and earth. There was never any indulgence in such petty rationalizing as marked China, but when suddenly these teachings were transmitted here from abroad, they quickly spread, for the men of old in their simplicity took them for the truth. In Japan there had been generation after generation, extending back to the remote past, which had known prosperity, but no sooner were these Confucian teachings propagated here than in the time of Temmu[2] a great rebellion occurred. Later. . . the palace, dress, and ceremonies were [made to look Chinese] and everything took on a superficial elegance; under the surface, however,

---

[1]Yao and Shun are mythical rulers from China's ancient past who were perceived as models of enlightened rule. Xia (Hsia), Yin, and Zhou (Chou) are the names of the first three Chinese dynasties described in historical records. The Yin Dynasty is also known as the Shang.

[2]Emperor Temmu (r. 631–686) assumed the throne after raising an army and defeating the forces of his nephew and reigning emperor, Kōbun.

contentiousness and dishonesty became more prevalent.

Confucianism made men crafty, and led them to worship the ruler to such an excessive degree that the whole country acquired a servant's mentality. . . .

Just as roads are naturally created when people live in uncultivated woodlands or fields, so the Way of the Age of the Gods spontaneously took hold in Japan. Because it was a Way indigenous to the country it caused our emperors to wax increasingly in prosperity. However, the Confucian teachings had not only repeatedly thrown China into disorder, but they now had the same effect in Japan. Yet there are those unwitting of these facts who reverence Confucianism and think that it is the Way to govern the country! This is a deplorable attitude. . . .

When ruling the country a knowledge of Chinese things is of no help in the face of an emergency. In such a situation some man will spontaneously come forth to propose things which are wise and true. In the same way, doctors often study and master Chinese texts, but very seldom do they cure any sickness. On the other hand, medicines which have been transmitted naturally in this country with no reasons or theoretical knowledge behind them, infallibly cure all maladies. It is good when a man spontaneously devotes himself to these things. It is unwise to become obsessed with them. I would like to show people even once what is good in our Way. The fact that the Confucian scholars know very little about government is obvious from the frequent disorders which arise in China whenever the government is left to them. . . .

People also tell me, "We had no writing in this country and therefore had to use Chinese characters. From this one fact you can know everything about the relative importance of our countries." I answer, "I need not recite again how troublesome, evil, turbulent a country China is. To mention just one instance — there is the matter of their picture-writing. There are about 38,000 characters in common use, as someone has determined. . . . Every place name and plant name has a separate character for it which has no other use but to designate that particular place or plant. Can any man, even one who devotes himself to the task earnestly, learn all these many characters? Sometimes people miswrite characters, sometimes the characters themselves change from one generation to the next. What a nuisance, a waste of effort, and a bother! In India, on the other hand, fifty letters suffice for the writing of the more than 5,000 volumes of the Buddhist scriptures. . . . In Holland, I understand, they use twenty-five letters. In this country there should be fifty. The appearance of letters used in all countries is in general the same, except for China where they invented their bothersome system.". . . As long as a few teachings were carefully observed and we worked in accordance with the Will of Heaven and earth, the country would be well off without any special instruction. Nevertheless, Chinese doctrines were introduced and corrupted men's hearts. Even though these teachings resembled those of China itself, they were of the kind which heard in the morning are forgotten by evening. Our country in ancient times was not like that. It obeyed the laws of Heaven and earth. The emperor was the sun and moon and the subjects the stars. If the subjects as stars protect the sun and moon, they will not hide it as is now the case. Just as the sun, moon, and stars have always been in Heaven, so our imperial sun and moon, and the stars his vassals, have existed without change from ancient days, and have ruled the world fairly. . . .

The Social Ills of Tokugawa Japan

46 ▾ Honda Toshiaki, A SECRET PLAN OF GOVERNMENT

Honda Toshiaki, born in northern Japan in 1721, was a perceptive critic of late Tokugawa society and a prophet of Japan's future. After studying and teaching mathematics, astronomy, and fencing in Edo, he devoted most of his life to observing and analyzing the state of contemporary Japan. In his travels he was particularly interested in examining conditions among the poor and learning the reasons for their misery. He concluded that as a small island nation, Japan needed to expand commerce and colonize, rather than concentrate on agriculture, as a large continental country like China could do. He believed Japan should abandon its seclusion policy and make efforts to learn modern navigation and weaponry. Honda publicized his ideas among his students and correspondents, but his influence on Japan's political leaders came only after his death. His only government service was as advisor to the lord of Kaga, a minor aristocrat. Honda died in Edo in 1821.

Honda's *A Secret Plan for Government*, written in 1798, is his most important work. In it he outlines an economic and political plan for Japan based on what he calls the "four imperative needs": to learn the effective use of gunpowder; to develop metallurgy; to increase trade; and to colonize nearby islands and distant lands. The following excerpt, in which Honda analyzes the roots of Japan's problems, comes at the end of a long discourse on Japanese history.

QUESTIONS FOR ANALYSIS

1. What is Honda's view of the daimyo?
2. How do merchants contribute to Japan's problems, according to Honda?
3. How does Honda justify his assertion that fifteen-sixteenths of all Japanese rice production goes to the merchants? Are his arguments plausible?
4. According to Honda, why is Europe rather than China the better model for Japan's revival?
5. What Confucian influence is evident in Honda's *Plan*? In what ways does Honda reject Confucianism?
6. In your view what would Kamo Mabuchi (source 45) have thought of Honda's ideas?

Not until Tokugawa Ieyasu[1] used his power to control the strong and give succor to the weak did the warfare that had lasted for three hundred years without a halt suddenly abate. Arrows were left in their quivers and spears in their racks. . . . It must have been because he realized

[1]The founder of the Tokugawa Shogunate, he seized power in 1600, received appointment as shogun in 1603, abdicated from office in 1605, but remained in power until his death in 1616 (see source 19).

how difficult it would be to preserve the empire for all ages to come if the people were not honest in their hearts that Ieyasu, in his testament, exhorted shoguns who would succeed him to abstain from any irregularities in government, and to rule on a basis of benevolence and honesty. It was his counsel that the shoguns should serve as models to the people, and by their honesty train the people in the ways of humanity and justice. He taught that the shogun should not compel obedience merely by the use of force, but by his acts of benevolence should keep the nation at peace. . . .

He taught the daimyo that the duties of a governor consisted in the careful attempt to guide the people of their domains in such a way as both to bring about the prosperity of the land and to encourage the literary and military arts.

However, in recent days there has been the spectacle of lords confiscating the allocated property of their retainers[2] on the pretext of paying back debts to the merchants. The debts do not then decrease, but usually seem rather to grow larger. One daimyo with an income of 60,000 *koku*[3] so increased his borrowings that he could not make good his debts, and there was a public suit. . . . Even if repayment had been attempted on the basis of his income of 60,000 koku, the debt would not have been completely settled for fifty or sixty years, so long a time that it is difficult to imagine the day would actually come.

All the daimyo are not in this position, but there is not one who has not borrowed from the merchants. Is this not a sad state of affairs? The merchant, watching this spectacle, must feel like a fisherman who sees a fish swim into his net. Officials of the daimyo harass the farmers for money, which they claim they need to repay the daimyo's debts, but the debts do not diminish. Instead, the daimyo go on contracting new ones year after year. The [daimyo's] officials are blamed for this situation, and are dismissed as incompetent. New officials then harass and afflict the farmers in much the same way as the old ones, and so it goes on. . . .

No matter how hard the daimyo and their officials rack their brains, they do not seem to be able to reduce the debts. The lords are "sunk in a pool of debts," as it is popularly said, a pool from which their children and grandchildren will be unable to escape. Everything will be as the merchants wish it. The daimyo turn over their domains to the merchants, receiving in return an allowance with which to pay their public and private expenses. . . .

Many fields have turned into wasteland since the famine of 1783, when thousands of farmers starved to death.[4] Wherever one goes . . . , one hears people say, "There used to be a village here. . . . The land over there was once part of such-and-such a county, but now there is no village and no revenue comes from the land." . . . When so many farmers starved, reducing still further their already insufficient numbers, the amount of uncultivated land greatly increased. If the wicked practice of infanticide, now so prevalent, is not stopped, the farming population will dwindle until it tends to die out altogether. Generous protective and relief measures must be put into effect immediately if this evil practice is to be stamped out. . . .

The Confucian scholars of ancient and modern times have talked a great deal about benevolence and compassion, but they possess neither in their hearts. Officials and authorities talk about benevolent government, but they have no understanding of what that means. Whose fault is it that the farmers are dying of starvation and that good fields are turning into wasteland? The fault lies entirely with the ruler. . . .

▷ There follows an enthusiastic but often inaccurate account of Europe's accomplishments.

[2]A reference to the *samurai*, lesser members of the military aristocracy.

[3]A *koku* is approximately five bushels of rice and was used to measure daimyo income.

[4]A reference to the Temmei famine (1783–1786), one of the three major famines that occurred in eighteenth-century Japan. The famines had various causes, including flooding, drought, typhoons, and insect damage.

Because astronomy, calendar making, and mathematics are considered the ruler's business, the European kings are well versed in celestial and terrestrial principles, and instruct the common people in them. Thus even among the lower classes one finds men who show great ability in their particular fields. The Europeans as a result have been able to establish industries with which the rest of the world is unfamiliar. It is for this reason that all the treasures of the world are said to be attracted to Europe. There is nowhere the Europeans' ships do not go in order to obtain the different products and treasures of the world. They trade their own rare products, superior implements, and unusual inventions for the precious metals and valuable goods of others, which they bring back to enrich their own countries. Their prosperity makes them strong, and it is because of their strength that they are never invaded or pillaged, whereas for their part they have invaded countless non-European countries. . . .

There is no place in the world to compare with Europe. It may be wondered in what way this supremacy was achieved. In the first place, the European nations have behind them a history of five to six thousand years. In this period they have delved deep into the beauties of the arts, have divined the foundations of government, and have established a system based on a thorough examination of the factors that naturally make a nation prosperous. Because of their proficiency in mathematics, they have excelled also in astronomy, calendar making, and surveying. They have elaborated laws of navigation such that there is nothing simpler for them than to sail the oceans of the world. . . .

In spite of this example, however, the Japanese do not look elsewhere than to China for good or beautiful things, so tainted are the customs and temperament of Japan by Chinese teachings. . . .

China is a mountainous country that extends as far as Europe and Africa. It is bounded by the ocean to the south, but water communication within the country is not feasible. Since it is impossible to feed the huge population of cities when transport can be effected only by human or animal strength, there are no big cities in China away from the coast. China is therefore a much less favored country than Japan, which is surrounded by water, and this factor shows in the deficiencies and faults of Chinese state policies. China does not merit being used as a model. Since Japan is a maritime nation, shipping and trade should be the chief concerns of the ruler. Ships should be sent to all countries to obtain products needed for national consumption and to bring precious metals to Japan. A maritime nation is equipped with the means to increase her national strength.

By contrast, a nation that attempts to get along on its own resources will grow steadily weaker. . . . To put the matter more bluntly, the policies followed by the various ruling families until now have determined that the lower classes must lead a hand-to-mouth existence. The best part of the harvests of the farmers who live on the domains of the empire is wrenched away from them. The lords spend all they take within the same year, and if they then do not have enough, they oppress the farmers all the more cruelly in an effort to obtain additional funds. This goes on year after year. . . .

Soon all the gold and silver currency will pass into the hands of the merchants, and only merchants will be deserving of the epithets "rich" and "mighty." Their power will thus grow until they stand first among the four classes. When I investigated the incomes of present-day merchants, I discovered that fifteen-sixteenths of the total income of Japan goes to the merchants, with only one-sixteenth left for the samurai. As proof of this statement, I cite the following case. When there are good rice harvests at Yonezawa in Dewa or in Semboku-gun in Akita[5] the price is five or six *mon* for one *sho.*[6] The rice is sold to merchants who ship it to Edo, where the price is about 100 mon, regardless of the original cost. At this rate, if one bought 10,000 ryos[7] worth of

[5]Dewa and Akita are provinces in northern Honshu.

[6]A *mon* was a copper coin; a *sho* was about 3.2 pints.

[7]Also known as a *koban*, a *ryo* was a Japanese gold coin.

rice in Dewa, sent it to Edo, and sold it there, one's capital would be increased to 160,000 ryo. If the 160,000 ryo in turn were used as capital, the return in Edo would be 2,560,000 ryo. With only two exchanges of trade it is possible to make enormous profits.

It may be claimed that of this sum part must go for shipping expenses and pack-horse charges, but the fact remains that one gets back sixteen times what one has paid for the rice. It is thus apparent that fifteen-sixteenths of the nation's income goes to the merchants. In terms of the production of an individual farmer, out of thirty days a month he works twenty-eight for the merchants and two for the samurai; or, out of 360 days in a year, he works $337^1/_2$ for the merchants and $22^1/_2$ for the samurai. Clearly, then, unless the samurai store grain it is impossible for them to offer any relief to the farmers in years of famine. This may be why they can do no more than look on when the farmers are dying of starvation. And all this because the right system has not been established. It is a most lamentable state of affairs that the farmers have to shoulder the weight of this error and die of starvation as inevitably as "water collecting in a hollow."

By means of the plans outlined in the account of the four imperative needs . . . the present corrupt and jejune society could be restored to its former prosperity and strength. The ancient glories of the warrior-nation of Japan would be revived. Colonization projects would gradually be commenced and would meet with great success. . . . Then, under enlightened government, Japan could certainly be made the richest and strongest country in the world.

Multiple Voices IV
Two Emperors: Portraits and Power

BACKGROUND

Portraits — pictorial representations of individuals — are usually thought of as paintings, but they also can be photographs, sculptures, drawings, medallions, coins, or engravings. They can depict their subjects sitting, standing, involved in an activity, or as part of a group. Portraits can be as large as the sixty-foot colossal busts of the four American presidents sculpted into Mount Rushmore in South Dakota, or as tiny as photographs encased in lockets and worn as jewelry. They can be as priceless as the *Mona Lisa*, on display at the Louvre in Paris behind a bulletproof, nonreflecting, temperature-controlled, airtight glass case, or as ordinary as the image of Lincoln on a U.S. penny. Not all cultures value portraiture. Africa, for example, has a rich tradition of mask-making, but its masks do not portray chieftains or kings, but rather deities, ancestral spirits, mythological beings, the dead, animal spirits, and other beings and forces believed to have power over humanity. In Jewish and Islamic cultures, portraiture smacks of idolatry and hence is rare. However, in China and Europe, where portraiture has been valued for centuries, it can offer valuable insights into the past.

More so than most sources, portraits need to be "read" with care. Although portraiture is associated with the idea of "likeness," and to its detractors is little more than the mechanical duplication of a person's features, in fact each portrait is the result of a long series of decisions made by the artist, the subject (who in most cases "sits" for the portrait), and the patron (who in many cases is also the subject). How will the subject be posed and in what setting? What will be the subject's facial expression? What will he or she be wearing? What props and other human figures will be included? Answers to these questions are based on yet other considerations: What is the portrait's intended audience, and what message is it meant to convey about the subject's physical characteristics, values, social status, and personality?

The paintings in this section provide an opportunity to analyze portraits of two contemporary rulers living on opposite sides of Eurasia: Qianlong, emperor of China from 1736 to 1796; and Napoleon Bonaparte, first consul and emperor of France from 1799 to 1814 and emperor once more from March 20 to June 22, 1815, after a return from exile. Not surprisingly, given the dissimilarities between China and Europe, there were many differences between the two emperors' views of themselves and their roles as rulers. But there were also similarities, including their use of paintings and portraits to solidify their authority.

During his fifty-year reign, Qianlong supported a large studio of painters — among them, several Europeans — who produced hundreds of paintings that went into the emperor's private collection and were displayed at various sites within the palace grounds in Beijing. A frequent visitor to the studio, Qianlong suggested themes for paintings, monitored his painters' efforts, and often had his own comments or scraps of poetry printed on their completed works. Aside from landscapes, most of the paintings produced by the imperial artists featured Qianlong — on his throne, on horseback, in hunting scenes, with his family, or at his desk. Almost all of them had a political message. Some sought to convey a sense of his power, benevolence, and wisdom, while others were meant to appeal to one of the various ethnic and religious groups among his subjects. For his Buddhist subjects in Tibet and newly conquered western lands, for example, he was portrayed in several paintings as the incarnation of a Buddhist saint sitting on a throne surrounded by figures representing deities, saints, and teachers. For members of his own ethnic group — the "barbarian" Manchus who had conquered China in the mid seventeenth century and made up only 2 percent of China's population — he was depicted as a warrior, a skilled horseman, or a fearless hunter. For his Chinese subjects, especially members of the scholar-gentry class, he was depicted as a supporter of the Confucian values of scholarship, filial piety, and traditional court ceremony.

Like Qianlong, Napoleon Bonaparte also was the subject of numerous paintings, all with political messages. Most of these paintings were paid for with government funds and commissioned by Napoleon himself; even for those commissioned by private individuals, Napoleon had a say about their content. Like the paintings of Qianlong, many paintings of Napoleon were meant to convey his authority and power. These include coronation scenes and portraits showing him in ceremonial dress and surrounded by symbols of imperial rule. Many other paintings celebrated Napoleon's generalship and his battlefield victories. Napoleon, however, wanted to be known as more than a great general, so many paintings depicted him in other roles — as the defender of the revolution, the sage statesman, the champion of science and progress, the enlightened lawgiver, and the man of destiny ordained to introduce a new European order based on reason.

THE SOURCES

All three Chinese paintings we have chosen are attributed to Giuseppe Castiglione (1688–1766), a skilled painter and Jesuit missionary who went to China in 1715 and took the Chinese name Lang Shining. He developed a style that blended European techniques and Chinese subject matter. He produced hundreds of paintings, some in collaboration with Chinese artists, and also designed a number of buildings on the palace grounds. The first painting shown here is *Qianlong at Leisure on New Year's Eve*, painted around 1738. In this painting Castiglione depicts Qianlong in a happy family scene dressed in traditional Chinese garb. Behind him stand two concubines, while on his lap and at his side are his three sons. The other six boys are thought to be cousins. The event is a traditional Chinese celebration of New Year's Eve, the culmination of a fifteen-day period in which the Chinese bid farewell to the old year and welcome the new. It is a time for family reunions, thanksgiving, and honoring the memory of ancestors. Outside the pavilion, one cousin is bringing in fruit, a frequent New Year's gift; another is distributing dried sesame stalks, which as symbols of the old year are either trampled on or burned; and a third is lighting firecrackers to welcome the new year. Aside from Qianlong himself, depicted as the dutiful father, the most important figure in the painting is his eldest son, shown holding a halberd. In the Chinese language, the halberd is represented by the same character as "good fortune"; the musical stone attached to it has the same character as "felicity"; and the two fish below the musical stone have the same character as "plentifulness."

The next painting, also attributed to Castiglione, is entitled *Taking a Stag with a Mighty Arrow*. Completed around 1760, it shows Qianlong wearing a loosely fitted Manchu-style robe for ease in mounting a horse. The pouches at his side are in the style favored by northeastern tribal hunters. Already having released one arrow, he reaches back for another being offered by a young woman. Although there is controversy about the identification of the woman, in all likelihood it is Princess Hexaio, Qianlong's tenth daughter. Manchu women, unlike their Han counterparts, were encouraged to ride, learn archery, and hunt, and Hexaio was famous for her skill in such undertakings.

The final painting, *Qianlong in His Study*, is attributed to Castiglione in collaboration with Jin Tingbaiao and was completed around 1767. Qianlong is depicted in the garb of a Confucian scholar with the distinctive wispy beard often connected with sagehood. He is sitting at his desk contemplating the words he is about to write, with his window open to the outside world of nature. On his desk are the basic Chinese writing tools — rice paper, writing brush, ink stick, and ink stone. Thus, he shows himself as a ruler interested in endeavors dear to the hearts of his Confucian officials — literature, calligraphy, and scholarship.

The two paintings of Napoleon are both by Jacques-Louis David (1748–1825), the most prominent painter of his age and an ardent supporter of the French Revolution. As a member of the National Convention, he voted for the execution of King Louis XVI (causing his royalist wife to divorce him) and organized dozens of revolutionary ceremonies and festivals inspired by his close friend, the radical Jacobin Robespierre. Imprisoned after the fall of Robespierre, he was released in 1797 (with the help of his ex-wife, whom he remarried) and gained the notice of Napoleon, whom David came to admire. After Napoleon became first consul, he asked David to paint his crossing of the Alps in 1800 at Great Saint Bernard Pass, a feat that enabled the French to surprise the Austrian army and win the Battle of Marengo on June 14, 1800. To curry the favor of Napoleon, the king of Spain, Charles IV, also commissioned David to paint the same scene. Both versions were exhibited in Paris in 1801, with the painting commissioned by Charles IV shown here. Although leading an army of 60,000 through the snow and mud of the Alps in May was an impressive achievement, David embellished it in his painting. As Napoleon's soldiers trudge by in the background, the first consul is shown on a rearing horse (not the mule he actually rode) and dressed in tights and a flowing cape (not the mud-spattered coat he wore). On stones below the horse's front legs are inscribed the names of Hannibal (247–183 B.C.E.), the Carthaginian general who famously led an army replete with elephants through the Saint Bernard Pass to attack Rome in the Second Punic War, and Charlemagne, who as king of the Franks also led an army through the pass in 773 C.E. when he attacked the Lombards.

The second painting of Napoleon, also by David, is entitled *The Emperor Napoleon in His Study at the Tuileries* (1812). It shows Napoleon rising from his desk after a long night of work to leave his office and review his troops. Napoleon is dressed in a military uniform and, as is suggested by the maps on his desk, has been giving some thought to military campaigns. But as can be seen by the words on the paper on top of the pile, he also has been working on the Civil Code, the mammoth codification of French law that was one of his regime's lasting achievements. David's painting is deceptive in this regard in that most of the work on the Civil Code was done by a panel of experts Napoleon appointed. Other notable features of the painting are the copy on the floor of Plutarch's *Lives*, biographical sketches of eminent ancient Greek statesmen written in the first century C.E., and the medallion he is wearing. It is the medallion of the Legion of Honor, an organization founded by Napoleon to honor outstanding military achievement or other service to the state. Although the painting was commissioned by a wealthy British admirer of the emperor and Napoleon did not pose for it, after he saw it, Napoleon told the painter, "You have understood me well, my dear David."

QUESTIONS FOR ANALYSIS

1. In regard to the three paintings of Qianlong, what impression does each painting convey, and what characteristics of Qianlong does each one communicate?
2. In the hunting scene, why does the artist include a woman?

3. In ***Qianlong at Leisure on New Year's Eve***, what is significant about the painting's setting and the placement and interaction of the various figures?
4. For the painting of Napoleon crossing the Alps, why did the artist include the soldiers in the background and the stone with the names of Hannibal and Charlemagne? What is significant about the bearing of the horse, the posture of Napoleon, his gestures, his gaze, and his dress? What impressions of Napoleon is David trying to communicate?
4. In David's painting of Napoleon in his study, what clues does the artist provide to show that Napoleon has been working through the night? Why did he include the book by Plutarch, the sword, the maps, and the papers scattered across the desk? What significance do you find in the glimpse of the library shown on the far left?
5. Thinking about the Chinese and French paintings together, what similarities and differences can you see in presentation and style? How effective is each of the works in communicating its message? And finally, what does this exercise reveal about the usefulness of paintings as sources for the historian?

I ▾ Giuseppe Castiglione, *QIANLONG AT LEISURE ON NEW YEAR'S EVE*

2 ▾ *Giuseppe Castiglione, TAKING A STAG WITH A MIGHTY ARROW*

3 ▾ *Giuseppe Castiglione and Jin Tingbaiao, QIANLONG IN HIS STUDY*

4 ▾ *Jacques-Louis David, BONAPARTE CROSSING THE ALPS AT SAINT-BERNARD*

5 ▾ *Jacques-Louis David, THE EMPEROR NAPOLEON IN HIS STUDY AT THE TUILERIES*

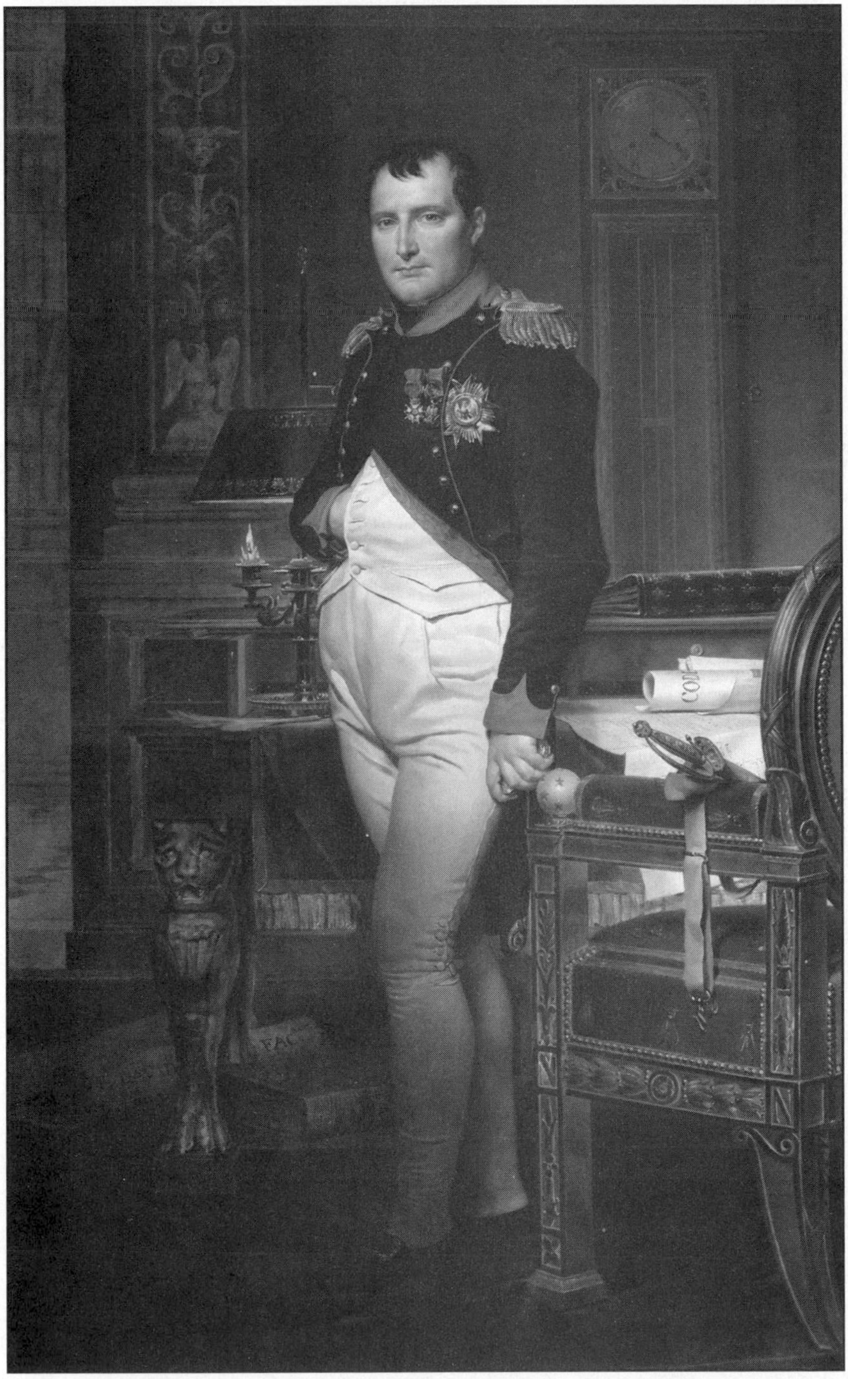

Part Three

The World in the Age of Western Dominance: 1800–1914

THE DIRECTION OF WORLD HISTORY during the nineteenth century is perhaps best symbolized by the experience of Africa. In 1800, except for the far southern regions settled by the Dutch and the areas on the west and east coasts where slaves were traded, Africa was largely untouched by Europeans. A century later, except for Ethiopia and Liberia, the continent was under the political control of European powers, who accomplished their takeover with scant regard for the interests and wishes of the Africans. In 1884 and 1885, rules for dividing up Africa were established at the Berlin West Africa Conference, whose rule-makers represented fourteen European nations and the United States. They agreed that each power had to give the others proper notice if it intended to annex African lands and, in doing so, could not simply stamp its name on a map. It had to have real troops or administrators on the scene. Only three decades later, in World War I, Africa's colonial masters dispatched thousands of Africans to battlefronts in Africa, Europe, and the Middle East, where many died fighting for their European overlords.

The Europeans' land grab in Africa was striking in its speed and magnitude, but it was not unique. Burma, India, Vietnam, Cambodia, Laos, the Malay Peninsula, the East Indies, and hundreds of South Pacific islands also came under direct European or U.S. control in the nineteenth century. Independent states, such as Cuba, Nicaragua, Haiti, the Dominican Republic, the Ottoman Empire, Egypt, and China, were forced to accept varying degrees of Western control of their finances and foreign policy. Australia and New Zealand became European settler colonies. Canada, South Africa, the Philippines, and most of the West Indies remained parts of pre-nineteenth-century empires, although Canada in 1867 and South Africa in 1910 were granted extensive powers of self-government and the Philippines in 1898 changed masters from Spain to the United States. Mexico and most Central and South American nations retained full political sovereignty but saw many of their economic assets — banks, railroads, mines, and grazing lands — taken over by Western investors. Only Japan, by adopting the technology, military organization, and industrial economy of the West, avoided subservience to the West and became an imperialist power itself.

Never had world economic and political relationships been as one-sided as they were when World War I began in 1914. A handful of nations led by Great Britain, France, and the newly emerging powers, Germany and the United States, wielded political influence throughout the world. These same nations controlled much of the world's economy and channeled a disproportionate amount of the world's wealth and resources to their own societies.

The West's expansion resulted in part from the inner dynamics of capitalism, with its drive for new markets, resources, and investment opportunities. It also resulted from nationalist rivalries among the Western powers themselves, most of whose leaders and citizens believed that prestige and prosperity depended on empire-building and overseas investment. It also resulted from the huge disparity between the military and economic strength of Europe and the United States and that of the rest of the world. During the nineteenth century, once powerful states such as the Ottoman Empire and China faced formidable internal problems, and others, such as Mughal India, had already collapsed. Europe and the United States, however, continued to industrialize, develop new technologies, and build the most powerful armies and navies in history. Thus, the Western nations faced no effective resistance when they sought to extend their economic grasp and political authority throughout the world.

The people of Asia and Africa now faced questions and, to the degree it was within their power to do so, made choices similar to those confronting the Russians during and after the reign of Peter the Great. Do we want to Westernize? If so, how thoroughly? At what human cost? How? How quickly? People found no easy answers to these questions, but ignoring the West was no longer an option.

Chapter 8

The West in the Age of Industrialization and Imperialism

As far-reaching as the transformation of Western civilization since the Renaissance had been, no one in 1800 could have predicted the even greater changes about to occur in the nineteenth century. When Napoleon met defeat at Waterloo in 1815, Europe's population was 200 million, with as many as 25 million people of European descent living in the rest of the world. By 1914 these numbers had increased to 450 million and 150 million, respectively. In 1815 a large majority of Europeans and Americans lived in rural villages and worked the land; by 1914, in highly industrialized nations such as Great Britain, a majority of the population lived in cities and worked in factories or offices. In 1815, despite two decades of revolution, most governments were still aristocratic and monarchical; in 1914 representative government and universal manhood suffrage were the norms in Europe, the United States, and the British dominions of Canada, Australia, and New Zealand. In 1815 most governments limited their activities to defense, the preservation of law and order, and some economic regulation; in 1914 governments subsidized education, sponsored scientific research, oversaw public health, monitored industry, provided social welfare care, maintained huge military establishments, and, as a result, had grown enormously.

Europe's global role also changed dramatically in these 100 years. In 1815 European political authority around the world appeared to be declining. Great Britain no longer ruled its thirteen American colonies; Portugal and Spain were losing their American colonies; and France recently had lost its prime West Indian colony, Saint Domingue, and sold 800,000 square miles of North American territory to the United States through the Louisiana Purchase. Great Britain's decision to outlaw the slave trade in 1807 seemed to be a step toward a diminished European role in Africa, and there was little to suggest that Western nations had the ability or inclination to extend their power in the Middle East or East Asia. Only the expansion of Great Britain in India hinted at what the nineteenth century would bring: the Western nations' takeover of Africa and Southeast Asia, their interference in the politics of China and the Middle East, and their dominance of the world's economy.

Many factors contributed to the West's transformation and expansion. The most important cause, however, was the Industrial Revolution — a series of wide-ranging economic changes involving the application of new technologies and energy sources to manufacturing, communication, and transportation. This revolution began in England in the late eighteenth century when a number of inventions transformed the textile industry. By 1914 industrialization had taken root in Europe, Japan, and the United States and was spreading to Canada, Russia, and parts of Latin America. Just as the discovery of agriculture had done many centuries earlier, industrialization profoundly altered the human condition.

Industrialization and the Working Class in Europe

The English were the first and, for many decades, the only people in the world to experience the material benefits and social costs of industrialization. With an abundant labor supply, strong domestic and foreign markets, rich coal deposits, plentiful capital, a sound banking system, good transportation, a favorable business climate, and government stability, England began to industrialize in the eighteenth century. By the 1760s mechanical devices for spinning and weaving were transforming the textile industry, and by the early 1800s coal-burning steam engines were being applied not only to textile manufacture but also to iron smelting, brewing, milling, and a host of other industrial processes. In 1830 the first public railroad line opened between Liverpool and Manchester, and within two decades railroads were moving people and goods throughout England.

During the nineteenth century, industrialization spread from England to continental Europe, the United States, and Japan, and in the process changed considerably. In the late nineteenth century, small family-owned businesses gave way to large corporations, monopolies, and cartels; new energy sources such as petroleum and electricity were introduced; and, most important, scientific discoveries, especially in chemistry, transformed thousands of industrial processes.

The Industrial Revolution was a revolution in every sense of the term. It affected politics, work, people's standards of living, marriage patterns, child-rearing, leisure, and the structure of society itself. In preindustrial Europe landowning aristocrats dominated society and politics, and peasants were the largest socioeconomic group. Preindustrial cities consisted of a middle class, or bourgeoisie, made up of merchants and professionals at the top and artisans and small shopkeepers below them. They also contained numerous servants and unskilled workers who earned wages as porters and laborers.

Industrial society looked quite different. Cities grew enormously, especially industrial centers like Birmingham, England, which increased in population from 73,000 to 250,000 between 1801 and 1850, and Liverpool, which increased from 77,000 to 400,000 in the same half century. Europe in 1800 had twenty-one cities with populations over 100,000. By 1900 the number of such cities had reached 120. Within these cities there emerged a new class of factory workers, the "proletariat," who took their place in the working class alongside skilled tradesmen, servants, and day laborers. Industrialization and urbanization also increased the size, diversity, and wealth of the middle class. To the ranks of merchants, lawyers, doctors, and shopkeepers, there were added industrialists, managers, government officials, white-collar workers, and skilled professionals in such fields as engineering, architecture, accounting, the sciences, and higher education.

This new and expanding middle class dominated the nineteenth century. Its members controlled Europe's liberal, parliamentary governments; set the standards of taste in literature, music, and art; and drove forward and reaped the benefits from Europe's industrialization. They considered themselves responsible for the material and moral progress of the age. To others, however, the rise of the middle class had a different meaning. Karl Marx, the German socialist, viewed the bourgeoisie as selfish materialists, exploiters and oppressors of the workers; he held them responsible for the poverty and squalor of the industrial age. Marx and his followers looked forward to the coming revolution in which workers would rise up and destroy the bourgeoisie, end class exploitation, and initiate a new era of cooperation, harmony, and equality.

English Workers in the Early Industrial Revolution

▼▼▼

47 ▾ *TESTIMONY BEFORE PARLIAMENTARY COMMITTEES ON WORKING CONDITIONS IN ENGLAND*

A key to England's early industrial growth was a large pool of workers willing to accept low wages for long hours of labor in factories and mines. Many of these workers were displaced farmers or farm workers forced from rural areas because of population growth and the consolidation of small farms into large estates by wealthy landowners. Rural families moved to cities or coal-mining towns, where they provided the workforce for the early Industrial Revolution. On arrival few avoided poverty, crowded housing, and poor health.

Eventually, the British government responded with legislation to protect workers, especially children, from exploitation. When considering such legislation, parliamentary committees held hearings to gather testimony from workers, employers, physicians, clergy, and local officials. Their statements, some of which are included in the following excerpts, provide a vivid picture of working-class conditions and middle-class values in the first half of the nineteenth century.

Section 1 includes testimony from the records of the Sadler Committee, chaired by Michael Thomas Sadler in 1831 and charged with investigating child labor in cotton and linen factories; section 2 includes testimony taken by a parliamentary commission appointed in 1833 to investigate working conditions in other textile industries; section 3 presents evidence taken in 1842 by a committee investigating conditions in coal mines.

QUESTIONS FOR ANALYSIS

1. What differences were there between working conditions in the mines and those in the cotton factories?
2. As revealed by the questions they asked, what did the committee members consider the worst abuses of working conditions in the factories and mines?
3. What does the testimony of Hannah Richardson and George Armitage reveal about (a) the economic circumstances of working-class families and (b) the attitudes of working-class families toward their children?
4. Consider the testimony of the workers themselves. Do the workers express anger? Do they demand changes? What might explain their attitudes?
5. For what reasons do William Harter and Thomas Wilson oppose factory laws? In what ways do their views reflect the economic philosophy of Adam Smith in *The Wealth of Nations* (source 31)?

▷ 1. Testimony before the Sadler Committee, 1831

ELIZABETH BENTLEY

What age are you? — Twenty-three. . . .

What time did you begin to work at a factory? — When I was six years old. . . .

What kind of mill is it? — Flax-mill. . . .

What was your business in that mill? — I was a little doffer.[1]

What were your hours of labor in that mill? — From 5 in the morning till 9 at night, when they were thronged [busy]. . . .

What were your usual hours of labor when you were not so thronged? — From 6 in the morning till 7 at night.

What time was allowed for your meals? — Forty minutes at noon.

[1]A worker, usually a young child, whose job was to clean the machines used in textile manufacturing.

Had you any time to get your breakfast or drinking? — No, we got it as we could.

And when your work was bad, you had hardly any time to eat it at all? — No; we were obliged to leave it or take it home, and when we did not take it, the overlooker took it, and gave it to his pigs.

Do you consider doffing a laborious employment? — Yes.

Explain what it is you had to do. — When the frames are full, they have to stop the frames, and take the flyers off, and take the full bobbins off, and carry them to the roller; and then put empty ones on, and set the frames on again.

Does that keep you constantly on your feet? — Yes, there are so many frames and they run so quick.

Your labor is very excessive? — Yes; you have not time for any thing.

Suppose you flagged a little, or were too late, what would they do? — Strap us.

Are they in the habit of strapping those who are last in doffing? — Yes.

Constantly? — Yes.

Girls as well as boys? — Yes.

Have you ever been strapped? — Yes.

Severely? — Yes. . . .

Did you live far from the mill? — Yes, two miles.

Had you a clock? — No, we had not.

Supposing you had not been in time enough in the morning at the mills, what would have been the consequence? — We should have been quartered.

What do you mean by that? — If we were a quarter of an hour too late, they would take off half an hour; we only got a penny an hour, and they would take a halfpenny more. . . .

Were you generally there in time? — Yes, my mother has been up at 4 o'clock in the morning, and at 2 o'clock in the morning; the colliers used to go to their work about 3 or 4 o'clock, and when she heard them stirring she has got up out of her warm bed, and gone out and asked them the time, and I have sometimes been at Hunslet Car at 2 o'clock in the morning, when it was streaming down with rain, and we have had to stay till the mill was opened. . . .

▷ 2. *Commission for Inquiry into the Employment of Children in Factories*, Second Report, 1833

JOHN WRIGHT [A silk mill worker in his mid thirties]

Are silk-mills clean in general? — They are; they are swept every day, and whitewashed once a year.

What is the temperature of silk-mills? — I don't know exactly the temperature, but it is very agreeable. . . .

Why, then, are those employed in them said to be in such a wretched condition? — In the first place, the great number of hands congregated together, in some rooms forty, in some fifty, in some sixty, and I have known some as many as 100, which must be injurious to both health and growing. In the second place, the privy is in the factory, which frequently emits an unwholesome smell; and it would be worth while to notice in the future erection of mills, that there be betwixt the privy door and the factory wall a kind of a lobby of cage-work. 3dly, The tediousness and the everlasting sameness in the first process preys much on the spirits, and makes the hands spiritless. 4thly, the extravagant number of hours a child is compelled to labor and confinement, which for one week is seventy-six hours, which makes 3,952 hours for one year, we deduct 208 hours for meals within the factory which makes the net labor for one year 3,744; but the labor and confinement together of a child between ten years of age and twenty is 39,520 hours, enough to fritter away the best constitution. 5thly, About six months in the year we are obliged to use either gas, candles, or lamps, for the longest portion of that time, nearly six hours a day, being obliged to work amid the smoke and soot of the same; and also a large portion of oil and grease is used in the mills.

What are the effects of the present system of labor? — From my earliest recollections, I have found the effects to be awfully detrimental to the well-being of the operative; I have observed frequently children carried to factories, unable to walk, and that entirely owing to excessive labor and confinement. . . .

WILLIAM HARTER [The owner of silk mill in Manchester]

What effect would it have on your manufacture to reduce the hours of labor to ten? — It would instantly much reduce the value of my mill and machinery, and consequently far prejudice my manufacture.

How so? — They are calculated to produce a certain quantity of work in a given time. Every machine is valuable in proportion to the quantity of work which it will turn off in a given time. It is impossible that the machinery could produce as much work in ten hours as in twelve. If the tending of the machines were a laborious occupation, the difference in the quantity of work might not always be in exact proportion to the difference of working time; but in my mill, and silk-mills in general, the work requires the least imaginable labor; therefore it is perfectly impossible that the machines could produce as much work in ten hours as in twelve. The produce would vary in about the same ratio as the working time.

What may be said about the sum invested in your mill and machinery? — It is not yet near complete, and the investment is a little short of 20,000 pounds.

Then to what extent do you consider your property would be prejudiced by a bill limiting the working hours to ten? — All other circumstances remaining the same, it is obvious that any property in the mill and machinery would be prejudiced to the extent of one-sixth its value, or upwards of 3,000 pounds.

How would the reduction in the hours of labor affect the cost of your manufactures? — The cost of our manufactures consists in the price of the raw material and of the expense of putting that said material into goods. Now the mere interest of the investment in buildings and machinery, and the expense of keeping the same in repair, forms a large item in the cost of manufacturing. Of course it follows, that the *gross* charge under this head would be the same upon a production of 10,000 pounds and 12,000 pounds, and this portion of the cost of manufacturing would consequently be increased by about 16%.

Do you mean to say, that to produce the same quantity of work which your present mill and machinery is capable of, it requires an additional outlay of upwards of 3,000 pounds? — I say distinctly, that to produce the same quantity of work under a ten-hours bill will require an additional outlay of 3,000 or 4,000 pounds; therefore a ten-hours bill would impose upon me the necessity of this additional outlay in such perishable property as buildings and machinery, or I must be content to relinquish one-sixth portion of my business.

▷ *3. Testimony before the Ashley Committee on the Conditions in Mines, 1842*

EDWARD POTTER

I am a coal viewer, and the manager of the South Hetton colliery. We have about 400 bound people [contract laborers], and in addition our bank people [foremen], men and boys about 700. In the pits 427 men and boys; of these, 290 men. . . .

Of the children in the pits we have none under eight, and only three so young. We are constantly beset by parents coming making application to take children under the age, and they are very anxious and very dissatisfied if we do not take the children; and there have been cases in times of brisk trade, when the parents have threatened to leave the colliery, and go elsewhere if we did not comply. . . . In point of fact, we would rather not have boys until nine years of age complete. If younger than that, they are apt to fall asleep and get hurt: some get killed. It is no interest to the company to take any boys under nine. . . .

HANNAH RICHARDSON

[A mine employee]

I've one child that works in the pit; he's going on ten. He is down from 6 to 8. . . . He's not much tired with the work, it's only the confinement that tires him. He likes it pretty well, for he'd rather be in the pit than go to school. There is not much difference in his health since he went into the pit. He was at school before, and can read pretty well, but can't write. He is used pretty well; I never hear him complain. I've another son in the pit, 17 years old. . . . He went into the pit at eight years old. It's not hurt his health nor his appetite, for he's a good size. It would hurt us if children were prevented from working till 11 or 12 years old, because we've not jobs enough to live now as it is. . . .

MR. GEORGE ARMITAGE

I am now a teacher at Hoyland school; I was a collier at Silkstone until I was 22 years old and worked in the pit above 10 years. . . . I hardly know how to reprobate the practice sufficiently of girls working in pits; nothing can be worse. I have no doubt that debauchery is carried on, for which there is every opportunity; for the girls go constantly, when hurrying, to the men, who work often alone in the bank-faces apart from every one. I think it scarcely possible for girls to remain modest who are in pits, regularly mixing with such company and hearing such language as they do — it is next to impossible. I dare venture to say that many of the wives who come from pits know nothing of sewing or any household duty, such as women ought to know — they lose all disposition to learn such things; they are rendered unfit for learning them also by being overworked and not being trained to the habit of it. . . . I think, if girls were trained properly, as girls ought to be, that there would be no more difficulty in finding suitable employment for them than in other places. Many a collier spends in drink what he has shut up a young child the whole week to earn in a dark cold corner as a trapper. . . .

THE REV. ROBERT WILLAN, CURATE OF ST. MARY'S, BARNSLEY

I have been resident here as chief minister for 22 years. I think the morals of the working classes here are in an appalling state. . . . The ill manners and conduct of the weavers are daily presented to view in the streets, but the colliers work under ground and are less seen, and we have less means of knowing. . . . The master-sin among the youths is that of gambling; the boys may be seen playing at pitch-and-toss on the Sabbath and on week-days; they are seen doing this in all directions. The next besetting sin is promiscuous sexual intercourse; this may be much induced by the manner in which they sleep — men, women, and children often sleeping in one bed-room. I have known a family of father and mother and 12 children, some of them up-grown, sleeping on a kind of sacking and straw bed, reaching from one side of the room to the other, along the floor; they were an English family. Sexual intercourse begins very young. This and gambling pave the way; then drinking ensues, and this is the vortex which draws in every other sin.

THOMAS WILSON, ESQ., OWNER OF THREE COLLIERIES

I object on general principles to government interference in the conduct of any trade, and I am satisfied that in the mines it would be productive of the greatest injury and injustice. The art of mining is not so perfectly understood as to admit of the way in which a colliery shall be conducted being dictated by any person, however experienced, with such certainty as would warrant an interference with the management of private business. I should also most decidedly object to placing collieries under the present provisions of the Factory Act[2] with respect to the education of children employed therein. First, because, if it is contended that coal-owners, as employers of children, are bound to attend to their education, this obligation extends equally to all other employers, and therefore it is unjust to single out one class only; secondly, because, if the legislature asserts a right to interfere to secure education, it is bound to make that interference general; and thirdly, because the mining population is in this neighborhood so intermixed with other classes, and is in such small bodies in any one place, that it would be impossible to provide separate schools for them.

[2]The Factory Act of 1833, which regulated employment of children and women, applied to textile factories.

A Working-Class Family in Berlin

48 ▾ *Otto von Leixner, LETTERS FROM BERLIN, WITH SPECIAL REFERENCE TO SOCIAL-DEMOCRATIC MOVEMENTS*

One should not assume that working conditions described in early English sources were the norm in Europe throughout the nineteenth century. As a result of trade unions, socialist political parties, the extension of the franchise, legislation, and the realization by many factory owners that improved working conditions meant increased productivity, skilled workers made solid gains in wages, hours, and housing. Nevertheless, even relatively well-paid workers in the late 1800s needed regular employment and self-discipline to avert economic failure.

The following description of a Berlin working-class family in 1890 is taken from a book published in 1891 by Otto von Leixner (1847–1907), a German writer of poetry, short fiction, literary criticism, and political commentary. In his *Letters from Berlin*, based largely on personal interviews, he describes the living and working conditions of Berlin factory workers. The following excerpt portrays the situation of a brass factory worker and his family.

QUESTIONS FOR ANALYSIS

1. What percentage of the German family's expenditures falls into the categories of housing, clothing, food, entertainment, and health care?
2. Based on von Leixner's description, how does the situation of this late-nineteenth-century Berlin working-class family differ from family conditions described in the parliamentary hearings (source 47)?
3. What circumstances may explain these differences?
4. How does this document shed light on the status of women in late-nineteenth-century German working-class families?

The first question to be answered is: "Can a Berlin, working class family really live on the wages of the father?" On the basis of my experiences, I can answer that question "Yes," even if that "Yes" must be qualified in certain circumstances.

As is the case with other social classes, there also exists among workers gradations in income from "master" and foreman to the young apprentice; and even among the former are differences according to various branches of industry. But the most fundamental difference is in moral character. If the husband is sober and decent, the wife frugal and hard-working, then a small salary suffices. If these characteristics are lacking, then even a larger salary is inadequate. This is the same for every class. . . .

To prove this, I refer to my visits to families. . . .

The first household belongs to a relatively well-paid worker. He is employed as a molder in a bronze ware workshop, and is a hard-working, respectable man, and a worthy spouse and father. . . . He hardly attends political meetings, the tavern very rarely. His wife, who previously was a servant girl, is, despite her infirmities, very industrious and thrifty. Their apartment consists of a rather sizable room, with an attached kitchen. Although the husband, wife, and two children live and sleep here, everything is meticulously clean. Colorful calico curtains hang on the two windows, and plants are growing on the window sills. Two beds and a simple sleeping sofa for the children occupy one long wall; the others are taken up by a cupboard, a wardrobe, and a washstand. A table and some chairs complete the furnishings.

The average income is 1700 marks.[1] In many years it is larger, but also occasionally smaller. The work is difficult, and when there is much to do at the shop, exhaustion sets in for the father, and he sometimes takes to bed for a week. 259 marks must be paid for rent. The small apartments are expensive, despite their deficiencies, because of high demand. . . .

When the molder is paid on Saturday, he puts aside a part for the rent that must be paid every month. The wife receives 18 marks for household costs per week, in other words, 2.57 marks per day or 64 pfennig for each person; from this the bill for lighting must be paid. The husband pays for heating, specifically in the following manner: in winter, in other words for five months, 20 small coal briquettes are purchased (6 marks per 100) and a few pieces of kindling wood; they have to make do with this. When needed, they sit by the cookstove in the kitchen. . . .

Their daily food consumption is instructive. The following sketch is an average, and the menu is not always the same. The use of dried peas and lentils, potatoes, flour, bread, and milk is high. Meat products, except for some cheap sausage — spread on bread, not put on in slices — is mostly chopped beef or lungs, in the form of meatballs (*Klops*) or meatloaf (ground meat mixed with bread crumbs or spices and baked in a little fat). To plan ahead for Sunday and holidays, the family cuts back on workdays. . . .

. . . Not even the smallest item is purchased on credit. This is a prime requirement if the small household is to remain on a sound footing. When larger expenses are necessary, then each week a partial amount is put aside, so that the expense can be paid for.

The husband takes coffee with him in the morning in a tin container, and in the evening and at midday he drinks at the most three glasses of beer, with each costing 10 pfennig (he hardly ever drinks anything stronger). On weekdays he smokes two cigars, on Sundays, three, at three pfennig each. He goes to the tavern perhaps once a week, but when he does, he is home by 10:30.

---

[1]The basic unit of the German currency. One mark equals 100 pfennig.

I now summarize what I could ascertain about their expenses in the following numbers:

	Marks
Income	1700
Expenses	
Rent	259
Housekeeping	924
Taxes	30
Health insurance and other premiums	13
Heating, on average	45
Winter coat for the husband	30
Hat	2.50
Boots for the husband	16
Boots for the wife	11
Boots for the children	10
Clothing for wife and children	23
Physician and pharmacist for wife	20
Newspaper, shared with another	3
Miscellaneous (mending, washing, amusements)	64
Husband (drinks, tobacco, donations, etc.)	162
	1612.50

In 1889 savings totaled 82 marks. A glance at expenditures shows how much thriftiness is needed not to exceed the amount of income. Husband and wife have to draw upon all their moral strength in order to make it through, and must know how to keep their expenses within the limits of economic reality. Amusements which cost money are rare. They consist of excursions to the zoo, where they take a lunch-basket, or to a country park. That is it. Very rarely, once every several years, they go to a cheap vaudeville theater. . . . The husband makes do; he borrows books from the public library and reads them in the evening if he is not too tired; the wife is satisfied with serialized novels and local news in the daily press, or she chats with neighbors after the children have gone to sleep.

So long as things remain on even keel, then a better paid worker, if he lives decently, can get by. . . . But even this requires above-average moral strength. . . . But if the husband and wife are frivolous, or irresponsible, then disaster begins. . . .

New Perspectives on Humanity and Society

In October 1873 the English naturalist Charles Darwin wrote a letter to the German philosopher and revolutionary Karl Marx in which he stated, "I believe we both earnestly desire the extension of human knowledge; and this in the long run is sure to add to the happiness of mankind." Whether Marx and Darwin added to human happiness is difficult to judge, but there is no doubting their enormous influence. Although nineteenth-century Europe produced more scientists, philosophers, artists, composers, novelists, poets, historians, critics, and social theorists than ever before, and although these intellectuals produced an abundance of provocative new ideas, none matched the wide-ranging influence of these two men.

Darwin (1809–1882) did not invent the theory of evolution. Several Europeans before him had hypothesized that species were mutable and that all plants and animals, including humans, evolved. Darwin's contribution was the wealth of scientific data he marshaled to support the idea of evolution and his theory that

evolution took place as a result of natural selection, not God's plan. Thus, Darwin cast doubt on the biblical creation story, in which God creates the whole universe, including the first humans, Adam and Eve, in seven days. Darwinism outraged biblical literalists and even today continues to be at the center of debates between science and religion. Darwinism also forced philosophers and other intellectuals to re-examine long-accepted notions about nature, morality, permanence versus change, and, of course, humanity itself. Finally, Darwinism had important political ramifications. Imperialists, free traders, nationalists, and fascists were just a few of the groups who used (or misused) Darwinism to bolster their beliefs.

Just as Darwin was not the first proponent of evolution, neither was Marx the first socialist. The first socialists were early-nineteenth-century visionaries, called "utopians" by Marx, whose dreams of equality and justice lacked philosophical rigor and practical political sense. Marx shared the utopians' moral outrage over the social damage caused by the Industrial Revolution, but he also was an academically trained philosopher knowledgeable in history, economics, and science. His goal was to establish the intellectual foundation of *scientific socialism* and to describe the mechanism by which socialism would ultimately replace capitalism. Through class conflict, in a process Marx referred to as the *dialectic*, society develops through stages until it reaches the age of industrial capitalism, when the oppressor class, the bourgeoisie, clashes with the factory workers, the proletariat. The proletariat will triumph, argues Marx, because capitalism itself, an intrinsically flawed system, will create the conditions for the proletarian revolution, the end of the dialectic, and a classless society.

Even the most dedicated disciples of Marx and Darwin concede that much of what they wrote was incomplete, incorrect, or hypothetical. Well before the collapse of most of the world's Marxist governments in the late twentieth century, critics could point out many ways in which Marx misjudged capitalism, workers' attitudes, and the causes of revolution. Opponents of Darwinism contend that its theories are unprovable and that natural selection is incapable of explaining the miraculous complexity of living thing. Nonetheless, Darwin and Marx remain a part of that small group of nineteenth-century European thinkers whose work has left an indelible mark on history.

The Marxist Critique of Industrial Capitalism

▼▼▼

49 ▼ *Karl Marx and Friedrich Engels, THE COMMUNIST MANIFESTO*

Karl Marx (1818–1883) was born in Trier, a German city on the Rhine River that was assigned to the Kingdom of Prussia at the Congress of Vienna in 1815. Marx's parents were Jewish, but in 1817 his father converted the family to Christianity and changed its name to Marx to protect his career as a lawyer. Young Marx studied law at the University of Bonn before enrolling at the University of Berlin, where he was influenced by the thought of the famous philosopher G. W. F. Hegel (1770–1831), especially his theory that history unfolds toward a specific goal in a process driven by the clash and resolution of antagonistic forces. After losing his job as a journalist for a Cologne newspaper because of his political views, Marx moved in 1844 to Paris, where he argued about capitalism and revolution with other radicals and continued his studies of economics and history. He also made the acquaintance of another German, Friedrich Engels (1820–1895), an ardent critic of capitalism despite the fortune he amassed from managing a textile mill in Manchester, England. In 1847 Marx and Engels joined the Communist League, a revolutionary society dominated by German political exiles in France and England. In 1848, a year of revolution in much of Europe, the two men wrote *The Communist Manifesto* to publicize the League's program. It became the most widely read socialist tract in history.

After 1848 Marx and Engels remained friends, with Engels giving Marx enough money to continue his writing and political activities while living in London. Both men continued to write on behalf of socialism, but Marx's works, especially his masterpiece, *Das Kapital* (*Capitalism*), assumed the far greater role in shaping modern socialist thought. Furthermore, Marx's views of history, human behavior, and social conflict have influenced not only politics but also philosophy, religion, literature, and all the social sciences.

QUESTIONS FOR ANALYSIS

1. How do Marx and Engels define class, and what do they mean by the "class struggle"?
2. According to Marx and Engels, how does the class struggle in nineteenth-century Europe differ from class struggles in previous eras?
3. According to Marx and Engels, what are the characteristics of the bourgeoisie?
4. Marx and Engels believe that bourgeois society is doomed and that the bourgeoisie will be the cause of their own destruction. Why?
5. The authors dismiss the importance of ideas as a force in human affairs. On what grounds? Ultimately, what is the cause of historical change in their view?
6. What may explain the popularity and influence of *The Communist Manifesto* among workers and those who sympathized with their plight?

I. THE BOURGEOISIE AND PROLETARIAT

The history of all hitherto existing society is the history of class struggles.

Freeman and slave, patrician and plebeian, lord and serf, guild-master and journeyman, in a word, oppressor and oppressed, stood in constant opposition to one another, carried on an uninterrupted, now hidden, now open fight, a fight that each time ended, either in a revolutionary reconstitution of society at large, or in the common ruin of the contending classes. . . .

Our epoch, the epoch of the bourgeoisie, possesses, however, this distinctive feature: It has simplified the class antagonisms. Society as a whole is more and more splitting up into two great hostile camps, into two great classes directly facing each other — bourgeoisie and proletariat.

From the serfs of the Middle Ages sprang the chartered burghers of the earliest towns. From these burgesses the first elements of the bourgeoisie were developed.

The discovery of America, the rounding of the Cape, opened up fresh ground for the rising bourgeoisie. The East-Indian and Chinese markets, the colonization of America, trade with the colonies, the increase in the means of exchange and in commodities generally, gave to commerce, to navigation, to industry, an impulse never before known, and thereby, to the revolutionary element in the tottering feudal society, a rapid development.

The feudal system of industry, in which industrial production was monopolized by closed guilds, now no longer sufficed for the growing wants of the new markets. The manufacturing system took its place. The guild-masters were pushed aside by the manufacturing middle class; division of labor between the different corporate guilds vanished in the face of division of labor in each single workshop.

Meantime the markets kept ever growing, the demand ever rising. Even manufacture[1] no longer sufficed. Thereupon, steam and machinery revolutionized industrial production. The place of manufacture was taken by the giant, modern industry, the place of the industrial middle class by industrial millionaires, the leaders of whole industrial armies, the modern bourgeois. . . .

The bourgeoisie, wherever it has got the upper hand, has put an end to all feudal, patriarchal, idyllic relations. It has pitilessly torn asunder the motley feudal ties that bound man to his "natural superiors," and has left no other nexus between man and man than naked self-interest, than callous "cash payment." . . . In one word, for exploitation, veiled by religious and political illusions, it has substituted naked, shameless, direct, brutal exploitation. . . .

We see then: the means of production and of exchange, on whose foundation the bourgeoisie built itself up, were generated in feudal society. At a certain stage in the development of these means of production and of exchange, the conditions under which feudal society produced and exchanged, the feudal organization of agriculture and manufacturing industry . . . became no longer compatible with the already developed productive forces; they became so many fetters. They had to be burst asunder; they were burst asunder. . . .

A similar movement is going on before our own eyes. Modern bourgeois society with its relations of production, of exchange and of property, a society that has conjured up such gigantic means of production and of exchange, is like the sorcerer who is no longer able to control the powers of the nether world whom he has called up by his spells. . . . It is enough to mention the commercial crises that by their periodical return put the existence of the entire bourgeois society on its trial, each time more threateningly. In these crises a great part not only of the existing products, but also of the previously created productive forces, are periodically destroyed. In these crises there breaks out an epidemic that, in all earlier epochs, would have seemed an absurdity — the epidemic of overproduction.

And how does the bourgeoisie get over these crises? On the one hand, by enforced destruction of a mass of productive forces; on the other, by the conquest of new markets, and by the more thorough exploitation of the old ones. That is to say, by paving the way for more extensive and more destructive crises, and by diminishing the means whereby crises are prevented.

The weapons with which the bourgeoisie felled feudalism to the ground are now turned against the bourgeoisie itself.

But not only has the bourgeoisie forged the weapons that bring death to itself; it has also called into existence the men who are to wield those weapons — the modern working class — the proletarians. . . .

---

[1]"Manufacture" is used here in the sense of making goods by hand rather than machines.

. . . Masses of laborers, crowded into the factory, are organized like soldiers. As privates of the industrial army they are placed under the command of a perfect hierarchy of officers and sergeants. Not only are they slaves of the bourgeois class, and of the bourgeois state; they are daily and hourly enslaved by the machine, by the overseer, and, above all, by the individual bourgeois manufacturer himself. . . .

The lower strata of the middle class — the small tradespeople, shopkeepers, and retired tradesmen generally, the handicraftsmen and peasants — all these sink gradually into the proletariat, partly because their diminutive capital does not suffice for the scale on which modern industry is carried on, . . . partly because their specialized skill is rendered worthless by new methods of production. Thus the proletariat is recruited from all classes of the population.

But with the development of industry the proletariat not only increases in number; it becomes concentrated in greater masses, its strength grows, and it feels that strength more. The various interests and conditions of life within the ranks of the proletariat are more and more equalized, in proportion as machinery obliterates all distinctions of labor, and nearly everywhere reduces wages to the same low level. The growing competition among the bourgeois, and the resulting commercial crises, make the wages of the workers ever more fluctuating. The unceasing improvement of machinery . . . makes their livelihood more and more precarious; the collisions between individual workmen and individual bourgeois take more and more the character of collisions between two classes. Thereupon the workers begin to form combinations (trade unions) against the bourgeois. . . . Here and there the contest breaks out into riots.

Now and then the workers are victorious, but only for a time. The real fruit of their battle lies, not in the immediate result, but in the ever expanding union of the workers. This union is helped on by the improved means of communication that are created by modern industry, and that place the workers of different localities in contact with one another. It was just this contact that was needed to centralize the numerous local struggles, all of the same character, into one national struggle between classes. . . .

Finally, in times when the class struggle nears the decisive hour, the process of dissolution going on within the ruling class, in fact within the whole range of old society, assumes such a violent, glaring character, that a small section of the ruling class cuts itself adrift, and joins the revolutionary class, the class that holds the future in its hands. Just as, therefore, at an earlier period, a section of the nobility went over to the bourgeoisie, so now a portion of the bourgeoisie goes over to the proletariat, and in particular, a portion of the bourgeois ideologists, who have raised themselves to the level of comprehending theoretically the historical movement as a whole.

II. PROLETARIANS AND COMMUNISTS

The distinguishing feature of communism is not the abolition of property generally, but the abolition of bourgeois property. But modern bourgeois private property is the final and most complete expression of the system of producing and appropriating products that is based on class antagonisms, on the exploitation of the many by the few.

In this sense, the theory of the Communists may be summed up in the single sentence: Abolition of private property. . . .

You are horrified at our intending to do away with private property. But in your existing society, private property is already done away with for nine-tenths of its population; its existence for the few is solely due to its nonexistence in the hands of those nine-tenths. . . .

The Communists are further reproached with desiring to abolish countries and nationality.

The working men have no country. We cannot take from them what they have not got. . . .

National differences and antagonism between peoples are daily more and more vanishing, owing to the development of the bourgeoisie, to freedom of commerce, to the world market, to uniformity in the mode of production and in the conditions of life corresponding thereto.

The supremacy of the proletariat will cause them to vanish still faster. United action of the leading civilized countries at least, is one of the first conditions for the emancipation of the proletariat.

. . . In proportion as the antagonism between classes within the nation vanishes, the hostility of one nation to another will come to an end. . . .

We have seen above that the first step in the revolution by the working class is to raise the proletariat to the position of ruling class, to win the battle for democracy.

The proletariat will use its political supremacy to wrest, by degrees, all capital from the bourgeoisie, to centralize all instruments of production in the hands of the State, i.e., of the proletariat organized as the ruling class; and to increase the total of productive forces as rapidly as possible.

Of course, in the beginning, this cannot be effected except by means of despotic inroads on the rights of property, and on the conditions of bourgeois production; by means of measures which . . . are unavoidable as a means of entirely revolutionizing the mode of production.

These measures will of course be different in different countries.

Nevertheless, in the most advanced countries, the following will be pretty generally applicable.

1. Abolition of property in land and application of all rents of land to public purposes.

2. A heavy progressive or graduated income tax.

3. Abolition of all right of inheritance.

4. Confiscation of the property of all emigrants and rebels.[2]

5. Centralization of credit in the hands of the State, by means of a national bank with State capital and an exclusive monopoly.

6. Centralization of the means of communication and transport in the hands of the State.

7. Extension of the number of State factories and instruments of production: the bringing into cultivation of waste lands, and the improvement of the soil generally in accordance with a common plan.

8. Equal obligation of all to work. Establishment of industrial armies, especially for agriculture.

9. Combination of agriculture with manufacturing industries; gradual abolition of the distinction between town and country, by a more equable distribution of the population over the country.

10. Free education for all children in public schools. Abolition of children's factory labor in its present form. . . .

When, in the course of development, class distinctions have disappeared, and all production has been concentrated in the hands of a vast association of the whole nation, the public power will lose its political character. . . . If, by means of a revolution, [the proletariat] makes itself the ruling class, and as such sweeps away by force the old conditions of production, then it will, along with these conditions, have swept away the conditions for the existence of class antagonisms and of classes generally, and will thereby have abolished its own supremacy as a class. . . .

The Communists disdain to conceal their views and aims. They openly declare that their ends can be attained only by the forcible overthrow of all existing social conditions. Let the ruling classes tremble at a Communist revolution. In it the proletarians have nothing to lose but their chains. They have a world to win.

WORKING MEN OF ALL COUNTRIES, UNITE!

---

[2]Presumably individuals who are resisting the new regime or fled during the revolution.

The Principles of Darwinism

50 ▾ Charles Darwin, *ON THE ORIGIN OF SPECIES and THE DESCENT OF MAN*

After pursuing his university education at Edinburgh and Cambridge, Charles Darwin (1809–1882) spent five years on the HMS *Beagle* as chief naturalist on a scientific expedition to the South Pacific and the western coast of South America. Darwin observed the bewildering variety of nature and began to speculate on how millions of species of plants and animals had come into existence. On his return to England, he developed his theory of evolution, basing his hypothesis on his own formidable biological knowledge, recent discoveries in geology, work on the selective breeding of plants and animals, and the theories of several authors that competition was the norm for all living things. In 1859 he published his theories in *On the Origin of Species*, followed in 1871 by *The Descent of Man*.

QUESTIONS FOR ANALYSIS

1. What does Darwin mean by the terms *struggle for existence* and *natural selection*?
2. How does Darwin defend himself from religiously motivated attacks on his work?
3. What were some implications of Darwin's work for nineteenth-century views of progress? Of nature? Of human nature?
4. Defenders of laissez-faire capitalism sometimes drew upon Darwinian concepts in their arguments against socialism. Which concepts might they have used?
5. Similarly, Darwinian concepts were used to defend militarism and late-nineteenth-century Western imperialism. Which of Darwin's theories might have proved useful in such a defense?

ON THE ORIGIN OF SPECIES

Chapter III Struggle for Existence

It has been seen in the last chapter that amongst organic beings in a state of nature there is some individual variability. . . . But the mere existence of individual variability and of some few well-marked varieties, . . . helps us but little in understanding how species arise in nature. How have all those exquisite adaptations of one part of the organization to another part, and to the conditions of life, and of one organic being to another being, been perfected? . . .

Again, . . . how is it that varieties, which I have called incipient species, become ultimately converted into good and distinct species, which in most cases obviously differ from each other far more than do the varieties of the same species? . . . All these results . . . follow from the struggle for life. Owing to this struggle, variations, however slight and from whatever cause proceeding, if they be in any degree profitable to the individuals of a species, in their infinitely complex relations to other organic beings and to their physical conditions of life, will tend to the preservation of such individuals, and will generally be inherited by the offspring. The offspring, also, will thus have a better chance of surviving, for, of the many individuals of any species which are periodically born, but a small number can survive. I have called this principle, by which each slight variation, if useful, is preserved, by the term Natural Selection, in order to mark its relation to man's power of selection. But the expression . . . Survival of the Fittest is more accurate, and is sometimes equally convenient. . . .

I should premise that I use this term in a large and metaphorical sense including . . . not only the life of the individual, but success in leaving progeny. Two canine animals, in a time of dearth, may be truly said to struggle with each other which shall get food and live. But a plant on the edge of a desert is said to struggle for life against the drought. . . . A plant which annually produces a thousand seeds, of which only one of an average comes to maturity, may be more truly said to struggle with the plants of the same and other kinds which already clothe the ground. . . . In these several senses, which pass into each other, I use for convenience's sake the general term of Struggle for Existence.

A struggle for existence inevitably follows from the high rate at which all organic beings tend to increase. Every being, which during its natural lifetime produces several eggs or seeds, must suffer destruction during some period of its life, and during some season or occasional year, otherwise . . . its numbers would quickly become so inordinately great that no country could support the product. Hence, as more individuals are produced than can possibly survive, there must in every case be a struggle for existence, either one individual with another of the same species, or with the individuals of distinct species, or with the physical conditions of life. . . . Although some species may be now increasing, more or less rapidly, in numbers, all cannot do so, for the world would not hold them.

THE DESCENT OF MAN

Chapter II On the Manner of Development of Man from Some Lower Form

In this chapter we have seen that as man at the present day is liable, like every other animal, to multiform individual differences or slight variations, so no doubt were the early progenitors [ancestors] of man; the variations being formerly induced by the same general causes, and governed by the same general and complex laws as at present. As all animals tend to multiply beyond their means of subsistence, so it must have been with the progenitors of man; and this would inevitably lead to a struggle for existence and to natural selection. . . .

Chapter VI On the Affinities and Genealogy of Man

Now as organisms have become slowly adapted to diversified lines of life by means of natural selection, their parts will have become more and more differentiated and specialized for various functions, from the advantage gained by the division of physiological labor. The same part appears often to have been modified first for one purpose, and then long afterwards for some other and quite distinct purpose; and thus all the parts are rendered more and more complex. But each organism still retains the general type of structure of the progenitor from which it was aboriginally derived. In accordance with this view it seems, if we turn to geological evidence, that organization on the whole has advanced throughout the world by slow and interrupted steps. In the great kingdom of the Vertebrata it has culminated in man. . . .

The most ancient progenitors in the kingdom of the Vertebrata, at which we are able to obtain an obscure glance, apparently consisted of a group of marine animals, resembling the larvae of existing Ascidians.[1] These animals probably gave rise to a group of fishes, as lowly organized

[1]Marine animals with a rodlike primitive backbone.

as the lancelet;[2] and from these the Ganoids,[3] and other fishes must have developed. From such fish a very small advance would carry us on to the Amphibians. We have seen that birds and reptiles were once intimately connected together; and the Monotremata[4] now connect mammals with reptiles in a slight degree. But no one can at present say by what line of descent the three higher and related classes, namely, mammals, birds, and reptiles, were derived from the two lower vertebrate classes, namely, amphibians and fishes. In the class of mammals the steps are not difficult to conceive which led from the ancient Monotremata to the ancient Marsupials,[5] and from these to the early progenitors of the placental mammals. We may thus ascend to the Lemuridae,[6] and the interval is not very wide from these to the Simiadae.[7] The Simiadae then branched off into two great stems, the New World and Old World monkeys; and from the latter, at a remote period, Man, the wonder and glory of the Universe, proceeded.

Chapter XXI General Summary and Conclusion

I am aware that the conclusions arrived at in this work will be denounced by some as highly irreligious; but he who denounces them is bound to show why it is more irreligious to explain the origin of man as a distinct species by descent from some lower form, through the laws of variation and natural selection, than to explain the birth of the individual through the laws of ordinary reproduction. The birth both of the species and of the individual are equally parts of that grand sequence of events, which our minds refuse to accept as the result of blind chance. The understanding revolts at such a conclusion, whether or not we are able to believe that every slight variation of structure, — the union of each pair in marriage, — the dissemination of each seed, — and other such events, have all been ordained for some special purpose. . . .

Man may be excused for feeling some pride at having risen, though not through his own exertions, to the very summit of the organic scale; and the fact of his having thus risen, instead of having been aboriginally placed there, may give him hope for a still higher destiny in the distant future. But we are not here concerned with hopes or fears, only with the truth as far as our reason permits us to discover it; and I have given the evidence to the best of my ability. We must, however, acknowledge, as it seems to me, that man with all his noble qualities, with sympathy which feels for the most debased, with benevolence which extends not only to other men but to the humblest living creature, with his god-like intellect which has penetrated into the movements and constitution of the solar system — with all these exalted powers — Man still bears in his bodily frame the indelible stamp of his lowly origin.

[2]Boney fish such as the sturgeon and gar, covered with large armorlike scales.
[3]Any of small translucent marine animals related to vertebrates.
[4]Order of egg-laying mammals such as the platypus.
[5]Mammals, such as the kangaroo, whose females lack placentas and carry their young in an abdominal pouch.
[6]Largely nocturnal tree-dwelling mammals distinct from monkeys.
[7]Apes and monkeys.

The Fight for Women's Political Rights

Women's political and legal rights emerged as a subject of public debate during the French Revolution, an event in which women played a prominent role. In October 1789 thousands of women marched from Paris to the palace grounds at Versailles, where their demonstrations forced the king and the National Assembly

to relocate to Paris, the center of revolutionary agitation. In 1790 women began to form their own political clubs and demand an end to laws and customs that were the foundation of France's patriarchal society. In response, legislators passed laws giving women the right to own property, marry without parental consent, initiate divorce, and take legal action against fathers of illegitimate children. In 1793, however, Jacobin revolutionaries outlawed women's political clubs and flatly rejected women's demands for political equality with men. Having women vote, hold public office, and serve in the army would, so it was argued, undermine the family and divert women from their calling as wives and mothers. Women experienced further setbacks in the late 1790s when more conservative revolutionary leaders rescinded most of the laws that had improved women's legal status. Under Napoleon, the Civil Code of 1804, later known as the Napoleonic Code, unequivocally reaffirmed women's legal inferiority to men.

In the conservative atmosphere of the 1820s and 1830s, women's political activism in Europe diminished, and prevailing opinion consigned middle-class women to a domestic role centered on child care, housekeeping, supervising servants, and providing husbands with a tranquil home. By midcentury, however, women on both sides of the Atlantic, many of whom were veterans of the temperance and antislavery movements, once more began to speak out and organize on behalf of women's political and legal rights. A landmark in the history of nineteenth-century feminism (a word coined in France in the 1830s) was the women's rights convention held in the upstate New York town of Seneca Falls in 1848, which adopted resolutions demanding for women the vote, divorce and property rights, and equal employment and educational opportunities. Such issues also became the focus of feminists in England in the 1850s and in France and Germany later in the century.

By the end of the nineteenth century, women had made some gains, especially in the areas of education and legal rights. In addition, professions such as nursing and teaching provided new opportunities for many middle-class women, and a few women established careers as doctors and lawyers. Despite the efforts of women's suffrage organizations, however, giving women the vote met stiff resistance, and only minor gains were made before World War I. By then only Australia, New Zealand, Finland, Norway, and several states in the western United States had granted women full voting privileges.

American Women Demand Equality

▼▼▼

51 ▼ *Ohio Women's Convention of 1850, RESOLUTIONS*

In 1850, two years after the first U.S. women's rights convention in Seneca Falls, a group of Ohio women met in Salem, in eastern Ohio, to draw up resolutions on the status of women for submission to a forthcoming convention that was to consider amendments to the state constitution. The Salem meeting has a special place in the history of feminist movements because, although men attended, they were not allowed to speak, vote, or make proposals. At the close of the meeting, the men in attendance organized their own association and, as their first act, voted to endorse the resolutions the women had just approved. The resolutions were received less favorably at the constitutional convention, where the delegates, all men, ignored them.

QUESTIONS FOR ANALYSIS

1. What specific demands do the resolutions make in the areas of political rights, employment, education, and the family?
2. For the authors of the resolutions, *dependence* is a key concept in their views of women's place in society. What do they mean by this term, and what social and political practices contribute to it?
3. The authors admit that not all women share their views. How do they view women who are content to accept their "idle lives" and "sterile submission"? How do they explain these women's indifference to women's plight?

Whereas, all men are created equal and endowed with certain God-given rights, and all just government is derived from the consent of the governed; and whereas, the doctrine that "man shall pursue his own substantial happiness" is acknowledged by the highest authority to be the great precept of Nature; and whereas, this doctrine is not local, but universal, being dictated by God himself; therefore,

Resolved, That the prohibition of Woman from participating in the enactment of the laws by which she is governed is a direct violation of this precept of Nature, as she is thereby prevented from occupying that position which duty points out, and from pursuing her own substantial happiness by acting up to her conscientious convictions; and that all statutes and constitutional provisions which sanction this prohibition are null and void.

Resolved, That all rights are *human* rights, and pertain to human beings, without distinction of sex; therefore justice demands that all laws shall be made, not for man, or for woman, but for mankind, and that the same legal protection be afforded to the one sex as to the other.

Resolved, That the servile submission and quiet indifference of the Women of this country in relation to the unequal and oppressive laws by which they are governed, are the fruit either of ignorance or degradation, both resulting legitimately from the action of those laws.

Resolved, That the evils arising from the present social, civil, and religious condition of women proclaim to them in language not to be misunderstood, that not only their *own* welfare, but the highest good of the race demands of them, as an imperative duty, that they should secure to themselves the elective franchise.

Resolved, That in those laws which confer on man the power to control the property and person of woman, and to remove from her at will the children of her affection, we recognize only the modified code of the slave plantation; and that thus we are brought more nearly in sympathy with the suffering slave, who is despoiled of all his rights.

Resolved, That we, as human beings, are entitled to claim and exercise all the rights that belong by nature to any members of the human family.

Resolved, That all distinctions between men and women in regard to social, literary, pecuniary, religious or political customs and institutions, based on a distinction of sex, are contrary to the laws of Nature, are unjust, and destructive to the purity, elevation and progress in knowledge and goodness of the great human family, and ought to be at once and forever abolished.

Resolved, That the practice of holding women amenable to a different standard of propriety and morality from that to which men are held amenable, is unjust and unnatural, and highly detrimental to domestic and social virtue and happiness.

Resolved, That the political history of Woman demonstrates that tyranny, the most degrading, cruel and arbitrary, can be exercised and produced the same in effect under a mild and republican form of government as by an hereditary despotism.

Resolved, That while we deprecate thus earnestly the political oppression of Woman, we see in her social condition, the regard in which she is held as a moral and intellectual being, the fundamental cause of that oppression.

Resolved, That amongst the principal causes of such social condition we regard the public sentiment which withholds from her all, or almost all, lucrative employment, and enlarged spheres of labor.

Resolved, That in the difficulties thus cast in the way of her self-support, and in her consequent *dependence* upon man, we see the greatest influence at work in imparting to her that tone of character which makes her to be regarded as the "weaker vessel." . . .

Resolved, That we regard those women who content themselves with an idle, aimless life, as involved in the guilt as well as the suffering of their own oppression; and that we hold those who go forth into the world, in the face of the frowns and the sneers of the public, to fill larger spheres of labor, as the truest preachers of the cause of Woman's Rights.

Whereas, one class of society dooms woman to a life of drudgery, another to one of dependence and frivolity; and whereas, the education she generally receives is calculated to cultivate vanity and dependence, therefore,

Resolved, That the education of woman should be in accordance with responsibility in life, that she may acquire the self-reliance and true dignity so essential to the proper fulfillment of the important duties devolving on her.

Resolved, That as woman is not permitted to hold office, nor have any voice in the government, she should not be compelled to pay taxes out of her scanty wages to support men who get eight dollars a-day for *taking* the right to *themselves* to enact laws *for* her.

Resolved, That we, the Women of Ohio, will hereafter meet annually in Convention to consult upon and adopt measures for the removal of various disabilities — political, social, religious, legal and pecuniary — to which women as a class are subjected, and from which results so much misery, degradation, and crime.

Violence and Women's Suffrage in England

52 ▾ *Emmeline Pankhurst, WHY WE ARE MILITANT*

Organized efforts by Englishwomen to gain the vote began in 1847, when a group of Sheffield women founded the Female Political Association and collected signatures on a prosuffrage petition they submitted to the House of Lords. Four years later, in 1851, Harriet Hardy Mill (1807–1858), the wife of philosopher John Stuart Mill, wrote a widely read pamphlet titled "Enfranchisement of Women." In 1867, nine years after her death, John Stuart Mill, then a member of the House of Commons, proposed an amendment to a voting reform bill that would have given

women the vote. It was rejected 194 to 73, a setback that led to the founding of the National Society for Women's Suffrage in 1868. In the following decades, women sought to advance their cause by making resolutions, publicizing their views, and performing symbolic acts such as appearing at polling places and requesting the vote, even though they knew they would be turned away.

In the early 1900s, however, the feminist movement became militant and confrontational. By 1900, Englishwomen could vote in local elections and stand for election to school boards and municipal offices. This was not enough for Emmeline Pankhurst (1858–1928), who since the 1870s had been a strong advocate for women's suffrage and better treatment for working-class and poor women. In 1903 she founded the Women's Social and Political Union (WSPU). Under the leadership of Pankhurst and her daughters, Christabel (1880–1958) and Sylvia (1882–1960), the WSPU tried to advance the cause of women's suffrage first by heckling politicians and then by smashing windows, slashing paintings in museums, burning letters in mailboxes, and finally martyrdom, when in May 1913 a young woman threw herself under the hooves of the king's racehorse at Epsom Downs and was killed before thousands of shocked spectators. When arrested, many suffragettes, as they were called, went on hunger strikes. The government responded by approving the forced feeding of prisoners and enforcing the "Cat and Mouse Bill," by which fasting women were released from prison until they had eaten and then were rearrested.

By 1913, however, Englishwomen still could not vote in parliamentary elections. This was the year in which Emmeline Pankhurst visited the United States and delivered the following speech to an audience in Madison Square Garden in New York City on October 21. It was attended by a disappointing crowd of only 3,000, mainly owing to a last-minute change in the time of the event — Mrs. Pankhurst had been held up by immigration authorities for two days after her arrival because of pending legal cases involving her in England.

QUESTIONS FOR ANALYSIS

1. In Pankhurst's view, what was the condition of the women's suffrage movement in the first years of the 1900s?
2. According to Pankhurst, why had "nonmilitant" efforts on behalf of women's suffrage failed?
3. What event sparked the new militancy of the WSPU?
4. According to Pankhurst, why was it so important for women to gain the right to vote in parliamentary elections?
5. How does Pankhurst explain the difficulty women encountered in their efforts to win the vote?

I know that in your minds there are questions like these; you are saying, "Woman Suffrage is sure to come; the emancipation of humanity is an evolutionary process, and how is it that some women, instead of trusting to that evolution, instead of educating the masses of people of their country, instead of educating their own sex to prepare them for citizenship, how is it that these militant women are using violence and upsetting the business arrangements of the country in their undue impatience to attain their end?"

Let me try to explain to you the situation. . . .

The extensions of the franchise to the men of my country have been preceded by very great violence, by something like a revolution, by something like civil war. In 1832,[1] you know we were on the edge of a civil war and on the edge of revolution, and it was at the point of the sword — no, not at the point of the sword — it was after the practice of arson on so large a scale that half the city of Bristol[2] was burned down in a single night, it was because more and greater violence and arson were feared that the Reform Bill of 1832 was allowed to pass into law. In 1867[3] . . . rioting went on all over the country, and as the result of that rioting, as the result of that unrest, . . . as a result of the fear of more rioting and violence the Reform Act of 1867 was put upon the statute books.

In 1884 . . . rioting was threatened and feared, and so the agricultural laborers got the vote.[4]

Meanwhile, during the '80's, women, like men, were asking for the franchise. Appeals, larger and more numerous than for any other reform, were presented in support of Woman's Suffrage. . . . More meetings were held, and larger, for Woman Suffrage than were held for votes for men, and yet the women did not get it. Men got the vote because they were and would be violent. The women did not get it because they were constitutional and law-abiding. . . .

Well, we in Great Britain, on the eve of the General Election of 1905, a mere handful of us— why, you could almost count us on the fingers of both hands — set out on the wonderful adventure of forcing the strongest Government of modern times to give the women the vote. . . .

The Suffrage movement was almost dead. The women had lost heart. You could not get a Suffrage meeting that was attended by members of the general public. . . .

Two women[5] changed that in a twinkling of an eye at a great Liberal demonstration in Manchester, where a Liberal leader, Sir Edward Grey, was explaining the program to be carried out during the Liberals' next turn of office. The two women put the fateful question, "When are you going to give votes to women?" and refused to sit down until they had been answered. These two women were sent to jail, and from that day to this the women's movement, both militant and constitutional, has never looked back. We had little more than one moribund society for Woman Suffrage in those days. Now we have nearly 50 societies for Woman Suffrage, and they are large in membership, they are rich in money, and their ranks, are swelling every day that passes. That is how militancy has put back the clock of Woman Suffrage in Great Britain. . . .

We are fighting to get the power to alter bad laws; but some people say to us, "Go to the representatives in the House of Commons, point out to them that these laws are bad, and you will find them quite ready to alter them."

Ladies and gentlemen, there are women in my country who have spent long and useful lives trying to get reforms, and because of their voteless condition, they are unable even to get the ear of Members of Parliament, much less are they able to secure those reforms.

Our marriage and divorce laws are a disgrace to civilization. I sometimes wonder, looking back from the serenity of past middle age, at the courage of women. I wonder that women have the courage to take upon themselves the responsibilities of marriage and motherhood when I see

---

[1]Through much of 1831 and 1832, public excitement over voting reform peaked, as parliament considered proposals to extend representation to new industrial towns and cities and the right to vote to the middle class.

[2]On October 31, 1831, a large crowd in Bristol protested against the House of Lords' decision to turn down the Reform Act by burning down 100 houses, including the Bishop's Palace. The mob looted and burned unpopular citizens' houses and released prisoners from the jails. Soldiers attacked the crowd, and hundreds were killed or severely wounded. Under pressure, Parliament did pass the Reform Act of 1832, the first of three major voting laws passed in the 1800s.

[3]The Reform Bill of 1867 extended the right to vote to working-class men.

[4]This was the result of the Reform Bill of 1884, which gave the vote to male agricultural workers.

[5]One of these women was Emmeline Pankhurst's elder daughter, Christabel.

how little protection the law of my country affords them. I wonder that a woman will face the ordeal of childbirth with the knowledge that after she has risked her life to bring a child into the world she has absolutely no parental rights over the future of that child. Think what trust women have in men when a woman will marry a man, knowing, if she has knowledge of the law, that if that man is not all she in her love for him thinks him, he may even bring a strange woman into the house, bring his mistress into the house to live with her, and she cannot get legal relief from such a marriage as that. . . .

Take the industrial side of the question: have men's wages for a hard day's work ever been so low and inadequate as are women's wages today? Have men ever had to suffer from the laws, more injustice than women suffer? Is there a single reason which men have had for demanding liberty that does not also apply to women?

Why, if you were talking to the *men* of any other nation you would not hesitate to reply in the affirmative. There is not a man in this meeting who has not felt sympathy with the uprising of the men of other lands when suffering from intolerable tyranny, when deprived of all representative rights. You are full of sympathy with men in Russia. You are full of sympathy with nations that rise against the domination of the Turk. You are full of sympathy with all struggling people striving for independence. How is it, then, that some of you have nothing but ridicule and contempt . . . for women who are fighting for exactly the same thing?

All my life I have tried to understand why it is that men who value their citizenship as their dearest possession seem to think citizenship ridiculous when it is to be applied to the women of their race. . . . A thought came to me . . . and it was this: that to men women are not human beings like themselves. Some men think we are superhuman; they put us on pedestals; they revere us; they think we are too fine and too delicate to come down into the hurly-burly of life. Other men think us sub-human; they think we are a strange species unfortunately having to exist for the perpetuation of the race. They think that we are fit for drudgery, but that in some strange way our minds are not like theirs, our love for great things is not like theirs, and so we are a sort of sub-human species.

We are neither superhuman nor are we sub-human. We are just human beings like yourselves.

Our hearts burn within us when we read the great mottoes which celebrate the liberty of your country; when we go to France and we read the words, liberty, fraternity and equality, don't you think that we appreciate the meaning of those words? And then when we wake to the knowledge that these things are not for us, they are only for our brothers, then there comes a sense of bitterness into the hearts of some women, and they say to themselves, "Will men never understand?" . . .

Nationalism and Imperialism in the Late Nineteenth Century

Nationalism emerged as a powerful force in Europe during the French Revolution, when the French people came to see the wars against Austria, Great Britain, Prussia, and Russia as a patriotic crusade to save their revolution and spread its ideals across the continent. In 1792 and 1793, the fervor of French troops saved the revolution, and in the early 1800s it contributed to stunning victories under Napoleon and the extension of French control over much of Europe by 1810. French con-

quests in turn aroused nationalism among Germans, Italians, Poles, and Russians, who fought to throw off French rule and reassert their independence.

Although successful in defeating France on the battlefield, nationalists had their hopes dashed in 1815 at the Congress of Vienna. Diplomats gave Norway to Sweden, Belgium to the Netherlands, and much of Italy to Austria; divided Poland among Russia, Prussia, and Austria; and kept Germany fragmented. But nationalism could not be eradicated by redrawing maps and making diplomatic compromises. Strengthened by romanticism, Darwin-inspired notions of competition and struggle, economic rivalries, and popular journalism, nationalism intensified in the nineteenth century, not only in areas of foreign rule and political fragmentation but also in long-established states such as Great Britain and France. It contributed to some of the nineteenth century's most important political developments, including the revolutions of 1830 and 1848, the unification of Italy in 1870 and of Germany in 1871, runaway militarism among the Great Powers, the emergence of new states in the Balkans, and what concerns us in this section, late-nineteenth-century imperialism.

Unlike nationalism, which dates from the 1790s, European imperialism goes back to the medieval crusades and sixteenth-century conquests of the Americas. Europe's overseas expansion continued in the late eighteenth and early nineteenth centuries despite the loss of American colonies by France, Great Britain, Portugal, and Spain. The British extended their authority in India; the French subdued Algeria between 1830 and 1847; and the European powers, led by England, forced China to open its ports to foreign trade after the Opium War (1839–1842). Then in the closing decades of the 1800s — the Era of Imperialism — the long history of Western expansion culminated in an unprecedented land grab. Between 1870 and 1914, Great Britain added 4.25 million square miles of territory and 66 million people to its empire; France, 3.5 million square miles of territory and 26 million people; Germany, 1 million square miles and 13 million people; and Belgium, 900,000 square miles and 13 million people. Italy, the United States, and the Netherlands also added colonial territories and subjects.

Technological innovation made these acquisitions possible and practical. The replacement of sailing vessels by metal-hulled steamships reduced two-month ocean voyages to two weeks; undersea telegraph lines enabled government officials and businessmen to communicate in minutes, not weeks or months; medical advances and new drugs protected Europeans from tropical diseases; and rapid-fire rifles and machine guns gave Western troops an insurmountable advantage over any Africans or Asians who offered resistance.

Technological capability alone, however, cannot explain the expansionist fever that gripped the West in the late 1800s. Anticipated economic gains, missionary fervor, racism, and a faith in the West's civilizing mission all contributed. But the most important cause was nationalism. Politicians, journalists, and millions of people from every walk of life were convinced that foreign conquests brought respect, prestige, and a sense of national accomplishment. To have colonies was a mark of Great Power status.

Racism, Militarism, and the New Nationalism

▼▼▼

53 ▼ *Heinrich von Treitschke, Extracts from HISTORY OF GERMANY IN THE NINETEENTH CENTURY and HISTORICAL AND POLITICAL WRITINGS*

As nationalism intensified in nineteenth-century Europe, it also changed. In the first half of the century, when nationalists saw conservative monarchical governments as the main obstacle to national self-determination, nationalism was linked to republicanism and liberalism. During the middle of the century, especially in Germany and Italy, nationalism was championed by pragmatic and moderate leaders who believed that hard-headed politics, not romantic gestures and lofty republican ideals, would bring about national unification and self-rule. By century's end nationalism was increasingly associated with conservative if not reactionary groups that used it to justify large military outlays, imperialism, and aggressive foreign policies and to lure the masses away from socialism and democracy.

The German historian Heinrich von Treitschke (1834–1896) represents this later link between nationalism and militarism, racism, and authoritarianism. The son of a Prussian general, Treitschke taught history at several universities, including the University of Berlin. He also was a member of the German parliament, the Reichstag, from 1871 to 1884. His best-known work is his seven-volume *History of Germany in the Nineteenth Century*. In this and his numerous other writings, lectures, and speeches, Treitschke advocated militarism, authoritarianism, and war as the paths to national greatness. His views struck a responsive chord among many Germans who feared socialism and democracy and yearned for the day when Germany would be recognized as the world's most powerful nation.

QUESTIONS FOR ANALYSIS

1. According to Treitschke, what is the relationship between the state and the individual?
2. In Treitschke's view, why is monarchy superior to democracy?
3. What qualities of Germans set them apart from other peoples, especially the English and the Jews, according to Treitschke?
4. Early-nineteenth-century nationalists believed that all nations had a contribution to make to human progress. What is Treitschke's view?
5. According to Treitschke, what is the value of war for a nation?

ON THE GERMAN CHARACTER

Depth of thought, idealism, cosmopolitan views; a transcendent philosophy which boldly oversteps (or freely looks over) the separating barriers of finite existence, familiarity with every human thought and feeling, the desire to traverse the world-wide realm of ideas in common with the foremost intellects of all nations and all times. All that has at all times been held to be characteristic of the Germans and has always been praised as the essence of German character and breeding.

The simple loyalty of the Germans contrasts remarkably with the lack of chivalry in the English character. This seems to be due to the fact that in England physical culture is sought, not in the exercise of noble arms, but in sports like boxing, swimming, and rowing, sports which undoubtedly have their value, but which obviously tend to encourage a brutal and purely athletic point of view, and the single and superficial ambition of getting a first prize.[1]

ON THE STATE

The state is a moral community, which is called upon to educate the human race by positive achievement. Its ultimate object is that a nation should develop in it, a nation distinguished by a real national character. To achieve this state is the highest moral duty for nation and individual alike. All private quarrels must be forgotten when the state is in danger.

At the moment when the state cries out that its very life is at stake, social selfishness must cease and party hatred be hushed. The individual must forget his egoism, and feel that he is a member of the whole body.

The most important possession of a state, its be-all and end-all, is power. He who is not man enough to look this truth in the face should not meddle in politics. The state is not physical power as an end in itself, it is power to protect and promote the higher interests. Power must justify itself by being applied for the greatest good of mankind. It is the highest moral duty of the state to increase its power. . . .

Only the truly great and powerful states ought to exist. Small states are unable to protect their subjects against external enemies; moreover, they are incapable of producing genuine patriotism or national pride and are sometimes incapable of *Kultur*[2] in great dimensions. Weimar produced a Goethe and a Schiller;[3] still these poets would have been greater had they been citizens of a German national state.

ON MONARCHY

The will of the state is, in a monarchy, the expression of the will of one man who wears the crown by virtue of the historic right of a certain family; with him the final authority rests. Nothing in a monarchy can be done contrary to the will of the monarch. In a democracy, plurality, the will of the people, expresses the will of the state. A monarchy excels any other form of government, including the democratic, in achieving unity and power in a nation. It is for this reason that monarchy seems so natural, and that it makes such an appeal to the popular understanding. We Germans had an experience of this in the first years of our new empire.[4] How wonderfully the idea of a united Fatherland was embodied for us in the person of the venerable Emperor! How much it meant to us that we could feel once more: "That man is Germany; there is no doubting it!"

---

[1]Treitschke is correct in drawing a distinction between English and German sports. The English prized competitive athletic contests, while the Germans favored group calisthenics and exercises.

[2]German for "culture" or "civilization."

[3]Johann Wolfgang von Goethe (1749–1832) and Johann von Schiller (1759–1805) were poets and dramatists who lived before Germany became a unified state. They both spent much of their adult lives in Weimar, the capital of the Duchy of Saxe-Weimar.

[4]When Germany became a unified state in 1871, the king of Prussia, Wilhelm I, became emperor of Germany.

ON WAR

The idea of perpetual peace is an illusion supported only by those of weak character. It has always been the weary, spiritless, and exhausted ages which have played with the dream of perpetual peace. A thousand touching portraits testify to the sacred power of the love which a righteous war awakes in noble nations. It is altogether impossible that peace be maintained in a world bristling with arms, and even God will see to it that war always recurs as a drastic medicine for the human race. Among great states the greatest political sin and the most contemptible is feebleness. . . .

War is elevating because the individual disappears before the great conception of the state. The devotion of the members of a community to each other is nowhere so splendidly conspicuous as in war.

Modern wars are not waged for the sake of goods and resources. What is at stake is the sublime moral good of national honor, which has something in the nature of unconditional sanctity, and compels the individual to sacrifice himself for it. . . .

The grandeur of war lies in the utter annihilation of puny man in the great conception of the State, and it brings out the full magnificence of the sacrifice of fellow-countrymen for one another. In war the chaff is winnowed from the wheat. Those who have lived through 1870 cannot fail to understand Niebuhr's[5] description of his feelings in 1813, when he speaks of how no one who has entered into the joy of being bound by a common tie to all his compatriots, gentle and simple alike, can ever forget how he was uplifted by the love, the friendliness, and the strength of that mutual sentiment.

It is war which fosters the political idealism which the materialist rejects. What a disaster for civilization it would be if mankind blotted its heroes from memory. The heroes of a nation are the figures which rejoice and inspire the spirit of its youth, and the writers whose words ring like trumpet blasts become the idols of our boyhood and our early manhood. He who feels no answering thrill is unworthy to bear arms for his country. To appeal from this judgment to Christianity would be sheer perversity, for does not the Bible distinctly say that the ruler shall rule by the sword, and again that greater love hath no man than to lay down his life for his friend? To Aryan[6] races, who are before all things courageous, the foolish preaching of everlasting peace has always been in vain. They have always been man enough to maintain with the sword what they have attained through the spirit. . . .

ON THE ENGLISH

The hypocritical Englishman, with the Bible in one hand and a pipe of opium[7] in the other, possesses no redeeming qualities. The nation was an ancient robber-knight, in full armor, lance in hand, on every one of the world's trade routes.

The English possess a commercial spirit, a love of money which has killed every sentiment of honor and every distinction of right and wrong. English cowardice and sensuality are hidden behind unctuous, theological fine talk which is to us free-thinking German heretics among all the sins of English nature the most repugnant. In England

[5]Barthold Georg Niebuhr (1776–1831) was a Prussian civil servant and historian. He lectured for a time at the University of Berlin and is best known for his three-volume history of Rome.

[6]Today, the term *Aryan*, or Indo-Iranian, refers to a branch of the Indo-European family of languages, which also includes Baltic, Slavic, Armenian, Greek, Celtic, Latin, and Germanic. Indo-Iranian includes Bengali, Persian, Punjabi, and Hindi. In Treitschke's day *Aryan* was used to refer not only to the prehistoric language from which all these languages derive but also to the racial group that spoke the language and migrated from its base in central Asia to Europe and India in the distant past. In the racial mythology that grew in connection with the term and later was embraced by Hitler and the Nazis, the Aryans provided Europe's original racial stock.

[7]Treitschke is making a point about what he considers the hypocrisy of the British, professed Christians who nonetheless sell opium to the Chinese.

all notions of honor and class prejudices vanish before the power of money, whereas the German nobility has remained poor but chivalrous. That last indispensable bulwark against the brutalization of society — the duel — has gone out of fashion in England and soon disappeared, to be supplanted by the riding whip.[8] This was a triumph of vulgarity. The newspapers, in their accounts of aristocratic weddings, record in exact detail how much each wedding guest has contributed in the form of presents or in cash; even the youth of the nation have turned their sports into a business, and contend for valuable prizes, whereas the German students wrought havoc on their countenances for the sake of a real or imaginary honor.[9]

ON JEWS

The Jews at one time played a necessary role in German history, because of their ability in the management of money. But now that the Aryans have become accustomed to the idiosyncrasies of finance, the Jews are no longer necessary. The international Jew, hidden in the mask of different nationalities, is a disintegrating influence; he can be of no further use to the world. It is necessary to speak openly about the Jews, undisturbed by the fact that the Jewish press befouls what is purely historical truth.

[8]Aristocratic males frequently settled disputes concerning their honor by dueling. To Treitschke, abandoning the duel for less manly pursuits such as hunting and horseback riding was a sign of decadence.

[9]Treitschke is again using examples from sports to underscore the differences between the Germans and the English. English sports such as rugby and football (American soccer) were organized into professional leagues; the Germans were still willing to be scarred in duels to defend their honor.

A Defense of French Imperialism

54 ▾ *Jules Ferry, SPEECH BEFORE THE FRENCH NATIONAL ASSEMBLY*

Jules Ferry (1832–1893), a French politician and ardent imperialist, twice served as premier of France. During his premierships (1880–1881, 1883–1885), France annexed Tunisia and parts of Indochina and directed French explorations in the Congo and of the Niger region of Africa. In debates in the French National Assembly, he frequently defended his policies against socialist and conservative critics who opposed French imperialism. In the following selection from a speech on July 28, 1883, he summarizes his reasons for supporting French expansionism; it also sheds light on his opponents' views.

QUESTIONS FOR ANALYSIS

1. **According to Ferry, what recent developments in world trade have made France's need for colonies more urgent?**
2. **What arguments against imperialism are proposed by Ferry's critics? How does Ferry counter them?**
3. **Aside from providing markets for French goods, what other economic advantages do colonies offer, according to Ferry?**
4. **How does Ferry's appeal for colonies reflect nineteenth-century nationalism?**

M. JULES FERRY Gentlemen, it embarrasses me to make such a prolonged demand upon the gracious attention of the Chamber, but I believe that the duty I am fulfilling upon this platform is not a useless one: It is as strenuous for me as for you, but I believe that there is some benefit in summarizing and condensing, in the form of arguments, the principles, the motives, and the various interests by which a policy of colonial expansion may be justified; it goes without saying that I will try to remain reasonable, moderate, and never lose sight of the major continental interests which are the primary concern of this country. What I wish to say, to support this proposition, is that in fact, just as in word, the policy of colonial expansion is a political and economic system; I wish to say that one can relate this system to three orders of ideas: economic ideas, ideas of civilization in its highest sense, and ideas of politics and patriotism.

In the area of economics, I will allow myself to place before you, with the support of some figures, the considerations which justify a policy of colonial expansion from the point of view of that need, felt more and more strongly by the industrial populations of Europe and particularly those of our own rich and hard working country: the need for export markets. . . . I will formulate only in a general way what each of you, in the different parts of France, is in a position to confirm. Yes, what is lacking for our great industry, drawn irrevocably on to the path of exportation by the (free trade) treaties of 1860,[1] what it lacks more and more is export markets. Why? Because next door to us Germany is surrounded by [tariff] barriers, because beyond the ocean, the United States of America has become protectionist, protectionist in the most extreme sense, because not only have these great markets, I will not say closed but shrunk, and thus become more difficult of access for our industrial products, but also these great states are beginning to pour products not seen heretofore into our own markets. . . . It is not necessary to pursue this demonstration any further. . . .

. . . Gentlemen, there is a second point, a second order of ideas to which I have to give equal attention, but as quickly as possible, believe me; it is the humanitarian and civilizing side of the question. On this point the honorable M. Camille Pelletan[2] has jeered in his own refined and clever manner; he jeers, he condemns, and he says "What is this civilization which you impose with cannon-balls? What is it but another form of barbarism? Don't these populations, these inferior races, have the same rights as you? Aren't they masters of their own houses? Have they called upon you? You come to them against their will, you offer them violence, but not civilization." There, gentlemen, is the thesis; I do not hesitate to say that this is not politics, nor is it history: it is political metaphysics. ("Ah, Ah" *on far left.*)[3]

. . . Gentlemen, I must speak from a higher and more truthful plane. It must be stated openly that, in effect, superior races have rights over inferior races. *(Movement on many benches on the far left.)*

M. JULES MAIGNE Oh! You dare to say this in the country which has proclaimed the rights of man!

M. DE GUILLOUTET This is a justification of slavery and the slave trade!

M. JULES FERRY If M. Maigne is right, if the declaration of the rights of man was written for the blacks of equatorial Africa, then by what right do you impose regular commerce upon them? They have not called upon you.

M. RAOUL DUVAL We do not want to impose anything upon them. It is you who wish to do so!

M. JULES MAIGNE To propose and to impose are two different things!

---

[1]Refers to a treaty between Great Britain and France that lowered tariffs between the two nations.

[2]Pelletan (1846–1915) was a radical republican politician noted for his strong patriotism.

[3]Going back to a tradition begun in the legislative assemblies of the French Revolution, democrats and republicans sat on the left, moderates in the center, and conservatives on the right. By the 1880s the "left" also included socialists.

M. Georges Perin[4] In any case, you cannot bring about commerce by force.

M. Jules Ferry I repeat that superior races have a right, because they have a duty. They have the duty to civilize inferior races. . . .

That is what I have to answer M. Pelletan in regard to the second point upon which he touched.

He then touched upon a third, more delicate, more serious point, and upon which I ask your permission to express myself quite frankly. It is the political side of the question. The honorable M. Pelletan, who is a distinguished writer, always comes up with remarkably precise formulations. I will borrow from him the one which he applied the other day to this aspect of colonial policy.

"It is a system," he says, "which consists of seeking out compensations in the Orient with a circumspect and peaceful seclusion which is actually imposed upon us in Europe."

I would like to explain myself in regard to this. I do not like this word "compensation," and, in effect, not here but elsewhere it has often been used in a treacherous way. If what is being said or insinuated is that a republican minister could possibly believe that there are in any part of the world compensations for the disasters which we have experienced,[5] an injury is being inflicted . . . and an injury undeserved by that government. *(Applause at the center and left.)* I will ward off this injury with all the force of my patriotism! *(New applause and bravos from the same benches.)*

Gentlemen, there are certain considerations which merit the attention of all patriots. The conditions of naval warfare have been profoundly altered. ("Very true! Very true!")

At this time, as you know, a warship cannot carry more than fourteen days' worth of coal, no matter how perfectly it is organized, and a ship which is out of coal is a derelict on the surface of the sea, abandoned to the first person who comes along. Thence the necessity of having on the oceans provision stations, shelters, ports for defense and revictualling. *(Applause at the center and left. Various interruptions.)* And it is for this that we needed Tunisia, for this that we needed Saigon and the Mekong Delta, for this that we need Madagascar, that we are at Diégo-Suarez and Vohemar[6] and will never leave them! *(Applause from a great number of benches.)* Gentlemen, in Europe as it is today, in this competition of so many rivals which we see growing around us, some by perfecting their military or maritime forces, others by the prodigious development of an ever growing population; in a Europe, or rather in a universe of this sort, a policy of peaceful seclusion or abstention is simply the highway to decadence! Nations are great in our times only by means of the activities which they develop; it is not simply "by the peaceful shining forth of institutions" *(Interruptions on the extreme left and right)* that they are great at this hour. . . .

(The Republican Party) has shown that it is quite aware that one cannot impose upon France a political ideal conforming to that of nations like independent Belgium and the Swiss Republic; that something else is needed for France: that she cannot be merely a free country, that she must also be a great country, exercising all of her rightful influence over the destiny of Europe, that she ought to propagate this influence throughout the world and carry everywhere that she can her language, her customs, her flag, her arms, and her genius. *(Applause at center and left.)*

---

[4]Maigne, Guilloutet, Duval, and Perin were all members of the assembly.

[5]Refers to France's defeat by Prussia and the German states in the Franco-Prussian War of 1870–1871.

[6]Madagascar port cities.

Images of Imperialism in Great Britain

55 ▾ *ADVERTISEMENTS AND ILLUSTRATIONS FROM BRITISH BOOKS AND PERIODICALS*

Although late-nineteenth-century imperialism had many critics, there is no doubt that in the major imperialist states it had broad support, not just from investors, missionary groups, and civil servants who had direct interests in Africa and Asia but also from the general populace. For many of its supporters, imperialism confirmed their faith in progress and their belief in the superiority of white, Christian Europe over the rest of the world. For ardent nationalists, it was a test and demonstration of the nation's strength and vigor. For those who found their lives in industrial society drab and tedious, it provided vicarious adventure, excitement, and a sense of the exotic.

Late-nineteenth-century popular culture provides ample evidence of the public's enthusiasm for imperialism. Especially in Great Britain, the premier imperialist power, novels, poetry, plays, children's books, advertisements, music hall entertainment, and publications of missionary societies were filled with positive imperialist images, themes, and motifs. Youth organizations such as the Boy Scouts (f. 1908) and Girl Guides (f. 1910) taught the value of service to Britain's imperial cause. The public's exposure to such material reinforced imperialism's appeal and strengthened support for the government's expansionist policies.

The selections in this section are examples of how British popular culture propagated imperial values. The first group of illustrations (page 272) appeared in *An ABC for Baby Patriots* by Mrs. Earnest Ames. Designed to be read to young children, it was published in 1898 in London and went through several printings. The illustration that accompanies the letter *N* depicts a British naval officer showing off a flotilla of Royal Navy ships on maneuvers off Spithead in the English Channel. The foreigners are a German on the left and a Frenchman on the right.

The second illustration (page 273) is taken from *The Kipling Reader*, a collection of stories written for young adults by Rudyard Kipling (1865–1936); the book was published in 1908 and illustrated by J. Macfarlane. Kipling, one of the most popular British writers of the era, is best remembered for his strong support of imperialism and his glorification of the heroism of the British soldier in India and Burma. This particular illustration depicts Scott, a character in the story "William the Conqueror." Set in India during a famine, the story centers on the romance between Scott and a young woman nicknamed "William" while they toil to save Indians from starvation. Scott has saved hundreds of babies by feeding them milk from a herd of goats he has managed to maintain. In this illustration he approaches William, who sees "a young man, beautiful as Paris, a god in a halo of gold dust, walking slowly at the head of his flocks, while at his knee ran small naked Cupids."

The third illustration (page 273) is an advertisement for Lipton Teas that appeared in 1897 in the *Illustrated London News*. The Lipton Company was founded in Glasgow, Scotland, by the son of a poor Irish shopkeeper, Thomas Lipton

(1850–1931). He opened a small food shop in Glasgow in 1871 and by 1890 owned 300 food stores throughout Great Britain. In 1890 the multimillionaire decided to cash in on the British taste for tea. Growing tea on plantations he owned in India and Ceylon and marketing it in inexpensive small packets that guaranteed freshness, the Lipton Company soon became synonymous with tea drinking throughout Europe and the United States. Lipton advertisements appeared regularly in the *Illustrated London News* in the 1890s and early 1900s.

The fourth and fifth illustrations (page 274) are cartoons published in the humor magazine *Punch*, founded in 1841. Although it was noted for its early political radicalism, by the late nineteenth century *Punch* had adopted a more moderate political stance, one that reflected the perspectives of its largely middle-class readers. The first cartoon, "On the Swoop," was published in 1894, a time when the European powers were consolidating their territorial claims in Africa. It shows an eagle representing Germany about to pounce on an African village. By then it was clear that the German acquisition of Tanganyika had ruined the British imperialists' dream of establishing a string of contiguous colonies in east Africa that stretched from Cairo in Egypt to Cape Town in South Africa. The second cartoon, "Britannia and Her Suitors," was published in 1901, when Great Britain was still studiously avoiding entanglements in the diplomatic alliances then taking shape among the continental powers. It shows Britannia dancing with a figure representing its colonies, while in the background the German emperor Wilhelm II, then allied only with weak Austria-Hungary, looks on unhappily. Farther in the background, Tsar Nicholas II of Russia dances with a figure representing France, with which Russia had been allied since 1894.

QUESTIONS FOR ANALYSIS

1. What views of Africans and Asians are being communicated in each of the illustrations?
2. What message is being communicated about the benefits colonial subjects are accruing from their status?
3. What images are being communicated about the British in their role as imperialists?
4. What concrete examples of nationalism can you see in the various illustrations?
5. How many of the justifications for imperialism presented in Jules Ferry's speech (source 54) can you find represented in the illustrations?
6. Using evidence in the illustrations alone, what conclusions can you draw about the reasons for imperialism's popularity within the general British population?

From *An ABC for Baby Patriots*

N.

N is the Navy
We keep at Spithead,
It's a sight that makes foreigners
Wish they were dead.

I.

I is for India,
Our land in the East
Where everyone goes
To shoot tigers and feast.

W.

W is the Word
Of an Englishman true;
When given, it means
What he says, he will do.

From The Kipling Reader

Advertisement for Lipton Teas, which appeared in the Illustrated London News, *a weekly publication*

PARTNERS.

Britannia. "AFTER ALL, MY DEAR, WE NEEDN'T TROUBLE OURSELVES ABOUT THE OTHERS."
Colonia. "NO; WE CAN ALWAYS DANCE TOGETHER, YOU AND I!"

"Britannia and Her Suitors," from Punch, *1901*

ON THE SWOOP!

"On the Swoop," from Punch, *1894*

Multiple Voices V
The American Response to Chinese Immigration, 1870s to the Early 1900s

BACKGROUND

Migration has always been a part of human history, but more people were on the move in the late 1800s than ever before. Taking advantage of cheap long-distance travel and lured by economic opportunities created by industrialization and the opening of the Americas, millions of human beings left their homes for new lives in new locales. Most of these migrants were Europeans, and most of them went to the Americas, where between 1900 and 1914 no fewer than 9 million immigrants arrived in the United States alone and no less than 60 percent of the U.S. labor force was foreign born. Migration was not limited to Europeans, however. Indians left their homes for Southeast Asia, the Caribbean, Africa, and South America, and Chinese and smaller numbers of Japanese emigrated to Malaya, Indonesia, Singapore, and the Americas.

Many immigrants were welcomed in their new homelands as a source of cheap labor and new skills. Many others, however, became targets of discrimination, bigotry, and violence, especially when they threatened the economic interests of certain groups or were perceived as being too "different" to be acceptable.

Such ambivalence is a pervasive theme in the history of the United States, despite its image as a haven for the world's poor and oppressed regardless of their origins. Anti-immigrant sentiment swelled in the 1850s, when the American Party, whose supporters were known as "Know-Nothings," ran on a platform directed at recently arrived German and Irish Catholics, who supposedly caused urban crime and made poor citizens because of their blind obedience to the pope. The Know-Nothings won control of the Massachusetts legislature in 1854 and received 22 percent of the popular vote for their presidential candidate, Millard Fillmore, in 1856. Anti-immigrant sentiment diminished during the Civil War and the 1870s but reemerged in the late 1800s, when the arrival of millions of Hungarians, Poles, Italians, Greeks, and Jews kindled fears that America would be ruined by people of poor racial stock and with no understanding of democracy. Despite widespread unease over the flood of new immigrants, legislative efforts to drastically limit or ban immigration failed, with one notable exception. The exception was immigration from China.

Chinese migration to the United States began in the late 1840s in response to population pressures and lawlessness in China and the lure of instant wealth in California, where gold had been discovered in 1848. Most emigrants were young men who planned to return to China after making their fortune. Only a few "struck it rich," but immigration continued, with approximately 130,000 Chinese arriving between 1850 and 1880. They worked on farms, labored on building the transcontinental railroad, and congregated in Chinatowns in cities on the Pacific coast from Los Angeles to Seattle, where they ran laundries and other small businesses and worked as servants and laborers. Some traveled east to work in Philadelphia, New York, and Boston.

Anti-Chinese sentiment emerged in the 1870s, especially in California. Convinced that the Chinese depressed wages and stole jobs from qualified Americans, labor unions campaigned to halt Chinese immigration and to deport the Chinese who already were in the United States. In response the California legislature approved special immigration taxes and laundry-operation fees. Such legislation was opposed by members of the Chinese American community and many native-born politicians, businessmen, clergy, and journalists. In 1882, however, the U.S. Congress passed and President Chester A. Arthur signed the Chinese Exclusion Act, which banned the immigration of Chinese laborers for ten years, required passes for all resident Chinese, and barred Chinese from citizenship.

Controversy over Chinese immigrants did not stop, however. Immigration continued, since relatives of Chinese residents in the United States, teachers, officials, merchants, and travelers could still enter the country. Furthermore, since the Exclusion Act lapsed after ten years, new legislation was debated and passed again in 1892 and 1902, when Congress finally made the ban permanent. Chinese immigration remained illegal until 1943, when Congress approved limited immigration in view of the Chinese-U.S. alliance during World War II.

THE SOURCES

The first two excerpts represent the views of opponents of Chinese immigration. The first is taken from a 100-page booklet published in 1873 titled *The Coming Struggle: What People of the Pacific Coast Think about the Coolie Invasion*. It was written by M. B. Starr, about whom nothing is known except what can be inferred from this, his only book. We learn that he was an ardent Protestant with a deep antipathy for Mormonism and appears to have had ties with San Francisco's small-business community. Several such businesses subsidized Starr's book, including Mendel's Havana and Domestic Cigars, which advertised that its cigars were made "by the white delicate hands of ladies," not "Chinamen." Clearly, Starr was no friend of the "coolies," the derogatory term for cheap Asian, especially Chinese, labor. The second excerpt was written in 1901, when Congress was about to reconsider the renewal of the Chinese exclusion law. It is a declaration adopted by the delegates to a Chinese exclusion convention sponsored by the American Federation of Labor in San Francisco.

Arguments against limiting Chinese immigration are also represented by two written sources. The first contains testimony taken at special hearings held in 1876 in San Francisco by a Joint Special Congressional Committee appointed to "investigate the character, extent and effect of Chinese immigration." The excerpts represent the views of farmers and businessmen who were questioned by two Caucasian lawyers representing the Chinese Consolidated Benevolent Association, a Chinatown-based organization that dealt with the city and state governments on issues pertaining to the Chinese community.

The last excerpt is taken from ***Chinese Immigration in Its Social and Economical Aspects***, published in 1881 by George F. Seward. Born in New York in 1840 and the nephew of Lincoln's secretary of state, William H. Seward, Seward served in the U.S. consulate in Shanghai between 1860 and 1876 and was U.S. ambassador to China from 1876 to 1880. He resigned under a cloud of scandal in 1880. After returning to the United States, he had a successful career as an insurance executive in New York, where he died in 1910.

The final sources are two political cartoons. "The Chinese Question" is the work of the most famous of all American political cartoonists, Thomas Nast (1840–1902). A German immigrant, Nast studied art in New York City and took a position at *Harper's Weekly* in 1859. There he became famous for cartoons that skewered Democrats, Irish, and the Roman Catholic Church but defended blacks, Native Americans, and Chinese immigrants. His cartoon "The Chinese Question" was published in 1871 in response to a bill proposed in the New York legislature to prohibit businesses contracting with the state from employing Chinese laborers. The legislation was a response to the importation in 1870 of seventy-five Chinese laborers from San Francisco to break a shoe workers' strike in North Adams, Massachusetts. Nast's cartoon shows Columbia, the feminine symbol of the United States, shielding a Chinese man from thugs. The imagery in the upper right background refers to the New York City draft riots of 1863, during which largely Irish American mobs protested the military draft and Lincoln's Emancipation Proclamation by burning the Colored Orphan Asylum and lynching blacks.

A different message is provided by George F. Keller's cartoon "The Coming Man," which appeared in the San Francisco weekly *The Wasp* in 1881. In the 1880s and 1890s, *The Wasp* carried on a relentless campaign against Chinese immigrants, who in this cartoon are represented by an ominous Chinese figure who has achieved a monopoly on the laundry business and employment in the cigar-making and clothes-making industries.

QUESTIONS FOR ANALYSIS

1. What do the documents reveal about the economic activities of the Chinese immigrants?
2. Among Americans, who stood to gain from the availability of Chinese immigrants and who stood to lose?
3. For the opponents of Chinese immigration, what qualities of the Chinese made them so threatening to the fabric of American society?
4. How did the supporters of Chinese immigration counter these arguments? What qualities of the immigrants did they emphasize?
5. Both the opponents and defenders of Chinese immigration appealed to "American values" to support their position. What do the documents tells us about how each side defined these values?
6. Overall, which side, the defenders or proponents of immigration, make the stronger arguments?

1 ▾ M. B. Starr, THE COMING STRUGGLE; OR WHAT THE PEOPLE ON THE PACIFIC COAST THINK OF THE COOLIE INVASION

What encouragement are we now offering to the millions of children who are doomed to get their living by doing the legitimate work of their fathers, if their fathers substitute an equal number of barbarians to do the work cheaper than they can? . . . What work have we for the boys to do when they come home from the schools, perfected in the arts and trades? Where then will be the dignity of hands, and where the dignity of *heads*? Let Satan, who always has work for idle hands, reply: "In the liquorshop and gambling saloon; in the hoodlum's gang, locked up in jail; in the gang of thieves and houses of imported cheap women; in the gang of robbers and chained in State's prison; on the criminal's scaffold and in the drunkard's grave. But if in addition to intellectual culture and industrial habits we preserve the work of the nation for them . . . the boys and girls will go forth from the school and workshop, with an ever-present sense of the dignity of *hands* as well as heads.

. . . But if our selfish love of money and power shall change this traditional custom . . . ; if we close all the avenues of living against them and employ serfs because it costs less to feed and clothe them, whom we can treat as slaves; if we turn a deaf ear to the appeals of our own countrymen for work, and give every opportunity to make a living to the heathen — they will remember us with a retaliation that will be more disastrous to the whole country than was the late rebellion [the Civil War].

But the earnestness and spirit displayed by all classes of people at the present time is continued, we may hope to check the further importation of coolies into the United States. . . . The moment that is done the feeling of disquietude and insecurity that now alarms the people will be allayed. That which has checked our prosperity, retarded the increase of American population and growth of cities, will vanish. . . . Then, instead of swarming, unfranchised serfs to eat out the substance of the land, reducing its inhabitants slowly to poverty and shame, five times that number of intelligent citizens will come in to drive out the savages, prostrate the forests, cultivate fertile fields, build railroads and manufactories, thriving villages and busy cities, with their schools of learning, renowned for their industry and commerce, swarming with a prosperous and happy, free and Christian people, who have sworn an eternal allegiance to the noblest institutions, the most prolific soil and genial clime on the face of the globe.

2 ▾ American Federation of Labor, SOME REASONS FOR CHINESE EXCLUSION

Until this year no statute had been passed by the State forbidding their intermarriage with the whites, and yet during their long residence but few intermarriages have taken place, and the offspring has been invariably degenerate. It is well established that the issue of the Caucasian and the Mongolian does not possess the virtues of either, but develops the vices of both. So physical assimilation is out of the question. . . . Their practical status among us has been that of single men competing at low wages against not only men of our race, but men who have been brought up by our civilization to family life and civic duty. They pay little taxes; they support no institutions, neither school, church, nor theater; they remain steadfastly, after all these years, a permanently foreign element . . . and now it has been clearly demonstrated that they can not, for the deep and ineradicable reasons of race and mental organization, assimilate with our own people and be molded as are other races into strong and composite American stock.

▾ ▾ ▾

It has been urged that the Chinese are unskilled and that they create wealth in field, mine, and forest, which ultimately redounds to the benefit of the white skilled workingman. The Chinese are skilled, and are capable of almost any skilled employment. They have invaded the cigar, shoe, broom, chemical, clothing, fruit canning, match making, woolen manufacturing industries, and have displaced more than 4,000 white men in these several employments in the city of San Francisco. As common laborers they have throughout California displaced tens of thousands of men. . . .

The home market should grow with the population. But the Chinese, living on the most meager food, having no families to support, inured to deprivation, and hoarding their wages for use in their native land, whither they invariably return, can not in any sense be regarded as consumers. Their earnings do not circulate nor are they reinvested, contrary to those economic laws which make for the prosperity of nations.

▾ ▾ ▾

Civilization in Europe has been frequently attacked and imperiled by the barbaric hordes of Asia. . . . But a peaceful invasion is more dangerous than a war-like attack. We can meet and defend ourselves against an open foe, but an insidious foe under our generous laws would be in possession of the citadel before we were aware. The free immigration of Chinese would be for all purposes an invasion by Asiatic barbarians, against whom civilization in Europe has been frequently defended, fortunately for us. It is our inheritance to keep it pure and uncontaminated, as it is our purpose and destiny to broaden and enlarge it. We are trustees for mankind.

---

3 ▾ *TESTIMONY FROM JOINT SPECIAL CONGRESSIONAL COMMITTEE ON CHINESE IMMIGRATION*

Donald McLennan sworn and examined.

By Mr. Bee:

Question. You are connected with the Mission Woolen Mills, I believe? — Answer. I am.

Q. How long have you been in that business? — A. Sixteen or seventeen years.

Q. How long have you been in this country? — A. About nineteen years.

Q. How many operatives have you? — A. We have about 600, altogether — about 300 Chinamen and the rest white.

Q. How do you look upon them for honesty? — A. I never found a case of theft among them. It is possible that such things might take place and we not know it; but still we have never discovered anything of the kind or noticed that anything was taken away.

Q. The Chinese, therefore, you regard as steady and reliable? — A. Yes, sir; they are a very steady people. I have never seen a drunken Chinaman in my life.

Q. Do they ever strike for higher wages? — A. Never. I never knew them to do so.

Q. What is the difference in the rate of wages that you pay to the two races? — A. We pay our white men from $1.75 to $6 a day, and we pay the Chinamen 90 cents a day.

Herman Heynemann sworn and examined.

By Mr. Brooks:

Question. What is your business? — A. A merchant.

Q. How long have you been engaged in that business here? — A. Fifteen years.

Q. What is the character of your business? — A. I am engaged in importing goods, also in manufacturing.

Q. What character of manufacturing? — A. I am president of the Pioneer Woolen Factory and agent of the Pacific Jute Factory.

Q. Why do you employ Chinese in your factory? — A. Originally we could not get any others at all. At that time it would have been an absolute impossibility to have run the factory upon white labor, simply because we could not get white operatives.

Q. Would the factory have been established with white labor? — A. No, sir. As a matter of fact, even with the Chinese labor, competition has been so active that we have had no dividends whatever.

By the Chairman:

Q. What is their character for industry and fidelity? — A. I have found in our factory during the last fifteen years, that we have not had a single case before the police court. All these Chinese laborers live on the premises. They have a building there; and we have not had a single case of any kind before the police court of murder, or rows among themselves, or theft upon the proprietors. I think that speaks well for them. I think there are few factories run entirely by white labor where the laborers live on the premises that could say that much.

Q. What is the cause, in your judgment, of the hostility to the Chinese? — A. The same cause that has been prevalent all over the earth, strangeness of manners. It used to be in England than any man who did not speak English was a "bloody foreigner." It did not make any difference whether he was the best man in the world, he was a "bloody foreigner," and it was the height of contempt to use that expression. I am just of the opinion . . . if this race, instead of keeping themselves in their peculiar dress, were to drink whisky and patronize the bar rooms to-day just like others do, the prejudice would disappear immediately.

4 ▾ George F. Seward, *CHINESE IMMIGRATION IN ITS SOCIAL AND ECONOMICAL ASPECTS*

But what, after all, is meant by the vague phrase that the Chinese will not assimilate. It has been iterated and reiterated, but is it entirely certain that any one knows what is meant? . . .

We have seen that the Chinese work in our fields, in our factories and upon our public works. They have been described for us as free men, as industrious, patient, pains taking, faithful, skillful, frugal, peaceable freemen. Can one ask more in these directions? Their competition is dreaded because they possess many of the qualities which make laborers useful to others and to themselves. They might lose some of these valuable characteristics and assimilate more closely in doing so to a part of the population of California. Would we have them do this ?

We have seen that their merchants are shrewd, enterprising and honorable. We have found them upon 'change respected, even courted. In business relations, then, as in labor, they have not failed.

We have seen that they are open to the truths of revealed religion. . . .

We have seen that in face of many special temptations crime is not more rampant among them than among ourselves.

We have seen that they care for their own sick and needy.

We have seen that they settle their differences and difficulties by friendly negotiation and arbitration. . . .

Do we ask more than this? Do we demand that men of a race whose traditions are different from ours, whose education and training are peculiar to themselves, should suddenly cast off devotion to their past and meet us on a common ground of social intercourse, their heads unshaven, their cues cut off, their bodies encased in tight fitting garments, that they shall eat potatoes rather than rice, and drink wine instead of tea? What then are these externals that we should pay so much attention to them? If the Chinese fulfill the purposes of life, . . . must we still show discontent because their dress and some of their customs indicate their origin?

5 ▾ Thomas Nast, "THE CHINESE QUESTION"

6 ▾ George Keller, "THE COMING MAN"

THE COMING MAN.

Allee samee 'Melican Man Monopoleeee.

Chapter 9

Western Pressures, Nationalism, and Reform in Africa, Southwest Asia, and India in the 1800s

AFRICA, SOUTHWEST ASIA, and India all shared a common experience in the nineteenth century: All three were caught up in a tidal wave of change set off by the political, economic, and cultural onslaught of Europe. Until the 1800s, European contact for the peoples and rulers of these regions had meant mainly contact with merchants, who stayed on the coast and traded with the permission of local rulers who often benefited from their activities. Only in the case of the Ottoman Empire were relations with Europeans marked by territorial conflict and war. And only in India were Europeans, in this instance the British in the late eighteenth century, able to establish political authority.

By the early twentieth century all three regions had been deeply affected — politically, economically, and culturally — by European penetration. In the 1800s the British extended their Indian empire until it encompassed most of the Indian subcontinent. Virtually the whole African continent also lost its independence. The main difference was that India had but one colonial master, while Africa had half a dozen. Persia experienced growing British and Russian interference in its affairs, culminating in the Anglo-Russian Agreement of 1907, which divided the country into a Russian-dominated north, a British-dominated south, and a nominally independent center. The Ottoman Empire survived but lost thousands of square miles of territory. In North Africa, which was still part of the Ottoman Empire despite the near independence of its rulers, Algeria and Tunisia became French colonies, and Egypt became a British protectorate. In southeastern Europe,

Greece, Serbia, Romania, Bulgaria, Montenegro, and Albania all gained their independence from Ottoman rule. In addition, Europeans compromised the sovereignty of the Ottoman state itself. Foreign businessmen, who controlled the empire's banks, railroads, and mines, regulated Ottoman tariff policy and were exempt from many of the empire's laws and taxes. Beginning in 1881, Europeans supervised the collection and disbursement of state revenues through the Ottoman Public Debt Administration, an agency established mainly to guarantee payment of government debts to European creditors.

In all three regions, European penetration threatened ruling elites and traditional political institutions, making some irrelevant, destroying others, and inspiring reform in a few. It also undermined these regions' traditional economies. Europeans built railroads and telegraph lines, undertook huge engineering projects such as the Suez Canal, created new demands for raw materials and agricultural goods, and aggressively marketed their own manufactured products. Europeans also introduced unsettling new ideas and values through intensified missionary activity, the introduction of the printing press, and the promotion of Western education and science. In a matter of decades, the peoples of Africa, Southwest Asia, and India were wrenched from their past and forced to face uncertain futures.

The European Assault on Africa

Paradoxically, the century that saw the nearly total submission of Africa to European rule began with an effort by Europeans to outlaw their main business in Africa, the slave trade. Responding to religious, humanitarian, and economic arguments, Great Britain and the United States both banned the slave trade in 1807, followed by Sweden, Denmark, the Netherlands, and, in 1848, France. Unexpectedly, this led to more, not less, European involvement in Africa. Palm oil, ivory, cocoa, coffee, rubber, and other goods replaced slaves as items of trade, and by the 1850s this "legitimate" trade was more profitable for the British than the old slave trade. Then, in the closing decades of the nineteenth century, African-European relations underwent a radical transformation, and the entire African continent except Liberia and Ethiopia succumbed to European rule.

The takeover took just over two decades. It began in earnest in the 1870s, a decade that saw the intensification of Catholic and Protestant missionary activity; the discovery of gold and diamonds in South Africa; heightened commercial competition among British, French, German, and African merchants in West Africa and the Niger delta region; and growing interest in Africa on the part of the European public because of explorers' accounts. Most important, in 1878 King

Leopold II of Belgium and his business associates dispatched the Welsh-American explorer Henry M. Stanley (1841–1904) to the Congo River basin, where he secured treaties with Africans that were the foundation for the Congo Free State, a territory of 900,000 square miles that was the monarch's personal property until taken over by the Belgian government in 1908. In 1880 the Italian-born explorer Pierre Savorgnan de Brazza (1853–1905) signed the first of hundreds of treaties with African chieftains that laid the basis for the French colonies in equatorial Africa. In 1881, the French established a protectorate over Tunisia, and in 1882 the British occupied Egypt. The Germans annexed Togo in 1883 and Cameroon in 1884. In 1884 and 1885, thirteen European nations and the United States attended the Berlin West Africa Conference, which established guidelines for the further colonization of Africa. By 1914, when World War I began, Africa was a vast European colony.

Africans did not passively acquiesce to the European onslaught. Many Africans fought back, but the Europeans' artillery, high-explosive shells, and machine guns doomed their efforts. In 1898 the Battle of Omdurman in present-day Sudan resulted in some 11,000 casualties for the Sudanese and 40 for the British and their Egyptian troops.

"With the View of Bettering . . . Our Country"

56 ▾ *Royal Niger Company, STANDARD TREATY*

During the partition of Africa, African chieftains signed hundreds of treaties that effectively gave control of their lands and resources to European states or trading companies. The "standard treaty" that follows was used in the late 1880s by the Royal Niger Company, the brainchild of Sir George Taubman Goldie, a British merchant who dreamed of adding the regions of the lower and middle Niger River to the British Empire. After he and his partners bought out French competitors, the Royal Niger Company was chartered by Queen Victoria in 1886 and given a trade monopoly and the right to exercise political authority in the Niger River region. On receiving the charter, the company's representatives drew up a set of standard treaties in which one needed only to fill in the blanks. Using such templates, they concluded no fewer than 373 treaties with chieftains of the region between 1886 and 1892. The company administered the region until 1900, when it sold its right to the British government for £865,000, thereby laying the basis for the British colony of Nigeria.

QUESTIONS FOR ANALYSIS

1. By accepting this treaty, what were the chieftains giving up?
2. What benefits were the Africans to receive by signing the treaty?
3. What does use of the standard treaty signify about British attitudes toward and knowledge of the Africans?
4. What does the treaty indicate about the motives of the British in Africa?

We, the undersigned Chiefs of ____, with the view to the bettering of the condition of our country and people, do this day cede to the Royal Niger Company, for ever, the whole of our territory extending from ____.

We also give to the said Royal Niger Company full power to settle all native disputes arising from any cause whatever, and we pledge ourselves not to enter into any war with other tribes without the sanction of the said Royal Niger Company.

We understand that the said Royal Niger Company have full power to mine, farm, and build in any portion of our country.

We bind ourselves not to have any intercourse with any strangers or foreigners except through the said Royal Niger Company.

In consideration of the foregoing, the said Royal Niger Company (Chartered and Limited) bind themselves not to interfere with any of the native laws or customs of the country, consistently with the maintenance of order and good government.

The said Royal Niger Company agree to pay native owners of land a reasonable amount for any portion they may require.

The said Royal Niger Company bind themselves to protect the said Chiefs from the attacks of any neighboring aggressive tribes.

The said Royal Niger Company also agree to pay the said Chiefs ____ measures native value.

We, the undersigned witnesses, do hereby solemnly declare that the ____ Chiefs whose names are placed opposite their respective crosses have in our presence affixed their crosses of their own free will and consent, and that the said ____ has in our presence affixed his signature.

Done in triplicate at ____, this ____ day of ____, 188____.

Declaration by interpreter I, ____, of ____, do hereby solemnly declare that I am well acquainted with the language of the country, and that on the ____ day of ____, 188____, I truly and faithfully explained the above Agreement to all the Chiefs present, and that they understood its meaning.

The Fate of the Ndbele

▼▼▼

57 ▾ *Ndansi Kumalo, HIS STORY*

In the early nineteenth century, the Ndebele were pastoralists living in southeastern Africa, a region experiencing political turmoil and economic hardship caused by overpopulation and drought. In the 1820s they fled from the warriors of the Zulu chieftain Shaka, who had created a formidable Zulu state in southeastern Africa. The Ndebele moved to a region north of the Vaal River but ten years later were forced off their land by Boer *trekkers*, Dutch pioneers from the south seeking grazing land for their cattle. The Ndebele moved north of the Limpopo River to a region that is part of present-day Zimbabwe. Despite their years of flight, here they established a sizable kingdom with a population of 100,000.

But the Ndebele could not escape danger. This time it came from the British, who, under the famous imperialist Cecil Rhodes, were anxious to exploit the region's mineral wealth. In 1888 the Ndebele chieftain, Lobengula, signed an agreement with Rhodes that gave the South Africa Company mining rights in exchange for 1,000 rifles and a monthly stipend of £100. Friction grew when European settlers began establishing farmsteads around 1890, and war broke out in 1893. The Ndebele were defeated, and they were defeated again when they rose up against

the British in 1897 and 1898. The Ndebele then made one last journey to a vast but arid reservation provided by their new masters.

One of the Ndebele who made this journey was Ndansi Kumalo. Born in the late 1870s, he was raised as a warrior. He fought against the British in the 1890s and took up farming after the Ndebele's defeat. In 1932 he caught the attention of a British filmmaker who was in Southern Rhodesia to make *Rhodes of Africa*, on the life of Cecil Rhodes. Ndansi Kumalo was recruited to play the part of Lobengula, the Ndebele chieftain. To complete the film, he traveled to England, where he took in the sights of London and flew for the first time. He also related his life story to the English Africanist Margery Perham, whose transcription of it serves as the basis for the following excerpt. *Rhodes of Africa* was a modest success, and after it opened, Ndansi Kumalo returned to Africa. In the following excerpt, he describes events of the 1890s.

QUESTIONS FOR ANALYSIS

1. What led to the outbreak of hostilities between the Ndebele and the British in 1893?
2. How did conditions following the war lead to the 1897 rebellion?
3. The condition of the Ndebele rapidly deteriorated after the suppression of the rebellion. Why?
4. Aside from raising revenue, what might the British have hoped to achieve by imposing, and then raising, taxes on the Ndebele?
5. What economic changes did the Ndebele experience as a result of their subjection to the Europeans?
6. Do you agree with Ndansi Kumalo that the arrival of Europeans was a mixed blessing? Why?

We were terribly upset and very angry at the coming of the white men, for Lobengula . . . was under her . . . [The Queen's] protection and it was quite unjustified that white men should come with force into our country.[1] . . . Lobengula had no war in his heart: he had always protected the white men and been good to them. If he had meant war, would he have sent our regiments far away to the north at this moment? As far as I know the trouble [in 1893] began in this way. Gandani, a chief who was sent out, reported that some of the Mashona[2] had taken the king's cattle; some regiments were detailed to follow and recover them. . . . Gandani had strict instructions not to molest the white people established in certain parts and to confine himself to the people who had taken the cattle. The commander was given a letter which he had to produce to the Europeans and tell them what the object of the party was. But the members of the party were restless and went without reporting to the white people and killed a lot of Mashonas. The pioneers were very angry and said, "You have trespassed into our part. . . . You have done wrong, you

[1]In the agreement Lobengula signed with Rhodes in 1888, the British government (Her Majesty's government) guaranteed there would be no English settlers on Ndebele land and no decrease in Lobengula's authority.

[2]Pastoralists subject to the Ndebele. Also known as Shona.

should have brought the letter first and then we should have given you permission to follow the cattle." The commander received orders from the white people to get out, and up to a certain point which he could not possibly reach in the time allowed. A force followed them up and they defended themselves. When the pioneers turned out there was a fight at Shangani and at Bembezi. . . .

The next news was that the white people had entered Bulawayo; the King's kraal[3] had been burnt down and the King had fled. Of the cattle very few were recovered; most fell into the hands of the white people. Only a very small portion were found and brought to Shangani where the King was, and we went there to give him any assistance we could. . . . Three of our leaders mounted their horses and followed up the King and he wanted to know where his cattle were; they said they had fallen into the hands of the whites, only a few were left. He said, "Go back and bring them along." But they did not go back again; the white forces had occupied Bulawayo and they went into the Matoppos. Then the white people came to where we were living and sent word round that all chiefs and warriors should go into Bulawayo and discuss peace, for the King had gone and they wanted to make peace. . . . The white people said, "Now that your King has deserted you, we occupy your country. Do you submit to us?" What could we do? "If you are sincere, come back and bring in all your arms, guns, and spears." We did so. . . .

So we surrendered to the white people and were told to go back to our homes and live our usual lives and attend to our crops. But the white men sent native police who did abominable things; they were cruel and assaulted a lot of our people and helped themselves to our cattle and goats. These policemen were not our own people; anybody was made a policeman. We were treated like slaves. They came and were overbearing and we were ordered to carry their clothes and bundles. They interfered with our wives and our daughters and molested them. In fact, the treatment we received was intolerable. We thought it best to fight and die rather than bear it. How the rebellion [of 1897] started I do not know; there was no organization, it was like a fire that suddenly flames up. We had been flogged by native police and then they rubbed salt water in the wounds. There was much bitterness because so many of our cattle were branded and taken away from us; we had no property, nothing we could call our own. We said, "It is no good living under such conditions; death would be better — let us fight." . . . We knew that we had very little chance because their weapons were so much superior to ours. But we meant to fight to the last, feeling that even if we could not beat them we might at least kill a few of them and so have some sort of revenge.

I fought in the rebellion. We used to look out for valleys where the white men were likely to approach. We took cover behind rocks and trees and tried to ambush them. We were forced by the nature of our weapons not to expose ourselves. I had a gun, a breech-loader. They — the white men — fought us with big guns and Maxims[4] and rifles.

I remember a fight in the Matoppos when we charged the white men. There were some hundreds of us; the white men also were as many. We charged them at close quarters: we thought we had a good chance to kill them but the Maxims were too much for us. We drove them off at the first charge, but they returned and formed up again. We made a second charge, but they were too strong for us. I cannot say how many white people were killed, but we think it was quite a lot. . . . Many of our people were killed in this fight: I saw four of my cousins shot. One was shot in the jaw and the whole of his face was blown away — like this — and he died. One was hit between the eyes; another here, in the

---

[3]The stockade where the king lived.

[4]Invented by the American-born engineer Hiram S. Maxim, the Maxim gun was an early machine gun.

shoulder; another had part of his ear shot off. We made many charges but each time we were beaten off, until at last the white men packed up and retreated. But for the Maxims, it would have been different. . . .

So peace was made. Many of our people had been killed, and now we began to die of starvation; and then came the rinderpest[5] and the cattle that were still left to us perished. We could not help thinking that all these dreadful things were brought by the white people. We struggled, and the Government helped us with grain; and by degrees we managed to get crops and pulled through. Our cattle were practically wiped out, but a few were left and from them we slowly bred up our herds again. We were offered work in the mines and farms to earn money and so were able to buy back some cattle. At first, of course, we were not used to going out to work, but advice was given that the chief should advise the young people to go out to work, and gradually they went. At first we received a good price for our cattle and sheep and goats. Then the tax came. It was 10s.[6] a year. Soon the Government said, "That is too little, you must contribute more; you must pay £1." We did so. Then those who took more than one wife were taxed; 10s. for each additional wife. The tax is heavy, but that is not all. We are also taxed for our dogs; 5s. for a dog. Then we were told we were living on private land; the owners wanted rent in addition to the Government tax; some 10s. some £1, some £2 a year. . . .

Would I like to have the old days back? Well, the white men have brought some good things. For a start, they brought us European implements — plows; we can buy European clothes, which are an advance. The Government has arranged for education and through that, when our children grow up, they may rise in status. We want them to be educated and civilized and make better citizens. . . . But, under the white people, we still have our troubles. Economic conditions are telling on us very severely. We are on land where the rainfall is scanty, and things will not grow well. In our own time we could pick our own country, but now all the best land has been taken by the white people. We get hardly any price for our cattle; we find it hard to meet our money obligations. If we have crops to spare we get very little for them . . . but all the same our taxes do not diminish. We see no prosperous days ahead of us. There is one thing we think an injustice. When we have plenty of grain the prices are very low, but the moment we are short of grain and we have to buy from Europeans at once the price is high. If when we have hard times and find it difficult to meet our obligations some of these burdens were taken off us it would gladden our hearts. As it is, if we do raise anything, it is never our own: all, or most of it, goes back in taxation. We can never save any money. If we could, we could help ourselves: we could build ourselves better houses; we could buy modern means of traveling about, a cart, or donkeys or mules. . . .

There are five schools in our district. Quite a number of people are Christians, but I am too old to change my ways. In our religion we believe that when anybody dies the spirit remains and we often make offerings to the spirits to keep them good-tempered. But now the making of offerings is dying out rapidly, for every member of the family should be present, but the children are Christians and refuse to come, so the spirit-worship is dying out. A good many of our children go to the mines in the Union, for the wages are better there. Unfortunately a large number do not come back at all. And some send money to their people — others do not. Some men have even deserted their families, their wives, and children. If they cannot go by train they walk long distances.

---

[5]An acute infectious disease of cattle.

[6]s. = shilling, one-twentieth of a pound.

Imperialist Economics and Rebellion in German East Africa

▼▼▼

58 ▾ RECORDS OF THE MAJI-MAJI REBELLION

The Germans were latecomers to imperialism, but after they gained control of territories in Africa and Oceania, they were quick to adopt the view that colonies existed to serve the economic interests of the colonial master. This clearly was the principle that underlay their policies in German East Africa, a large and politically diverse region on Africa's east coast, surrounded by Kenya to the north, the Belgian Congo to the west, and Northern Rhodesia and Mozambique to the south. At first administered in the 1880s by the German East Africa Company, the colony came under direct control of the German government in 1890. German economic policy lacked direction in the 1880s and 1890s as the Germans struggled to overcome African resistance and experimented with several strategies to force Africans to grow crops the Germans needed for their home industries, especially cotton.

In 1902 the Germans implemented a plan to increase cotton cultivation in the coastal and southern sections of the colony. It required each village to provide a quota of laborers to work cultivating cotton a certain number of days a year on government estates, settler plantations, or village fields. To encourage Africans to accept these low-paying jobs, the Germans instituted a head tax payable in cash only. African opposition to the plan led to rebellion in 1905. Encouraged by religious leaders who supplied the rebels with *maji*, a magic water that supposedly made warriors impervious to bullets, the rebellion spread throughout the colony's central and southern regions. The Germans fought back with Maxim guns, mass executions, and the burning of villages. The rebellion ended in 1907, at a cost of 75,000 African deaths, many the result of famine.

The following testimony was gathered by German officials in the wake of the rebellion. Most of the information deals with the experiences of the Matumbi, highlanders who lived in the southeastern part of the colony.

QUESTIONS FOR ANALYSIS

1. What do these records and testimonies reveal about Germany's administration of its colony?
2. Why did the Africans object so strongly to German agricultural policy?
3. What other aspects of German rule did the Africans find objectionable?
4. What does the source reveal about German views of Africans and Germany's African colonies?
5. What information does the source provide about the role of women in the African village?

[RECOLLECTION OF AMBROSE NGOMBALE MWIRU CONCERNING THE ARRIVAL OF A GERMAN AGENT IN 1897]

Then when that European arrived he asked, "Why did you not answer the call by drum to pay tax?" And they said, "We do not owe you anything. We have no debt to you. If you as a stranger want to stay in this country, then you will have to ask us [for permission]. Then we will ask of you an offering to propitiate the gods. You will offer something and we will propitiate the gods on your behalf; we will give you land and you will get a place to stay in. But it is not for us as hosts to give you the offering. That is quite impossible."

[RECOLLECTIONS OF NDUNDULE MANGAYA]

The cultivation of cotton was done by turns. Every village was allotted days on which to cultivate at Samanga Ndumbo [a coastal town] and at the Jumbe's[1] plantation. One person came from each homestead, unless there were very many people. Thus you might be told to work for five or ten days at Samanga. So a person would go. Then after half the number of days another man came from home to relieve him. . . . It was also like this at the Jumbe's. If you returned from Samanga then your turn at the Jumbe's remained, or if you began at the Jumbe's you waited for the turn at Samanga after you had finished. No woman went unless her husband ran away; then they would say she had hidden him. Then the woman would go. When in a village a former clan head was seized to go to cultivate he would offer his slave in his stead. Then after arriving there you all suffered very greatly. Your back and your buttocks were whipped, and there was no rising up once you stooped to dig. The good thing about the Germans was that all people were the same before the whip. If a Jumbe or akida[2] made a mistake he received the whip as well. Thus there were people whose job was to clear the land of trees and undergrowth; others tilled the land; others would smooth the field and plant; another group would do the weeding and yet another the picking; and lastly others carried the bales of cotton to the coast. . . . We did not get anything. In addition, people suffered much from the cotton, which took three months to ripen and was picked in the fourth. Now digging and planting were in the months of Ntandatu and Nchimbi, and this was the time of very many wild pigs[3] in this country. If you left the chasing of the pigs to the women she could not manage well at night. In addition, the pigs are very stubborn at that period and will not move even if you go within very close range. Only very few women can assist their husbands at night and these are the ones with very strong hearts. There were just as many birds, and if you did not have children it was necessary to help your wife drive away the birds, while at the same time you cleared a piece of land for the second maize crop, because your wife would not have time. And during this very period they still wanted you to leave your home and go to Samanga or to work on the jumbe's plantation. This was why people became furious and angry. The work was astonishingly hard and full of grave suffering, but its wages were the whip on one's back and buttocks. And yet he [the German] still wanted us to pay him the tax. Were we not human beings? And Wamatumbi . . . since the days of old, did not want to be troubled or ruled by any person. They were really fierce, ah! Given such grave suffering they thought it better for a man to die rather than live in such torment.

Thus they hated the rule which was too cruel. It was not because of agriculture, not at all. If it had been good agriculture which had meaning and profit, who would have given himself up to

[1]A chief or headman given low-level administrative responsibilities by the Germans.

[2]Usually Muslims recruited from coastal towns who functioned as overseers or guards.

[3]A threat to cultivated crops.

die? Earlier they had made troubles as well, but when he [the Germans] began to cause us to cultivate cotton for him and to dig roads and so on, then people said, "This has now become an absolute ruler. Destroy him."

[RECOLLECTION OF NDULI NJIMBWI CONCERNING WORK ON A PLANTATION OWNED BY A GERMAN SETTLER NAMED STEINHAGEN]

During the cultivation there was much suffering. We, the labor conscripts, stayed in the front line cultivating. Then behind us was an overseer whose work it was to whip us. Behind the overseer there was a jumbe, and every jumbe stood behind his fifty men. Behind the line of jumbes stood Bwana Kinoo [Steinhagen] himself. . . . [T]he overseer had a whip, and he was extremely cruel. His work was to whip the conscripts if they rose up or tried to rest, or if they left a trail of their footprints behind them.[4] Ah, brothers, God is great — that we have lived like this is God's Providence! And on the other side Bwana Kinoo had a bamboo stick. If the men of a certain jumbe left their footprints behind them, that jumbe would be boxed on the ears and Kinoo would beat him with the bamboo stick using both hands, while at the same time the overseer lashed out at us laborers.

[EXCERPTS FROM AN INTERVIEW WITH A GERMAN OFFICIAL VON GEIBLER CONCERNING THE COMMUNAL PLOTS]

Village plots were set up in each headman's area early in 1902 (September–October). Bushland was mainly chosen. . . . Each headman made a plot for his area in the neighborhood of his headquarters. The principle was that every 30–50 men were to cultivate $2\frac{1}{2}$ acres. . . . Where possible, the advice of the natives was obtained as to the crop to be grown. So far as possible, one crop was to be grown on each plot, according to the type of soil. Some 2,000 acres were cleared and cultivated. . . .

In 1903–04 it was ordered that each village plot should be extended by at least a quarter. The total area in that year came to 3,215 acres. Maize, millet, simsim [sesame], groundnuts, rice, and coconut palms were grown during 1902–03. Cotton was added in 1903–04.

No extension took place in 1904–05, but the cultivation of other crops was abandoned in favor of cotton.

What was the labor situation and the supervision?

. . . According to returns by the headmen, the number of able-bodied men amounted to:

1902–03	c. 25,000 men
1903–04	c. 26,000 men
1904–05	c. 25,000 men

During the last year, women and children had to be brought in to help, since the men frequently refused to work. . . .

The akidas were relied upon to report on the condition of the plots, and they were also responsible for punishing those whom the headmen reported as refractory workers. There was no European control of this — who among the natives worked, and for how many days — although agricultural students (some of them children) were sent out, each with a note-book, to judge the condition of the plots and the work performed, and to report to the District Officer. Only once a year did a European visit the plots, to measure them out and select the land. No lists of workers were kept anywhere; the profits were distributed only according to the total numbers. Work on most of the plots was *flatly* refused during 1904–05. The headmen complained that

[4]Such a trail would have meant the person had walked away from his assigned work.

they no longer had the people in hand. The officials of the Commune believed at the time that they could detect a state of ferment.

Were refractory workers punished, and by whom?

Last year (1904–05), the following reports from the akidas and from Sergeant Holzhausen, who was sent to inspect the headmen, numerous headmen were punished by the District Office with imprisonment in chains or solitary confinement for totally neglecting their village plots as a result of the natives' refusal to work. The last, in June, was headman Kibasila, who got one month in chains.

Southwest Asia Under Siege

The nineteenth century confirmed what had been apparent for at least a century, namely that misgovernment, economic stagnation, and military neglect had enfeebled the once-powerful and culturally sophisticated Persian and Ottoman empires. The Ottoman Empire lost its territories in North Africa and southeastern Europe, and it escaped military defeats by Russia and its onetime province, Egypt, only because Great Britain and France dreaded the consequences of its disintegration and intervened. Persia lost territory on each side of the Caspian Sea to Russia and lands around the Persian Gulf to Great Britain. At times Russian and British consular officials in Tehran, not the shah, appeared to be in charge of Persian affairs. Economic development in the region mainly benefited European businessmen. Ottoman, Persian, and Egyptian governments all welcomed European investors and borrowed heavily from European financiers, who then "rescued" them from their debts in return for monopolies, control of governmental expenditures, and a cut of tax revenues.

Intellectuals, military men, and religious leaders in the region debated the causes and significance of these developments, and government officials, especially within the Ottoman state, took action by implementing reforms. Such reformers loosely fit into one of two categories. Moderates sought to reorganize the army, end corruption, improve tax collection, and reform the judiciary while preserving the authority of traditional rulers. These were the goals, for example, of Ottoman reforms under Selem III (1789–1807) and during the so-called era of *Tanzimat* (restructuring), which took place under Sultan Abdul Majid (r. 1839–1861). Reformers in this camp cautiously approved greater intellectual and cultural contacts with the West and accepted the need for European investment. By the 1870s in the Ottoman Empire and the 1890s in Persia, reformers went further; they advocated acceptance of Western science and secularism and demanded parliaments, written constitutions, elections, and guarantees of individual freedoms.

Reformers in both camps faced formidable obstacles. Powerful families and well-placed officials who benefited from the status quo naturally opposed them. So did many religious leaders, who feared that all reforms at some level were European-inspired and thus threatened Islam by encouraging secularization. True reform, they believed, would come not from modern weapons and new law codes, but from rededication to Islam.

The reformers' biggest obstacle was lack of money. The costs of modern armies, schools, roads, telegraph lines, bridges, and steamships outstripped revenues, forcing governments to rely on European loans and investments and accept European control of taxes and expenditures. In other words, the reformers' policies fostered greater economic dependency on the West, one of the things they most wished to avoid.

In the end, reformers in the Middle East were unable to halt Western intervention or stave off political disaster. Egypt remained a British protectorate. In 1907 Persia was divided into a Russian north and a British south, with only the central portion under the control of the Qajars, who were overthrown by a military coup in 1925. The Ottoman Empire lost all but a tiny sliver of its European territories as a result of the Balkan Wars of 1912 and 1913 and lost its Arab provinces during World War I. It disappeared altogether when the sultan's government was overthrown by Turkish nationalists in 1920 and replaced by the present-day state of Turkey.

Persian Opposition to the Tobacco Concession

59 ▾ *Sayyid Jamal ad-Din, LETTER TO HASAN SHIRAZI*

European imperialism did not always involve gunboats, invading armies, and control by colonial administrators. It frequently had more to do with economics than politics. The Ottoman Empire and Persia, for example, remained independent states in the 1800s, but their finances and economies were increasingly controlled and manipulated by European bondholders, bankers, businessmen, and speculators. Their experiences are as much a part of the West's imperialist expansion as those of India, Africa, and Southeast Asia.

For Persia, economic imperialism was epitomized by the numerous concessions granted to foreign businessmen by the shah's government. These agreements gave Europeans control of a sector of the nation's economy, usually in return for a one-time payment and a percentage of profits. Viewed as a painless way to attract foreign capital, solve budget problems, and generate bribes, such arrangements were irresistible to Persian officials. Hundreds of concessions were granted for activities ranging from railroad construction to the administration of a national lottery.

As the number of concessions mounted in the 1870s and 1880s, many Persians became increasingly frustrated over their inability to dissuade their autocratic and concession-loving ruler, Shah Nasir al-Din, from selling off the nation's economic future to foreigners. This changed, however, in 1891, when for the first time in history a government abandoned an unpopular policy after the population "kicked the habit" and (temporarily) gave up tobacco smoking.

In 1891 Persians learned of a new concession granted to the British Imperial Tobacco Corporation for the purchase, processing, and sale of tobacco throughout Persia, for which it paid the shah £15,000 and promised him 25 percent of the profits. The English expected profits of approximately £500,000 per year, while the

Persian faced the prospect of paying inflated prices for a product they grew, used heavily, and previously had marketed themselves. Persia erupted with demonstrations, angry sermons, calls for boycotts, destruction of tobacco warehouses, and denunciations of the shah. Then in December Persia's most prominent Shia religious leader, Hasan Shirazi, ordered Persians to stop smoking until the concession was lifted. The nation obeyed, and the concession was soon canceled.

A key figure in the campaign against the tobacco concession was the intellectual Sayyid Jamal ad-Din. Born in 1838 or 1839 in Persia and raised as a Shia, he was educated in Persia, learned of the West while visiting British India and Europe, and traveled and taught throughout the Middle East. In his many writings and speeches, Jamal ad-Din blended Islamic traditionalism with a selective acceptance of Western science, technology, and values. He taught that only a religious and intellectual revival that transcended state boundaries and sectarian differences could save Islam from subservience to the West.

After he moved to Tehran in 1889, Jamal ad-Din became a vocal critic of the shah. Fearing arrest, he sought sanctuary at a religious shrine, but the shah's soldiers forcefully removed him in January 1891 and deported him to Ottoman territory. From exile, in April 1891 he wrote the following letter to the Shia leader Hasan Shirazi. It is unclear how much influence the letter had, but as Jamal ad-Din had hoped, Shirazi did abandon his apolitical stance by denouncing the shah and issuing the antismoking decree.

The shah stayed in power and the foreigners remained, but for the first time in their modern history, all Persians, rural and urban, religious and secular, had united for a political end. Such unity of purpose reappeared in the Persian Revolution of 1906, which briefly established a parliamentary government.

QUESTIONS FOR ANALYSIS

1. What strategies does Jamal ad-Din use to convince Hasan Shirazi that he should speak out against the shah? What does he claim would be the consequences of inaction?
2. According to Jamal ad-Din, what are the personal faults of the shah? Are his criticisms based more on religious or nonreligious considerations?
3. What has been the result of the shah's fiscal and economic policies, according to the author?
4. What view of the West is expressed in the letter?
5. What seems to be Jamal ad-Din's vision of Persia's future?
6. What does the letter reveal about the prospects for and progress of reform in Persia?

Your Reverence . . . Hasan Shirazi — may God protect by your means the fold of Islam, and avert the plots of the vile unbelievers!—

God has set you apart . . . and has committed to your hands the reins to guide the people obediently to the most luminous Law, and thus to protect their rights, and to guard their hearts from errors and doubts. He has entrusted to you out of all mankind (so that you have become the heir of the Prophet) the care of those weighty interests by which the people shall prosper in this world and attain happiness in the hereafter. He has assigned to you the throne of authority, and has bestowed on you such supremacy over his people as empowers you to save and defend their country and testify for them to the ways of those who have gone before. . . .

O most mighty Religious Guide! Verily the Shah's purpose wavers, his character is impure, his perceptions are failing and his heart is corrupt. He is incapable of governing the land, or managing the affairs of his people, and has entrusted the reins of government in all things great and small to the hands of a wicked freethinker,[1] a tyrant and usurper, who reviles the Prophets openly, and heeds not God's Law, who counts for nothing the religious authorities, curses the doctors of the Law, rejects the pious, . . . and treats preachers as one would treat the vilest of mankind. Moreover since his return from Europe he has taken the bit between his teeth, drinks wine openly,[2] associates with unbelievers and displays enmity toward the virtuous. Such is his private conduct; but in addition to this he has sold to the foes of our Faith the greater part of the Persian lands and the profits derived from them, for example, the mines, the roads leading to them, the roads connecting them with the frontiers of the country, the inns about to be built by the side of these extensive means of travel which will spread out through all parts of the kingdom, and the gardens and fields surrounding them. Also the river Karun[3] and the guesthouses which will arise on its banks up to its very source, and the gardens and meadows which adjoin it, and the highway from Ahwaz to Tehran, with the buildings, inns, gardens, and fields surrounding it. Also tobacco, with the chief centers of its cultivation, the lands on which it is grown, and the warehouses, carriers, and sellers, wherever these are found. He has similarly disposed of the grapes used for making wine, and the shops, factories, and winepresses pertaining to this trade throughout the whole of Persia; and so likewise soap, candles, and sugar, and the factories connected with their manufacture. Lastly there is the Bank:[4] what must you understand about the Bank? It means the complete handing over of the reins of government to the enemy of Islam, the enslaving of the people to that enemy, the surrendering of them and of all dominion and authority into the hands of the foreign foe.

After this the ignorant traitor, desiring to pacify the people by his futile arguments, pretended that these agreements were temporary, and these compacts were only for a limited period which would not exceed a hundred years! God! what an argument, the weakness of which amazed even the traitors! . . .

In short this criminal has offered the provinces of Persia to auction among the Powers [of Europe], and is selling the realms of Islam and the abodes of Muhammad and his household (on whom be greeting and salutation) to foreigners. But by reason of the vileness of his nature and meanness of his understanding he sells them for a paltry sum and at a wretched price. (Yea, thus it is when meanness and avarice are mingled with treason and folly!)

And you, . . . if you will not arise to help this people, and will not unite them in purpose, and pluck them forth, by the power of the Holy Law from the hands of this sinner, verily the realms of Islam will soon be under the control of foreigners, who will rule . . . as they please and do what they will. If this opportunity is lost . . . and this thing happens while you are alive, verily you will not leave behind . . . a fair record in the register of time and on the pages of history. And you know that the *ulama*[5] of Persia and the Persian people . . . with one accord . . . await a word from you with which they shall behold their happiness and by which their deliverance shall be effected. How then can it seem that one on

[1]Amin al-Sultan, the shah's grand vizier.

[2]A forbidden act according to the Quran.

[3]In 1888 an Englishman had been granted a concession to open steamship traffic on the Karun River.

[4]The Imperial Bank of Persia had been granted a sixty-year concession to issue bank notes and carry on other banking activities.

[5]Those learned in religion.

whom God has bestowed such power as this to be so reluctant to use it or to leave it suspended?

I further assure Your Eminence, speaking as one who knows and seeks, that the Ottoman Government will rejoice in your undertaking of this effort and will aid you in it, for it is well aware that the intervention of Europeans in the Persian domains and their ascendancy there will assuredly prove injurious to its own dominions. Moreover all the ministers and lords of Persia will rejoice in a word in this sense uttered by you, seeing that all of them naturally detest these innovations and are constitutionally opposed to these agreements, which your actions will give them the opportunity to annul, that perhaps they may restrain this evil of covetousness which has been sanctioned and approved. . . . All is from you, by you and in you, and you are responsible for all before God and men. . . .

As for my own story and what that ungrateful tyrant did to me . . . the wretch [the shah] commanded me to be dragged, when I was in sanctuary in the shrine of Shah 'Abdu'l-'Azim and grievously ill, through the snow to the capital with such circumstances of disrespect, humiliation and disgrace as cannot be imagined for wickedness (and all this after I had been plundered and despoiled). Verily we belong to God and verily unto Him do we return!

Thereafter his miserable lackeys placed me, despite my illness, on a pack-saddle, loading me with chains, and this in the winter season, amid the snow-drifts and bitter, icy blasts, and a company of horsemen conveyed me to Khaniqin,[6] guarded by an escort. And he had previously written to the . . . Turkish governor, requesting him to remove me to Basra, knowing well that, if he left me alone, I should come to you, . . . and inform you of his doings and of the state of the people, and explain to you what had befallen the lands of Islam through the evil deeds of this infidel, and would invoke your help, . . . for the True Faith, and convince you to come to the assistance of the Muslims. For he knew for a certainty that, should I succeed in meeting you, it would not be possible for him to continue in his office, involving as it does the ruin of the country, the destruction of the people, and the encouragement of unbelief. . . . What is this weakness? What this cowardice? How is it possible that a low-born vagabond and contemptible fool should be able to sell the Muslims and their lands for a vile price and a paltry sum . . . ? Is there no hand able to pluck up this evil root and so to appease the wrathful indignation of the Muslims, and avenge the descendants of the Chief of God's Apostles (upon whom and whose household be blessings and salutation)? . . .

Peace be upon thee, and the Mercy of God, and His Blessings.

[6]A Turkish frontier post on the road from Persia to Baghdad.

The Beginnings of Arab Nationalism

▼▼▼

60 ▾ *ANNOUNCEMENT TO THE ARABS, SONS OF QAHTAN*

Of all the non-Turkish ethnic groups in the Ottoman Empire, the Arabs were the sultan's least troublesome. Attached to the Ottoman state through habits of loyalty and their perception that the sultan/caliph was the protector of the Islamic community, the Arabs — unlike Kurds, Armenians, and Balkan Christians — experienced no surge of nationalism and made no demands for independence or greater autonomy. This changed, however, in the early 1900s, when Arab nationalism suddenly emerged. It gained strength during the Arab revolt against the Turks in World War I and has played a significant role in the region's politics to the present day.

Although Arab nationalism emerged on the eve of World War I, its roots go back to the nineteenth century, when publications of Arabic-language printing houses and the establishment of schools and universities in major Arab cities by French Jesuit and American Protestant missionaries sparked interest in Arab history and literature. These schools also introduced Arab students to Western scientific and political ideas. At the same time, continued Ottoman misrule and military losses in the Balkans weakened Arabs' faith in Ottoman rule. The empire, some suggested, was no longer capable of defending the interests of Islam, and a few went further to suggest that the Islamic community would continue to decline until its founders and natural leaders, the Arabs, regained control.

A key event in the history of Arab nationalism was the Young Turk Revolution of 1908. Although many Arabs had supported the Young Turks' political agenda before the revolution, they turned against the new regime after it replaced Arab officials with Turks, stripped many old Arab families of their local authority, mandated the use of Turkish throughout the empire, and encouraged the secularization of education and the law. Arab political organizations formed in Cairo, Beirut, Damascus, Baghdad, and Aleppo, with some advocating greater Arab autonomy within the empire, and others demanding Arab independence.

Independence clearly was the goal of the author or authors of the following "announcement" to the Arabs, which appeared in Cairo in the summer of 1914. It may have been written by a supporter of Major Aziz Ali-al-Misri, a decorated Arab officer in the Ottoman army and founder of the Covenant, an organization of Arab officers dedicated to Arab independence. Arrested and condemned to death by Ottoman officials in early 1914, he was released later in the year and allowed to go to Cairo as a result of foreign pressure and public outcry among the Arabs.

QUESTIONS FOR ANALYSIS

1. The author's nationalism is directed against both the Turks and the West. What, specifically, are his views of each?
2. Does he have a deeper aversion for the Turks or for the Western nations? Why?

3. **In the author's view, what lessons can the Arabs learn from the Armenians?**
4. **How does the author define "Arab"?**
5. **What role does religion play in connection with the author's nationalism? How committed is he to Islam?**
6. **What are the author's goals for the Arab people? How does he believe these goals can be attained?**

O Sons of Qahtan! O Descendants of Adnan![1] Are you asleep? And how long will you remain asleep? . . . When will you realize the truth? When will you know that your country has been sold to the foreigner? See how your natural resources have been alienated from you and have come into the possession of England, France, and Germany. Have you no right to these resources? You have become humiliated slaves in the hands of the usurping tyrant; the foreigner unjustly dispossesses you of the fruit of your work and labor and leaves you to suffer the pangs of hunger. How long will it be before you understand that you have become a plaything in the hand of him who has no religion but to kill the Arabs and forcibly to seize their possessions? The Country is yours, and they say that rule belongs to the people, but those who exercise rule over you . . . do not consider you part of the people, for they inflict on you all kinds of suffering, tyranny, and persecution. How, then, can they concede to you any political rights? In their eyes you are but a flock of sheep whose wool is to be clipped, whose milk is to be drunk, and whose meat is to be eaten. . . .

The Armenians, small as their numbers are when compared to yours, have won their administrative autonomy in spite of the opposition of the Turkish state, and they will presently become independent.[2] Their people will then become self-governing, free and advanced, free and active in the social organization of humanity, in contrast to you, who will remain ever enslaved to the descendants of Genghis and Hulagu[3] who brought to an end your advanced Arab government in Baghdad, the Abode of Peace; and to the descendants of Tamerlane[4] who built a tower composed of the heads of eighty thousand Arabs in Aleppo. Till when will you go on acquiescing in this utter humiliation, when your honor is made free of, your wives raped, your children orphaned, your habitations destroyed, . . . your money taken to be spent in the palaces of Constantinople, full as they are with intoxicating drink, musical instruments, and all kinds of wealth and luxury, and your young men driven to

---

[1]Qahtan, or Kahtan, was supposedly the ancient ancestor of all south Arabs; Adnan was the ancestor of north Arabs.

[2]These claims are exaggerated. Slightly more than 1 million Armenians were Ottoman subjects, with most of them living in eastern Anatolia. An upsurge in Armenian nationalism at the end of the nineteenth century led to a proliferation of Armenian political groups, antigovernment terrorism, and public demonstrations against Turkish rule. Abdul Hamid's government responded by ordering, or at least condoning, massacres of perhaps as many as 100,000 Armenians by Ottoman troops and mobs between 1894 and 1897. Another massacre of approximately 20,000 Armenians took place in 1909. Such atrocities outraged world opinion, and European governments pressured the Ottomans to implement reforms on behalf of the Armenians. In 1914 the Ottoman government and the European powers agreed on a plan to establish two large provinces with heavy Armenian populations in eastern Anatolia and to place them under the administrative authority of Europeans. With the outbreak of World War I, however, the plan was dropped. During the war, government-ordered evacuations of Armenians from their homelands and attacks on Armenian communities resulted in more than 1 million Armenian deaths.

[3]Chinggis Khan (1167–1227) was the Mongol ruler who conquered northern China, central Asia, and Persia; his grandson Hulagu, or Hülegü, led the armies that sacked Baghdad in 1258, killing an estimated 200,000 inhabitants and bringing an end to the Abbasid Dynasty.

[4]Tamerlane (ca. 1336–1405) was a conqueror of Turko-Mongol ancestry. His armies carved out a short-lived empire that stretched from Asia Minor to India. His most notorious custom was to pile his victims' skulls in huge pyramids after a city had been sacked.

fight your Arab brethren. . . . Has your Arab blood become congealed in your veins, and has it changed into dirty water? You have become, by God, a byword among the nations, a laughing-stock of the world, a subject of mockery and derision among the peoples. You have almost become proverbial in your humility, weakness, and acquiescence in great loss.

Compare how well the Turks treat the Armenians and how they seek to humor them, with the harsh treatment which they reserve for you Arabs. See how the Turkish government adopts the stance of obedience before them, how it humbly begs them to accept more than their due share of parliamentary representation. As for you, O how we grieve for you! The government directs against you those armies which had been defeated on the Russian front and in the Balkans,[5] in order to kill you, destroy your liberty, destroy your noble Arab race, and finally to finish you off, as though it can have no power but over you. . . .

O sons of Qahtan! Do you not know that man is meant to live here on earth a goodly life, in honor and prosperity, a life full of spiritual values . . . ? What, then, is the value of life, when honor is stained, possessions robbed, and souls destroyed? What is the meaning of a life spent in humiliation and subjection, without honor, without possessions, without enjoyment of liberty and independence? . . .

O ye Arabs! Warn the people of the Yemen, of Asir, of Nejd, and of Iraq[6] against the intrigues of your enemies. Be united, in the Syrian and Iraqi provinces, with the members of your race and fatherland. Let the Muslims, the Christians, and the Jews be as one in working for the interest of the nation and of the country. You all dwell in one land, you speak one language, so be also one nation and one land. Do not become divided against yourselves according to the designs and purposes of the troublemakers who feign Islam, while Islam is really innocent of their misdeeds. . . .

Unite then and help one another, and do not say, O ye Muslims: This is a Christian, and this is a Jew, for you are all God's dependents, and religion is for God alone. God has commanded us . . . to follow justice and equality, to deal faithfully with him who does not fight us, even though his religion is different, and to fight him who uses us tyrannously. Who, then, have tyrannized over the Arabs? . . . Is it not the band of Constantinople who fight you and seek to exterminate some of the Arabs by means of sword and fire, and others by means of quarrels and dissensions, following the maxim "divide and rule" . . . ?

Every tyrannical government is an enemy and a foe to Islam; how more so, then, if the government destroys Islam, considers it lawful to shed the blood of the people of the Prophet of Islam, and seeks to kill the language of Islam in the name of Islamic government and the Islamic caliphate? . . . Therefore, he who supports these unionists[7] because he considers them Muslims is in clear error, for none of them have done a good deed for Islam. . . . Fanatic in its cause, they fight the Quran and the tradition of the Arabic Prophet. Is this the Islam which it is incumbent on them to respect? It is not notorious that they seek to kill the Arabic language? Did they not write books to show that it must be abandoned, and that prayers and the call to prayers should be made in Turkish? And if Arabic dies, how can the Quran and the traditions live? And if the Book and the traditions cease to be known, what remains of Islam?

---

[5]The Ottoman government had been fighting and losing wars in the Balkans since the 1820s; their most recent defeat had come in the Balkan War of 1912–1913. The last major war with Russia had been fought in 1877 and 1878, with disastrous results for the Ottomans.

[6]Yemen, Asir, and Nejd are all regions of the Arabian Peninsula; Iraq was a province centered on the Tigris/Euphrates rivers. The Ottoman government had sent troops to all these regions to quell disturbances or control local Arab rulers.

[7]Refers to the Committee of Union and Progress, the political party of the Young Turks.

And O ye Christian and Jewish Arabs, combine with your brethren the Muslim Arabs, and do not follow in the footsteps of him who says to you, whether he be one of you or not: The Arab Muslims are sunk in religious fanaticism, therefore we prefer the irreligious Turks. This is nonsensical speech which proceeds from an ignorant man who knows neither his own nor his people's interest. . . . Our ancestors were not fanatical in this sense, for Jews and Christians used to study in the mosques of Baghdad and the Andalus like brethren. Let them, both sides, aim at tolerance and at the removal of these ugly fanaticisms. . . . Combine with your fellow countrymen and your kin, and know that ugly fanaticism will inevitably disappear. A day will come when fanaticism will disappear from our country, leaving no trace, and that day shall be when our affairs will be in our own hands, and when our affairs, our learning, and the verdicts of our courts will be conducted in our own language. If we are united, such a day is not far off. . . .

The reform of which we speak is not on the principle of decentralization coupled with allegiance to the minions of Constantinople, but on the principle of complete independence and the formation of a decentralized Arab state which will revive our ancient glories and rule the country on autonomous lines, according to the needs of each province.

India Under British Domination

As Great Britain took control of India during the nineteenth century, British administrators, policymakers, and the general public all agreed that this new colony should serve the economic interests of the mother country. It would be a source of raw materials, an area for investment, and a market for British manufactured goods. Other issues, however, sparked debate. Most of the British realized that at some point they would leave India and that their colony would become a self-governing, independent state. They had no timetable for leaving, however, and they disagreed about how to prepare their subjects for independence. They would bring some Indians into the colonial administration, but how many and at what levels? They would provide India with schools and colleges, but would they offer Western or traditional Indian learning? They would attempt to "civilize" the Indians, but in doing so, how much traditional Indian culture should be suppressed?

The debate was complicated by sharp disagreements among Indians about their relationship with their colonial masters. At first, many Indians considered British rule a blessing that would enable them to benefit from Western science, constitutional government, and economic development. Such views persisted into the twentieth century, but by the late 1800s only a small minority embraced them unequivocally. Many Indians came to resent the British assumption that Western ways were superior to centuries-old Indian beliefs and practices. They also were offended by Britain's one-sided economic policies, which drained India's resources, stifled development, and damaged traditional industries. Finally, they were angered by Great Britain's reluctance to seriously consider Indian self-rule.

As the following documents reveal, an evaluation of the benefits and the harm of British rule in India is no simple matter. Historians continue to debate the issue down to the present day.

The Case for Western Schools

61 ▾ *Rammohun Roy, LETTER TO LORD AMHERST; Thomas Babington Macaulay, MINUTE ON EDUCATION*

From the 1770s onward, directors of the East India Company, missionaries, and the London government all agreed that Britain had ethical and pragmatic reasons to support schools for their Indian subjects. What they could not agree on was what these schools should teach. At first, the East India Company, in the interest of not disturbing traditional Indian culture and social relationships, sponsored studies in Persian, Arabic, and Sanskrit, the ancient language of India. Such an approach was favored by influential British scholars and intellectuals known as "Orientalists," who greatly admired Indian culture and literature, and most missionaries, who accommodated their Indian audience by learning Indian dialects and translating the Bible into native languages. By the early 1800s, however, many Indians began to demand schools that taught English and Western curricula to prepare them for employment in the civil service. Their views were supported by a growing number of Englishmen, including some missionaries, who saw little or no value in Indian culture or religions and sought to establish schools that would be agents of anglicization. The debate between the two sides began in earnest in 1813, when Parliament voted funds "for the revival and promotion of literature and the encouragement of the learned natives of India" and appointed a Committee on Public Instruction to decide how the funds should be spent.

What follows are excerpts from the writings of two prominent "Anglicists," the Indian Rammohun Roy and the Englishman Thomas Babington Macaulay. Roy, sometimes referred to as "the father of modern India," was born into a devout high-caste Hindu family in 1772. He showed an early genius for languages and a keen interest in religions. By the age of twenty, he had learned Arabic, Persian, Greek, and Sanskrit and had spent five years traveling across India seeking religious enlightenment. He then learned English and entered the service of the East India Company, ultimately attaining the highest administrative rank possible for an Indian. In 1814, at the age of forty-two, he retired to Calcutta, where he founded several newspapers and a number of schools, and campaigned to abolish the practice of widow burning, or *sati*. He also established the Society of God, dedicated to combining Christian ethical teaching with certain Hindu beliefs. He wrote the following letter in 1823 to the British governor-general of India, Lord Amherst (1773–1857), to oppose a British plan to sponsor a school in Calcutta to teach Sanskrit and Hindu literature.

Thomas Babington Macaulay (1800–1859), a noted politician and historian, entered the debate on Indian education in 1833 when he was appointed to the Governor-General's Council after a career in Parliament, in which he fought for voting reform and full religious toleration for Jews. In 1835 he submitted a "minute" (report) to the Committee on Public Instruction in which he made a case for a British-style educational system for India. Although not all of his ideas were implemented until the 1850s, Macaulay's ideas prevailed.

QUESTIONS FOR ANALYSIS

1. **How would you characterize Roy's attitude toward the British? Conversely, how would characterize Macaluay's attitude toward the Indians?**
2. **What do Macaulay and Roy agree upon when they describe the value of Western learning and literature? On what point do they disagree?**
3. **According to both men, what will be the weaknesses of an education based on traditional Indian learning?**
4. **According to Roy, what implications would a Hindu-based educational system have for India's political future?**
5. **What role does Macaulay envision for the Indian students educated in the Western-style schools he advocates?**

RAMMOHOUN ROY, LETTER TO LORD AMHERST (1823)

The establishment of a new Sanskrit School in Calcutta evinces the laudable desire of government to improve the natives of India by education — a blessing for which they must ever be grateful, and every well-wisher of the human race must be desirous that the efforts made to promote it should be guided by the most enlightened principles, so that the stream of intelligence may flow in the most useful channels.

When this seminary of learning was proposed, we understood that the government in England had ordered a considerable sum of money to be annually devoted to the instruction of its Indian subjects. We were filled with sanguine hopes that this sum would be laid out in employing European gentlemen of talent and education to instruct the natives of India in mathematics, natural philosophy, chemistry, anatomy, and other useful sciences, which the natives of Europe have carried to a degree of perfection that has raised them above the inhabitants of other parts of the world. . . .

We find that the government are establishing a Sanskrit school under Hindu pandits[1] to impart such knowledge as is already current in India. This seminary (similar in character to those which existed in Europe before the time of Lord Bacon)[2] can only be expected to load the minds of youth with grammatical niceties and metaphysical distinctions of little or no practical use to the possessors or to society. The pupils will there acquire what was known two thousand years ago with the addition of vain and empty subtleties since then produced by speculative men such as is already commonly taught in all parts of India.

The Sanskrit language, so difficult that almost a lifetime is necessary for its acquisition, is well known to have been for ages a lamentable check to the diffusion of knowledge, and the learning concealed under this almost impervious veil is far from sufficient to reward the labor of acquiring it. . . .

Neither can much improvement arise from such speculations as the following which are the themes suggested by the Vedanta.[3] In what manner is the soul absorbed in the Deity? What relation does it bear to the Divine Essence? Nor will youths be fitted to be better members of society by the Vedantic doctrines which teach them to believe that all visible things have no real existence, that as father, brother, etc., have no real entity, they consequently deserve no real affec-

---

[1]Wise and learned men of Hindu India.

[2]A reference to the English philosopher and prophet of science, Francis Bacon (1561–1626). Excerpts from his New Organon are included in source 8.

[3]A major school of Hindu philosophy based on the study and analysis of three ancient texts, the *Upanishads*, the *Vedanta-sutras*, and the *Bhagavad Gita*.

tion, and therefore the sooner we escape from them and leave the world the better. . . .

If it had been intended to keep the British nation in ignorance of real knowledge, the Baconian philosophy would not have been allowed to displace the system of the schoolmen which was the best calculated to perpetuate ignorance. In the same manner the Sanskrit system of education would be the best calculated to keep this country in darkness, if such had been the policy of the British legislature. But as the improvement of the native population is the object of the government, it will consequently promote a more liberal and enlightened system of instruction, embracing mathematics, natural philosophy, chemistry, anatomy, with other useful sciences, which may be accomplished with the sums proposed by employing a few gentlemen of talent and learning educated in Europe and providing a college furnished with necessary books, instruments, and other apparatus.

In presenting this subject to your Lordship, I conceive myself discharging a solemn duty which I owe to my countrymen, and also to that enlightened sovereign and legislature which have extended their benevolent care to this distant land, actuated by a desire to improve the inhabitants, and therefore humbly trust you will excuse the liberty I have taken in thus expressing my sentiments to your Lordship.

THOMAS MACAULAY, MINUTE ON EDUCATION (1835)

All parties seem to be agreed on one point, that the dialects commonly spoken among the natives of this part of India [Bengal] contain neither literary nor scientific information, and are, moreover, so poor and rude that, until they are enriched from some other quarter, it will not be easy to translate any valuable work into them. It seems to be admitted on all sides that the intellectual improvement of those classes of the people who have the means of pursuing higher studies can at present be effected only by means of some language not vernacular amongst them. . . .

I have no knowledge of either Sanscrit or Arabic. But I have done what I could to form a correct estimate of their value. I have read translations of the most celebrated Arabic and Sanscrit works. I have conversed both here and at home with men distinguished by their proficiency in the Eastern tongues. I am quite ready to take the Oriental learning at the valuation of the Orientalists themselves. I have never found one among them who could deny that a single shelf of a good European library was worth the whole native literature of India and Arabia. . . . It is, I believe, no exaggeration to say, that all the historical information which has been collected from all the books written in the Sanscrit language is less valuable than what may be found in the most paltry abridgments used at preparatory schools in England. In every branch of physical or moral philosophy, the relative position of the two nations is nearly the same. . . .

. . . The claims of our own language it is hardly necessary to recapitulate. It stands preeminent even among the languages of the West. . . . Whoever knows that language has ready access to all the vast intellectual wealth, which all the wisest nations of the earth have created and hoarded in the course of ninety generations. It may safely be said that the literature now extant in that language is of far greater value than all the literature which three hundred years ago was extant in all the languages of the world together. . . .

The question now before us is simply whether, when it is in our power to teach this language, we shall teach languages in which, by universal confession, there are no books on any subject which deserve to be compared to our own; whether, when we can teach European science, we shall teach systems which, by universal confession, whenever they differ from those of Europe, differ for the worse; and whether, when we can patronize sound philosophy and true history, we shall countenance, at the public expense, medical doctrines which would disgrace an English farrier, astronomy which would move laughter in girls at an English boarding school, history abounding with kings thirty feet high and reigns thirty thousand years long, and geography, made up of seas of treacle and seas of butter. . . .

In one point I fully agree with the gentlemen to whose general views I am opposed. I feel with them, that it is impossible for us, with our limited means, to attempt to educate the body of the people. We must at present do our best to form a class who may be interpreters between us and the millions whom we govern; a class of persons, Indian in blood and color, but English in taste, in opinions, in morals, and in intellect. To that class we may leave it to refine the vernacular dialects of the country, to enrich those dialects with terms of science borrowed from the Western nomenclature, and to render them by degrees fit vehicles for conveying knowledge to the great mass of the population. . . .

The Pros and Cons of British Rule

62 ▾ *Dadabhai Naoroji, 1871 LONDON SPEECH*

The man who best symbolized India's growing ambivalence about British rule in the late 1800s was Dadabhai Naoroji (1825–1917). Born into a prosperous Bombay (present-day Mumbai) family, he abandoned a promising career as a mathematician at the age of thirty and moved to London, where he believed he could work effectively for the improvement of conditions in India. In 1892, running as a candidate for the Liberal Party, he became the first Indian to be elected to the British Parliament. In 1885, during one of his many return visits to India, he was instrumental in the founding of the Indian National Congress, an organization of moderate, largely middle-class Indians who sought more governmental responsibility and a greater say in policy-making.

Naoroji made the following evaluation of Britain's impact on India in response to a question following a speech he delivered in 1871 to a learned society in London. It later was published in a collection of his works that appeared in 1887. He begins by discussing the "credit," or benefit, of British rule.

QUESTIONS FOR ANALYSIS

1. **What does Naoroji regard as Britain's most important contributions to India's development?**
2. **In his view, in what areas have the British failed India?**
3. **According to Naoroji, how can India's problems be solved, short of independence?**
4. **To what extent would Naoroji's remarks have pleased Rammohun Roy?**

Credit — *In the Cause of Humanity:* Abolition of suttee [sati] and infanticide.

Destruction of Dacoits, Thugs, Pindarees,[1] and other such pests of Indian society.

Remarriage of Hindu widows, and charitable aid in time of famine.

Glorious work all this, of which any nation may well be proud, and such as has not fallen to the lot of any people in the history of mankind.

[1]Thieves, highway murderers, and robber bands.

In the Cause of Civilization: Education, both male and female. Though yet only partial, an inestimable blessing as far as it has gone, and leading gradually to the destruction of superstition, and many moral and social evils. Resuscitation of India's own noble literature, modified and refined by the enlightenment of the West. . . .

Politically: Peace and order. Freedom of speech and liberty of the press. Higher political knowledge and aspirations. Improvement of government in the native States. Security of life and property. Freedom from oppression caused by the caprice or avarice of despotic rulers, and from devastation by war. Equal justice between man and man (sometimes vitiated by partiality to Europeans). Service of highly educated administrators, who have achieved the above-mentioned good result.

Materially: Loans for railways and irrigation. . . . The development of a few valuable products, such as indigo, tea, coffee, silk, &c. Increase of exports. Telegraphs.

Generally: A slowly growing desire of late to treat India equitably, and as a country held in trust. Good intentions.

No nation on the face of the earth has ever had the opportunity of achieving such a glorious work as this. I hope in this credit side of the account I have done no injustice, and if I have omitted any item which anyone may think of importance, I shall have the greatest pleasure in inserting it. I appreciate, and so do my countrymen, what England has done for India, and I know that it is only in British hands that her regeneration can be accomplished. Now for the debit side.

Debit — *In the Cause of Humanity:* Nothing. Everything, therefore, is in your favor under this head.

In the Cause of Civilization: As I have said already, there has been a failure to do as much as might have been done, but I put nothing to the debit. . . .

Politically: Repeated breach of pledges to give the natives a fair and reasonable share in the higher administration of their own country, which has much shaken confidence in the good faith of the British word. Political aspirations and the legitimate claim to have reasonable voice in the legislation and the imposition and disbursement of taxes, met to a very slight degree, thus treating the natives of India not as British subjects, to whom representation is a birthright. . . .

Consequent on the above, an utter disregard of the feelings and views of the natives. The great moral evil of the drain of the wisdom and practical administration and statesmanship, leaving none to guide the rising generation. . . .

Financially: All attention is engrossed in devising new modes of taxation, without any adequate effort to increase the means of the people to pay; and the consequent vexation and oppressiveness of the taxes imposed, imperial and local. Inequitable financial relations between England and India, i.e., the political debt of £100,000,000 clapped on India's shoulders, and all home charges also, though the British exchequer contributes nearly £3,000,000 to the expenses of the colonies. . . .

Materially: The political drain,[2] up to this time, from India to England, of above £500,000,000 at the lowest computation, in principal alone, which with interest would be some thousands of millions. The further continuation of this drain at the rate, at present, of above £12,000,000, with a tendency to increase. . . .

The consequent continuous impoverishment and exhaustion of the country, except so far as it has been very partially relieved and replenished by the railway and irrigation loans, and the windfall of the consequences of the American war, since 1850.[3] Even with this relief, the material condition of India is such that the great mass of the poor people have hardly *2d* a day and a few rags, or a scanty subsistence.

[2]A reference to the taxes and other fees paid by Indians to support the colonial administration and the wealth taken out of the Indian economy by British businesses.

[3]A reference to the U.S. Civil War, which disrupted world cotton markets by limiting exports from the Confederate states.

The famines that were in their power to prevent, if they had done their duty, as a good and intelligent government. The policy adopted during the last fifteen years of building railways, irrigation works, etc., is hopeful, has already resulted in much good to your credit, and if persevered in, gratitude and contentment will follow.

[An] increase of exports [without adequate compensation]; [a] loss of manufacturing industry and skill. Here I end the debit side. . . .

To sum up the whole, the British rule has been — morally, a great blessing; politically peace and order on one hand, blunders on the other, materially, impoverishment (relieved as far as the railway and other loans go). The natives call the British system "Sakar ki Churi," the knife of sugar. That is to say there is no oppression, it is all smooth and sweet, but it is the knife, notwithstanding. I mention this that you should know these feelings. Our great misfortune is that you do not know our wants. When you will know our real wishes, I have not the least doubt that you would do justice. The genius and spirit of the British people is fair play and justice. The great problems before the English statesmen are two: 1) To make the foreign rule self-supporting, either by returning to India, in some shape or other, the wealth that has been, and is being, drawn from it, or by stopping that drain in some way . . . 2) How to satisfy reasonably the growing political aspirations and just rights of a people called British subjects to have a fair share in the administration and legislation of their own country. If the Select Committee solve these two problems, before which all other difficulties, financial or others, are as nothing, they will deserve the blessings of 200,000,000 of the human race.

Chapter 10

East and Southeast Asia Confront the West

During the nineteenth century, ancient patterns of life in East and Southeast Asia were irrevocably altered by upheavals that felled governments, intensified social conflict, introduced new ideas and technologies, and transformed long-standing relationships among states. These changes were caused in part by social and political forces generated from within these societies themselves, but most resulted from new pressures from the West. Until the nineteenth century, Western involvement in the region had been limited to commerce and modest and generally ineffectual missionary activity. The only exceptions were the Philippines, which since the sixteenth century had been ruled by Spain, and Java, where in the eighteenth century the Dutch had established indirect and informal control in cooperation with indigenous rulers. Only the Filipinos converted to Catholicism in large numbers. Elsewhere the region's rulers remained politically independent, and neither they nor their subjects were significantly affected by Western culture.

This changed in the nineteenth century. In Southeast Asia, by the time World War I began in 1914, Burma, Laos, Cambodia, Vietnam, Singapore, the states of the Malay Peninsula, and many islands of the East Indies had all joined the Philippines and Java as parts of Western empires. Thailand remained independent but lost territory to France and Great Britain.

China faced severe internal problems and experienced relentless economic and military pressures from Britain, France, Russia, Germany, the United States, and Japan. Previous Chinese regimes had survived domestic turbulence and foreign threats, but this time China's problems proved fatal, not just to the Qing Dynasty but also to China's 2,000-year tradition of imperial rule. When the last Qing emperor was overthrown in the Revolution of 1911, no new dynasty was established, and China faced a future without the authority of an emperor, the rule of scholar-officials, or the guidance of official Confucian ideology.

Japan also faced internal conflict and foreign threats, but its experience sharply differed from China's. After an intense debate over Japan's future sparked by the "opening" of Japan by American Commodore Matthew Perry in 1853, a group of patriotic aristocrats overthrew the Tokugawa shogunate in 1867, restored the emperor, and began laying plans for Japan's modernization. By the 1890s Japan had escaped becoming a victim of imperialism and was well on its way to becoming an imperialist power itself.

The Disintegration of Imperial China

In 1842, only a half century after the Qianlong emperor sent King George III of England his condescending rejection of the British appeal for trade concessions (see source 44), the Daoguang emperor (r. 1821–1850) was forced to approve the Treaty of Nanjing, which required his government to open five ports to British merchants, cede Hong Kong to the British, lower tariffs, pay Britain an indemnity of $21 million, and free all British prisoners. Acceptance of these humiliating terms followed defeat in the Opium War (1839–1842), the climax of Chinese efforts to halt the British sale of opium to China.

The Treaty of Nanjing was only a foretaste of the galling indignities the Chinese experienced during the rest of the nineteenth century. As a result of foreign pressures and military defeats, the government agreed to open additional ports to foreign trade, lost control of Korea, granted foreigners the right to collect customs duties, lost legal authority over resident foreigners, and promised to protect the lives and property of Christian missionaries. In 1899 and 1900, resentment of the hated "foreign devils" inspired the Boxer Rebellion, an uprising in which rebels murdered foreigners and Chinese Christians and besieged foreign embassies in Beijing. After a force of British, French, German, Russian, U.S., and Japanese troops crushed the rebellion, the government was forced to sign yet another punitive treaty, which among other things demanded an indemnity payment of $333 million, to be paid over a forty-year period with terms of interest that more than doubled the amount.

Even without the foreign onslaught, China faced enormous problems, many of them resulting from its spiraling population. By midcentury its population reached an estimated 430 million, an increase of more than 100 million since 1800. The inevitable results were land shortages, famines, and deepening poverty among the peasantry. Heavy taxes, inflation, and bureaucratic corruption compounded the peasants' woes. Meanwhile the government neglected public works and the military, and as bureaucratic efficiency declined, landowners, secret societies, and military strongmen took over local affairs by default. Reform programs such as the Self-Strengthening Movement and the One Hundred Days' Reforms were frustrated by conservative opposition, money shortages, and the difficulty of blending Confucian values with modern technology and Western political ideas. Rebellion, lawlessness, and foreign exploitation continued to plague the Qing regime until the Revolution of 1911 caused the regime, and China's ancient imperial tradition, to pass into history.

The Curse of Opium

▼▼▼

63 ▾ *Lin Zexu,* *LETTER TO QUEEN VICTORIA, 1839*

Although opium derivatives had been used in Chinese medicine for centuries, smoking opium as a narcotic dates only from the seventeenth century, shortly after Europeans introduced tobacco smoking to the Chinese. Opium use increased dramatically in the late 1700s when British and Indian merchants with access to one of the world's largest poppy-growing areas in north and northwest India began to sell large amounts of opium in China. By the early 1800s, millions of Chinese at every social and economic level were addicted to opium, and almost 2 million pounds of opium were being sold in China every year.

Chinese officials viewed the epidemic of opium smoking with alarm, but they could not agree on how to stop it. Some advocated the legalization of opium and the expansion of poppy growing in China to lessen the country's dependence on imports. Others, who favored more drastic measures, won the support of the Daoguang emperor, who banned opium use in 1838. One year later he sent one of his officials, Lin Zexu (1785–1850), to Guangzhou to confiscate the foreign merchants' stock of opium and halt their trade in opium altogether. Lin had served in the Hanlin Academy, China's leading center for Confucian studies in Beijing, and had held various provincial posts, including terms in Hubei and Hunan, where he had tried to suppress opium smoking. In Guangzhou he launched a campaign of moral persuasion and force to enforce the emperor's ban. Insight into his thinking is provided by a letter he wrote to Great Britain's Queen Victoria in 1839, imploring her to halt her subjects' sale of opium.

Nothing came of his letter, and the noncooperation of British merchants in Guangzhou drove Lin to take more drastic steps. He arrested the leading English opium trader and blockaded the foreign quarter until its merchants agreed to hand over 20,000 chests of opium. On receiving the opium, he had it mixed with water, salt, and lime and flushed into the sea. In response, the British government dispatched a fleet to Chinese waters and mobilized Indian troops to protect its interests. While the flotilla of almost fifty vessels was en route in late 1839, fighting had already started around Guangzhou. The Opium War was under way.

QUESTIONS FOR ANALYSIS

1. What does Lin's letter reveal about Chinese views of foreign relations and the relationship between the Chinese emperor and other rulers?
2. What differences does Lin see in the motives of Chinese and those of Europeans in regard to trade?
3. What moral arguments does Lin use to persuade Victoria to order the end of opium trading? What other arguments does he use?
4. What seems to be Lin's understanding of the powers that Victoria has as queen of England?
5. How does Lin view the world outside of China? How do his views differ from and resemble those of the Qianlong emperor (source 44)?

A communication: magnificently our great Emperor soothes and pacifies China and the foreign countries, regarding all with the same kindness. If there is profit, then he shares it with the peoples of the world; if there is harm, then he removes it on behalf of the world. This is because he takes the mind of heaven and earth as his mind.

The kings of your honorable country by a tradition handed down from generation to generation have always been noted for their politeness and submissiveness. We have read your successive tributary memorials saying, "In general our countrymen who go to trade in China have always received His Majesty the Emperor's gracious treatment and equal justice," and so on. Privately we are delighted with the way in which the honorable rulers of your country deeply understand the grand principles and are grateful for the Celestial grace. For this reason the Celestial Court in soothing those from afar has redoubled its polite and kind treatment. The profit from trade has been enjoyed by them continuously for two hundred years. This is the source from which your country has become known for its wealth.

But after a long period of commercial intercourse, there appear among the crowd of barbarians both good persons and bad, unevenly. Consequently there are those who smuggle opium to seduce the Chinese people and so cause the spread of the poison to all provinces. Such persons who only care to profit themselves, and disregard their harm to others, are not tolerated by the laws of heaven and are unanimously hated by human beings. . . .

We find that your country is sixty or seventy thousand *li*[1] from China. Yet there are barbarian ships that strive to come here for trade for the purpose of making a great profit. The wealth of China is used to profit the barbarians. That is to say, the great profit made by barbarians is all taken from the rightful share of China. By what right do they then in return use the poisonous drug to injure the Chinese people? Even though the barbarians may not necessarily intend to do us harm, yet in coveting profit to an extreme, they have no regard for injuring others. Let us ask, where is your conscience? I have heard that the smoking of opium is very strictly forbidden by your country; that is because the harm caused by opium is clearly understood. Since it is not permitted to do harm to your own country, then even less should you let it be passed on to the harm of other countries — how much less to China! Of all that China exports to foreign countries, there is not a single thing which is not beneficial to people: they are of benefit when eaten, or of benefit when used, or of benefit when resold: all are beneficial. Is there a single article from China which has done any harm to

---

[1]One *li* equals approximately one-third of a mile.

foreign countries? Take tea and rhubarb,[2] for example; the foreign countries cannot get along for a single day without them. If China cuts off these benefits with no sympathy for those who are to suffer, then what can the barbarians rely upon to keep themselves alive? . . . As for other foodstuffs, beginning with candy, ginger, cinnamon, and so forth, and articles for use, beginning with silk, satin, chinaware, and so on, all the things that must be had by foreign countries are innumerable. On the other hand, articles coming from the outside to China can only be used as toys. We can take them or get along without them. Since they are not needed by China, what difficulty would there be if we closed the frontier and stopped the trade? Nevertheless our Celestial Court lets tea, silk, and other goods be shipped without limit and circulated everywhere without begrudging it in the slightest. This is for no other reason but to share the benefit with the people of the whole world. . . .

Suppose there were people from another country who carried opium for sale to England and seduced your people into buying and smoking it; certainly your honorable ruler would deeply hate it and be bitterly aroused. We have heard heretofore that your honorable ruler is kind and benevolent. Naturally you would not wish to give unto others what you yourself do not want. . . .

We have further learned that in London, the capital of your honorable rule, and in Scotland, Ireland, and other places, originally no opium has been produced. Only in several places of India under your control . . . has opium been planted from hill to hill, and ponds have been opened for its manufacture. For months and years work is continued in order to accumulate the poison. The obnoxious odor ascends, irritating heaven and frightening the spirits. Indeed you . . . can eradicate the opium plant in these places, hoe over the fields entirely, and sow in its stead the five grains [millet, barley, wheat, etc.]. Anyone who dares again to plant and manufacture opium should be severely punished. This will really be a great, benevolent goverment policy that will increase the common weal and get rid of evil. For this, Heaven must support you and the spirits must bring you good fortune, prolonging your old age and extending your descendants. All will depend on this act. . . .

Suppose a man of another country comes to England to trade, he still has to obey the English laws; how much more should he obey in China the laws of the Celestial Dynasty?

Now we have set up regulations governing the Chinese people. He who sells opium shall receive the death penalty and he who smokes it also the death penalty. Now consider this: if the barbarians do not bring opium, then how can the Chinese people resell it, and how can they smoke it? The fact is that the wicked barbarians beguile the Chinese people into a death trap. How then can we grant life only to these barbarians? He who takes the life of even one person still has to atone for it with his own life; yet is the harm done by opium limited to the taking of one life only? Therefore in the new regulations, in regard to those barbarians who bring opium to China, the penalty is fixed at decapitation or strangulation. This is what is called getting rid of a harmful thing on behalf of mankind. . . .

May you check [restrain] your wicked and sift [separate out] your vicious people before they come to China, in order to guarantee the peace of your nation, to show further the sincerity of your politeness and submissiveness, and to let the two countries enjoy together the blessings of peace. How fortunate, how fortunate indeed! After receiving this dispatch will you immediately give us a prompt reply regarding the details and circumstances of your cutting off the opium traffic. Be sure not to put this off.

[2]Rhubarb roots were used in medicines.

The Self-Strengthening Movement

64 ▾ Feng Guifen, *PERSONAL PROTESTS FROM THE STUDY OF JIAOBIN*

Feng Guifen was a native of Suzhou who entered government service in 1840 after performing brilliantly on the provincial civil service examination in 1832 and the metropolitan examination held under the auspices of the emperor in Beijing in 1840. Over the next two decades, he prepared policy memoranda for the emperor as a member of the prestigious Hanlin Academy, organized and led troops against rebel armies, and served as director of scholarly academies in Suzhou and Shanghai. During his service he became well aware of the government's failures — neglect of waterways, corruption in tax collection, inadequate military planning, and indifference to the poor. He came to appreciate how these failures drove millions of the emperor's subjects to support the cause of rebellion in the 1850s, including the massive Taiping Rebellion (1850–1864), which cost 20 to 30 million lives. Finally, he fully realized the extent of Chinese impotence in the face of Western military power. Like other Chinese he was shamed by Chinese defeats in the Opium War (1839–1842) and the Arrow War (1856–1860) and humiliated by the treaties that came in their wake.

Despite these failures and indignities, when Feng Guifen retired from government service in 1859 to direct a school in Suzhou, as a dedicated Confucianist he still believed in China's time-honored governing principles. He was convinced, furthermore, that China could overcome the twin threats of rebellion and foreign encroachment, but only if it embraced reform. He outlined his thoughts in a collection of essays, ***Personal Protests from the Study of Jiaobin***, which he distributed among government officials in 1861. Here he outlined a policy of ***Ziqiang***, or "self-strengthening," a traditional Chinese term to describe what a declining dynasty needed to do in order to recover. Feng specifically defined self-strengthening as selective borrowing from the West, especially in military matters, and an affirmation of essential Confucian principles. His essays caught the attention of one of China's leading statesmen, Li Hongzhang (1823–1901), who invited Feng to join his staff between 1862 and 1865, and who as prime spokesman for the self-strengthening movement over the next thirty years drew inspiration from Feng's ideas.

In 1898, twenty-four years after Feng's death, his contributions to the cause of moderate reform were recognized by the Guangzhou emperor, who ordered 1,000 copies of Feng's essays to be printed and distributed to government offices, where they were to be read and discussed.

QUESTIONS FOR ANALYSIS

1. Feng argues that the Chinese have only themselves to blame for their "inferiority." In his view, how and why have they failed?

2. **According to Feng, who will need to take the initiative to implement the reforms he is proposing?**
3. **What specific reforms does Feng propose for Chinese education and the civil service examinations?**
4. **According to Feng, why is the study of European languages of critical importance?**
5. **What role does Feng envision for Confucianism once self-strengthening is achieved?**
6. **According to Feng, if his proposals are implemented, how will China's standing in the world be affected?**

According to a general geography compiled by an Englishman, the territory of China is eight times that of Russia, ten times that of the United States, one hundred times that of France, and two hundred times that of Great Britain. . . . Yet we are shamefully humiliated by the four nations, not because our climate, soil, or resources are inferior to theirs, but because our people are inferior. . . . Now, our inferiority is not due to our allotment [i.e., our inherent nature] from Heaven, but is rather due to ourselves. If it were allotted us by Heaven, it would be a shame but not something we could do anything about. Since the inferiority is due to ourselves, it is a still greater shame but something we can do something about. And if we feel ashamed, there is nothing better than self-strengthening. . . .

Why are the Western nations small and yet strong? Why are we large and yet weak? We must search for the means to become their equal, and that depends solely on human effort. With regard to the present situation, several observations may be made: in not wasting human talents, we are inferior to the barbarians; in not wasting natural resources, we are inferior to the barbarians; in allowing no barrier to come between the ruler and the people, we are inferior to the barbarians; and in the matching of words with deeds, we are also inferior to the barbarians. The remedy for these four points is to seek the causes in ourselves. They can be changed at once if only the emperor would set us in the right direction. There is no need to learn from the barbarians in these matters.

We have only one thing to learn from the barbarians, and that is strong ships and effective guns. . . . Funds should be allotted to establish a shipyard and arsenal in each trading port. A few barbarians should be employed, and Chinese who are good in using their minds should be selected to receive instruction so that in turn they may teach many craftsmen. When a piece of work is finished and is as good as that made by the barbarians, the makers should be rewarded with an official *juren* degree[1] and be permitted to participate in the metropolitan examinations on the same basis as other scholars. Those whose products are of superior quality should be rewarded with the *jinshi* degree and be permitted to participate in the palace examinations like others. The workers should be paid double so that they will not quit their jobs.

Our nation's emphasis on civil service examinations has sunk deep into people's minds for a long time. Intelligent and brilliant scholars have exhausted their time and energy in such useless

---

[1]The *juren* degree was awarded to successful candidates in the provincial civil service examinations held every three years in major provincial cities; the *jinshi* degree, China's highest degree, was awarded to successful candidates in the metropolitan examination held every three years in Beijing.

things as the stereotyped examination essays, examination papers, and formal calligraphy. . . . We should now order one-half of them to apply themselves to the manufacturing of instruments and weapons and to the promotion of physical studies. . . . The intelligence and ingenuity of the Chinese are certainly superior to those of the various barbarians; it is only that hitherto we have not made use of them. . . . There ought to be some people of extraordinary intelligence who can have new ideas and improve on Western methods. At first they may take the foreigners as their teachers and models; then they may come to the same level and be their equals; finally they may move ahead and surpass them. Herein lies the way to self-strengthening.

It may be argued: "Guan Zhong repelled the barbarians and Confucius acclaimed his virtue; the state of Chu adopted barbarian ways and [Confucius in] the *Spring and Autumn Annals*[2] condemned them. Is not what you are proposing contrary to the Way of the sages?" No, it is not. When we speak of repelling the barbarians, we must have the actual means to repel them, and not just empty bravado. If we live in the present day and speak of repelling the barbarians, we should ask with what instruments we are to repel them. . . . [The answer is that] we should use the instruments of the barbarians but not adopt the ways of the barbarians. We should use them so that we can repel them.

Some have asked why we should not just purchase the ships and man them with [foreign] hirelings, but the answer is that this will not do. If we can manufacture, repair, and use them, then they are our weapons. . . . In the end the way to avoid trouble is to manufacture, repair, and use weapons by ourselves. Only thus can we pacify the empire; only thus can we become the leading power in the world; only thus can we restore our original strength, redeem ourselves from former humiliations, and maintain the integrity of our vast territory so as to remain the greatest country on earth.

ON THE ADOPTION OF WESTERN LEARNING

Western books on mathematics, mechanics, optics, light, and chemistry contain the best principles of the natural sciences. In the books on geography, the mountains, rivers, strategic points, customs, and native products of the hundred countries are fully listed. Most of this information is beyond the reach of the Chinese people. . . .

If we wish to use Western knowledge, we should establish official translation bureaus in Guangzhou and Shanghai. Brilliant students not over fifteen years of age should be selected from those areas to live and study in these schools on double allowances. Westerners should be appointed to teach them the spoken and written languages of the various nations, and famous Chinese teachers should be engaged to teach them classics, history, and other subjects. At the same time they should learn mathematics. . . . China has many brilliant people. There must be some who can learn from the barbarians and surpass them.

It is from learning that the principles of government are derived. In discussing good government, the great historian Sima Qian[3] said, "Take the latter-day kings as your models." This was because they were nearer in time; their customs had changed from the past and were more similar to the present; and their ideas were not so lofty as to be impracticable. It is my opinion that today we should also take the foreign nations as our examples. They live at the same time and in the same world with us; they have attained pros-

[2]*The Spring and Autumn Annals* is a chronicle of the state of Lu from 722 to 481 B.C.E. Traditionally ascribed to Confucius, it came to be included as one of the Five Classics of Chinese literature. Guang Zhang, who died in 645 B.C.E., was prime minister for the state of Qi. Chu was a state in South China.

[3]Sima Qian (ca. 145–90 B.C.E.), the author of *Shiji*, a wide-ranging account of early Chinese history, laid the foundation for later Chinese historical writing.

perity and power by their own efforts. Is it not fully clear that they are similar to us and that their methods can easily be put into practice? If we let Chinese ethics and Confucian teachings serve as the foundation, and let them be supplemented by the methods used by the various nations for the attainment of prosperity and power, would it not be the best of all solutions?

Moreover, during the past twenty years since the opening of trade, a great number of foreign chiefs have learned our written and spoken language, and the best of them can even read our classics and histories. They are generally able to speak on our dynastic regulations and civil administration, on our geography and the condition of our people. On the other hand, our officials from the governors down are completely ignorant of foreign countries. In comparison, should we not feel ashamed? The Chinese officials have to rely upon stupid and preposterous interpreters as their eyes and ears. The mildness or severity of the original statement, its sense of urgency or lack of insistence, may be lost through their tortuous interpretations. Thus frequently a small grudge may develop into a grave hostility. At present the most important political problem of the empire is to control the barbarians, yet the pivotal function is entrusted to such people. No wonder that we understand neither the foreigners nor ourselves and cannot distinguish fact from untruth. Whether in peace negotiations or in deliberating for war, we are unable to grasp the essentials. This is indeed the underlying trouble of our nation.

The Emergence of Modern Japan

In the late nineteenth century, Japan accomplished what no other nation had, or has since, been able to do. In only four decades and without recourse to foreign loans or investments, it changed from a secluded, preindustrial society vulnerable to foreign exploitation into a powerful, industrialized nation that shocked the world by winning wars against China in 1895 and Russia in 1905. What made this transformation even more remarkable was that it was accompanied by little social upheaval and that despite its magnitude the Japanese retained many of their hallowed ideals and beliefs.

Japan's transformation began in 1867 when a faction of aristocrats overthrew the Tokugawa shogunate and then orchestrated the move of the previously secluded and ceremonial emperor from Kyoto to Edo, where he assumed titular authority over a government that they controlled. These events are known as the Meiji Restoration, based on the Japanese word *meiji* ("brilliant rule"), chosen by Emperor Mutsuhito as his reign name.

The Meiji Restoration came after a century in which the foundations of Tokugawa society had been weakened by population growth, urbanization, intellectual ferment, social change, and the erosion of Confucian values. Peasant revolts, urban riots, and bolder and more frequent denunciations of the shogun by restive aristocrats all were signs of a troubled regime. Then in July 1853 an event that many Japanese had feared for decades finally occurred. After four U.S. naval vessels mounting sixty-one guns and carrying 967 men sailed into Edo Bay, their commander, Commodore Perry, presented the shogun's officials a list of demands: opening of two ports to American trading ships; help for any American ships and their crews wrecked on the Japanese coast; and permission for American ships to buy coal provisions in Japanese ports. He also sent the Japanese negotiator several white flags. The reason, he explained, was that if Japan rejected the U.S. demands, there would be a war that Japan would certainly lose, and in that case white flags would come in handy. When Perry returned the following February, the Japanese acquiesced and within a decade also granted similar privileges to the Netherlands, Russia, Great Britain, and France. Japan was open to the world.

In response, patriotic Japanese bitterly turned against a government lacking the will, strength, and broad-based support to protect them from such indignities. Opponents of the shogun raised the cry, "Honor the emperor, expel the barbarians!" They were convinced that only the semidivine emperor could inspire the national effort needed to overcome the foreigners. On January 3, 1868 (by the Japanese calendar, the ninth day of the twelfth month of 1867), forces led by the Satsuma and Chosu clans seized the shogun's palace and declared the restoration of the emperor. Mutsuhito accepted the rebels' invitation to head the government, and after his supporters crushed the shogun's resistance, more than 250 years of Tokugawa rule ended. Japan now entered the Meiji Era, a period of transformation unparalleled in recent history.

Eastern Ethics and Western Science

▼▼▼

65 ▼ *Sakuma Shozan, REFLECTIONS ON MY ERRORS*

After Commodore Perry left Tokyo in the summer of 1853, promising to return within a year to receive answers to his demands, government officials, daimyo, samurai, intellectuals, merchants, and courtiers entered into an intense debate about the crisis at hand and their nation's future. Although the immediate reaction was to reject all things Western and "expel the barbarians," many soon realized that threats were no match for superior ships and firepower. Thus, as the debate went on (ending only in 1868 with the collapse of the shogunate), increasing numbers of Japanese were willing to consider the ideas of Sakuma Shozan, whose philosophy is summarized by the motto he made famous: "Eastern ethics and Western science."

Born into a samurai family in 1811, Sakuma received a Confucian education before entering the service of one of Japan's leading aristocrats, Sanada Yukitsura. When the shogun put Sanada in charge of Japan's coastal fortifications in 1841, Sakuma entered the world of artillery, naval strategy, and shipbuilding. He learned Dutch, read all he could of Western science, and became an advocate of adopting Western weaponry. In the 1840s such views were unpopular within the shogun's government, and as a result both Sakuma and his lord were dismissed from the shogun's service. Sakuma experienced more problems in 1854, when at his urging a student of his attempted to stow away on one of Perry's ships as it left Japan but was captured. Sakuma, along with his student, was imprisoned, and although Sakuma was released after several months, he remained under house arrest for eight years.

Sakuma wrote his deceptively titled *Reflections on My Errors* on his release from prison. Far from being an apology for his "errors," it was a vigorous defense of his opinions, made up of fifty-two brief commentaries on various issues. Although he claimed that the work was to be "locked up in a box" and shown only to his descendants, it was widely circulated among Japan's military and political leaders.

After completing *Reflections*, Sakuma continued to call for the opening of Japan and cooperation between shogun and emperor. He died because of his convictions. In 1864 he was murdered by an antiforeign zealot because he was riding a horse with a Western-style saddle.

QUESTIONS FOR ANALYSIS

1. What is the meaning of the parable about the "man who is grieved by the illness of his lord or his father"? What is the meaning of the story concerning Zao Wei?
2. What does Sakuma mean by Eastern ethics? Does he see any difficulty reconciling them with Western science?
3. What does Sakuma see as the weaknesses of Japan's military leaders and Confucian scholars? How can their deficiencies be rectified?
4. Why does Sakuma consider the study of mathematics and science to be so important?
5. Aside from his admiration of Western science, how would you characterize Sakuma's attitude toward the West?
6. What similarities and differences do you see between Sakuma's ideas and those of Honda Toshiaki (source 46)? How do his ideas resemble and differ from those of Feng Guifen (source 64)?

Take, for example, a man who is grieved by the illness of his lord or his father, and who is seeking medicine to cure it. If he is fortunate enough to secure the medicine, and is certain that it will be efficacious, then, certainly, without questioning either its cost or the quality of its name, he will beg his lord or father to take it. Should the latter refuse on the grounds that he dislikes the name, does the younger man make various schemes to give the medicine secretly, or does he simply sit by and wait for his master to die? There is no question about it: the feeling of genuine sincerity and heartfelt grief on the part of the subject or son makes it absolutely impossible for him to sit idly and watch his master's anguish; consequently, even if he knows that he will later have to face his master's anger, he cannot but give the medicine secretly. . . .

▾ ▾ ▾

The gentleman has five pleasures, but wealth and rank are not among them. That his house understands decorum and righteousness and remains free from family rifts — this is one pleasure. That exercising care in giving to and taking from others, he provides for himself honestly, free, internally, from shame before his wife and children, and externally, from disgrace before the public — this is the second pleasure. That he expounds and glorifies the learning of the sages, knows in his heart the great Way, and in all situations contents himself with his duty, in adversity as well as in prosperity — this is the third pleasure. That he is born after the opening of the vistas of science by the Westerners, and can therefore understand principles not known to the sages and wise men of old — this is the fourth pleasure. That he employs the ethics of the East and the scientific technique of the West, neglecting neither the spiritual nor material aspects of life, combining subjective and objective, and thus bringing benefit to the people and serving the nation — this is the fifth pleasure. . . .

▾ ▾ ▾

The principal requisite of national defense is that it prevents the foreign barbarians from holding us in contempt. The existing coastal defense installations all lack method; the pieces of artillery that have been set up are improperly made; and the officials who negotiate with the foreigners are mediocrities who have no understanding of warfare. The situation being such, even though we wish to avoid incurring the scorn of the barbarians, how, in fact, can we do so? . . .

▾ ▾ ▾

Of the men who now hold posts as commanders of the army, those who are not dukes or princes or men of noble rank, are members of wealthy families. As such, they find their daily pleasure in drinking wine, singing, and dancing; and they are ignorant of military strategy and discipline. Should a national emergency arise, there is no one who could command the respect of the warriors and halt the enemy's attack. This is the great sorrow of our times. For this reason, I have wished to follow in substance the Western principles of armament, and, by banding together loyal, valorous, strong men of old, established families not in the military class — men of whom one would be equal to ten ordinary men — to form a voluntary group which would be made to have as its sole aim that of guarding the nation and protecting the people. Anyone wishing to join the society would be tested and his merits examined; and, if he did not shirk hardship, he would then be permitted to join. Men of talent in military strategy, planning, and administration would be advanced to positions of leadership, and then, if the day should come when the country must be defended, this group could be gathered together and organized into an army to await official commands. It is to be hoped that they would drive the enemy away and perform greater service than those who now form the military class. . . .

▾ ▾ ▾

Mathematics is the basis for all learning. In the Western world after this science was discovered military tactics advanced greatly, far outstripping that of former times. . . . In the *Art of War*[1] of Sunzi, the statement about "estimation, determination of quantity, calculation, judgment, and victory" has reference to mathematics. However, since Sunzi's time neither we nor the Chinese have ceased to read, study, and memorize his teachings, and our art of war remains exactly as it was then. It consequently cannot be compared with that of the West. There is no reason for this other than that we have not devoted ourselves to basic studies. At the present time, if we wish really to complete our military preparations, we must develop this branch of study. . . .

▾ ▾ ▾

What do the so-called scholars of today actually do? . . . Do they, after having learned the rites and music, punishment and administration, the classics and governmental system, go on to discuss and learn the elements of the art of war, of military discipline, of the principles of machinery? Do they make exhaustive studies of conditions in foreign countries? Of effective defense methods? Of strategy in setting up strongholds, defense barriers, and reinforcements? Of the knowledge of computation, gravitation, geometry, and mathematics? If they do, I have not heard of it! Therefore I ask what the so-called scholars of today actually do. . . .

▾ ▾ ▾

[1]A classic work on military strategy written during the early fourth century B.C.E.

In order to master the barbarians there is nothing so effective as to ascertain in the beginning conditions among them. To do this, there is no better first step than to be familiar with barbarian tongues. Thus, learning a barbarian language is not only a step toward knowing the barbarians, but also the groundwork for mastering them. . . .

▼▼▼

Last summer the American barbarians arrived in the Bay of Uraga[2] with four warships, bearing their president's message. Their deportment and manner of expression were exceedingly arrogant, and the resulting insult to our national dignity was not small. Those who heard could but gnash their teeth. A certain person on guard in Uraga suffered this insult in silence, and, having been ultimately unable to do anything about it, after the barbarians had retired, he drew his knife and slashed to bits a portrait of their leader, which they had left as a gift. Thus he gave vent to his rage. In former times Zao Wei of Song,[3] having been demoted, was serving as an official in Shensi, and when he heard of the character of Chao Yuanhao, he had a person skillful in drawing paint Chao's image. Zao looked at this portrait and knew from its manly appearance that Chao would doubtless make trouble on the border in the future. Therefore Zao wished to take steps toward preparing the border in advance, and toward collecting together and examining men of ability. Afterwards, everything turned out as he had predicted. Thus, by looking at the portrait of his enemy, he could see his enemy's abilities and thereby aid himself with his own preparations. It can only be regretted that the Japanese guard did not think of this. Instead of using the portrait, he tore it up. In both cases there was a barbarian; in both cases there was a portrait. But one man, lacking the portrait, sought to obtain it, while the other, having it, destroyed it. Their depth of knowledge and farsightedness in planning were vastly different.

---

[2]A small bay at the mouth of Tokyo Bay.

[3]The Chinese Song Dynasty ruled from 960 to 1279 C.E.

Patriotic Duty and Business Success

▼▼▼

66 ▼ Iwasaki Yataro, *LETTER TO MITSUBISHI EMPLOYEES*

From the moment the Meiji reformers seized power, they sought to modernize Japan's economy, especially in industries on which modern military power depended. After a rocky start in the 1870s, Japanese industrialization proceeded rapidly, and by 1900 the nation had become a major economic power through a combination of government subsidies and individual entrepreneurship.

The greatest success story in Japan's economic transformation was Iwasaki Yataro (1835–1885), the founder of one of the nation's most powerful business conglomerates, Mitsubishi. Born into a poor farming family, Iwasaki gained a rudimentary education and held several low-level business jobs before he found employment as an official in the service of the aristocratic Tosa family in the mid 1860s. He was given the task of managing and reducing the Tosa domain's huge debt, which had resulted from purchases of firearms and artillery. His policies, which included paying some debtors with counterfeit money, quickly eliminated the domain's deficit. In 1871, when the domain abandoned its direct ownership of business enterprises, it gave Iwasaki eleven steamships and all the assets

connected with its enterprises in the silk, coal, tea, and lumber industries. In return, Iwasaki was expected to pay off some new Tosa debts and provide employment for former samurai. With this to build on, he systematically wiped out foreign and domestic competition and, through a series of shrewd (and frequently cutthroat) business moves, turned Mitsubishi into Japan's second-largest conglomerate, with interests in shipbuilding, mining, banking, insurance, and manufacturing.

Iwasaki wrote the following letter to his employees in 1876 during Mitsubishi's battle with the British Peninsular and Oriental Steam Navigation Company over control of Japanese coastal trade. He had just cut fares in half but had also reduced wages by a third.

QUESTIONS FOR ANALYSIS

1. Why does Iwasaki believe that the Japanese must prevent foreigners from becoming involved in the coastal trade?
2. According to Iwasaki, what is at stake in the competition for control of Japan's coastal trade?
3. What advantages and disadvantages does Iwasaki's company have in its rivalry with the Peninsular and Oriental Steam Navigation Company?
4. How does Iwasaki attempt to inspire greater dedication and effort from his workers?
5. To what extent is Iwasaki's letter similar in spirit to Sakuma Shozan's *Reflections on My Errors* (source 65)?

Many people have expressed differing opinions concerning the principles and advantages of engaging foreigners or Japanese in the task of coastal trade. Granted, we may permit a dissenting opinion which suggests that in principle both foreigners and Japanese must be permitted to engage in coastal trade, but once we look into the question of advantages, we know that coastal trade is too important a matter to be given over to the control of foreigners. If we allow the right of coastal navigation to fall into the hands of foreigners in peacetime it means loss of business opportunities and employment for our own people, and in wartime it means yielding the vital right of information to foreigners. In fact, this is not too different from abandoning the rights of our country as an independent nation.

Looking back into the past, in Japan at the time when we abandoned the policy of seclusion and entered into an era of friendly intercourse and commerce with foreign nations, we should have been prepared for this very task. However, due to the fact that our people lack knowledge and wealth, we have yet to assemble a fleet sufficient to engage in coastal navigation. Furthermore, we have neither the necessary skills for navigation nor a plan for developing maritime transportation industry. This condition is the cause of attracting foreign shipping companies to occupy our major maritime transport lines. Yet our people show not a sense of surprise at it. Some people say that our treaties with foreign powers contain an express provision allowing foreign ships to proceed from Harbor A to Harbor B, and others claim that such a provision must not be regarded as granting foreign ships the right to coastal navigation inasmuch as it is intended not to impose unduly heavy taxes on them. While I am not qualified to discuss it, the issue remains an important one.

I now propose to do my utmost, and along with my 35 million compatriots, perform my duty as a citizen of this country. That is to recover the right of coastal trade in our hands, and not to delegate that task to foreigners. Unless we propose to do so, it is useless for our government to revise the unequal treaties[1] or to change our entrenched customs. We need people who can respond, otherwise all the endeavors of the government will come to naught. This is the reason why the government protects our company, and I know that our responsibilities are even greater than the full weight of Mt. Fuji[2] thrust upon our shoulders. There have been many who wish to hinder our progress in fulfilling our obligations. However, we have been able to eliminate one of our worst enemies, the Pacific Mail Company of the United States, from contention by application of appropriate means.[3] Now, another rival has emerged. It is the Peninsular & Oriental Steam Navigation Company of Great Britain which is setting up a new line between Yokohama and Shanghai, and is attempting to claim its right over the ports of Nagasaki, Kobe, and Yokohama. The P & O Company comes to compete for the right of coastal navigation with us. How can we decline the challenge? Heretofore, our company has received protection from the government, support from the nation, and hard work from its employees through which it has done its duty. However, our company is young and not every phase of its operation is well conducted. In contrast, the P & O Company is backed by its massive capital, its large fleet of ships, and by its experiences of operations in Oriental countries. In competing against this giant, what methods can we employ?

I have thought about this problem very carefully and have come to one conclusion. There is no other alternative but to eliminate unnecessary positions and unnecessary expenditures. This is a time-worn solution and no new wisdom is involved. Even though it is a familiar saying, it is much easier said than done, and this indeed has been the root cause of difficulties in the past and present times. Therefore, starting immediately I propose that we engage in this task. By eliminating unnecessary personnel from the payroll, eliminating unnecessary expenditures, and engaging in hard and arduous work, we shall be able to solidify the foundation of our company. If there is a will there is a way. Through our own effort, we shall be able to repay the government for its protection and answer our nation for its confidence shown in us. Let us work together in discharging our responsibilities and not be ashamed of ourselves. Whether we succeed or fail, whether we can gain profit or sustain loss, we cannot anticipate at this time. Hopefully, all of you will join me in a singleness of heart to attain this cherished goal, forebearing and undaunted by setbacks to restore to our own hands the right to our own coastal trade. If we succeed it will not only be an accomplishment for our company alone but also a glorious event for our Japanese Empire, which shall let its light shine to all four corners of earth. We can succeed or fail, and it depends on your effort or lack of effort. Do your utmost in this endeavor!

[1]The various commercial treaties the shogunate signed after Commodore Perry's mission.

[2]The highest mountain in Japan, near Tokyo.

[3]The American firm abandoned its effort to crack the Japanese market when it found it could not compete with Mitsubishi's low prices, made possible largely by government subsidies.

Images of the West in Late Tokugawa and Meiji Japan

67 ▾ *PRINTS AND DRAWINGS, 1853–1887*

Following the Europeans' arrival in Japan in 1542, their ideas, dress, weapons, and religion proved attractive to many Japanese. As many as 500,000 Japanese converted to Catholicism, military leaders put European firearms to use, and some Japanese showed an interest in European fashion and cuisine. After the Tokugawa suppressed Christianity and implemented the seclusion policy in the seventeenth century, however, knowledge of the West was limited to merchants who traded with the Dutch in Nagasaki and a handful of intellectuals interested in European thought. For most Japanese, memory of the South Sea Barbarians disappeared.

The opening of Japan to foreign trade in 1854 changed this dramatically. Inspired by a mixture of fear, awe, and curiosity, the Japanese developed a deep interest in the West, and a flood of printed material about Europe and the United States appeared in the 1850s and 1860s. After the Meiji Restoration, imitation of the West became a patriotic duty. Employing Western science, technology, military organization, and government practices would make Japan strong and prosperous; adopting Western fashion, etiquette, grooming habits, and architecture would make the Japanese respected and admired. In the late 1880s, however, a reaction against overzealous Westernization set in. Since then, the Japanese have managed to strike a balance between borrowing from the West and preserving the essentials of their traditional culture.

The following six illustrations provide insights into changing Japanese views of the West. The first two (page 325) are tile prints that appeared soon after the arrival of Commodore Perry. Forerunners of modern newspapers, tile prints were produced quickly and anonymously after newsworthy events and sold for a few cents. The first print depicts one of Perry's "black ships," so called because of the dark smoke that belched from their smokestacks. The text provides information on the ship's dimensions and its voyage to Japan. The second print depicts Commander Henry Adams, Perry's second-in-command.

The next two illustrations appeared when the drive to emulate Europeans was under way. The first (page 326) is part of a series of woodblock prints published in the 1880s entitled *Self-Made Men Worthy of Emulation*. The individual depicted is Fukuchi Gen'ichiro (1841–1909), a journalist who served as editor-in-chief of Tokyo's first daily newspaper. He is shown covering the Satsuma Rebellion of 1877, a failed rebellion by disgruntled samurai against the new Meiji order. The artist is Kobayashi Kiyochika (1847–1911), a self-taught painter whose numerous woodblock prints show the influence of Western painting and perspective. The accompanying text (with an erroneous birthdate) reads:

> Fukuchi Gen'ichiro was born in Nagasaki in 1844. An exceptionally bright child, he could recognize characters at the age of five and had begun to read and write at about the age of seven. He resolved to enter the service of the shogunate and, upon coming of age, entered the government, in the service of which he traveled three times to Europe.

One of Commodore Perry's Black Ships

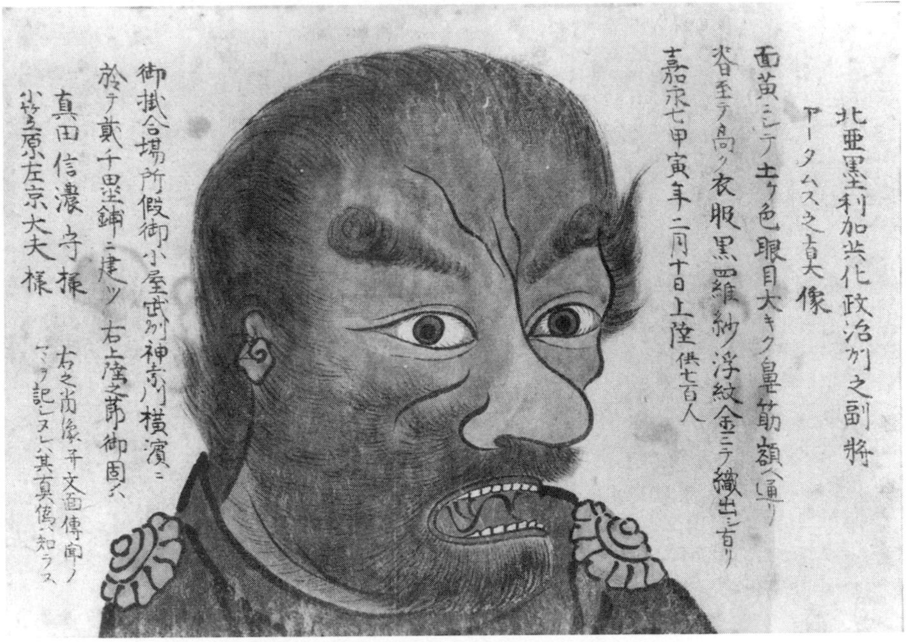

Commodore Perry's Second-in-Command, Commander Henry Adams

Kobayashi Kiyochika, *Fukuchi Gen'ichiro*

> He then entered into a successful business career. In 1874 he became president of the Reporters' Association. He personally covered the Satsuma Rebellion in the south. Received by the emperor, he respectfully reported his observations to the throne. His style seemed almost supernatural in its logic, force, and lucidity. He is one of the truly great men of Meiji.

The next illustration (page 327) appeared in a popular book by Kanagaki Robun published in serial form in the 1870s. *Hiking through the West* relates the adventures of two Japanese travelers during a trip to London and back. The illustration depicts, from right to left, an "unenlightened man," dressed as a samurai; a "half-enlightened man"; and an "enlightened man."

Even as Japanese enthusiasm for things Western was peaking, some opposed Japan's rush to Westernize. Government censorship silenced most of these critics, but a few managed to get their ideas into print. Cartoonists Honda Kinkichiro and

Kanagaki Robun, *Hiking through the West*

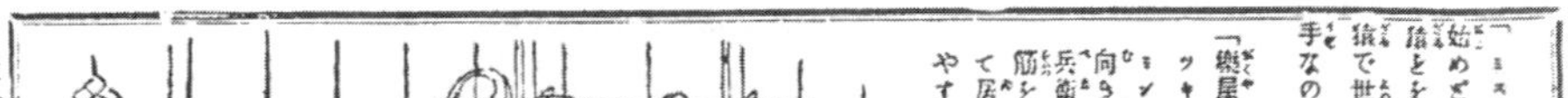

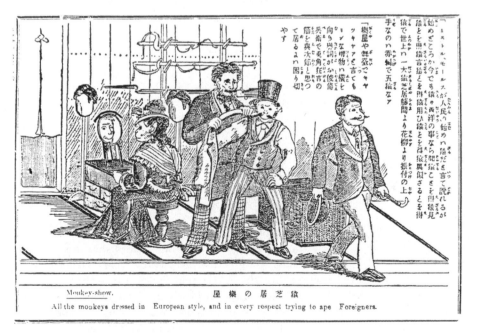

Honda Kinkichiro, *"Monkey Show Dressing Room"*

Kobayashi Kiyochika, *"Hands Dance, Feet Stomp, Call Out Hurrah!"*

Kobayashi Kyochika were two such individuals. Honda's cartoons, usually with English captions and a Japanese text, appeared in the 1870s and 1880s in the weekly humor magazine *Marumara Chimbun*. "Monkey Show Dressing Room" (page 327) was published in 1879, shortly after Dr. Edward S. Morse introduced Darwin's theory of evolution in a series of lectures at the newly founded Department of Zoology at Tokyo University. The text reads, "Mr. Morse explains that all human beings were monkeys in the beginning. In the beginning — but even now aren't we still monkeys? When it comes to Western things we think the red beards [Westerners] are the most skillful at everything."

Kobayashi, the artist who made the print of Fukuchi Gen'ichiro and who contributed cartoons to *Marumara Chimbun* in the 1880s, published his cartoon (page 328) in the *Tokyo Daily News* in 1891. It depicts a New Year's Dance held in the Rokumeikan, a pavilion built by the government in 1883 to serve as a venue for fancy-dress balls and other entertainments involving Westerners and Japan's elite. Above the dance floor, filled with ill-matched Western and Japanese couples, is a sign that reads, "Hands Dance, Feet Stomp, Call Out Hurrah!"

QUESTIONS FOR ANALYSIS

1. What impression of the West is conveyed by the prints of Perry's ship and his second-in-command, Commander Adams? What specific details help convey this impression?
2. In the top illustration on page 327, what are the most significant differences between the three figures? How does the artist convey a sense of the "enlightened man's" superiority?
3. What is there in the drawing of Fukuchi Gen'ichiro and in the accompanying text that makes him "a man worthy of emulation"?
4. Why do you think the artist chose to depict Fukuchi while he was covering the Satsuma Rebellion?
5. What messages are Honda and Kobayashi attempting to convey about Japan's campaign to Westernize?
6. Compare and contrast the depiction of Westerners in "Hands Dance . . ." with the earlier depiction of Commander Adams.

Southeast Asia in the Era of Imperialism

The Western takeover of Southeast Asia was more gradual than the European seizure of Africa but was motivated by the same mixture of nationalism, anticipated economic benefits, missionary zeal, and perceived strategic imperatives. The British move into Burma, which took place in three stages following wars in the 1820s, 1850s, and 1880s, was to prevent Burmese interference in India and head off French influence. In contrast, economic motives inspired the British takeover of the Malay Peninsula. The British annexed Singapore in 1819 after they discovered that Melaka, taken from the Dutch in 1795, had lost much of its commercial prominence. They gradually extended their authority over the rest of the peninsula to protect their interests in the region's tin mines and rubber plantations. The French subjugation of Vietnam, which began in 1862 with the takeover of Saigon and the southern provinces, was ostensibly to protect Vietnamese Christians and European Catholic missionaries from persecution by the Vietnamese government. The French subsequently took over northern Vietnam, Laos, and Cambodia and combined these territories into French Indochina. The Dutch extended their political authority in the East Indies in the late nineteenth century to head off European competitors and to exploit the islands' tin, oil, rubber, and agricultural products. Finally, the United States became an imperialist power in the region when it took over the Philippines from Spain after the Spanish-American War of 1898.

Western colonialism in most of Southeast Asia was relatively brief, lasting on average only a century or less, but it was still significant. In politics it brought administrative cohesion to diverse island groupings such as the East Indies, and elsewhere it weakened or eliminated the authority of traditional leaders. It also altered the region's economy by stimulating enterprises such as tin mining and rubber production, introducing new crops such as the oil palm, improving communications, and promoting the construction of new harbors and rail systems. In part because of economic development, the region's population soared from approximately 26 million in 1830 to 123 million in the 1940s. Western colonialism also expanded education and introduced the ideologies of nationalism, liberalism, and democracy. Inevitably, these developments inspired anticolonial movements that after World War II led to the emergence of independent states throughout the region.

Reform from Above in Thailand

▼▼▼

68 ▾ *King Chulalongkorn, EDICTS AND PROCLAMATIONS*

Unlike the rulers of Burma, who underestimated the British threat, and those of Vietnam, who provoked the French by persecuting Christians, the kings of Thailand pursued a policy of compromise with the West and a program of European-inspired reform. As a result, Thailand lost territory in the imperialist era, but not its independence.

Since the 1600s, contacts between Thailand and the West had been minimal, but in the 1820s British merchants began to seek trading privileges, and missionaries, many of them American Protestants, became active. Missionaries made few converts among Thailand's Buddhists, but they introduced Western medicine, science, and the country's first printing press. They also influenced King Mongkut (r. 1851–1868), who oversaw Thailand's early response to the West. Before becoming king, Mongkut spent twenty-seven years in a Buddhist monastery, where in addition to his religious studies he learned Western languages and developed an interest in Western science and mathematics. As king, he sought to modernize Thailand's army and economy and accommodate Western powers by opening Thailand to trade.

Mongkut's policies were continued under his son Chulalongkorn (one of the eighty children Mongkut fathered after abandoning monastic celibacy at age forty-seven), who reigned from 1868 to 1910. Chulalongkorn's experiences included trips to India, Java, and Malaya and two visits to Europe. He delicately balanced his diplomatic relations with Great Britain, which controlled Burma and the Malay Peninsula, and France, which dominated Indochina. He also introduced railroad, postal, and telegraph systems; founded schools; and abolished slavery.

The following excerpts from Chulalongkorn's speeches and writings provide insights into his motives and style as a reformer. The first two sections deal with education, the expansion of which was important to Chulalongkorn's plans to modernize his country. The third excerpt is from a speech in 1864 on the subject of slavery, a centuries-old institution in Thailand. Large numbers of Thais sold themselves into slavery to cancel debts or escape poverty, and by doing so also consigned their children to slavery. The state put a value on slaves at various ages, and slaves could gain their freedom if they paid their master their worth. Few could do this, so most slaves were slaves for life. Chulalongkorn gradually liberalized Thailand's slavery laws and in 1895 abolished slavery altogether.

QUESTIONS FOR ANALYSIS

1. What were Chulalongkorn's convictions about education, and how were they linked to his strategy for ending slavery?
2. According to Chulalongkorn, what kind of person should Thailand's educational system seek to produce?
3. In Chulalongkorn's view, what are the major deficiencies of missionary schools?
4. What motivated Chulalongkorn to improve the lot of slaves in Thailand?
5. Why does he believe that immediately ending slavery would be a mistake?
6. How does Chulalongkorn's approach to reform resemble and differ from that of Russia's Peter the Great (source 28)?

ROYAL PROCLAMATION ON EDUCATION

. . . Chulalongkorn, Lord of Siam, considers that, though the long-established practice in education in Siam has been to use the monastery as the seat of learning and the home as the center of vocational training in the family, in modern times the increasing tempo of international communications by means of steamers at sea and railways on land and the increasing international contacts caused by the necessity of nations to exchange commodities, have dictated a reorientation of academic and technical training in a correct and useful manner and also a proper adjustment of outmoded disciplines and arts. . . .

The Government has for some time maintained schools; but the original purpose of training people for the needs of the civil service has misled some into thinking that learning is meant exclusively for those destined for the civil service and that it is no part of the masses' duty to seek knowledge. . . .

In actual fact, education leads to intelligence and proper behavior and skill in earning one's living. No matter what a person's career is, whether it be in teaching, medicine, trade or mechanics, prior learning is essential for success in life. . . .

From now on it shall be the duty of parents and guardians to teach their children and afford them such opportunity for education as their status and financial means allow. . . . The purpose of such education and training shall be to inculcate the following qualities: inquisitiveness for knowledge to whet intelligence and capability, good and righteous behavior, concern for family welfare, generosity to relatives, unity and harmony with spouses, faithfulness to friends, economy, kindness to others, regard for the public good, compliance with laws, willingness to serve the country with courage, loyalty to the throne in times of need, and gratefulness and loyalty to the throne at all times.

LETTER TO THE THAI MINISTER OF EDUCATION, 1910

Dear Praya Paisal,

I have one more thing to tell you. At the celebration of my birthday the Kulstree School[1] for royal ladies sent me 6 copies of the Wadhana Widhaya magazine, which is a monthly and which you may have seen yourself. . . .

My reaction as I went through the magazine was initially that these missionaries had a working knowledge of Siamese and that our girl students

[1]A school sponsored by the Church of England, England's state church, for educating princesses and daughters of the high nobility.

had a working knowledge of English. On reflection, however, it was seen that the knowledge of contributors was confined to narrow limits, since there were many errors in respect, for instance, to geography and history about which nothing was known. . . .

My conclusion from this was that, though the teaching of missionaries could bring about knowledge and intelligence in some matters, it could hardly foster patriotism, since the basic approach was already destructive of this. . . . In one place mention was made of liberty, which the Siamese were unlikely to understand. . . . This is something we are not accustomed to and must be a novelty. . . . I think it should be our principle to think out the approach to education that will promote the welfare of that part of the globe in which we live rather that which missionaries set up. What they preach will be different from the principles of learning in particular countries. Do they all preach this in all places and do they succeed elsewhere? I do not think they do. They can only deceive softhearted and ignorant women into following them. Even then these people [those who follow the missionaries' teachings] are in the minority and in an embarrassing position. They feel abashed to pay respect to Buddhist monks in the presence of Europeans, and are equally ashamed to let the Siamese know their European faith. There are many such Siamese, and it is not in the nature of our good citizens to be so. . . .

SPEECH ON SLAVERY (1864)

I wish to see whatever is beneficial to the people accomplished gradually according to circumstances and unjust, though well-established, customs abolished. But, as it is impossible to change everything overnight, steady pruning is necessary to lighten the burden. If this practice is adopted, things will proceed smoothly and satisfactorily as time goes by. As far as slavery is concerned, children born to slaves in their creditors' houses are considered by present legislation to be slaves. For this purpose, male slaves born in such circumstances from the age of 26 to 40 are worth each, according to present legislation, 14 *tamlungs*,[2] while female ones are worth each 12 *tamlungs*. In the case of male slaves of more than 40 and female ones of more than 30, value declines gradually with advancing age until at 100 male slaves are worth 1 *tamlung* while female ones 3 *baht*.

I feel that children born to slaves in their creditor's houses, who are slaves as from the time of delivery and are worth something even beyond 100, have not been treated kindly. Children thus born have nothing to do with their parents' wrongdoing. The parents have not only sold themselves into slavery but also dragged their innocent children into lifetime slavery and suffering on their behalf. But to emancipate them straight away now would put them into the danger of being neglected and being left to die by themselves, since unkind creditors, seeing no use in letting mothers look after their children, will put these mothers to work. It is therefore felt that, if these children are of no use to their parents' creditors, they will meet with no kindness. If the burden borne at present is so reduced as to allow them to become free, it seems advisable. Slaves' children aged from 8 upwards can be depended upon to work, and thus their full worth should be calculated as from this age. With advancing years their worth should be reduced until at 21 they are emancipated just in time for ordination as priests and for embarking on their careers. Similarly, female slaves are emancipated just in time to get married and have children. . . . Thus at 21 they are emancipated, and, in view of the fact that they have served their masters up to 20, enough advantage has been derived by their masters. . . .

▷ Chulalongkorn expresses his hope that all slavery might be abolished.

[2]A unit of Thai currency; one tamlung equaled four baht.

However, I do not think that my proposal can be carried to its logical conclusions, since pressure exists in the direction of making people want to become slaves despite our desire to see the contrary. Slaves do not have to pay high State taxes and do not have to engage in any regular occupation, since they are maintained by their masters. They work when work comes to them; otherwise they are unoccupied. When there is nothing to do and they happen to come by a bit of money, they gamble, since there is no risk of losing their means of subsistence. . . . If my proposal really succeeds, I can think of one other thing which can effectively liberate slaves' children from slavery. Slaves' children are compelled to serve their masters from an early age and know nothing other than what pleases their masters. Instead of getting vocational training, they spend their free time in gambling from early childhood so that this habit becomes ingrained, thereby preventing them from seeing any value in having a career. If they really have to quit slavery, they do not possess sufficient knowledge to improve their status and are compelled to return to slavery. It is because of this that there should be an institution for education similar to the old almshouse where, by royal command, education was given to children. There have been a good many men educated in this manner, and many available clerks at the time came from such institution. . . . At the present time, there are not enough clerks [literate people] to go round. Literate people are in great demand among the noblemen and will not readily remain slaves. This is why I feel that education can really free slaves. . . . Once they can read and write, various subjects including those derived from translated European texts can be taught. At 17 or 18 they should be able to apply their knowledge to various branches of the civil service as petty officials or clerks, or secure employment outside the civil service. . . . But school education is an increasingly expensive undertaking, and should begin in a small way with possibilities of gradual expansion. This will not only reduce the number of slaves but will also bring prosperity to the country, paving the way for a more drastic reform in the future. . . .

The Fall of Vietnam

69 ▾ Phan Thanh Gian, LETTER TO EMPEROR TU DUC and LAST MESSAGE TO HIS ADMINISTRATORS

In 1802 decades of civil war ended in Vietnam when Nguyen Anh unified the country after his conquest of Hanoi. Taking the name Emperor Gia Long, he and his successors sought to govern the country according to the principles of Confucianism, which had influenced Vietnamese politics and thought for many centuries. The Nguyen emperors' efforts to stabilize Vietnam and turn it into a model Confucian society led to the persecution of Vietnamese Catholics, who, as a result mainly of French missionary efforts, numbered 300,000 by the nineteenth century. When Catholics were implicated in a rebellion in 1833, Emperor Minh Mang ordered the imprisonment and execution of converts and European missionaries. Three years later he closed Vietnamese ports to European shipping. In response, the French sent naval vessels and troops to Vietnam, ostensibly to protect Christianity but also to advance French imperialism. Fighting broke out in earnest in 1858, and although the Vietnamese staunchly resisted, Emperor Tu Duc accepted

a settlement in 1862 by which he ceded to the French three southern provinces around Saigon.

Four years later an anti-French rebellion broke out west of Saigon, then under the governorship of Phan Thanh Gian (1796–1867), one of Vietnam's leading statesmen. When he failed to suppress the revolts, the French sent in troops and demanded control of the provinces. In 1867 Phan Thanh Gian acquiesced and then committed suicide, but not before he wrote the following two letters, one to Emperor Tu Duc and the other to administrators in his district.

QUESTIONS FOR ANALYSIS

1. What is the basis of Phan Thanh Gian's hope that the emperor can save Vietnam from further humiliation at the hands of the French?
2. What is Phan Thanh Gian's view of the French?
3. What evidence of Phan Thanh Gian's Confucian training do you see in the letter?
4. Why did Phan Thanh Gian decide to acquiesce to the French?

LETTER TO EMPEROR TU DUC

8, July 1867

I, Phan Thanh Gian, make the following report, in expressing frankly, with my head bowed, my humble sentiments, and in soliciting, with my head raised, your discerning scrutiny.

During the period of difficulties and misfortunes that we are presently undergoing, rebellion is rising around the capital, the pernicious [French] influence is expanding on our frontiers. . . .

My duty compels me to die. I would not dare to live thoughtlessly, leaving a heritage of shame to my Sovereign and my Father. Happily, I have confidence in my Emperor, who has extensive knowledge of ancient times and the present and who has studied profoundly the causes of peace and of dissension: . . . In respectfully observing the warnings of Heaven and in having pity on the misery of man . . . in changing the string of the guitar, in modifying the track of the governmental chariot, it is still possible for you to act in accordance with your authority and means.

At the last moment of life, the throat constricted, I do not know what to say, but, in wiping my tears and in raising my eyes toward you affectionately, I can only ardently hope that this wish will be realized. With respect, I make this report, Tu Duc, twentieth year, sixth moon, seventh day, Phan Thanh Gian.

LAST MESSAGE TO HIS ADMINISTRATORS

It is written: He who lives in accordance with the will of Heaven lives in virtue; he who does not live according to the will of Heaven lives in evil. To work according to the will of Heaven is to listen to natural reason. . . . Man is an intelligent animal created by Heaven. Every animal lives according to his nature, as water flows to low ground, as fire goes out on dry ground. . . .

The empire of our king is ancient. Our gratitude toward our kings is complete and always ardent; we cannot forget them. Now, the French are come, with their powerful weapons of war to cause dissension among us. We are weak against them; our commanders and our soldiers have been vanquished. Each battle adds to our misery. . . . The French have immense warships, filled with soldiers and armed with huge cannons. No one can resist them. They go where they want, the strongest ramparts fall before them.

I have raised my spirit toward Heaven and I have listened to the voice of reason. And I have said: "It would be as senseless for you to wish to defeat your enemies by force of arms as for a young fawn to attack a tiger. You attract uselessly great misfortunes upon the people whom Heaven has confided to you. I have thus written to all the mandarins and to all the war commanders to break their lances and surrender the forts without fighting.

"But, if I have followed the Will of Heaven by averting great evils from the head of the people, I am a traitor to our king in delivering without resistance the provinces which belong to him. . . . I deserve death. Mandarins and people, you can live under the command of the French, who are only terrible during the battle, but their flag must never fly above a fortress where Phan Thanh Gian still lives."

Multiple Voices VI ▾▾▾ The Loosening of Tradition: Feminist Voices in Egypt, Iran, China, and Japan

BACKGROUND

By the early 1900s, feminism was an important force in Western societies. Drawing on the natural-rights philosophy of the Enlightenment and the egalitarian principles of the French Revolution, nineteenth-century women had campaigned for political and economic rights, access to education, and greater vocational opportunities. They made modest gains. In much of Europe, the United States, Canada, Australia, and New Zealand, girls had access to primary and secondary education, and small numbers of women were able to attend universities and enter professions in medicine, law, and science. As result of urbanization and industrialization, more women were entering the paid work force as teachers, office workers, factory laborers, and nurses. Legal changes gave married women more control of their property and easier access to divorce. In Norway, Finland, and the states of Wyoming, Colorado, and Utah, women could vote in national elections.

Women's lives also were changing in non-Western societies in the nineteenth and early twentieth centuries, in many cases as a result of contacts with the West through colonialism. British rule in India, for example, led to the ban of *sati*, the ritual suicide of widows by burning, in a series of measures taken between 1798 and 1846. Colonial rule also altered the status of women in Algeria, Tunisia, and Libya, countries in which European legal systems superseded Islamic law.

In both colonies and semicolonial areas such as China and the Ottoman Empire, Christian missionary schools created new opportunities for female education. Missionary schools were open to boys and girls alike, and they introduced all their students to Western concepts of equality and individualism. In Egypt, India, and Southeast Asia, increasing numbers of upper-class families hired tutors to teach their daughters European languages and culture as part of their efforts to emulate Europeans. Around 1900 the growing number of women authors in these regions and most of their female readers were products of these new educational experiences.

Nationalism in non-Western lands also encouraged movements to improve women's status. Nationalists in Turkey, Arab lands, India, China, Japan, and Thailand came to see the oppression and abuse of women as an impediment to modernization and a source of embarrassment. They supported greater freedom, education, and job opportunities for women and sought to end perceived symbols of their society's backwardness, such as foot binding in China and the veiling and seclusion of women in Islamic lands.

Non-Western feminists faced formidable obstacles. Their audience was small, and their views were bitterly opposed by conservatives who considered their demands subversive to religion and morality. Patriarchy remained strong despite feminist challenges. But new issues had been raised, positions staked out, and agendas clarified. As much as in Europe and the United States, the efforts of non-Western feminists before World War I prepared the way for greater future changes.

THE SOURCES

The first source is an unsigned editorial entitled "Girls' Education Is the Basis of Civilization and Moral Refinement," published in the Persian newspaper ***The Dawn*** in 1907. Although state-controlled newspapers and journals had been published in Persia since the early 1800s, freedom of the press arrived only in 1907. This was the result of the Revolution of 1906–1907, which created a new constitution that instituted a parliament and guaranteed basic freedoms. ***The Dawn*** was one of dozens of newspapers, journals, and magazines that flourished briefly in the wake of these changes.

The second excerpt is drawn from a speech delivered in 1909 by the Egyptian feminist Malak Hifni Nasif, better known by her pen name, Bahithat al-Badiya (Arabic for "Seeker in the Desert"). Born into a prosperous family in Cairo, a city with a significant European population and many cultural ties with Europe, she was educated by private tutors and then at a private girls' school. On graduating, she became a teacher at her former school and a frequent contributor of essays and poems to various Cairo publications. In her writings and speeches, which were published in 1910, she addressed a wide range of issues pertaining to Egyptian women, including attire, education, marriage, and paid work.

In the following remarks, Bahithat al-Badiya discusses the issue of acceptable dress for Egyptian women. As can be seen, she rejects the traditional practice of restricting women to the home and requiring strict adherence to ***hijab***, the code that requires that a woman must cover everything but her face and her hands in the presence of nonrelated men. This attire includes a headscarf that covers a woman's hair, ears, neck, and upper chest and a voluminous cotton outergarment, or *izar*, that covers her to her throat, wrist, and ankle. Bahithat al-Badiya does not, however, recommend imitating the European style of dress.

The third source was written by the leading Chinese feminist of the early twentieth century, Qiu Jin (1875–1907), who devoted her life to women's liberation and the overthrow of the Qing Dynasty. Raised in a moderately wealthy family and well educated, Qiu was married to an older man but left China in 1903 to study in Japan. On her return in 1906, she founded a magazine and served as the principal for a girls' school. In 1907 she and her cousin were arrested and beheaded for revolutionary activity. In the following speech, probably delivered in 1906, she denounces the oppression of Chinese women, especially the practice of foot binding, the painful and injurious practice in which Chinese girls as young as four or five had their feet tightly wrapped and gradually bent until the arch was broken and all toes but the big toe were bent under. When the wrappings were removed seven to ten years later, the teenage girl was a semicripple with feet half their normal size, but she would be ready for matrimony. Girls with "big feet" were considered unmarriageable.

The fourth and final source is the work of Hiratsuka Raicho (1886–1971), a Japanese writer, journalist, and political activist, best known for her advocacy of women's rights. Born Hiratsuka Haruko into the family of a high-ranking government official in Tokyo, she attended Japan's Women's University, where her father required her to major in home economics, but she spent most of her time auditing courses on Western art and literature. On graduation she continued her studies of English and Zen Buddhism, but ruined her chance for a conventional marriage when the details of her affair with a married man became known. In 1911 she, along with a number of other Japanese female writers, founded a new literary magazine, *Seito* (Bluestocking), which soon became outspoken in its advocacy of women's rights. Under her pen name Raicho (Thunderbird), she gave the journal its motto, "In the beginning, woman was the sun," the title of her lead editorial in the journal's first issue. Although *Seito* ceased publication in 1916, it nonetheless made an important contribution to Japan's nascent feminist movement, and its founder, Hiratsuka Raicho, who continued to speak out on a wide range of social and political issues until her death in 1971, remains one of the movement's most important voices.

QUESTIONS FOR ANALYSIS

1. What specific issue or issues pertaining to women does each author address?
2. Taken as a whole, what do the four sources reveal about the status of women in Middle Eastern and East Asian societies around 1900?
3. Whom or what do the authors blame for the problems faced by women in their societies?
4. To what degree has the four authors' thinking been influenced by Western ideas and practices?
5. What role or roles do the authors envision for women once their "liberation" is achieved? How will their status compare with that of men?

1 ▾ "GIRLS' EDUCATION IS THE BASIS OF CIVILIZATION AND MORAL REFINEMENT"

The best path to civilization is the education, training of girls. The first necessity of moral refinement for girls is to be educated, trained, and cultured. Every nation that wants to become civilized has to begin educating and training girls from an early age. Each nation, according to their own religious laws and practices, should provide it [education] for them with any means possible.

Indeed, these girls will become mothers themselves, and their children will socialize with one another and their habits and disposition will spread among each other. But if they have all been educated in a good manner and with moral refinement, then there can be established in that nation a higher civilization. In this manner, the nation will develop and complete its march of progress by becoming civilized.

On the other hand, if the girls (children) are trained and raised by an uneducated mother, then the bad moods, habits, and disposition will have a bad effect on the children. Along with the growth and mental maturity, an indecent manner will be formed and become a habit; and it will also spread among the children. Therefore, barbarism will develop among the people and they will never become a civilized nation. . . .

Every character and manner, good or bad, when experienced by a child will develop inside him and will be there. When Confucius, a Chinese savant, saw the moral refinement that resulted from educating girls, he understood that it is the greatest and most desired outcome from their education. He took advantage of this idea and instituted it as a law in the Chinese nation. Thus, each girl that is educated and trained in decent manner and has not committed a sin will receive a specific amount of money from government.[1]

One day Napoleon arrived in one of the schools in France, and told the teachers: "I have provided the best necessities for education in France. I have made any resources available for learning by any means, so why is public instruction not improving, and why are the children not learning or advancing in their knowledge?" The teachers replied: "The home school teachers in France are not educated. The reason for retrogression and the lack of children's learning is because of the uneducated and untrained mothers."

Therefore, our nation, which has taken off the tattered garment of barbarism and savagery, and has put on the sash of honor and civilization, should not neglect the importance of girls' education and culture.

[1]It is unclear where the author got her information about Confucius. He was not an advocate of women's education and never was in a position to institute laws on this or other matters. It is also unclear where the author found the anecdote about Napoleon.

2 ▾ *Bahithat al-Badiya,* LECTURE IN THE CLUB OF THE UMMA PARTY

Men criticize the way we dress in the street. They have a point because we have exceeded the bounds of custom and propriety. We claim we are veiling but we are neither properly covered nor unveiled. I do not advocate a return to the veils of our grandmothers because it can rightly be called being buried alive, not *hijab*, correct covering. The woman used to spend her whole life within the walls of her house not going out into the street except when she was carried to her grave. I do not, on the other hand, advocate unveiling, like Europeans, and mixing with men, because they are harmful to us. . . .

If we had been raised from childhood to go unveiled and if our men were ready for it I would approve of unveiling for those who want it. But the nation is not ready for it now. Some of our prudent women do not fear to mix with men, but we have to place limits on those who are less prudent because we are quick to imitate and seldom find our authenticity in the veil. Don't you see that diamond tiaras were originally meant for queens and princesses and now they are worn by singers and dancers. . . .

The way we wear the *izar* now imitates the dress of Europeans, but we have outdone them in display. The European woman wears the simplest dress she has when she is outside and wears whatever she wishes at home or when invited to soirées. But our women are just the opposite. In front of her husband she wears a simple tunic and when she goes out she wears her best clothes, loads herself down with jewelry and pours bottles of perfume on herself. . . . She walks swaying like bamboo in a way that entices passersby or at least they pretend to be enticed. I am sure that most of these showy women do this without bad intentions, but how can the onlooker understand good intentions when appearances do not indicate it?

Veiling should not prevent us from breathing fresh air or going out to buy what we need if no one can buy it for us. It must not prevent us from gaining an education or cause our health to deteriorate. When we have finished our work and feel restless and if our house does not have a spacious garden why shouldn't we go to the outskirts of the city and take the fresh air that God has created for everyone and not just put in boxes exclusively for men. But, we should be prudent and not take promenades alone and we should avoid gossip. We should not saunter moving our heads right and left. . . .

The imprisonment in the home of the Egyptian woman of the past is detrimental while the current freedom of the European is excessive. I cannot find a better model [than] today's Turkish woman. She falls between the two extremes and does not violate what Islam prescribes. She is a good example of decorum and modesty.

I have heard that some of our high officials are teaching their girls European dancing and acting. I consider both despicable — a detestable crossing of boundaries and a blind imitation of Europeans. Customs should not be abandoned except when they are harmful. European customs should not be taken up by Egyptians except when they are appropriate and practical. What good is there for us in women and men holding each other's waists dancing or daughters appearing on stage before audiences acting with bare bosoms in love scenes? This is contrary to Islam and a moral threat we must fight as much as we can. . . .

---

3 ▾ *Qiu Jin,* AN ADDRESS TO TWO HUNDRED MILLION FELLOW COUNTRYWOMEN

Alas! The greatest injustice in this world must be the injustice suffered by our female population of two hundred million. If a girl is lucky enough to have a good father, then her childhood is at least tolerable. But if by chance her father is an ill-tempered and unreasonable man, he may curse her birth: "What rotten luck: another useless thing." Some men go as far as killing baby girls while most hold the opinion that "girls are eventually someone else's property" and treat them with coldness and disdain. In a few years, without thinking about whether it is right or wrong, he[2] forcibly binds his daughter's soft, white feet with white cloth so that even in her sleep she cannot find comfort and relief until the flesh becomes rotten and the bones broken. What is all this misery for? Is it just so that on the girl's wedding day friends and neighbors will compliment him, saying, "Your daughter's feet are really small"? Is that what the pain is for?

But that is not the worst of it. When the time for marriage comes, a girl's future life is placed in the hands of a couple of shameless matchmakers and a family seeking rich and powerful in-laws. A match can be made without anyone ever inquiring whether the prospective bridegroom is honest, kind, or educated. . . . After her marriage, if the man doesn't do her any harm, she is told that she should thank Heaven for her good fortune. But if the man is bad or he ill-treats her, she is told that her marriage is retribution for some sin committed in her previous existence. If she complains at all or tries to reason with her husband, he may get angry and beat her. When other people find out they will criticize, saying, "That woman is bad; she doesn't know how to behave like a wife.". . . Why is there no justice for women? We constantly hear men say, "The human mind is just and we must treat people with fairness and equality." Then why do they greet women like black slaves from Africa? How did inequality and injustice reach this state?

Dear sisters, you must know that you'll get nothing if you rely upon others. You must go out and get things for yourselves. In ancient times when decadent scholars came out with such nonsense as "men are exalted, women are lowly," "a virtuous woman is one without talent," and "the husband guides the wife," ambitious and spirited women should have organized and opposed them. . . . Men feared that if women were educated they would become superior to men, so they did not allow us to be educated. Couldn't the women have challenged the men and refused to submit? It seems clear now that it was we women who abandoned our responsibilities to ourselves and felt content to let men do everything for us. As long as we could live in comfort and leisure, we let men make all the decisions for us. When men said we were useless, we became useless; when they said we were incapable, we stopped questioning them even when our entire female sex had reached slave status. . . . When we heard that men liked small feet, we immediately bound them just to please them, just to keep our free meal tickets. As for their forbidding us to read and write, well, that was only too good to be true. . . .

. . . Let us all put aside our former selves and be resurrected as complete human beings. Those of you who are old, do not call yourselves old and useless. If your husbands want to open schools, don't stop them; if your good sons want to study abroad, don't hold them back. Those among us who are middle-aged, don't hold back your husbands lest they lose their ambition and spirit and fail in their work. After your sons are born, send them to schools. You must do the same for your daughters and, whatever you do, don't bind their feet. As for you young girls among us, go to school if you can. If not, read and study at home. . . . You must know that when a country is near destruction, women cannot rely on the men any more because they aren't even able to protect themselves. If we don't take heart now and shape up, it will be too late when China is destroyed.

---

[2]Although Qiu uses the male pronoun, the actual work of binding feet was performed by female members of the girl's family, usually mothers or grandmothers.

4 ▾ Hiratsuka Raicho, "IN THE BEGINNING WOMAN WAS THE SUN" (1911)

In the beginning, woman was truly the sun, and a true being. Now woman is the moon. She lives by others, and shines through the light of others. Her countenance is pale, like a patient.

We must now restore the sun, which has been hidden from us. . . .

Freedom and Liberation! Oftentimes we have heard the term "liberation of women." But what is it then? Are we not seriously misunderstanding the term freedom or liberation? Even if we call the problem the liberation of women, are there not many other issues involved? Assuming that women are freed from external oppression, liberated from constraint, given so-called higher education, employed in various occupations, given [the] franchise, and provided an opportunity to be independent from the protection of their parents and husbands, and to be freed from the little confinement of their homes, can all of these be called liberation of women? They may provide proper surroundings and opportunities to let us fulfill the true goal of liberation. Yet they remain merely the means, and do not represent our goal or ideals.

However, I am unlike many intellectuals in Japan who suggest that higher education is not necessary for women. Men and women are endowed by nature to have equal faculties. Therefore, it is odd to assume that one of the sexes requires education while the other does not. This may be tolerated in a given country and in a given age, but it is fundamentally a very unsound proposition.

I bemoan the fact that there is only one private college for women in Japan, and that there is no tolerance on man's part to permit entrance of women into many universities maintained for men. However, what benefit is there when the intellectual level of women becomes similar to that of men? . . .

Now, what is the true liberation which I am seeking? It is none other than to provide an opportunity for women to develop fully their hidden talents and hidden abilities. We must remove all the hindrances that stand in the way of women's development, whether they be external oppression or lack of knowledge. And above and beyond these factors, we must realize that we are the masters in possession of great talents. . . .

▲▲▲

Part Four

The Global Community and Its Challenges in the Twentieth and Twenty-First Centuries

WHAT WILL FUTURE HISTORIANS say about the last 100 years of human history? How will they interpret the wars, revolutions, economic transformations, new ideologies, technological breakthroughs, population trends, cultural changes, and countless other events and developments that took place? How will they explain the seeming contradiction between humankind's stupendous achievements and its abysmal failures? From the perspective of the early twenty-first century, no one can answer such questions. Future historians' views of our past will be shaped by events that have not yet occurred and by values and concerns unique to their own era. What seems of great consequence to us, therefore, may be insignificant to them, while developments we barely notice may be important parts of their stories.

It would be surprising, however, if future historians did not note the importance of the dramatic shift in world political relationships that took place after World War II. The world of the early 1900s was a Eurocentric world. Europeans and people of European descent living elsewhere were the best-educated and wealthiest people on earth. When one spoke of the Great Powers, they all were European states or European offshoots such as Russia and the United States. They were the political masters of Africa and much of Asia and dominated the global economy. After World War II, Europe's primacy ended. The Europeans' colonial empires disintegrated, their paramount role in international relations ended, and their economic importance declined in the face of global competition.

Future historians undoubtedly also will highlight the phenomenon of globalization, a word and concept that came into common usage at the end of the twentieth century to describe the unprecedented scale of integration and interaction that had come to dominate relationships among the world's peoples. Human interaction, of course, was nothing new. Long-distance trade, migration, travel, missionary activity, wars of conquest, and the diffusion of new ideas and technologies had been parts of history for thousands of years. Interaction on a global scale increased markedly in the fifteenth and sixteenth centuries, when Europeans opened sea routes to Africa, the Americas, and Asia and launched a new era in commerce, migration, and biological exchange. During the twentieth century, however, breakthroughs in communications and transportation virtually obliterated the limitations of time and space, and the exchange of goods and ideas among the world's peoples reached undreamed-of levels. It became the age of *world* wars, *multinational* corporations, *global* communication networks, the *World Wide Web*, and thousands of *international* organizations.

Historians assuredly will note other developments: the ongoing rush of scientific, medical, and technological discoveries; the spectacular expansion of the world's population (from approximately 1.7 billion in 1900 to 6.8 billion in 2007); the relative decline of the world's rural population and the growth of cities, best represented by megacities such as Tokyo, Mexico City, São Paulo, and Mumbai; and the emergence of a shared global culture, symbolized by the unlimited possibilities of the Internet and the ubiquity of McDonald's restaurants, Japanese automobiles, blue jeans, twenty-four-hour cable news networks, and Chinese manufactured goods of every imaginable sort.

What else historians will say about the last 100 years is open to conjecture. They undoubtedly will take note of our recent history's inhumanities and cruelties: its appalling war casualties, its use of torture, and its genocides, not just against Jews in World War II but also against Armenians in World War I; Cambodians in the 1970s; Bosnians, Kosovars, and Tutsi in the 1990s; and the Fur, Zaghawa, and Massaleit peoples of Darfur in the early 2000s. Will such developments be described as aberrations or the beginning of a new trend toward brutality and callousness in human relationships? Historians surely will discuss the emergence of more than 100 new independent states in Africa and Asia after the demise of colonialism. Will their stories be celebrations of economic and political achievement or tales of failure and disillusionment? They will note that the twentieth and early twenty-first centuries were marked by signs of both growing religious fervor and indifference; environmental disasters and growing environmental consciousness; and the globalization of culture and the continued appeal of nationalism and ethnic identification.

In looking to the future, optimists affirm their faith in progress, holding fast to the dream that reasonable human beings are capable of shaping a future of peace, harmony, and a just sharing of the world's wealth. Pessimists ponder population projections, inevitable energy shortages, worsening pollution, global warming, and the persistence of intractable political conflicts and warn of the coming of a new "dark age." However things develop, recent history has launched humankind on new paths that will determine its future for years to come.

Chapter 11

The Industrialized World in Crisis

IN 1922 THE FRENCH INTELLECTUAL Paul Valéry spoke these words in a speech to a university audience in Switzerland:

> The storm has died away, and still we are restless, uneasy, as if the storm is about to break. Almost all the affairs of men remain in terrible uncertainty. We think of what has disappeared, we are almost destroyed by what has been destroyed; we do not know what will be born, and we fear the future, not without reason. We hope vaguely, we dread precisely; . . . we confess that the charm of life is behind us, abundance is behind us, but doubt and disorder are in us and with us. There is no thinking man, however shrewd or learned he may be, who can hope to overcome this anxiety, to escape this darkness, to measure the probable duration of this period when the vital relations of humanity are disturbed profoundly.[1]

How stark a contrast between Valéry's despondency and the optimism that preceded World War I. Before the war the West's wealth and power reached unimagined heights, and most Americans and Europeans were self-satisfied, proud, and confident. They took for granted their moral and intellectual superiority and were convinced that their world dominance would last indefinitely. The people of Japan, a new entrant into the ranks of industrialized nations, imagined a different future, but like the people of the West they looked forward to that future with high expectations. Only a few years later, assurance gave way to doubt, hope to despair, and moderation to fanaticism.

The turning point, especially for Europe, was World War I — the four-year exercise in death that resulted in 30 million casualties, billions of squandered dollars, and a disturbing realization that human inventiveness could have dark and devastating

[1]Paul Valéry, *Variety* (New York: Harcourt Brace, 1927), p. 252.

consequences. The war and the postwar treaties set the stage for three decades marked by worldwide economic depression, totalitarianism, diplomatic failure, contempt for human rights, and, finally, a second world war with a legacy of 50 to 60 million dead, the attempted annihilation of Europe's Jews, and the dropping of the first atomic bombs.

Interwar intellectuals who shared Paul Valéry's anxiety and gloom prophesied the fall of Western civilization and drew analogies between the decline of the West in the twentieth century and the fatal problems of fifth-century Rome. Post–World War II developments discredited much of their pessimism. The industrialized nations, even devastated Germany and Japan, recovered from the wars, affirmed a commitment to liberal democracy, and rebuilt their economies. What changed was their role in the world. Empires disappeared, and formerly colonial peoples reestablished their political independence. The traumatic events that unfolded between 1914 and 1945 were largely responsible for these changes.

The Trauma of World War I

Why did Europeans find World War I so demoralizing, so unsettling, so devoid of any quality or result that might have justified its appalling costs and casualties? War, after all, was nothing new for Europeans. Dynastic wars, religious wars, commercial wars, colonial wars, civil wars, wars to preserve or destroy the balance of power, wars of every conceivable variety fill the pages of European history books. Some of these wars involved dozens of states, and some can even be considered world wars. The Seven Years' War (1756–1763) was fought in Europe, the Americas, and India. The wars of the French Revolution and Napoleonic Era spilled over from Europe into Egypt and had reverberations in the Americas, South Africa, and Southeast Asia. Yet none of these experiences prepared Europeans for the war they fought between 1914 and 1918.

The sheer number of battlefield casualties goes far to explain the war's devastating impact. The war's thirty-two belligerents mobilized approximately 65 million men, of whom just under 10 million were killed and slightly more than 20 million were wounded. To present these statistics in another way, this means that for approximately 1,500 consecutive days, on average 6,000 men were killed every day. Losses were high on both the eastern and western fronts, but those in the west were more troubling. Here, after the Germans almost took Paris in the early weeks of fighting, the war became a stalemate until the armistice on November 11, 1918. Along a 400-mile front stretching from the English Channel through

Belgium and France to the Swiss border, defense — a combination of trenches, barbed wire, land mines, poison gas, and machine guns — proved superior to offense — massive artillery barrages followed by charges of troops sent over the top across no man's land to overrun enemy lines. Such attacks produced unbearably long casualty lists but minuscule gains of territory.

Such losses would have been easier to endure if the war had led to a secure and lasting peace. But the hardships and antagonisms of the postwar years rendered such sacrifice meaningless. After the war, winners and losers alike faced inflation, high unemployment, and, after a few years of prosperity in the 1920s, the affliction of the Great Depression. Embittered by their defeat and harsh treatment in the Versailles Treaty, the Germans abandoned their democratic Weimar Republic for Hitler's Nazi dictatorship in 1933. Japan and Italy, though on the winning side, were disappointed with their territorial gains, and this resentment played into the hands of ultranationalist politicians. The Arabs, who had fought against Germany's ally, the Turks, in the hope of achieving nationhood, were embittered when Great Britain and France denied their independence. The United States, disillusioned with war and Great Power wrangling, withdrew into diplomatic isolation, leaving Great Britain and France to enforce the postwar treaties. Britain and France expanded their colonial empires in Africa and the Middle East, but this was scant compensation for their casualties, expenditures, and postwar problems. There were no true victors in World War I.

The Romance of War

70 ▾ *POPULAR ART AND POSTER ART FROM GERMANY, ENGLAND, AND AUSTRALIA*

When war came in 1914, crowds cheered, men rushed to enlist, and politicians promised that "the boys would be home by Christmas." Without having experienced a general war since the defeat of Napoleon in 1815 and with little thought to the carnage in the American Civil War, Europeans saw the war as a glorious adventure — an opportunity to fight for the flag or the kaiser or the king; to wear splendid uniforms; and to win glory in battles decided by élan, spirit, and bravery. The war they fought was nothing like the war they imagined, and the disparity between expectations and reality was one of many reasons why World War I brought forth such despair and disillusionment.

The four illustrations shown here portray both the eagerness and the optimism of all belligerents at the war's start as well as their efforts to sustain this enthusiasm as the war dragged on. *The Departure* (page 349, left) shows German troops departing for the battlefront in late summer 1914. The work of a Swedish artist, B. Hennerberg, it appeared in the German periodical *Simplicissimus* in August 1914. Noted before the war for its irreverent satire and criticism of German militarism, *Simplicissimus* lent its full support to the war effort once the fighting began.

The second illustration (page 349, right) is one of a series of war-related cards included by the Mitchell Tobacco Company in its packs of Golden Dawn Cigarettes in 1914 and early 1915. It shows a sergeant offering smokes to the soldiers under his command before battle. Tobacco advertising with military themes reached a saturation point in England during the war years.

The third illustration (page 350, left) is an Australian recruitment poster issued in 1915. Although Australia, like Canada, controlled its internal affairs by the time the war started, its foreign policy was still controlled by Great Britain. Hence when Great Britain went to war, so did Australia. The Australian parliament refused to approve conscription, however, so the government had to work hard to encourage volunteers. This particular poster appeared when Australian troops were heavily involved in the Gallipoli campaign, the allied effort to knock the Ottoman Empire out of the war. Directing its message to the many young men who were members of sports clubs, the recruitment poster promised them an opportunity to enlist in a battalion made up entirely of fellow sportsmen.

The fourth illustration (page 350, right) is a poster that was produced and distributed by the newly formed British Ministry of Munitions in early 1917 to encourage women to accept jobs in the munitions industry. This is an example of the effort from 1915 onward to enlist women in the war effort as medical workers, police, agricultural workers, porters, drivers, foresters, members of the Women's Auxiliary Army Corps, and, most important, factory laborers. It shows a young and attractive Englishwoman offering a jaunty salute to a passing soldier as she arrives for work. It gives no hint of the dangers of munitions work. During the war approximately 300 "munitionettes" were killed in explosions or from chemical-related sicknesses. Women who worked with TNT came to be known as "canaries" because of their yellowish skin. Despite such hazards and relatively low pay, approximately 950,000 women were working in munitions factories by war's end.

QUESTIONS FOR ANALYSIS

1. What message about the war does each of the four illustrations seek to convey?
2. In what specific ways does each illustration romanticize the life of a soldier or female munitions worker?
3. What impression of battle does the English tobacco card communicate?
4. What does a comparison of Hennerberg's painting and the English poster of the munitions worker suggest about changing views of women's role during the war and in society at large?

B. Hennerberg, *The Departure*

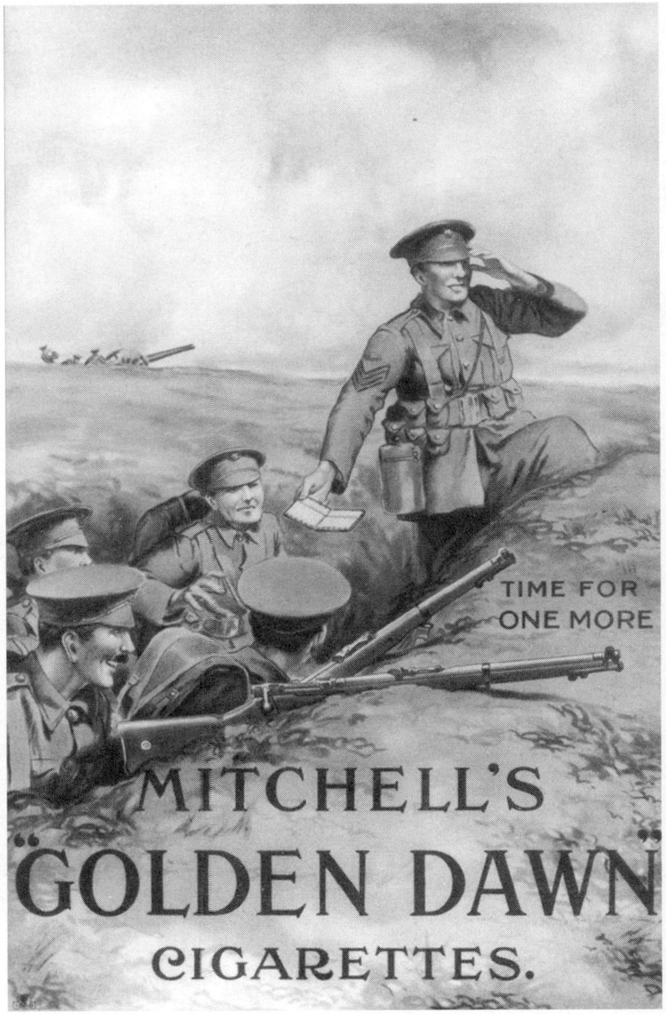

Advertisement card from Golden Dawn Cigarettes

Australian recruitment poster

Septimus Scott, *These Women Are Doing Their Bit*

Twenty-Four Hours on the Western Front

▼▼▼

71 ▼ Henry S. Clapham, *MUD AND KHAKI, MEMOIRS OF AN INCOMPLETE SOLDIER*

Until 1914 Henry S. Clapham led a conventional life. Born in 1875 in the town of Hull, he graduated from Queen's College in Taunton, a boarding school for the sons of well-to-do families. After clerking in a law office, he married and began a career as a solicitor in London. His favorite entertainment was playing the card game bridge. In the fall of 1914, however, he answered the call to enlist and by January 1915 was a British soldier fighting to hold back the Germans in northern Belgium. Clapham fought there until October 1915, when a hand wound made him unfit for service. On his return to England, he resumed his career as a lawyer and, like many returning soldiers, prepared his diary notes for publication as a book, which appeared in 1917 with the title *Mud and Khaki*. It went through several printings and was republished in 1930.

Clapham's book describes his experiences fighting in and around Ypres, a Belgian city of some 200,000 in the low, wet, largely unforested region that abuts the English Channel. It was the site of three major battles, one in the fall of 1914, another in 1915, and the last and bloodiest in 1917. Clapham fought in the so-called Second Battle of Ypres, which began in April 1915 when General Erich von Falkenhayn ordered a German attack on the entrenched English, Canadian, French, and French colonial troops to firm up German lines and divert allied troops from an anticipated offensive farther south. After the Germans abandoned their offensive in late May, fighting continued in the region, as Clapham's memoir clearly shows.

The Second Battle of Ypres saw the introduction of poison gas on the Western Front. Chlorine gas, a product of the German dyestuff industry and developed by the German chemical company IG Farben, could be released from cylinders or delivered by artillery shells. It stimulated the lungs to produce fluid, causing the victim to drown. Thousands of soldiers around Ypres died as a result of German gas attacks, but the effectiveness of the new weapon diminished when soldiers were supplied with respirators, or gas masks, and learned that holding a wet (often urine-soaked) handkerchief over one's nose and mouth provided some protection. Such countermeasures stimulated both sides to develop other types of poison gas, including phosgene, which causes asphyxiation, and mustard gas, which causes severe blistering.

QUESTIONS FOR ANALYSIS

1. As far as can be determined by Clapham's account, what were the actual results of the one day of fighting he describes?
2. What aspects of the fighting did Clapham and the other men find most unnerving?

3. **Wars inevitably cause immense human suffering. But the suffering in World War I for soldiers and civilians alike was especially traumatic and unbearable. What is there in Clapham's account that may explain this phenomenon?**

JUNE 19, 1915

We started again at dusk and passed down the railway cutting, but, instead of turning off into the fields, we went on as far as the Menin Road, at what is known as "Hell Fire Corner." A few hundred yards down the road we found a resting place for the night in some shallow "jumping off" trenches, a few yards back from the front line. It was very dark, and the trench was small, and sitting in a huddle I got a cramp and felt miserable.

The Huns[1] started by putting over big crumps[2] all around us. They seemed to aim for the relics of a building a hundred yards in the rear, and there the bricks were flying. . . . Then at 2:50 A.M. our own guns started and kept up a heavy bombardment of the trenches in front until 4:15, by which time it was quite light. . . .

At 4.15 a whistle blew. The men in the front line went over the top, and we scrambled out and took their places in the front trench. In front of us was a small field . . . split diagonally by an old footpath. On the other side of the field was a belt of trees in which lay the Hun trench.

In a few moments flags went up there, to show that it had been captured and that the troops were going on. Another whistle, and we ourselves scrambled over the parapet[3] and sprinted across the field. Personally I was so overweighted that I could only amble. . . . I took the diagonal path, as the line of least resistance, and most of my section did the same.

When I dropped into the Hun trench I found it a great place, only three feet wide, and at least eight deep, and beautifully made of white sandbags, back and front. At that spot there was no sign of any damage by our shells, but a number of dead Huns lay in the bottom. There was a sniper's post just where I fell in, a comfortable little square hole, fitted with seats and shelves, bottles of beer, tinned meats, and a fine helmet hanging on a hook.

Our first duty was to change the [barbed] wire, so . . . I slipped off my pack, and, clambering out again, started to move the wire from what was now the rear, to the new front of the trench. It was rotten stuff, most of it loose coils. . . . What there was movable of it, we got across without much difficulty, and we had just finished when we were ordered to move down the trench, as our diagonal advance had brought us too far to the right.

We moved down along the belt of woodland, which was only a few yards broad, to a spot where one of our companies was already hard at work digging a communication trench[4] back to our old front line. Here there was really no trench at all. One or more of our own big shells had burst in the middle, filling it up for a distance of ten yards and practically destroying both parapet and parados.[5] Some of us started building up the parapet with sandbags, and I saw the twins [two men in Clapham's unit] merrily at work hauling out dead Huns at least twice their own size.

---

[1]A derogatory term for German soldiers in World War I. The Huns were a nomadic people of Central Asia whose invasions of the fourth and fifth century C.E. contributed to the fall of the Western Roman Empire. The Huns were legendary for their cruelty and ferocity.

[2]A heavy German shell that exploded with a cloud of black smoke.

[3]A mound built to protect the front of a trench.

[4]A shallow trench built from the front line to a relatively safe area in the rear. Used to supply front-line troops with food and ammunition and to transport killed and wounded soldiers away from the fighting.

[5]A mound built to protect the rear of a trench.

There was a hedge along the back of the trench, so I scrambled through a hole in it, piled my pack, rifle, and other things, including the helmet, on the farther side, and started again on the wire. Hereabouts it was much better stuff, and it took us some time to get it across and pegged down. We had just got the last knife-rest across, when I saw a man who was placing sandbags on the parapet from the farther side swivel round, throw his legs into the trench, and collapse in a heap in the bottom. Several others were already lying there, and for the first time I realized that a regular hail of machine-gun bullets was sweeping over the trench.

. . . We all started work at a feverish pace, digging out the trench and building up some sort of shelter in front. One chap, a very nice kid, was bowled over almost at once with a bullet in the groin, and lay in the trench, kicking and screaming while we worked. . . .

The attacking battalions had carried several more trenches and we were told that two at least had been held, but our own orders were to consolidate and hold on to the trench we were in at all costs. . . .

I had just filled a sandbag and placed it on the top of the parapet when I happened to glance down, and saw a slight movement in the earth between my feet. I stooped and scraped away the soil with my fingers and found what seemed like palpitating flesh. It proved to be a man's cheek, and a few minutes' work uncovered his head. I poured a little water down his throat, and two or three of us dug out the rest of him. He was undamaged except for his feet and ankles, which were a mass of pulp, and he recovered consciousness as we worked. The first thing he said was in English: "What Corps are you?" He was a big man, and told us he was forty-five and had only been a soldier for a fortnight.

We dragged him out and laid him under the hedge. There was nothing else we could do for him. He had another drink later, but he must have died in the course of the day. I am afraid we forgot all about him, but nothing could have lived there until evening.

The Captain was the next to go. He insisted on standing on the parados, directing operations, and got a bullet in the lungs. He could walk, and two men were detailed to take him down to the dressing-station. One came back, to be killed later in the day, but the other stopped a bullet *en route*, and followed the Captain.

When we had got our big Hun out, he left a big hole in the ground, and we found a dead arm and hand projecting from the bottom. We dug about, but did not seem to be able to find the body, and when I seized the sleeve and pulled, the arm came out of the ground by itself. We had to dig deeper for our own sake, but there was nothing else left, except messy earth, which seemed to have been driven into the side of the trench. The man helping me turned sick, for it wasn't pretty work. . . .

About 5.30 A.M. the Huns started shelling, and the new communication trench soon became a death-trap. A constant stream of wounded who had come down another trench from the north, passed along the rear. The Huns made a target of the two traverses (unluckily including our own), from which the communication trench opened, and numbers of the wounded were caught just behind us. The trench itself was soon choked with bodies. . . .

The shelling got worse as the day wore on and several more of our men went down. They plastered us with crumps, shrapnel, and whizz-bangs.[6] One of the latter took off a sandbag from the top of the parapet and landed it on my head. It nearly broke my neck and I felt ill for some time after. . . .

The worst of it was the inaction. Every minute several shells fell within a few yards and covered us with dust, and the smell of the explosives poisoned

[6]*Shrapnel* were hollow shells filled with bullets or pieces of metal that scattered on explosion. *Whizzbangs* were shells fired by light German field guns.

my mouth. All I could do was to crouch against the parapet and pant for breath, expecting every moment to be my last. And this went on for hours. I began to long for the shell which would put an end to everything, but in time my nerves became almost numbed, and I lay like a log until roused.

I think it must have been midday when something happened. An alarm was given and we manned the parapet, to see some scores of men retreating at a run from the trench in front. They ran right over us, men of half a dozen battalions, and many dropped on the way. As they passed, something was said of gas, but it appeared that nearly all the officers in the two front trenches had been killed or wounded, someone had raised an alarm of gas, and the men had panicked and run.

A lot of the runaways insisted on gathering by the hedge just behind us, in spite of our warnings not to do so, and I saw at least twenty hit by shrapnel within a few yards of us.

The Brigade-Major arrived, cursing, and called upon some of our own men to advance and reoccupy the trench in front. He led them himself, and they made a very fine dash across. I do not think more than twenty fell, and they reoccupied the trench and, I believe, the third also, before the Huns realized that they were empty. . . .

Soon the runaways began to return. They had been turned back, in some cases, at the point of the revolver, but when their first panic had been overcome, they came back quite willingly, although they must have lost heavily in the process. They crowded into our trench, and there was hardly room to move a limb.

It was scorchingly hot and no one could eat, although I tried to do so. All day long we were constantly covered with debris from the shell-bursts. Great pieces fell all about us, and, packed like herrings, we crowded in the bottom of the trench. Hardly anything could be done for the wounded. If their wounds were slight, they generally risked a dash to the rear. Every now and then we stood to in expectation of a counter-attack, but none developed.

About 6 P.M. the worst moment of the day came. The Huns started to bombard us with a shell which was quite new to us. It sounded like a gigantic fire-cracker, with two distinct explosions. These shells came over just above the parapet, in a flood, much more quickly than we could count them. After a quarter of an hour of this sort of thing, there was a sudden crash in the trench and ten feet of the parapet, just beyond me, was blown away and everyone around blinded by the dust. With my first glance I saw what looked like half a dozen bodies, mingled with sandbags, and then I smelt gas and realized that these were gas-shells. I had my respirator on in a hurry and most of our own men were as quick. The others were slower and suffered for it. One man was sick all over the sandbags and another was coughing his heart up. We pulled four men out of the debris unharmed. One man was unconscious, and died of gas later. Another was hopelessly smashed up and must have got it full in the chest.

We all thought that this was the end and almost hoped for it, but luckily the gas-shells stopped, and after a quarter of an hour we could take off our respirators. I started in at once to build up the parapet again, for we had been laid open to the world in front, but the gas lingered about the hole for hours, and I had to give up delving in the bottom for a time. As it was it made me feel very sick.

A counter-attack actually commenced as soon as the bombardment ceased, and we had to stand to again. . . . As we leaned over the parapet, I saw the body of a Hun lying twenty yards out in front. It commenced to writhe and finally half-sat up. I suppose the gas had caught him. The man standing next me — a corporal in a county battalion — raised his rifle, and before I could stop him, sent a bullet into the body. It was a rotten thing to see, but I suppose it was really a merciful end for the poor chap, better than his own gas, at any rate.

The men in the front trenches had got it as badly as we had, and if the counter-attack was pressed, it did not seem humanly possible, in the condition we were in, to offer a successful defence. . . . Fortunately, our own guns started and apparently caught the Huns massing. The counter-attack accordingly crumpled up.

In the midst of it all, someone realized that the big gap in the parapet could not be manned, and four of us, including myself, were ordered to lie down behind what was left of the parados and cover the gap with our rifles. It was uncomfortable work, as . . . the place was a jumble of dead bodies. We could not stand up to clear them away, and in order to get a place at all, I had to lie across the body of a gigantic Hun. . . .

We managed to get some sort of parapet erected in the end. It was more or less bullet-proof, at any rate. At dusk some scores of men came back from the front line, wounded or gassed. They had to cross the open at a run or a shamble, but I did not see any hit. Then the Brigade-Major appeared, and cheered us by promising a relief that night. It still rained shells, although not so hard as before dusk, and we did not feel capable of standing much more of it.

The Russian Revolution and the Foundation of the Soviet State

One of the most important results of World War I was the downfall of Russia's tsarist regime and its replacement by a Bolshevik dictatorship inspired by the doctrines of Karl Marx. Tsar Nicholas II, facing battlefield defeat, army defections, and rioting in St. Petersburg, abdicated in March 1917. Tsarist rule was replaced by a liberal provisional government charged with governing Russia until a constituent assembly could meet and write a new constitution. Seven months later, the Bolsheviks wrested power from the provisional government, and after four years of civil war they established the world's first communist state.

Nicholas II's Russia was full of discontent. Its millions of peasants were no longer serfs, but they still lived in abysmal poverty. Some moved to Moscow or St. Petersburg to work in Russia's factories, but without political power or unions, most exchanged the squalor of the rural village for the squalor of the urban slum. Meanwhile, many intellectuals, mostly from Russia's small middle class, became further alienated from the tsar's regime and threw their support to political causes ranging from anarchism to constitutional monarchy. With the fervor of religious zealots, for decades they had argued, organized parties, hatched plots, planned revolution, assassinated government officials (including Tsar Alexander II in 1881), published pamphlets by the thousands, and tried, not always successfully, to stay one step ahead of the secret police.

Nicholas II raised his subjects' hopes in 1905, when after rioting in St. Petersburg he promised constitutional reforms and a parliament. Russians soon realized, however, that he had no intention of surrendering control of such crucial areas as finance, defense, and ministerial appointments. Meanwhile, workers and peasants cursed their government, and revolutionaries continued to plot. World War I provided the final push to a regime teetering on the brink of collapse.

Once in power, the Bolsheviks faced the challenge of establishing the world's first Marxist state. After a decade of experiment and controversy, in the 1930s Soviet leaders created a framework of government that lasted until the breakup of the Soviet Union in the late 1980s. The Soviet Union became a major industrial power and a highly centralized, one-party dictatorship that tolerated no dissent. Freedom and individual initiative played no role in this new society, based, so their leaders claimed, on the principles of Karl Marx.

The Basic Tenets of Leninism

▼▼▼

72 ▾ *Lenin, WHAT IS TO BE DONE?*

The founder of the Soviet Union was Vladimir Ilyich Ulyanov (1870–1924), better known by his adopted revolutionary name, Lenin. The son of a government official, Lenin dedicated himself to revolution after the government executed his brother for plotting the assassination of Tsar Alexander III. He joined the Marxist-inspired Social-Democratic Party, founded in 1898, and in 1903 he became the leader of the "majority men," or Bolsheviks, who, in opposition to the "minority men," or Mensheviks, demanded highly centralized party leadership, noncooperation with middle-class liberals, and single-minded devotion to revolution.

Lenin outlined his ideas about revolutionary tactics in 1902 in the pamphlet "What Is to Be Done?" It was directed at ideological enemies he called "Economists," Marxists who believed that because Russia had just begun to industrialize, it was not ready for socialism. Social-Democrats, the Economists believed, should seek short-term economic gains for workers rather than revolution. Published in Germany, smuggled into Russia, and read by thousands of Social-Democrats, "What Is to Be Done?" established Lenin as a major party theoretician and a man to be reckoned with in the Social-Democratic Party. It marked the beginning of that distinctive variant of Marxism known as Leninism.

QUESTIONS FOR ANALYSIS

1. According to Lenin, how does the "critical Marxism" of men such as Bernstein endanger the socialist movement?
2. In Lenin's view, how are the goals and purposes of trade unionism similar to and different from those of the Social-Democratic Party?
3. Why, according to Lenin, have the workers been unable to develop true revolutionary consciousness? What does he believe must be done to change this?
4. What advantages does Lenin see in restricting the party to a small corps of dedicated revolutionaries?
5. What kinds of activities will these professional revolutionaries carry on to further the cause of revolution?
6. Compare and contrast the views of Lenin and Marx (see source 49) on the following topics: revolution, the working class, the role of the party.

[THE WORKERS AND REVOLUTION]

We have said that *there could not have been* Social-Democratic consciousness among the workers. It would have to be brought to them from without. The history of all countries shows that the working class, exclusively by its own effort, is able to develop only trade-union consciousness, i.e., the conviction that it is necessary to combine in unions, fight the employers, and strive to compel the government to pass necessary labor legislation, etc. . . .

The overwhelming majority of Russian Social-Democrats have of late been almost entirely absorbed by this work of organising the exposure of factory conditions. . . . — so much so, indeed, that they have lost sight of the fact that this, *taken by itself*, is in essence still not Social-Democratic work, but merely trade union work. As a matter of fact, the exposures merely dealt with the relations between the workers *in a given trade* and their employers, and all they achieved was that the sellers of labor-power learned to sell their "commodity" on better terms and to fight the purchasers over a purely commercial deal. These exposures could have served . . . as a beginning and a component part of Social-Democratic activity; but they could also have led . . . to a "purely trade union" struggle and to a non-Social-Democratic working-class movement. Social-Democracy leads the struggle of the working class, not only for better terms for the sale of labor-power, but for the abolition of the social system that compels the propertyless to sell themselves to the rich. Social-Democracy represents the working class, not in its relation to a given group of employers alone, but in its relation to all classes of modern society and to the state as an organised political force. . . . We must take up actively the political education of the working class and the development of its political consciousness. . . .

Why do the Russian workers still manifest little revolutionary activity in response to the brutal treatment of the people by the police, the persecution of religious sects, the flogging of peasants, the outrageous censorship, the torture of soldiers, the persecution of the most innocent cultural undertakings, etc.? . . . We must blame ourselves, our lagging behind the mass movement, for still being unable to organize sufficiently wide, striking, and rapid exposures of all the shameful outrages. When we do that (and we must and can do it), the most backward worker will understand, *or will feel*, that the students and religious sects, the peasants and the authors are being abused and outraged by those same dark forces that are oppressing and crushing him at every step of his life. Feeling that, he himself will be filled with an irresistible desire to react, and he will know how to heckle the censors one day, on another day to demonstrate outside the house of a governor who has brutally suppressed a peasant uprising . . . etc. As yet we have done very little, almost nothing, *to bring* before the working masses prompt exposures on all possible issues. Many of us as yet do not recognize this as our *bounden duty* but trail spontaneously in the wake of the "drab everyday struggle," in the narrow confines of factory life. . . .

[THE PARTY AND ITS PURPOSES]

If we begin with the solid foundation of a strong organisation of revolutionaries, we can ensure the stability of the movement as a whole and carry out the aims both of Social-Democracy and of trade unions proper. If, however, we begin with a broad workers' organisation, which is supposedly most "accessible" to the masses (but which is actually most accessible to the gendarmes and makes revolutionaries most accessible to the police), we shall achieve neither the one aim nor the other. . . .

"A dozen wise men can be more easily wiped out than a hundred fools." This wonderful truth (for which the hundred fools will always applaud you) appears obvious only because in the very midst of the argument you have skipped from one question to another. You [the skeptical reader] began by talking and continued to talk of the unearthing of a "committee," of the unearthing of an "organization," and now you skip to the question of unearthing the movement's "roots" in their "depths." The fact is, of course, that our movement cannot be unearthed, for the very reason that it has countless thousands of roots deep down among the masses. . . . But since you raise the question of *organizations* being unearthed and persist in your opinion, I assert that it is far more difficult to unearth a dozen wise men than a hundred fools. This position I will defend, no matter how much you instigate the masses against me for my "anti-democratic" views, etc. As I have stated repeatedly, by "wise men," in connection with organization, I mean *professional revolutionaries*. . . . I assert: (1) that no revolutionary movement can endure without a stable organization of leaders maintaining continuity; (2) that the broader the popular mass drawn spontaneously into the struggle, which forms the basis of the movement and participates in it, the more urgent the need for such an organization, and the more solid this organization must be (for it is much easier for all sorts of demagogues to side-track the more backward sections of the masses); (3) that such an organization must consist chiefly of people professionally engaged in revolutionary activity; (4) that in an autocratic state, the more we *confine* the membership of such an organization to people who are professionally engaged in revolutionary activity and who have been professionally trained in the art of combating the political police, the more difficult will it be to unearth the organization; and (5) the *greater* will be the number of people from the working class and from the other social classes who will be able to join the movement and perform active work in it.

I shall deal only with the last two points. The question as to whether it is easier to wipe out "a dozen wise men" or "a hundred fools" reduces itself to the question, above considered, whether it is possible to have a mass *organization* when the maintenance of strict secrecy is essential. . . . To concentrate all secret functions in the hands of as small a number of professional revolutionaries as possible does not mean that the latter will "do the thinking for all" and that the rank and file will not take an active part in the *movement*. . . . Centralization of the secret functions of the *organization* by no means implies centralization of all the functions of the *movement*. . . . The active and widespread participation of the masses will not suffer; on the contrary, it will benefit by the fact that a "dozen" experienced revolutionaries, trained professionally no less than the police, will centralize all the secret aspects of the work — the drawing up of leaflets, the working out of approximate plans; and the appointing of bodies of leaders for each urban district, for each factory district, and for each educational institution. . . . Centralization of the most secret functions in an organization of revolutionaries will not diminish, but rather increase the extent and enhance the quality of the activity of a large number of other organizations, that are intended for a broad public and are therefore as loose and as non-secret as possible, such as workers' trade unions; workers' self-education circles[1] and circles for reading illegal literature; and socialist, as well as democratic, circles among *all* other sections of the population; etc., etc. We must have such circles, trade unions, and organizations everywhere in *as large a number as possible* and with the widest variety of functions; but it would be absurd and harmful *to confound* them with the organization of *revolutionaries*, . . . to make still more hazy the all too faint recognition of the fact that in order to "serve" the mass movement we must have people who will devote themselves exclusively to Social-Democratic activities, and that such people must train themselves patiently and steadfastly to be professional revolutionaries.

Yes, this recognition is incredibly dim. Our worst sin with regard to organization consists in the fact that *by our primitiveness we have lowered the prestige of revolutionaries in Russia*. A person who is

[1]Regular meetings of workers, intellectuals, or students to discuss and plan strategies to overcome Russia's social and political problems.

flabby and shaky on questions of theory, who has a narrow outlook, who pleads the spontaneity of the masses as an excuse for his own sluggishness, who resembles a trade-union secretary more than a spokesman of the people, who is unable to conceive of a broad and bold plan that would command the respect even of opponents, and who is inexperienced and clumsy in his own professional art — the art of combating the political police — such a man is not a revolutionary, but a wretched amateur!

Let no active worker take offense at these frank remarks, for as far as insufficient training is concerned, I apply them first and foremost to myself. I used to work in a study circle that set itself very broad, all-embracing tasks; and all of us, members of that circle, suffered painfully and acutely from the realization that we were acting as amateurs at a moment in history when we might have been able to say, varying a well-known statement: "Give us an organization of revolutionaries, and we will overturn Russia!" . . .

Forging the Soviet State

73 ▾ *COMMUNIST DECREES AND LEGISLATION, 1917–1918*

On October 25, 1917, with the Bolsheviks in control of public buildings and other key points in Petrograd (as St. Petersburg was then called), Lenin confidently opened the Second Congress of Soviets with the words, "We shall now proceed to construct the Socialist order." As Lenin soon found out, building that new socialist order proved difficult. For one thing, while the Bolsheviks had a broad set of revolutionary aspirations for Russia, they had no blueprint for how to govern the country or how to restructure Russian society. Furthermore, the Bolsheviks were a minority party, as shown by the results of the elections for the Constituent Assembly in November 1917: The Bolsheviks received only 29 percent of the vote, as opposed to 58 percent for the Social Revolutionaries. Finally, they faced formidable problems — a ruined economy, continuing involvement in World War I until March 1918, and civil war from 1918 to 1921.

Despite these challenges, the Bolsheviks had no choice but to plunge ahead. In their first year in power, they issued hundreds of decrees that touched every aspect of Russian life and government and initiated programs and policies that in some cases lasted until the Soviet Union's demise in 1991.

What follows is a sample of the decrees issued by the Bolsheviks in 1917 and 1918. The Decree on Land, issued on October 26 by the Second Congress of Soviets only hours after the Bolsheviks seized power, recognized land seizures that peasants had already carried out.

The Decree on Suppression of Hostile Newspapers and the Decree Dissolving the Constituent Assembly were both steps toward one-party dictatorship. The Bolsheviks, both before and after seizing power, had supported convening a popularly elected Constituent Assembly. But the election of November 1917 resulted in only 168 Bolshevik deputies out of 703 and a clear Social Revolutionary majority. The Assembly convened on January 5, 1918, only to be dissolved by the Bolsheviks on January 7. It was the Soviet Union's last democratically elected parliament until 1989.

The Edict on Child Welfare, issued in January 1918, was the brainchild of Alexandra Kollontai (1873–1952), a leading Social Democrat who fled Russia in 1908 to escape arrest and, like Lenin, returned to St. Petersburg (renamed Petrograd under the Bolsheviks) after the fall of the tsar's government. She became a member of the executive committee of the Petrograd Soviet and played a leading role in the events leading up to the Bolshevik coup. As commissioner of social welfare under the Bolsheviks, she was responsible for laws that legalized abortion, liberalized marriage and divorce, and granted women equal standing with men.

The Decree on Nationalization of Large-Scale Industries was issued in June 1918 after the beginning of the civil war. Until then, industry had remained under private ownership, supposedly subject to "workers' control." Now it was nationalized without compensation to the owners.

QUESTIONS FOR ANALYSIS

1. What rationale is provided in these documents for the "undemocratic" steps taken by the Bolsheviks to dissolve the Constituent Assembly and close down hostile newspapers?
2. What are the economic ramifications of the decrees on land use and the nationalization of industry? Who benefits, and who is hurt?
3. How will these decrees change essential features of Russian society and social relationships?
4. To what extent do the steps taken by the Bolsheviks as reflected in these decrees reflect Marx and Engels's views in *The Communist Manifesto* (source 49), especially in the section in which they discuss the first steps to be taken by the proletariat after its seizure of power (p. 253)?
5. In what specific ways do these decrees increase the role of the state? What implications might this have for the Soviet Union's future?

DECREE ON LAND, OCTOBER 26, 1917

1. *Private ownership of land shall be abolished forever . . .*

   All land . . . *shall be alienated without compensation* and become the property of the whole people, and pass into the use of all those who cultivate it. . . .
2. All mineral wealth, e.g., ore, oil, coal, salt, etc., as well as all forests and waters of state importance, shall pass into the exclusive use of the state. All the small streams, lakes, woods, etc., shall pass into the use of the communities, to be administered by the local self-government bodies.
3. Lands on which *high-level scientific* farming is practised, e.g., orchards, plantations, seed plots, nurseries, hot-houses, etc. *shall not be divided up, but shall be converted into model farms*, to be turned over for exclusive use *to the state or to the communities*, depending on the size and importance of such lands. . . .
6. The right to use the land shall be accorded to all citizens of the Russian state (without distinction of sex) desiring to cultivate it by their own labor, with the help of their families, or in partnership, but only as long as they are able to cultivate it. . . .

DECREE ON SUPPRESSION OF HOSTILE NEWSPAPERS, OCTOBER 27, 1917

Everyone knows that the bourgeois press is one of the most powerful weapons of the bourgeoisie. Especially in this critical moment when the new authority, that of the workers and peasants, is in process of consolidation, it was impossible to leave this weapon in the hands of the enemy at a time when it is not less dangerous than bombs and machine guns. This is why temporary and extraordinary measures have been adopted for the purpose of cutting off the stream of mire and calumny in which the . . . press would be glad to drown the young victory of the people.

As soon as the new order will be consolidated, all administrative measures against the press will be suspended; full liberty will be given it within the limits of responsibility before the laws, in accordance with the broadest and most progressive regulations in this respect. . . .

DECREE DISSOLVING THE CONSTITUENT ASSEMBLY, JANUARY 7, 1918

The October Revolution, by giving the power to the Soviets, and through the Soviets to the toiling and exploited classes, aroused the desperate resistance of the exploiters, and in the crushing of this resistance it fully revealed itself as the beginning of the socialist revolution. The toiling classes learnt by experience that the old bourgeois parliamentarism had outlived its purpose and was absolutely incompatible with the aim of achieving Socialism, and that not national institutions, but only class institutions (such as the soviets), were capable of overcoming the resistance of the propertied classes and of laying the foundations of a socialist society. To relinquish the sovereign power of the Soviets, to relinquish the Soviet republic won by the people, for the sake of bourgeois parliamentarism and the Constituent Assembly, would now be a retrograde step and cause the collapse of the October workers' and peasants' revolution. . . .

The Right Socialist Revolutionary and Menshevik parties are in fact waging outside the walls of the Constituent Assembly a most desperate struggle against the Soviet power, calling openly in their press for its overthrow and characterizing as arbitrary and unlawful the crushing by force of the resistance of the exploiters by the toiling classes, which is essential in the interests of emancipation from exploitation. They are defending the saboteurs, the servitors of capital, and are going to the length of undisguised calls to terrorism, which certain "unidentified groups" have already begun to practice. It is obvious that under such circumstances the remaining part of the Constituent Assembly could only serve as a screen for the struggle of the counterrevolutionaries to overthrow the Soviet power.

Accordingly, the Central Executive Committee resolves: The Constituent Assembly is hereby dissolved.

EDICT ON CHILD WELFARE, JANUARY 1918

After a search that has lasted centuries, human thought has at last discovered the radiant epoch where the working class, with its own hands, can freely construct that form of maternity protection which will preserve the child for the mother and the mother for the child. . . .

The new Soviet Russia calls all you working women, you working mothers with your sensitive hearts, you bold builders of a new social life, you teachers of the new attitudes, you children's doctors and midwives, to devote your minds and emotions to building the great edifice that will provide social protection for future generations. From the date of publication of this decree, all large and small institutions under the commissariat of social welfare that serve the child, from the children's home in the capital to the modest village creche [a day nursery], shall be merged into one government organization and placed under the department for the protection of maternity and childhood. As an integral part of the total number of institutions connected with pregnancy and maternity, they shall continue to fulfil the single common task of creating citizens who are strong both mentally and physically. . . .

For the rapid elaboration and introduction of the reforms necessary for the protection of childhood in Russia, commissions are being organized under the auspices of the departments of maternity and childhood. . . . The commissions must base their work on the following main principles:

1. The preservation of the mother for the child: milk from the mother's breast is invaluable for the child.
2. The child must be brought up in the enlightened and understanding atmosphere provided by the socialist family.
3. Conditions must be created which permit the development of the child's physical and mental powers and the child's keen comprehension of life.

DECREE ON NATIONALIZATION OF LARGE-SCALE INDUSTRIES, JUNE 28, 1918

For the purpose of combating decisively the economic disorganization and the breakdown of the food supply, and of establishing more firmly the dictatorship of the working class and the village poor, the Soviet of People's Commissars has resolved:

1. To declare all of the following industrial and commercial enterprises which are located in the Soviet Republic, with all their capital and property, whatever they may consist of, the property of the Russian Socialist Federated Soviet Republic. [A long list of mines, mills, and factories follows.]
2. The administration of the nationalized industries shall be organized . . . by the different departments of the Supreme Council of National Economy. . . .
4. Beginning with the promulgation of this decree, the members of the administration, the directors, and other responsible officers of the nationalized industries will be held responsible to the Soviet Republic both for the intactness and upkeep of the business and for its proper functioning. . . .
5. The entire personnel of every enterprise — technicians, workers, members of the board of directors, and foremen — shall be considered employees of the Russian Socialist Federated Soviet Republic; their wages shall be fixed in accordance with the scales existing at the time of nationalization and shall be paid out of the funds of the respective enterprises. . . .
6. All private capital belonging to members of the boards of directors, stockholders, and owners of the nationalized enterprises will be attached [taken by state authority] pending the determination of the relation of such capital to the turnover capital and resources of the enterprises in question. . . .

Ultranationalism in Germany and Japan

Nationalism, the most important single cause of World War I, became even more potent in the 1920s and 1930s, leading to a second world war many times more costly and horrifying than the first. In Italy and Germany, nationalism fueled right-wing, antidemocratic movements personified by Benito Mussolini, whose Fascists seized power in Italy in 1922, and Adolf Hitler, whose National Socialists took over Germany in 1933. In Japan ultranationalists never completely subverted the limited democracy established by the 1890 constitution, but in the 1930s their views inspired millions and became dogma to Japan's military and political leaders.

Germany, Italy, and Japan were similar in several respects. All three were recent political creations: Italy completed its national unification when Rome and its environs joined the Kingdom of Italy in 1870; Germany became a unified nation-state in 1871; and a new Japan was created after the Meiji Restoration of 1868. All three had weak parliamentary governments, lacked democratic experience, and resented their treatment after World War I. The Germans were humiliated by the Versailles Treaty, and the Italians and Japanese were insulted by the refusal of Great Britain and France to recognize all their territorial claims. Finally, all three faced severe postwar economic problems — problems that extreme nationalists promised to eliminate by expansion and conquest.

Ultranationalism in each state also had the same tragic result: It led all three into catastrophic wars. After conquering Manchuria in 1931, invading China in 1937, attacking the United States at Pearl Harbor in 1941, and expanding into Southeast Asia, Japan conceded defeat when atomic bombs devastated Hiroshima and Nagasaki in August 1945. Germany launched World War II in Europe with its attack on Poland in September 1939, but after conquering much of Western Europe and invading the Soviet Union in 1941, its armies were steadily pushed back until the leaders of a devastated land surrendered in May 1945. Italy entered World War II as an ally of Germany in 1940, but its armies performed poorly, and only massive German support prevented its rapid collapse. Italian anti-Fascists captured Mussolini and shot him without trial on April 28, 1945, just a few days before Adolf Hitler committed suicide in his bunker under the rubble of what had been Berlin.

Hitler's Dreams

▾▾▾

74 ▾ *Adolf Hitler, MEIN KAMPF*

Born to an Austrian customs official and his German wife in 1889, Adolf Hitler moved to Vienna at the age of nineteen to seek a career as an artist or architect. His efforts failed, however, and he lived at the bottom of Viennese society, drifting from one low-paying job to another. In 1912 he moved to Munich, where his life fell into the same purposeless pattern. Enlistment in the German army in World War I rescued Hitler, giving him comradeship and a sense of direction he had lacked. After the war a shattered Hitler returned to Munich, where in 1919 he joined the small German Workers' Party, which in 1920 changed its name to the National Socialist German Workers' Party, or Nazis.

After becoming leader of the National Socialists, Hitler staged an abortive coup d'état against the government of the German state of Bavaria in 1923. For this he was sentenced to a five-year prison term (serving only nine months), during which time he wrote the first volume of *Mein Kampf (My Struggle)*. To a remarkable degree, this work, which he completed in 1925, provided the ideas that inspired his millions of followers and guided the National Socialists until their destruction in 1945.

QUESTIONS FOR ANALYSIS

1. What broad purpose does Hitler see in human existence?
2. How, in Hitler's view, are the Aryans and Jews dissimilar?
3. What is Hitler's view of political leadership?
4. What role do parliaments play in a "folkish" state, according to Hitler?
5. How does Hitler plan to reorient German foreign policy? What goals does he set for Germany, and how are they to be achieved?
6. Based on these excerpts, what can you infer about his objections to the ideologies of democracy, liberalism, and socialism?
7. How do Hitler's views of race compare to those of von Treitschke (source 53)?

NATION AND RACE

There are some truths that are so plain and obvious that for this very reason the everyday world does not see them or at least does not apprehend them. . . .

So humans invariably wander about the garden of nature, convinced that they know and understand everything, yet with few exceptions are blind to one of the fundamental principles Nature uses in her work: the intrinsic segregation of the species of every living thing on the earth. . . . Each beast mates with only one of its own species: the titmouse with titmouse, finch with finch, stork with stork, field mouse with field mouse, house mouse with house mouse, wolf with wolf. . . . This is only natural.

Any cross-breeding between two not completely equal beings will result in a product that is in between the level of the two parents. That means that the offspring will be superior to the parent who is at a biologically lower level of being but inferior to the parent at a higher level. This means the offspring will be overcome in the struggle for existence against those at the higher level. Such matings go against the will of Nature for the higher breeding of life.

A precondition for this lies not in the blending of beings of a higher and lower order, but rather the absolute victory of the stronger. The stronger must dominate and must not blend with the weaker orders and sacrifice their powers. Only born weaklings can find this cruel, but after all, they are only weaker and more narrow-minded types of men; unless this law dominated, then any conceivable higher evolution of living organisms would be unthinkable. . . .

Nature looks on this calmly and approvingly. The struggle for daily bread allows all those who are weak, sick, and indecisive to be defeated, while the struggle of the males for females gives to the strongest alone the right or at least the possibility to reproduce. Always this struggle is a means of advancing the health and power of resistance of the species, and thus a means to its higher evolution.

As little as nature approves the mating of higher and lower individuals, she approves even less the blending of higher races with lower ones; for indeed otherwise her previous work toward higher development perhaps over hundreds of thousands of years might be rendered useless with one blow. If this were not the case, progressive development would stop and even deterioration might set in. . . .

All the great civilizations of the past died out because contamination of their blood caused them to become decadent. . . . In other words, in order to protect a certain culture, the type of human who created the culture must be preserved. But such preservation is tied to the inalterable law of the necessity and the right of victory of the best and the strongest.

Whoever would live must fight. Whoever will not fight in this world of endless competition does not deserve to live. . . . He interferes with the victory path of the best race and with it, the precondition for all human progress. . . .

It is an idle undertaking to argue about which race or races were the original standard-bearers of human culture and were therefore the true founders of everything we conceive by the word humanity. It is much simpler to deal with the question as it pertains to the present, and here the answer is simple and clear. What we see before us today as human culture, all the yields of art, science, and technology, are almost exclusively the creative product of the Aryans.[1] Indeed this fact alone leads to the not unfounded conclusion that the Aryan alone is the founder of the higher type of humanity, and further that he represents the prototype of what we understand by the word: MAN. He is the Prometheus[2] from whose brow the bright spark of genius has forever burst forth, time and again rekindling the fire, which as knowledge has illuminated the night full of silent mysteries, and has permitted humans to ascend the path of mastery over the other beings of the earth. Eliminate him — and deep darkness will again descend on the earth after a few thousand years; human civilization will die out and the earth will become a desert. . . .

The Jew provides the greatest contrast to the Aryan. With no other people of the world has the instinct for self-preservation been so developed as by the so-called chosen race.[3] The best proof of this statement rests in the fact that this race still exists. Where can another people be found in the past 2,000 years that has undergone so few changes in its inner qualities, character, etc. as the Jews? What people has undergone upheavals as great as this one — and nonetheless has emerged unchanged from the greatest catastrophes of humanity? What an infinitely tenacious will to live and to preserve one's kind is revealed in this fact. . . .

Since the Jew . . . never had a civilization of his own, others have always provided the foundations of his intellectual labors. His intellect has always developed by the use of those cultural achievements he has found ready at hand around him. Never has it happened the other way around.

For though their drive for self-preservation is not smaller, but larger than that of other people, and though their mental capabilities may easily give the impression that their intellectual powers are equal to those of other races, the Jews lack the most basic characteristic of a truly cultured people, namely an idealistic spirit.

It is a remarkable fact that the herd instinct brings people together for mutual protection only so long as there is a common danger that makes mutual assistance necessary or unavoidable. The same pack of wolves that an instant ago combined to overcome their prey will soon after satisfying their hunger again become individual beasts. . . . It goes the same way with the Jews. His sense of self sacrifice is only apparent. It lasts only so long as it is strictly necessary. . . . Jews act together only when a common danger threatens them or a common prey attracts them. When these two things are lacking, then their characteristic of the crassest egoism returns as a force, and out of this once unified people emerges in a flash a swarm of rats fighting bloodily against one another. . . .

That is why the Jewish state — which should be the living organism for the maintenance and improvement of the race — has absolutely no borders. For the territorial definition of a state always demands a certain idealism of spirit on

[1]*Aryan*, strictly speaking, is a linguistic term referring to a branch of the Indo-European family of languages known as Indo-Iranian. It also is used to refer to a people who as early as 4000 B.C.E. began to migrate from their homeland in the steppes of western Asia to Iran, India, Mesopotamia, Asia Minor, and Europe. In the nineteenth century, *Aryan* was used to refer to the racial group that spoke Indo-European languages. According to Hitler and the Nazis, the Aryans provided Europe's original racial stock and stood in contrast to other peoples such as the Jews, who spoke Semitic languages.

[2]In Greek mythology Prometheus was the titan (titans were offspring of Uranus, Heaven, and Gaea, Earth) who stole fire from the gods and gave it to humans, along with all other arts and civilization.

[3]A reference to the Jewish belief that God had chosen the Jews to enter into a special covenantal relationship in which God promised to be the God of the Hebrews and favor them in return for true worship and obedience.

the part of the race which forms the state and especially an acceptance of the idea of work. . . . If this attitude is lacking then the prerequisite for civilization is lacking.

▷ Hitler describes the process by which Jews in concert with communists have come close to subverting and controlling the peoples and nations of Europe.

Here he stops at nothing, and his vileness becomes so monstrous that no one should be surprised if among our people the hateful figure of the Jew is taken as the personification of the devil and the symbol of evil. . . .

How close they see their approaching victory can be seen in the frightful way that their dealings with members of other races develop.

The black-haired Jewish youth, with satanic joy on his face, lurks in wait for hours for the innocent girls he plans to defile with his blood, and steal the young girl from her people. With every means at hand he seeks to undermine the racial foundations of the people they would subjugate. . . .

Around those nations which have offered sturdy resistance to their internal attacks, they surround them with a web of enemies; thanks to their international influence, they incite them to war, and when necessary, will plant the flag of revolution, even on the battlefield.

In economics he shakes the foundations of the state long enough so that unprofitable business enterprises are shut down and come under his financial control. In politics he denies the state its means of self-preservation, destroys its means of self-maintenance and defense, annihilates faith in state leadership, insults its history and traditions, and drags everything that is truly great into the gutter.

Culturally, he pollutes art, literature and theater, makes a mockery of natural sensibilities, destroys every concept of beauty and nobility, the worthy and the good, and instead drags other men down to the sphere of its own lowly type of existence.

Religion is made an object of mockery, morality and ethics are described as old-fashioned, until finally the last props of a people for maintaining their existence in this world are destroyed.

PERSONALITY AND THE IDEAL OF THE FOLKISH[4] STATE

. . . The folkish state must care for the well-being of its citizens by recognizing in everything the worth of the person, and by doing so direct it to the highest level of its productive capability, thus guaranteeing for each the highest level of participation.

Accordingly, the folkish state must free the entire leadership, especially those in political leadership, from the parliamentary principle of majority rule by the multitude, so that the right of personality is guaranteed without any limitation. From this is derived the following realization. *The best state constitution and form is that which with unquestioned certainty raises the best minds from the national community to positions of leading authority and influence.* . . .

There are no majority decisions, rather only responsible individuals, and the word "advice" will once again have its original meaning. Each man will have advisers at his side, *but the decision will be made by one man.*

The principle that made the Prussian army in its time the most splendid instrument of the German people will have to become someday the foundation for the construction of our completed state: *authority of every leader downward and responsibility upward.* . . .

This principle of binding absolute responsibility with absolute authority will gradually bring forth an elite group of leaders which today in an era of irresponsible parliamentarianism is hardly thinkable.

---

[4]The word Hitler uses, *völkisch*, is an adjective derived from *Volk*, meaning "people" or "nation," which Hitler defined in a racial sense; thus a "folkish" state is one that expresses the characteristics of and furthers the interests of a particular race, in this case, the Aryans.

THE DIRECTION AND POLITICS OF EASTERN EUROPE

The foreign policy of the folkish state has as its purpose to guarantee the existence on this planet of the race that it gathers within its borders. With this in mind it must create a natural and healthy ratio between the number and growth of the population and the extent and quality of the land and soil. The balance must be such that it accords with the vital needs of the people. . . . Only a sufficiently large space on the earth can assure the independent existence of a people. . . .

The National Socialist movement must seek to eliminate the disproportion between our people's population and our territory — viewing this as a source of food as well as a basis for national power — and between our historical past and our present hopeless impotence. While doing so it must remain conscious of the fact that we as protectors of the highest humanity on earth are bound also by the highest duty that will be fulfilled only if we inspire the German people with the racial ideal, so that they will occupy themselves not just with the breeding of good dogs, horses, and cats but also show concern about the purity of *their own* blood. . . .

State boundaries are made by man and can be changed by man.

. . . And only in force lies the right of possession. If today the German people are imprisoned within an impossible territorial area and for that reason are face to face with a miserable future, this is not the commandment of fate, any more than a revolt against such a situation would be a violation of the laws of fate; . . . the soil on which we now live was not bestowed upon our ancestors by Heaven; rather, they had to conquer it by risking their lives. So with us, in the future we will win soil and with it the means of existence of the people not through some sort of folkish grace but only through the power of the triumphant sword.

But we National Socialists must go further: *The right to land and soil will become an obligation if without further territorial expansion a great people is threatened with its destruction.* And that is particularly true when the people in question is not some little nigger people, but the German mother of life, which has given cultural shape to the modern world. *Germany will either become a world power or will no longer exist. . . .*

And so we National Socialists consciously draw a line below the direction of our foreign policy before the war. We take up where we broke off six hundred years ago. We put a stop to the eternal pull of the Germans toward the south and western Europe and turn our gaze to the lands of the east. We put an end to the colonial and commercial policy of the prewar period and shift to the land-oriented policy of the future.

When today we speak of new territory and soil in Europe, we think primarily of *Russia* and her subservient border states.

The Destiny of Japan

▾▾▾

75 ▾ THE WAY OF SUBJECTS

In 1941, only a few months before the bombing of Pearl Harbor, the Japanese Ministry of Education issued "The Way of Subjects," a pamphlet that became required reading for high school and university students. It reflects the principles of Japanese ultranationalism, a growing force in the 1920s and 1930s.

Racial and cultural pride had characterized the Japanese for centuries and was a major reason for their wholehearted support of modernization during the Meiji Period. In the 1930s and 1940s, nationalism intensified and, as in Germany and Italy, became identified with antidemocratic and antisocialist movements. It grew in response to resentment of the West for its treatment of Japan after World War I, fears of a reunified China under Chiang Kai-shek and the Nationalists, concerns

about economic fluctuations and social tensions caused by the Great Depression, opposition to "dangerous" ideologies such as socialism and communism, and anxieties about Western influence on Japan.

The ultranationalists denounced democracy, socialism, and the influence of big business on Japanese life. They praised Japanese virtues of harmony and duty, idealized the past, demanded absolute obedience to the emperor, and called for the revival of warrior values. They also clamored for Japanese imperialist expansion, claiming that only this could save Japan from overpopulation and economic isolation.

With strong support in the rural population and army, ultranationalism peaked between 1931 and 1936, when its disciples assassinated business leaders and government officials, including a prime minister, and plotted to overthrow the government. The most serious coup attempt took place in February 1936, when officers and troops of the Fifteenth Division attacked and held downtown Tokyo for three days before authorities suppressed their rebellion. The government survived, but to satisfy the extremists it cracked down on leftist politicians and acceded to many of the army's demands. The balance of Japanese politics had shifted to right-wing militarists, setting the stage for the invasion of China in 1937 and the bombing of Pearl Harbor in 1941.

QUESTIONS FOR ANALYSIS

1. What is the stated purpose of "The Way of Subjects"?
2. According to the authors, what are the distinguishing characteristics of Western nations, and how is the West threatening Japan?
3. According to the authors, how do the Japanese differ from other people? What do they see as Japan's special mission?
4. What, according to the authors, is the role of individual Japanese in fulfilling the nation's mission?
5. To what extent do the authors' views of Japan's future resemble Hitler's dreams for Germany (source 74)?

The way of the subjects of the Emperor issues from the polity of the Emperor, and is to guard and maintain the Imperial Throne coexistent with the Heavens and the Earth. This is not an abstract principle, but a way of daily practices based on history. The life and activities of the nation are all attuned to the task of strengthening the foundation of the Empire.

Looking to the past, this country has been widely seeking knowledge in the world since the Meiji Restoration, thereby fostering and maintaining the prosperity of the state. With the influx of European and American culture into this country, however, individualism, liberalism, utilitarianism, and materialism began to assert themselves, so that the traditional character of the country was much impaired and the virtuous habits and customs bequeathed by our ancestors were affected unfavorably.

With the outbreak of the Manchurian Affair[1] and further occurrence of the China Affair,[2] the national spirit started to be elevated gradually,

[1]The Japanese invasion of Manchuria in 1931.

[2]The invasion of China in 1937.

but there is still much to be desired in point of the people's understanding the fundamental principle of polity as a whole and their consciousness as subjects of the Emperor. . . .

If this situation is left unremedied, it will be difficult to eradicate the evils of European and American thought that are deeply penetrating various strata of Japan's national life, and to achieve the unprecedentedly great tasks by establishing a structure of national solidarity of guarding and maintaining the prosperity of the Imperial Throne. Herein lies an urgent need to discard the self-centered and utilitarian ideas and to elevate and practice the way of the Emperor's subjects based on state service as the primary requisite.

▾ ▾ ▾

The thoughts that have formed the foundation of Western civilization since the early period of the modern age are individualism, liberalism, materialism, and so on. These thoughts regard the strong preying on the weak as reasonable, unstintedly promote the pursuit of luxury and pleasure, encourage materialism, and stimulate competition for acquiring colonies and securing trade, thereby leading the world to a veritable hell of fighting and bloodshed. . . . The self-destruction in the shape of the World War finally followed. It was only natural that cries were raised even among men of those countries after the war that Western civilization was crumbling. A vigorous movement was started by Britain, France, and the United States to maintain the status quo by any means. Simultaneously, a movement aiming at social revolution through class conflict on the basis of thoroughgoing materialism like Communism also vigorously developed. On the other hand, Nazism and Fascism arose with great force. The basic principles of the totalitarianism in Germany and Italy are to remove the evils of individualism and liberalism.

That these principles show great similarity to Eastern culture and spirit is a noteworthy fact that suggests the future of Western civilization and the creation of a new culture. Thus, the orientation of world history has made the collapse of the old world order a certainty. Japan has hereby initiated the construction of a new world order based on moral principles.

The Manchurian Affair was a violent outburst of Japanese national life long suppressed. Taking advantage of this, Japan in the glare of all the Powers made a step toward the creation of a world based on moral principles and the construction of a new order. This was a manifestation of the spirit, profound and lofty, embodied in the founding of Empire, and an unavoidable action for its national life and world mission.

Japan's position was raised suddenly to the world's forefront as a result of the Russo-Japanese War of 1904–05. . . . The general tendency of world domination by Europe and America has begun to show signs of a change since then. Japan's victory attracted the attention of the entire world, and this caused a reawakening of Asiatic countries, which had been forced to lie prostrate under British and American influence, with the result that an independence movement was started.

Hopes to be free of the shackles and bondage of Europe and America were ablaze among the nations of India, Turkey, Arabia, Thailand, Vietnam, and others. This also inspired a new national movement in China. Amid this stormy atmosphere of Asia's reawakening, Japan has come to be keenly conscious of the fact that the stabilization of East Asia is her mission, and that the emancipation of East Asian nations rests solely on her efforts. . . .

▾ ▾ ▾

Viewed from the standpoint of world history, the China Affair is a step toward the construction of a world of moral principles by Japan. The building up of a new order for securing lasting world peace will be attained by the completion of the China Affair as a steppingstone. In this regard the China Affair would not and should not end with the mere downfall of the Chiang Kai-shek regime.[3] Until the evils of European and American influences in East Asia that have led China astray are eliminated, until Japan's cooperation with New China as one of the links in the chain of the Greater East Asian Coprosperity Sphere[4] yields satisfactory results, and East Asia and the rest of the world are united as one on the basis of moral principles, Japan's indefatigable efforts are sorely needed. . . .

Japan has a political mission to help various regions in the Greater East Asian Coprosperity Sphere, which are reduced to a state of quasi-colony by Europe and America, and rescue them from their control. Economically, this country will have to eradicate the evils of their exploitation and then set up an economic structure for coexistence and coprosperity. Culturally, Japan must strive to fashion East Asian nations to abandon their following of European and American culture and to develop Eastern culture for the purpose of contributing to the creation of a just world. . . . It is natural that unusual difficulties attend the establishment of a new order and the creation of a new culture. Overcoming these difficulties will do much to help in establishing a world dominated by morality, in which all nations can co-operate and all people can secure their proper positions. . . .

It is urgent for Japan to achieve the establishment of a structure of national unanimity in politics, economy, culture, education, and all other realms of national life. Defense is absolutely necessary for national existence. A nation without defense is one that belongs to a dream world. Whether defense is perfected or not is the scale that measures the nation's existence or ruin. . . .

With the change of war from a simple military matter to a complicated total affair, the distinction between wartime and peacetime has been clouded. When the world was singing peace, a furious economic and cultural war was staged behind the scenes, among nations. Unless a country is organized even in time of peace, so that the total struggle of the state and the people is constantly concentrated on the objective of the country, and the highest capacity is displayed, the country is predestined to be defeated before taking to arms. . . .

▾ ▾ ▾

The cardinal objective of strengthening the total war organism is solely to help the Imperial Throne, and this can be attained by all the people fulfilling their duty as subjects through their respective positions in society. . . .

Standing on the national principle of blood and soil, Germany aims at destroying the world domination of the Anglo-Saxon race and the prevailing condition of pressure brought to bear upon Germany. . . . And for this she has succeeded in achieving thoroughgoing popular confidence in, and obedience to, the dictatorship of the Nazis, and is adopting totalitarianism. Italy's ideals are the restoration of the great Roman Empire, and her policy for realizing them is not different from that of Germany. . . .

The ideals of Japan are to manifest to the entire world the spirit of her Empire-founding. . . . There is virtually no country in the world other than Japan having such a superb and lofty mission bearing world significance. So it can be said that the construction of a new structure and an armed state is all so that Japan may revive her proper national standing and return to her original status of supporting the Throne by the myriad subjects, thereby perfecting the workings of national strength and leaving no stone unturned in displaying her total power to the fullest extent.

▾ ▾ ▾

The Imperial Family is the fountain source of the Japanese nation, and national and private lives issue from this. . . . Here is the reason for the present glorious state, in which the Emperor

---

[3]Chiang Kai-shek (1887–1975), successor to Sun Yat-sen as head of the Nationalist Party, was the recognized leader of wartime China, even though the communists under Mao Zedong controlled large parts of the country.

[4]The Japanese term for their Asian empire.

and his subjects are harmonized into one great unit. . . .

The great duty of the Japanese people to guard and maintain the Imperial Throne has lasted to the present . . . and will last forever and ever. To serve the Emperor is its key point. Our lives will become sincere and true when they are offered to the Emperor and the state. Our own private life is fulfillment of the way of the subjects; in other words, it is not private, but public, insofar as it is held by the subjects supporting the Throne.

The Legacy of World War II

In the two decades after World War I, weapons became more destructive, nationalism more fanatical, and leaders' ambitions more fantastic. As a result, the war that began in Asia in 1937 and in Europe in 1939 — World War II — became the most devastating and destructive war in history. Modern communication and transportation systems enabled generals to plan and execute massive campaigns such as the German invasion of the Soviet Union in 1941 and the Allies' Normandy invasion in 1944. The airplane, only a curiosity in World War I, became an instrument of destruction in World War II, making possible the German assault on English cities in 1940, the Japanese attack on Pearl Harbor in 1941, the around-the-clock bombing of Germany by Britain and the United States from 1943 to 1945, and the American fire-bombing of Tokyo in 1945.

Only the closing months of the war, however, fully revealed the destructive possibilities of modern technology and large bureaucratic states. As Allied armies liberated Europe in the winter and spring of 1945, they found in the Third Reich's concentration and extermination camps the horrifying results of the Nazi assault on political enemies, religious dissidents, prisoners of war, Gypsies, Slavs, and especially Jews. Then on August 6 the United States dropped an atomic bomb on Hiroshima, Japan. It killed nearly 80,000 people, seriously injured twice that number, and obliterated three-fifths of the city. On August 9 the United States dropped a second atomic bomb on Nagasaki, intending to destroy the Mitsubishi shipyards. It missed its target but destroyed half the city and killed 75,000 people.

A half century later the names Hiroshima and Nagasaki still evoke nightmares in a world where thousands of nuclear warheads exist and many nations have the capacity to manufacture nuclear weapons many times more powerful than those dropped on Japan. Similarly, the Holocaust, the Nazi attempt to exterminate the Jews, continues to haunt the imagination. Racism and ethnic hatreds are universally condemned, but they flourish in many parts of the world. Anti-Semitism has resurfaced in Central and Eastern Europe, the Serbs have bombed and starved Bosnian and Kosovar towns and cities in the name of ethnic cleansing, Tutsi and Hutu have slaughtered one another in Central Africa, and racial tensions continue to plague the United States and dozens of other societies.

Was the Holocaust an aberration resulting from the unique prejudices of the Germans and the perverse views of a handful of their leaders? Or was something much more basic in human nature involved? These are just two of the many disturbing questions raised by the Nazi campaign to exterminate the Jews.

"Führer, You Order. We Obey"

76 ▾ Rudolf Höss, MEMOIRS

On gaining power, the Nazis began to implement the anti-Jewish policies Hitler and the Nazis had promised in *Mein Kampf* and thousands of books, pamphlets, and speeches. Jewish shops were plundered while police looked the other way, Jewish physicians were excluded from hospitals, Jewish judges lost their posts, Jewish students were denied admission to universities, and Jewish veterans were stripped of their benefits. In 1935 the Nazis promulgated the Nuremberg Laws, which deprived Jews of citizenship and outlawed marriage between Jews and non-Jews. In November 1938 the regime organized nationwide violence against Jewish synagogues and shops in what came to be known as *Kristallnacht*, or "night of the broken glass."

After the war began in late 1939, conquests in Eastern Europe gave the Nazis new opportunities to address the "Jewish problem." In early 1941 they began to deport Jews from Germany and conquered territories to Poland and Czechoslovakia, where Jews were employed as slave laborers or placed in concentration camps. In June 1941 special units known as *Einsatzgruppen* ("special action forces") were organized to exterminate Jews in territories conquered on the eastern front. In eighteen months they gunned down more than 1 million Jews and smaller numbers of Gypsies and Slavs. Then in January 1942 at the Wannsee Conference outside Berlin, the Nazi leadership approved the Final Solution to the so-called Jewish problem. Their goal was the extermination of European Jewry, and to reach it they constructed special camps where their murderous work could be done efficiently and quickly. When World War II ended, the Nazis had not achieved their goal of annihilating Europe's 11 million Jews. They did, however, slaughter close to 6 million, thus earning themselves a permanent place in the long history of man's inhumanity to man.

The following excerpt comes from the memoirs of Rudolf Höss (1900–1947), the commandant of the Auschwitz concentration camp in Poland from 1940 to 1943. After serving in World War I, Höss abandoned plans to become a priest and became involved in a number of right-wing political movements, including the Nazi Party, which he joined in the early 1920s. After serving a jail sentence for participating in the murder of a teacher suspected of "treason," Höss became a farmer and then, in 1934, a member of the Nazi SS, or *Schutzstaffel* (Guard Detachment). The SS, under its leader Heinrich Himmler, grew from a small security force to guard Hitler and other high-ranking Nazis into a powerful party organization involved in police work, state security, intelligence gathering, administration of conquered territories, and management of the concentration camps. After postings at the Dachau and Sachsenhausen camps, Höss was appointed commandant of Auschwitz, a huge, sprawling complex where more than a million Jews were gassed or shot and tens of thousands of prisoners served as slave laborers in nearby factories. In 1943 Höss became overseer of all the Third Reich's concentration camps, but he returned to Auschwitz in 1944 to administer the murder of 400,000 Hungarian Jews. After his capture in 1946, he was tried and convicted for crimes against humanity by the international military tribunal at Nuremberg. He was hanged on April 16, 1947, within sight of the villa where he and his family had lived while he served as commandant at Auschwitz.

While awaiting trial, Höss was encouraged to compose a memoir to sharpen his recollection of his experiences. In the following passage, he discusses his views of the Jews and his reaction to the mass killings he planned and witnessed.

QUESTIONS FOR ANALYSIS

1. What does Höss claim to have been his attitude toward the Jews?
2. How do his statements about the Jews accord with his assertion that he was a fanatic National Socialist?
3. Does Höss make any distinction between the Russians and the Jews that he had exterminated?
4. What was Höss's attitude toward the Final Solution? How does Höss characterize his role in the mass extermination of the Jews?
5. How did his involvement in the Holocaust affect him personally? How, according to Höss, did it affect other German participants?
6. What would you describe as the key components of Höss's personality? To what extent was his personality shaped by the Nazi philosophy to which he was dedicated?
7. What insight does this excerpt provide about the issue of how much the German people knew of and participated in the Holocaust?

Since I was a fanatic National Socialist, I was firmly convinced that our idea would take hold in all countries, modified by the various local customs, and would gradually become dominant. This would then break the dominance of international Jewry. Anti-Semitism was nothing new throughout the whole world. It always made its strongest appearance when the Jews had pushed themselves into positions of power and when their evil actions became known to the general public. . . . I believed that because our ideas were better and stronger, we would prevail in the long run. . . .

I want to emphasize here that I personally never hated the Jews. I considered them to be the enemy of our nation. However, that was precisely the reason to treat them the same way as the other prisoners. I never made a distinction concerning this. Besides, the feeling of hatred is not in me, but I know what hate is, and how it manifests itself. I have seen it and I have felt it.

The original order . . . to annihilate all the Jews stated, "All Jews without exception are to be destroyed." It was later changed by Himmler so that those able to work were to be used in the arms factories. This made Auschwitz the assembly point for the Jews to a degree never before known. . . .

When he gave me the order personally . . . to prepare a place for mass killings and then carry it out, I could never have imagined the scale, or what the consequences would be. Of course, this order was something extraordinary, something monstrous. However, the reasoning behind the order of this mass annihilation seemed correct to me. At the time I wasted no thoughts about it. I had received an order; I had to carry it out. I could not allow myself to form an opinion as to whether this mass extermination of the Jews was necessary or not. At the time it was beyond my frame of mind. Since the Führer himself had ordered "The Final Solution of the Jewish Question," there was no second guessing for an old National Socialist, much less an SS officer. "Führer, you order. We obey" was not just a phrase or a slogan. It was meant to be taken seriously.[1]

Since my arrest I have been told repeatedly that I could have refused to obey this order, and even that I could have shot Himmler dead. I do not believe that among the thousands of SS officers there was even one who would have had even a glimmer of such a thought. . . . Of course, many SS officers moaned and groaned about the many harsh orders. Even then, they carried out every order. . . . As leader of the SS, Himmler's person was sacred. His fundamental orders in the name of the Führer were holy. There was no reflection, no interpretation, no explanation about these orders. They were carried out ruthlessly, regardless of the final consequences, even if it meant giving your life for them. Quite a few did that during the war.

It was not in vain that the leadership training of the SS officers held up the Japanese as shining examples of those willing to sacrifice their lives for the state and for the emperor, who was also their god. SS education was not just a series of useless high school lectures. It went far deeper, and Himmler knew very well what he could demand of his SS. . . .

Whatever the Führer or Himmler ordered was always right. Even democratic England has its saying, "My country, right or wrong," and every patriotic Englishman follows it.

Before the mass destruction of the Jews began, all the Russian politruks[2] and political commissars were killed in almost every camp during 1941 and 1942. According to the secret order given by Hitler, the Einsatzgruppen searched for and picked up the Russian politruks and commissars from all the POW camps. They transferred all they found to the nearest concentration camp for liquidation. . . . The first small transports were shot by firing squads of SS soldiers.

While I was on an official trip, my second in command, Camp Commander Fritzsch, experimented with gas for killings. He used a gas called Cyclon B, prussic acid,[3] which was often used as an insecticide in the camp to exterminate lice and vermin. There was always a supply on hand. When I returned Fritzsch reported to me about how he had used the gas. We used it again to kill the next transport.

The gassing was carried out in the basement of Block 11. I viewed the killings wearing a gas mask for protection. Death occurred in the crammed-full cells immediately after the gas was thrown in. Only a brief choking outcry and it was all over. . . .

At the time I really didn't waste any thoughts about the killing of the Russian POWs. It was ordered; I had to carry it out. But I must admit openly that the gassings had a calming effect on me, since in the near future the mass annihilation of the Jews was to begin. Up to this point it was not clear to me . . . how the killing of the expected masses was to be done. Perhaps by gas? But how, and what kind of gas? Now we had discovered the gas and the procedure. I was always horrified of death by firing squads, especially when I thought of the huge numbers of women and children who would have to be killed. Now I was at ease. We were all saved from these bloodbaths, and the victims would be

[1]All SS members swore the following oath: "I swear to you Adolf Hitler, as Führer and Chancellor of the Reich, loyalty and bravery. I vow to you and to the authorities appointed by you obedience unto death, so help me God."

[2]Communist Party members.

[3]Cyclon (or Zyklon) B is a blue crystalline substance; its active ingredient, hydrocyanic acid, sublimates into a gas upon contact with air. It causes death by combining with the red blood cells and preventing them from carrying oxygen.

spared until the last moment. That is what I worried about the most when I thought of Eichmann's[4] accounts of the mowing down of the Jews with machine guns and pistols by the Einsatzgruppen. Horrible scenes were supposed to have occurred: people running away even after being shot, the killing of those who were only wounded, especially the women and children. Another thing on my mind was the many suicides among the ranks of the SS Special Action Squads who could no longer mentally endure wading in the bloodbath. Some of them went mad. Most of the members of the Special Action Squads drank a great deal to help get through this horrible work. According to [Captain] Höfle's accounts, the men of Globocnik's[5] extermination section drank tremendous quantities of alcohol.

In the spring of 1942 the first transports of Jews arrived from Upper Silesia. All of them were to be exterminated. They were led from the ramp across the meadow, later named section B-II of Birkenau,[6] to the farmhouse called Bunker I. Aumeier, Palitzsch, and a few other block leaders led them and spoke to them as one would in casual conversation, asking them about their occupations and their schooling in order to fool them. After arriving at the farmhouse they were told to undress. At first they went very quietly into the rooms where they were supposed to be disinfected. At that point some of them became suspicious and started talking about suffocation and extermination. Immediately a panic started. Those still standing outside were quickly driven into the chambers, and the doors were bolted shut. In the next transport those who were nervous or upset were identified and watched closely at all times. As soon as unrest was noticed these troublemakers were inconspicuously led behind the farmhouse and killed with a small-caliber pistol, which could not be heard by the others. . . .

I also watched how some women who suspected or knew what was happening, even with the fear of death all over their faces, still managed enough strength to play with their children and to talk to them lovingly. Once a woman with four children, all holding each other by the hand to help the smallest ones over the rough ground, passed by me very slowly. She stepped very close to me and whispered, pointing to her four children, "How can you murder these beautiful, darling children? Don't you have any heart?"

Another time an old man hissed while passing me, "Germany will pay a bitter penance for the mass murder of the Jews." His eyes glowed with hatred as he spoke. In spite of this he went bravely into the gas chamber without worrying about the others. . . .

Occasionally some women would suddenly start screaming in a terrible way while undressing. They pulled out their hair and acted as if they had gone crazy. Quickly they were led behind the farmhouse and killed by a bullet in the back of the neck from a small-caliber pistol. . . . As the doors were being shut, I saw a woman trying to shove her children out the chamber, crying out, "Why don't you at least let my precious children live?" There were many heartbreaking scenes like this which affected all who were present.

In the spring of 1942 hundreds of people in the full bloom of life walked beneath the budding fruit trees of the farm into the gas chamber to their death, most of them without a hint of what was going to happen to them. To this day I can still see these pictures of the arrivals, the selections, and the procession to their death. . . .

---

[4]Adolf Eichmann (1906–1962) was a bureaucrat originally in charge of Jewish emigration. After the Wannsee Conference, he was given the responsibility for organizing the deportation of Jews to the death camps. He fled to Argentina in 1946 but was captured by Israeli agents, who took him to Israel, where he was tried and executed.

[5]Odilio Globocnik was the officer responsible for organizing and training SS units in Eastern Europe.

[6]Birkenau was the German name for the town where a large addition to the Auschwitz complex was built in late 1941 and early 1942.

. . . Many of the men often approached me during my inspection trips through the killing areas and poured out their depression and anxieties to me, hoping that I could give them some reassurance. During these conversations the question arose again and again, "Is what we have to do here necessary? Is it necessary that hundreds of thousands of women and children have to be annihilated?" And I, who countless times deep inside myself had asked the same question, had to put them off by reminding them that it was Hitler's order. I had to tell them that it was necessary to destroy all the Jews in order to forever free Germany and the future generations from our toughest enemy.

. . . However, secret doubts tormented all of us. Under no circumstances could I reveal my secret doubts to anyone. I had to convince myself to be like a rock when faced with the necessity of carrying out this horribly severe order, and I had to show this in every way, in order to force all those under me to hang on mentally and emotionally. . . .

Hour upon hour I had to witness all that happened. I had to watch day and night, whether it was the dragging and burning of the bodies, the teeth being ripped out, the cutting of the hair,[7] I had to watch all this horror. For hours I had to stand in the horrible, haunting stench while the mass graves were dug open, and the bodies were dragged out and burned. I also had to watch the procession of death itself through the peephole of the gas chamber because the doctors called my attention to it. I had to do all of this because I was the one to whom everyone looked, and because I had to show everybody that I was not only the one who gave the orders and issued the directives, but that I was also willing to be present at whatever task I ordered my men to perform. . . .

And yet, everyone in Auschwitz believed the Kommandant really had a good life. Yes, my family had it good in Auschwitz, every wish that my wife or my children had was fulfilled. The children could live free and easy. My wife had her flower paradise. The prisoners tried to give my wife every consideration and tried to do something nice for the children. By the same token no former prisoner can say that he was treated poorly in any way in our house. My wife would have loved to give a present to every prisoner who performed a service for us. The children constantly begged me for cigarettes for the prisoners. The children especially loved the gardeners. In our entire family there was a deep love for farming and especially for animals. Every Sunday I had to drive with them across all the fields, walk them through the stables, and we could never skip visiting the dog kennels. Their greatest love was for our two horses and our colt. The prisoners who worked in the household were always dragging in some animal the children kept in the garden. Turtles, martens, cats, or lizards; there was always something new and interesting in the garden. The children splashed around in the summertime in the small pool in the garden or the Sola River. Their greatest pleasure was when daddy went into the water with them. But he had only a little time to share all the joys of childhood.

Today I deeply regret that I didn't spend more time with my family. I always believed that I had to be constantly on duty. Through this exaggerated sense of duty I always had made my life more difficult than it actually was. My wife often urged me, "Don't always think of your duty, think of your family too." But what did my wife know about the things that depressed me? She never found out.[8]

[7]Teeth extracted from the corpses were soaked in muriatic acid to remove muscle and bone before the gold fillings were extracted. Some of the gold was distributed to dentists who used it in fillings for SS men and their families; the rest was deposited in the Reichsbank. Hair was used to make felt and thread.

[8]In an interview with a court-appointed psychiatrist during the Nuremberg trials in 1946, Höss stated that his wife actually did learn of his participation in the mass executions at the camp, and that afterward they became estranged and ceased having sexual relations.

August 6, 1945

77 ▾ *Iwao Nakamura and Atsuko Tsujioka, RECOLLECTIONS*

In 1951 Dr. Arata Osada, a professor of education at the University of Hiroshima, sponsored a project in which young Japanese from primary grades through the university level were asked to write down their memories of the August 6 bombing and its aftermath. Moved by their recollections, he arranged to have published a sample of their compositions in 1951. His stated purpose was to reveal the horrors of nuclear war and thereby encourage nuclear disarmament. An English translation appeared in 1980.

QUESTIONS FOR ANALYSIS

Readers are encouraged to formulate their own questions about the events and experiences described in these memoirs.

IWAO NAKAMURA

11th Grade Boy (5th Grade at the Time)

Today, as I begin to write an account of my experiences after five years and several months have passed, the wretched scenes of that time float up before my eyes like phantoms. And as these phantoms appear, I can actually hear the pathetic groans, the screams.

In an instant it became dark as night, Hiroshima on that day. Flames shooting up from wrecked houses as if to illuminate this darkness. Amidst this, children aimlessly wandering about, groaning with pain, their burned faces twitching and bloated like balloons. An old man, skin flaking off like the skin of a potato, trying to get away on weak, unsteady legs, praying as he went. A man frantically calling out the names of his wife and children, both hands to his forehead from which blood trickled down. Just the memory of it makes my blood run cold. This is the real face of war. . . .

I, who cannot forget, was in the fifth year of primary school when it happened. To escape the frequent air raids, I and my sisters had been evacuated to the home of our relatives in the country, but on August 2, I returned to my home at Naka Kakomachi (near the former Prefectural Office) during the summer vacation, to recover from the effects of a summer illness that had left me very weak. . . .

It was after eight on August 6 and the midsummer sun was beginning to scorch down on Hiroshima. An all-clear signal had sounded and with relief we sat down for breakfast a little later than usual. Usually by this time, my father had left the house for the office and I would be at the hospital for treatment.

I was just starting on my second bowl of rice. At that moment, a bluish-white ray of light like a magnesium flare hit me in the face, a terrific roar tore at my eardrums and it became so dark I could not see anything. I stood up, dropping my rice bowl and chopsticks. I do not know what happened next or how long I was unconscious. When I came to, I found myself trapped under what seemed like a heavy rock, but my head was free. It was still dark but I finally discovered that I was under a collapsed wall. It was all so sudden that I kept wondering if I was dreaming. I tried very hard to crawl free, but the heavy wall would not budge. A suffocating stench flooded the area and began to choke me. My breathing became short, my ears began to ring, and my heart was pounding as if it were about to burst. "I can't last much longer," I said to myself, and then a draft of cold air flowed past me and some light appeared. The taste of that fresh air is something I shall never forget. I breathed it in with all my might. This fresh air and the brighter surroundings gave me renewed vigor and I somehow managed to struggle out from under the wall. . . .

Nothing was left of the Hiroshima of a few minutes ago. The houses and buildings had been destroyed and the streets transformed into a black desert, with only the flames from burning buildings giving a lurid illumination to the dark sky over Hiroshima. Flames were already shooting out of the wreckage of the house next door. We couldn't see my two brothers. My mother was in tears as she called their names. My father went frantic as he dug among the collapsed walls and scattered tiles. It must have been by the mercy of God that we were able to rescue my brothers from under the wreckage before the flames reached them. They were not hurt, either. The five of us left our burning home and hurried toward Koi. Around us was a sea of flames. The street was filled with flames and smoke from the burning wreckage of houses and burning power poles which had toppled down blocked our way time after time, almost sending us into the depths of despair. It seems that everyone in the area had already made their escape, for we saw no one but sometimes we heard moans, a sound like a wild beast. . . . As we passed Nakajima Primary School area and approached Sumiyoshi Bridge, I saw a damaged water tank in which a number of people had their heads down, drinking. I was so thirsty and attracted by the sight of people that I left my parents' side without thinking, and approached the tank. But when I got near and was able to see into the tank, I gave an involuntary cry and backed away. What I saw reflected in the blood-stained water were the faces of monsters. They had leaned over the side of the tank and died in that position. From the burned shreds of their sailor uniforms, I knew they were schoolgirls, but they had no hair left and their burned faces were crimson with blood; they no longer appeared human. After we came out on the main road and crossed Sumiyoshi Bridge, we finally came across some living human beings — but maybe it would be more correct to say that we met some people from Hell. They were naked and their skin, burned and bloody, was like red rust and their bodies were bloated up like balloons. . . . The houses on both sides of this street, which was several dozen yards wide, were in flames so that we could only move along a strip in the center about three or four yards wide. This narrow passage was covered with seriously burned and injured people, unable to walk, and with dead bodies, leaving hardly any space for us to get through. At places, we were forced to step over them callously, but we apologized in our hearts as we did this. Among them were old people pleading for water, tiny children seeking help, students unconsciously calling for their parents, brothers, and sisters, and there was a mother prostrate on the ground, moaning with pain but with one arm still tightly embracing her dead baby. But how could we help them when we ourselves did not know our own fate?

When we reached the Koi First Aid Station, we learned that we were among the last to escape from the Sumiyoshi Bridge area. After my father had received some medical treatment, we hurried over Koi Hill to our relatives at Tomo Village in Asa County. When we were crossing the hill late that evening, we could see Hiroshima lying far below, now a mere smoldering desert. After offering a silent prayer for the victims, we descended the hill toward Tomo.

ATSUKO TSUJIOKA

Student, Hiroshima Women's Junior College

It happened instantaneously. I felt as if my back had been struck with a big hammer, and then as if I had been thrown into boiling oil. I was unconscious for a while. When I regained my senses, the whole area was covered with black smoke. . . . I lay on the ground with my arms pressed against my chest, and called for help, again and again: "Mother! Mother! Father!"

But, of course, neither Mother nor Father answered me. . . . I could hear the other girls shouting for their mothers in the hellish darkness, and I sensed that they were getting away. I got up and just ran after them desperately. Near Tsurumi Bridge, a red hot electric wire got wrapped around my ankles. I pulled free of it somehow, without thinking, and ran to the foot of the Tsurumi Bridge. By that time, there was white smoke everywhere. I had been working in a place called Tanaka-cho, about 600 yards from the blast center. I seemed to have been blown quite a bit north and had to take a completely different route to the bridge, which would have been straight ahead of me if I was where I should have been.

There was a large cistern at the foot of the bridge. In the tank were some mothers, one holding her naked, burned baby above her head, and another crying and trying to give her baby milk from her burned breast. Also in the tank were schoolchildren, with only their heads, and their hands clasped in prayer, above the surface of the water. They were sobbing for their parents, but everyone had been hurt, so there was no one to help them. People's hair was white with dust, and scorched; they did not look human. "Surely not me," I thought, and I looked down at my own hands. They were bloody and what looked like rags hung from my arms, and inside was fresh-looking flesh, all red, white and black. I was shocked and reached for the handkerchief I carried in the pocket of my trousers, but there was no handkerchief or pocket. The lower part of the trousers had been burned away. I could feel my face swelling up, but there was nothing I could do about it. I and some friends decided to try to get back to our houses in the suburbs. Houses were blazing on both sides of the street as we walked along, and my back started hurting worse.

We heard people calling for help inside wrecked buildings, and then saw the same buildings go up in flames. A boy of about six, covered in blood, was jumping up and down in front of one of the burning houses, holding a cooking pot in his hands and yelling something we could not understand. . . . I wonder what happened to those people? And the ones trapped in the buildings. In our rush to get home quickly, the four of us were proceeding toward the center of the atomic explosion, in the opposite direction from everyone else. However, when we reached Inari-machi, we could not go any further because the bridge had been destroyed, so we headed for Futaba Hill, instead. My legs gave out near Futaba, and I almost crawled the last part of the way to the foot of the hill, saying, "Wait for me! Please wait for me!"

Luckily for us, we met some kind soldiers in white coats there, who took us to a place we could lie down and rest, and treated our wounds. They dug around and told me that they had removed pieces of tile from the back of my head. They bandaged my head for me and tried to console us by saying, "Rest here now. Your teacher is bound to come and get you soon." . . .

That first night ended. There were cries for water from early morning. I was terribly thirsty. There was a puddle in the middle of the barracks. I realized that the water was filthy, but I scooped up some of it with my shoe and drank it. It looked like coffee with milk. . . . I found out that there was a river just behind the barracks and went out with my shoes and drank to my heart's content. After that, I went back and forth many times to get water for those lying near me, and for the injured soldiers. . . . Mercurochrome had been painted on my burns once, and they got black and sticky. I tried to dry them out in the sun. My friends and the other people were no longer able to move. The skin had peeled off of their burned arms, legs, and backs. I wanted to move them, but there was no place on their bodies that I could touch. Some people came around noon on the second day and gave us some rice balls. Our faces were burned and swollen so badly that we could hardly open our mouths, so we got very little of the rice into them. My eyes had swollen up by the third day, and I could not move around. I lay down in the barracks with my friends. I remember being in a kind of dream world, talking on and on with my delirious friends. . . .

Another time, I must have been dreaming: I thought that my father and sister were coming up the hill to get me. I was so glad that I forced my eyes open with my fingers to see, but it was dark and I could not see anything. People who came to the barracks would call out the names and addresses of the people they were looking for. My father and four or five of our neighbors had been searching for me since the bombing. They found me in a corner of the barracks at the foot of Futaba Hill, on the evening of the third day. They were able to find me because the wooden name tag my father had written for me was on my chest. The writing on the tag had been burned all the way through it, as if it had been etched.

"Atsuko! This is your father!"

I was so happy I couldn't speak. I only nodded my head. My eyes were swollen closed. I could not see my father, but I was saved.

I still have the scars from that day; on my head, face, arms, legs, and chest. There are reddish black scars on my arms and the face that I see in the mirror does not look as if it belongs to me. It always saddens me to think that I will never look the way I used to. I lost all hope at first. I was obsessed with the idea that I had become a freak and did not want to be seen by anyone. I cried constantly for my good friends and kind teachers who had died in such a terrible way.

My way of thinking became warped and pessimistic. Even my beautiful voice, that my friends had envied, had turned weak and hoarse. When I think of the way it was then, I feel as if I were being strangled. But I have been able to take comfort in the thought that physical beauty is not everything, that a beautiful spirit can do away with physical ugliness. This has given me new hope for the future. I am going to study hard and develop my mind and body, to become someone with culture and inner beauty.

Multiple Voices VII ▾▾▾ The Decision to Drop the Atomic Bomb

BACKGROUND

The chain of events and decisions that led to the dropping of atomic bombs on Hiroshima and Nagasaki on August 6 and August 9, 1945, began with a letter sent to President Franklin D. Roosevelt in 1939 by Albert Einstein, the world-famous physicist who had fled Nazi Germany in 1932 to escape the scourge of Nazi anti-Semitism. Written at the urging of another distinguished European-born physicist, Leo Szilard, the letter warned that German scientists were pursuing research on nuclear chain reactions with the goal of producing weapons of enormous power. It recommended that the U.S. government fund and coordinate similar research. In response, Roosevelt appointed a committee of scientists to investigate the possibility of uranium chain reactions. Only in 1941, however, after hearing the results of promising nuclear research in England, did he order an all-out effort

to produce an atomic weapon. A year later the project was placed under the control of the army and code-named the Manhattan Project.

Under the direction of Brigadier General Leslie Groves, the Manhattan Project became a huge, desperate enterprise, employing more than 100,000 persons, who worked under the direction of the country's leading nuclear physicists and engineers at thirty-seven installations and a dozen university laboratories. Success was achieved on July 16, 1945, when the first atomic bomb, equal in force to 20,000 tons of TNT and 20,000 times more powerful than the largest conventional bomb, was exploded in the New Mexico desert. In less than a month, atomic bombs reduced Hiroshima and Nagasaki to ashes, and World War II was over.

President Truman, unaware of the Manhattan Project as a senator from Missouri and as Roosevelt's vice president, first learned of the new weapon at his first cabinet meeting on April 13, a day after Roosevelt's death, and received a full briefing from Secretary of War Henry R. Stimson on April 25. In response, Truman appointed a small committee, known as the Interim Committee, to advise him on the use of atomic weapons during and after the war. Chaired by Stimson, it consisted of seven other members: George Harrison, Stimson's special assistant; James Byrnes, a presidential advisor; Ralph Bard, undersecretary of the navy; William Clayton, undersecretary of state; and Vannevar Bush, Karl Compton, and James Conant, three prominent academic scientists who during the war worked for the National Defense Research Council, an agency created by President Roosevelt to oversee and fund scientific research for military purposes. Throughout the late spring and summer, the committee met frequently, discussing and making recommendations on a wide range of issues, including whether and how atomic bombs should be used. Their recommendations were communicated to the president by Stimson. In its deliberations the committee was advised by high-ranking military officers, business leaders, and a small committee of scientists, known as the Scientific Panel.

The events and decisions that occurred in the late spring and summer of 1945 are discussed in connection with the description of the sources that follows.

THE SOURCES

The first source is an excerpt from a summary of comments made by General George Marshall in a meeting with Secretary of War Henry Stimson on May 29, 1945. Marshall was sworn in as army chief of staff by President Roosevelt on September 1, 1939, the day Germany invaded Poland, and still was serving in the closing weeks of the war. With Germany having surrendered on May 8, at the May 29 meeting the two men discussed the final campaign against Japan.

The second source is an excerpt from a memoir written by Arthur Compton, a member of the Scientific Panel. A Nobel Prize winner for his work on x-rays, Compton was director of the Metallurgical Laboratory at the University of Chicago, where the world's first nuclear chain reaction was produced in December 1942. Here Compton describes a meeting of the Interim Committee on May 31, 1945.

Both the third and fourth sources were written by scientists who had participated in the Manhattan Project. The Franck Report, submitted to the Interim Committee on June 11, 1945, was prepared by the Committee on the Social and Political Implications of Atomic Energy, a group of scientists from the University of Chicago Metallurgical Laboratory who had reservations about the military use of atomic weapons. Its chairperson was James Franck, a German-born chemist and Nobel laureate (1925) for his work on the bombardment of atoms by electrons. A notable feature of the report is its consideration of the ramifications of using the atomic bomb for the postwar world. The next source is excerpted from a petition circulated by Leo Szilard, a Hungarian-born physicist, and signed by sixty-nine other scientists. Szilard, who, with Enrico Fermi, designed the first successful nuclear reactor, was deeply moved by the wartime destruction he had seen as a young man in Hungary during World War I. Although Szilard had urged Einstein to write President Roosevelt about the need for research on the military uses of atomic energy in 1939 and had made major contributions to the Manhattan Project, he became increasingly dismayed as scientists lost control of the research to the military. In May and June of 1945, he sought to discourage the U.S. government from using the bomb. Szilard was one of the signatories of the Franck Report and was the inspiration for the petition sent to President Truman on June 17.

The Interim Committee dismissed the key recommendations of the Franck Report, and in all likelihood President Truman never read Szilard's petition. On July 16, while attending the Potsdam Conference in Germany, Truman learned of the successful test of the atomic bomb in New Mexico and received a full report on July 21. On July 25 he ordered the U.S. military to prepare for an atomic attack on Japan sometime after August 1. On July 26 the United States, China, and Great Britain issued the Potsdam Declaration, which urged Japan to surrender unconditionally or face "the prompt and complete destruction of the Japanese armed forces and just as inevitably the utter devastation of the Japanese homeland." No mention was made of a new and terrible weapon. Although some Japanese civilian leaders continued to work for an agreement that would end the war, in the end Japan refused the terms of the Potsdam Declaration, and attacks on Hiroshima and Nagasaki followed.

The last sources were written by the two men who were most responsible for the decision to use atomic weapons, President Truman and Secretary of War Stimson. The first document is a brief letter dated August 11 from President Truman to Samuel Cavert, general secretary of the Federal Council of Churches, an ecumenical organization representing some thirty major Protestant and Orthodox denominations in the United States. On August 9 Cavert had sent a telegram to President Truman stating, "Many Christians are deeply disturbed over use of atomic bombs against Japanese cities because of their necessarily indiscriminate destructive effects and because their use sets extremely dangerous precedent for future of mankind." The last source is an excerpt from an article Stimson wrote for *Harper's Magazine* in 1947 after his retirement from public service. In it he describes the work of the Interim Committee and his reasons for advising the president to use the bomb.

QUESTIONS FOR ANALYSIS

1. How many different ideas for using the atomic bomb as a means for ending the war can you find in the sources?
2. What were the arguments made by individuals who cautioned against the use of the atomic bomb or who thought it should be "demonstrated" rather than used against the enemy?
3. What points were made against such arguments?
4. What were the main arguments of those who believed that the bomb should be used against Japanese targets without prior warning?
5. Inevitably, the question must be asked: What would you have decided if you had been president?

I ▾ MEMORANDUM OF CONVERSATION WITH GENERAL MARSHALL

The Secretary [Stimson] referred to the burning of Tokyo and the possible ways and means of employing the larger bombs. . . .

General Marshall said he thought these weapons might first be used against straight military objectives such as a large naval installation and then if no complete result was derived from the effect of that, he thought we ought to designate a number of large manufacturing areas from which the people would be warned to leave — telling the Japanese that we intended to destroy such centers. There would be no individual designations so that the Japs would not know exactly where we were to hit — a number should be named and the hit should follow shortly after. Every effort should be made to keep our record of warning clear. We must offset by such warning methods the opprobrium which might follow from an ill considered employment of such force.

The General then spoke of his stimulation of the new weapons and operations people to the development of new weapons and tactics to cope with the care and last ditch defense tactics of the suicidal Japanese. He sought to avoid the attrition we were now suffering from such fanatical but hopeless defense methods — it requires new tactics. He also spoke of gas and the possibility of using it in a limited degree, say on the outlying islands where operations were now going on or were about to take place. . . . It did not need to be our newest and most potent — just drench them and sicken them so that the fight would be taken out of them — saturate an area, possibly with mustard [gas], and just stand off. . . . There would be the matter of public opinion which we had to consider, but that was something which might also be dealt with. The character of the weapon was no less humane than phosporous and flame throwers and need not be used against dense populations or civilians — merely against these last pockets of resistance which had to be wiped out but had no other military significance. . . .

2 ▾ *Arthur Compton, RECOLLECTION OF INTERIM COMMITTEE MEETING*

Throughout the morning's discussions it seemed to be a foregone conclusion that the bomb would be used. It was regarding only the details of strategy and tactics that differing views were expressed. At the luncheon following the morning meeting, I was seated at Mr. Stimson's left. In the course of the conversation I asked the Secretary whether it might not be possible to arrange a nonmilitary demonstration of the bomb in such a manner that the Japanese would be so impressed that they would see the uselessness of continuing the war. The Secretary opened this question for general discussion by those at the table. Various possibilities were brought forward. One after the other it seemed necessary that they should be discarded.

It was evident that everyone would suspect trickery. If a bomb were exploded in Japan with previous notice, the Japanese air power was still adequate to give serious interference. An atomic bomb was an intricate device, still in the developmental stage. Its operation would be far from routine. If during the final adjustments of the bomb the Japanese defenders should attack, a faulty move might easily result in some kind of failure. Such an end to an advertised demonstration of power would be much worse than if the attempt had not been made. It was now evident that when the time came for the bombs to be used we should have only one of them available, followed afterwards by others at all-too-long intervals. We could not afford the chance that one of them might be a dud. If the test were made on some neutral territory, it was hard to believe that Japan's determined and fanatical military men would be impressed. If such an open test were made first and failed to bring surrender, the chance would be gone to give the shock of surprise that proved so effective. On the contrary, it would make the Japanese ready to interfere with an atomic attack if they could. Though the possibility of a demonstration that would not destroy human lives was attractive, no one could suggest a way in which it could be made so convincing that it would be likely to stop the war.

Ten days later, at Oppenheimer's invitation, Lawrence, Fermi, and I spent a long week end at Los Alamos. . . . We were determined to find; it we could, some effective way of demonstrating the power of an atomic bomb without loss of life that would impress Japan's warlords. If only this could be done!

Ernest Lawrence was the last one of our group to give up hope for finding such a solution. The difficulties of making a purely technical demonstration that would carry its impact effectively into Japan's controlling councils were indeed great. We had to count on every possible effort to distort even obvious facts. Experience with the determination of Japan's fight[ing] men made it evident that the war would not be stopped unless these men themselves were convinced of its futility.

3 ▾ *THE FRANCK REPORT*

Certain and perhaps important tactical results undoubtedly can be achieved, but we nevertheless think that the question of the use of the very first available atomic bombs in the Japanese war should be weighed very carefully, not only by military authority, but by the highest political leadership of this country. If we consider international agreement on total prevention of nuclear warfare as the paramount objective, and believe that it can be achieved, this kind of introduction of atomic weapons to the world may easily destroy all our chances of success. Russia, and even allied countries which bear less mistrust of our ways and intentions, as well as neutral countries, will be deeply shocked. It will be very difficult to persuade the world that a nation which was capable of secretly preparing and suddenly releasing a weapon, as indiscriminate as the rocket bomb and a thousand times more destructive, is to be trusted in its proclaimed desire of having such weapons abolished by international agreement. We have large accumulations of poison gas, but do not use them, and recent polls have shown that public opinion in this country would disapprove of such a use even if it would accelerate the winning of the Far Eastern war. It is true, that some irrational element in mass psychology makes gas poisoning more revolting than blasting by explosive, even though gas warfare is in no way more "inhuman" than the war of bombs and bullets. Nevertheless, it is not at all certain that the American public opinion, if it could be enlightened as to the effect of atomic explosives, would support the first introduction by our own country of such an indiscriminate method of wholesale destruction of civilian life.

Thus, from the "optimistic" point of view — looking forward to an international agreement on prevention of nuclear warfare — the military advantages and the saving of American lives, achieved by the sudden use of atomic bombs against Japan, may be outweighed by the ensuing loss of confidence and wave of horror and repulsion, sweeping over the rest of the world, and perhaps dividing even the public opinion at home.

From this point of view a demonstration of the new weapon may best be made before the eyes of representatives of all United Nations, on the desert or a barren island. The best possible atmosphere for the achievement of an international agreement could be achieved if America would be able to say to the world, "You see what weapon we had but did not use. We are ready to renounce its use in the future and to join other nations in working out adequate supervision of the use of this nuclear weapon."

This may sound fantastic, but then in nuclear weapons we have something entirely new in the order of magnitude of destructive power, and if we want to capitalize fully on the advantage which its possession gives us, we must use new and imaginative methods. After such a demonstration the weapon could be used against Japan if a sanction of the United Nations (and of the public opinion at home) could be obtained, perhaps after a preliminary ultimatum to Japan to surrender or at least to evacuate a certain region as an alternative to the total destruction of this target. . . .

4 ▾ THE SZILARD PETITION

. . . We, the undersigned scientists, have been working in the field of atomic power. Until recently, we have had to fear that the United States might be attacked by atomic bombs during this war and that her only defense might lie in a counterattack by the same means. Today, with the defeat of Germany, this danger is averted and we feel impelled to say what follows:

The war has to be brought speedily to a successful conclusion and attacks by atomic bombs may very well be an effective method of warfare. We feel, however, that such attacks on Japan could not be justified, at least not unless the terms which will be imposed after the war on Japan were made public in detail and Japan were given an opportunity to surrender.

If such public announcement gave assurance to the Japanese that they could look forward to a life devoted to peaceful pursuits in their homeland and if Japan still refused to surrender our nation might then, in certain circumstances, find itself forced to resort to the use of atomic bombs. Such a step, however, ought not to be made at any time without seriously considering the moral responsibilities which are involved.

The development of atomic power will provide the nations with new means of destruction. The atomic bombs at our disposal represent only the first step in this direction, and there is almost no limit to the destructive power which will become available in the course of their future development. Thus a nation which sets the precedent of using these newly liberated forces of nature for purposes of destruction may have to bear the responsibility of opening the door to an era of devastation on an unimaginable scale. . . .

5 ▾ *President Harry Truman, LETTER TO SAMUEL CAVERT*

August 11, 1945

My dear Mr. Cavert,

I appreciated very much your telegram of August 9. Nobody is more disturbed over the use of Atomic bombs than I am but I was greatly disturbed by the unwarranted attack by the Japanese on Pearl Harbor and their murder of our prisoners of war. The only language they seem to understand is the one we have been using to bombard them.

When you have to deal with a beast you have to treat him as a beast. It is regrettable but nevertheless true.

Sincerely yours,
Harry S. Truman

6 ▾ *Henry Stimson, THE DECISION TO USE THE ATOMIC BOMB*

In the middle of July 1945, the intelligence section of the War Department General Staff estimated Japanese military strength as follows: in the home islands, slightly under 2,000,000; in Korea, Manchuria, China proper, and Formosa, slightly over 2,000,000; in French Indo-China, Thailand, and Burma, over 200,000; in the East Indies area, including the Philippines, over 500,000; in the by-passed Pacific islands, over 100,000. The total strength of the Japanese Army was estimated at about 5,000,000 men. . . .

As we understood it in July, there was a very strong possibility that the Japanese government might determine upon resistance to the end, in all the areas of the Far East under its control. In such an event the Allies would be faced with the enormous task of destroying an armed force of five million men and five thousand suicide aircraft, belonging to a race which had already amply demonstrated its ability to fight literally to the death.

The strategic plans of our armed forces for the defeat of Japan, as they stood in July, had been prepared without reliance upon the atomic bomb, which had not yet been tested in New Mexico. We were planning an intensified sea and air blockade, and greatly intensified strategic air bombing, through the summer and early fall, to be followed on November 1 by an invasion of the southern island of Kyushu. This would be followed in turn by an invasion of the main island of Honshu in the spring of 1946. The total U.S. military and naval force involved in this grand design was of the order of 5,000,000 men; if all those indirectly concerned are included, it was larger still.

We estimated that if we should be forced to carry this plan to its conclusion, the major fighting would not end until the latter part of 1946, at the earliest. I was informed that such operations might be expected to cost over a million casualties to American forces alone. Additional large losses might be expected among our allies, and, of course, if our campaign were successful and if we could judge by previous experience, enemy casualties would be much larger than our own.

It was already clear in July that even before the invasion we should be able to inflict enormously severe damage on the Japanese homeland by the combined application of "conventional" sea and air power. The critical question was whether this kind of action would induce surrender. It therefore became necessary to consider very carefully the probable state of mind of the enemy, and to assess with accuracy the line of conduct which might end his will to resist.

▼▼▼

The face of war is the face of death; death is an inevitable part of every order that a wartime leader gives. The decision to use the atomic bomb was a decision that brought death to over a hundred thousand Japanese. . . . But this deliberate, premeditated destruction was our least abhorrent choice. The destruction of Hiroshima and Nagasaki put an end to the Japanese war. It stopped the fire raids and the strangling blockade; it ended the ghastly specter of a clash of great land armies. . . .

▲▲▲

Chapter 12

Anticolonialism, Nationalism, and Revolution in Africa, Asia, and Latin America

DURING THE NINETEENTH CENTURY, the industrialized nations of Europe and the United States — "the West" — achieved unprecedented global dominance. For India and most of Africa and Southeast Asia, this meant colonial status and outright political control by Western nations. For China and many states in the Middle East and Latin America, it meant the subordination of their economic interests to those of the West and erosion of their political sovereignty. The great majority of people in Europe and the United States viewed these developments as just and inevitable. Their preponderance confirmed their intellectual and moral superiority to black-, yellow-, and brown-skinned people, whom the English writer Rudyard Kipling had depicted in his poem "The White Man's Burden" as "half devil and half child."

In the first half of the twentieth century, however, Africans, Asians, and Latin Americans challenged the West's ascendancy and self-proclaimed superiority. In areas ruled by the West as colonies, mounting anticolonialism gave rise to organized parties and movements that demanded more political power and ultimately, independence. Such movements were strongest in India, where opposition to British rule escalated from polite requests by educated Indians for greater political responsibility to nationwide boycotts and mass demonstrations for independence. Despite French, British, and Dutch repression in Southeast Asia, dozens of political parties and secret organizations worked for the peaceful end or violent overthrow of colonial regimes. In Africa — although colonized only in the late 1800s and despite its ethnic and linguistic diversity — articulate and forceful proponents of Pan-Africanism, anticolonialism, and nationalism also emerged. In the Arab Middle East, where nationalist aspirations after World War I were dashed by the mandate system and the continuation of the British protectorate in Egypt, opponents of Anglo-French political control sought independence for Egypt, Iraq, Lebanon, and Syria.

While nationalism in colonial areas was directed against foreign rule, in those parts of Asia and Latin America where states were independent but nonetheless subservient to U.S. and European interests, it focused on overcoming economic dependency and political weakness. In Turkey this meant a sharp break from its past and implementation of a program of secularization and modernization under Mustafa Kemal Atatürk, the father of modern Turkey. In China nationalism resulted in a struggle to rebuild the country and end foreign interference in the face of warlordism, civil war between Nationalists and Communists, and the Japanese invasions of Manchuria in 1931 and China itself in 1937. In Latin America nationalism inspired new plans for economic development after the Great Depression of the 1930s ruined the worldwide market for the region's agricultural and mineral products. Such efforts intensified political struggles between entrenched elites and populist leaders who promised the masses social reforms.

When World War II ended in 1945, many Western leaders thought they could return to the world they had dominated before the war. In the immediate postwar years, the Dutch, French, and British all used force to maintain their empires but soon realized the futility of their efforts. Based on developments in the first half of the twentieth century, Asian and African demands for independence proved irresistible.

African Society and Identity Under Colonial Rule

Compared with the experience of India, the unfolding of colonialism in Africa resembles watching a film shown at high speed. Europeans arrived in force at the end of the nineteenth century, and after overcoming resistance and deciding among themselves who controlled what, they gave serious thought to the policies that would determine the future of their new acquisitions. Not long after these issues had been resolved, World War II was fought, and independence movements swept through Africa. In 1957 the Gold Coast, a British colony, became the independent nation of Ghana, and this in turn sparked a chain of events that resulted in the establishment of dozens of new independent states within the next decade and a half.

So brief was Africa's colonial experience, and so rapid was the Europeans' exit, that nationalism in Africa never became the broad popular movement that emerged in India during its long struggle against British rule. In addition, nationalist movements in Africa were hampered by other factors: the indifference of many chieftains, farmers, and petty traders who benefited from European rule; the paucity of Africans with formal education and political experience; the gap between educated city-dwellers and the rural masses; and rivalries among ethnic groups. Nevertheless, Africans in the interwar years found ways to express their opposition to colonial rule. They demonstrated against labor conscription, new taxes, and government-mandated land confiscations. They organized political associations, published journals, wrote books and newspaper editorials, joined independent African Christian churches, attended international meetings, and sent representatives to European capitals to state their grievances. Despite many obstacles, voices of African nationalism multiplied before World War II, and a growing audience listened to what they had to say.

The results of colonialism in Africa went well beyond politics and the birth of nationalism. Colonialism also fostered population growth, encouraged urbanization, undermined traditional religions, altered gender relationships, introduced new sports and pastimes, and changed how people dressed and what languages they spoke. Most important, it forced Africans to consider new ways of looking at themselves and their place in the world. Inevitably many features of old Africa — traditional names, music, art, marriage customs, and systems of inheritance — were weakened or lost. Whether such changes were beneficial or harmful for Africa is still debated among Africans today. There was less debate among Africans who actually lived under colonialism. With few exceptions, they found their colonial experience unsettling, dispiriting, and demeaning.

Eagles into Chickens

78 ▾ James Aggrey, PARABLE OF THE EAGLE

James Aggrey, an educator and clergyman who was among the most prominent Africans of his day, was born in 1875 in the Gold Coast, a British colony. He was educated in a Protestant mission school, became a convert to Christianity, and at age twenty-three traveled to the United States to study for the ministry. He remained in the United States for twenty years, studying economics and agriculture, speaking out against racial prejudice, and working among poor blacks of South Carolina. He returned to Africa in 1918 and died in 1927. "Parable of the Eagle" was written in the early 1920s.

QUESTIONS FOR ANALYSIS

1. According to the lesson of Aggrey's parable, what psychological and emotional damage results from colonialism?
2. If the lessons of Aggrey's parable had been translated into actual policy by colonial administrators, what aspects of colonial rule would have been affected?

A certain man went through a forest seeking any bird of interest he might find. He caught a young eagle, brought it home and put it among his fowls and ducks and turkeys, and gave it chickens' food to eat even though it was an eagle, the king of birds.

Five years later a naturalist came to see him and, after passing through his garden, said: "That bird is an eagle, not a chicken."

"Yes," said its owner, "but I have trained it to be a chicken. It is no longer an eagle, it is a chicken, even though it measures fifteen feet from tip to tip of its wings."

"No," said the naturalist, "it is an eagle still: it has the heart of an eagle, and I will make it soar high up to the heavens."

"No," said the owner, "it is a chicken, and it will never fly."

They agreed to test it. The naturalist picked up the eagle, held it up, and said with great intensity: "Eagle, thou art an eagle; thou dost belong to the sky and not to this earth; stretch forth thy wings and fly."

The eagle turned this way and that, and then, looking down, saw the chickens eating their food, and down he jumped.

The owner said: "I told you it was a chicken."

"No," said the naturalist, "it is an eagle. Give it another chance tomorrow."

So the next day he took it to the top of the house and said: "Eagle, thou art an eagle; stretch forth thy wings and fly." But again the eagle, seeing the chickens feeding, jumped down and fed with them.

Then the owner said: "I told you it was a chicken."

"No," asserted the naturalist, "it is an eagle, and it still has the heart of an eagle; only give it one more chance, and I will make it fly tomorrow."

The next morning he rose early and took the eagle outside the city, away from the houses, to the foot of a high mountain. The sun was just rising, gilding the top of the mountain with gold, and every crag was glistening in the joy of that beautiful morning.

He picked up the eagle and said to it: "Eagle, thou art an eagle; thou dost belong to the sky and not to this earth; stretch forth thy wings and fly!"

The eagle looked around and trembled as if new life were coming to it; but it did not fly. The naturalist then made it look straight at the sun. Suddenly it stretched out its wings and, with the screech of an eagle, it mounted higher and higher and never returned. It was an eagle, though it had been kept and tamed as a chicken!

My people of Africa, we were created in the image of God, but men have made us think that we are chickens, and we still think we are; but we are eagles. Stretch forth your wings and fly! Don't be content with the food of chickens!

The Value of African Tradition

▼▼▼

79 ▼ *Kabaka Daudi Chwa,* *EDUCATION, CIVILIZATION, AND "FOREIGNIZATION" IN BUGANDA*

The Great Lakes region of east-central Africa, dominated by the kingdom of Buganda, was one of the earliest areas of European missionary activity in the nineteenth century. British Protestant missionaries arrived in the region in 1877 and were followed by French Catholic missionaries in 1879. With the hold of traditional Baganda religion already weakened by conversions to Islam, the missionaries made numerous converts, especially among young courtiers in the entourage of the hereditary Baganda ruler, known as the *kabaka*. In the 1880s Protestant-Catholic rivalries among the chiefs led to civil war, the weakening of the kabaka's power, and the establishment of a British protectorate in 1894. In 1900 British authorities and the Baganda chiefs signed the Buganda Agreement, which recognized Baganda dominance over other peoples in the Uganda protectorate and maintained the chiefs' traditional powers as a means of carrying out British policy. Uganda itself was divided into twenty chieftaincies, of which ten were Protestant, eight were Catholic, and two were Muslim.

Daudi Chwa (1897–1939) as a two-year-old was named kabaka of Buganda after his father was deposed and exiled for leading a campaign against the British. A convert to Christianity, he was a figurehead, since the British gave his major chiefs a free hand to administer the colony. He did play an active and successful role in opposing the plan to consolidate Uganda, Kenya, and Tanganyika in the 1930s. Toward the end of his life, Daudi Chwa developed reservations about the effects of colonial rule, especially in the cultural and religious spheres. In 1935, four years before his death, he published his views in a pamphlet, "Education, Civilization, and 'Foreignization' in Buganda." In it, he deplored how Christianity had replaced traditional beliefs and practices.

QUESTIONS FOR ANALYSIS

1. How would you characterize the traditional system of justice of the Baganda? By what means did this system try to deter behavior that was counter to the people's rules and customs?

2. **According to the kabaka, in what ways do traditional Baganda moral values resemble those of Christianity?**
3. **According to the kabaka, what have the Baganda gained and lost as a result of European colonization?**
4. **What sort of thinking about the "backwardness" of the Baganda does the kabaka try to counter in his letter?**
5. **In the kabaka's view, what should be the proper balance between traditional and European beliefs and practices?**

Everyone knows that education and civilization were started simultaneously in this country in their respective rudimentary forms by the kind efforts of the members of the various Missionary Societies and have now been enhanced largely due to the assistance rendered by the Protectorate Government.

Naturally, Education and Civilization gained tremendous favour among the Baganda,[1] and as a consequence there are numerous Schools in remote villages in Buganda Kingdom for the Education of the young generations. . . .

Now my fears are that instead of the Baganda acquiring proper and legitimate education and civilization there is possible danger that they may be drifting to "foreignization.". . . To be more explicit, what I mean by the word "foreignization" is that instead of the Baganda acquiring proper education at the various Schools and of availing themselves of the legitimate amenities of civilization, I am very much afraid the young generation of this country is merely drifting wholesale towards "foreignization" of their natural instincts and is discarding its native and traditional customs, habits and good breeding. . . .

I am well aware that it has been said more than once that the Baganda have neither morals nor public opinion. . . . I do not wish to be considered in this article to uphold the Baganda as a Nation of Angels — But what I do maintain is that prior to the advent of the Europeans the Baganda had a very strict moral code of their own which was always enforced by a constant and genuine fear of some evil or incurable or even fatal disease being suffered invariably by the breaker of this moral code. In fact I maintain the Baganda observed most strictly the doctrine of the Ten Commandments in spite of the fact that Christianity and the so-called Christian morals were absolutely unknown to the Baganda. . . .

(a) Theft was always punished very severely, invariably by the loss of the right hand of the offender, so as to render him incapable of committing the same offense again.

(b) Adultery was almost unknown among the Baganda and any man found guilty of such offense was always ostracized from Society.

(c) Murder was invariably followed by a very severe vendetta between the members of the family or clan of the victim and those of the offender.

(d) Filial obedience was most honored among the Baganda and disobedience or disrespect of one's parents was always supposed to be punished by some higher power by the infliction of some horrible or incurable disease upon the offender.

(e) False evidence was looked upon with contempt. The person who bore false evidence and the person against whom it was given were both subjected to a very severe test by forcing them to drink a certain kind of strong drug known as "Madudu," which was supposed to result in making one of the parties who was in the wrong unconscious.

In this connection I should like to point out that although polygamy was universally recognized among the Baganda and was never considered as immoral yet prostitution was absolutely unheard

---

[1]The Baganda are the people of the kingdom of Buganda.

of. Civilization, education and freedom are the direct causes of the appalling state of affairs as regards prostitution and promiscuous relationships between the Baganda men and women. . . . As an illustration of the strictness of the old moral code of the Baganda I should like to point out here one of the most important native custom of looking after the daughters in a Muganda's[2] home. It was one of the worst filial offenses for a daughter to become pregnant while living with her parents. As soon as she was discovered in that condition she was at once expelled from her parents' house, and was absolutely cut off from them. She could not eat with them nor would her parents touch her until the child was born and some rites had been gone through which necessitated a great deal of hardship and shame on the part of the girl and her seducer. This custom was intended to stimulate morality among the Baganda girls, since any girl who went astray before she was given in marriage suffered this indignity and was always looked upon with contempt by all her relatives and friends. Furthermore any girl who was given in marriage and was found not to be a virgin merited unspeakable disfavor in the eyes of her parents, relations and friends. All this, however, is of course, no longer the case. The present so-called education and civilization prevailing in this country has completely destroyed this moral code by removing the constant fear just referred to above from the minds of the young generation of the Baganda by the freedom and liberty which are the natural consequences of the present World civilization.

. . . Whilst . . . apart from their ignorance of Christianity and their practice of polygamy I am strongly of opinion that most of the traditional customs and etiquette of the Baganda . . . were quite consistent with the principles of Christianity. In support of this argument it is only necessary to mention a few customs of the Baganda to show that they unconsciously possessed a sense of the modern Christian morality:

(a) It was one of the most important behaviors among the Baganda for one's neighbor to be considered as his own relative and to share with him in his happiness or unhappiness. . . .

(b) It was the recognized etiquette for a Muganda to salute every one that he met on the road, whether he knew him or not.

(c) When a Muganda was taking his meal and any one passed by, it was always the custom to invite him to share it with him.

(d) It was always the duty of every one who hears an alarm at any time of day or night or a cry for help to go at once and render assistance to the party in distress or danger. . . .

(e) It was the duty of every Muganda, when requested, to assist any traveller in directing him to his destination, or to give him food or water, and even to give him shelter from rain or for the night. . . .

My intention therefore in this article is to emphasize the fact that while boasting of having acquired Western education and civilization in an amazingly short period, we have entirely and completely ignored our native traditional customs. In other words we have "foreignized" our native existence by acquiring the worst foreign habits and customs of the Western people. I am only too well aware that this is inevitable in all countries where Western civilization has reached, so I have considered it my duty in this article to warn very strongly all members of the young generation of the Baganda that while they are legitimately entitled to strive to acquire education and civilization they should also take a very great care that acquisition of Western Education and Civilization does not automatically destroy their best inherent traditions and customs which, in my own opinion, are quite as good as those found among the Western Civilized countries but which only require developing and remodelling where necessary on the lines and ideas of western civilization.

---

[2]Muganda is the word (singular) for an individual living in the kingdom of Buganda.

Political and Religious Currents in the Middle East

The aftermath of World War I brought political disaster to the Middle East. The Turks, who had fought on Germany's side, were forced in 1920 to accept the humiliating Treaty of Sèvres, which stripped Turkey of its Arab territories; limited the Turkish army to 50,000 men; gave France, Britain, and Italy control of its finances; and proposed to cede parts of Turkey itself to Italy, Greece, and the new states of Kurdistan and Armenia. The sultan, overwhelmed by problems of lawlessness, army desertions, and inflation, not only accepted the treaty but also offered no resistance when the Greeks landed troops in western Anatolia in May 1919.

The Turks' former subjects, the Arabs, also experienced bitter disappointment, even though they had been on the winning side in the war. Promised self-rule for joining the Anglo-French alliance and fighting against their Ottoman overlords, they learned in 1919 that the British and French had agreed in 1916 to divide Arab lands between them and that this, rather than the promises of Arab independence, would determine the postwar settlement. In 1920 Iraq, Syria, Palestine, Lebanon, and Jordan all became British or French mandates, a status that differed from old-style colonialism in name only.

Arabs also were incensed by the continuation of the British protectorate in Egypt and by the British commitment to honor their wartime promises to support the establishment of a national homeland in Palestine for the Jewish people. Farther east, another major Islamic state, Persia (Iran), under the decrepit rule of the Qajar Dynasty, also seemed on the verge of becoming a British protectorate.

Efforts to reverse the postwar settlements were most successful in Turkey and Persia. Under Mustafa Kemal, the Turks rallied to drive out the Greeks and smash the nascent Armenian state between 1919 and 1922. In 1922 the Turks abolished the sultanate, and in 1923 the European powers agreed to replace the Treaty of Sèvres with the Treaty of Lausanne, which recognized the integrity and independence of the new Turkish republic. Mustafa Kemal now had an opportunity to transform Turkey into a modern secular state. In Persia, which barely avoided becoming a British protectorate in 1919, Colonel Reza Khan (1878–1944) was named shah in 1925 and, like his hero, Kemal, sought to build up his country through economic development, educational reform, and Westernization.

Arab efforts to achieve independence and prevent Jewish immigration to Palestine were less successful. Of the twenty Arab states that stretched from Morocco in the west to Iraq in the east, only Saudi Arabia and Yemen were truly independent in the interwar years. Egypt and Iraq attained limited self-rule, but the presence of British troops and the continuing British influence over foreign and military affairs were sources of friction and anger in both countries. The drive for independence was even more frustrating in French-controlled Lebanon and Syria. In the 1930s the French reneged on promises to relinquish their authority, and

Lebanon remained a mandate until 1943 and Syria until 1945. Arabs throughout the Middle East also were angered by growing Jewish migration to Palestine, especially in the 1930s, when mounting anti-Semitism in Europe created a mass of new immigrants.

While confronting these immediate postwar diplomatic and political problems, the people and leaders of the region faced other difficult issues. What could be done to end poverty and illiteracy? How could the teachings and expectations of Islam be reconciled with the realities and demands of modernization? Was modernization itself desirable, and, if so, how was it to be achieved? Was the goal of Arab nationalism the expulsion of the British and French and the stifling of Zionism, or was it the attainment of a single united Arab state? Questions such as these were not new to the people of the Middle East. But in the face of the changes that swept through the region in the first half of the twentieth century, finding answers to them became more urgent and more difficult.

Secularism and Nationalism in Republican Turkey

80 ▾ *Mustafa Kemal, SPEECH TO THE CONGRESS OF THE PEOPLE'S REPUBLICAN PARTY*

The archsymbol of secularism and nationalism in the Muslim world in the interwar years was Mustafa Kemal (1881–1938), a military hero during World War I who went on to serve as the first president of the Turkish republic. Disgusted by the Ottoman sultan's acquiescence to the Greek occupation of the Turkish port of Smyrna (Izmir) in 1919, Kemal assumed leadership of a resistance movement that by 1923 had overthrown the sultan, defeated the Greeks, and won the annulment of the punitive Treaty of Sèvres. Exercising broad powers as president of Turkey until his death in 1938, Kemal sought to transform Turkey into a modern secular nation-state. To accomplish this, he broke the power of Islam over education and the legal system, encouraged industrialization, accorded women full legal rights, mandated the use of a new Turkish alphabet, and ordered Turks to adopt Western-style dress. Directing all Turks to adopt hereditary family names, he took for himself the name *Atatürk*, or "Great Turk."

Having consolidated his authority, Kemal decided in 1927 to review his accomplishments and impress upon his subjects the need for continued support. He chose as the occasion the meeting of the People's Republican Party, which he had founded and was Turkey's only legal political party. Here he delivered an extraordinary speech. Having worked on it for three months (in the process exhausting dozens of secretaries), he delivered it over a period of six days.

In these excerpts he discusses Turkey's past and future; explains his reasons for abolishing the caliphate, the ancient office by virtue of which Turkish sultans had been the theoretical rulers of all Muslims; and justifies his suppression of the Progressive Republican Party, which despite its name was a party of conservatives who opposed Turkey's modernization.

QUESTIONS FOR ANALYSIS

1. **According to Kemal, what were the "erroneous ideas" that had guided the Ottoman state in the past?**
2. **Why does Kemal argue that nation-states, not empires, are the most desirable form of political organization?**
3. **What is Kemal's view of the West?**
4. **What are his views of Islam?**
5. **What arguments does Kemal offer against the continuation of the caliphate?**
6. **How does Kemal justify his suppression of the Progressive Republicans? What, in his view, were the positive results of this step?**

[NATIONALISM AND EMPIRE]

. . . Among the Ottoman rulers there were some who endeavored to form a gigantic empire by seizing Germany and Western Europe. One of these rulers hoped to unite the whole Islamic world in one body, to lead it and govern it. For this purpose he obtained control of Syria and Egypt and assumed the title of Caliph.[1] Another Sultan pursued the twofold aim, on the one hand of gaining the mastery over Europe, and on the other of subjecting the Islamic world to his authority and government. The continuous counterattacks from the West, the discontent and insurrections in the Muslim world, as well as the dissensions between the various elements which this policy had artificially brought together within certain limits, had the ultimate result of burying the Ottoman Empire, in the same way as many others, under the pall of history. . . .

To unite different nations under one common name, to give these different elements equal rights, subject them to the same conditions and thus to found a mighty State is a brilliant and attractive political ideal; but it is a misleading one. It is an unrealizable aim to attempt to unite in one tribe the various races existing on the earth, thereby abolishing all boundaries. Herein lies a truth which the centuries that have gone by and the men who have lived during these centuries have clearly shown in dark and sanguinary events.

There is nothing in history to show how the policy of Panislamism[2] could have succeeded or how it could have found a basis for its realization on this earth. As regards the result of the ambition to organize a State which should be governed by the idea of world-supremacy and include the whole of humanity without distinction of race, history does not afford examples of this. For us, there can be no question of the lust of conquest. . . .

In order that our nation should be able to live a happy, strenuous, and permanent life, it is necessary that the State should pursue an exclusively national policy and that this policy should be in perfect agreement with our internal organization and be based on it. When I speak of national policy, I mean it in this sense: To work within our national boundaries for the real happiness and welfare of the nation and the country by, above all, relying on our own strength in order to retain our existence. But not to lead the people to follow fictitious aims, of whatever nature, which could only bring them misfortune, and expect from the civilized world civilized human treatment, friendship based on mutuality. . . .

---

[1]A reference to Selim I, who conquered Egypt and Syria in 1515–1516; it is doubtful that he actually considered himself caliph, that is, leader and protector of all Muslims.

[2]The program of uniting all Muslims under one government or ruler.

[THE ISSUE OF THE CALIPHATE]

I must call attention to the fact that Hodja Shukri, as well as the politicians who pushed forward his person and signature, had intended to substitute the sovereign bearing the title of Sultan or Padishah by a monarch with the title of Caliph.[3] The only difference was that, instead of speaking of a monarch of this or that country or nation, they now spoke of a monarch whose authority extended over a population of three hundred million souls belonging to manifold nations and dwelling in different continents of the world. Into the hands of this great monarch, whose authority was to extend over the whole of Islam, they placed as the only power that of the Turkish people, that is to say, only from 10 to 15 millions of these three hundred million subjects. The monarch designated under the title of Caliph was to guide the affairs of these Muslim peoples and to secure the execution of the religious prescriptions which would best correspond to their worldly interests. He was to defend the rights of all Muslims and concentrate all the affairs of the Muslim world in his hands with effective authority. . . .

If the Caliph and Caliphate, as they maintained, were to be invested with a dignity embracing the whole of Islam, ought they not to have realized in all justice that a crushing burden would be imposed on Turkey, on her existence; her entire resources and all her forces would be placed at the disposal of the Caliph? . . .

I made statements everywhere, that were necessary to dispel the uncertainty and anxiety of the people concerning this question of the Caliphate. . . . I gave the people to understand that neither Turkey nor the handful of men she possesses could be placed at the disposal of the Caliph so that he might fulfill the mission attributed to him, namely, to found a State comprising the whole of Islam. The Turkish nation is incapable of undertaking such an irrational mission.

For centuries our nation was guided under the influence of these erroneous ideas. But what has been the result of it? Everywhere they have lost millions of men. "Do you know," I asked, "how many sons of Anatolia have perished in the scorching deserts of the Yemen? Do you know the losses we have suffered in holding Syria and Iraq and Egypt and in maintaining our position in Africa? And do you see what has come out of it? Do you know?. . .

"New Turkey, the people of New Turkey, have no reason to think of anything else but their own existence and their own welfare. She has nothing more to give away to others." . . .

[THE SUPPRESSION OF THE PROGRESSIVE REPUBLICANS]

As you know, it was at the time that the members of the opposition had founded a party under the name of "Republican Progressive Party" and published its program. . . .

Under the mask of respect for religious ideas and dogmas the new Party addressed itself to the people in the following words:

"We want the re-establishment of the Caliphate; we do not want new laws; we are satisfied with the religious law; we shall protect the Medressas, the Tekkes, the pious institutions, the Softahs, the Sheikhs[4] and their disciples. Be on our side; the party of Mustafa Kemal, having abolished the Caliphate, is breaking Islam into ruins; they will make you into unbelievers. . . ."

Read these sentences, Gentlemen, from a letter written by one of the adherents of this program: . . . "They are attacking the very principles

---

[3]These events took place in January 1923. After Sultan Mehmed V was deposed on November 1, 1922, his cousin was designated caliph. Because of their long rule and vast territories, Ottoman sultans by the nineteenth century were viewed by many Muslims as caliphs, that is, successors of the prophet Muhammad, with jurisdiction over all of Islam. Shukri was a *hodja* (or *hojja*), a Turkish religious leader; he hoped that the new Turkish state would continue to support the caliphate even after the sultanate was abolished. In 1924, however, Kemal abolished the caliphate.

[4]A *medressa* is an advanced school of Islamic learning; a *tekke* is a small teaching mosque usually built over the tomb of a saint; a *softah* is a student in an Islamic school; a *sheikh*, or *shaykh*, is a master of a religious order of Sufis, who adopted a mystical approach to Islam.

which perpetuate the existence of the Muslim world. . . . The assimilation with the Occident means the destruction of our history, our civilization. . . ." Gentlemen, facts and events have proved that the program of the Republican Progressive Party has been the work emanating from the brain of traitors. This Party became the refuge and the point of support for reactionary and rebellious elements. . . .

The Government and the Committee found themselves forced to take extraordinary measures. They caused the law regarding the restoration of order to be proclaimed, and the Independence Courts to take action. For a considerable time they kept eight or nine divisions of the army at war strength for the suppression of disorders, and put an end to the injurious organization which bore the name "Republican Progressive Party."

The result was, of course, the success of the Republic. . . .

Gentlemen, it was necessary to abolish the fez,[5] which sat on our heads as a sign of ignorance, of fanaticism, of hatred to progress and civilization, and to adopt in its place the hat, the customary headdress of the whole civilized world, thus showing, among other things, that no difference existed in the manner of thought between the Turkish nation and the whole family of civilized mankind. We did that while the law for the Restoration of Order was still in force. If it had not been in force we should have done so all the same; but one can say with complete truth that the existence of this law made the thing much easier for us. As a matter of fact the application of the law for the Restoration of Order prevented the morale of the nation being poisoned to a great extent by reactionaries.

Gentlemen, while the law regarding the Restoration of Order was in force there took place also the closing of the Tekkes, of the convents, and of the mausoleums, as well as the abolition of all sects[6] and all kinds of titles such as Sheikh, Dervish, . . . Occultist, Magician, Mausoleum Guard, etc.[7]

One will be able to imagine how necessary the carrying through of these measures was, in order to prove that our nation as a whole was no primitive nation, filled with superstitions and prejudices.

Could a civilized nation tolerate a mass of people who let themselves be led by the nose by a herd of Sheikhs, Dedes, Seids, . . . Babas and Emirs,[8] who entrusted their destiny and their lives to chiromancers,[9] magicians, dice-throwers and amulet sellers? Ought one to conserve in the Turkish State, in the Turkish Republic, elements and institutions such as those which had for centuries given the nation the appearance of being other than it really was? Would one not therewith have committed the greatest, most irreparable error to the cause of progress and reawakening?

If we made use of the law for the Restoration of Order in this manner, it was in order to avoid such a historic error; to show the nation's brow pure and luminous, as it is; to prove that our people think neither in a fanatical nor a reactionary manner.

Gentlemen, at the same time the new laws were worked out and decreed which promise the most fruitful results for the nation on the social and economic plane, and in general in all the forms of the expression of human activity . . . the Citizens' Legal Code, which ensures the liberty of women and stabilizes the existence of the family.

Accordingly we made use of all circumstances only from one point of view, which consisted therein: to raise the nation on to that step on which it is justified in standing in the civilized world, to stabilize the Turkish Republic more and more on steadfast foundations . . . and in addition to destroy the spirit of despotism for ever.

---

[5]The fez was a brimless hat popular among Turkish men during the nineteenth century; its lack of a brim allowed the wearer to touch his forehead to the ground while kneeling during prayer without removing the hat.

[6]Islamic religious orders.

[7]A *dervish*, or *darvish*, was a member of an Islamic sect famous for its whirling dances that symbolized the movement of the heavenly spheres; an *occultist* was a Sufi who achieved a state of withdrawal from the world; a *mausoleum guard* guarded the tomb of a saint or holy person.

[8]A *dede* was head of a Sufi order; *seids*, or *sayyids*, were descendants of the prophet Muhammad through his daughter Fatima; *baba* was a popular surname among Sufi preachers; in this context *emir* is an honorary Turkish title.

[9]People who told the future by reading palms.

A Call for Islamic Social and Political Action

81 ▾ The Muslim Brotherhood, TOWARD THE LIGHT

Although Mustafa Kemal's commitment to modernization had supporters throughout the Middle East, it also had staunch opponents. Many Muslims — from all classes and across all educational levels — were alarmed by the prospect of a secularized, Westernized future and sought instead to establish a true Islamic society guided by the Quran and conforming to Islamic law. In the interwar years, their hopes were best represented by the Muslim Brotherhood, founded in 1929 by an Egyptian schoolteacher, Hasan al-Banna (1906–1949).

Born in a small town in the Nile Delta, Hasan al-Banna as a student in Cairo after World War I was deeply troubled by the factionalism, social conflict, poverty, and religious indifference he observed in Egypt. He concluded that British colonialism and the broad acceptance of Western values had caused these ills and that a return to fundamental Islamic teachings would cure them. In 1927 he became a schoolteacher in the Sinai town of Ismailia, where he organized religious study groups and committed himself to Islamic renewal. In 1929 he founded the Muslim Brotherhood, an organization dedicated to the realization of Islamic government in Egypt and other Muslim lands.

In the 1930s the Brotherhood grew into a tightly knit, disciplined organization with a million members and a network of branches made up of numerous secret cells. It built mosques, schools, and small hospitals; sponsored youth programs, social clubs, and light industries; and publicized its religious message through preaching and publications. In the 1940s, with a greater commitment to political activism, it clashed with British authorities and the Egyptian government itself. Linked to the assassination of several officials, the Brotherhood was outlawed by the Egyptian government in 1949, and Hasan al-Banna himself was assassinated by government agents that same year.

The Brotherhood regained legal status in Egypt in 1950 and since then has continued to be an important religious and political force in the Arab Middle East. It has branches in Sudan, Syria, and other Arab states; vast financial resources; and an estimated membership of 2 million, despite attempts by the Egyptian government to suppress the organization on two occasions in the 1950s and 1960s after its members were implicated in assassination plots. The organization also has experienced bitter internal divisions. In Egypt the Brotherhood officially rejected violence in the 1980s in favor of winning elected office and increasing its commitment to social service activities. Such moderation caused defections to more militant groups. Islamic Jihad and Hamas, which are committed to the cause of Palestinian nationhood and oppose compromise with Israel, are both offshoots of the Muslim Brotherhood.

The following excerpt is drawn from a pamphlet issued by the Brotherhood in 1936. Directed to King Faruk of Egypt and other Arab leaders, it summarizes the Brotherhood's early goals.

QUESTIONS FOR ANALYSIS

1. How would you characterize the Brotherhood's views on the purposes and goals of government?
2. According to this document, what was the Brotherhood's conception of the ideal government official?
3. What does the document reveal about the Brotherhood's attitude toward the West? Are there aspects of Western culture that the Brotherhood finds acceptable?
4. What role does the Brotherhood envision for women in Islamic society?
5. According to the Brotherhood, what are the goals of education? How are they to be achieved?
6. What policies does the Brotherhood propose to help the poor?
7. What is there in the statement that might help account for the widespread support of the Brotherhood among Middle Eastern Muslims?

After having studied the ideals which ought to inspire a renascent nation on the spiritual level, we wish to offer, in conclusion, some practical suggestions. We will list here only the chapter headings because we know very well that each suggestion will require profound study as well as the special attention of experts; we know also that the needs of the nation are enormous; we do not believe that the fulfilling of the needs and the aspirations of the country will be easy; what is more, we do not think that these goals can be reached in one journey or two. . . . The task will require a great deal of patience, a great deal of ability, and a willing tenacity.

But one thing is certain: resolve will lead to success. A dedicated nation, working to accomplish the right, will certainly reach, with God's help, the goals toward which it strives.

The following are the chapter headings for a reform based upon the true spirit of Islam:

I. In the political, judicial, and administrative fields:

1. To prohibit political parties and to direct the forces of the nation toward the formation of a united front;
2. To reform the law so that it will be entirely in accordance with Islamic legal practice;
3. To build up the army, to increase the number of youth groups; to instill in youth the spirit of holy struggle, faith, and self-sacrifice;
4. To strengthen the ties among Islamic countries and more particularly among Arab countries which is a necessary step toward serious examination of the question of the defunct Caliphate;[1]
5. To propagate an Islamic spirit within the civil administration so that all officials will understand the need for applying the teachings of Islam;
6. To supervise the personal conduct of officials because the private life and the administrative life of these officials form an indivisible whole;
7. To advance the hours of work in summer and in winter so that the accomplishment of religious obligations will be eased . . . ;
8. To condemn corruption and influence peddling; to reward only competence and merit;
9. Government will act in conformity to the law and to Islamic principles; the carrying

[1]The office of caliph, or successor of Muhammad as head of the Muslim community, had been held by the Ottoman sultans but was abolished by Kemal in 1924.

out of ceremonies, receptions, and official meetings, as well as the administration of prisons and hospitals should not be contrary to Islamic teachings. The scheduling of government services ought to take account of the hours set aside for prayer.

10. To train and to use . . . graduates of Al-Azhar University,[2] for military and civil roles;

II. In the fields of social and everyday practical life:

1. The people should respect public morality; this ought to be the object of special attention — to strongly condemn attacks upon public mores and morality;
2. To find a solution for the problems of women, a solution that will allow her to progress and which will protect her while conforming to Islamic principles. This very important social question should not be ignored because it has become the subject of polemics and of more or less unsupported and exaggerated opinion;
3. To root out . . . prostitution and to consider fornication as a reprehensible crime the authors of which should be flogged;
4. To prohibit all games of chance (gaming, lotteries, races, gambling clubs);
5. To stop the use of alcohol and intoxicants — these obliterate the painful consequences of people's evil deeds;
6. To campaign against ostentation in dress and loose behavior. To instruct women in what is proper with particular strictness as regards female teachers, pupils, students, and doctors;
7. To prepare instructional programs for girls . . . a program different from the one for boys;
8. Male students should not be mixed with female students — any private meetings between unmarried men and women is considered to be wrong until it is approved;
9. To encourage marriage and procreation — to develop legislation to safeguard the family and to solve marriage problems;
10. To close dance halls; to forbid dancing;
11. To censor theater productions and films; to be rigorous in approving films;
12. To rigorously censor and select music;
13. To approve programs, songs, and subjects before they are broadcast to the nation; to use radio to encourage national education;
14. To confiscate provocative articles and books as well as magazines that plant seeds of skepticism or spread immorality;
15. To carefully organize vacation centers;
16. To change the hours when public cafes are opened or closed, to watch the activities of those who habituate them — to direct these people towards wholesome pursuits, to prevent people from spending too much time in these cafes;
17. To use the cafes as centers to teach reading and writing to illiterates, to seek help in this task from primary school teachers and students; . . .
19. To bring to trial those who break the laws of Islam, who do not fast, who do not pray, and who insult religion;
20. To transfer village primary schools to the mosque. . . .
21. Religious teaching should constitute the essential subject matter to be taught in all educational establishments and faculties;
22. To memorize the Quran in state elementary schools — this will be required in order to obtain diplomas with a religious or philosophical specialty. . . .
24. The cultivation of teaching the Arabic language in all grades — absolute priority to be given to Arabic over foreign languages;
25. To study the history of Islam, the nation, and Muslim civilization;
26. To study the best way to arrive at a uniform mode of dress for the nation;
27. To combat foreign customs (in the realm of vocabulary, customs, dress, nursing) and to Egyptianize all of these (one finds these

[2]An educational institution in Cairo specializing in Islamic studies.

customs among the well-to-do members of society); . . .

29. To safeguard public health through every kind of publicity — increasing the number of hospitals, doctors, and out-patient clinics;
30. To call particular attention to the problems of village life (administration, hygiene, water supply, education, recreation, morality).

III. The economic field:

1. Organization of the zakat tax[3] according to Islamic precepts, using zakat proceeds for welfare projects such as aiding the indigent, the poor, orphans; the zakat should also be used to strengthen the army;
2. To prevent the practice of usury, to direct banks to implement this policy; the government should provide an example by giving up the interest fixed by banks for servicing a personal loan or an industrial loan, etc.;
3. To encourage economic projects and to employ the jobless, to employ for the nation's benefit the skills possessed by the foreigners in these enterprises; . . .
5. Aid for low-ranking employees and enlargement of their pay, lowering the income of high-ranking employees; . . .
7. To encourage agricultural and industrial works, to improve the situation of the peasants and industrial workers;
8. To give special attention to the technical and social needs of the workers, to raise their level of life and aid their class;
9. Utilization of certain natural resources (uncultivated land, neglected mines, etc.). . . .

[3]A fixed share of income or property that all Muslims must pay as a tax for the welfare of the needy or other charitable purposes.

Anticolonialism in India and Southeast Asia

During the late nineteenth century, when Indians were already in a full-scale debate about their relationship with Great Britain and some were demanding independence, many Southeast Asians were experiencing direct European political control for the first time. Nonetheless, in the first half of the twentieth century, developments in both areas showed some marked similarities. Nationalism swept through the Indian population, and despite their many differences in religion, education, and caste status, millions of Indians came to agree that Great Britain should "quit India" and allow Indian self-rule. Nationalism also intensified in Southeast Asia, especially in Vietnam and the Dutch East Indies, where force was needed to suppress anticolonial movements in both areas in the 1920s and 1930s.

The reasons for this upsurge of anti-European sentiment included religious revivals of Hinduism in India, Buddhism in Burma, and Islam in Southeast Asia, all of which heightened people's awareness of their differences from the West; the emergence of Japan, which demonstrated that an Asian nation could become a great power; the carnage of World War I, which raised doubts about the Europeans' "superiority"; and the spread of Western education and political ideologies. Most telling, however, was anger over the disparity between the Europeans' stated good intentions about their colonies' futures and their actual record of economic exploitation, racial prejudice, and opposition to self-rule.

To these factors were added the extraordinary influence of charismatic leaders such as Mohandas Gandhi, who drew the Indian masses into the nationalist

movement; Jawaharlal Nehru, who guided the Indian Congress Party in the 1930s and 1940s; Ho Chi Minh, who built a strong nationalist coalition in Vietnam in the face of French persecution; and Achmed Sukarno, who rallied Indonesian nationalists despite opposition from the Dutch.

World War II was the catalyst for the creation of independent nations throughout the region in the late 1940s and the 1950s. But events and leaders of the first half of the twentieth century set the stage.

Gandhi's Vision for India

▼▼▼

82 ▾ *Mohandas Gandhi, INDIAN HOME RULE*

Mohandas Gandhi, the outstanding figure in modern Indian history, was born in 1869 in a village north of Mumbai on the Arabian Sea. His father was a government official who presided over an extended family with strict Hindu practices. Gandhi studied law in England, and after failing to establish a legal practice in Mumbai, he moved to South Africa in 1893 to serve the area's large Indian population.

In South Africa he became incensed over discriminatory laws against Indians, many of whom were indentured servants employed by whites or petty Indian merchants. During his struggle to improve the lot of South Africa's Indian population, Gandhi developed his philosophy of *satyagraha*, usually translated into English as "soul force." Satyagraha sought justice not through violence but through love, a willingness to suffer, and conversion of the oppressor. Central to his strategy was nonviolent resistance: Gandhi's followers disobeyed unjust laws and accepted the consequences — even beatings and imprisonment — to reach the hearts of the British and change their thinking.

Gandhi first wrote about his theories of satyagraha in 1908 after meeting with a group of Indians in England who favored force to oust the British. In response, he composed a pamphlet, "Hind Swaraj," or "Indian Home Rule," in which he explains his theory of nonviolent resistance and his doubts about the benefits of modern civilization. Written as a dialogue between a "reader" and an "editor" (Gandhi), "Indian Home Rule" was printed in hundreds of editions and still serves as the best summary of Gandhi's philosophy.

QUESTIONS FOR ANALYSIS

1. What does Gandhi see as the major deficiency of modern civilization?
2. According to Gandhi, how has civilization specifically affected women?
3. Why does Gandhi have faith that Hindus and Muslims will be able to live in peace in India?
4. What, according to Gandhi, is true civilization, and what is India's role in preserving it?
5. What leads Gandhi to his conviction that love is stronger than force?
6. Why did Gandhi's attack on civilization gain him support among the Indian masses?

CHAPTER VI

Civilization

READER: Now you will have to explain what you mean by civilization. . . .

EDITOR: Let us first consider what state of things is described by the word "civilization." Its true test lies in the fact that people living in it make bodily welfare the object of life. We will take some examples: The people of Europe today live in better-built houses than they did a hundred years ago. This is considered an emblem of civilization, and this is also a matter to promote bodily happiness. Formerly, they wore skins, and used as their weapons spears. Now, they wear long trousers, and for embellishing their bodies they wear a variety of clothing, and, instead of spears, they carry with them revolvers containing five or more chambers. If people of a certain country, who have hitherto not been in the habit of wearing much clothing, boots, etc., adopt European clothing, they are supposed to have become civilized out of savagery. Formerly, in Europe, people plowed their lands mainly by manual labor. Now, one man can plow a vast tract by means of steam-engines, and can thus amass great wealth. This is called a sign of civilization. Formerly, the fewest men wrote books, that were most valuable. Now, anybody writes and prints anything he likes and poisons people's minds. Formerly, men traveled in wagons; now they fly through the air, in trains at the rate of four hundred and more miles per day. This is considered the height of civilization. It has been stated that, as men progress, they shall be able to travel in airships and reach any part of the world in a few hours. Men will not need the use of their hands and feet. They will press a button, and they will have their clothing by their side. They will press another button, and they will have their newspaper. A third, and a motor-car will be in waiting for them. They will have a variety of delicately dished up food. Everything will be done by machinery. Formerly, when people wanted to fight with one another, they measured between them their bodily strength; now it is possible to take away thousands of lives by one man working behind a gun from a hill. This is civilization. Formerly, men worked in the open air only so much as they liked. Now, thousands of workmen meet together and for the sake of maintenance work in factories or mines. Their condition is worse than that of beasts. They are obliged to work, at the risk of their lives, at most dangerous occupations, for the sake of millionaires. Formerly, men were made slaves under physical compulsion, now they are enslaved by temptation of money and of the luxuries that money can buy. There are now diseases of which people never dreamed before, and an army of doctors is engaged in finding out their cures, and so hospitals have increased. This is a test of civilization. Formerly, special messengers were required and much expense was incurred in order to send letters; today, anyone can abuse his fellow by means of a letter for one penny. True, at the same cost, one can send one's thanks also. Formerly, people had two or three meals consisting of homemade bread and vegetables; now, they require something to eat every two hours, so that they have hardly leisure for anything else. What more need I say? All this you can ascertain from several authoritative books. These are all true tests of civilization. And, if any one speaks to the contrary, know that he is ignorant. This civilization takes note neither of morality nor of religion. . . .

This civilization is irreligion, and it has taken such a hold on the people in Europe that those who are in it appear to be half mad. They lack real physical strength or courage. They keep up their energy by intoxication. They can hardly be happy in solitude. Women, who should be the queens of households, wander in the streets, or they slave away in factories. For the sake of a pittance, half a million women in England alone are laboring under trying circumstances in factories or similar institutions. This awful fact is one of the causes of the daily growing suffragette movement.

This civilization is such that one has only to be patient and it will be self-destroyed.

CHAPTER X

The Hindus and the Muslims

READER: But I am impatient to hear your answer to my question. Has the introduction of Islam not unmade the nation?

EDITOR: India cannot cease to be one nation because people belonging to different religions live in it. The introduction of foreigners does not necessarily destroy the nation, they merge in it. A country is one nation only when such a condition obtains in it. That country must have a faculty for assimilation. India has ever been such a country. In reality, there are as many religions as there are individuals, but those who are conscious of the spirit of nationality do not interfere with one another's religion. If they do, they are not fit to be considered a nation. If the Hindus believe that India should be peopled only by Hindus, they are living in dreamland. The Hindus, the Muslims, the Parsees[1] and the Christians who have made India their country are fellow-countrymen, and they will have to live in unity if only for their own interest. In no part of the world are one nationality and one religion synonymous terms; nor has it ever been so in India.

READER: But what about the inborn enmity between Hindus and Muslims?

EDITOR: That phrase has been invented by our mutual enemy.[2] When the Hindus and Muslims fought against one another, they certainly spoke in that strain. They have long since ceased to fight. How, then, can there be any inborn enmity? Pray remember this too, that we did not cease to fight only after British occupation. The Hindus flourished under Muslim sovereigns and Muslims under the Hindu. Each party recognized that mutual fighting was suicidal, and that neither party would abandon its religion by force of arms. Both parties, therefore, decided to live in peace. With the English advent the quarrels recommenced. . . .

Hindus and Muslims own the same ancestors, and the same blood runs through their veins. Do people become enemies because they change their religion? Is the God of the Muslim different from the God of the Hindu? Religions are different roads converging to the same point. What does it matter that we take different roads, so long as we reach the same goal? Wherein is the cause for quarreling?

CHAPTER XIII

What Is True Civilization?

READER: You have denounced railways, lawyers and doctors. I can see that you will discard all machinery. What, then, is civilization?

EDITOR: The answer to that question is not difficult. I believe that the civilization India has evolved is not to be beaten in the world. Nothing can equal the seeds sown by our ancestors. Rome went, Greece shared the same fate, the might of the Pharaohs was broken, Japan has become westernized, of China nothing can be said, but India is still, somehow or other, sound at the foundation. The people of Europe learn their lessons from the writings of the men of Greece or Rome, which exist no longer in their former glory. In trying to learn from them, the Europeans imagine that they will avoid the mistakes of Greece and Rome. Such is their pitiable condition. In the midst of all this, India remains immovable, and that is her glory. It is a charge against India that her people are so uncivilized, ignorant, and stolid, that it is not possible to induce them to adopt any changes. It is a charge really against our merit. What we have tested and found true on the anvil of experience, we dare not change. Many thrust their advice upon India, and she remains steady. This is her beauty; it is the sheet-anchor of our hope.

---

[1]Followers of the Zoroastrian religion who fled India when Islamic armies conquered Persia in the seventh century C.E.

[2]The British.

Civilization is that mode of conduct which points out to man the path of duty. Performance of duty and observance of morality are convertible terms. To observe morality is to attain mastery over our mind and our passions. So doing, we know ourselves. The Gujarati[3] equivalent for civilization means "good conduct." If this definition be correct, then India, as so many writers have shown, has nothing to learn from anybody else, and this is as it should be.

CHAPTER XVII

Passive Resistance

READER: Is there any historical evidence as to the success of what you have called soul-force or truth-force? No instance seems to have happened of any nation having risen through soul-force. I still think that the evil-doers will not cease doing evil without physical punishment.

EDITOR: . . . The force of love is the same as the force of the soul or truth. We have evidence of its working at every step. The universe would disappear without the existence of that force. But you ask for historical evidence. It is, therefore, necessary to know what history means. . . .

The fact that there are so many men still alive in the world shows that it is based not on the force of arms but on the force of truth or love. Therefore the greatest and most unimpeachable evidence of the success of this force is to be found in the fact that, in spite of the wars of the world, it still lives on.

Thousands, indeed, tens of thousands, depend for their existence on a very active working of this force. Little quarrels of millions of families in their daily lives disappear before the exercise of this force. Hundreds of nations live in peace. History does not and cannot take note of this fact. History is really a record of every interruption of the even working of the force of love or of the soul. . . . Soul-force, being natural, is not noted in history.

READER: According to what you say, it is plain that instances of the kind of passive resistance are not to be found in history. It is necessary to understand this passive resistance more fully. It will be better, therefore, if you enlarge upon it.

EDITOR: Passive resistance is a method of securing rights by personal suffering; it is the reverse of resistance by arms. When I refuse to do a thing that is repugnant to my conscience, I use soul-force. For instance, the government of the day has passed a law which is applicable to me: I do not like it; if, by using violence, I force the government to repeal the law, I am employing what may be termed body-force. If I do not obey the law and accept the penalty for its breach, I use soul-force. It involves sacrifice of self.

Everybody admits that sacrifice of self is infinitely superior to sacrifice of others. Moreover, if this kind of force is used in a cause that is unjust, only the person using it suffers. He does not make others suffer for his mistakes. Men have before now done many things which were subsequently found to have been wrong. No man can claim to be absolutely in the right, or that a particular thing is wrong, because he thinks so, but it is wrong for him so long as that is his deliberate judgment. It is, therefore, meet [proper] that he should not do that which he knows to be wrong, and suffer the consequence whatever it may be. This is the key to the use of soul-force. . . .

READER: From what you say, I deduce that passive resistance is a splendid weapon of the weak but that, when they are strong, they may take up arms.

EDITOR: This is gross ignorance. Passive resistance, that is, soul-force, is matchless. It is superior to the force of arms. How, then, can it be considered only a weapon of the weak? Physical-force men are strangers to the courage that is requisite in a passive resister. Do you believe that a coward can ever disobey a law that he dislikes? Extremists are considered to be advocates of brute-force. Why do they, then, talk about

[3]An Indian dialect spoken in Gujarat, in northwest India.

obeying laws? I do not blame them. They can say nothing else. When they succeed in driving out the English, and they themselves become governors, they will want you and me to obey their laws. And that is a fitting thing for their constitution. But a passive resister will say he will not obey a law that is against his conscience, even though he may be blown to pieces at the mouth of a cannon.

What do you think? Wherein is courage required — in blowing others to pieces from behind a cannon or with a smiling face to approach a cannon and to be blown to pieces? Who is the true warrior — he who keeps death always as a bosom-friend or he who controls the death of others? Believe me that a man devoid of courage and manhood can never be a passive resister.

This, however, I will admit: that even a man, weak in body, is capable of offering this resistance. One man can offer it just as well as millions. Both men and women can indulge in it. It does not require the training of an army; it needs no Jiu-jitsu. Control over the mind is alone necessary, and, when that is attained, man is free like the king of the forest, and his very glance withers the enemy.

Passive resistance is an all-sided sword; it can be used anyhow; it blesses him who uses it and him against whom it is used. Without drawing a drop of blood, it produces far-reaching results.

A Vietnamese Condemnation of French Rule

83 ▾ *Nguyen Thai Hoc, LETTER TO THE FRENCH CHAMBER OF DEPUTIES*

Having taken control of Vietnam's southern region, known as Cochin China, in the 1860s, the French extended their authority over Tongking (northern Vietnam) and Annam (central Vietnam) in the mid 1880s. Convinced of their civilizing mission, the French sought to undermine Vietnam's Confucian culture by creating a French-trained Vietnamese elite willing to cooperate with the colonial regime. Although some members of Vietnam's upper class resisted French rule (including the young emperor Duy-tan, whose plot to overthrow the French was uncovered in 1916), most at first sought some sort of compromise between Western culture and Confucianism.

Revolutionary nationalistic movements gained adherents in the 1920s, however, as more and more Vietnamese became incensed over continued exploitation and repression, even though 90,000 Vietnamese troops and laborers had helped the French during World War I. The leading nationalist organization was the Viet Nam Quoc Dan Dang (Vietnamese Nationalist Party, or VNQDD), founded in 1927 by Nguyen Thai Hoc, a teacher from Hanoi. As a young man, he sought to improve conditions in Vietnam through moderate reforms but became disillusioned with the French and turned to revolution. The VNQDD was modeled on Sun Yat-sen's Nationalist Party and was dedicated to achieving an independent and democratic-socialist Vietnam. In 1929, with VNQDD membership at about 1,500, its leaders plotted an anti-French insurrection. The uprising, known as the Yen Bay Revolt, was crushed in 1930, and the VNQDD leaders were arrested and executed.

While awaiting his execution, Nguyen Thai Hoc wrote the following letter to France's parliament, the Chamber of Deputies. A defense of his actions and a denunciation of French colonialism, the letter was also released to the Vietnamese public.

QUESTIONS FOR ANALYSIS

1. **In Nguyen Thai Hoc's view, what are French intentions in Vietnam, and what has been the effect of French occupation?**
2. **How did Nguyen Thai Hoc evolve from a moderate reformer to a revolutionary?**
3. **If implemented, how would his suggestions to Governor General Varenne have improved the lot of the Vietnamese people?**
4. **What does the French response to the Yen Bay uprising reveal about the nature of French colonial rule?**
5. **What do you suppose Nguyen Thai Hoc hoped to accomplish by writing this letter?**

Gentlemen:

I, the undersigned, Nguyen Thai Hoc, a Vietnamese citizen, twenty-six years old, chairman and founder of the Vietnamese Nationalist Party, at present arrested and imprisoned at the jail of Yen Bay, Tongking, Indochina, have the great honor to inform you of the following facts:

According to the tenets of justice, everyone has the right to defend his own country when it is invaded by foreigners, and according to the principles of humanity, everyone has the duty to save his compatriots when they are in difficulty or in danger. As for myself, I have assessed the fact that my country has been annexed by you French for more than sixty years. I realize that under your dictatorial yoke, my compatriots have experienced a very hard life, and my people will without doubt be completely annihilated, by the naked principle of natural selection. Therefore, my right and my duty have compelled me to seek every way to defend my country which has been invaded and occupied, and to save my people who are in great danger.

At the beginning, I had thought to cooperate with the French in Indochina in order to serve my compatriots, my country and my people, particularly in the areas of cultural and economic development. As regards economic development, in 1925 I sent a memorandum to Governor General Varenne,[1] describing to him all our aspirations concerning the protection of local industry and commerce in Indochina. I urged strongly in the same letter the creation of a Superior School of Industrial Development in Tongking. In 1926 I again addressed another letter to the then Governor General of Indochina in which I included some explicit suggestions to relieve the hardships of our poor people. In 1927, for a third time, I sent a letter to the Résident Supérieur[2] in Tongking, requesting permission to publish a weekly magazine with the aim of safeguarding and encouraging local industry and commerce. With regard to the cultural domain, I sent a letter to the Governor General in 1927, requesting (1) the privilege of opening tuition-free schools for the children of the lower classes, particularly children of workers and peasants; (2) freedom to

---

[1]Alexandre Varenne was governor general of Indochina from 1925 to 1929.

[2]The *résident supérieur* of Tongking was the chief French administrator for northern Vietnam.

open popular publishing houses and libraries in industrial centers.

It is absolutely ridiculous that every suggestion has been rejected. My letters were without answer; my plans have not been considered; my requests have been ignored; even the articles that I sent to newspapers have been censored and rejected. From the experience of these rejections, I have come to the conclusion that the French have no sincere intention of helping my country or my people. I also concluded that we have to expel France. For this reason, in 1927, I began to organize a revolutionary party, which I named the Vietnamese Nationalist Party, with the aim of overthrowing the dictatorial and oppressive administration in our country. We aspire to create a Republic of Vietnam, composed of persons sincerely concerned with the happiness of the people. My party is a clandestine organization, and in February 1929, it was uncovered by the security police. Among the members of my party, a great number have been arrested. Fifty-two persons have been condemned to forced labor ranging from two to twenty years. Although many have been detained and many others unjustly condemned, my party has not ceased its activity. Under my guidance, the Party continues to operate and progress towards its aim.

During the Yen Bay uprising someone succeeded in killing some French officers. The authorities accused my party of having organized and perpetrated this revolt. They have accused me of having given the orders for the massacre. In truth, I have never given such orders, and I have presented before the Penal Court of Yen Bay all the evidence showing the inanity of this accusation. Even so, some of the members of my party completely ignorant of that event have been accused of participating in it. The French Indochinese government burned and destroyed their houses. They sent French troops to occupy their villages and stole their rice to divide it among the soldiers. Not just members of my party have been suffering from this injustice — we should rather call this cruelty than injustice — but also many simple peasants, interested only in their daily work in the rice fields, living miserable lives like buffaloes and horses, have been compromised in this reprisal. At the present time, in various areas there are tens of thousands of men, women, and children, persons of all ages, who have been massacred.[3] They died either of hunger or exposure because the French Indochinese government burned their homes. I therefore beseech you in tears to redress this injustice which otherwise will annihilate my people, which will stain French honor, and which will belittle all human values.

I have the honor to inform you that I am responsible for all events happening in my country under the leadership of my party from 1927 until the present. You only need to execute me. I beg your indulgence for all the others who at the present time are imprisoned in various jails.

[3]Many civilian deaths resulted from French actions following the revolt, but Nguyen Thai Hoc's estimate of 10,000 or more deaths is an exaggeration.

Latin America in an Era of Economic Challenge and Political Change

A popular slogan among Latin America's politicians, business leaders, and landowners in the late nineteenth century was "order and progress," and to an extent exceptional in the region's history, they achieved both. Around 1870 Latin America's economy entered a period of export-driven expansion that lasted until the 1920s. The region became a major supplier of wheat, beef, mutton, coffee, raw rubber, nitrates, copper, tin, bananas, and a host of other primary products to Europe and the United States and a major market for European and U.S. manufactured goods. Land prices soared, and English and U.S. capital flowed into Latin America as investments in railroads, banks, food-processing facilities, and mining operations and as loans to governments for the construction of roads, bridges, and public buildings.

Latin America's boom took place in a climate of relative political stability. In Argentina, Chile, and Brazil, this meant republican governments controlled by an oligarchy of landowning families, sometimes in alliance with businessmen in the import-export trade; in Mexico, Peru, Ecuador, and Venezuela, it meant rule by a strongman or dictator (*caudillo*), who also usually represented the interests of landowners. Oligarchs and dictators alike sought economic growth by maintaining law and order, approving land confiscations from the Church and peasantry, and keeping foreign business interests happy by maintaining low taxes and tariffs.

Latin America in these years is often viewed as an example of ***neocolonialism***. Although the region had achieved independence from Spain and Portugal in the early 1800s, economic relationships reminiscent of the colonial era persisted. Latin America still depended on the export of primary products to industrialized Europe and the United States, and depended on those same regions for manufactured goods and capital. The beneficiaries of this system were Latin America's landowning elite, European and U.S. bondholders, and foreign businesses with investments in construction, railroads, shipping, and mining. Dependency on foreign markets, capital, and manufactured goods made Latin American governments vulnerable to diplomatic arm-twisting by their powerful economic "partners." In the Caribbean and Central America, it also led to U.S. military intervention.

By the 1930s the neocolonial economy and the political order it supported were both in shambles. The cause of the breakdown was the worldwide economic depression of the 1930s. Demand for Latin America's agricultural products and raw materials plummeted, driving millions into unemployment and depriving the region of the foreign exchange needed to buy manufactured goods from abroad. Foreign loans and investments dried up after the international banking system and stock markets collapsed. Governments faced insolvency, and capital shortages crippled plans to end the economic slump through industrialization. Latin Americans increasingly resented European and especially U.S. ownership of tin and copper mines, oil fields, railroads, banks, processing plants, and prime agricultural land. Once welcomed as a means of attracting capital and encouraging growth, foreign ownership now was condemned as imperialist plunder.

As the Great Depression spread economic misery across Latin America, one government after another fell in an epidemic of election swings, revolts, military coups, and countercoups. While most of these short-lived regimes had no lasting political impact, in Brazil and Mexico political changes in the 1930s were more significant. In Brazil Gétulio Vargas created his *Estado Nova* (New State), a mixture of dictatorship, repression, anticolonialism, economic planning, nationalism, industrialization, and government-sponsored programs for housing, improved wages, and medical care, all of which provided Latin America with an authoritarian model for entry into the era of mass politics. In Mexico similarly important changes took place during the presidency of Lázaro Cárdenas, who between 1934 and 1940 sought to rekindle the spirit of Mexico's Revolution of 1911 through educational reform, land redistribution, and nationalization of foreign-owned businesses.

Economic Dependency and Its Dangers

▼▼▼

84 ▼ *Francisco García Calderón, LATIN AMERICA: ITS RISE AND PROGRESS*

For most of the nineteenth century, the United States had relatively little involvement in Latin America. The foundation of its policy was the Monroe Doctrine, announced by President James Monroe in 1823, which warned European powers that the United States would not tolerate attempts to re-establish their authority over the newly independent states in the Western Hemisphere. U.S. interests in the region focused almost exclusively on Mexico, whose territories in Texas, California, and New Mexico became part of the United States after the U.S. victory in the Mexican War of 1846–1848. Other schemes to annex Cuba, Nicaragua, and the Mexican provinces of Yucatán and Lower California proved impractical or failed to generate support.

U.S.–Latin American relations changed dramatically beginning in the 1880s, however. As the United States became an industrial power, it gradually replaced Great Britain as the region's main purchaser of exports and supplier of manufactured goods. By 1910 the United States purchased 30 percent of Latin America's exports and provided it with 25 percent of its imports. By then U.S. investments had increased to $1.6 billion, almost all of it "new money" invested since the end of the Civil War in 1865. As U.S. businesses expanded their operations in Latin America, successive administrations in Washington encouraged their efforts and pledged to protect their interests. In 1905 President Theodore Roosevelt announced the Roosevelt Corollary to the Monroe Doctrine. The corollary stated that the United States reserved the right to intervene in the internal affairs of any state in the Western Hemisphere that was guilty of "chronic wrongdoing," a euphemism for a failure to pay its debts or maintain law and order. Roosevelt's successor, William Howard Taft, was even more explicit. He stated that his foreign policy would include "active intervention to secure our merchandise and our capitalists' opportunity for profitable investment." These were not idle words. Between 1898 and 1934, the United States annexed Puerto Rico and intervened militarily in Cuba, Mexico, Guatemala, Honduras, Nicaragua, Panama, Colombia, and the Dominican Republic.

Condemnation of Latin America's economic dependence on foreigners and denunciations of "Yankee imperialism" became commonplace with the onset of the Great Depression, but such criticisms began earlier. One of the first such critics was the Peruvian diplomat and author Francisco García Calderón. Born into a wealthy and politically prominent family in Lima in 1883, García Calderón entered the Peruvian foreign service soon after graduating from the University of San Marcos. A career diplomat with postings to London and Paris and ambassadorships to Belgium and Portugal, he authored numerous essays and books on Latin America and its place in the world. His most widely read book was ***Latin America: Its Rise and Progress***, which ranged over the region's history and discussed a number of contemporary issues, including immigration, the state of the economy, and Latin America's foreign relations. First published in 1912, it remained in print until the 1920s, having gone through numerous editions in several languages.

QUESTIONS FOR ANALYSIS

1. According to García Calderón, how has U.S. foreign policy toward Latin America evolved since the time of the Monroe Doctrine?
2. How does he explain these changes?
3. According to García Calderón, what benefits have accrued to Latin America as a result of foreign investments? How has Latin America been hurt by such investments?
4. How does García Calderón characterize Latin Americans, and how do they differ from the "Anglo-Saxons" of the United States?
5. How have the Latin American states contributed to their own economic problems?
6. If one accepts the premises of García Calderón's arguments, what would the Latin American states have had to do to overcome the problems connected with foreign economic dependency?

The nation [the United States] which was peopled by nine millions of men in 1820 now numbers eighty millions — an immense demographic power; in the space of ten years, from 1890 to 1900, this population increased by one-fifth. By virtue of its iron, wheat, oil, and cotton, and its victorious industrialism, the democracy aspires to a world-wide significance of destiny; the consciousness of its powers is creating fresh international duties. Yankee pride increases with the endless multiplication of wealth and population, and the patriotic sentiment has reached such an intensity that it has become transformed into imperialism. . . .

Interventions have become more frequent with the expansion of frontiers. The United States have recently intervened in the territory of Acre [in western Brazil], there to found a republic of rubber gatherers; at Panama, there to develop a province and construct a canal; in Cuba, under cover of the Platt amendment,[1] to maintain order in the interior; in San Domingo, to support the civilising revolution and overthrow the tyrants; in Venezuela, and in Central America, to enforce upon these nations, torn by intestine disorders, the political and financial tutelage of the imperial democracy. In Guatemala and Honduras the loans concluded with the monarchs of North American finance have reduced the people to a new slavery. Supervision of the customs and the dispatch of pacificatory [peace-keeping] squadrons to defend the interests of the Anglo-Saxon[2] have enforced peace and tranquility: such are the means employed. . . . Mr. Pierpont Morgan[3] proposes to encompass the finances of Latin America by a vast network of Yankee banks. Chicago merchants and Wall Street financiers created the Meat Trust in the Argentine. . . . It has even been announced, although the news hardly appears probable, that a North American syndicate wished to buy enormous belts of land in Guatemala. . . . The fortification of the Panama Canal, and the possible acquisition of the Galapagos Islands in the Pacific, are fresh manifestations of imperialistic progress.

▾▾▾

Unexploited wealth abounds in [Latin] America. Forests of rubber, as in the African Congo; mines of gold and diamonds, which recall the treasures of the Transvaal and the Klondike; rivers which flow over beds of auriferous [gold-bearing] sand . . . coffee, cocoa, and wheat, whose abundance is such that these products are enough to glut the markets of the world. But there is no national capital [for investment]. This contrast between the wealth of the soil and the poverty of the States gives rise to serious economic problems. . . .

Since the very beginnings of independence the Latin democracies, lacking financial reserves, have had need of European gold. . . . The necessities of the war with Spain and the always difficult task of building up a new society demanded the assistance of foreign gold; loans accumulated. . . . The lamentable history of these bankrupt democracies dates from this period.

For geographical reasons, and on account of its very inferiority, South America cannot dispense with the influence of the Anglo-Saxon North, with its exuberant wealth and its industries. South America has need of capital, of enterprising men, of bold explorers, and these the United States supply in abundance. The defence of the South should consist in avoiding the establishment of privileges or monopolies, whether in favor of North Americans or Europeans.

▾▾▾

The descendants of the prodigal Spanish conquerors, who knew nothing of labor or thrift, have incessantly resorted to fresh loans in order to fill the gaps in their budgets. Politicians knew of only one solution of the economic disorder — to borrow, so that little by little the Latin-American countries became actually the financial colonies of Europe.

Economic dependence has a necessary corollary — political servitude. French intervention in Mexico[4]

[1]The Platt Amendment refers to a series of provisions sponsored by Senator Orville Platt of Connecticut and approved by the U.S. Congress that was attached to Cuba's constitution in 1901. It limited Cuba's treaty-writing capacity, restricted its right to contract public debt, gave the United States the right to maintain naval bases, and provided for U.S. intervention in Cuba if an unstable government failed to protect "life, liberty, and property."

[2]A loosely used term, Anglo-Saxon usually refers to people of English descent.

[3]John Pierpont Morgan (1837–1913), founder of the investment bank J. P. Morgan and Company, was one of the wealthiest and most powerful financiers in the United States.

[4]In 1861 Spain, Great Britain, and France sent troops to Mexico to force the government to pay its debts. After gaining assurances of future payments, Spain and Great Britain withdrew their troops, but Emperor Napoleon III of France went forward with a plan to establish a new Mexican government under French protection. The French-sponsored candidate for emperor of Mexico was Archduke Ferdinand Maximilian of Hapsburg, brother of Austrian emperor Franz Josef. Maximilian served as emperor from 1863 to 1865, when the threat of U.S. intervention convinced Napoleon III to abandon his Mexican project.

was originally caused by the mass of unsatisfied financial claims; foreigners, the creditors of the State, were in favor of intervention. England and France, who began by seeking to ensure the recovery of certain debts, finally forced a monarch upon the debitor nation. The United States entertained the ambition of becoming the sole creditor of the American peoples: this remarkable privilege would have assured them of an incontestable hegemony over the whole continent.

In the history of Latin America loans symbolise political disorder, lack of foresight, and waste. . . . Old debts are liquidated by means of new, and budgetary deficits are balanced by means of foreign gold. . . .

The budgets of various States complicate still further a situation already difficult. They increase beyond all measure, without the slightest relation to the progress made by the nation. They are based upon taxes which are one of the causes of the national impoverishment, or upon a protectionist tariff which adds greatly to the cost of life. The politicians, thinking chiefly of appearances, neglect the development of the national resources for the immediate augmentation of the fiscal revenues; thanks to fresh taxes, the budgets increase. These resources are not employed in furthering profitable undertakings, such as building railroads or highways, or increasing the navigability of the rivers. The bureaucracy is increased in a like proportion, and the budgets, swelled in order to dupe the outside world, serve only to support a nest of parasites. In the economic life of these countries the State is a kind of beneficent providence which creates and preserves the fortune of individual persons, increases the common poverty by taxation, display, useless enterprises, the upkeep of military and civil officials, and the waste of money borrowed abroad. . . .

To sum up, the new continent, politically free, is economically a vassal. This dependence is inevitable; without European capital there would have been no railways, no ports, and no stable government in [Latin] America. But the disorder which prevails in the finances of the country changes into a real servitude what might otherwise have been a beneficial relation.

Economic Nationalism in Mexico

85 ▾ Lázaro Cárdenas, SPEECH TO THE NATION

Following the overthrow of dictator Porfirio Díaz in 1911, conflict among aspiring leaders marked the first decade of Mexico's revolution, and it was unclear whether the revolutionary movement would survive. In 1917, however, a constitutional convention drafted a new charter that confirmed the principles of free speech, religious toleration, universal suffrage, the separation of powers, and the protection of private property. It also committed the government to social reform and greater control over foreign corporations.

Little changed, however, until the presidency of Lázaro Cárdenas from 1934 to 1940. In a series of bold steps, he confiscated millions of acres of land from large estates for redistribution to peasants, introduced free and compulsory elementary education, and sponsored legislation to provide medical and unemployment insurance. His most audacious step, however, was the nationalization of Mexico's oil industry. In 1936 a dispute between Mexican labor unions and U.S. and British oil companies erupted into a strike, and in the ensuing legal battle, seventeen oil companies refused to accept the pro-union ruling of an arbitration board appointed by Cárdenas, even after the Mexican Supreme Court upheld the decision. In response,

Cárdenas ordered the government seizure of the oil companies' property. Cárdenas announced his decision on March 18, 1938, in a radio speech to the nation. In the following excerpt, Cárdenas comments on the role of the oil companies in Mexico's economic and social development.

QUESTIONS FOR ANALYSIS

1. **In the account of Cárdenas, which actions by the foreign oil companies forced him to nationalize the oil industry?**
2. **According to Cárdenas, what truth is there in the oil companies' claims that they have benefited Mexico?**
3. **According to Cárdenas, who is ultimately responsible for the actions of the oil companies?**
4. **Which political activities of the oil companies does Cárdenas condemn?**
5. **What hardships does Cárdenas anticipate for the Mexican people as a result of his decision?**
6. **In what ways is Cárdenas's speech an appeal to Mexican nationalism?**

In each and every one of the various attempts of the Executive to arrive at a final solution of the conflict within conciliatory limits . . . the intransigence of the companies was clearly demonstrated.

Their attitude was therefore premeditated and their position deliberately taken, so that the Government, in defense of its own dignity, had to resort to application of the Expropriation Act, as there were no means less drastic or decision less severe that might bring about a solution of the problem. . . .

It has been repeated *ad nauseam* that the oil industry has brought additional capital for the development and progress of the country. This assertion is an exaggeration. For many years throughout the major period of their existence, oil companies have enjoyed great privileges for development and expansion, including customs and tax exemptions and innumerable prerogatives; it is these factors of special privilege, together with the prodigious productivity of the oil deposits granted them by the Nation often against public will and law, that represent almost the total amount of this so-called capital.

Potential wealth of the Nation; miserably underpaid native labor; tax exemptions; economic privileges; governmental tolerance — these are the factors of the boom of the Mexican oil industry.

Let us now examine the social contributions of the companies. In how many of the villages bordering on the oil fields is there a hospital, or school or social center, or a sanitary water supply, or an athletic field, or even an electric plant fed by the millions of cubic meters of natural gas allowed to go to waste?

What center of oil production, on the other hand, does not have its company police force for the protection of private, selfish, and often illegal interests? These organizations, whether authorized by the Government or not, are charged with innumerable outrages, abuses, and murders, always on behalf of the companies that employ them.

Who is not aware of the irritating discrimination governing construction of the company camps? Comfort for the foreign personnel; misery, drabness, and insalubrity for the Mexicans. Refrigeration and protection against tropical insects for the former; indifference and neglect, medical service and supplies always grudgingly provided, for the latter; lower wages and harder, more exhausting labor for our people.

The tolerance which the companies have abused was born, it is true, in the shadow of the ignorance, betrayals, and weakness of the country's rulers; but the mechanism was set in motion by investors lacking in the necessary moral resources to give something in exchange for the wealth they have been exploiting.

Another inevitable consequence of the presence of the oil companies, strongly characterized by their anti-social tendencies, and even more harmful than all those already mentioned, has been their persistent and improper intervention in national affairs.

The oil companies' support to strong rebel factions against the constituted government in the Huasteca region of Veracruz and in the Isthmus of Tehuantepec during the years 1917 to 1920 is no longer a matter for discussion by anyone. Nor is anyone ignorant of the fact that in later periods and even at the present time, the oil companies have almost openly encouraged the ambitions of elements discontented with the country's government, every time their interests were affected either by taxation or by the modification of their privileges or the withdrawal of the customary tolerance. They have had money, arms, and munitions for rebellion, money for the anti-patriotic press which defends them, money with which to enrich their unconditional defenders. But for the progress of the country, for establishing an economic equilibrium with their workers through a just compensation of labor, for maintaining hygienic conditions in the districts where they themselves operate, or for conserving the vast riches of the natural petroleum gases from destruction, they have neither money, nor financial possibilities, nor the desire to subtract the necessary funds from the volume of their profits.

Nor is there money with which to meet a responsibility imposed upon them by judicial verdict, for they rely on their pride and their economic power to shield them from the dignity and sovereignty of a Nation which has generously placed in their hands its vast natural resources and now finds itself unable to obtain the satisfaction of the most elementary obligations by ordinary legal means.

As a logical consequence of this brief analysis, it was therefore necessary to adopt a definite and legal measure to end this permanent state of affairs in which the country sees its industrial progress held back by those who hold in their hands the power to erect obstacles as well as the motive power of all activity and who, instead of using it to high and worthy purposes, abuse their economic strength to the point of jeopardizing the very life of a Nation endeavoring to bring about the elevation of its people through its own laws, its own resources, and the free management of its own destinies.

With the only solution to this problem thus placed before it, I ask the entire Nation for moral and material support sufficient to carry out so justified, important, and indispensable a decision. . . .

It is necessary that all groups of the population be imbued with a full optimism and that each citizen, whether in agricultural, industrial, commercial, transportation, or other pursuits, develop a greater activity from this moment on, in order to create new resources which will reveal that the spirit of our people is capable of saving the nation's economy by the efforts of its own citizens.

And, finally, as the fear may arise among the interests now in bitter conflict in the field of international affairs[1] that a deviation of raw materials fundamentally necessary to the struggle in which the most powerful nations are engaged might result from the consummation of this act of national sovereignty and dignity, we wish to state that our petroleum operations will not depart a single inch from the moral solidarity maintained by Mexico with the democratic nations, whom we wish to assure that the expropriation

[1]World War II in Europe was still more than a year away, but the Japanese invasion of China was in full swing, Spain was in the midst of its civil war, and Hitler had just annexed Austria.

now decreed has as its only purpose the elimination of obstacles erected by groups who do not understand the evolutionary needs of all peoples and who would themselves have no compunction in selling Mexican oil to the highest bidder, without taking into account the consequences of such action to the popular masses and the nations in conflict.

China in an Era of Political Disintegration and Revolution

The overthrow of the Qing Dynasty in 1911 failed to produce China's long-awaited national revival. In the aftermath of the revolution, Sun Yat-sen and his dreams of democracy were pushed aside by General Yuan Shikai, who ruled the Chinese "republic" as a dictator between 1912 and 1916 and was planning to have himself declared emperor when he died in 1916. After his death China was carved up by dozens of generally unscrupulous and irresponsible warlords — military strongmen whose local authority was based on their control of private armies and whose grip on China was not completely broken until after the Communists took power in 1949. With a weak national government, the Chinese endured continued Western domination of their coastal cities and were able to offer only feeble resistance when the Japanese conquered Manchuria in 1931 and invaded China itself in 1937. Massive flooding of the Yellow River and widespread famine in north China in the 1920s deepened the people's misery.

With Confucian certainties shattered and China falling into political ruin, intellectuals intensely debated China's predicament. The 1920s were years of intellectual experiment and inquiry, in which members of study groups, journalists, poets, fiction writers, academics, and students scrutinized what it meant to be Chinese and debated the country's future. Most of these intellectuals rejected traditional Chinese values, customs, and education, arguing that only a sharp break from the past would enable China to stand up to Japan and the West. Most of them believed that China needed to model itself on the West, although what specific Western values and institutions should be borrowed was a matter of debate.

In politics, two revolutionary parties — the Nationalist Party, or Guomindang, and the Chinese Communist Party — competed for support. The Guomindang, led by Sun Yat-sen until his death in 1925, was theoretically dedicated to Sun's "three principles of the people": democracy, nationalism, and livelihood. The party came to be identified with the educated, Western-oriented bourgeoisie of China's coastal cities and in practice, under General Chiang Kai-shek (1887–1975), concentrated less on social reform and democracy than on fighting warlords in the 1920s and Communists in the 1930s. The Chinese Communist Party, founded in 1921, was dedicated to Marxism-Leninism, with its leadership provided by intellectuals and its major support eventually coming from China's rural masses.

Aided by agents of the Soviet Union, the Guomindang and the Communists formed a coalition in 1923 to destroy the warlords. Their combined forces launched the Northern Expedition against the warlords in 1926, but the alliance disintegrated in 1927 when Chiang Kai-shek, buoyed by his early victories and generous financial support from Chinese businessmen, purged the Communists from the army and ordered Guomindang troops in Shanghai to kill Communist leaders who had gathered there. Communist troops and their leaders fled to the countryside, where, under the leadership of Mao Zedong (1893–1976), they rebuilt the party into a formidable military and political force. After a long struggle against the Guomindang and the Japanese, the Communists gained control of China in 1949.

The May 4th Movement and the Birth of Chinese Nationalism

▾▾▾

86 ▾ *Deng Yingchao, THE SPIRIT OF THE MAY 4th MOVEMENT*

On May 4, 1919, word reached Beijing that the diplomats at the Paris Peace Conference had rejected Chinese demands that the prewar German concessions in Shandong province be returned to Chinese control; instead, they were to be retained by Japan. Incensed by this rebuff from the Western powers, which had welcomed China as an ally in World War I, and resentful of Japan for taking one more piece of Chinese territory, university students in Beijing erupted in anger. Three thousand of them descended on Tiananmen Square, where they shouted slogans, waved banners, attacked a pro-Japanese official, and burned the house of a cabinet minister. The movement quickly spread. Students at other universities joined in, and with support from journalists, merchants, and well-known politicians such as Sun Yat-sen, they organized a national boycott of Japanese goods. After the Beijing warlord government attempted to crack down by arresting some 1,500 students in Beijing, the movement gained even more support, with whole factories going on strike and students refusing to attend classes. In response, the arrested Beijing students were released, the cabinet fell, and China refused to sign the Versailles Treaty. This was more than a one-time victory for China's students. The "May 4th incident" became a truly national movement, one that made nationalism a part of China's political landscape.

Deng Yingchao was a sixteen-year-old student at a women's teachers' college in Tianjin when the May 4th demonstrations in Beijing spread to her university. The experience changed her life. Not only did she turn into a political activist, but she also met her future husband, Zhou Enlai, who served as China's premier and foreign minister after the Communist revolution. She joined the Communist Party in 1924 and was one of the few women who was part of the Long March, the 6,000-mile trek of Mao Zedong's followers from Jiangxi province to Shaanxi in 1934–1935. After the Communist victory in 1949, she was revered as the nation's "elder sister" and became a member of the party's Central Committee. She weathered numerous political storms and died in Beijing at age eighty-eight.

The following excerpt comes from an article written by Deng in 1949 in commemoration of the events of May 4, 1919. It captures the hopeful enthusiasm of the young participants in the May 4th movement and conveys the broad significance of the events.

QUESTIONS FOR ANALYSIS

1. What does Deng Yingchao's article reveal about the level of enthusiasm among the student protesters? What does it tell us about the students' goals?
2. Aside from the immediate impact of the demonstrations in Beijing, what were the deeper causes of the student protests, according to Deng?
3. What can be gathered from Deng's article about the level of public support for the student protesters in Tianjin?
4. According to Deng, what was the long-term significance of the May 4th movement?
5. Writing from the perspective of 1949, Deng suggests that the Communist movement in China can be traced back to the May 4th movement. To what degree does her recounting of events affirm such an interpretation?

On May 4, 1919, students in Beijing held a demonstration asking the government to refuse to sign the Versailles Peace Treaty and to punish the traitors at home. . . . The following day, when the news reached Tainjin, it aroused the indignation of students there who staged their own demonstrations of May 7th. They then started organizing such patriotic societies as the Tianjin Students Union, the Tianjin Women's Patriotic Society, and the Tianjin Association of National Salvation. We had no political theory to guide us at that time, only our strong patriotic enthusiasm. In addition to the Beijing students' demands, we demanded "Abolish the Twenty-one Demands!"[1] "Boycott Japanese Goods!" "Buy Chinese-Made Goods!" Furthermore, we emphatically refused to become slaves to foreign powers!

Despite the fact that it was a patriotic students' demonstration, the Northern Warlord government resorted to force to quell the protest. The police dispersed the march with rifles fixed with bayonets and sprayed us with hoses; and later resorted to rifle butts and even arrests. However, our political awareness awakened a new spirit in us in our new struggle with the government. New European ideas and culture poured into China after World War I. Also the success of the 1917 October Revolution in Russia brought progressive Marxism-Leninism to China. . . .

What we did know intuitively was that alone, we students did not have enough strength to save China from foreign powers. Therefore, we knew that we "must awaken all our compatriots."

We therefore organized many speakers' committees to spread propaganda among the people. I became the head of the speakers' group in the Tianjin Women's Patriotic Society and in the Tianjin Students Union. Frequently we gave

---

[1]The Twenty-one Demands, presented to China by Japan in 1915, required China to confirm Japan's claim to the former German concessions in Shandong and various economic concessions in Manchuria and Mongolia. They also demanded extensive Japanese rights in China itself, including the appointment of Japanese advisors to the Chinese government. The Chinese successfully resisted these latter demands but did acquiesce to the claims in Shandong for economic concessions.

speeches outside the campus. At first, we women dared not to give speeches on the street due to the feudalistic tradition that existed in China then. So the female students went instead to the places where people gathered either for an exhibition or to see a show, while the male students gave speeches in the street to passersby. There were always a lot of listeners. We told them why we should be united to save our country; that traitors in the government must be punished; and that people should have the right to freedom of assembly and association. We talked about the suffering of the Korean people after their country was conquered; and we publicly lodged our protests against the Northern Warlord government that persecutes progressive students. Usually tears streamed down our cheeks when we gave our speeches and our listeners were often visibly moved.

In addition to making speeches we also made home visits to out-of-the-way places or to slum areas. We went door-to-door to give our pleas, and some families gave us a warm welcome, but others just slammed the door on us. However, nothing could discourage us.

We delivered handbills and published newspapers to spread our patriotic enthusiasm even further. *The Paper of the Students Union*, for example, was run by the Tianjin Students Union and each issue sold more than 20,000 copies — a considerable number at that time! It was originally published every three days; however, later it was expanded into a daily newspaper. . . .

The Women's Patriotic Society also published a weekly. Both papers reported foreign and national current events, students' movements across the country, student editorials, progressive articles, and cultural and art news.

The reactionary Northern Warlord government, however, turned a deaf ear to us. They ultimately bowed to Japanese powers, shielded the traitors, and tried to suppress the students' movement. At that time people were denied expressing their patriotic views. So what we then struggled most urgently for was freedom of assembly and association; the right to express one's political views; and for freedom of the press. United under this common goal, we struggled bravely.

▷ After describing the numerous clashes between students and university and governmental authorities in 1919 and 1920, Deng comments on the broad significance of the May 4th movement.

The women's liberation movement was greatly enhanced by the May 4th Movement; this became an important part of the movement. And slogans such as "sexual equality," "freedom of marriage," "co-educational universities," "social contacts for women," and "job opportunity for women," were put forward.

In Tianjin we merged the men's students union with the women's. Fearing ridicule and that public opinion would be against it, some of the women were hesitant at first. However, the male and female activists among us took the lead and we worked together bravely to overcome all obstacles. In our work, we were equal and we respected each other. . . . Women students, particularly the more progressive ones, worked especially hard for we knew we were pioneers among Chinese women to show that women are not inferior to men. Inspired by the new ideals, among the progressive students men broke with the tradition of sexual discrimination and treated us with respect. . . .

At this time cultural movements were developing rapidly and students were receptive to publications which promoted new ideas. In Beijing, for example, there were *New Youth, Young China*, and *New Tide* magazines. In Tianjin, the Students Union every week would invite a progressive professor . . . to give us an academic lecture on new literary ideas such as how to write in vernacular Chinese rather than in classical stereotyped writings.

Today these things are commonplace, but then it was very new and important.

As more scientific subjects and new ideas poured into China, we felt an urgency to learn, discuss, study, and understand them. Thus by the end of that summer, a smaller and well-organized group — the Awakening Society — was established by 20 of the more progressive activists among us students. . . .

At that time we didn't have a definite political conviction, nor did we know much about Communism. We just had a vague idea that the principle of distribution in the most advantageous society was "from each according to his ability, to each according to his needs." We knew only that a revolution led by Lenin in Russia had been successful; and that the aim of that revolution was to emancipate the majority of the people who were oppressed, and to established a classless society.

How we did long for such a society! But at that time we could not learn about such a society because we could scarcely find any copy of Lenin's ideas or information about the October Revolution.

The Maoist Version of Marxism

▾▾▾

87 ▾ *Mao Zedong, REPORT ON AN INVESTIGATION OF THE PEASANT MOVEMENT IN HUNAN and STRATEGIC PROBLEMS OF CHINA'S REVOLUTIONARY WAR*

Mao Zedong, born into a well-to-do peasant family in Hunan province in 1893, was a university student when he participated in the anti-Qing revolution of 1911. During the next several years, while serving as a library assistant at Beijing University, he embraced Marxism and helped organize the Chinese Communist Party, which was officially founded in 1921. Originally given the task of organizing urban labor unions, Mao came to believe that the peasants, whose capacity for class revolution was discounted by orthodox Marxist-Leninists, would lead China to socialism.

After the break from the Guomindang, the Communists took their small army to the remote and hilly region on the Hunan-Jiangxi border, where in 1931 they proclaimed the Chinese Soviet Republic. In 1934 Chiang Kai-shek's troops surrounded the Communists' forces, but as they moved in for the kill, more than 100,000 Communist troops and officials broke their encirclement and embarked on the Long March. This legendary trek lasted more than a year and covered 6,000 miles before a remnant found safety in the remote mountains around Yan'an in northern Shaanxi province. It was here that Mao, now the party's recognized leader, rebuilt his army and readied himself and his followers for what would be fourteen more years of struggle against the Japanese and the Guomindang.

The following excerpts are drawn from two of Mao's most important writings. The first, his "Report on an Investigation of the Peasant Movement in Hunan," was written in 1927 after he visited Hunan province to study the activities and accomplishments of peasant associations, groups of peasants who, with the help of Communist organizers, had seized land, humiliated or killed landlords, and taken control of their communities. In it Mao seeks to convince other party members that the peasants are the main source of revolution in China. The second excerpt, from his "Strategic Problems of China's Revolutionary War," is based on a series of lectures delivered at the Red Army College in late 1936. In it Mao assesses China's military situation and outlines his strategy for victory over the Guomindang through guerrilla warfare.

QUESTIONS FOR ANALYSIS

1. What specific developments in Hunan province reinforced Mao's convictions about the peasantry as a revolutionary force?
2. What criticisms have been made of the Hunan peasant movement, and how does Mao attempt to counter these criticisms?
3. What can be learned from these two writings about Mao's views of the role of the Communist Party in China's revolutionary struggle?
4. According to Mao, what have been the sources of oppression of the Chinese people? Once these sources of oppression are removed, what will China look like?
5. According to Mao, what are the four unique characteristics of China's revolutionary war, and how do they affect Mao's military strategy?
6. What are the characteristics of Mao's "active defense" as opposed to "passive defense"?
7. How do Mao's ideas about revolution resemble and differ from those of Marx (source 49)? How do they resemble and differ from those of Lenin (source 72)?

REPORT ON AN INVESTIGATION OF THE PEASANT MOVEMENT IN HUNAN [1927]

. . . All talk directed against the peasant movement must be speedily set right. All the wrong measures taken by the revolutionary authorities concerning the peasant movement must be speedily changed. Only thus can the future of the revolution be benefited. For the present upsurge of the peasant movement is a colossal event. In a very short time, in China's central, southern and northern provinces, several hundred million peasants will rise like a mighty storm, like a hurricane, a force so swift and violent that no power, however great, will be able to hold it back. They will smash all the trammels that bind them and rush forward along the road to liberation. They will sweep all the imperialists, warlords, corrupt officials, local tyrants and evil gentry into their graves. Every revolutionary party and every revolutionary comrade will be put to the test, to be accepted or rejected as they decide. There are three alternatives. To march at their head and lead them? To trail behind them, gesticulating and criticizing? Or to stand in their way and oppose them? Every Chinese is free to choose, but events will force you to make the choice quickly. . . .

"Yes, peasant associations are necessary, but they are going rather too far." This is the opinion of the middle-of-the-roaders. But what is the actual situation? True, the peasants are in a sense "unruly" in the countryside. Supreme in authority, the peasant association allows the landlord no say and sweeps away his prestige. This amounts to striking the landlord down to the dust and keeping him there. . . . People swarm into the houses of local tyrants and evil gentry who are against the peasant association, slaughter their pigs and consume their grain. They even loll for a minute or two on the ivory-inlaid beds belonging to the young ladies in the households of the local tyrants and evil gentry. At the slightest provocation they make arrests, crown the arrested with tall paper-hats, and parade them through the villages, saying, "You dirty landlords, now you know who we are!" . . . This is what some people call "going too far," or "exceeding the proper limits in righting a wrong," or "really too much." Such talk may seem plausible, but in fact it is wrong. First, the local tyrants, evil gentry and lawless landlords have themselves driven the peasants to this. For ages they have used their power to tyrannize over the peasants and trample them underfoot; that is why the peasants have reacted so strongly. . . . Secondly, a revolution is not a dinner party, or writing an essay, or painting a picture, or doing embroidery; it cannot be so refined, so leisurely and gentle, so temperate, kind, courteous, restrained and magnanimous. A revolution is an insurrection, an act of violence by which one class overthrows another. A rural revolution is a revolution by which the peasantry overthrows the power of the feudal landlord class. Without using the greatest force, the peasants cannot possibly overthrow the deep-rooted authority of the landlords which has lasted for thousands of years. . . . To put it bluntly, it is necessary to create terror for a while in every rural area. . . .

▾ ▾ ▾

A man in China is usually subjected to the domination of three systems of authority: (1) the state system, . . . ranging from the national, provincial and county government down to that of the township; (2) the clan system, . . . ranging from the central ancestral temple and its branch temples down to the head of the household; and (3) the supernatural system (religious authority), ranging from the King of Hell down to the town and village gods belonging to the nether world, and from the Emperor of Heaven down to all the various gods and spirits belonging to the celestial world. As for women, in addition to being dominated by these three systems of authority, they are also dominated by the men (the authority of the husband). These four authorities — political, clan, religious and masculine — are the embodiment of the whole feudal-patriarchal system and ideology, and are the four thick ropes binding the Chinese people, particularly the peasants. . . .

The political authority of the landlords is the backbone of all the other systems of authority. With that overturned, the clan authority, the religious authority and the authority of the husband all begin to totter. . . . In many places the peasant associations have taken over the temples of the gods as their offices. Everywhere they advocate the appropriation of temple property in order to start peasant schools and to defray the expenses of the associations, calling it "public revenue from superstition." In Liling County, prohibiting superstitious practices and smashing idols have become quite the vogue. . . .

In places where the power of the peasants is predominant, only the older peasants and the women still believe in the gods, the younger peasants no longer doing so. Since the latter control the associations, the overthrow of religious authority and the eradication of superstition are going on everywhere. As to the authority of the husband, this has always been weaker among the poor peasants because, out of economic necessity, their womenfolk have to do more manual labour than the women of the richer classes and therefore have more say and greater power of decision in family matters. . . . With the rise of the peasant movement, the women in many places have now begun to organize rural women's associations; the opportunity has come for them to lift up their heads, and the authority of the husband is getting shakier every day. In a word, the whole feudal-patriarchal system and ideology is tottering with the growth of the peasants' power.

STRATEGIC PROBLEMS OF CHINA'S REVOLUTIONARY WAR [1936]

What then are the characteristics of China's revolutionary war?

I think there are four.

The first is that China is a vast semi-colonial country which is unevenly developed both politically and economically. . . .

The unevenness of political and economic development in China — the coexistence of a frail capitalist economy and a preponderant semi-feudal economy; the coexistence of a few modern industrial and commercial cities and the boundless expanses of stagnant rural districts; the coexistence of several millions of industrial workers on the one hand and, on the other, hundreds of millions of peasants and handicraftsmen under the old regime; the coexistence of big warlords controlling the Central government and small warlords controlling the provinces; . . . and the coexistence of a few railway and steamship lines and motor roads on the one hand and, on the other, the vast number of wheel-barrow paths and trails for pedestrians only, many of which are even difficult for them to negotiate. . . .

The second characteristic is the great strength of the enemy.

What is the situation of the Guomindang, the enemy of the Red Army? It is a party that has seized political power and has relatively stabilized it. It has gained the support of the principal counter-revolutionary countries in the world. It has remodeled its army, which has thus become different from any other army in Chinese history and on the whole similar to the armies of the modern states in the world; its army is supplied much more abundantly with arms and other equipment than the Red Army, and is greater in numerical strength than any army in Chinese history. . . .

The third characteristic is that the Red Army is weak and small. . . .

Our political power is dispersed and isolated in mountainous or remote regions, and is deprived of any outside help. In economic and cultural conditions the revolutionary base areas are more backward than the Guomindang areas. The revolutionary bases embrace only rural districts and small towns. . . .

The fourth characteristic is the Communist Party's leadership and the agrarian revolution.

This characteristic is the inevitable result of the first one. It gives rise to the following two features. On the one hand, China's revolutionary war, though taking place in a period of reaction in China and throughout the capitalist world, can yet be victorious because it is led by the Communist Party and supported by the peasantry. Because we have secured the support of the peasantry, our base areas, though small, possess great political power and stand firmly opposed to the political power of the Guomindang which encompasses a vast area; in a military sense this creates colossal difficulties for the attacking Guomindang troops. The Red Army, though small, has great fighting capacity, because its men under the leadership of the Communist Party have sprung from the agrarian revolution and are fighting for their own interests, and because officers and men are politically united.

On the other hand, our situation contrasts sharply with that of the Guomindang. Opposed to the agrarian revolution, the Guomindang is deprived of the support of the peasantry. Despite the great size of its army it cannot arouse the bulk of the soldiers or many of the lower-rank officers. . . . Officers and men are politically disunited and this reduces its fighting capacity. . . .

Military experts of new and rapidly developing imperialist countries like Germany and Japan positively boast of the advantages of strategic offensive and condemn strategic defensive. Such an idea is fundamentally unsuitable for China's revolutionary war. Such military experts point out that the great shortcoming of defense lies in the fact that, instead of gingering up [enlivening] the people, it demoralizes them. . . . Our case is different. Under the slogan of safeguarding the revolutionary base areas and safeguarding China, we can rally the greatest majority of the people to fight single-mindedly, because we are the victims of oppression and aggression. . . .

In military terms, our warfare consists in the alternate adoption of the defensive and the offensive. . . . It remains a defensive until a campaign of "encirclement and annihilation" is smashed, and then it immediately begins as an offensive; they are but two phases of the same thing, as one campaign of "encirclement and annihilation" of the enemy is closely followed by another. Of the two phases, the defensive phase is more complicated and more important than the offensive phase. It involves numerous problems of how to smash the campaign of "encirclement and annihilation." . . .

In the civil war, when the Red Army surpasses the enemy in strength, there will no longer be any use for strategic defensive in general. Then our only directive will be strategic offensive. Such a change depends on an overall change in the relative strength of the enemy and ourselves. The only defensive measures that remain will be of a partial character.

Chapter 13

The Global Community Since 1945

WRITING THE HISTORY of the recent past presents a unique challenge for early twenty-first century historians. Their most basic task — getting the facts right and determining "what happened" — is relatively easy. Although the inability of historians to examine certain sealed documents in government archives is an obstacle, this is offset by many advantages. Historians of the recent past have lived through many of the events they are describing, can interview eyewitnesses and participants, and have access not only to information contained in books, newspapers, and government documents but also in films, video recordings, and photographs. Many important documents have been digitized, making it possible to do historical research in front of one's computer screen rather than in distant archives and libraries.

Writing history, however, requires more than factual accuracy and telling "what happened." It also entails making interpretations, judging what's important and what's trivial, and determining how events fit into long-term patterns and trends. To do these tasks well, historians need a perspective that includes knowledge of what preceded and what followed the events they are describing. Historians of the recent past, without knowledge of the future, will always lack this perspective and thus can make only educated guesses about the meaning of events that have recently taken place.

Consider, for example, the sudden disintegration of the Soviet Union in the late 1980s and early 1990s. Politicians, journalists, and historians — indeed, everyone who had anything to say about it — agreed at the time that a historic turning point had occurred. The demise of the Soviet Union, they argued, ended the Cold War, diminished the threat of nuclear holocaust, revealed fatal flaws in communism, confirmed the triumph of capitalism, and opened up new possibilities for world peace and cooperation. The U.S. political scientist

Francis Fukuyama went even further. To him it meant the "end of history." Liberal democracy and capitalism had cleared the field of all competitors and would dominate human societies around the globe forever.

From the perspective of the early twenty-first century, it is unclear, however, how many of these judgments will prove correct. In post-Soviet Russia, democracy survived the tumultuous and wrenching "shock therapy" that converted the economy from state control to market capitalism in the 1990s, but millions of Russians remain disenchanted with this new economic system that has brought unimagined wealth to a handful of "oligarchs" but pain and insecurity to countless others. Many have also become disenchanted with democracy. Under the presidency of Vladimir Putin, who took power in 2000, the government took control of much of the media, stifled unfriendly journalists, and harassed and prosecuted liberal and communist critics of Putin's regime. Although such steps were widely criticized in the West, public opinion polls have suggested that Russians have fewer reservations. Meanwhile, relations between Russia and the United States and, to a lesser degree, between Russia and the states of Western Europe have deteriorated in recent years. Russian leaders have resented Western carping about Russia's democratic failings. They also have strongly opposed the expansion of the North Atlantic Treaty Organization to include many formerly communist states in Eastern Europe and the plan announced by President George W. Bush in 2007 to build a missile-defense system in Central Europe. For their part, U.S. leaders have been aggravated by Russia's meddling in its neighbors' politics, its tepid support for their Middle East policies, and its willingness to use its vast gas and oil reserves as a political weapon.

Will the Cold War return? Will Russia return to its ancient pattern of authoritarian rule? Will some future leader tap the wellsprings of Russian nationalism to launch post-Soviet Russia on a path of conquest and expansion? Will the governments of Russia and the United States fail to make good on their promises to further reduce their stockpiles of nuclear weapons? If the answer to any of these questions is "yes," then the demise of the Soviet empire and the humbling of Russia that took place in the late 1980s and early 1990s will no longer be viewed as turning points but as temporary interruptions of long-term patterns.

What is true of the fall of the Soviet Union also applies to many other recent events and developments. Is the intensification of Islamic fundamentalism in the late twentieth century a prelude to a "battle of civilizations" between the West and Islam or a passing phase in Islam's history? Are the recent gains made by Western women in education, job opportunities, and legal status the first stage toward greater gender equality worldwide or an early indication that feminism will be a uniquely Western phenomenon? Will the environmental movement that emerged in the 1970s be hailed as a triumph of human foresight or mourned as something that came too late and accomplished too little? Will China's hothouse economic growth be considered the first step in its emergence as a new superpower or the prelude to some unforeseen economic or political upheaval? Will recent population increases be sustainable or catastrophic? Will Africa lift itself from the curse of economic underdevelopment? No one will be able to answer these and countless other questions for another fifty years or more, and until then no definitive history of the post–World War II era can be written.

Perhaps the greatest challenge for historians of the recent past is making sense of the combination of recent economic, political, technological, and cultural changes described by globalization, a word with several layers of meaning. It refers, first of all, to a world of free trade, open markets, and capitalist competition in which goods, services, and capital flow across seamless international borders. It also refers to a world in which a remarkable series of technological breakthroughs — computers, communications satellites, fiber-optic cable, and especially the Internet — have destroyed the barriers of time and space. It refers, finally, to a world of increasing cultural homogeneity in which tastes in music, art, architecture, personal dress, and countless other areas of life have become increasingly standardized and, for better or worse, westernized.

Historians can safely agree that globalization represents an acceleration and intensification of a trend that has been a key feature of world history for thousands of years. Where it will take us is impossible to predict. Its supporters see universal benefits from worldwide economic growth, strengthened democracies through better-informed citizenry, increased capacity to deal with global environmental problems, and even a heightened sense of human community. Its detractors, of which there are many, see a widening divide between haves and have-nots, dangerous political transitions, the triumph of an ethos of corporate greed, and a bland uniformity in world culture. Whichever side is correct, understanding the roots and meaning of globalization will be a primary challenge for future historians.

From World War II to the Cold War

In the spring of 1945, the Allies, led by Great Britain, the United States, and the Soviet Union, defeated Hitler and were making plans for victory over Japan. Less than a year later, however, in March 1946, the British wartime leader Winston Churchill warned that an "iron curtain" was descending across Soviet-dominated Eastern Europe, and he called for an Anglo-American alliance to halt Soviet expansion. One year after that, in March 1947, President Harry Truman in an address to Congress denounced the Soviet Union as a menace to world peace and committed the United States to support "free peoples who are resisting attempted subjugation by armed minorities or by outside pressures." Truman's aide, Clark Clifford, described the speech as "the opening gun in a campaign to bring the people up to the realization that the war isn't over by any means." In April 1947 another presidential aide, Bernard Baruch, gave the war its name. It was a "cold war," a war that would dominate international politics until the close of the twentieth century.

Historians have minutely explored the causes of the Cold War and have written a great deal about which side — the Soviet Union or the United States — was to blame for bringing it about. One thing is certain, however: Each side deeply distrusted the other's motives and ambitions, and each side saw the other as a threat to its very existence. As a result, postwar disputes between the Soviet Union and the United States came to be viewed as the first skirmishes in a new struggle for world domination rather than disagreements amenable to compromise. Two documents written in the immediate postwar years illustrate this perspective. The first, a telegram written in September 1946 by the Soviet ambassador to the United States, Nikolai Novikov, warned Soviet leaders that the U.S. government was intent on crippling the Soviet Union and achieving world dominance. The second, a report prepared for President Truman by the National Security Council in early 1950, is titled "United States Objectives and Programs for National Security," and usually is referred to as NSC-68. Together they provide revealing insights into the thinking that led to four decades of struggle and competition between the world's two superpowers.

Cold War Origins: A Soviet Perspective

88 ▾ *Nikolai Novikov, TELEGRAM*

Nikolai Novikov was trained at Leningrad State University in the early 1930s in Middle Eastern economics and languages but abandoned plans for an academic career when he was drafted into the foreign service because of his knowledge of the Middle East. In 1941 he was named ambassador to Egypt, where he also served as liaison to the Yugoslav and Greek governments in exile, both of which were located in Cairo. Early in 1945 he was named deputy chief of the Soviet mission in Washington, D.C.; in April he became Soviet ambassador to the United States. He resigned from the foreign service in 1947 and returned to the Soviet Union, where he wrote his memoirs and otherwise lived in obscurity.

Novikov's telegram was unknown to scholars until a Soviet official revealed it to a group of Soviet and U.S. historians attending a meeting on the origins of the Cold War in Washington in 1990. According to Novikov's memoir, while he and the Soviet foreign minister Vyacheslav Molotov (1890–1986) were attending the Paris foreign ministers' conference in August 1946, Molotov requested that he write an analysis of U.S. foreign policy goals. Also according to Novikov, Molotov examined an early outline of the document in Paris and made several suggestions for improvements. This information lends credence to the theory that Molotov, who favored a hard line against the West, wanted Novikov's report to present a dark and perhaps exaggerated picture of U.S. goals to strengthen his hand against rivals who favored caution and compromise.

We know that Molotov read Novikov's final version of the cable. The underlined passages in the printed text represent underlinings that Molotov himself made on the original document. What happened next to the telegram is unclear. Did Molotov show it to Stalin and other high-ranking officials? Did it contribute to the atmosphere of confrontation that was building in 1946? The answer to both questions is probably yes, but until historians gain further access to Soviet archives, no one will know exactly how important Novikov's telegram was in the Cold War's murky beginnings.

QUESTIONS FOR ANALYSIS

1. What specific evidence does Novikov cite to prove his assertion that the goal of U.S. foreign policy is world domination?
2. In his view, how does the United States propose to achieve its goal?
3. What is Novikov's evaluation of U.S. strengths and weaknesses?
4. How does he view the prospects of Anglo-American cooperation? Is this something the Soviet Union should fear? Why or why not?
5. What implications might Novikov's analysis have had on actual Soviet policy?

The enormous relative weight of the USSR in international affairs in general and in the European countries in particular, the independence of its foreign policy, and the economic and political assistance that it provides to neighboring countries, both allies and former enemies, has led to the growth of the political influence of the Soviet Union in these countries and to the further strengthening of democratic tendencies in them.

Such a situation in Eastern and Southeastern Europe cannot help but be regarded by the American imperialists as an obstacle in the path of the expansionist policy of the United States. . . .

One of the stages in the achievement of dominance over the world by the United States is its understanding with England concerning the partial division of the world on the basis of mutual concessions. The basic lines of the secret agreement between the United States and England regarding the division of the world consist, as shown by facts, in their agreement on the inclusion of Japan and China in the sphere of influence of the United States in the Far East, while the United States, for its part, has agreed not to hinder England either in resolving the Indian problem or in strengthening its influence in Siam and Indonesia. . . .

The American policy in China is striving for the complete economic and political submission of China to the control of American monopolistic capital. Following this policy, the American government does not shrink even from interference in the internal affairs of China. At the present time in China, there are more than 50,000 American soldiers. . . .

China is gradually being transformed into a bridgehead for the American armed forces. American air bases are located all over its territory. . . . The measures carried out in northern China by the American army show that it intends to stay there for a long time.

In Japan, despite the presence there of only a small contingent of American troops, control is in the hands of the Americans. . . .

Measures taken by the American occupational authorities in the area of domestic policy and intended to support reactionary classes and groups, which the United States plans to use in the struggle against the Soviet Union, also meet with a sympathetic attitude on the part of England. . . .

▾▾▾

Obvious indications of the U.S. effort to establish world dominance are also to be found in the increase in military potential in peacetime and in the establishment of a large number of naval and air bases both in the United States and beyond its borders.

In the summer of 1946, for the first time in the history of the country, Congress passed a law on the establishment of a peacetime army, not on a volunteer basis but on the basis of universal military service. The size of the army, which is supposed to amount to about one million persons as of July 1, 1947, was also increased significantly. The size of the navy at the conclusion of the war decreased quite insignificantly in comparison with war-time. At the present time, the American navy occupies first place in the world, leaving England's navy far behind, to say nothing of those of other countries.

Expenditures on the army and navy have risen colossally, amounting to 13 billion dollars according to the budget for 1946–47 (about 40 percent of the total budget of 36 billion dollars). This is more than ten times greater than corresponding expenditures in the budget for 1938, which did not amount to even one billion dollars. . . .

The establishment of American bases on islands that are often 10,000 to 12,000 kilometers from the territory of the United States and are on the other side of the Atlantic and Pacific oceans clearly indicates the offensive nature of the strategic concepts of the commands of the U.S. army and navy. This interpretation is also confirmed by the fact that the American navy is intensively studying the naval approaches to the boundaries of Europe. For this purpose, American naval vessels in the course of 1946 visited the ports of Norway, Denmark, Sweden, Turkey, and Greece. In addition, the American navy is constantly operating in the Mediterranean Sea.

All of these facts show clearly that a decisive role in the realization of plans for world dominance by the United States is played by its armed forces.

▾▾▾

In recent years American capital has penetrated very intensively into the economy of the Near Eastern countries, in particular into the oil industry. At present there are American oil concessions in all of the Near Eastern countries that have oil deposits (Iraq, Bahrain, Kuwait, Egypt, and Saudi Arabia). American capital, which made its first appearance in the oil industry of the Near East only in 1927, now controls about 42 percent of all proven reserves in the Near East, excluding Iran. . . .

In expanding in the Near East, American capital has English capital as its greatest and most stubborn competitor. The fierce competition between them is the chief factor preventing England and the United States from reaching an understanding on the division of spheres of influence in the Near East, a division that can occur only at the expense of direct British interests in this region. . . .

The irregular nature of relations between England and the United States in the Near East is manifested in part also in the great activity of the American naval fleet in the eastern part of the Mediterranean Sea. Such activity cannot help but be in conflict with the basic interests of the British Empire. These actions on the part of the U.S. fleet undoubtedly are also linked with American oil and other economic interests in the Near East. . . .

. . . The strengthening of U.S. positions in the Near East and the establishment of conditions for basing the American navy at one or more points on the Mediterranean Sea will therefore signify the emergence of a new threat to the security of the southern regions of the Soviet Union.

The ruling circles of the United States obviously have a sympathetic attitude toward the idea of a military alliance with England, but at the present time the matter has not yet culminated in an official alliance. Churchill's speech in Fulton[1] calling for the conclusion of an Anglo-American military alliance for the purpose of establishing joint domination over the world was therefore not supported officially by Truman or Byrnes,[2] although Truman by his presence [during the "iron curtain" speech] did indirectly sanction Churchill's appeal.

Even if the United States does not go so far as to conclude a military alliance with England just now, in practice they still maintain very close contact on military questions. The combined Anglo-American headquarters in Washington continues to exist, despite the fact that over a year has passed since the end of the war. . . .

▾▾▾

One of the most important elements in the general policy of the United States, which is directed toward limiting the international role of the USSR in the postwar world, is the policy with regard to Germany. In Germany, the United States is taking measures to strengthen reactionary forces for the purpose of opposing democratic reconstruction. Furthermore, it displays special insistence on accompanying this policy with completely inadequate measures for the demilitarization of Germany. . . . Instead, the United States is considering the possibility of terminating the Allied occupation of German territory before the main tasks of the occupation — the demilitarization and democratization of Germany — have been implemented. This would create the prerequisites for the revival of an imperialist Germany, which the United States plans to use in a future war on its side. One cannot help seeing that such a policy has a clearly outlined anti-Soviet edge and constitutes a serious danger to the cause of peace.

The numerous and extremely hostile statements by American government, political, and military figures with regard to the Soviet Union and its foreign policy are very characteristic of the current relationship between the ruling circles of the United States and the USSR. These statements are echoed in an even more unrestrained tone by the overwhelming majority of the American press organs. Talk about a "third war," meaning a war against the Soviet Union, and even a direct call for this war — with the threat of using the atomic bomb — such is the content of the statements on relations with the Soviet Union by reactionaries at public meetings and in the press. . . .

[1]A reference to Winston Churchill's "iron curtain" speech, delivered at Westminster College in Fulton, Missouri, in March 1946.

[2]James Byrnes (1879–1972), secretary of state from 1945 to 1947.

The basic goal of this anti-Soviet campaign of American "public opinion" is to exert political pressure on the Soviet Union and compel it to make concessions. Another, no less important goal of the campaign is the attempt to create an atmosphere of war psychosis among the masses, who are weary of war, thus making it easier for the U.S. government to carry out measures for the maintenance of high military potential. . . .

Of course, all of these measures for maintaining a high military potential are not goals in themselves. They are only intended to prepare the conditions for winning world supremacy in a new war, the date for which, to be sure, cannot be determined now by anyone, but which is contemplated by the most bellicose circles of American imperialism.

Careful note should be taken of the fact that the preparation by the United States for a future war is being conducted with the prospect of war against the Soviet Union, which in the eyes of American imperialists is the main obstacle in the path of the United States to world domination. This is indicated by facts such as the tactical training of the American army for war with the Soviet Union as the future opponent, the siting of American strategic bases in regions from which it is possible to launch strikes on Soviet territory, intensified training and strengthening of Arctic regions as close approaches to the USSR, and attempts to prepare Germany and Japan to use those countries in a war against the USSR.

The Soviet Threat: A U.S. Perspective

▼▼▼

89 ▼ *National Security Council, UNITED STATES OBJECTIVES AND PROGRAMS FOR NATIONAL SECURITY*

Of the many thousands of papers, memoranda, reports, and policy statements produced by U.S. officials in the opening stages of the Cold War, two stand out as particularly important. The first, the so-called "Long Telegram," was written in 1946 by the career diplomat George Kennan while serving in Moscow as a special assistant to the U.S. ambassador to the Soviet Union, Averill Harriman. In his telegram to the State Department, Kennan argued that Soviet expansionism and hostility to the outside world were rooted less in Marxism than in a deep sense of Russian inferiority and insecurity. He argued further that the USSR's influence had to be "contained" in areas of vital strategic importance to the United States.

Of equal importance was a report entitled "United States Objectives and Programs for National Security," which was submitted to the president in April 1950. It was prepared by the National Security Council, an advisory body to the president that in 1950 consisted of the president himself; the vice-president; the secretaries of state, defense, and the treasury; and the chairman of the National Security Resources Board. Its function was to advise the president on the integration of domestic, foreign, and military policies relating to national security and to facilitate interagency cooperation.

In early 1950, when the report was being prepared, many of the key events in what we perceive as the Cold War had already occurred. The Truman Doctrine of

1947 pledged military aid to Greece and Turkey and any other country resisting a communist takeover; the Marshall Plan (1947) sought to blunt the appeal of communism by allocating millions of dollars to rebuild the economies of Western Europe; and the North Atlantic Treaty Organization (NATO) was established in 1949 to counter Soviet military strength in Eastern Europe. Although no European countries became communist after Czechoslovakia in 1947, American anxiety over international communism sharpened in 1949 when the Communists under Mao Zedong took over China and the Soviets detonated their first atomic bomb. Against this background, President Truman gave his approval to the formation of an ad hoc committee chaired by the Department of State's Policy Planning head Paul Nitze to prepare a position paper on a suitable U.S. response to the perceived communist threat. The paper, a blueprint for U.S. Cold War strategy, was released in April 1950, just two months before the onset of the Korean War.

QUESTIONS FOR ANALYSIS

1. According to this document, how did World War II fundamentally alter diplomatic relationships?
2. What view of the Soviet Union does this document present?
3. According to the report, what is the Soviet strategy for subverting the free world?
4. What does "containment" mean?
5. What must be done to ensure containment's effectiveness?

Within the past thirty-five years the world has experienced two global wars of tremendous violence. . . . During the span of one generation, the international distribution of power has been fundamentally altered. For several centuries it had proved impossible for any one nation to gain such preponderant strength that a coalition of other nations could not in time face it with greater strength. The international scene was marked by recurring periods of violence and war, but a system of sovereign and independent states was maintained, over which no state was able to achieve hegemony.

Two complex sets of factors have now basically altered this historical distribution of power. First, the defeat of Germany and Japan and the decline of the British and French Empires have interacted with the development of the United States and the Soviet Union in such a way that power has increasingly gravitated to these two centers. Second, the Soviet Union, unlike previous aspirants to hegemony, is animated by a new fanatic faith, antithetical to our own, and seeks to impose its absolute authority over the rest of the world. Conflict has, therefore, become endemic and is waged, on the part of the Soviet Union, by violent or non-violent methods in accordance with the dictates of expediency. . . .

On the one hand, the people of the world yearn for relief from the anxiety arising from the risk of atomic war. On the other hand, any substantial further extension of the area under the domination of the Kremlin would raise the possibility that no coalition adequate to confront the Kremlin with greater strength could be assembled. It is in this context that this Republic and its citizens in the ascendancy of their strength stand in their deepest peril.

The issues that face us are momentous, involving the fulfillment or destruction not only of this Republic but of civilization itself. They are issues which will not await our deliberations.

With conscience and resolution this Government and the people it represents must now take new and fateful decisions. . . .

Our overall policy at the present time may be described as one designed to foster a world environment in which the American system can survive and flourish. It therefore rejects the concept of isolation and affirms the necessity of our positive participation in the world community.

This broad intention embraces two subsidiary policies. One is a policy which we would probably pursue even if there were no Soviet threat. It is a policy of attempting to develop a healthy international community. The other is the policy of "containing" the Soviet system. . . .

As for the policy of "containment," it is one which seeks by all means short of war to (1) block further expansion of Soviet power, (2) expose the falsities of Soviet pretensions, (3) induce a retraction of the Kremlin's control and influence and (4) in general, so foster the seeds of destruction within the Soviet system that the Kremlin is brought at least to the point of modifying its behavior to conform to generally accepted international standards.

It was and continues to be cardinal in this policy that we possess superior overall power in ourselves or in dependable combination with other like-minded nations. One of the most important ingredients of power is military strength. In the concept of "containment," the maintenance of a strong military posture is deemed to be essential for two reasons: (1) as an ultimate guarantee of our national security and (2) as an indispensable backdrop to the conduct of the policy of "containment." . . .

At the same time, it is essential to the successful conduct of a policy of "containment" that we always leave open the possibility of negotiation with the U.S.S.R. A diplomatic freeze — and we are in one now — tends to defeat the very purposes of "containment" because it raises tensions at the same time that it makes Soviet retractions and adjustments in the direction of moderated behavior more difficult. It also tends to inhibit our initiative and deprives us of opportunities for maintaining a moral ascendancy in our struggle with the Soviet system. . . .

It is quite clear from Soviet theory and practice that the Kremlin seeks to bring the free world under its dominion by the methods of the cold war. The preferred technique is to subvert by infiltration and intimidation. Every institution of our society is an instrument which it is sought to stultify and turn against our purposes. Those that touch most closely our material and moral strength are obviously the prime targets, labor unions, civil enterprises, schools, churches, and all media for influencing opinion. The effort is not so much to make them serve obvious Soviet ends as to prevent them from serving our ends, and thus to make them sources of confusion in our economy, our culture, and our body politic. The doubts and diversities that in terms of our values are part of the merit of a free system, the weaknesses and the problems that are peculiar to it, the rights and privileges that free men enjoy, and the disorganization and destruction left in the wake of the last attack in our freedoms, all are but opportunities for the Kremlin to do its evil work. Every advantage is taken of the fact that our means of prevention and retaliation are limited by those principles and scruples which are precisely the ones that give our freedom and democracy its meaning for us. None of our scruples deter those whose only code is, "morality is that which serves the revolution."

At the same time the Soviet Union is seeking to create overwhelming military force, in order to back up infiltration with intimidation. In the only terms in which it understands strength, it is seeking to demonstrate to the free world that force and the will to use it are on the side of the Kremlin, that those who lack it are decadent and doomed. In local incidents it threatens and encroaches both for the sake of local gains and to increase anxiety and defeatism in all the free world.

The possession of atomic weapons at each of the opposite poles of power, and the inability (for different reasons) of either side to place any trust in the other, puts a premium on a surprise attack against us. It equally puts a premium on a more violent and ruthless prosecution of its design by cold war, especially if the Kremlin is sufficiently objective to realize the improbability of our prosecuting a preventive war. It also puts a premium on piecemeal aggression against others, counting on our unwillingness to engage in atomic war unless we are directly attacked. We run all these risks and the added risk of being confused and immobilized by our inability to weigh and choose, and pursue a firm course based on a rational assessment of each. . . .

Our position as the center of power in the free world places a heavy responsibility upon the United States for leadership. We must organize and enlist the energies and resources of the free world in a positive program for peace which will frustrate the Kremlin design for world domination by creating a situation in the free world to which the Kremlin will be compelled to adjust. Without such a cooperative effort, led by the United States, we will have to make gradual withdrawals under pressure until we discover one day that we have sacrificed positions of vital interest. . . .

In summary, we must, by means of a rapid and sustained build-up of the political, economic, and military strength of the free world, and by means of an affirmative program intended to wrest the initiative from the Soviet Union, confront it with convincing evidence of the determination and ability of the free world to frustrate the Kremlin design of a world dominated by its will. Such evidence is the only means short of war which eventually may force the Kremlin to abandon its present course of action and to negotiate acceptable agreements on issues of major importance.

The whole success of the proposed program hangs ultimately on recognition by this Government, the American people, and all free peoples, that the cold war is in fact a real war in which the survival of the free world is at stake. Essential prerequisites to success are consultations with Congressional leaders designed to make the program the object of nonpartisan legislative support, and a presentation to the public of a full explanation of the facts and implications of the present international situation. The prosecution of the program will require of us all the ingenuity, sacrifice, and unity demanded by the vital importance of the issue and the tenacity to persevere until our national objectives have been attained.

The End of Europe's Empires

In 1939, when World War II began in Europe, a handful of nations — the United States, Belgium, Italy, the Netherlands, Portugal, and especially Great Britain and France — controlled colonial empires that contained approximately one-third of the world's population and area. Although the United States, never fully comfortable as an imperialist power, had granted the Philippines self-rule in 1935 with the promise of complete independence ten years later, other colonial powers during and after World War II were intent on maintaining their colonies. In 1943 British cabinet officials spoke of "many generations" before its colonial subjects were ready for self-government. At the Brazzaville Conference on the future of the French empire in Africa, held in 1944 in French Equatorial Africa, the forty French officials who attended declined even to discuss independence for France's African colonies since it was so far in the future.

By the mid 1970s, however, most African and Asian colonies had become independent states. Although this sweeping change is often referred to by a single word, *decolonization*, it was a complex and variegated process that defies easy generalizations. What caused it, how it unfolded, and what it left behind depended on many variables, including the strength of indigenous nationalist movements, the effects of World War II, the extent of European settlement, differences in colonial policy, and the nature of the colonial societies themselves. Decolonization in India, in which a broadly based nationalist movement had existed since the late 1800s, was different from decolonization in Africa, where nationalism was just taking root at the time of independence. Decolonization in Africa differed in French, British, Belgian, and Portuguese colonies, and it differed in British colonies such as Rhodesia, where 250,000 whites had settled, and the Gold Coast, where most British residents were administrators.

It is easier to generalize about decolonization's significance. It was, first of all, another symptom of Europe's shrinking political influence after World War II. It was, in addition, the beginning of a new chapter in the Cold War. Having begun as a conflict over the political future of postwar Europe, the Cold War in the 1950s and 1960s expanded to include the new states of Asia and Africa. To win their support, the Soviet Union and the United States extended economic and military aid, sponsored cultural exchanges, and worked behind the scenes to prop up favored politicians. In the case of Vietnam, a former French colony, Great Power involvement went much further. From the late 1950s until 1973, the United States sent 2 million troops to Southeast Asia and spent billions of dollars to prevent the unification of Vietnam under communism. The United States failed and, in doing so, learned painful lessons about the limits of power and the strength of nationalism in the postcolonial era.

Great Britain Lets Go of India

▼▼▼

90 ▼ *DEBATE IN THE HOUSE OF COMMONS*

A turning point in the dismantling of Europe's empires took place in August 1947 when the Indian people gained independence from Great Britain and the new states of India and Pakistan were created. After the greatest imperial power released its hold on the "jewel in the crown" of its empire, nationalist leaders throughout Asia and Africa demanded equal treatment, and European politicians found it more difficult to justify continued colonial rule.

British and Indian leaders had debated the timing and framework of Indian independence for decades, but World War II brought the issue to a head. Many Indians, still embittered by the meager benefits they had received for their sacrifices in World War I, showed little enthusiasm for the British cause in World War II. In

1942, after Japan's conquest of Southeast Asia, the British government sent Sir Stafford Cripps to Delhi to offer India dominion status after the war if India would support the war against Japan. Negotiations broke down, however, leading Gandhi to launch the "Quit India" movement, his last nationwide passive resistance campaign against British rule. Anti-British feeling intensified in 1943 when a disastrous famine took between 1 million and 3 million lives and the pro-Japanese Indian National Army, organized by Subhas Bose, declared war on Great Britain.

A shift in postwar British politics also affected India's future. The 1945 elections initiated six years of rule by the Labour Party, which had less enthusiasm for the idea of empire than the Conservatives. In the face of mounting restiveness in India, Prime Minister Clement Attlee dispatched a three-person mission to India charged with preserving Indian unity in the face of Hindu-Muslim enmity and arranging for India's independence as soon as possible. Although Hindus and Muslims could not reconcile their differences, on February 20, 1947, the Labour government went ahead and announced that British rule would end in India no later than June 1948.

This led to an emotional two-day debate in Parliament in which Conservatives and some Liberals argued that independence should be delayed. The Labour Party had a strong majority, however, and in March 1947 Parliament approved its plan. At midnight on August 14–15, 1947, predominantly Hindu India and predominantly Muslim Pakistan became independent states.

The following excerpts are from the parliamentary debates of March 4 and 5, 1947. All the speakers are opposing a proposal by Sir John Anderson, a Liberal representing the Scottish universities, that Great Britain should promise independence by June 1948 but withdraw the offer and require further negotiations if a suitable Hindu-Muslim agreement could not be achieved.

QUESTIONS FOR ANALYSIS

1. What were the points of disagreement among members of Parliament about the benefits and harm of British colonial rule in India?
2. Some speakers who believed that British colonialism had benefited India still supported independence. Why?
3. The critics of British rule in India supported immediate independence. What was their line of argument?
4. According to the speakers, what military and economic realities make it impractical to continue British rule in India?
5. How do the speakers view developments in India as part of broader historical trends?
6. Most of the speakers were members of the Labour Party and thus sympathetic to socialism. What examples of socialist perspectives can you find in their speeches?

MR. CLEMENT DAVIES[1] (MONTGOMERY) It is an old adage now, that "the old order changeth, yielding place to new," but there has been a more rapid change from the old to the new in our time than ever before. We have witnessed great changes in each one of the five Continents, and for many of those changes this country and its people have been directly or indirectly responsible. . . . In all the lands where the British flag flies, we have taught the peoples the rule of law and the value of justice impartially administered. We have extended knowledge, and tried to inculcate understanding and toleration.

Our declared objects were twofold — first, the betterment of the conditions of the people and the improvement of their standard of life; and, second, to teach them the ways of good administration and gradually train them to undertake responsibility so that one day we could hand over to them the full burden of their own self-government. Our teachings and our methods have had widespread effect, and we should rejoice that so many peoples in the world today are awake, and aware of their own individualities, and have a desire to express their own personalities and their traditions, and to live their own mode of life. . . . Our association with India during two centuries has been, on the whole — with mistakes, as we will admit — an honorable one. So far as we were able we brought peace to this great sub-continent; we have introduced not only a system of law and order, but also a system of administration of justice, fair and impartial, which has won their respect. . . . We have tried to inculcate into them the feeling that although they are composed of different races, with different languages, customs, and religions, they are really part of one great people of India.

The standard of life, pathetically low as it is, has improved so that during the last 30 years there has been an increase in the population of 100 million and they now number 400 million people. We have brought to them schools, universities, and teachers, and we have not only introduced the Indians into the Civil Service but have gradually handed over to them, in the Provinces and even in the Central Government, the administration and government of their own land and their own people. . . . Then in 1946, there was the offer of complete independence, with the right again, if they so chose, of contracting in and coming back within the British Commonwealth of Nations.[2]

I agree that these offers were made subject to the condition that the Indian peoples themselves would co-operate to form a Central Government and draw up not only their own Constitution, but the method of framing it. Unfortunately, the leaders of the two main parties in India have failed to agree upon the formation of even a Constituent Assembly, and have failed, therefore, to agree upon a form of Constitution. . . .

What are the possible courses that could be pursued? . . . The first of the courses would be to restore power into our own hands so that we might not only have the responsibility but the full means of exercising that responsibility. I believe that that is not only impossible but unthinkable at this present stage. . . . Secondly, can we continue, as we do at present, to wait until an agreement is reached for the formation of a Central Government with a full Constitution, capable of acting on behalf of the whole of India? The present state of affairs there and the deterioration which has already set in — and which has worsened — have shown us that we cannot long continue on that course.

The third course is the step taken by His Majesty's Government — the declaration made by the Government that we cannot and do not intend in the slightest degree to go back upon our word, that we do not intend to damp the

[1] A London lawyer (1884–1962) who was a Liberal member of Parliament from 1929 until the time of his death.

[2] The British Commonwealth of Nations was founded by Parliament in 1931 through the Statute of Westminster. It is a free association of nations comprised of Great Britain and a number of its former dependencies that have chosen to maintain ties of friendship and practical cooperation. Members acknowledge the British monarch as the symbolic head of their association. Since 1946 it has been known as the Commonwealth of Nations.

hopes of the Indian peoples but rather to raise them, and that we cannot possibly go on indefinitely as we have been going on during these past months; that not only shall they have the power they now really possess but after June 1948, the full responsibility for government of their own peoples in India. . . .

MR. SORENSEN[3] (LEYTON, WEST) I have considerable sympathy with the hon. and gallant Member for Ayr Burghs (Sir T. Moore),[4] because, politically, he has been dead for some time and does not know it. His ideas were extraordinarily reminiscent of 50 years ago, and I do not propose, therefore, to deal with so unpleasant and decadent a subject. When he drew attention to the service we have rendered to India — and we have undoubtedly rendered service — he overlooked the fact that India has had an existence extending for some thousands of years before the British occupation, and that during that period she managed to run schools, establish a chain of rest houses, preserve an economy, and reach a high level of civilization, when the inhabitants of these islands were in a condition of barbarism and savagery. One has only to discuss such matters with a few representative Indians to realize that they can draw up a fairly powerful indictment of the evil we have taken to India as well as the good. . . .

Whatever may have been the origin of the various problems in India, or the degree of culpability which may be attached to this or that party or person, a situation now confronts us which demands decision. . . . That is why, in my estimation, the Government are perfectly right to fix a date for the transference of power. . . . Responsibility is ultimately an Indian matter. Acute problems have existed in India for centuries, and they have not been solved under our domination. Untouchability, the appalling subjugation of women, the division of the castes, the incipient or actual conflict between Muslim and Hindu — all those and many others exist.

I do not forget what is to me the most terrible of all India's problems, the appalling poverty. It has not been solved by us, although we have had our opportunity. On the contrary, in some respects we have increased that problem, because, despite the contributions that we have made to India's welfare, we have taken a great deal of wealth from India in order that we ourselves might enjoy a relatively higher standard of life. Can it be denied that we have benefited in the past substantially by the ignorant, sweated labor of the Indian people? We have not solved those social problems. The Indians may not solve them either. There are many problems that the Western world cannot solve, but at least, those problems are India's responsibility. Indians are more likely, because they are intimate with their own problems, to know how to find their way through those labyrinths than we, who are, to the Indian but aliens and foreigners.

Here I submit a point which surely will receive the endorsement of most hon. Members of this House. It is that even a benevolent autocracy can be no substitute for democracy and liberty. . . .

I would therefore put two points to the House tonight. Are we really asked by hon. Members on the other side to engage in a gamble, first by continuing as we are and trying to control India indefinitely, with the probability that we should not succeed and that all over India there would be rebellion, chaos, and breakdown? Secondly, are we to try to reconquer India and in doing so, to impose upon ourselves an economic burden which we could not possibly afford? How many men would be required to keep India quiet if the great majority of the Indians were determined to defy our power? I guarantee that the number would not be fewer than a million men, with all the necessary resources and munitions of war.

[3]Reginald Sorensen (1884–1971) was a clergyman who served in Parliament as a member of the Labour Party from 1929 to 1931 and from 1939 to 1954.

[4]Lieutenant Colonel Thomas Moore (1888–1971) was a Conservative member of Parliament from 1929 to 1962. He had just spoken against the government's plan for Indian independence.

Are we to do this at a time when we are crying out for manpower in this country, when in the mines, the textile industry, and elsewhere we want every man we can possibly secure? There are already 1,500,000 men under arms. To talk about facing the possibility of governing and policing India and keeping India under proper supervision out of our own resources is not only nonsense, but would provide the last straw that breaks the camel's back. . . .

FLIGHT-LIEUTENANT CRAWLEY[5] (BUCKINGHAM) Right hon. and hon. Members opposite, who envisage our staying in India, must have some idea of what type of rule we should maintain. A fact about the Indian services which they seem to ignore is that they are largely Indianized. Can they really expect the Services, Indianized to the extent of 80 or 90 percent, to carry out their policy any longer? Is it not true that in any situation that is likely to arise in India now, if the British remain without a definite date being given for withdrawal, every single Indian member of the Services, will, in the mind of all politically conscious Indians become a political collaborator? We have seen that in Palestine where Arab hates Arab and Jew hates Jew if they think they are collaborating with the British.[6] How could we get the Indianized part of the Services to carry out a policy which, in the view of all political Indians, is anti-Indian? The only conceivable way in which we could stay even for seven years in India would be by instituting a type of rule which we in this country abhor more than any other — a purely dictatorial rule based upon all the things we detest most, such as an informative police, not for an emergency measure, but for a long period and imprisonment without trial. . . .

MR. HAROLD DAVIES[7] (LEEK) . . . I believe that India is the pivot of the Pacific Ocean area. All the peoples of Asia are on the move. Can we in this House, by wishful thinking, sweep aside this natural desire for independence, freedom, and nationalism that has grown in Asia from Karachi to Peking,[8] from Karachi to Indonesia and Indo-China? That is all part of that movement, and we must recognize it. I am not a Utopian. I know that the changeover will not be easy. But there is no hon. Member opposite who has given any concrete, practical alternative to the decision, which has been made by my right hon. friends. What alternative can we give?

This little old country is tottering and wounded as a result of the wars inherent in the capitalist system. Can we, today, carry out vast commitments from one end of the world to another? Is it not time that we said to those for whom we have spoken so long, "The time has come when you shall have your independence. That time has come; the moment is here"? I should like to recall what Macaulay[9] said:

> Many politicians of our times are in the habit of laying it down as a self-evident proposition, that no people ought to be free until they are fit to use their freedom. This maxim is worthy of the fool in the old story who resolved not to go into the water until he had learned to swim.

India must learn now to build up democracy. . . .

---

[5]Aidan Crawley (1908–1992) was an educator and journalist who served in the Royal Air Force during World War II. He was a Labour member of Parliament from 1945 to 1951.

[6]The British were attempting to extricate themselves from Palestine, which they had received as a mandate after World War I and was the scene of bitter Arab-Jewish rivalry.

[7]Harold Davies (1904–1984) was an author and educator who served in Parliament as a member of the Labour Party from 1959 to 1964.

[8]Karachi, a port city on the Arabian Sea, was soon to become Pakistan's first capital city. *Peking* is a variant spelling of *Beijing*.

[9]Thomas B. Macaulay (1800–1859) was an English essayist, historian, and statesman.

Colonialism's Legacy: An African Perspective

91 ▾ Patrice Lumumba, *INDEPENDENCE DAY SPEECH*

Among the many independence-day ceremonies that occurred after World War II, few matched the drama of June 30, 1960, when Belgian rule ended in the Congo. By previous arrangement, speeches were to be delivered by young King Baudouin of Belgium and the president-elect of the new Congo Republic, Joseph Kasavubu. The king's speech, paternalistic and patronizing to the extreme, praised King Leopold II, the greedy founder of the Belgian Congo, and congratulated the Belgians for their contributions to Congolese development. Baudouin's speech angered the Congolese in attendance, and in his speech Kasavubu skipped the parts where he had planned to compliment the Belgians. Then the microphone was handed to Patrice Lumumba, the nationalist leader who had been chosen to be the Congo Republic's first prime minister. His fiery words stunned his listeners and revealed the deep wounds caused by eight decades of colonial rule.

Lumumba, born in 1925 and educated in Stanleyville, had been a postal clerk and a sales manager for a brewery before entering politics in the late 1950s. Founder of the Congolese National Movement in 1958, Lumumba was the sole Congolese leader who could claim a truly national rather than regional following. Tragically, only months after delivering his speech, Lumumba was captured by political enemies working in concert with Belgian troops. He was beaten, tortured, and shot to death, and then his body was cut in pieces and dissolved in concentrated sulfuric acid to destroy the evidence. He is one of thousands who died in the Congolese civil wars that followed independence.

QUESTIONS FOR ANALYSIS

1. What does Lumumba find to be the most repugnant aspect of Belgian imperialism?
2. What goals does Lumumba hope an independent Congo will achieve?
3. After achieving independence the new nation disintegrated almost immediately into chaos. What in Lumumba's speech hints of this imminent political turmoil?

Your Majesty, Excellencies, Ladies and Gentlemen, Congolese men and women, fighters for independence who today are victorious, I salute you in the name of the Congolese government.

I ask of you all, my friends who have ceaselessly struggled at our side, that this thirtieth of June, 1960, may be preserved as an illustrious date etched indelibly in your hearts, a date whose meaning you will teach proudly to your children, so that they in turn may pass on to their children and to their grandchildren the glorious story of our struggle for liberty.

For if independence of the Congo is today proclaimed in agreement with Belgium, a friendly nation with whom we are on equal footing, yet no Congolese worthy of the name can ever forget that it has been by struggle that this independence has been gained, a continuous and prolonged struggle, an ardent and idealistic struggle, a struggle in which we have spared neither our strength nor our privations, neither our suffering nor our blood.

Of this struggle, one of tears, fire, and blood, we are proud to the very depths of our being, for it was a noble and just struggle, absolutely necessary in order to bring to an end the humiliating slavery which had been imposed upon us by force.

This was our fate during eighty years of colonial rule; our wounds are still too fresh and painful for us to be able to erase them from our memories.

We have known the back-breaking work exacted from us in exchange for salaries which permitted us neither to eat enough to satisfy our hunger, nor to dress and lodge ourselves decently, nor to raise our children as the beloved creatures that they are.

We have known the mockery, the insults, the blows submitted to morning, noon and night because we were "nègres."[1] Who will forget that to a Negro one used the familiar term of address, not, certainly, as to a friend, but because the more dignified forms were reserved for Whites alone?

We have known that our lands were despoiled in the name of supposedly legal texts which in reality recognized only the right of the stronger.

We have known the law was never the same, whether dealing with a White or a Negro; that it was accommodating for the one, cruel and inhuman to the other.

We have known the atrocious suffering of those who were imprisoned for political opinion or religious beliefs: exiles in their own country, their fate was truly worse than death itself.

We have known that in the cities there were magnificent houses for the Whites and crumbling hovels for the Negroes, that a Negro was not admitted to movie theaters or restaurants, that he was not allowed to enter so-called "European" stores, that when the Negro traveled, it was on the lowest level of a boat, at the feet of the White man in his de luxe cabin.

And, finally, who will forget the hangings or the firing squads where so many of our brothers perished, or the cells into which were brutally thrown those who escaped the soldiers' bullets — the soldiers whom the colonialists made the instruments of their domination?

From all this, my brothers, have we deeply suffered.

But all this, however, we who by the vote of your elected representatives are directed to guide our beloved country, we who have suffered in our bodies and in our hearts from colonialist oppression, we it is who tell you — all this is henceforth ended.

The Republic of the Congo has been proclaimed, and our beloved country is now in the hands of its own children.

Together, my brothers, we are going to start a new struggle, a sublime struggle, which will lead our country to peace, prosperity and greatness.

Together we are going to establish social justice and ensure for each man just remuneration for his work.

We are going to show the world what the black man can do when he works in freedom, and we are going to make the Congo the hub of all Africa.

We are going to be vigilant that the lands of our nation truly profit our nation's children.

We are going to re-examine all former laws, and make new ones which will be just and noble.

We are going to put an end to suppression of free thought and make it possible for all citizens fully to enjoy the fundamental liberties set down in the declaration of the Rights of Man.[2]

We are going to succeed in suppressing all discrimination — no matter what it may be — and give to each individual the just place to

[1]*Nègres*, the French word for Negroes, when used in certain contexts or phrases had racist, derogatory connotations.

[2]The statement of the basic principles adopted on August 26, 1789, in France.

which his human dignity, his work and his devotion to his country entitle him.

We shall cause to reign not the peace of guns and bayonets, but the peace of hearts and good will.

And for all this, dear compatriots, rest assured that we shall be able to count upon not only our own enormous forces and immense riches, but also upon the assistance of numerous foreign countries whose collaboration we shall accept only as long as it is honest and does not seek to impose upon us any political system, whatever it may be.

In this domain, even Belgium, who finally understanding the sense and direction of history has no longer attempted to oppose our independence, is ready to accord us its aid and friendship, and a treaty to this effect has just been signed between us as two equal and independent countries. This cooperation, I am sure, will prove profitable for both countries. For our part, even while remaining vigilant, we shall know how to respect commitments freely consented to.

Thus, in domestic as well as in foreign affairs, the new Congo which my government is going to create will be a rich country, a free and prosperous one. But in order that we may arrive at this goal without delay, I ask you all, legislators and Congolese citizens, to help me with all your power.

I ask you all to forget tribal quarrels which drain our energies, and risk making us an object of scorn among other nations.

I ask the parliamentary minority to help my government by constructive opposition, and to remain strictly within legal and democratic bounds.

I ask you all not to demand from one day to the next unconsidered raises in salary before I have had the time to set in motion an over-all plan through which I hope to assure the prosperity of the nation.

I ask you all not to shrink from any sacrifice in order to assure the success of our magnificent enterprises.

I ask you all, finally, to respect unconditionally the life and the property of your fellow citizens and of the foreigners established in our country. If the behavior of these foreigners leaves something to be desired, our justice will be prompt in expelling them from the territory of the Republic; if, on the other hand, their conduct is satisfactory, they must be left in peace, for they also are working for the prosperity of our country.

And so, my brothers in race, my brothers in conflict, my compatriots, this is what I wanted to tell you in the name of the government, on this magnificent day of our complete and sovereign Independence.

Our government — strong, national, popular — will be the salvation of this country.

Homage to the Champions of National Liberty!

Long Live Independent and Sovereign Congo!

New Nations and Their Challenges

As one colony after another achieved independence in the 1950s and 1960s, euphoria swept across Africa and Asia. All the ways that colonialism had branded subject peoples with the mark of inferiority could now be forgotten. With a unity of purpose forged in the struggle for independence and with constitutions guaranteeing parliamentary government and basic freedoms, leaders and common people alike were ready to show the world they could govern themselves effectively.

Their economic aspirations were equally optimistic. With the heavy hand of the colonial master lifted from their economies, they anticipated economic development and the alleviation of poverty.

A few new states achieved their dreams, but many others experienced difficulties and disappointments. Many were nations in name only, with boundaries drawn by European colonial administrations without regard for cultural affinities, ethnic groupings, religious traditions, or economic viability. Independent India has maintained its status as the world's most populous constitutional democracy despite religious tensions and formidable social problems. In most of Africa and in other parts of Asia, however, shallow national loyalties were undermined by regionalism and ethnic conflict, and soon civil wars and military coups took their toll on democratic governments. Democracies gave way to dictatorships, which at their best were controlled by nationalist leaders with the interests of their countrymen at heart, but at their worst were dominated by venal, shortsighted, even genocidal leaders who enriched themselves and their henchmen while their nations' economies crumbled. In some cases, lawlessness, random violence, and warlordism overwhelmed even the dictators, and central governments virtually disappeared.

The economic records of the new states varied widely but overall were disappointing. Taiwan and South Korea, former colonies of Japan, and Singapore, Malaysia, and Hong Kong, former colonies of Great Britain, emerged as industrial, commercial, and financial powers. Oil-rich states in the Persian Gulf, the Middle East, and parts of Africa benefited from the surge in oil prices in the 1970s but struggled to develop the balanced economies needed to improve their people's standard of living or provide a foundation for lasting economic growth. Elsewhere economic development was at best mediocre or at worst catastrophic. Political instability was but one of many causes of poor economic performance. The lack of capital, poorly implemented economic development plans, low educational levels, droughts, inadequate infrastructure, and fluctuations in the world market for commodities also were contributing factors. The greatest obstacle to economic development was population growth. India, for example, experienced modest industrialization and substantial increases in food production in its first four decades of independence, but not enough to keep pace with its growing numbers. In 1947 India's population was 350 million; in 1990 it was 844 million, the great majority of whom remained desperately poor.

By the end of the 1980s, one thing was clear. For the new states of Africa and Asia, the end of colonial rule was no panacea. Economic development was more difficult to achieve and democratic government more difficult to maintain than anyone had imagined on that exhilarating day when independence had been achieved.

The Challenge of Ethnic Tensions

92 ▾ C. Odumegwu Ojukwu, SPEECHES AND WRITINGS

Political challenges for the newly independent states of sub-Saharan Africa were daunting: poor communications, low literacy levels, peasant societies' resistance to taxation by distant governments, underdeveloped economies, arbitrary national boundaries, and unrealistically high expectations. Overshadowing everything else, however, was the persistence of strong local and ethnic loyalties that led most people to judge national policies by the narrow standard of how they benefited one's region or tribe. In the Republic of Congo (soon to be renamed the Democratic Republic of Congo and later Zaire), rebellion and civil war broke out in January 1960, literally within hours of the formal end of Belgian rule. Newly independent Nigeria held together longer, but it too fell victim to civil war in 1967 when the eastern province of Biafra declared its independence.

When Nigeria became independent in 1960, its constitution was the product of protracted deliberations involving British administrators and representatives of the colony's major ethnic groups, the Hausa-Fulani, the Yoruba, and the Igbo. It established a central government with a prime minister and legislature and three provinces with extensive powers: the Northern Region, which was dominated by the Hausa-Fulani and was overwhelmingly Muslim; the Western Region, which was dominated by the Yoruba and was Protestant; and the Eastern Region, which was dominated by the Igbo and was mainly Roman Catholic. Denouncing corruption and the government's failure to address mounting economic problems, army officers, mostly Igbo, led a coup d'état in 1966 and then created a strong centralized national government at the expense of Nigeria's provinces. This angered the Hausa-Fulani and the Yoruba, who feared that the more highly educated and economically sophisticated Igbo would dominate the new regime. The result was another coup, led by Yakuba Gowon, an army officer from the Northern Region, and massacres of Igbo living outside the Eastern Region. The Eastern Region refused to recognize the new government and declared itself the independent Republic of Biafra in May 1967.

The leader of the Biafran independence movement was Chukwuemeka Odumegwu Ojukwu, who was born into a wealthy Igbo family and educated in England, where he received a master's degree in history from Oxford. He rose through the ranks of the Nigerian army and in 1967 became head of state and army commander-in-chief of newly independent Biafra. Immediately attacked by Nigerian forces, Biafra held out until 1970, when Ojukwu capitulated and fled to Guinea. Yakuba Gowon now ruled a reunited Nigeria, which he divided into twelve provinces rather than three to defuse ethnic conflict. For the next two decades, except between 1979 and 1983, Nigeria was ruled by military dictators.

The following excerpts are from General Ojukwu's speeches and writings from 1966 to 1969. They reveal his views of Nigeria's history and politics and his thoughts on the meaning of the Biafran independence movement.

QUESTIONS FOR ANALYSIS

1. **In Ojukwu's opinion, how did the British and the Northern Nigerians contribute to the problems of the Nigerian state?**
2. **What characteristics define the people of Eastern Nigeria, in Ojukwu's view?**
3. **According to Ojukwu, what have been the major flaws of the Nigerian government since independence? How will the new state of Biafra avoid these shortcomings?**
4. **What specific reasons does Ojukwu provide for the decision of Eastern Nigerians to secede?**
5. **What does Ojukwu see as the broader significance of the Biafran independence movement?**

THE BACKGROUND OF A CRISIS

The constitutional arrangements of Nigeria, as imposed upon the people by the erstwhile British rulers, were nothing but an implicit acceptance of the fact that there was no basis for Nigerian unity

It was Britain, first, that amalgamated the country in 1914, unwilling as the people of the North were.[1] It was Britain that forced a federation of Nigeria, even when the people of the North objected to it very strongly. It was Britain, while keeping Nigeria together, that made it impossible for the people to know themselves and get close to each other, by maintaining an apartheid policy in Northern Nigeria which herded all Southerners into little reserves, barring them from Northern Nigerian schools, and maintaining different systems of justice in a country they claimed to be one.[2]

It was Britain, for her economic interest, that put the various nations in Nigeria side by side and called it a federation, so as to have a large market. . . .

On October 1, 1960, independence was granted to the people of Nigeria in a form of "federation," based on artificially made units. The Nigerian Constitution installed the North in perpetual dominance over Nigeria. . . . Thus were sown, by design or by default, the seeds of factionalism and hate, of struggle for power at the center, and of the worst types of political chicanery and abuse of power. One of two situations was bound to result from that arrangement: either perpetual domination of the rest of the country by the North, not by consent but by force and fraud, or a dissolution of the federation bond. . . .

Nigeria in the end came to be run by compromises made and broken between the Northerners and consenting Southern politicians. This led to interminable violent crises, to corruption and nepotism, and to the arbitrary use of power. . . .

Key projects in the National Development Plan were not pursued with necessary vigor. Instead of these, palaces were constructed for the indulgence of ministers and other holders of public offices — men supposed to serve the interest of the common man. Expensive fleets of flamboyant and luxurious cars were purchased. Taxpayers' money was wasted on unnecessary foreign travel by ministers, each competing with the other only in their unbridled excesses.

This has disrupted the economy, depressed the standard of living of the toiling masses, spiraled prices, and made the rich richer and the poor

---

[1]The provinces of Northern and Southern Nigeria were brought under a common administration by Sir Frederick Lugard, the governor-general of Nigeria between 1912 and 1919.

[2]Many Eastern Nigerians had moved to other parts of the country, mainly to pursue business opportunities. Many believed they were treated as second-class citizens, especially in the Muslim north.

poorer. Internal squabbles for parochial and clannish patronage took the place of purposeful coordinated service of the people. Land, the basic heritage of the people, was converted into the private estates of rapacious individuals who, thus trampling on the rights of the people, violated their sacred trust under this system. The public service was being increasingly demoralized. Nepotism became rife. Tribalism became the order of the day. In appointments and promotions mere lip service was paid to honesty and hard work.

Under the system, efficiency inevitably declined. All this led inevitably to the complete loss of moral and political authority by the former regime. . . .

GRIEVANCES OF THE EASTERN NIGERIANS

In the old Federation some of you here will remember quite vividly what the contribution of the people from this area, now known as Biafra, was to the betterment of the areas in which we chose to reside and believed was our country. Socially we gave our best in Nigeria. Politically, we led the struggle for independence and sustained it. Economically, the hope of Nigeria was embedded deeply in this area and we contributed everything for the common good of Nigeria.

Our people moved from this area to all parts of the old Federation, and particularly to Northern Nigeria. Where there was darkness we gave them light! In Northern Nigeria, where they had no shelter we gave them houses. Where they were sick, as indeed most Northerners are, we brought them health. Where there was backwardness we brought progress. And where there was ignorance we brought them education. As a result of all this, we became people marked out in the various communities in which we lived.

Initially we were marked out as people who were progressive. Next, as people who were successful. Finally as people who should be the object of jealousy — people who were to be hated, and this hatred arose as a result of our success. . . . Nigerians hate us simply because where they failed, the Biafran succeeded. . . . We were relegated to the position of second-class citizens and later to slavery — yes, slavery — because as we worked, our masters enjoyed the fruits of our labor.

We reached a stage where the people from this part were fast losing their identity. They hid away the fact that they came from this area. . . .

How many of you looked in dismay at our own sons slowly shaving off their hair and putting on Northern Nigerian robes and passing as Northerners? Some of our senior men in public office considered very seriously whether to go to Mecca[3] or not even though they were not Muslims. It became shameful to be an Eastern Nigerian! Those of you who lived in Lagos[4] would probably remember that if you wanted to be able to ride over the law with impunity, all you had to do was to put on the Northern Nigerian gown and pretend to be a Northerner. . . . You all remember that if a Northern Nigerian ran into your car and damaged it the police would release the Northerner who was at fault and arrest you whose car was damaged by the careless Northerner. This was the state of affairs in the old Nigeria.

The Northern attitude is the attitude of horse and rider. . . . We were carrying the North physically, economically, and in every other way. For all that we received no thanks. They only got furious if we did not travel fast enough. Then they would kick. But, for every mule there comes a time when it bucks and says, "No, I will carry no more." We have bucked. We will carry Northern Nigeria no more!

[3]Pilgrimage to Mecca, the home of the prophet Muhammad on the Arabian Peninsula, was a religious act to be performed if possible once in one's life by all Muslims.

[4]At the time, Nigeria's capital.

THE NEW BIAFRAN SOCIETY

Born out of the gruesome murders and vandalism of yesterday, Biafra has come to stay as a historical reality. We believe that the future we face and our battle for survival cannot be won by bullets alone, but by brainpower, modern skills, and the determination to live and succeed. . . .

Nepotism and tribalism are twin evils. I believe that these can be avoided if we set about making sure that every appointment in our society is based on one and only one criterion — merit. We should ensure that this term "merit" is no mumbo-jumbo. It should be something that is obvious for everyone to see: that is, when you have given somebody a job, the reason for giving that job to that person in preference to others must be generally clear. . . .

Tribalism is, perhaps, more deeply rooted. . . . When I first came to this area as the military governor, one of the first things I did was to erase tribe from all public documents. We are all Biafrans. "Where do you come from?" you are asked, and the answer is simple: "I come from Biafra." The government must not emphasize tribal origin if it is trying to stamp out tribalism. . . .

Every effort should be made by future governments to educate our people away from tribalism. I would like to see movement of people across tribal frontiers. The government should encourage people to move from their own areas to be educated elsewhere. Yes, I would even go further to support government measures to encourage intertribal marriages. . . . It is only a gesture, but if the government really believes that tribalism could be wiped out, something like a bounty should be given to that young man who marries across tribe, to show that the government appreciates what he has done. . . .

I see a new breed of men and women, with new moral and spiritual values, building a new society — a renascent and strong Biafra.

I see the realization of all our cherished dreams and aspirations in a revolution which will not only guarantee our basic freedoms but usher in an era of equal opportunity and prosperity for all.

I see the evolution of a new democracy in Biafra as we advance as partners in our country's onward march to her destiny.

When I look into the future, I see Biafra transformed into a fully industrialized nation, wastelands and slums giving way to throbbing industrial centers and cities. . . .

I see agriculture mechanized by science and technology. . . .

I see a Republic knit with arteries of roads and highways; a nation of free men and women dedicated to the noble attributes of justice and liberty for which our youth have shed their blood; a people with an art and literature rich and unrivaled.

I am sure all Biafrans share these hopes for our country's future and destiny. . . . We are building a society which will destroy the myth that the black man cannot organize his own society.

. . . We are taking our rightful place in the world as human beings. . . . The black man cannot progress until he can point at a progressive black society. Until a society, a virile society entirely black, is established, the black man, whether he is in America, whether he is in Africa, will never be able to take his place side by side with the white man. We have the unique opportunity today of breaking our chains.

. . . We owe it, therefore, to Africa not to fail. Africa needs a Biafra. Biafra is the breaking of the chains. . . .

The Challenge of Religious Conflict

93 ▾ *Girilal Jain, EDITORIAL ON THE HINDU STATE*

India since independence has never been free of religious tensions. Even after Muslims were given their own state of Pakistan in 1947, religious pluralism characterized India's population: According to its most recent census (2001), India is composed of approximately 80.5 percent Hindus, 13.4 percent Muslims, 2.3 percent Christians, slightly more than 1.9 percent Sikhs, and smaller numbers of Jains, Parsis, and Buddhists. None of these groups has been completely satisfied with India's constitution, which states that India is a secular state with partiality toward no religious group. Many Hindus are convinced that the government bends over backward to protect Muslims and Sikhs; Muslims and Sikhs, conversely, are equally certain that the government panders to Hindus. In the early 1980s, religious tensions intensified as Muslims began to make converts among low-caste Hindus in the south, Sikhs agitated for an independent Punjab, and Hindus organized their own political party, the Bharatiya Janata (Indian People's Party), or BJP, whose goal was the "Hinduization" of India. Founded in 1982, the BJP increased its representation in parliament from 2 members in 1984 to 185 members in 1996, 50 more than that of the Congress Party, which had enjoyed a parliamentary majority in all but four years since 1947. A BJP-led coalition led the Indian government briefly in 1996 and from March 1998 to May 2004, when it experienced a surprising election setback and failed to achieve a parliamentary majority.

An important spokesman for Hindu nationalism and the BJP before his death in 1993 was the journalist Girilal Jain, who was editor-in-chief of the New Delhi *Times of India* between 1978 and 1988. Born into a poor rural family in 1922 and educated at Delhi University, Jain was jailed by the British during the 1942 "Quit India" campaign. As a journalist he was best known for his impassioned support of Indira Gandhi, prime minister from 1966 to 1970 and from 1980 to 1984. During the 1980s he was drawn to Hindu nationalism and the BJP.

The following editorial was written in 1990, when Hindu-Muslim tensions were peaking over the Babri mosque in the city of Ayodhya, built in the sixteenth century on the site of a Hindu temple believed to be the birthplace of the Hindu god-king Ram. Hindus demanded the destruction of the mosque, which was no longer used, so that a temple in honor of Ram could be built. In December 1992, Hindus stormed the mosque and destroyed it, precipitating a government crisis and causing violence that took thousands of lives. The government, with its commitment to religious pluralism and democracy, survived, but religious tensions remained high.

QUESTIONS FOR ANALYSIS

1. What are the reasons for Jain's disenchantment with India's government?
2. What does Jain mean when he says that the issues that concern the BJP have to do with "civilization," not religion?
3. How does Jain define the West? How does he view the West's role in Indian history?
4. Why, according to Jain, is the controversy over the Ayodhya mosque so significant for India's future?
5. In Jain's view, why have the Muslims been satisfied to go along with the secularist policies of the Indian state?
6. What is Jain's vision of India's future?

A specter haunts dominant sections of India's political and intellectual elites — the specter of a growing Hindu self-awareness and self-assertion. Till recently these elites had used the bogey of Hindu "communalism" and revivalism as a convenient device to keep themselves in power and to "legitimize" their slavish imitation of the West. Unfortunately for them, the ghost has now materialized.

Millions of Hindus have stood up. It will not be easy to trick them back into acquiescing in an order which has been characterized not so much by its "appeasement of Muslims" as by its alienness, rootlessness and contempt for the land's unique cultural past. Secularism, a euphemism for irreligion and repudiation of the Hindu ethos, and socialism, a euphemism for denigration and humiliation of the business community to the benefit of ever expanding rapacious bureaucracy, . . . have been major planks of this order. Both have lost much of their old glitter and, therefore, capacity to dazzle and mislead. . . .

The Hindu fight is not at all with Muslims; the fight is between Hindus anxious to renew themselves in the spirit of their civilization, and the state, Indian in name and not in spirit and the political and intellectual class trapped in the debris the British managed to bury us under before they left. The proponents of the Western ideology are using Muslims as auxiliaries and it is a pity Muslim "leaders" are allowing themselves to be so used. . . .

Secularist-versus-Hindu-Rashtra[1] controversy is, of course, not new. In fact, it has been with us since the twenties when some of our forebears began to search for a definition of nationalism which could transcend at once the Hindu-Muslim divide and the aggregationist approach whereby India was regarded as a Hindu-Muslim-Sikh-Christian land. But it has acquired an intensity it has not had since partition.

This intensity is the result of a variety of factors which have cumulatively provoked intense anxiety among millions of Hindus regarding their future and simultaneously given a new sense of strength and confidence to the proponents of Hindu Rashtra. The first part of this story begins, in my view, with the mass conversion of Harijans to Islam in Meenakshipuram in Tamil Nadu in 1981[2] and travels via the rise of Pakistan-backed armed secessionist movements in Punjab and Jammu and Kashmir,[3] and the second part with the spectacular success of the Bharatiya Janata Party (BJP) in the last polls. . . .

---

[1]Hindi for "state" or "polity."

[2]Hindus were incensed when large numbers of low-caste Hindus, or Harijans, were converted to Islam in 1981. It was believed that the missionary campaign was financed by Saudi Arabians.

[3]The Indian states of Punjab, Jammu, and Kashmir were created at the time of independence. With mixed populations of Hindus, Muslims, and Sikhs, they have been plagued by religious conflict and have been a source of bitter conflict between India and Pakistan.

India, to put the matter brusquely, has been a battleground between two civilizations (Hindu and Islamic) for well over a thousand years, and three (Hindu, Muslim and Western) for over two hundred years. None of them has ever won a decisive enough and durable enough victory to oblige the other two to assimilate themselves fully into it. So the battle continues. This stalemate lies at the root of the crisis of identity the intelligentsia has faced since the beginning of the freedom movement in the last quarter of the nineteenth century. . . .

The more resilient and upwardly mobile section of the intelligentsia must, by definition, seek to come to terms with the ruling power and its mores, and the less successful part of it to look for its roots and seek comfort in its cultural past. This was so during the Muslim period; this was the case during the British Raj;[4] and this rule has not ceased to operate since independence.

Thus in the medieval period of our history there grew up a class of Hindus in and around centers of Muslim power who took to the Persian-Arabic culture and ways of the rulers; similarly under the more securely founded and far better organized and managed Raj there arose a vast number of Hindus who took to the English language, Western ideas, ideals, dress and eating habits; . . . they, their progeny and other recruits to their class have continued to dominate independent India.

They are the self-proclaimed secularists who have sought, and continue to seek, to remake India in the Western image. The image has, of course, been an eclectic one; if they have stuck to the institutional framework inherited from the British, they have been more than willing to take up not only the Soviet model of economic development,[5] but also the Soviet theories on a variety of issues such as the nationalities problem and the nature of imperialism and neo-colonialism.

Behind them has stood, and continues to stand, the awesome intellectual might of the West, which may or may not be anti-India, depending on the exigencies of its interests, but which has to be antipathetic to Hinduism. . . .

Some secularists may be genuinely pro-Muslim, . . . because they find high Islamic culture and the ornate Urdu[6] language attractive. But, by and large, that is not the motivating force in their lives. They are driven, above all, by the fear of what they call regression into their own past which they hate and dread. Most of the exponents of this viewpoint have come and continue to come understandably from the Left, understandably because no other group of Indians can possibly be so alienated from the country's cultural past as the followers of Lenin, Stalin and Mao, who have spared little effort to turn their own countries into cultural wastelands.

The state in independent India has, it is true, sought, broadly speaking, to be neutral in the matter of religion. But this is a surface view of the reality. The Indian state has been far from neutral in civilizational terms. It has been an agency, and a powerful agency, for the spread of Western values and mores. It has willfully sought to replicate Western institutions, the Soviet Union too being essentially part of Western civilization. It could not be otherwise in view of the orientation and aspirations of the dominant elite of which Nehru[7] remains the guiding spirit.

Muslims have found such a state acceptable principally on three counts. First, it has agreed to leave them alone in respect of their personal law (the Shariat). . . . Secondly, it has allowed them to expand their traditional . . . educational system in madrasahs[8] attached to mosques.

---

[4]*Raj* Hindi for "reign" or "rule."

[5]Beginning in 1951 the government adopted a series of five-year plans for the nation's economic development in imitation of the five-year plans initiated by Stalin in 1928. The plans featured central planning and state ownership of major enterprises.

[6]Urdu is the primary language of Pakistan and northern India.

[7]Jawaharlal Nehru (1889–1964), India's first prime minister, was a major target of Jain because of his commitment to socialism and secularism.

[8]Madrasahs are advanced schools of learning, or colleges, devoted to Islamic studies.

Above all, it has helped them avoid the necessity to come to terms with Hindu civilization in a predominantly Hindu India. This last count is the crux of the matter. . . .

In the past up to the sixteenth century, great temples have been built in our country by rulers to mark the rise of a new dynasty or to mark a triumph. . . . In the present case, the proposal to build the Rama temple has also helped produce an "army" which can in the first instance achieve the victory the construction can proclaim.

The raising of such an "army" in our democracy, however flawed, involves not only a body of disciplined cadres, which is available in the shape of the RSS,[9] a political organization, which too is available in the Bharatiya Janata Party, but also an aroused citizenry. . . . The Vishwa Hindu Parishad[10] and its allies have fullfilled this need in a manner which is truly spectacular.

The BJP-VHP-RSS leaders have rendered the country another great service. They have brought Hindu interests, if not the Hindu ethos, into the public domain where they legitimately belong. But it would appear that they have not fully grasped the implications of their action. Their talk of pseudo-secularism gives me that feeling. The fight is not against what they call pseudosecularism; it is against secularism in its proper definition whereby man as animal usurps the place of man as spirit. . . .

[9]RSS stands for the Rashtriya Swayamsevak Sangh, a militant Hindu organization founded in 1925 dedicated to the strengthening of Hindu culture.

[10]The Vishwa Hindu Parishad (VHP), or World Hindu Society, was founded in 1964. It is dedicated to demolishing mosques built on Hindu holy sites.

Communism's Retreat

The Cold War era was a time of moral and ideological absolutes. On one side was the communist world, characterized by authoritarian, one-party governments, centralized economic planning, and a commitment to the worldwide triumph of Marxism over capitalism. On the other side was the "free world," a bloc of nations led by the United States, with the goal of defending capitalism and spreading liberal democracy. For more than forty years, these two blocs formed formidable military alliances, built up huge nuclear arsenals, supported giant intelligence establishments, and competed for support among nonaligned nations. For both sides the dualisms of the Cold War — communism versus capitalism, the United States versus the Soviet Union, NATO versus the Warsaw Pact — gave direction and meaning to international politics.

In reality, the Cold War was never completely about ideology. From its start, the United States and its allies propped up dictators when it served their purposes of containing communism. Furthermore, cracks and fissures appeared in both coalitions as early as the 1950s. Anti-Soviet revolts took place in Eastern Europe in 1956 and 1968, and relations between China and the Soviet Union cooled in the mid 1960s. Also in the 1960s, the prospering, stable democracies of Western Europe, inspired by the independent course of France's leader, Charles de Gaulle, no longer unquestioningly accepted U.S. policies concerning military deployment in Europe and U.S. involvement in Vietnam.

There were times when the Cold War seemed about to end, but on each occasion old tensions returned. Peaceful coexistence in the late 1950s gave way to renewed acrimony after the downing of a U.S. spy plane over Soviet territory in 1960, the building of the Berlin Wall in 1961, and the Cuban missile crisis of 1962. U.S.–Soviet relations improved in the 1970s but again deteriorated after the Soviet invasion of Afghanistan in 1979. In the early 1980s, President Ronald Reagan branded the Soviet Union an "evil empire," and Soviet suspicions of the United States deepened. Leaders on both sides showed no sign that they expected anything other than continuing U.S.–Soviet conflict.

By 1991, however, the Cold War was over. In one state after another, communist regimes in Eastern Europe either collapsed or were voted out of power and replaced by democracies. Within the Soviet Union, Premier Mikhail Gorbachev in 1985 initiated policies of glasnost (openness) and perestroika (restructuring) to rejuvenate Soviet society. But his efforts to save communism by democratization and economic liberalization had unexpected results. By the end of 1991, communist rule and the Soviet Union itself had ceased to exist.

Profound changes also took place in communist China. After the death of Mao Zedong in 1976, China, under the leadership of Deng Xiaoping, deemphasized ideology and egalitarianism in favor of pragmatism and economic development. Deng ordered the opening of small private businesses, fostered a market economy in agriculture, opened China to foreign investment, supported scientific and technological education, and encouraged Chinese exports of manufactured goods. The result was economic growth rates of 12 percent annually in the early 1990s. China remained authoritarian and officially communist, but with its commitment to "market socialism," it was far different from the isolated, ideology-driven China of previous decades.

China's New Course

94 ▾ Deng Xiaoping, SPEECHES AND WRITINGS

Of all the events of the late twentieth century, China's full entry into the global economy and its decision to commit itself to economic development may prove to be the most significant. For centuries China was the world's most successful state in terms of size, wealth, technological sophistication, and the continuity of its political institutions. This was easy to forget in the nineteenth and twentieth centuries, when China became a pawn of the Western powers and a victim of political breakdown, military defeat, and deepening poverty. In the 1980s, however, China's leaders set a new course that seems destined to restore China to its preeminence in Asia, if not its primacy among the world's powers.

The man who launched China on its new path was Deng Xiaoping. Born into the family of a well-off landowner in 1904, Deng studied in China and then in France after World War I. He worked in a French factory before returning to China by way of the Soviet Union, where he studied in 1925–1926. On his return to China, he joined the Communist Party and became one of Mao's most loyal followers in the struggle against the Guomindang and the Japanese.

After 1949 Deng became a member of the politburo and party secretary general, with responsibilities for overseeing economic development in southwest China. He supported the strategy of developing China's economy by following the Stalinist model of agricultural collectivization, centralized planning, and investment in heavy industry. This was scrapped in 1958 when Mao instituted the Great Leap Forward. In a little more than two years, some 24,000 People's Communes were established, each containing approximately 30,000 people who performed industrial and agricultural work, received political indoctrination, and participated in various social experiments. The Great Leap Forward was a spectacular failure, and in its wake Deng and other moderates dismantled the communes and reintroduced centralized planning.

This made Deng a prime candidate for vilification after Mao launched the Great Cultural Revolution in 1966. Designed to revive revolutionary fervor and rescue China from materialism and Soviet-style bureaucratization, the revolution unleashed the energies of millions of young people who were urged to rise up and smash "bourgeois" elements throughout society. Deng fell from power, was paraded through the streets in a dunce cap, and was put to work in a mess hall and a tractor repair shop. As the intensity of the Cultural Revolution faded, Deng was reinstated as a party official, and after Mao's death he led the moderates in their struggle with the radical faction led by Mao's widow, Jiang Qing. Deng's faction won, and in December 1978 the Central Committee of the Chinese Communist Party officially abandoned Mao's emphasis on ideology and class struggle in favor of a moderate, pragmatic policy designed to achieve the Four Modernizations in agriculture, industry, science and technology, and the military.

To encourage economic growth, the government fostered free markets, competition, and private incentives. Although Deng claimed that China had entered its "second revolution," it was an economic revolution only. When millions of Chinese demonstrated for democracy in the spring of 1989, the government crushed the demonstration in Beijing with soldiers and tanks, thus assuring the continuation of the party dictatorship. After 1989 Deng withdrew from public life and died in early 1997. The following excerpts are from speeches and interviews given by Deng between 1983 and 1986.

QUESTIONS FOR ANALYSIS

1. According to Deng, what had been the shortcomings of China's economic development planning under Mao Zedong?
2. According to Deng, how is China's new economic policy truly Marxist and truly socialist?
3. How does Deng view China's role in the world? What implications will China's new economic priorities have for its foreign policy?
4. What is Deng's rationale for opposing democracy in China?

MAOISM'S FLAWS

Comrade Mao Zedong was a great leader, and it was under his leadership that the Chinese revolution triumphed. But he made the grave mistake of neglecting the development of the productive forces. I do not mean he didn't want to develop them. The point is, not all of the methods he used were correct. For instance, the people's communes were established in defiance of the laws governing socio-economic development. The most important lesson we have learned, among a great many others, is that we must be clear about what socialism is and how to build it.

The fundamental principle of Marxism is that the productive forces must be developed. The goal for Marxists is to realize communism, which must be built on the basis of highly developed productive forces. What is a communist society? It is a society in which there is vast material wealth and in which the principle of from each according to his ability, to each according to his needs is applied. . . .

Our experience in the 20 years from 1958 to 1978 teaches us that poverty is not socialism, that socialism means eliminating poverty. Unless you are developing the productive forces and raising people's living standards, you cannot say that you are building socialism.

After the Third Plenary Session[1] we proceeded to explore ways of building socialism in China. Finally we decided to develop the productive forces and gradually expand the economy. The first goal we set was to achieve comparative prosperity by the end of the century. . . . So taking population increase into consideration, we planned to quadruple our GNP, which meant that per capita GNP would grow from $250 to $800 or $1,000. We shall lead a much better life when we reach this level, although it is still much lower than that of the developed countries. That is why we call it comparative prosperity. When we attain that level, China's GNP will have reached $1,000 billion, representing increased national strength. And the most populous nation in the world will have shaken off poverty and be able to make a greater contribution to mankind. With a GNP of $1,000 billion as a springboard, within 30 or 50 more years — 50, to be more accurate — China may reach its second goal, to approach the level of the developed countries. How are we to go about achieving these goals? . . . We began our reform in the countryside. The main point of the rural reform has been to bring the peasants' initiative into full play by introducing the responsibility system and discarding the system whereby everybody ate from the same big pot. Why did we start in the countryside? Because that is where 80 per cent of China's population lives. If we didn't raise living standards in the countryside, the society would be unstable. Industry, commerce and other sectors of the economy cannot develop on the basis of the poverty of 80 per cent of the population. After three years of practice the rural reform has proved successful. I can say with assurance it is a good policy. The countryside has assumed a new look. The living standards of 90 per cent of the rural population have been raised. . . .

After our success in rural reform we embarked on urban reform. Urban reform is more complicated and risky. This is especially true in China, because we have no experience in this regard. Also, China has traditionally been a very closed society, so that people lack information about what's going on elsewhere. . . .

It is our hope that businessmen and economists in other countries will appreciate that to help China develop will benefit the world. China's foreign trade volume makes up a very small portion of the world's total. If we succeed in quadrupling the GNP, the volume of our foreign trade will increase considerably, promoting China's economic relations with other countries and expanding its

[1]The Third Plenary Session of Eleventh Central Committee of the Chinese Communist Party, held in December 1978, approved the Four Modernizations Program favored by Deng.

market. Therefore, judged from the perspective of world politics and economics, China's development will benefit world peace and the world economy. . . .

TRUE SOCIALISM

Our modernization programme is a socialist programme, not anything else. All our policies for carrying out reform, opening to the outside world and invigorating the domestic economy are designed to develop the socialist economy. We allow the development of individual economy, of joint ventures with both Chinese and foreign investment and of enterprises wholly owned by foreign businessmen, but socialist public ownership will always remain predominant. The aim of socialism is to make all our people prosperous, not to create polarization. If our policies led to polarization, it would mean that we had failed; if a new bourgeoisie emerged, it would mean that we had strayed from the right path. In encouraging some regions to become prosperous first, we intend that they should help the economically backward ones to develop. Similarly, in encouraging some people to become prosperous first, we intend that they should help others who are still in poverty to become better off, so that there will be common prosperity rather than polarization. A limit should be placed on the wealth of people who become prosperous first, through the income tax, for example. In addition, we should encourage them to contribute money to run schools and build roads, although we definitely shouldn't set quotas for them. We should encourage these people to make donations, but it's better not to give such donations too much publicity.

In short, predominance of public ownership and common prosperity are the two fundamental socialist principles that we must adhere to. We shall firmly put them into practice. And ultimately we shall move on to communism.

SPECIAL ECONOMIC ZONES

In establishing special economic zones[2] and implementing an open policy, we must make it clear that our guideline is just that — to open and not to close.

I was impressed by the prosperity of the Shenzhen[3] Special Economic Zone during my stay there. The pace of construction in Shenzhen is rapid. It is particularly fast in Shekou, because the authorities there are permitted to make their own spending decisions up to a limit of U.S. $5 million. Their slogan is "time is money, efficiency is life." In Shenzhen, it doesn't take long to erect a tall building; the workers complete a storey in a couple of days. The construction workers there are from inland cities. Their high efficiency is due to the "contracted responsibility system," under which they are paid according to their performance, and to a fair system of rewards and penalties.

A special economic zone is a medium for introducing technology, management and knowledge. It is also a window for our foreign policy. Through the special economic zone we can import foreign technology, obtain knowledge and learn management, which is also a kind of knowledge. . . . Public order in Shenzhen is reportedly better than before, and people who slipped off to Hongkong have begun to return. One reason is that there are more job opportunities and people's incomes and living standards are rising, all of which proves that cultural and ideological progress is based on material progress.

[2]The Special Economic Zones were restricted areas where foreign firms could set up businesses and house foreign personnel.

[3]A district next to Hong Kong.

CHINA'S FOREIGN RELATIONS

Reviewing our history, we have concluded that one of the most important reasons for China's long years of stagnation and backwardness was its policy of closing the country to outside contact. Our experience shows that China cannot rebuild itself with its doors closed to the outside and that it cannot develop in isolation from the rest of the world. It goes without saying that a large country like China cannot depend on others for its development; it must depend mainly on itself, on its own efforts. Nevertheless, while holding to self-reliance, we should open our country to the outside world to obtain such aid as foreign investment capital and technology. . . .

CHINA'S POLITICAL FUTURE

The recent student unrest[4] is not going to lead to any major disturbances. But because of its nature it must be taken very seriously. Firm measures must be taken against any student who creates trouble at Tiananmen Square. . . . In the beginning, we mainly used persuasion, which is as it should be in dealing with student demonstrators. But if any of them disturb public order or violate the law, they must be dealt with unhesitatingly. Persuasion includes application of the law. When a disturbance breaks out in a place, it's because the leaders there didn't take a firm, clear-cut stand. This is not a problem that has arisen in just one or two places or in just the last couple of years; it is the result of failure over the past several years to take a firm, clear-cut stand against bourgeois liberalization. It is essential to adhere firmly to the Four Cardinal Principles;[5] otherwise bourgeois liberalization will spread unchecked — and that has been the root cause of the problem. . . .

In developing our democracy, we cannot simply copy bourgeois democracy, or introduce the system of a balance of three powers. I have often criticized people in power in the United States, saying that actually they have three governments. Of course, the American bourgeoisie uses this system in dealing with other countries, but when it comes to internal affairs, the three branches often pull in different directions, and that makes trouble. We cannot adopt such a system. . . .

Without leadership by the Communist Party and without socialism, there is no future for China. This truth has been demonstrated in the past, and it will be demonstrated again in future. When we succeed in raising China's per capita GNP to $4,000 and everyone is prosperous, that will better demonstrate the superiority of socialism over capitalism, it will point the way for three quarters of the world's population and it will provide further proof of the correctness of Marxism. Therefore, we must confidently keep to the socialist road and uphold the Four Cardinal Principles.

We cannot do without dictatorship. We must not only affirm the need for it but exercise it when necessary. Of course, we must be cautious about resorting to dictatorial means and make as few arrests as possible. But if some people attempt to provoke bloodshed, what are we going to do about it? We should first expose their plot and then do our best to avoid shedding blood, even if that means some of our own people get hurt. However, ringleaders who have violated the law must be sentenced according to law. Unless we are prepared to do that, it will be impossible to put an end to disturbances. If we take no action and back down, we shall only have more trouble down the road.

The struggle against bourgeois liberalization is also indispensable. We should not be afraid that it will damage our reputation abroad. China must take its own road and build socialism with Chinese characteristics — that is the only way China can have a future. We must show foreigners that

[4]Deng made these remarks in December 1986, when student demonstrations and speechmaking on behalf of the Pro-Democracy Movement had been going on in Tiananmen Square in Beijing for several years.

[5]Issued by Deng in 1979, the Four Cardinal Principles were (1) the socialist path, (2) the dictatorship of the proletariat, (3) party leadership, and (4) Marxism–Leninism–Mao Zedong thought.

China's political situation is stable. If our country were plunged into disorder and our nation reduced to a heap of loose sand, how could we ever prosper? The reason the imperialists were able to bully us in the past was precisely that we were a heap of loose sand.

A Plan to Save Communism in the Soviet Union

95 ▾ Mikhail Gorbachev, PERESTROIKA

Throughout the 1970s and early 1980s, the Soviet Union was one of the world's two superpowers, with an enormous army, a huge industrial establishment, an impressive record of technological achievement, and a seemingly unshakable authoritarian government. In reality, industrial and agricultural production were stagnating, the people's morale was plummeting, and the fossilized bureaucracy was mired in old policies and theories that no longer worked. Against this background Mikhail Gorbachev became general secretary of the Communist Party in March 1985 and began the task of rejuvenating Soviet communism by introducing policies based on glasnost, or openness, and perestroika, or restructuring.

Gorbachev, who was fifty-four years old when he took power, was born of peasant parents and had studied law and agricultural economics. After filling a variety of positions in the Communist Party, he became a member of the politburo in 1979. In 1987 he published a book, *Perestroika*, from which the following excerpt is taken. In it he describes his goals for Soviet communism. He fell from power in 1991, with his reforms having led not to communism's reform but to its demise and not to the Soviet Union's revival but to its collapse.

QUESTIONS FOR ANALYSIS

1. **What developments in the Soviet Union led Gorbachev to the conclusion that Soviet society and government were in need of reform?**
2. **In Gorbachev's analysis, what caused Soviet society to "lose its momentum"?**
3. **In Gorbachev's view, how will the "individual" in Soviet society be affected by his reforms?**
4. **To what extent is perestroika democratic?**
5. **What similarities and differences do you see between Gorbachev's statements about perestroika and Deng's comments about the needs of China (source 94)?**

Russia, where a great Revolution took place seventy years ago, is an ancient country with a unique history filled with searchings, accomplishments, and tragic events. It has given the world many discoveries and outstanding personalities.

However, the Soviet Union is a young state without analogues in history or in the modern world. Over the past seven decades — a short span in the history of human civilization — our country has traveled a path equal to centuries. One of the mightiest powers in the world rose up to replace the backward semi-colonial and semi-feudal Russian Empire. . . .

At some stage — this became particularly clear in the latter half of the seventies — something happened that was at first sight inexplicable. The country began to lose momentum. Economic failures became more frequent. Difficulties began to accumulate and deteriorate, and unresolved problems to multiply. Elements of what we call stagnation and other phenomena alien to socialism began to appear in the life of society. A kind of "braking mechanism" affecting social and economic development formed. And all this happened at a time when scientific and technological revolution opened up new prospects for economic and social progress. . . .

Analyzing the situation, we first discovered a slowing economic growth. In the last fifteen years the national income growth rates had declined by more than a half and by the beginning of the eighties had fallen to a level close to economic stagnation. A country that was once quickly closing on the world's advanced nations began to lose one position after another. . . .

. . . We spent, in fact we are still spending, far more on raw materials, energy, and other resources per unit of output than other developed nations. Our country's wealth in terms of natural and manpower resources has spoilt, one may even say corrupted, us. . . .

The presentation of a "problem-free" reality backfired: a breach had formed between word and deed, which bred public passivity and disbelief in the slogans being proclaimed. It was only natural that this situation resulted in a credibility gap: everything that was proclaimed from the rostrums and printed in newspapers and textbooks was put in question. Decay began in public morals; the great feeling of solidarity with each other that was forged during the heroic times of the Revolution, the first five-year plans, the Great Patriotic War,[1] and postwar rehabilitation was weakening; alcoholism, drug addiction, and crime were growing; and the penetration of the stereotypes of mass culture alien to us, which bred vulgarity and low tastes and brought about ideological barrenness, increased.

Political flirtation and mass distribution of awards, titles, and bonuses often replaced genuine concern for the people, for their living and working conditions, for a favorable social atmosphere. An atmosphere emerged of "everything goes," and fewer and fewer demands were made on discipline and responsibility. Attempts were made to cover it all up with pompous campaigns and undertakings and celebrations of numerous anniversaries centrally and locally. The world of day-to-day realities and the world of feigned prosperity were diverging more and more. . . .

By saying all this I want to make the reader understand that the energy for revolutionary change has been accumulating amid our people and in the Party for some time. And the ideas of perestroika have been prompted not just by pragmatic interests and considerations but also by our troubled conscience, by the indomitable commitment to ideals which we inherited from the Revolution and as a result of a theoretical quest which gave us a better knowledge of society and reinforced our determination to go ahead.

Today our main job is to lift the individual spiritually, respecting his inner world and giving him moral strength. We are seeking to make the whole intellectual potential of society and all the potentialities of culture work to mold a socially active person, spiritually rich, just, and conscientious. An individual must know and feel that his contribution is needed, that his dignity is not being infringed upon, that he is being treated with trust and respect. When an individual sees all this, he is capable of accomplishing much.

Of course, perestroika somehow affects everybody; it jolts many out of their customary state of calm and satisfaction at the existing way of life. Here I think it is appropriate to draw your attention to one specific feature of socialism. I have in mind the high degree of social protection in our society. On the one hand, it is, doubtless, a benefit and a major achievement of ours. On the other, it makes some people spongers.

[1]World War II.

There is virtually no unemployment. The state has assumed concern for ensuring employment. Even a person dismissed for laziness or a breach of labor discipline must be given another job. Also, wage-leveling has become a regular feature of our everyday life: even if a person is a bad worker, he gets enough to live fairly comfortably. The children of an outright parasite will not be left to the mercy of fate. We have enormous sums of money concentrated in the social funds from which people receive financial assistance. The same funds provide subsidies for the upkeep of kindergartens, orphanages, Young Pioneer[2] houses, and other institutions related to children's creativity and sport. Health care is free, and so is education. People are protected from the vicissitudes of life, and we are proud of this.

But we also see that dishonest people try to exploit these advantages of socialism; they know only their rights, but they do not want to know their duties: they work poorly, shirk, and drink hard. There are quite a few people who have adapted the existing laws and practices to their own selfish interests. They give little to society, but nevertheless managed to get from it all that is possible. . . .

The policy of restructuring puts everything in its place. We are fully restoring the principle of socialism. "From each according to his ability, to each according to his work," and we seek to affirm social justice for all, equal rights for all, one law for all, one kind of discipline for all, and high responsibilities for each. Perestroika raises the level of social responsibility and expectation. . . .

It is essential to learn to adjust policy in keeping with the way it is received by the masses, and to ensure feedback, absorbing the ideas, opinions, and advice coming from the people. The masses suggest a lot of useful and interesting things which are not always clearly perceived "from the top.". . .

The Plenary Meeting encouraged extensive efforts to strengthen the democratic basis of Soviet society, to develop self-government and extend glasnost, that is openness, in the entire management network. We see now how stimulating that impulse was for the nation. Democratic changes have been taking place at every work collective, at every state and public organization, and within the Party. More glasnost, genuine control from "below," and greater initiative and enterprise at work are now part and parcel of our life. . . .

Perestroika means overcoming the stagnation process, breaking down the braking mechanism, creating a dependable and effective mechanism for the acceleration of social and economic progress and giving it greater dynamism.

Perestroika means mass initiative. It is the comprehensive development of democracy, socialist self-government, encouragement of initiative and creative endeavor, improved order and discipline, more glasnost, criticism, and self-criticism in all spheres of our society. It is utmost respect for the individual and consideration for personal dignity.

Perestroika is the all-round intensification of the Soviet economy, the revival and development of the principles of democratic centralism in running the national economy, the universal introduction of economic methods, the renunciation of management by injunction and by administrative methods, and the overall encouragement of innovation and socialist enterprise.

Perestroika means a resolute shift to scientific methods, an ability to provide a solid scientific basis for every new initiative. It means the combination of the achievements of the scientific and technological revolution with a planned economy.

Perestroika means priority development of the social sphere aimed at ever better satisfaction of the Soviet people's requirements for good living and working conditions, for good rest and recreation, education, and health care. It means unceasing concern for cultural and spiritual wealth, for the culture of every individual and society as a whole.

---

[2]A youth organization sponsored by the Soviet regime.

Perestroika means the elimination from society of the distortions of socialist ethics, the consistent implementation of the principles of social justice. It means the unity of words and deeds, rights and duties. It is the elevation of honest, highly-qualified labor, the overcoming of leveling tendencies in pay and consumerism.

I stress once again: perestroika is not some kind of illumination or revelation. To restructure our life means to understand the objective necessity for renovation and acceleration. And that necessity emerged in the heart of our society. The essence of perestroika lies in the fact that it *unites socialism with democracy* and revives the Leninist concept of socialist construction both in theory and in practice. Such is the essence of perestroika, which accounts for its genuine revolutionary spirit and its all-embracing scope.

The goal is worth the effort. And we are sure that our effort will be a worthy contribution to humanity's social progress.

Terrorism in a Global Age

On the morning of September 11, 2001, four U.S. commercial airliners — two from Logan Airport in Boston, and one each from Dulles International Airport in Washington, D.C., and Newark International Airport in New Jersey — were hijacked shortly after departure by members of al-Qaeda, a terrorist organization founded in the 1980s by Osama bin Laden. One of the four jets was commandeered by passengers and crashed in a field in southwestern Pennsylvania with no survivors, but the other three found their targets. One was flown to Washington, D.C., where it crashed into the Pentagon, the symbol of U.S. military might; the other two were flown to New York City, where they smashed into the twin towers of the World Trade Center, the symbol of U.S. capitalism. The twin towers were destroyed, more than 3,000 people were killed, and fighting terrorism became the priority of governments around the world.

Terrorism as a political weapon has a long history. Many histories of the subject begin with the first century C.E., when Roman authorities financed dissidents and malcontents to murder enemies in subject territories or neighboring states, and members of a small Jewish sect assassinated officials and prominent individuals in and around Jerusalem to bring about the end of Roman rule in Palestine. Terrorism's history includes the Persian religious sect, the Assassins, who used murder to end the rule of the Seljuk Turks in Southwest Asia; Catholics who sought to undermine England's Protestant government by plotting to blow up the houses of Parliament in 1605; and European anarchists and radical socialists who assassinated some fifty prominent politicians and heads of state from the late 1800s through the early 1900s. The assassination of Austro-Hungarian Archduke Franz-Ferdinand in July 1914 by a member of the Serbian sect called "Union or Death" led directly to the outbreak of World War I one month later.

After subsiding during and after World War I, terrorism revived after World War II. Beginning in the late 1940s, terrorist acts have taken place in every part of the world and have been carried out by groups espousing many different causes:

anticolonialists in Africa and Asia; left-wing radicals in Europe; Arabs bent on the destruction of Israel; abortion foes in the United States; religious extremists in India, Northern Ireland, Indonesia, and Africa; enemies of apartheid in South Africa; and Chechen separatists in Russia, to name but a few. They also include obscure religious sects such as Aum Shinrikyo, whose members killed twelve and injured thousands when they released sarin gas in the Tokyo subway system in 1995; alienated individuals such as Theodore Kaczynski, the American opponent of technology whose letter bombs killed three and injured twenty-three before his arrest in 1997; and self-proclaimed patriots like Timothy McVeigh, who sought to strike a blow against the "tyranny" of the U.S. government in 1995 when his truck bomb destroyed the federal building in Oklahoma City and killed 168.

In recent decades, terrorism has been identified especially with the Middle East, whose peoples are both victims of terrorism and a major source of recruitment, organizational effort, and financing for terrorist activities around the world. Many Westerners equate terrorism with Islamic fundamentalism and Arab nationalism, but to many Muslims this is a false perception. To them, these "terrorists" are political heroes and martyrs, responding in kind to acts of violence perpetrated by the true terrorists, the leaders and agents of Israel and the United States.

Terrorist bombings, hijackings, kidnappings, and assassinations related to political and religious conflict in the Middle East took more than 1,000 lives from the 1970s through the 1990s, but it was the attack on the World Trade Center and the Pentagon on September 11, 2001, that caused a seismic shift in world politics and made the prevention of terrorism the twenty-first century's first great challenge. The two sources in this section seek to provide insight into the beliefs and values of those who were responsible for that attack.

The Worldview of Osama bin Laden

▼▼▼

96 ▾ Osama bin Laden, *DECLARATION OF JIHAD AGAINST AMERICANS OCCUPYING THE LAND OF THE TWO HOLY MOSQUES*

Osama bin Laden, the founder of al-Qaeda, was born in 1957 in Saudi Arabia, the son of a billionaire owner of a construction company and his tenth or eleventh wife, a cultured Syrian woman. Raised as a Wahhabi Muslim, young Osama led a privileged existence of private schooling, vacations in Scandinavia, and English lessons in Oxford. At seventeen, he enrolled as a civil engineering student at King Abdul Aziz University in Jidda, Saudi Arabia, where he became interested in Islamic theology and forged friendships with Islamic radicals. In 1980 he went to the Pakistani-Afghan border to aid Afghan holy warriors, or mujahideen, who were fighting Soviet troops who had invaded Afghanistan in late 1979 to prop up the pro-Soviet regime. Using his inheritance (perhaps as much as $300 million), he organized an office to provide money and weapons for the thousands of Muslim volunteers who flocked to Afghanistan to fight for their faith; from the mid 1980s onward, he became an active fighter himself. Out of these contacts and activities, al-Qaeda (meaning "the base" in Arabic) began to take shape under bin Laden's direction.

On his return to Saudi Arabia, bin Laden became an outspoken critic of the Saudi regime for its corruption, secularism, and acceptance of the U.S. military presence during and after the first Persian Gulf War. In 1991 he fled to Sudan, where he extended and expanded al-Qaeda to include as many as several thousand agents with cells ranging from the Philippines to the United States. Between 1992 and 1995, al-Qaeda was linked to attacks on U.S. troops in Yemen and Somalia, the bombing of an American-operated Saudi National Guard training center in Riyadh, and unsuccessful plots to assassinate Pope John Paul II, President Bill Clinton, and Egyptian president Hosni Mubarak. Under U.S. pressure the Sudanese government expelled bin Laden in 1996, forcing al-Qaeda to establish a new base in Afghanistan, which was coming under the control of the radical Islamic group known as the Taliban. Between 1996 and 2000, al-Qaeda was responsible for more acts of terrorism, including the car bombing of an apartment building in Dhahran, Saudi Arabia, that killed nineteen U.S. soldiers; the simultaneous bombings of U.S. embassies in Tanzania and Kenya that killed 234 and injured several thousand; and the attack on the USS *Cole* in Aden, Yemen, that killed seventeen U.S. sailors and wounded thirty-nine. After the attacks of September 11, 2001, the United States invaded Afghanistan, ended Taliban rule, and smashed al-Qaeda headquarters and training camps. Bin Laden eluded capture, however, presumably moving to the mountainous region straddling the Pakistani-Afghan border.

Bin Laden has published little and, as leader of a secret terrorist organization, has given few interviews or public speeches. One exception is the speech he delivered to his followers in Afghanistan in August 1996 in which he "declared war" on the United States. Printed in Arabic-language newspapers and audiotaped for worldwide distribution, bin Laden's speech describes his motives and priorities.

QUESTIONS FOR ANALYSIS

1. How does bin Laden perceive the Muslims' place in the world? Who are their main enemies?
2. Why does bin Laden oppose the existing government of Saudi Arabia?
3. What are the goals of the "Zionist-Crusaders alliance," according to bin Laden?
4. What lessons can be learned, according to bin Laden, by the U.S. response to terrorist attacks and military setbacks in Beirut, Aden, and Somalia?
5. Why is bin Laden convinced that Muslims will triumph in their struggle with the United States?
6. What do you perceive as bin Laden's ultimate political and religious goals?

It should not be hidden from you that the community of Islam has suffered from aggression, iniquity and injustice imposed on them by the Zionist-Crusaders alliance and their collaborators; to the extent that the Muslims' blood became the cheapest and their wealth as loot in the hands of the enemies. Their blood was spilled in Palestine and Iraq. The horrifying pictures of the massacre of Qana[1] in Lebanon are still fresh in our memory. Massacres in Tajikistan, Burma, Kashmir, Assam, the Philippines, Fatani, Ogadin, Somalia, Eritrea, Chechnya and in Bosnia Herzegovina[2] took place, massacres that send shivers in the body and shake the conscience. All of this and the world watched and listened, and not only didn't respond to these atrocities, but also with a conspiracy between the USA and its allies and under the cover of the iniquitous United Nations the dispossessed people were even prevented from obtaining arms to defend themselves.

The people of Islam awakened and realized that they are the main target for the aggression of the Zionist-Crusaders alliance. All false claims and propaganda about "Human Rights" were hammered down and exposed by the massacres that took place against the Muslims in every part of the world. The latest and the greatest of these aggressions experienced by the Muslims since the death of the Prophet is the occupation of the land of the two Holy Places,[3] the foundation of the house of Islam, the place of the revelation, the source of the message and the place of the noble Kabah, the Qiblah of all Muslims,[4] by the armies of the American Crusaders and their allies.

Today we work to lift the iniquity that had been imposed on the Umma [the Muslim community] by the Zionist-Crusaders alliance, particularly after they have occupied the blessed land of Jerusalem, route of the journey of the Prophet,[5] . . . and the land of the two Holy Places. . . . We wish to study the means by which we could return the situation [in Saudi Arabia] to its normal path and to return to the people their own rights, particularly after the large damages and the great aggression on the life and the religion of the people. . . .

Injustice had affected the people in industry and agriculture. It affected the people of the rural and urban areas. And almost everybody complains about something. The situation at the land of the two Holy Places became like a huge volcano at the verge of eruption that would destroy the Kuffar[6] and the corruption and its sources. . . .

People are fully concerned about their everyday living; everybody talks about the deterioration of the economy, inflation, ever increasing debts and jails full of prisoners. Government employees with limited income talk about debts of ten thousands and hundred thousands of Saudi Riyals. . . .

Through its course of actions the regime has torn off its legitimacy:

(1) Suspension of the Islamic Sharia law and exchanging it with man-made civil law. . . .

---

[1]In April 1996 the Israelis launched a two-week bombardment of territory in southern Lebanon where the terrorist group Hezbollah was located. On April 18, 100 civilians were killed when the Israelis shelled the battalion headquarters of a UN peacekeeping force where some 800 Lebanese had taken refuge. The Israelis blamed "technical and procedural errors," an explanation questioned by an official UN report.

[2]This is a rather wide-ranging list. The massacres in Assam, a province of northeastern India, were carried out by an Assam separatist group in 1990 and claimed several dozen victims, not all of whom were Muslims. Attacks on Burmese Muslims in the early 1990s were carried out by Buddhists.

[3]Mecca, the birthplace of Muhammad and the site of the Kabah, Islam's holiest shrine, and Medina, the city to which Muhammad and his followers fled in 622 C.E.

[4]The Kabah is the cube-shaped shrine in Mecca; the Qiblah is the direction pointing to the Kabah, toward which Muslims must pray.

[5]Muhammad's miraculous "night journey" took him and the angel Gabriel from Mecca to Jerusalem, from which they ascended into heaven and then returned to Mecca the following morning. They rode a horselike creature, or *Buraq*.

[6]Those who do not believe in God.

(2) The inability of the regime to protect the country and allowing the enemy of the Umma, the American crusader forces, to occupy the land for the longest of years. . . . As a result of the policy imposed on the country, especially in the oil industry where production is restricted or expanded and prices are fixed to suit the American economy, ignoring the economy of the country. Expensive deals were imposed on the country to purchase arms. People are asking what then is the justification for the very existence of the regime?

Quick efforts were made by individuals and by different groups in society to contain the situation and to prevent the danger. They advised the government both privately and openly; they sent letters and poems, reports after reports, reminders after reminders; they explored every avenue and enlisted every influential man in their movement of reform and correction. They wrote in a style of passion, diplomacy and wisdom asking for corrective measures . . . from the "great wrongdoings and corruption" that had engulfed even the basic principles of the religion and the legitimate rights of the people.

But to our deepest regret the regime refused to listen to the people. . . .

The regime is fully responsible for what has been incurred by the country and the nation; however, the occupying American enemy is the principal and the main cause of the situation. Therefore efforts should be concentrated on destroying, fighting and killing the enemy until, by the Grace of Allah, it is completely defeated. . . .

▾ ▾ ▾

It is incredible that our country is the world's largest buyer of arms from the USA and the area's biggest commercial partner of the Americans who are assisting their Zionist brothers in occupying Palestine and in evicting and killing the Muslims there, by providing arms, men and financial support. To deny these occupiers . . . the enormous revenues from their trade with our country is a very important help for our Jihad against them. . . .

We expect the women of the land of the two Holy Places and other countries to carry out their role in boycotting the American goods. If economic boycott is intertwined with the military operations of the Mujahideen [holy warriors], then defeating the enemy will be even nearer, by the Permission of Allah. . . .

▾ ▾ ▾

A few days ago the news agencies had reported that the Defense Secretary[7] of the Crusading Americans had said that "the explosions at Riyadh and Al Khobar[8] had taught him one lesson: that is, not to withdraw when attacked by coward terrorists."

We say to the Defense Secretary that his talk can induce a grieving mother to laughter! . . . Where was this false courage of yours when the explosion in Beirut took place in 1983? You were turned into scattered bits and pieces at that time; 241 marine soldiers were killed.[9] And where was this courage of yours when two explosions made you leave Aden in less than twenty-four hours![10]

But your most disgraceful case was in Somalia;[11] where you moved an international force, including twenty-eight thousand American soldiers. . . . However, when tens of your soldiers were killed in minor battles and one American pilot was dragged in the streets of Mogadishu

[7]William Perry, secretary of defense between 1994 and 1997.

[8]In November 1995 a car bomb in Riyadh at a Saudi National Guard training center killed five Americans; the bombing of Khobar Towers, a U.S. Air Force housing complex in Dhahran, Saudi Arabia, killed nineteen Americans.

[9]President Reagan ordered the withdrawal of marine peacekeepers after a bomb killed 241 marines and navy seamen in October 1983 in Beirut.

[10]The Pentagon withdrew 100 army personnel after the U.S. embassy in Aden was bombed in 1993.

[11]President Clinton ordered the withdrawal of U.S. peacekeepers from Somalia by March 1994 after a clash with Somali warlords in Mogadishu in October 1993 resulted in the deaths of eighteen army rangers.

you left the area carrying disappointment, humiliation, defeat and your dead with you. Clinton appeared in front of the whole world threatening and promising revenge, but these threats were merely a preparation for withdrawal. You have been disgraced by Allah and you withdrew; the extent of your impotence and weaknesses became very clear. . . .

Since the sons of the land of the two Holy Places feel and strongly believe that fighting against the nonbelievers in every part of the world is absolutely essential; then they would be even more enthusiastic, more powerful and larger in number upon fighting on their own land, the place of their births, defending the greatest of their sanctities, the noble Kabah. They know that the Muslims of the world will assist and help them to victory. To liberate their Holy Places is the greatest of issues concerning all Muslims; it is the duty of every Muslim in this world. I say to you William [Perry] that: These youths love death as you love life. They inherit dignity, pride, courage, generosity, truthfulness and sacrifice from father to father. They are most . . . steadfast at war. They inherit these values from their ancestors. . . .

These youths believe in what has been told by Allah and His messenger about the greatness of the reward for the Mujahideen martyrs. . . .

Those youths know that their reward in fighting you, the USA, is double their reward in fighting someone else. They have no intention except to enter paradise by killing you. . . .

In the heat of battle they do not care, and cure the insanity of the enemy by their "insane" courage. Terrorizing you, while you are carrying arms on our land, is a legitimate and morally required duty. It is a legitimate right well known to all humans and other creatures. Your example and our example is like a snake which entered into a house of a man and got killed by him. The coward is the man who lets you walk, while carrying arms, freely on his land and provides you with peace and security.

Those youths are different from your soldiers. Your problem will be how to convince your troops to fight, while our problem will be how to restrain our youths to wait for their turn in fighting. . . . The youths hold you responsible for all of the killings and evictions of the Muslims and the violation of the sanctities, carried out by your Zionist brothers in Lebanon; you openly supplied them with arms and finance. More than 600,000 Iraqi children have died due to lack of food and medicine and as a result of the unjustifiable aggression imposed on Iraq and its nation.[12]

The children of Iraq are our children. You, the USA, together with the Saudi regime are responsible for the shedding of the blood of these innocent children. Due to all of that, whatever treaty you have with our country is now null and void. . . .

It is a duty now on every tribe on the Arab Peninsula to fight in the cause of Allah and to cleanse the land from those occupiers. Allah knows that their blood is permitted to be spilled and their wealth is a booty; their wealth is a booty to those who kill them. . . . Our youths knew that the humiliation suffered by the Muslims as a result of the occupation of their Holy Places cannot be removed except by explosions and Jihad.

---

[12]The alleged victims of economic sanctions imposed on Iraq after the first Persian Gulf War.

The Final Step Toward Martyrdom

97 ▾ *Mohammed Atta, THE LAST NIGHT*

Mohammed Atta was born in a Cairo suburb on September 1, 1968, and died on September 11, 2001, when he flew a hijacked American Airlines passenger jet into one of the towers of the World Trade Center in lower Manhattan. The son of a lawyer, Atta graduated with a degree in architecture from Cairo University. He then moved to Hamburg, Germany, where he was a student at the Technical University and a part-time employee at a Hamburg consulting firm. Devoted to Islam, he made a pilgrimage to Mecca in 1995, and on his return to Hamburg began an Islamic prayer group. At some point he was recruited by al-Qaeda, and by the late 1990s his Hamburg apartment was a regular meeting place for the Hamburg al-Qaeda cell. Late in 1999 it is probable that he met Osama bin Laden at the al-Qaeda leader's base in Afghanistan. In June 2000 Atta entered the United States and attended a flight school in Venice, Florida. In 2001 he briefly visited Germany and Spain and then returned to Florida, where he took additional flying lessons. On the morning of September 11, he and another conspirator drove from their motel in South Portland, Maine, to Portland International Airport, flew to Boston, and boarded American Airlines Flight 11.

It was later discovered that Atta had left behind a bag containing airline uniforms, flight manuals, and a four-page document in Arabic, copies of which were also found in the effects of two of the other terrorists. The document is a list of instructions for the terrorists to review on the night of September 10. Excerpts from these instructions follow.

QUESTIONS FOR ANALYSIS

1. **According to Atta, how should the participants prepare themselves for what lies ahead of them?**
2. **Is Atta totally confident about the success of the mission? What might go wrong, and what can be done to prevent failure?**
3. **What rewards can the participants expect from their anticipated martyrdom?**
4. **What feelings does Atta express about the victims of their actions?**
5. **On the basis of this document, what conclusions can be drawn about Atta's and, by extension, the other participants' motives?**

---

1. Make an oath to die and renew your intentions. Shave excess hair from the body and wear cologne. Shower.[1]

2. Make sure you know all aspects of the plan well, and expect the response, or a reaction, from the enemy.

[1]These are ritual acts of self-purification to prepare oneself for martyrdom and salvation.

3. Read al-Tawba and Anfal[2] and reflect on their meanings and remember all of the things that God has promised for the martyrs.

4. Remind your soul to listen and obey and remember that you will face decisive situations that might prevent you from 100 percent obedience, so tame your soul, purify it, convince it, make it understand, and incite it.

5. Pray during the night and be persistent in asking God to give you victory, control and conquest, and that he may make your task easier and not expose us.

6. Remember God frequently, and the best way to do it is to read the Holy Quran. . . . It is enough for us that it are [*sic*] the words of the Creator of the Earth and the planets, the One that you will meet [on the Day of Judgment].

7. Purify your soul from all unclean things. Completely forget something called "this world." The time for play is over and the serious time is upon us. How much time have we wasted in our lives? Shouldn't we take advantage of these last hours to offer good deeds and obedience?

8. You should feel complete tranquility, because the time between you and your marriage [in heaven] is very short [soon to come]. Afterward begins the happy life, where God is satisfied with you, and eternal bliss "in the company of the prophets, the companions, the martyrs and the good people, who are all good company." Ask God for his mercy and be optimistic. . . .

9. Keep in mind that, if you fall into hardship, how will you act and how will you remain steadfast and remember that you will return to God and remember that anything that happens to you could never be avoided, and what did not happen to you could never have happened to you. . . .

10. Remember the words of Almighty God [lines from the Quran]: "You were looking to the battle before you engaged in it, and now you see it with your own two eyes." Remember: "How many small groups beat big groups by the will of God." And his words: "If God gives you victory, no one can beat you. And if he betrays you, who can give you victory without Him? So the faithful put their trust in God.". . .

12. Bless your body with some verses of the Quran [done by reading verses into one's hands and then rubbing the hands over whatever is to be blessed], the luggage, clothes, the knife, your personal effects, your ID, your passport, and all of your papers.

13. Check your weapon before you leave and long before you leave. (You must make your knife sharp and you must not discomfort your animal during the slaughter.) . . .

THE SECOND STEP

When the taxi takes you to (M) [this initial probably stands for *matar*, airport in Arabic] remember God constantly while in the car. . . .

When you have reached (M) and have left the taxi, say a supplication of place ["O Lord, I ask you for the best of this place, and ask you to protect me from its evils"], and everywhere you go say that prayer and smile and be calm, for God is with the believers. And the angels protect you without you feeling anything. Say this supplication: "God is more dear than all of his creation." And say: "O Lord, protect me from them as you wish." And say: "O Lord, take your anger out on them [the enemy] and we ask you to protect us from their evils." And say: "O Lord, block their vision from in front of them, so that they may not see." And say: "God is all we need, he is the best to rely upon.". . .

All of their equipment and gates and technology will not prevent, nor harm, except by God's will. The believers do not fear such things. The only ones that fear it are the allies of Satan, who are the brothers of the devil. . . . "This is only the Devil scaring his allies" who are fascinated with Western civilization, and have drunk the love [of the West] like they drink water . . . and have be-

[2]The ninth and eighth chapters (surahs) of the Quran, sometimes referred to as the "war chapters"; they describe the need for holy war against Islam's persecutors.

come afraid of their weak equipment "so fear them not, and fear Me, if you are believers.". . .

You must remember your brothers with all respect. No one should notice that you are making the supplication, "There is no God but God," because if you say it 1,000 times no one will be able to tell whether you are quiet or remember God. And among its miracles is what the prophet, peace be upon him, said: Whoever says, "There is no God but God," with all his heart, goes to heaven. The prophet, peace be upon him, said: "If you put all the worlds and universes on one side of the balance, and 'No God but God' on the other, 'No God but God' will weigh more heavily." You can repeat these words confidently, and this is just one of the strengths of these words. . . .

Also, do not seem confused or show signs of nervous tension. Be happy, optimistic, calm because you are heading for a deed that God loves and will accept [as a good deed]. It will be the day, God willing, you spend with the women of paradise. . . .

THE THIRD PHASE

When you ride the (T) [this initial probably stands for *tayyara*, airplane in Arabic], before your foot steps in it, and before you enter it, you make a prayer and supplications. Remember that this is a battle for the sake of God. . . . When the (T) moves, even slightly, toward (Q) [unknown reference], say the supplication of travel. Because you are traveling to Almighty God, so be attentive on this trip. . . .

And then it takes off. This is the moment that both groups come together. So remember God, as he said in his Book: "Oh Lord, pour your patience upon us and make our feet steadfast and give us victory over the infidels.". . . Pray for yourself and all of your brothers that they may be victorious and hit their targets and [unclear] and ask God to grant you martyrdom facing the enemy, not running away from it, and for him to grant you patience and the feeling that anything that happens to you is for him. . . .

When the confrontation begins, strike like champions who do not want to go back to this world. Shout, "Allahu Akbar" ["God is great"], because this strikes fear in the hearts of the nonbelievers. . . . Know that the gardens of paradise are waiting for you in all their beauty, and the women of paradise are waiting, calling out, "Come hither, friend of God." They have dressed in their most beautiful clothing.

If God decrees that any of you are to slaughter, you should dedicate the slaughter to your fathers . . . because you have obligations toward them. . . . If you slaughter, do not cause the discomfort of those you are killing, because this is one of the practices of the prophet, peace be upon him. . . .

Then implement the way of the prophet in taking prisoners. Take prisoners and kill them. As Almighty God said: "No prophet should have prisoners until he has soaked the land with blood. You want the bounties of this world [in exchange for prisoners] and God wants the other world [for you], and God is all-powerful, all-wise."

If everything goes well, every one of you should pat the other on the shoulder in confidence. . . . Remind your brothers that this act is for Almighty God. Do not confuse your brothers or distract them. He should give them glad tidings and make them calm, and remind them [of God] and encourage them. How beautiful it is for one to read God's words, such as: "'And those who prefer the afterlife over this world should fight for the sake of God." And his words: "Do not suppose that those who are killed for the sake of God are dead; they are alive. . . ." And others. Or they should sing songs to boost their morale, as the pious first generations did in the throes of battle, to bring calm, tranquility, and joy to the hearts of his brothers.

. . . When the hour of reality approaches, the zero hour . . . wholeheartedly welcome death for the sake of God. Always be remembering God. Either end your life while praying, seconds before the target, or make your last words: "There is no God but God, Muhammad is his messenger."

Afterward, we will all meet in the highest heaven, God willing. . . .

And may the peace of the God be upon the prophet.

The Promise and Pains of Globalization

Globalization, the process by which different regions of the world come to mutually affect one another economically, politically, or culturally, is nothing new. It began thousands of years ago but intensified in the last five centuries as a result of the European discovery of the Americas, the increase in world trade, European imperialism, the Industrial Revolution, and technological innovations ranging from the development of the caravel by European ship designers in the 1400s to the invention of the telephone and telegraph in the nineteenth century. Developments in the twentieth century accelerated globalization, especially in the 1990s, when the end of the Cold War signaled the triumph of free-market capitalism and when the Internet revolution made it possible for human beings around the globe to instantaneously find information, exchange ideas, transfer capital, make deals, and share cultures seven days a week, twenty-four hours a day.

Mainly a topic for politicians and academics in the 1990s, globalization grabbed international headlines in the fall of 1999 when tens of thousands of globalization opponents disrupted a meeting of the executive council of the World Trade Organization (WTO) being held in Seattle. Subsequent demonstrations against globalization took place at meetings of the WTO, the World Bank, the International Monetary Fund, the Group of Eight industrialized nations, and the World Economic Forum, an annual meeting of senior politicians and business leaders held in Davos, Switzerland. Antiglobalist protesters have an agenda with dozens of items, ranging from specific policies of the World Bank and WTO to exploited labor, job loss, environmental degradation, the ethos of corporate greed, gender inequality, genetically engineered food, Third World poverty, the rights of indigenous people, the plight of small farmers, and much else. More so than any other topic, however, one issue — free trade — has been at the center of the globalization debate.

Free trade has been advocated and opposed by economists ever since the Scottish moral philosopher Adam Smith made his famous defense of laissez faire in his *Wealth of Nations* (1776; see source 31). In the twentieth century, free trade was embraced by the economists, business leaders, and politicians who met at the Bretton Woods Conference in New Hampshire in July 1944 to lay the foundation for the postwar international economy. Convinced that protectionism in the early twentieth century had hindered growth, inflated prices, sharpened national rivalries through trade wars, and contributed to the Great Depression, the delegates sought to create an institutional framework that would achieve economic growth by unleashing capitalism's full potential through free trade. They created the International Monetary Fund, which promotes monetary cooperation and exchange; the World Bank, which makes loans for economic development; and the General Agreement on Tariffs and Trade (GATT), which, until it was replaced by the WTO in 1995, provided rules for settling trade disputes and negotiating reductions in tariffs and trade barriers.

Although tariffs decreased in the 1960s and 1970s as a result of a series of negotiations or "rounds" sponsored by GATT, free trade went out of favor in the 1970s and early 1980s when many states returned to protectionism in response to a worldwide economic slump. In the 1980s, however, with the backing of multinational corporations eager to tap into new markets and with the support of newly elected U.S. and European leaders dedicated to free-market principles, free trade made a comeback. In 1994 the eighth round of GATT-sponsored tariff discussions, the Uruguay Round, resulted in tariff reductions on a broad range of goods and services, including agricultural products. It also established the WTO, which was given authority to investigate grievances, settle disputes, and enforce rules. Also in 1994, Mexico, the United States, and Canada signed the North American Free Trade Agreement (NAFTA), which created a free-trade zone in North America.

Free trade was once more ascendant, and its supporters were confident that a new era of capitalist expansion was at hand. But free trade still had many opponents, and disagreements about its benefits and liabilities continue to be the focus of the larger debate about the future of globalization.

The first two selections in this section give a sense of the arguments made by the opponents and advocates of free trade. Both selections were written in the 1990s, but the issues they raised then continue to be at the center of the economic globalization debates of the twenty-first century. The third is a compilation of statistical data compiled by the World Bank that shed light on world economic development over the past four decades.

The Dangers of NAFTA, GATT, and Free Trade

▼▼▼

98 ▼ *Ralph Nader, FREE TRADE AND THE DECLINE OF DEMOCRACY*

During the nationwide debate preceding the congressional vote on the North American Free Trade Agreement in December 1993, opponents denounced the treaty's economic, political, and environmental implications. A leading critic was Ralph Nader, a lawyer from Connecticut who in the 1960s emerged as a prominent consumer advocate when he published a book, *Unsafe at Any Speed*, about the dangers of flawed automobile design. In the 1970s and 1980s, Nader rallied support for a wide range of consumer and environmental causes and helped found organizations such as the Center for Study of Responsive Law, the Public Interest Research Group, Congress Watch, and the Tax Reform Group. In 2000 he ran for president on the Green Party ticket, receiving 3 percent of the popular vote. The following article was published in 1993 in an anthology, *The Case Against "Free Trade."*

QUESTIONS FOR ANALYSIS

1. **According to Nader, why are multinational corporations so supportive of NAFTA and the new GATT proposals?**
2. **What will be the economic implications of NAFTA for the U.S. economy, according to Nader?**
3. **What, in Nader's view, are the potential political dangers of free trade?**
4. **Why is Nader convinced that there are "no winners" in free trade?**
5. **What is Nader's alternative to an international economy based on free trade?**

Citizens beware. An unprecedented corporate power grab is underway in global negotiations over international trade.

Operating under the deceptive banner of "free" trade, multinational corporations are working hard to expand their control over the international economy and to undo vital health, safety, and environmental protections won by citizen movements across the globe in recent decades.

The megacorporations are not expecting these victories to be gained in town halls, state offices, the U.S. Capitol, or even at the United Nations. They are looking to circumvent the democratic process altogether, in a bold and brazen drive to achieve an autocratic far-reaching agenda through two trade agreements, the U.S.-Mexico-Canada free trade deal (formally known as NAFTA, the North American Free Trade Agreement) and an expansion of the General Agreement on Tariffs and Trade (GATT), called the Uruguay Round.

The Fortune 200's GATT and NAFTA agenda would make the air you breathe dirtier and the water you drink more polluted. It would cost jobs, depress wage levels, and make workplaces less safe. It would destroy family farms and undermine consumer protections such as those ensuring that the food you eat is not compromised by unsanitary conditions or higher levels of pesticides and preservatives.

And that's only for the industrialized countries. The large global companies have an even more ambitious set of goals for the Third World. They hope to use GATT and NAFTA to capitalize on the poverty of Third World countries and exploit their generally low environmental, safety, and wage standards. At the same time, these corporations plan to displace locally owned businesses and solidify their control over developing countries' economies and natural resources. . . .

U.S. corporations long ago learned how to pit states against each other in "a race to the bottom" — to profit from the lower wages, pollution standards, and taxes. Now, through their NAFTA and GATT campaigns, multinational corporations are directing their efforts to the international arena, where desperately poor countries are willing and able to offer standards at 19th century American levels and below.

It's an old game: when fifty years ago the textile workers of Massachusetts demanded higher wages and safer working conditions, the industry moved its factories to the Carolinas and Georgia. If California considers enacting environmental standards in order to make it safer for people to breathe, business threatens to shut down and move to another state.

The trade agreements are crafted to enable corporations to play this game at the global level, to pit country against country in a race to see who can set the lowest wage levels, the lowest environmental standards, the lowest consumer safety standards. . . .

Enactment of the free trade deals virtually ensures that any local, state, or even national effort in the United States to demand that corporations pay their fair share of taxes, provide a decent standard of living to their employees, or limit their pollution of the air, water, and land will be met with the refrain, "You can't burden us like that. If you do, we won't be able to compete. We'll have to close down and move to a country that offers us a more hospitable business climate." This sort of threat is extremely powerful — communities already devastated by plant closures and a declining manufacturing base are desperate not to lose more jobs, and they know all too well from experience that threats of this sort are often carried out.

Want a small-scale preview of the post-GATT and NAFTA free trade world? Check out the U.S.-Mexico border region, where hundreds of U.S. companies have opened up shop during the last two decades in a special free trade zone made up of factories known as *maquiladoras*. . . .

- In Brownsville, Texas, just across the border from Matamoros, a *maquiladora* town, babies are being born without brains in record numbers; public health officials in the area believe there is a link between anencephaly (the name of this horrendous birth defect) and exposure of pregnant women to certain toxic chemicals dumped in streams and on the ground in the *maquiladoras* across the border. Imagine the effect on fetal health in Matamoros itself.
- U.S. companies in Mexico dump xylene, an industrial solvent, at levels up to 50,000 times what is allowed in the United States, and some companies dump methylene chloride at levels up to 215,000 times the U.S. standards, according to test results of a U.S. Environmental Protection Agency certified laboratory. . . .
- Working conditions inside the *maquiladora* plants are deplorable. The National Safe Workplace Institute reports that "most experts are in agreement that *maquila* workers suffer much higher levels of injuries than U.S. workers," and notes that "an alarming number of mentally retarded infants have been born to mothers who worked in *maquila* plants during pregnancies."

Worst of all, the corporate-induced race to the bottom is a game that no country or community can win. There is always some place in the world that is a little worse off, where the living conditions are a little bit more wretched. . . .

. . . "Non-tariff trade barriers," in fact, has become a code phrase to undermine all sorts of citizen-protection standards and regulations. Literally, the term means any measure that is not a tariff and that inhibits trade — for instance restrictions on trade in food containing too much pesticide residue or products that don't meet safety standards. Corporate interests focus on a safety, health, or environmental regulation that they don't like, develop an argument about how it violates the rules of a trade agreement, and then demand that the regulation be revoked. . . .

. . . Already, a Dutch and several U.S. states' recycling programs, the U.S. asbestos ban, the U.S. Delaney clause prohibiting carcinogenic additives to food, a Canadian reforestation program, U.S., Indonesian, and other countries' restrictions on exports of unprocessed logs . . . , the gas guzzler tax, driftnet fishing and whaling restrictions, U.S. laws designed to protect dolphins, smoking and smokeless tobacco restrictions, and a European ban on beef tainted with growth hormones have either been attacked as non-tariff barriers under existing free trade agreements or threatened with future challenges under the Uruguay Round when it is completed. . . .

U.S. citizen groups already have enough problems dealing in Washington with corporate lobbyists and indentured politicians without being told that decisions are going to be made in other countries, by other officials, and by other lobbies that have no accountability or disclosure requirements in the country. . . .

To compound the autocracy, disputes about non-tariff trade barriers are decided not by elected officials or their appointees, but by secretive panels of foreign trade bureaucrats. Only national government representatives are allowed to participate in the trade agreement dispute resolution; citizen organizations are locked out.

. . . As the world prepares to enter the twenty-first century, GATT and NAFTA would lead the planet in exactly the wrong direction. . . . No one denies the usefulness of international trade and commerce. But societies need to focus their attention on fostering community-oriented production. Such smaller-scale operations are more flexible and adaptable to local needs and environmentally sustainable production methods, and more susceptible to democratic controls. They are less likely to threaten to migrate, and they may perceive their interests as more overlapping with general community interests.

Similarly, allocating power to lower level governmental bodies tends to increase citizen power. Concentrating power in international organizations, as the trade pacts do, tends to remove critical decisions from citizen influence — it's a lot easier to get ahold of your city council representative than international trade bureaucrats.

"Globaphobia" Is No Answer

99 ▾ *Gary Burtless, Robert Z. Lawrence, Robert E. Litan, and Robert Shapiro, GLOBAPHOBIA: CONFRONTING FEARS ABOUT OPEN TRADE*

The following defense of free trade was published in 1998 by four economists connected with the Brookings Institution in Washington, D.C. Founded in 1916 and named after a St. Louis businessman who was an early benefactor of the organization, the Brookings Institution maintains a program of research and publication on public policy issues in the areas of foreign relations, economics, and governance. With financial backing from dozens of large corporations and private philanthropists, it supports the work of approximately 100 scholars. Centrist and nonpartisan, the Brookings Institution endeavors to improve the performance of U.S. institutions and the quality of public policy by linking scholarship and decision-making.

QUESTIONS FOR ANALYSIS

1. **What is the focus of the authors' arguments? Are there issues raised by Nader that they ignore?**
2. **Conversely, do the authors make points that Nader failed to mention in his commentary?**
3. **List and briefly explain the benefits that result from free trade, according to the authors.**
4. **The authors concede that some individuals will experience pain as a result of free trade. How and in what way will this occur?**
5. **In your view, who has made the stronger argument, Nader or the Brookings Institution scholars?**

We have written this book to demonstrate that the fear of globalization — or "globaphobia" — rests on very weak foundations. . . .

First, the United States globalized rapidly during the golden years before 1973, when productivity and wages were growing briskly and inequality was shrinking, demonstrating that living standards can advance at a healthy rate while the United States increases its links with the rest of the world. . . .

Second, even though globalization harms some American workers, the protectionist remedies suggested by some trade critics are, at best, short-term palliatives and, at worst, harmful to the interests of the broad class of workers that they are designed to help. Sheltering U.S. firms from imports may grant some workers a short reprieve from wage cuts or downsizing. But protection dulls the incentives of workers and firms to innovate and stay abreast of market developments. As a result, its benefits for individual workers and firms are often temporary. . . .

Third, erecting new barriers to imports also has an unseen boomerang effect in depressing exports. . . . While higher barriers to imports can temporarily improve the trade balance, this improvement would cause the value of the dollar on world exchange markets to rise, undercutting the competitive position of U.S. exports and curtailing job opportunities for Americans in export industries. Moreover, by increasing the costs of input (whether imported or domestic) that producers use to generate goods and services, protection further damages the competitive position of U.S. exporters. This is especially true in high-tech industries, where many American firms rely on foreign-made parts or capital equipment. The dangers of protection are further compounded to the extent it provokes retaliation by other countries. In that event, some Americans who work in exporting industries would lose their jobs, both directly and because higher barriers abroad would induce some of our exporting firms to move their plants (and jobs) overseas. In short, protection is not a zero-sum policy for the United States: it is a *negative sum* policy.

Fourth, globaphobia distracts policymakers and voters from implementing policies that would directly address the major causes of the stagnation or deterioration in the wages of less-skilled Americans. *The most significant problem faced by underpaid workers in the United States is not foreign competition. It is the mismatch between the skills that employers increasingly demand and the skills that many young adults bring to the labor market*. For the next generation of workers, the problem can be addressed by improvements in schooling and public and private training. The more difficult challenge is faced by today's unskilled adults, who find themselves unable to respond to the help wanted ads in daily newspapers, which often call for highly technical skills. It is easy to blame foreign imports for low wages, but doing so will not equip these workers with the new skills that employers need. The role of government is to help those who want to help themselves; most important, by maintaining a high-pressure economy that continues to generate new jobs, and secondarily, by facilitating training and providing effective inducements to displaced workers to find new jobs as rapidly as possible.

Fifth, Americans in fact have a vested interest in negotiating additional reductions of overseas barriers that limit the market for U.S. goods and services. These barriers typically harm the very industries in which America leads the world, including agriculture, financial services, pharmaceuticals, aircraft, and telecommunications. . . .

Sixth, it cannot be stressed too heavily that open trade benefits consumers. Each barrier to trade raises prices not only on the affected imports but also on the domestically produced goods or services with which they compete. Those who would nonetheless have the United States erect barriers to foreign goods — whether in the name of "fair trade," "national security," or some other claimed objective — must face the fact that they are asking the government to tax consumers in order to achieve these goals. . . . By contrast, lowering barriers to foreign goods delivers the equivalent of a tax cut to American consumers, while encouraging U.S. firms to innovate. The net result is higher living standards for Americans at home.

Finally, to ensure support for free trade, political leaders must abandon the argument traditionally used to advance the cause of trade liberalization: that it will generate *more* jobs. Proponents of freer trade should instead stick with the truth. Total employment depends on the overall macroeconomic environment (the willingness and capacity of Americans to buy goods and services) not on the trade balance. . . . We trade with foreigners for the same reasons that we trade among ourselves: to get better deals. Lower trade barriers in other countries mean *better* jobs for Americans. Firms in industries that are major exporters pay anywhere from 5 to 15 percent more than the average national wage. The "price" for gaining those trade opportunities — reducing our own trade barriers — is one that Americans should be glad to pay.

In spite of the enormous benefits of openness to trade and capital flows from the rest of the world and notwithstanding the additional benefits that Americans would derive from further liberalization, it is important to recognize that open borders create losers as well as winners. Openness exposes workers and company owners to the risk of major losses when new foreign competitors enter the U.S. market. Workers can lose their jobs. This has certainly occurred in a wide range of industries exposed to intense foreign competition — autos, steel, textiles, apparel, and footwear. . . . In some cases, workers are forced to accept permanent reductions in pay, either in the jobs they continue to hold in a trade-affected industry or in new jobs they must take after suffering displacement. Other workers, including mainly the unskilled and semiskilled, may be forced to accept small pay reductions as an indirect effect of liberalization. Indeed, the job losses of thousands of similar workers in traded goods industries may tend to push down the wages of *all* workers — even those in the service sector — in a particular skill category. . . .

Among the big winners are the stockholders, executives, and workers of exporting firms such as Boeing, Microsoft, and General Electric, as well as Hollywood (whose movies and television shows are seen around the world). There are many millions of more modest winners as well, including the workers, retirees, and nonworking poor, who benefit from lower prices and a far wider and better selection of products.

One problem in making the case for open borders is that few of the winners recognize the extent of the gains they enjoy as a result of free trade. The losses suffered by displaced workers in the auto, apparel, or shoemaking industries are vividly portrayed on the nightly news, but few Americans realize that cars, clothes, and shoes are cheaper, better made, or more varied as a result of their country's openness to the rest of the world. Workers who make products sold outside the United States often fail to recognize how much their jobs and wages depend on America's willingness to import as well as its capacity to export. People contributing to a pension fund seldom realize that their returns . . . are boosted by the fund's ability to invest overseas, and almost no borrower understands that the cost of a mortgage or car loan is lower because of America's attractiveness to foreigners as a place to invest their money. All of these benefits help improve the standard of living of typical Americans, and they can be directly or indirectly traced to our openness. They are nearly invisible to most citizens, however; certainly far less visible than the painful losses suffered by workers who lose their jobs when a factory is shut down.

Economic Development in the Era of Globalization

100 ▾ *World Bank, WORLD DEVELOPMENT INDICATORS*

The statistics in the following tables provide insight into world economic relationships, the meaning of poverty, and the nature and size of the gap between developed and developing nations from the mid 1960s to 2006. The data were compiled by the World Bank, also known as the International Bank for Reconstruction and Development, one of many international organizations concerned with alleviating world poverty by encouraging economic development. Founded at the Bretton Woods Conference held in New Hampshire in 1944, the World Bank soon became affiliated with the newly established United Nations. Using funds subscribed by United Nations members, the bank makes loans to nations and private businesses for projects that further economic development. Although most loans at first were allocated for post–World War II reconstruction projects, since the 1950s the bank has supported projects mainly in developing nations. Since 2000, the World Bank has sought to contribute to achieving the so-called Millennium Development Goals adopted by 189 member states of the United Nations in September 2000 at the Millennium Summit. Designed to "free all men, women, and children from the abject and dehumanizing conditions of extreme poverty," the eight goals to be achieved by 2015 include: eradicating extreme poverty and hunger; achieving universal primary education; promoting gender equality and empowering women; reducing child mortality; improving maternal health; combating HIV/AIDS, malaria and other diseases; ensuring environmental sustainability; and developing a global partnership for economic development.

Since 1978 the World Bank has published annually its *World Development Report*, which contains commentary on development strategy and statistics on economic, demographic, fiscal, and educational trends. Since 2001 most of the statistical data have been published separately as *World Development Indicators*.

The World Bank draws on a wide range of sources for the information in its annual reports, including reports from governments, United Nations agencies, and nongovernmental organizations. Inevitably, in any given year, some data may be missing due to a nation's refusal to cooperate or its inability to do so because of conflict. Furthermore, many factors affect the reliability of the submitted data, including weak statistical methods used by some governments, differences in coverage, and disagreements over key definitions. Despite such difficulties, the data provided by the World Bank allow us to make broad comparisons over time.

Of the more than 100 nations covered in the World Bank reports, 29 have been included in the following tables. They represent all the world's regions and range from some of the world's poorest states to the some of the richest. The tables provide data on eight topics:

1. Population.

2. Per capita Gross Domestic Product (GDP), a number calculated by dividing a country's population into the Gross Domestic Product (or Gross National Income), the value of all goods and services produced within a country in a given time. Such information gives a broad idea of a country's standard of living, but is not necessarily an accurate gauge of the prevalence of poverty. For this, further information about wealth distribution would be needed.

3. Life expectancy.

4. Infant mortality. This measures the number of infants per one thousand who die before their first birthday.

5. Literacy of adults aged fifteen years or older. Literacy is defined as the ability to read and write simple sentences about one's daily life experiences.

6. Per capita energy consumption, a number calculated by converting a country's total energy consumption into the equivalent of the energy produced by one kilogram of oil, and then dividing it by the country's population.

7. Percentage of population with access to an improved water source. An improved source of water refers to a household connection, public standpipe, borehole, protected well or spring, or rainwater collection able to provide a minimum of 20 liters of water a day not more than one kilometer from one's dwelling.

8. Percentage of population with access to improved sanitation facilities. Improved sanitation facilities are capable of effectively preventing human, animal, and insect contact with human waste. They may range from simple, protected pit latrines to flush toilets with sewerage connection.

QUESTIONS FOR ANALYSIS

1. What population trends are revealed in the tables?
2. To what extent do the tables reveal uneven development among the world's major regions?
3. Does the information in the tables suggest that the gap between rich and poor nations is getting larger or smaller?
4. For those nations that have not achieved significant economic progress, what insights do the tables provide into reasons for their lack of success?
5. What information do the tables provide on the relationship between economic growth and environmental quality?
6. On the basis of the information in the tables, would it appear that things are getting better or worse for humankind?

Table 1
Population (millions)

	1976	1990	2005
Brazil	110	150.4	186
Canada	23.2	26.5	32
Chile	10.5	13.2	16
China	835.8	1,337.7	1,305
Congo, Democratic Republic	25.4	37.3	58
Egypt	38.1	52.1	74
Ethiopia	28.7	51.2	71
Ghana	10.1	14.9	22
Guatemala	6.5	9.2	13
Haiti	4.7	6.5	9
India	620.4	849.5	1,095
Indonesia	135.2	178.2	221
Israel	3.6	3.9	7
Italy	56.2	57.7	57
Japan	112.8	123.5	128
Mali	5.8	8.5	14
Mexico	62	86.2	103
Nigeria	77.1	115.5	132
Poland	34.3	38.2	38
Sierra Leone	3.1	4.1	6
South Africa	26	35.9	45
South Korea	36	42.8	48
Switzerland	6.4	6.7	7
Syria	7.7	12.4	19
Thailand	43	55.8	64
Uganda	11.9	16.3	29
United Kingdom	56.1	57.4	60
United States	215.1	250	296
Zimbabwe	6.5	9.8	13

Table 2
GDP per Capita (U.S. dollars)

	1976	1990	2005
Brazil	1,140	2,680	3,550
Canada	7,510	20,440	32,590
Chile	1,050	1,770	5,870
China	410	370	1,740
Congo, Democratic Republic	140	220	120
Egypt	280	600	1,260
Ethiopia	100	120	160
Ghana	580	390	450
Guatemala	630	900	2,400
Haiti	150	370	450
India	150	350	730
Indonesia	240	570	1,280
Israel	3,920	9,700	18,580
Italy	3,050	18,520	30,250
Japan	4,910	26,930	38,950
Mali	100	270	380
Mexico	1,090	2,010	7,310
Nigeria	380	290	560
Poland	2,860	1,790	7,610
Sierra Leone	200	240	220
South Africa	1,340	2,560	4,960
South Korea	670	5,400	15,840
Switzerland	8,850	33,160	55,320
Syria	780	980	1,380
Thailand	380	1,420	2,720
Uganda	240	220	280
United Kingdom	4,020	9,790	37,740
United States	7,890	22,240	43,560
Zimbabwe	550	640	350

Table 3
Life Expectancy at Birth

	1960	1977	2005
Brazil	57	62	66
Canada	71	74	77
Chile	57	67	72
China	53	64	70
Congo, Democratic Republic	40	46	44
Egypt	46	54	71
Ethiopia	36	39	43
Ghana	40	48	55
Guatemala	47	57	63
Haiti	42	51	53
India	43	51	64
Indonesia	41	48	68
Israel	69	72	80
Italy	69	73	80
Japan	68	76	82
Mali	37	42	49
Mexico	58	65	75
Nigeria	39	48	44
Poland	66	71	75
Sierra Leone	37	46	41
South Africa	53	60	48
South Korea	54	63	78
Switzerland	71	74	81
Syria	48	57	74
Thailand	51	61	71
Uganda	44	53	49
United Kingdom	70	73	76
United States	70	73	76
Zimbabwe	45	52	59

Table 4
Adult Literacy Rate (% over 15 years old)

	1974	1990	2006	
			Males	Females
Brazil	64	81	88	89
Canada	98	95+	*[1]	*
Chile	90	93	96	96
China	[2]—	73	95	87
Congo, Democratic Republic	15	61[3]	81	54
Egypt	40	48	83	59
Ethiopia	—	—	—	—
Ghana	25	60	66	50
Guatemala	47	55	75	63
Haiti	20	53	—	—
India	36	48	73	48
Indonesia	62	77	94	87
Israel	84	—	*	*
Italy	98	95+	*	*
Japan	99	95+	*	*
Mali	10	32	27	12
Mexico	76	87	92	90
Nigeria	—	51	—	—
Poland	98	—	*	*
Sierra Leone	15	21	47	24
South Africa	—	—	84	81
South Korea	92	96	*	*
Switzerland	99	95+	*	*
Syria	53	64	86	74
Thailand	82	93	95	91
Uganda	25	48	77	58
United Kingdom	98	*	*	*
United States	99	*	*	*
Zimbabwe	—	63	—	—

[1]* = Literacy rates above 95%.
[2]— = No data available.
[3]1985 data.

Table 5

Infant Mortality Rate per 1,000 Live Births

	1970	1990	2005
Brazil	95	50	31
Canada	19	7	5
Chile	78	18	8
China	69	38	23
Congo, Democratic Republic	141	129	129
Egypt	158	71	76
Ethiopia	158	122	80
Ghana	111	75	68
Guatemala	100	60	32
Haiti	141	102	84
India	137	80	56
Indonesia	118	60	28
Israel	20	10	5
Italy	30	8	4
Japan	13	5	3
Mali	204	140	120
Mexico	72	37	22
Nigeria	139	120	100
Poland	33	19	6
Sierra Leone	197	175	165
South Africa	79	45	55
South Korea	51	8	5
Switzerland	15	7	4
Syria	96	31	14
Thailand	27	31	18
Uganda	109	93	79
United Kingdom	19	8	5
United States	20	9	6
Zimbabwe	96	53	81

[1]Figure for 1965.

Table 6

Per Capita Energy Consumption (kilograms of oil equivalent)

	1965	1990	2004
Brazil	286	897	1,114
Canada	6,007	7,534	8,411
Chile	652	1,067	1,732
China	178	763	1,242
Congo, Democratic Republic	74	425	274
Egypt	313	573	783
Ethiopia	10	296	303
Ghana	76	345	386
Guatemala	150	504	616
Haiti	24	231	262
India	100	426	531
Indonesia	91	548	800
Israel	1,574	2,599	3,049
Italy	1,568	2,610	3,171
Japan	1,474	3,610	4,173
Mali	14	—	—
Mexico	605	1,494	1,622
Nigeria	34	783	769
Poland	2,027	2,260	2,403
Sierra Leone	100	—	—
South Africa	1,744	2,592	2,829
South Korea	238	2,161	4,431
Switzerland	2,501	3,724	3,672
Syria	212	909	903
Thailand	82	803	1,524
Uganda	36	—	—
United Kingdom	3,481	3,686	3,906
United States	6,535	7,722	7,921
Zimbabwe	441	888	719

Table 7
Access to Improved Water Source (% of population)

	1990	2004
Brazil	83	89
Canada	100	100
Chile	90	95
China	70	77
Congo, Democratic Republic	43	46
Egypt	94	98
Ethiopia	23	22
Ghana	55	75
Guatemala	79	95
Haiti	47	54
India	70	86
Indonesia	72	77
Israel	100	100
Italy	100	100
Japan	100	100
Mali	34	50
Mexico	82	97
Nigeria	49	48
Poland	—	—
Sierra Leone	—	57
South Africa	83	88
South Korea	—	92
Switzerland	100	100
Syria	80	93
Thailand	95	98
Uganda	44	60
United Kingdom	100	100
United States	100	100
Zimbabwe	78	81

Table 8

Access to Improved Sanitation Facilities (% of population)

	1990	2004
Brazil	70	75
Canada	100	100
Chile	84	91
China	23	44
Congo, Democratic Republic	16	30
Egypt	54	70
Ethiopia	3	13
Ghana	58	83
Guatemala	50	61
Haiti	24	30
India	14	33
Indonesia	52	72
Israel	96	96
Italy	100	100
Japan	100	100
Mali	36	46
Mexico	58	79
Nigeria	39	44
Poland	—	—
Sierra Leone	—	39
South Africa	69	65
South Korea	69	95
Switzerland	100	100
Syria	73	90
Thailand	80	99
Uganda	42	43
United Kingdom	100	100
United States	100	100
Zimbabwe	50	33

Sources

Prologue

(1) From E. G. Ravenstein, ed. and trans., *A Journal of the First Voyage of Vasco da Gama, 1497–1499* (Hakluyt Society, 1898), First Series, No. 99. Reproduced by Burt Franklin, 1963, pp. 77–78. Modernized by A. J. Andrea. (2) *Travels in Asia and Africa, 1325–1354*, H. A. R. Gibb, trans. (New York: Robert M. McBride & Co., 1929), pp. 234–237, passim. Modernized by A. J. Andrea. (3) From Ma Huan, Ying-Yai Sheng-Lan, *The Overall Survey of the Ocean's Shores* [1433], J. V. G. Mills, trans. The Hakluyt Society at the University Press, 1970, pp. 138–143, passim. Romanization to Pinyin style from Wade Giles by A. J. Andrea. (4) *The Catalan World Atlas*, © British Library, London, UK / The Bridgeman Art Library.

Part One ▾ A New Era of Interaction and Exchange: The Fifteenth Through Seventeenth Centuries

Chapter 1

Source 1: From *The Reformation Writings of Martin Luther*, Vol. 1, *The Basis of the Protestant Reformation*, translated and edited by Bertram Lee Woolf (London: Lutterworth Press, 1953). Reprinted with permission of Lutterworth Press. **Source 2:** Lucas Cranach, *Two Kinds of Preaching: Evangelical and Papal*, Bildarchiv Preussischer Kulturbesitz / Art Resource, NY. **Source 3:** From Gerald Strauss, ed., *Manifestations of Discontent in Germany on the Eve of the Reformation*, Indiana University Press, 1971, pp. 21–23, 27, 28. Reprinted with permission. Martin Luther, *Selections from His Writings*, John Dillenberger, ed. (New York: Anchor Doubleday, 1962), 481, 482. **Source 4:** Lodorico Guicciardini, *Omnium Belgii sive inferioris Germaniae regionum descriptio* (Amsterdam: Guiljemus Jansonius, 1613). Overfield. **Source 5:** From *Della Famiglia*, Guido Guarino, trans. and editor, 1971, pp. 120–124, 216–219. Reprinted by permission of Bucknell University Press. **Source 6:** Courtesy of Schlossmuseum Gotha, Gotha, Germany. **Source 7:** From *Discoveries and Opinions of Galileo* by Galileo Galilei, translated by Stillman Drake, Copyright © 1957 by Stillman Drake. Used by permission of Doubleday, a division of Random House, Inc. **Source 8:** James Spedding, R. L. Ellis, and Douglas Heath, eds., *The Works of Francis Bacon* (New York: Hurd and Houghton, 1864), vol. 10, pp. 67–69, 72–75, 131–132, 140–142.

Multiple Voices I

(1) From Cecil Jane, ed. and trans., *Selected Documents Illustrating the Four Voyages of Columbus*, 2 vols. (London: Hakluyt Society, 1930–1933), 1: 2–18. The Hakluyt Society was established in 1846 for the purpose of printing rare or unpublished Voyages and Travels. For further information please see their website at: www.hakluyt.com. (2) Anonymous, Woodcut of 1505. Bayerische Staatsbibliothek, Munchen. (3) "Democrates Secundus, or the Just Causes of War Against the Indians," pp. 118–120 from *The Spanish Tradition in America*, edited by Charles Gibson. Compilation, Introduction, Notes, and Translations by the editor Copyright © 1968 by Charles Gibson. Reprinted by permission of HarperCollins Publishers. (4) From *In Defense of the Indians*, ed. and trans. by Stafford Poole, University of Northern Illinois Press, 1992. Reprinted with permission of Northern Illinois University Press. (5) Bibliotheque Nationale, Paris, France, Giraudon/The Bridgeman Art Library International.

Chapter 2

Source 9: Ogier Ghiselin de Busbecq, *The Life and Letters of Ogier Ghiselin de Busbecq* (London: Kegan Paul, 1881), pp. 113–120 (passim), 153–155, 218–220, 254. **Source 10:** Abbas I: Eskandar Beg Monshi, *History of Shah Abbas the Great*, Roger Savory, trans. (Boulder: Westview Press, 1978), 517–525. Reprinted with permission of the author. **Source 11:** David Price, trans., *Memoirs of the Emperor Jahangir Written by Himself* (London: Oriental Translation Society, 1928), pp. 8–12, 13–20, 33–36, 51–53, 65–66. **Source 12:** John J. Saunders, ed., *The Muslim World on the Eve of Europe's Expansion* (Englewood Cliffs, NJ: Prentice Hall, 1966), pp. 41–43. **Source 13:** Abul Fazl, *The Ain-I-Akari*, ed. and trans. by H. S. Jarrett (Calcutta, India: Baptist Mission Press, 1868–1894), vol. 3, pp. 8, 114–119, 159–160, 225–232, 279, 284, 285–286, 291–292. **Source 14:** From Judith E. Tucker, *In The House of the Law Gender and Islamic Law in Ottoman Syria and Palestine*, 1988, pp. 26, 47, 68, 69, 78, 83, and 165. Reprinted with permission of The University of California Press.

Chapter 3

Source 15: From *Self and Society & Ming Thought*, by William Theodore de Bary. Copyright © 1970 Columbia University Press. Reprinted with permission of the publisher. **Source 16:** David J. Lu, *Japan: A Documentary History* (New York: M. E. Sharpe, 1997), pp. 258–261. Translation copyright © 1997 by David J. Lu. Reprinted with permission of M. E. Sharpe, Inc. **Source 17:** Reprinted with the permission of The Free Press, a Division of Simon & Schuster Adult Publishing Group, from *Chinese Civilization and Society* by Patricia Buckley Ebrey. Copyright © 1981 by The Free Press. All rights reserved. **Source 18:** Reprinted with permission of The Free Press, a Division of Simon & Schuster Adult Publishing Group, from *Chinese Civilization and Society* by Patricia Buckley Ebrey. Copyright © 1993 by Patricia

Buckley Ebrey. All rights reserved. **Source 19:** From *Japan: A Documentary History*, ed. and trans. David J. Lu (Armonk, NY: M. E. Sharpe, 1997), p. 191. Translation copyright © 1997 by David J. Lu. Reprinted with permission of M. E. Sharpe, Inc.

Multiple Voices II

(1) Excerpted from George Ellison, *Deus Destroyed: The Image of Christianity in Early Modern Japan* (Cambridge: Harvard University Council on East Studies, 1988), pp. 115–118. Copyright © The President and Fellows of Harvard College, 1973. Reprinted with permission of the Harvard University Asian Center. **(2)** From *China in the Sixteenth Century* by Matthew Ricci, translated by Louis J. Gallagher S.J. Copyright 1942, 1953 and renewed 1970 by Louis J. Gallagher, S.J. Used by permission of Random House, Inc. **(3)** From *A Chronicle of the Carmelites in Persia and the Papal Mission of the XVII and XVII Centuries* (London: Eyre and Spottiswoode, 1939), 160, 161.

Chapter 4

Source 20: Basil Davidson, trans., *The African Past* (London: Curtis Brown, Ltd., 1964). **Source 21:** George McCall Theal, ed. and trans. *Records of South-Eastern Africa* (London: F. W. Clowes for the Government of the Cape Colony, 1898), vol. 7., pp. 293–300. **Source 22:** The selections here from Book Twelve are translated from the Nahuatl by James Lockhart and appear in the book he edited, *We People Here: Nahuatl Accounts of the Conquest of Mexico*, University of California Press, 1993. Reprinted with permission of the author. **Source 23:** From David Pieterzen DeVries, *Voyages from Holland to America* (New York: Billin and Brothers, 1853), pp. 114–117. **Source 24:** From "Life and Labor in Ancient Mexico," *The Brief and Summary Relation of the Lords of New Spain*, Benjamin Keen, ed. and trans., Rutgers University Press, 1963, pp. 203, 204, 207–212 (passim), 219, 220, 223, 237–240 (passim). Reprinted with permission of Patricia Keen and Gail Keen. **Source 25:** Excerpt from Antonio Vazquez de Espinosa, *Description of the Indies*, c. 1620, trans. by Charles Upson Clark, Smithsonian Institution Press, 1968.

Part Two ▾ A World of Transformation and Tradition: Mid Seventeenth to Early Nineteenth Century

Chapter 5

Source 26: From Bossuet, *Politique tirée des paroles de l'Ecriture sainte* in *Oeuvres choisies de Bossuet* 5 vols. (Paris: Hachette, 1897–1901), vol. 2. trans. by James H. Overfield. **Source 27:** *The Statutes: Revised Edition* (London: Eyre and Spottiswoode, 1871), vol. 1, pp. 10–12. **Source 28:** Marte Blinoff, *Life and Thought in Old Russia* (University Park: Pennsylvania State University Press, 1961), pp. 49–50; Eugene Schuyler, *Peter the Great*, vol. 2, pp. 176–177; L. Jay Oliva, *Peter the Great* (Englewood Cliffs, NJ: Prentice-Hall, 1970), p. 50; George Vernadsky et al., *A Source Book for Russian History from Early Times to 1917*, vol. 2 (New Haven and London: Yale University Press, 1972), pp. 347, 329, 357. **Source 29:** (1 and 2, illustrations) Sébastian Le Clerc, *The Royal Academy and Its Protectors* and *A Dissection at the Jardin des Plantes*. Courtesy of The Bancroft Library, University of California at Berkeley. **Source 30:** From *Les Philosophes* by Norman L. Torrey, Copyright © 1960 by Norman L. Torrey. Used by permission of G. P. Putnam's Sons, a division of Penguin Group (USA) Inc. **Source 31:** Adam Smith, *An Inquiry into the Nature and Causes of the Wealth of Nations* (Hartford, CT: Cooke and Hale, 1818), vol. 7, pp. 10–12, 40, 43, 299–304, 316, 317, 319, 330, 331. **Source 32:** "Declaration of the Rights of Man and of the Citizen," in J. B. Buchez and P.-C. Roux, *Histoire parlementaire de la revolution francaise* (Paris: Librarie Paulin, 1834), vol. 11, pp. 404–406. **Source 33:** (1) From Leo Gershoy, ed., *The Era of the French Revolution 1789–1799,* Van Nostrand, 1957, pp. 152, 156, 157, 161, 162, and 163. Reprinted with permission of Krieger Publishing Company. (2) Translated from original text: Rapport et décrêt, du 23 août, l'an II de la République, sur la requisition civique des jeunes citoyens pour la defense de la Patrie (Paris: 1793). (3) Translated from original text in F. A. Aulard, *Recueil des actes du Comite de salut public, avec la correspondance officielle des representants en mission et le registre du Conseil executif provisoire* (Paris, Imprimerie nationale, 1889–1951) XIII, 546. (4) Translated from *Rapport fait à la Convention nationale . . . dans la séance de du 13 prairial* (Paris: 1794). **Source 34:** Thomas Paine, *The Political Writings of Thomas Paine* (New York: Solomon King, 1830), vol. 1, pp. 21, 22, 25, 28, 29, 31, 33–35, 40–47. **Source 35:** From Simón Bolívar, *Selected Writings*, ed., Harold A. Bierck, Jr., trans. by Lewis Bertrand, 1951, pp. 103–122.

Multiple Voices III

(1) John Wesley, *Thoughts Upon Slavery,* in *The Works of John Wesley*, Thomas Jackson, ed. (14 vols.: 3rd ed.). London: Wesleyan Methodist Book Room, 1872, Volume XI, pp. 59–79. **(2)** Lynn Hunt, ed., *The French Revolution and Human Rights* (Boston: Bedford/St. Martin's, 1999), 107, 108. Reproduced with permission of Palgrave Macmillan. **(3)** W. S. van Ryneveld, Response to Governor Macartney's Questionnaire, November 29, 1797, reprinted in Andre Du Toit and Hermann Giliomee, eds., *Afrikaner Political Thought* (Berkeley: University of California Press, 1983), pp. 46–49. **(4)** Joseph Dupuis, *Journal of a Residence in Ashantee, Comprising Notes and Researches Relative to the Gold Coast, and the Interior of Western Africa*.... (London: Henry Colburn, 1824), 162–164.

Chapter 6

Source 36: Paul Edwards, ed. and trans., *Equiano's Travels* (Oxford: Heinemann Educational Books, 1967), pp. 25–42. **Source 37:** Thomas Phillips, "A Journal of a Voyage Made in the Hannibal of London in 1694," in Elizabeth Donnan, ed., *Documents Illustrative of the History of the Slave Trade to America* (Washington, D.C.: Carnegie Institute, 1930), pp. 399–410. **Source 38:** From Walter L. Wright, *The Book of Counsel for Viziers and Governors*. Princeton University Press, 1935, pp. 88–89, 95, 96, 102–106, 111, 112, and 126. Reprinted by permission of Princeton University Press. **Source 39:** (1) Joseph Francois Dupleix, "Memorandum to the Directors of the French East India Company" from Virginia Thompson, *Dupleix and His Letters* (New York: Baillou: 1933), 801–202. (2) Robert Clive in a letter to William Pitt, in John Malcolm, *The Life of Robert, Lord Clive* (London: John Murray, 1836), vol. 2, pp. 119–125. **Source 40:** J. O'Kinealy, "Translation of an Arabic Pamphlet on the History and Doctrines of the Wahhabis, Written by 'Abdullah, Grandson of 'Abdul Wahhab, the Founder of the Wahhabis," Journal of the Asiatic Society of Bengal, vol. 43 (1874), pp. 68–82. **Source 41:** Usman dan Fodio, "The Book of Differences," from M. Hiskett, "Kitab al-farq: A Work on the Habe Kingdoms Attributed to Uthmann dan Fodio," in *Bulletin of the School of Oriental and African Studies*, vol. 23 (1960); "Concerning the Government of Our Country," from Tanbih al-ikhwan, translation in Thomas Hodgkin, *Nigerian Perspectives* (Oxford: Oxford University Press, 1975), pp. 244, 245; "Light of Intellectuals," from Nur al-albab, in Hodgkin, pp. 254–255; "Dispatch to the Folk of the Sudan," from A. D. H. Bivar, "The Whatiqat ah al-Sudan: A Manifesto of the Fulani Jihad," in *The Journal of African History*, vol. 2 (1961).

Chapter 7

Source 42: From *Emperor of China* by Jonathan D. Spence, Copyright © 1974 by Jonathan D. Spence. Used by permission of Alfred A. Knopf, a division of Random House, Inc. **Source 43:** Sir Henry Dundas in a letter to Lord George Macartney, Cheng Pei-kai, and Michael Lestz, in *The Search for Modern China: A Documentary Collection* (New York: W. W. Norton & Co., 1999), pp. 92–98. **Source 44:** Emperor Qianlong, "Edict on Trade with Great Britain," in J. O. P. Brand, *Annals and Memoirs of the Court of Peking* (Boston: Houghton Mifflin, 1914), pp. 325–331. **Source 45:** From *Sources of Japanese Tradition*, by William Theodore de Bry. Copyright © 1966 Columbia University Press. Reprinted with permission of the publisher. **Source 46:** Excerpts from Donald Keene, *The Japanese Discovery of Europe, 1720–1830*, Revised Edition. Copyright © 1952 and 1969 by Donald Keene. Used with the permission of Stanford University Press, www.sup.org.

Multiple Voices IV

(1) illustration: *Qianlong at Leisure*, The Palace Museum, Beijing, China. (2) illustration: *Taking Stag*, The Palace Museum, Beijing, China. (3) illustration: *Qianlong in His Study*, The Palace Museum, Beijing, China. (4) *Bonaparte Crossing the Alps*, Musee Nat. du Chateau de Malmaison, Rueil-Malmaison, France, Lauros / Giraudon / The Bridgeman Art Library International. (5) *Napoleon in His Study*, Private Collection, Lauros / Giraudon / The Bridgeman Art Library International.

Part Three ▾ The World in the Age of Western Dominance: 1800–1914

Chapter 8

Source 47: "Report from the Committee on the Bill to Regulate the Labour of Children in the Mills and the Factories in the United Kingdom," *British Sessional Papers*, vol. 15 (London, 1832), pp. 195, 196; "Second Report of the Commission of Inquiry into the Employment of Children in Factories," *British Sessional Papers*, vol. 21, pt. D-3 (London, 1833), pp. 26–28; "First Report of the Commission of Inquiry into the Employment of Children in Mines," *British Sessional Papers*, vol. 16 (London, 1842), pp. 149, 230, 258, 263–264. **Source 48:** Otto von Leixner, *Soziale Briefe aus Berlin* (Berlin: F. Pfeilstücker, 1891), trans. James H. Overfield. **Source 49:** Karl Marx and Friedrich Engels, *The Manifesto of the Communist Party*, authorized English trans. by Samuel Moore (London: W. Reeves, 1888). **Source 50:** Charles Darwin, "On the Origin of Species" in Charles Darwin, *The Origin of Species* (New York: Appleton and Company, 1896), pp. 75–78; and Charles Darwin, *The Descent of Man* (New York: Appleton and Company, 1896), pp. 62–63, 164–165, 613, 616–617. **Source 51:** Gerda Lerner, ed., *The Female Experience: An American Documentation* (Indianapolis, IN: Bobbs Merrill, 1977), pp. 343–347. **Source 52:** Jane Marcus, ed., *Speech, Suffrage and the Pankhursts* (London: Routledge & Kegan Paul, 1987), 153–157, 159–161. **Source 53:** From Louis Snyder, *Documents of German History*, pp. 259–262. Copyright © 1958 by Rutgers, the State University. Reprinted by permission of Rutgers University Press. **Source 54:** Ralph Austen, ed., *Modern Imperialism* (Lexington, MA: D. C. Heath, 1969), pp. 70–73. Copyright © 1969. Used by permission. **Source 55:** illustrations: (1–3) Mrs. Ernest (Mary Frances) Ames, *An ABC for Baby Patriots* (London: Dean & Son, 1899), pp. "N," "I," "W." Courtesy of de Grummond Children's Literature Collection, University of Southern Mississippi. (4) From *The Kipling Reader* (London: Macmillan, 1908), illus. by J. MacFarlane. By permission of the Houghton Library, Harvard University. 12.08.6. (5) Lipton Teas ad from *Illustrated London News*, vol. XVI, no. 3058, November 27, 1897. Courtesy of The Illustrated London News Picture Library. (6–7) "On the Swoop," from *Punch*, 1894, Punch Cartoon Library & Archive and "Britannia and Her Suitors," from *Punch*, 1901.

Multiple Voices V

(1) M. B. Starr, *The Coming Struggle; or What the People on the Pacific Coast Think of the Coolie Invasion* (San Francisco: Bacon & Company, 1873). (2) American Federation of Labor, "Some Reasons for Chinese Exclusion. Meat Vs. Rice," Senate

Document No. 137, 57th Congress, 1st Session (Washington, D.C.: Government Printing Office, 1902). (3) *Memorial Six Companies... Testimony of California's' Leading Citizens Before the Joint Special Congressional Committee* (San Francisco: n.p., 1877), 21, 25. (4) George. F. Seward, *Chinese Immigration in Its Social and Economical Aspects* (New York: Scribner's, 1881), 252–253. (5) illustration: Thomas Nast, "The Chinese Question," *Harper's Weekly*, February 19, 1871, p. 149. Thomas Nast/HarpWeek, LLC. (6) illustration: George Keller, "The Coming Man," *The Wasp*, May 20, 1881. The Bancroft Library—University of California.

Chapter 9

Source 56: Edward Hertslet, ed., *The Map of Africa by Treaty*, 2nd ed. (Her Majesty's Stationery Office, 1896), vol. 1, pp. 467–268. **Source 57:** Margery Perham, ed., *Ten Africans*, Copyright © 1936 by Faber & Faber. **Source 58:** From C. G. K. Gwasa and John Iliffe, "Records of the Maji-Maji Rising" (Nairobi: East African Publishing House, 1967), pp. 4–8 (Historical Association of Tanzania, Paper Number 4). Modified for this edition. **Source 59:** Edward G. Brown, *The Persian Revolution of 1905*. Copyright © 1966 by Frank Cass & Co. Used by permission. **Source 60:** "Announcement to the Arabs" by Sylvia G. Haim, *Arab Nationalism: An Anthology* (Berkeley: University of California Press, 1962), 83–88. Selection and translation of text are made by her and copyrighted by her. **Source 61:** (1) Rammohun Roy, *The English Works of Rammohun Roy* (Allahabad, India: Panini Office, 1906), pp. 471–474. (2) Bureau of Education, *Selections from Educational Records*, Part I. ed. H. Sharp (Calcutta: Superintendent, Government Printing, 1920), 107–117, passim. **Source 62:** Dadabhai Naoroji, *Speeches, Addresses and Writings* (Bombay: Caxton Printing Works, 1887), 131–136.

Chapter 10

Source 63: Dun J. Li, ed., *China in Transition 1517–1911*, 1st edition. © 1969, pp. 64–67. Reprinted with permission of Wadsworth, a division of Thomson Learning: www.thomsonrights.com. Fax 800-730-2215. **Source 64:** From Wm. Theodore de Bry and Richard Lufarno, *Sources of Chinese Tradition*, second edition, vol. 2 (New York: Columbia University Press, 2000), 235–238. Copyright © 2000 Columbia University Press. Reprinted with permission of the publisher. **Source 65:** From Charles Terry, unpublished master's thesis published in *Sources of Japanese Tradition* by Tsunudo, de Bry, and Keene, pp. 609–615. Copyright © 1951 Columbia University Press. Reprinted with the permission of the publisher. **Source 66:** David John Lu, *Sources of Japanese History* (New York: McGraw-Hill, 1974), vol. 2, pp. 42–45. **Source 67:** illustrations: (1) *One of Commodore Perry's Black Ships*, Courtesy of the International Society for Educational Information (ISEI). (2) *Commodore Perry's Second-in-Command, Commander Henry Adams*, Anonymous, 1853, Japan. "Visit of American Ships in Shimoda Harbor, Kaei VI (1853) with Commodore Perry. Officers and Men, etc." Hand scroll in colors on paper. Gift of Mrs. Walter F. Dillingham (Given in Memory of Alice Perry Grew), 1960. Courtesy Honolulu Academy of Arts. (3) Kobayashi Kiyochika, *Fukuchi Gen'ichiro*, The Metropolitan Museum of Art, Gift of Lincoln Kirstein, 1962 (JP 3420). (4) Kanagaki Robun, *Hiking Through the West*, Courtesy of the Library of Congress. (5) Honda Kinkichiro, *Monkey Show Dressing Room*, Courtesy of the Library of Congress. (6) Kobayashi Kiyochika, *Hands Dance, Feet Stomp, Call Out Hurrah!* Courtesy of the Library of Congress. **Source 68:** From Chomchai Prachom, *Chulalongkorn the Great*, Tokyo: Centre for East Asian Cultural Studies, 1965, pp. 52–56, 90–95. Reprinted with permission of the Toyko Bunko. **Source 69:** Letter to Emperor Tu Doc and Last Message to His Administrators from *We the Vietnamese* by Francois Sully and Donald Kirk. Copyright © 1971 by Praeger Publishers Inc. Reprinted by permission of Henry Holt and Company, LLC.

Multiple Voices VI

(1) As seen in Akram F. Khater, *Sources in the History of the Modern Middle East*. Copyright © 2003 Houghton Mifflin. (2) Bahiththat al-Badiya, "Lecture in the Club of the Umma Party," in Margot Badran and miriam cooke, *Opening the Gates*, 2nd edition (Bloomington: Indiana University Press, 2004), 228–230. (3) "An Address to Two Hundred Million Fellow Countrywomen" (1906) from Patricia Embrey, *Chinese Civilization: A Sourcebook* (New York: The Free Press, a Division of Simon & Schuster). (4) "Women's Talents": David John Lu, *Sources of Japanese History*, vol. 2 (New York: McGraw-Hill, 1974), 118–119.

Part Four ▾ The Global Community and Its Challenges in the Twentieth and Twenty-First Centuries

Chapter 11

Source 70: illustrations: (1) B. Hennerberg, *The Departure*, Courtesy of Imperial War Museum, London. (2) *Advertisement card from Golden Dawn Cigarettes*, Courtesy of Imperial War Museum, London. (3) *Australian recruitment poster*, Courtesy of Imperial War Museum, London. (4) Septimus Scott, *These Women Are Doing Their Bit*, Courtesy of the Imperial War Museum, London. **Source 71:** H. S. Clapham, *Mud and Khaki: Memoirs of an Incomplete Soldier*, Hutchinson & Co., 1930, pp. 141–153. **Source 72:** V. L. Lenin, *Collected Works*, vol. 5 (London: Lawrence and Wishart, 1973), pp. 352–353, 375–376, 399–401, 413–414, 425, 454, 463–467. **Source 73:** V. I. Lenin, *Selected Works*, Vol. II, Book 1 (Moscow: Progress Publishers, 1964, 282–284. **Source 74:** Adolf Hitler, *Mein Kampf* (Munich: F. Eher Nachfolger, 1927), trans. by J. Overfield. **Source 75:** Excerpt from *Tokyo Record*, Copyright © 1943 by Otto D. Tolischus and renewed 1970 by Naya G. Tolischus. Reprinted by permission of Harcourt, Inc. **Source 76:** From Rudolf Höss, *Death Dealer: The Mem-*

oirs of the SS Kommandant at Auschwitz by Rudolf Höss, edited by Stephen Paskuly, translated by Andrew Pollinger (Amherst, NY: Prometheus Books, 1992), pp. 141–142, 153–159, 161–162, 164. Copyright © 1992 by Steven Paskuly. Reprinted with permission of the publisher. **Source 77:** Iwao Nakamura and Atsuko Tsujioka, "Recollections from Arata Osada," in *Children of Hiroshima* (London: Taylor and Francis, 1981), pp. 173–175, 265–269.

Multiple Voices VII

(1) Memorandum of Conversation with General Marshall, May 29, 1945, National Archives. **(2)** From Arthur Compton, *Atomic Quest* (New York: Oxford University Press, 1956), 238–241. Reprinted with permission of Oxford University Press. **(3)** The Franck Report (June 11, 1945), From U.S. National Archives, Washington, D.C.: Record Group 77, Manhattan Engineer District Records, Harrison-Bundy File, folder #76. **(4)** A Petition to the President of the United States, July 17, 1945: From U.S. National Archives, Record Group #77, Records of the Chief of Engineers, Manhattan Engineer District, Harrison-Bundy File, folder #76. **(5)** President Harry Truman, Letter to Samuel Cavert, August 11, 1945: From Harry S. Truman Presidential Library and Museum. **(6)** From Harry L. Stimson, "The Decision to Use the Atomic Bomb," *Harper's Weekly*, February 1947 by Harper's Magazine. Copyright © 1947 by *Harper's* Magazine. All rights reserved. Reproduced from the February issue by special permission.

Chapter 12

Source 78: James Aggrey, "Parable of the Eagle," in Edward Smith, *Aggrey of Africa* SCM Press (1929). **Source 79:** Donald A. Low, *The Mind of Buganda* (Berkeley: University of California Press, 1971), 134–138. Reprinted by permission of the University of California Press. **Source 80:** Mustafa Kemal, *A Speech Delivered by Ghazi Mustapha Kemal* (Leipzig: F. F. Koehler, 1929), pp. 376–379, 589–594, 717, 721–722. **Source 81:** From Hasan al-Banna, "Towards the Light," in Robert Langdon, *The Emergence of the Middle East*, Van Nostrand, 1970. Reprinted with permission of Robert Landen via Copyright Clearance Center. **Source 82:** Mohandas Gandhi, *Indian Home Rule* (Madras, India: Ganesh & Co., 1922), pp. 30–35, 47–50, 63, 64, 85, 68, 90, 91. Copyright © 1967 by Harper & Row, Publishers, Reprinted by permission of the authors. **Source 83:** Harry Benda and John Larkin, *The World of Southeast Asia* (New York: Harper & Row, 1967), pp. 182–185. Copyright © 1967 by Harper & Row, Publishers. Reprinted by permission of the authors. **Source 84:** From Francisco Garcia Calderón, *Latin America: Its Rise and Progress*, Bernard Miall, trans. (Charles Scribner's Sons and T. Fisher Unwin, Ltd., 1913). pp. 298, 301–303, 306, 311, 378–382. Reprinted with permission of A & C Black Publishers Limited. **Source 85:** Benjamin Keen, ed. and trans., *Readings in Latin American Civilization* (Boston: Houghton Mifflin, 1955), pp. 362–364. **Source 86:** Deng Yingchao, "The Spirit of the May 4th Movement," in *Women of China*, May, 1989, pp. 40–42. **Source 87:** Mao Zedong, *Selected Works* (New York: International Publishers, 1954). Reprinted by permission.

Chapter 13

Source 88: From Kenneth Jensen, ed., *Origins of the Cold War*, Kovikov, Kennan, and Roberts, "Long Telegrams," of 1946, 1991, pp. 3–31 passim. Reprinted with permission of Endowment of the U.S. Institute of Peace. **Source 89:** NSC-68: U.S. Department of State, Foreign Relations of the United States 1950, vol. 1. **Source 90:** *Parliamentary Debates*, 5th ser., vol. 434 (London: His Majesty's Printing Office, 1947). **Source 91:** From *Lumumba Speaks* by Patrice Lumumba. Copyright © 1963 by Editions Presence Africaine; Copyright © 1972 by Little, Brown and Company, Inc. (Translation). By permission of Little, Brown and Company. **Source 92:** From *Biafra*: Volume 1, Selected Speeches; Volume 2, Random Thoughts by C. Odumegwu Ojukwu. Copyright © 1969 by Chukwuemeka Odumegwu Ojukwu. Reprinted by permission of HarperCollins Publisher. **Source 93:** Giralal Jain, "On Hindu Rashtra," from Koenrad Elst, *Ayodhya and After* (New Delhi: Crescent Printing Works, 1991) pp. 364–367, 369–371, 373–375. Reprinted by permission of the author. **Source 94:** Deng Xiaoping, *Fundamental Issues in Present-Day China* (Beijing: Foreign Languages Press, 1987), 42–44, 69–72, 101–102, 105–109, 162–163. Pergamon Press. **Source 95:** From *Perestroika* by Mikhail Gorbachev, pp. 18–19, 21–25, 30–36. Copyright © 1987 by Mikhail Gorbachev. Reprinted by permission of HarperCollins Publishers. **Source 96:** "Declaration of Jihad Against Americans Occupying the Land of the Two Holy Mosques," from http://azzam.com/html/articlesdeclaration.htm. **Source 97:** The original letter was translated by Capital Communications Group, Inc., Washington, D.C. Reprinted with permission. **Source 98:** From *The Case Against Free Trade: GATT, NAFTA, and the Globalization of Corporate Power* by Ralph Nader et al., published by North Atlantic Books. Copyright © 1993 by Earth Island Press. Reprinted by permission of the publisher. **Source 99:** From Gary Burtless, Robert Z. Lawrence, Robert E. Litan, and Robert Shapiro, *Globaphobia: Confronting Fears About Open Trade*, Washington, D.C., The Brookings Institution, Progressive Policy Institute, and Twentieth Century Fund, 1988, pp. 6–11. Reprinted with permission of The Brookings Institution. **Source 100:** From *World Development Indicators* 2003 by World Bank. Copyright 2003 by World Bank. Reproduced with permission of World Bank via Copyright Clearance Center.